CIMA'S Official *Learning System*

Managerial Level

Management Accounting – Decision Management

Colin Wilks
Louise Burke

ELSEVIER

AMSTERDAM   BOSTON   HEIDELBERG   LONDON   NEW YORK   OXFORD
PARIS   SAN DIEGO   SAN FRANCISCO   SINGAPORE   SYDNEY   TOKYO

CIMA Publishing is an imprint of Elsevier
Linacre House, Jordan Hill, Oxford OX2 8DP, UK
30 Corporate Drive, Suite 400, Burlington, MA 01803, USA

First edition 2007

Copyright © 2007 Elsevier Ltd. All rights reserved

No part of this publication may be reproduced, stored in a retrieval system
or transmitted in any form or by any means electronic, mechanical, photocopying,
recording or otherwise without the prior written permission of the publisher

Permissions may be sought directly from Elsevier's Science & Technology Rights
Department in Oxford, UK: phone (+44) (0) 1865 843830; fax (+44) (0) 1865 853333;
e-mail: permissions@elsevier.com. Alternatively you can submit your request online by
visiting the Elsevier web site at http://elsevier.com/locate/permissions, and selecting
Obtaining permission to use Elsevier material

Notice
No responsibility is assumed by the publisher for any injury and/or damage to persons
or property as a matter of products liability, negligence or otherwise, or from any use
or operation of any methods, products, instructions or ideas contained in the material
herein.

British Library Cataloguing in Publication Data
A catalogue record for this book is available from the British Library

ISBN-13: 978 0 7506 8535 1

For information on all CIMA publications
visit our web site at books.elsevier.com

Typeset by Integra Software Services Pvt. Ltd, Pondicherry, India
www.integra-india.com
Printed and bound in the Netherlands
07 08 09 10   10 9 8 7 6 5 4 3 2 1

Working together to grow
libraries in developing countries

www.elsevier.com | www.bookaid.org | www.sabre.org

ELSEVIER   BOOK AID International   Sabre Foundation

Contents

The CIMA *Learning System*	xi
Acknowledgements	xi
How to use your CIMA *Learning System*	xi
Guide to the Icons used within this Text	xii
Study technique	xiii
Management Accounting – Decision Management Syllabus	xv
Transitional arrangements	xix

1 Revision of Basic Aspects, Classifications and Approaches to Cost Accounting — 1

	Learning Outcome	3
1.1	Introduction	3
1.2	What is meant by cost?	3
1.3	Cost units	4
	1.3.1 Composite cost units	4
1.4	Cost centres	5
1.5	Classification of costs	5
	1.5.1 Classification of costs according to their nature	5
	1.5.2 Classification of costs according to their purpose	6
	1.5.3 Other examples of cost classification	6
1.6	Cost behaviour	7
	1.6.1 Fixed cost	7
	1.6.2 Variable cost	8
	1.6.3 Semi-variable cost	10
	1.6.4 Analysing semi-variable costs	10
	1.6.5 Using historical data	13
1.7	The elements of cost	13
1.8	Summary	14

2 Absorption Costing, Activity-based Costing and Marginal Costing — 15

	Learning Outcome	17
2.1	Introduction	17
2.2	Overhead allocation and apportionment	17
2.3	Overhead absorption	18
2.4	Applying the overhead absorption rate	18
2.5	Selecting the most appropriate absorption rate	19

2.6		Predetermined overhead absorption rates	20
	2.6.1	Under- or over-absorption of overheads	20
	2.6.2	The reasons for under- or over-absorption	21
	2.6.3	Accounting for under- or over-absorbed overheads	21
	2.6.4	The problems caused by under- or over-absorption of overheads	22
2.7		Illustrative example	22
2.8		Recent developments in absorption costing methods	24
	2.8.1	The criticisms of the traditional approach	24
	2.8.2	Activity-based costing	24
2.9		The difference between marginal costing and absorption costing	26
2.10		Marginal costing and contribution	26
2.11		Preparing profit statements using marginal costing and absorption costing	27
	2.11.1	Profit statements using marginal costing	28
	2.11.2	Profit statements using absorption costing	28
2.12		Reconciling the profit figures	29
	2.12.1	Reconciling the profits given by the different methods	29
	2.12.2	Reconciling the profits for different periods	30
	2.12.3	Profit differences in the long term	30
2.13		Should marginal costing or absorption costing be used?	31
2.14		Summary	31

3 Breakeven Analysis 33

		Learning Outcomes	35
3.1		Introduction	35
3.2		Breakeven or cost–volume–profit analysis	35
	3.2.1	Calculating the breakeven point	35
3.3		The margin of safety	36
3.4		The contribution to sales (C/S) ratio	37
3.5		Drawing a basic breakeven chart	38
3.6		The contribution breakeven chart	39
3.7		The profit–volume chart	40
	3.7.1	The advantage of the profit–volume chart	41
3.8		The limitations of breakeven (or CVP) analysis	42
3.9		The economist's breakeven chart	43
3.10		Using costs for decision-making	43
	3.10.1	Short-term decision-making	44
3.11		Evaluating proposals	44
3.12		Multi-product CVP analysis	46
3.13		Summary	48
		Reading	49
		Revision Questions	53
		Solutions to Revision Questions	57

4 Relevant Cost and Short-term Decisions 63

		Learning Outcomes	65
4.1		Introduction	65
4.2		Relevant costs	65
	4.2.1	Non-relevant costs	65

	4.3	Opportunity costs		67
		4.3.1 Examples of opportunity costs		67
		4.3.2 Notional costs and opportunity costs		68
	4.4	Avoidable, differential and incremental costs		68
		4.4.1 Avoidable costs		68
		4.4.2 Differential/incremental costs		68
		4.4.3 Using incremental costs		68
		4.4.4 Incremental revenues		69
		4.4.5 Minimum price quotations for special orders		70
	4.5	Limiting factor decision-making		70
		4.5.1 Decisions involving a single limiting factor		70
	4.6	Further decision-making problems		73
	4.7	Summary		80
		Readings		81
		Revision Questions		89
		Solutions to Revision Questions		97
5	**Linear Programming**			**105**
		Learning Outcomes		107
	5.1	Introduction		107
	5.2	Basic linear programming		107
		5.2.1 Formulating the mathematical model		108
		5.2.2 The graphical method of solving linear programming models		109
		5.2.3 Further examples of the construction and graphing of constraints		113
		5.2.4 Multiple solutions		114
		5.2.5 Slack and surplus		117
		5.2.6 Shadow prices and opportunity costs		118
	5.3	The Simplex method		119
	5.4	Worth and relative loss		121
	5.5	Summary		122
		Reading		123
		Revision Questions		129
		Solutions to Revision Questions		133
6	**Pricing**			**139**
		Learning Outcomes		141
	6.1	Introduction		141
	6.2	Demand and the product life cycle		141
		6.2.1 Price elasticity of demand		141
		6.2.2 The product life cycle		145
		6.2.3 The profit-maximisation model		147
		6.2.4 Limitations of the profit-maximisation model		148
	6.3	Pricing strategies based on cost		148
		6.3.1 Total cost-plus pricing		148
		6.3.2 Marginal cost-plus pricing		151

6.4	Other pricing strategies		152
	6.4.1 Premium pricing		152
	6.4.2 Market skimming		152
	6.4.3 Penetration pricing		153
	6.4.4 Price differentiation		153
	6.4.5 Loss leader pricing		154
	6.4.6 Product bundling		154
	6.4.7 Pricing with additional features		155
	6.4.8 Using discounts in pricing		156
	6.4.9 Controlled pricing		157
6.5	Summary		157
	Reading		159
	Revision Questions		165
	Solutions to Revision Questions		169

7 Risk and Uncertainty 173

	Learning Outcomes	175
7.1	Introduction	175
7.2	Probability	175
	7.2.1 The probabilistic model and expected value	175
	7.2.2 Examples of expected value calculations	177
7.3	Decision trees	180
	7.3.1 Method and applications	180
	7.3.2 The value of perfect information	184
7.4	Uncertainty in investment appraisal	185
7.5	Standard deviations to measure risk and uncertainty	186
7.6	Maximin, Maximax and regret criteria	187
7.7	Summary	188
	Readings	189
	Revision Questions	199
	Solutions to Revision Questions	203

8 Investment Appraisal 209

	Learning Outcomes	211
8.1	Introduction	211
8.2	The different appraisal methods	211
	8.2.1 Introduction	211
	8.2.2 Net present value (NPV)	213
	8.2.3 Payback (PB)	215
	8.2.4 Discounted payback (DPB)	217
	8.2.5 Discounted payback index (DPBI) or profitability index	217
	8.2.6 Internal rate of return (IRR)	218
	8.2.7 Multiple IRRs	220
	8.2.8 Modified internal rate of return (MIRR)	221
	8.2.9 Accounting rate of return (ARR)	222

	8.2.10	Example comparing ARR and NPV	224
	8.2.11	Summary of the four investment appraisal methods	225
8.3	Making the cash flows and NPV model more realistic		226
	8.3.1	Using the annuity rate	226
	8.3.2	Unequal lives	226
	8.3.3	Asset replacement cycles	227
	8.3.4	Capital rationing	230
	8.3.5	The discount rate	231
	8.3.6	Sensitivity analysis	232
	8.3.7	Risk	235
	8.3.8	Inflation	236
	8.3.9	Incorporating the effect of taxation	238
8.4	Post-completion appraisal		242
	8.4.1	The investment cycle	242
	8.4.2	Benefits of post-completion appraisal	242
	8.4.3	Project abandonment	244
	8.4.4	Role of post-appraisal in project abandonment	247
8.5	Summary		248
	Readings		249
	Revision Questions		279
	Solutions to Revision Questions		287

9 The Value Chain – TQM 301

	Learning Outcomes	303
9.1	Introduction	303
9.2	Continuous improvement	303
9.3	Kaizen costing	304
9.4	Value analysis	304
9.5	Functional analysis	305
9.6	The value chain	305
9.7	Just-in-time concept	306
	9.7.1 JIT systems	308
	9.7.2 JIT and supplier relationships	309
9.8	Total quality management (TQM)	310
	9.8.1 Quality as a concept	310
	9.8.2 TQM in practice	312
9.9	Business process re-engineering	313
9.10	Summary	313
	Reading	315
	Revision Questions	319
	Solutions to Revision Questions	323

10 Activity-based Approaches 329

	Learning Outcomes	331
10.1	Introduction	331

10.2	The overhead problem		331
	10.2.1	Cost behaviour	331
	10.2.2	Absorption costing	332
	10.2.3	Direct product profitability (DPP)	333
10.3	Activity-based costing (ABC)		336
	10.3.1	Introduction	336
	10.3.2	Simple example of traditional absorption costing and ABC	339
	10.3.3	Activity-based management	341
	10.3.4	Activity-based management: cost management of activities	342
	10.3.5	Costing objects other than products	344
	10.3.6	Activity-based management: customer profitability analysis	344
	10.3.7	Distribution channel profitability	346
	10.3.8	Activity-based management: strategic activity management	347
	10.3.9	Using ABC in service industries and activities	348
	10.3.10	Problems with implementing ABC	349
10.4	Pareto analysis		350
	10.4.1	The rule	350
	10.4.2	Uses of Pareto analysis	351
10.5	Summary		354
	Readings		355
	Revision Questions		377
	Solutions to Revision Questions		385

11 Learning and Experience Curves — 399

	Learning Outcome		401
11.1	Introduction		401
11.2	The learning curve		401
	11.2.1	Introduction	401
	11.2.2	The nature of the learning curve	401
	11.2.3	Uses of the learning curve	405
	11.2.4	Learned behaviour	405
	11.2.5	Experience curves	406
11.3	Summary		408
	Reading		409
	Revision Questions		415
	Solutions to Revision Questions		417

12 Costing Systems — 421

	Learning Outcomes		423
12.1	Introduction		423
12.2	Costing systems and manufacturing philosophy		423
	12.2.1	Introduction	423
	12.2.2	Traditional manufacturing philosophy	424
	12.2.3	Modern manufacturing philosophy	426
	12.2.4	Volume versus variety	426

12.3	Pull systems		428
	12.3.1 Just-in-time (JIT)		428
	12.3.2 Backflush accounting		429
12.4	Throughput accounting		432
	12.4.1 The theory of constraints (TOC)		432
	12.4.2 Throughput accounting (TA)		433
	12.4.3 Throughput cost control and effectiveness measures		437
	12.4.4 Case – throughput accounting at Garrett Automotive Ltd UK		438
	12.4.5 Summary of throughput accounting		439
12.5	Cost planning and reduction over the life cycle		441
	12.5.1 Target costing: a strategic profit management system		441
	12.5.2 Using target costing in the concept and design stages		443
	12.5.3 Target costing for existing products		444
	12.5.4 Target costing support systems		445
12.6	Life cycle costing		446
	12.6.1 Life cycle costing – introduction		446
	12.6.2 Product life cycle costing		447
	12.6.3 Customer life cycle costing		450
12.7	Summary		451
	Readings		453
	Revision Questions		461
	Solutions to Revision Questions		467

Preparing for the Examination — 471

Revision technique — 473
  Planning — 473
  Getting down to work — 474
  Tips for the final revision phase — 474
Format of the examination — 475
  Structure of the paper — 475

Revision Questions — 477

Solutions to Revision Questions — 529

Index — 623

The CIMA Learning System

Acknowledgements

Every effort has been made to contact the holders of copyright material, but if any here have been inadvertently overlooked the publishers will be pleased to make the necessary arrangements at the first opportunity.

This text has been structured to be studied independently of the Performance Evaluation paper, therefore the reader will notice some unavoidable overlap between the two texts.

How to use your CIMA Learning System

This *Management Accounting – Decision Management Learning System* has been devised as a resource for students attempting to pass their CIMA exams, and provides:

- a detailed explanation of all syllabus areas;
- extensive 'practical' materials, including readings from relevant journals;
- generous question practice, together with full solutions
- an exam preparation section, complete with exam standard questions and solutions.

This Learning System has been designed with the needs of home-study and distance-learning candidates in mind. Such students require very full coverage of the syllabus topics, and also the facility to undertake extensive question practice. However, the Learning System is also ideal for fully taught courses.

The main body of the text is divided into a number of chapters, each of which is organised on the following pattern:

- *Detailed learning outcomes* expected after your studies of the chapter are complete. You should assimilate these before beginning detailed work on the chapter, so that you can appreciate where your studies are leading.
- *Step-by-step topic coverage*. This is the heart of each chapter, containing detailed explanatory text supported where appropriate by worked examples and exercises. You should work carefully through this section, ensuring that you understand the material being explained and can tackle the examples and exercises successfully. Remember that in many cases knowledge is cumulative: if you fail to digest earlier material thoroughly, you may struggle to understand later chapters.

- *Readings and activities.* Some chapters are illustrated by more practical elements, such as relevant journal articles or other readings, together with comments and questions designed to stimulate discussion.
- *Question practice.* The test of how well you have learned the material is your ability to tackle exam-standard questions. Make a serious attempt at producing your own answers, but at this stage do not be too concerned about attempting the questions in exam conditions. In particular, it is more important to absorb the material thoroughly by completing a full solution than to observe the time limits that would apply in the actual exam.
- *Solutions.* Avoid the temptation merely to 'audit' the solutions provided. It is an illusion to think that this provides the same benefits as you would gain from a serious attempt of your own. However, if you are struggling to get started on a question you should read the introductory guidance provided at the beginning of the solution, and then make your own attempt before referring back to the full solution.

Having worked through the chapters you are ready to begin your final preparations for the examination. The final section of this CIMA *Learning System* provides you with the guidance you need. It includes the following features:

- A brief guide to revision technique.
- A note on the format of the exam. You should know what to expect when you tackle the real exam, and in particular the number of questions to attempt, which questions are compulsory and which optional, and so on.
- Guidance on how to tackle the exam itself.
- A table mapping revision questions to the syllabus learning outcomes allowing you to quickly identify questions by subject area.
- Revision questions. These are of exam standard and should be tackled in exam conditions, especially as regards the time allocation.
- Solutions to the revision questions. As before, these indicate the length and the quality of solution that would be expected of a well-prepared candidate.

If you work conscientiously through this CIMA *Learning System* according to the guidelines above you will be giving yourself an excellent chance of exam success. Good luck with your studies!

Guide to the Icons used within this Text

Key term or definition

Equation to learn

Exam tip to topic likely to appear in the exam

Exercise

Question

Solution

Comment or Note

Study technique

Passing exams is partly a matter of intellectual ability, but however accomplished you are in that respect you can improve your chances significantly by the use of appropriate study and revision techniques. In this section we briefly outline some tips for effective study during the earlier stages of your approach to the exam. Later in the text we mention some techniques that you will find useful at the revision stage.

Planning

To begin with, formal planning is essential to get the best return from the time you spend studying. Estimate how much time in total you are going to need for each subject that you face. Remember that you need to allow time for revision as well as for initial study of the material. The amount of notional study time for any subject is the minimum estimated time that students will need to achieve the specified learning outcomes set out earlier in this chapter. This time includes all appropriate learning activities, for example face-to-face tuition, private study, directed home study, learning in the workplace, revision time, etc. You may find it helpful to read *Better Exam Results* by Sam Malone, CIMA Publishing, ISBN: 075066357X. This book will provide you with proven study techniques. Chapter by chapter it covers the building blocks of successful learning and examination techniques.

The notional study time for Managerial level *Decision Management* is 200 hours. Note that the standard amount of notional learning hours attributed to one full-time academic year of approximately 30 weeks is 1,200 hours.

By way of example, the notional study time might be made up as follows:

	Hours
Face-to-face study: up to	60
Personal study: up to	100
'Other' study – e.g. learning in the workplace, revision, etc.: up to	40
	200

Note that all study and learning-time recommendations should be used only as a guideline and are intended as minimum amounts. The amount of time recommended for face-to-face tuition, personal study and/or additional learning will vary according to the type of course undertaken, prior learning of the student, and the pace at which different students learn.

Now split your total time requirement over the weeks between now and the assessment. This will give you an idea of how much time you need to devote to study each week. Remember to allow for holidays or other periods during which you will not be able to study (e.g. because of seasonal workloads).

With your study material before you, decide which chapters you are going to study in each week, and which weeks you will devote to revision and final question practice.

Prepare a written schedule summarising the above – and stick to it!

The amount of space allocated to a topic in the study material is not a very good guide as to how long it will take you. For example, 'Summarising and Analysing Data' has a weight of 25 per cent in the syllabus and this is the best guide as to how long you should spend on it. It occupies 45 per cent of the main body of the text because it includes many tables and charts.

It is essential to know your syllabus. As your course progresses you will become more familiar with how long it takes to cover topics in sufficient depth. Your timetable may need to be adapted to allocate enough time for the whole syllabus.

Tips for effective studying

(1) Aim to find a quiet and undisturbed location for your study, and plan as far as possible to use the same period of time each day. Getting into a routine helps to avoid wasting time. Make sure that you have all the materials you need before you begin so as to minimise interruptions.

(2) Store all your materials in one place, so that you do not waste time searching for items around the house. If you have to pack everything away after each study period, keep them in a box, or even a suitcase, which will not be disturbed until the next time.

(3) Limit distractions. To make the most effective use of your study periods you should be able to apply total concentration, so turn off the TV, set your phones to message mode, and put up your 'do not disturb' sign.

(4) Your timetable will tell you which topic to study. However, before diving in and becoming engrossed in the finer points, make sure you have an overall picture of all the areas that need to be covered by the end of that session. After an hour, allow yourself a short break and move away from your books. With experience, you will learn to assess the pace you need to work at. You should also allow enough time to read relevant articles from newspapers and journals, which will supplement your knowledge and demonstrate a wider perspective.

(5) Work carefully through a chapter, making notes as you go. When you have covered a suitable amount of material, vary the pattern by attempting a practice question. Preparing an answer plan is a good habit to get into, while you are both studying and revising, and also in the examination room. It helps to impose a structure on your solutions, and avoids rambling. When you have finished your attempt, make notes of any mistakes you made, or any areas that you failed to cover or covered only skimpily.

(6) Make notes as you study, and discover the techniques that work best for you. Your notes may be in the form of lists, bullet points, diagrams, summaries, 'mind maps', or the written word, but remember that you will need to refer back to them at a later date, so they must be intelligible. If you are on a taught course, make sure you highlight any issues you would like to follow up with your lecturer.

(7) Organise your paperwork. There are now numerous paper storage systems available to ensure that all your notes, calculations and articles can be effectively filed and easily retrieved later.

Management Accounting – Decision Management Syllabus

First examined in May 2005

Syllabus outline

The syllabus comprises:

	Topic	Study Weighting
A	Financial Information for Short-term Decision-Making	30%
B	Financial Information for Long-term Decision-Making	25%
C	The Treatment of Uncertainty in Decision-Making	15%
D	Cost Planning and Analysis for Competitive Advantage	30%

Learning aims

Students should be able to:
- separate costs into their fixed and variable components and use these in break-even analysis and in decision-making under multiple constraints;
- establish relevant cash flows for decision making and apply these principles in a variety of contexts including process/product viability and pricing including evaluation of the tension between short-term, 'contribution based' pricing and long-term, 'return on investment' pricing;
- develop relevant cash flows for long-term projects taking account of inflation and taxation where appropriate, evaluate projects using discounting and traditional methods, critically assess alternative methods of evaluation and place evaluation techniques in the context of the whole process of investment decision making;
- apply learning curves in forecasting future costs and the techniques of activity-based management, target costing and value analysis in managing future costs and evaluate the actual and potential impacts of contemporary techniques such as JIT, TOC and TQM on efficiency, inventory and cost;
- undertake sensitivity analysis and assess the impact of risk in decision models using probability analysis, expected value tables and decision trees as appropriate;
- discuss externally oriented management accounting techniques and apply these techniques to the value chain, 'gain sharing' arrangements and customer/channel profitability analysis.

Assessment Strategy

There will be a written examination paper of three hours, with the following sections.
Section A – 20 marks

A variety of compulsory objective test questions, each worth between 2 and 4 marks. Mini-scenarios may be given, to which a group of questions relate.
Section B – 30 marks

Three compulsory medium answer questions, each worth 10 marks. Short scenarios may be given, to which some or all questions relate.

Section C – 50 marks

Two questions, from a choice of three, each worth 25 marks. Short scenarios may be given, to which questions relate.

Learning Outcomes and Syllabus Content

A – Financial Information for Short-term Decision-Making – 30%

Learning outcomes

On completion of their studies students should be able to:

(i) discuss the principles of decision making including the identification of relevant cash flows and their use alongside non-quantifiable factors in making rounded judgements;

(ii) explain the particular issues that arise in pricing decisions and the conflict between 'marginal cost' principles and the need for full recovery of all costs incurred;

(iii) apply an approach to pricing based on profit maximisation in imperfect markets and evaluate the financial consequences of alternative pricing strategies;

(iv) explain the possible conflicts between cost accounting for profit reporting and stock valuation and the convenient availability of information for decision-making;

(v) explain why joint costs must be allocated to final products for financial reporting purposes, but why this is unhelpful when decisions concerning process and product viability have to be taken;

(vi) discuss the usefulness of dividing costs into variable and fixed components in the context of short-term decision making;

(vii) apply variable/fixed cost analysis in multiple product contexts to break-even analysis and product mix decision making, including circumstances where there are multiple constraints and linear programming methods are needed to reach 'optimal' solutions;

(viii) discuss the meaning of 'optimal' solutions and show how linear programming methods can be employed for profit maximising, revenue maximising and satisfying objectives.

Syllabus content

- Relevant cash flows and their use in short-term decisions, typically concerning acceptance/rejection of contracts, pricing and cost/benefit comparisons.
- The importance of strategic, intangible and non-financial judgements in decision-making.
- Pricing decisions for profit maximising in imperfect markets. (Note: tabular methods of solution are acceptable).
- Pricing strategies and the financial consequences of market skimming, premium pricing, penetration pricing, loss leaders, product bundling/optional extras and product differentiation to appeal to different market segments.
- The allocation of joint costs and decisions concerning process and product viability based on relevant costs and revenues.
- Multi-product break-even analysis, including break-even and profit/volume charts, contribution/sales ratio, margin of safety etc.

- Simple product mix analysis in situations where there are limitations on product/service demand and one other production constraint.
- Linear programming for more complex situations involving multiple constraints. Solution by graphical methods of two variable problems, together with understanding of the mechanics of simplex solution, shadow prices etc. (Note: questions requiring the full application of the simplex algorithm will not be set although candidates should be able to formulate an initial tableau, interpret a final simplex tableau and apply the information it contained in a final tableau.)

B – Financial Information for Long-term Decision-Making – 25%

Learning outcomes

On completion of their studies students should be able to:

(i) explain the processes involved in making long-term decisions;
(ii) apply the principles of relevant cash flow analysis to long-run projects that continue for several years;
(iii) calculate project cash flows, accounting for tax and inflation, and apply perpetuities to derive 'end of project' value where appropriate;
(iv) apply activity-based costing techniques to derive approximate 'long-run' product or service costs appropriate for use in strategic decision making;
(v) explain the financial consequences of dealing with long-run projects, in particular the importance of accounting for the 'time value of money';
(vi) evaluate project proposals using the techniques of investment appraisal;
(vii) compare, contrast and evaluate the alternative techniques of investment appraisal;
(viii) evaluate and rank projects that might be mutually exclusive, involve unequal lives and/or be subject to capital rationing;
(ix) apply sensitivity analysis to cash flow parameters to identify those to which net present value is particularly sensitive;
(x) produce decision support information for management, integrating financial and non-financial considerations.

Syllabus content

- The process of investment decision making, including origination of proposals, creation of capital budgets, go/no go decisions on individual projects (where judgements on qualitative issues interact with financial analysis), and post audit of completed projects;
- Generation of relevant project cash flows taking account of inflation, tax, and 'final' project value where appropriate.
- Activity-based costing to derive approximate 'long-run' costs appropriate for use in strategic decision making.
- The techniques of investment appraisal: payback, discounted payback, accounting rate of return, net present value and internal rate of return.
- Application of the techniques of investment appraisal to project cash flows and evaluation of the strengths and weaknesses of the techniques.

- Sensitivity analysis to identify the input variables that most effect the chosen measure of project worth (payback, ARR, NPV or IRR).
- Methods of dealing with particular problems: the use of annuities in comparing projects with unequal lives and the profitability index in capital rationing situations.

C – The Treatment of Uncertainty in Decision-Making – 15%

On completion of their studies students should be able to:

(i) evaluate the impact of uncertainty and risk on decision models that may be based on CVP analysis, relevant cash flows, learning curves, discounting techniques etc.;
(ii) apply sensitivity analysis on both short- and long-run decision models to identify variables that might have significant impacts on project outcomes;
(iii) analyse risk and uncertainty by calculating expected values and standard deviations together with probability tables and histograms;
(iv) prepare expected value tables and ascertain the value of information;
(v) prepare and apply decision trees.

Syllabus content

- The nature of risk and uncertainty.
- Sensitivity analysis in decision modelling and the use of computer software for 'what if' analysis.
- Assignment of probabilities to key variables in decision models.
- Analysis of probabilistic models and interpretation of distributions of project outcomes.
- Expected value tables and the value of information.
- Decision trees for multi-stage decision problems.

D – Cost Planning and Analysis for Competitive Advantage – 30%

Learning outcomes

On completion of their studies students should be able to:

(i) compare and contrast value analysis and functional cost analysis;
(ii) evaluate the impacts of just-in-time production, the theory of constraints and total quality management on efficiency, inventory and cost;
(iii) explain the concepts of continuous improvement and Kaizen costing that are central to total quality management and prepare cost of quality reports;
(iv) explain and apply learning and experience curves to estimate time and cost for new products and services;
(v) apply the techniques of activity-based management in identifying cost drivers/ activities and explain how process re-engineering can be used to eliminate non-value adding activities and reduce activity costs;
(vi) explain how target costs can be derived from target prices and describe the relationship between target costs and standard costs;

(vii) explain the concept of life cycle costing and how life cycle costs interact with marketing strategies at each stage of the life cycle.
(viii) explain the concept of the value chain and discuss the management of contribution/profit generated throughout the chain;
(ix) discuss gain sharing arrangements whereby contractors and customers benefit if contract targets for cost, delivery etc. are beaten;
(x) apply activity-based costing ideas to analyse 'direct customer profitability and extend this analysis to distribution channel profitability;
(xi) apply Pareto analysis as a convenient technique for identifying key elements of data and in presenting the results of other analyses, such as activity-based profitability calculations.

Syllabus content

- Value analysis and quality function deployment.
- The benefits of just-in-time production, total quality management and theory of constraints and the implications of these methods for decision-making in the 'new manufacturing environment'.
- Kaizen costing, continuous improvement and cost of quality reporting.
- Learning curves and their use in predicting product/service costs, including derivation of the learning rate and the learning index.
- Activity-based management in the analysis of overhead and its use in improving the efficiency of repetitive overhead activities.
- Target costing.
- Life cycle costing and implications for marketing strategies.
- The value chain and supply chain management, including the trend to outsource manufacturing operations to Eastern Europe and the Far East.
- Gain sharing arrangements in situations where, because of the size of the project, a limited number of contractors or security issues (e.g. in defence work), normal competitive pressures do not apply.
- The use of direct and activity-based cost methods in tracing costs to 'cost objects', such as customers or distribution channels, and the comparison of such costs with appropriate revenues to establish 'tiered' contribution levels, as in the activity-based cost hierarchy.
- Pareto analysis.

Transitional arrangements

Students who have passed the Management Accounting – Decision Making paper under the Beyond 2000 syllabus will be given a credit for the Management Accounting – Decision Management paper under the new 2005 syllabus. For further details of transitional arrangements, please contact CIMA directly or visit their website at www.cimaglobal.com.

This text has been structured to be studied independently of the Performance Evaluation paper, therefore, the reader will notice some unavoidable overlap between the two texts.

Revision of Basic Aspects, Classifications and Approaches to Cost Accounting

Revision of Basic Aspects, Classifications and Approaches to Cost Accounting

LEARNING OUTCOME

▸ Discuss the usefulness of dividing costs into variable and fixed components in the context of short-term decision-making.

1.1 Introduction

In this chapter we will look at some of the fundamental aspects of cost accounting which you should recall from your earlier studies.

In particular, we will see how costs can be classified and coded to assist in cost collection and analysis. The most common cost behaviour patterns will be explained and analysed.

1.2 What is meant by cost?

The word 'cost' can be used in two contexts. It can be used as a noun, for example, when referring to the cost of an item. Alternatively it can be used as a verb, for example, we can say that we are attempting to cost an activity. CIMA's definition of cost used in these two contexts is as follows:

   As a noun: the amount of expenditure (actual or notional) incurred on, or attributable to, a specified thing or activity
As a verb: to ascertain the cost of a specified thing or activity.

The terminology goes on to explain that the word cost can rarely stand alone and should be qualified as to its nature and limitations. You will know from your earlier studies, and will be seeing throughout this text that there are many different types of cost and that each has its usefulness and limitations in different circumstances.

1.3 Cost units

You should already be able to explain what a cost unit is, using your earlier cost accounting knowledge. The CIMA *Terminology* defines a cost unit as 'a unit of product or service in relation to which costs are ascertained'.

This means that a cost unit can be anything for which it is possible to ascertain the cost. The cost unit selected in each situation will depend on a number of factors, including the purpose of the cost ascertainment exercise and the amount of information available.

Cost units can be developed for all kinds of organisations, whether manufacturing, commercial or public service based. Some examples from the CIMA *Terminology* are as follows:

Industry sector	*Cost unit*
Brick-making	1,000 bricks
Electricity	Kilowatt-hour (KwH)
Professional services	Chargeable hour
Education	Enrolled student

Activity	*Cost unit*
Credit control	Account maintained
Selling	Customer call

The list is not exhaustive. A cost unit can be anything which is measurable and useful for cost control purposes. For example with brick-making, 1,000 bricks is suggested as a cost unit. It would be possible to determine the cost per brick but perhaps in this case a larger measure is considered more suitable and useful for control purposes.

Notice that this list of cost units contains both tangible and intangible items. Tangible items are those which can be seen and touched, for example the 1,000 bricks. Intangible items cannot be seen and touched but they can be measured, for example, a chargeable hour of accounting service.

1.3.1 Composite cost units

The cost units for services are usually intangible and they are often composite cost units, that is, they are often made up of two parts. For example, if we were attempting to monitor and control the costs of a delivery service we might measure the cost per tonne delivered. However, 'tonne delivered' would not be a particularly useful cost unit because it would not be valid to compare the cost per tonne delivered from London to Edinburgh with the cost per tonne delivered from London to Brighton. The former journey is much longer and it will almost certainly cost more to deliver a tonne over the longer distance.

Composite cost units assist in overcoming this problem. We could perhaps use a 'tonne-mile' instead. This means that we would record and monitor the cost of carrying one tonne for one mile. The cost per tonne-mile would be a comparable measure whatever the length of journey and this is therefore a valid and useful cost unit for control purposes.

Other examples of composite cost units might be as follows:

Business	*Cost unit*
Hotel	Bed-night
Bus company	Passenger-mile
Hospital	In-patient day

1.4 Cost centres

 The CIMA *Terminology* defines a cost centre as 'a production or service location, function, activity or item of equipment for which costs are accumulated.'

A cost centre is used as a 'collecting place' for costs. The cost of operating the cost centre is determined for the period, and then this total cost is related to the cost units which have passed through the cost centre.

For instance, an example of a production cost centre could be the machine shop in a factory. The production overhead cost for the machine shop might be £100,000 for the period. If 1,000 cost units have passed through this cost centre we might say that the production overhead cost relating to the machine shop was £100 for each unit.

The CIMA definition of a cost centre also mentions a service location, a function, an activity or an item of equipment being used as a cost centre. Examples of these might be as follows but you should try to think of some others:

Type of cost centre	Examples
Service location	Stores, canteen
Function	Sales representative
Activity	Quality control
Item of equipment	Packing machine

If you are finding it difficult to see how a sales representative could be used as a cost centre, then work carefully through the following points:

1. What are the costs which might be incurred in 'operating' a sales representative for one period?

    Examples might be the representative's salary cost, the cost of running a company car, the cost of any samples given away by the representative and so on. Say these amount to £20,000.

2. Once we have determined this cost, the next thing which we need to know is the number of cost units which can be related to the sales representative.

    The cost unit selected might be £100 of sales achieved. If the representative has achieved £200,000 of sales, then we could say that the representative's costs amounted to £10 per £100 of sales. The representative has thus been used as a cost centre or collecting place for the costs, which have then been related to the cost units.

1.5 Classification of costs

You would have seen in your earlier studies that costs can be classified in many different ways. It is necessary to be able to classify all costs, that is, to be able to arrange them into logical groups, in order to devise an efficient system to collect and analyse the costs. The classifications selected and the level of detail used in the classification groupings will depend on the purpose of the classification exercise.

The CIMA *Terminology* defines classification as 'the arrangement of items in logical groups having regard to their nature (subjective classification) or purpose (objective classification)'.

1.5.1 Classification of costs according to their nature

This means grouping costs according to whether they are materials, labour or expense cost. Within each of these classifications there is a number of subdivisions;

for example, within the materials classification the subdivisions might include the following:

(a) Raw materials, that is, the basic raw material used in manufacture.
(b) Components, that is, complete parts which are used in the manufacturing process.
(c) Consumables, that is, cleaning materials, etc.
(d) Maintenance materials, that is, spare parts for machines, lubricating oils, etc.

The list of sub-divisions is not exhaustive, and there may even be further subdivisions of each of these groups. For example, the raw materials may be further divided according to the type of raw material, for instance, steel, plastic, glass, etc.

1.5.2 Classification of costs according to their purpose

When costs are classified having regard to their purpose, they are grouped according to the reason for which they have been incurred. The broadest classification of this type is to divide costs into direct costs and indirect costs.

It is important for you to realise that a particular cost may sometimes be a direct cost and sometimes an indirect cost. It depends on what we are trying to cost.

For example, the salary of the machining department supervisor is a direct cost of that department because it can be specifically identified with the department. However, it is an indirect cost of each of the cost units processed in the machining department because it cannot be specifically identified with any particular cost unit.

1.5.3 Other examples of cost classification

(a) *Fixed and variable costs*. This classification is made according to whether a cost varies in total when the activity level changes. A fixed cost remains unaltered when activity varies. The total expenditure on variable costs will change in line with changes in the level of activity. This particular classification can be particularly useful if we are classifying costs for decision-making purposes.
(b) *Production, selling and administration costs*. This classification is based on a functional analysis of costs. It groups costs according to the function of the business which has incurred them. This sort of analysis is particularly useful for stock valuation purposes. For example, selling overheads should not be included in the valuation of stock because an item which is still held in stock would not yet have incurred any selling overheads.
(c) *Controllable and non-controllable costs*. Costs may be classified in management reporting systems according to whether they are controllable or non-controllable. This means that the costs which are within the control of management are highlighted in the reports so that management action is directed where it is most worthwhile.
(d) *Normal and abnormal costs*. A normal cost is one which management were expecting to incur and which is of the expected order of magnitude. An abnormal cost is one which was not expected or which is larger or smaller than expected. This type of classification is used to draw managers' attention to the cost of abnormal events.
(e) *Relevant and non-relevant costs*. This method of classification divides costs according to whether they are relevant to a decision being taken, or not relevant to the decision. Examples of non-relevant costs are sunk costs or past costs, which you will be learning about in a later chapter.

1.6 Cost behaviour

Many factors affect the level of costs incurred; for instance, inflation will cause costs to increase over a period of time. In the field of cost accounting, when we talk about cost behaviour we are referring to the way in which costs of output are affected by fluctuations in the level of activity.

The level of activity can be measured in many different ways. For example, we can record the number of units produced, miles travelled, hours worked, percentage of capacity utilised and so on.

An understanding of cost behaviour patterns is essential for many management tasks, particularly in the areas of planning, decision-making and control. It would be impossible for managers to forecast and control costs without at least a basic knowledge of the way in which costs behave in relation to the level of activity.

In this section we will look at the most common cost behaviour patterns and we will consider some examples of each.

1.6.1 Fixed cost

The CIMA *Terminology* defines a fixed cost as 'a cost which is incurred for an accounting period, and which, within certain output or turnover limits, tends to be unaffected by fluctuations in the levels of activity (output or turnover)'.

Another term which can be used to refer to a fixed cost is a period cost. This highlights the fact that a fixed cost is incurred according to the time elapsed, rather than according to the level of activity.

A fixed cost can be depicted graphically as shown in Figure 1.1.

Examples of fixed costs are rent, rates, insurance and executive salaries.

The graph shows that the cost is constant (in this case at £5,000) for all levels of activity. However, it is important to note that this is only true for the relevant range of activity. Consider, for example, the behaviour of the rent cost. Within the relevant range it is possible to expand activity without needing extra premises and therefore the rent cost remains constant. However if activity is expanded to the critical point where further premises are needed, then the rent cost will increase to a new, higher level.

This cost behaviour pattern can be described as a stepped fixed cost (Figure 1.2).

The cost is constant within the relevant range for each activity level but when a critical level of activity is reached, the total cost incurred increases to the next step.

The possibility of changes occurring in cost behaviour patterns means that it is unreliable to predict costs for activity levels which are outside the relevant range. For example, our records

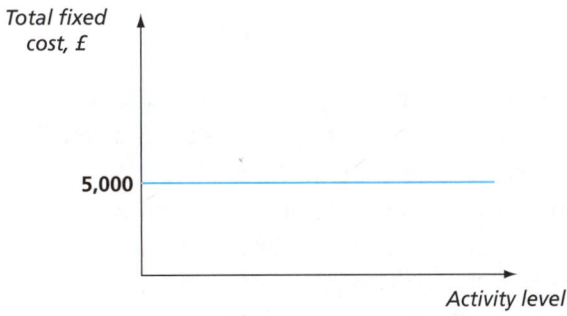

Figure 1.1 Fixed cost

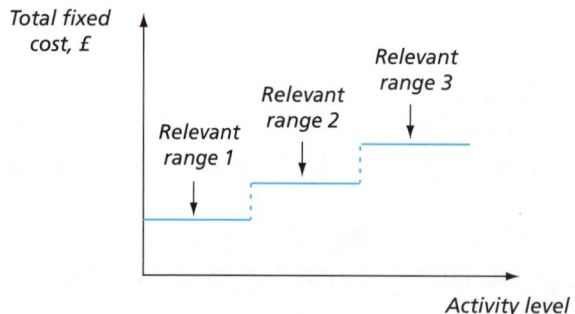

Figure 1.2 Stepped fixed cost

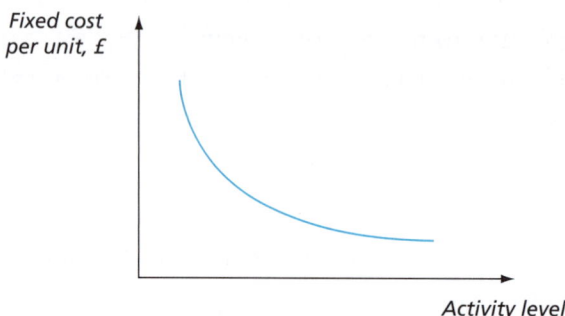

Figure 1.3 Fixed cost per unit

might show the cost incurred at various activity levels between 100 units and 5,000 units. We should therefore try to avoid using this information as the basis for forecasting the level of cost which would be incurred at an activity of, say, 6,000 units, which is outside the relevant range.

When you are drawing or interpreting graphs of cost behaviour patterns, it is important that you pay great attention to the label on the vertical axis. In Figures 1.1 and 1.2 the graphs depicted the total cost incurred. If the vertical axis had been used to represent the fixed cost per unit, then it would look like in Figure 1.3.

The fixed cost per unit reduces as the activity level is increased. This is because the same amount of fixed cost is being spread over an increasing number of units.

1.6.2 Variable cost

> The CIMA *Terminology* defines a variable cost as 'a cost which varies with a measure of activity'.

Examples of variable costs are direct material, direct labour.

The graph in Figure 1.4 depicts a linear variable cost. It is a straight line through the origin which means that the cost is nil at zero activity level. When activity increases the total variable cost increases in direct proportion, that is, if activity goes up by 10 per cent, then the total variable cost also increases by 10 per cent, as long as the activity level is still within the relevant range.

The gradient of the line will depend on the amount of variable cost per unit (Figure 1.5).

The straight line parallel to the horizontal axis depicts a constant variable cost per unit, within the relevant range.

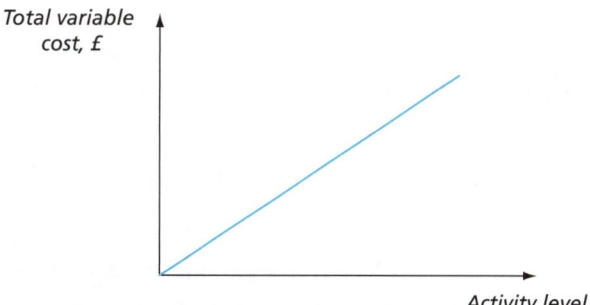

Figure 1.4 Linear variable cost

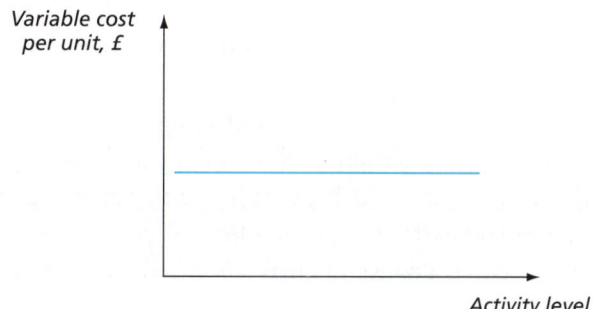

Figure 1.5 Variable cost per unit

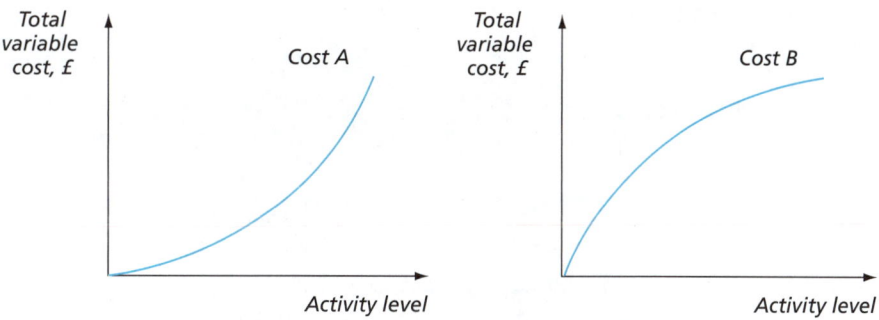

Figure 1.6 Non-liner variable costs

In most examination situations, and very often in practice, variable costs are assumed to be linear. Although many variable costs do approximate to a linear function this assumption may not always be realistic. A variable cost may be non-linear as depicted in either of the diagrams in Figure 1.6.

The graph of cost A becomes steeper as the activity level increases. This indicates that each successive unit of activity is adding more to the total variable cost than the previous unit. An example of a variable cost which follows this pattern could be the cost of direct labour where employees are paid an accelerating bonus for achieving higher levels of output. The graph of cost B becomes less steep as the activity level increases. Each successive unit of activity adds less to total variable cost than the previous unit. An example of a variable cost which follows this pattern could be the cost of direct material where quantity discounts are available.

The important point is that managers should be aware of any assumptions that have been made in estimating cost behaviour patterns. They can then use the information which is based on these assumptions with a full awareness of its possible limitations.

1.6.3 Semi-variable cost

> A semi-variable cost is also referred to as a semi-fixed or mixed cost. The CIMA *Terminology* defines it as 'a cost containing both fixed and variable components and which is thus partly affected by a change in the level of activity'.

A graph of a semi-variable cost might look like the one in Figure 1.7.

Examples of semi-variable costs are gas and electricity. Both of these expenditures consist of a fixed amount payable for the period, with a further variable amount which is related to the consumption of gas or electricity.

Alternatively, a semi-variable cost behaviour pattern might look like the one in Figure 1.8.

This cost remains constant up to a certain level of activity and then increases as the variable cost element is incurred. An example of such a cost might be the rental cost of a photocopier where a fixed rental is paid and no extra charge is made for copies up to a certain number. Once this number of copies is exceeded, a constant charge is levied for each copy taken.

1.6.4 Analysing semi-variable costs

The semi-variable cost behaviour pattern depicted in Figure 1.7 is most common in practice and in examination situations.

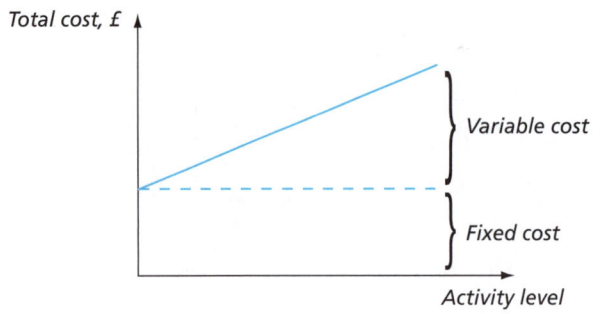

Figure 1.7 Semi-variable cost

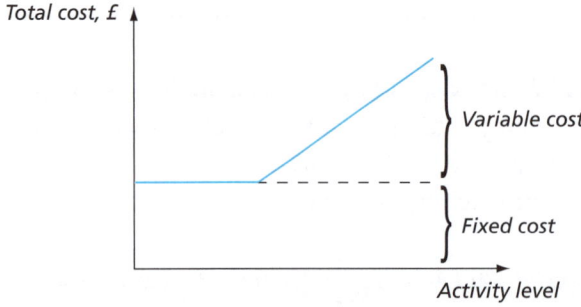

Figure 1.8 Semi-variable cost

When managers have identified a semi-variable cost they will need to know how much of it is fixed and how much is variable. Only when they have determined this will they be able to estimate the cost to be incurred at relevant activity levels. Past records of costs and their associated activity levels are usually used to carry out the analysis. The three most common methods used to separate the fixed and variable elements are as follows.

(a) The high–low method.
(b) The scattergraph method.
(c) The least squares method of regression analysis.

You will have learned about the least squares method in your earlier studies. If you do not recall the details of the method then you should refresh your memory. In this text we will look at methods (a) and (b) in more depth.

(a) The high–low method

This method picks out the highest and lowest activity levels from the available data and investigates the change in cost which has occurred between them. The highest and lowest points are selected to try to use the greatest possible range of data. This improves the accuracy of the result.

We will demonstrate how the method works by using two examples. The first example takes no account of inflation. The second example demonstrates how index numbers can be used to eliminate the effects of inflation.

Example: ignoring inflation A company has recorded the following data for a semi-variable cost:

Month	Activity level units	Cost incurred £
January	1,800	36,600
February	2,450	41,150
March	2,100	38,700
April	2,000	38,000
May	1,750	36,250
June	1,950	37,650

The highest activity level occurred in February and the lowest in May. Since the amount of fixed cost incurred in each month is constant, the extra cost resulting from the activity increase must be the variable cost.

	Activity level units	£
February	2,450	41,150
May	1,750	36,250
Increase	700	4,900

The extra variable cost for 700 units is £4,900. We can now calculate the variable cost per unit.

$$\text{Variable cost} = \frac{£4,900}{700} = £7 \text{ per unit}$$

Substituting back in the data for February, we can determine the amount of fixed cost:

February	£
– total cost	41,150
– variable cost (2,450 units × £7)	17,150
Therefore, fixed cost per month	24,000

Now that the fixed and variable cost elements have been identified, it is possible to estimate the total cost for any activity level within the range 1,750–2,450 units.

Example: taking account of inflation A transport company has recorded the following data for a semi-variable cost, together with the relevant price index relating to each year.

Year	'000 miles travelled	Cost incurred £	Price index
1	2,590	23,680	100
2	2,840	25,631	106
3	3,160	27,302	110
4	3,040	28,759	117

The managers wish to forecast the cost which will be incurred in year 5, when it is estimated that 3,100,000 miles will be travelled and the price index will be at 120.

The first step is to select the highest and lowest activity levels and then use the index numbers to eliminate the effects of inflation.

	'000 miles	£	Cost at year 1 prices, £
High – year 3	3,160	27,302 × 100/110	24,820
Low – year 1	2,590	23,680	23,680
Increase	570		1,140

Variable cost per '000 miles at year 1 prices = £1,140/570 = £2

Fixed cost, substituting in year 1 = £23,680 − (2,590 × £2) = 18,500 at year 1 prices
The cost for year 5 can now be estimated, using a price index of 120.

	£
Variable cost 3,100 × £2 × 120/100	7,440
Fixed cost £18,500 × 120/100	22,200
Total cost estimate	29,640

The major problem with the high–low method is that it takes account of only two sets of data. If these two measurements are not representative of the rest of the data then the estimate of fixed and variable costs may be very inaccurate.

(b) The scattergraph method

This method takes account of all available historical data and it is very simple to use. However, it is very prone to inaccuracies that arise due to subjectivity and the likelihood of human error.

1. First a scattergraph is drawn which plots all available pairs of data on a graph.
2. Then a line of best fit is drawn by eye. This is the line which, in the judgement of the user, appears to be the best representation of the gradient of the sets of points on the graph. This is demonstrated in Figure 1.9.

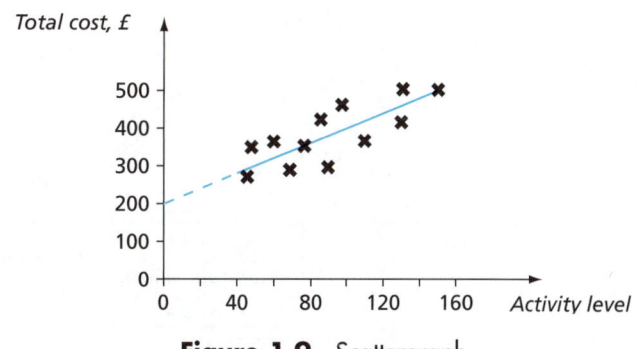

Figure 1.9 Scattergraph

3. The point where the extrapolation of this line cuts the vertical axis (the intercept) is then read off as the total fixed cost element. The variable cost per unit is given by the gradient of the line.

From Figure 1.9, the fixed cost contained within this set of data is adjudged to be £200. The variable cost is calculated as follows.

Cost for zero units = £200
Cost for 150 units = £500

$$\text{Gradient (i.e. variable cost)} = \frac{500 - 200}{150 - 0} = £2 \text{ per unit}$$

1.6.5 Using historical data

The main problem which arises in the determination of cost behaviour is that the estimates are usually based on data collected in the past. Events in the past may not be representative of the future and managers should be aware of this if they are using the information for planning and decision-making purposes.

1.7 The elements of cost

In your earlier studies you will have acquired a thorough knowledge of the build-up of costs using a conventional absorption approach. The following diagram (Figure 1.10) taken from the CIMA *Terminology* is a useful summary of the various cost elements which combine to form total cost.

You should recall from your earlier studies how material and labour costs are collected and analysed to form part of the prime cost of a product or service.

We will spend more time looking at the collection and analysis of overhead, building on your earlier knowledge and seeing how the techniques which you have learned can be applied to more complex situations. The analysis of overhead is the subject of the next chapter.

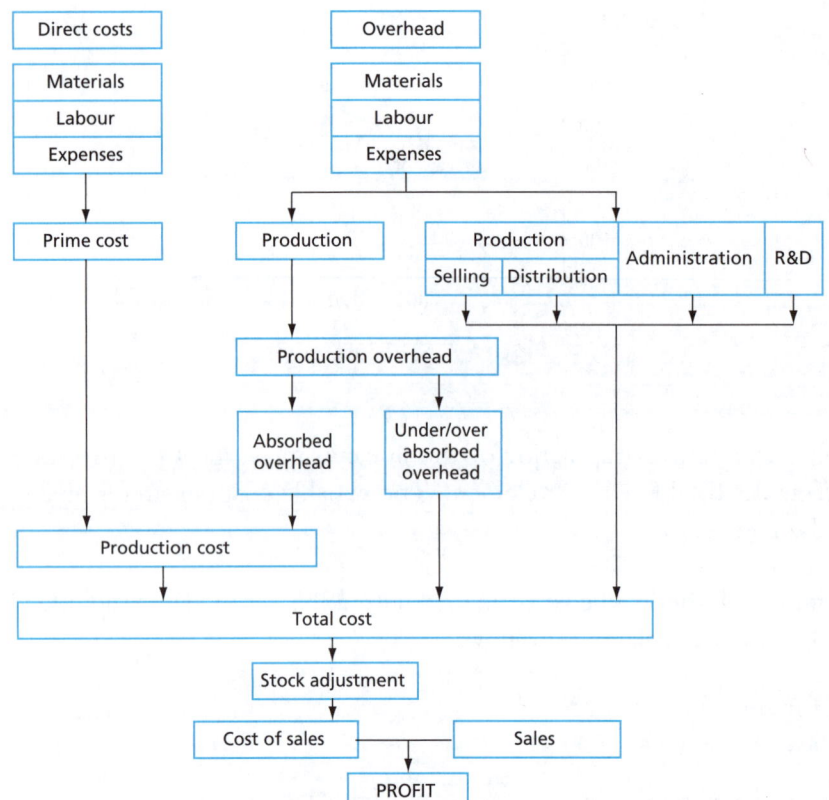

Figure 1.10 Elements of cost

1.8 Summary

In this chapter we have

- Reminded you of some basic cost accounting terms
- Reminded you of the alternative approaches to cost classification
- Revised the techniques of analysing costs according to their behaviour when activity levels change.

Absorption Costing, Activity-based Costing and Marginal Costing

Absorption Costing, Activity-based Costing and Marginal Costing

2

> **LEARNING OUTCOME**
>
> ▶ Explain the possible conflicts between cost accounting for profit reporting and stock valuation and the convenient availability of information for decision-making.

2.1 Introduction

In this chapter we will discuss and demonstrate the alternative cost accounting techniques of absorption costing, activity-based costing and marginal costing.

We will then recognise the alternative uses of cost accounting information and the appropriateness of each technique to those uses.

2.2 Overhead allocation and apportionment

Having selected suitable cost centres for the organisation, the first stage in the analysis of overheads is to determine the overhead cost for each cost centre. This is achieved through the process of allocation and apportionment.

Cost *allocation* is possible when we can identify a cost as specifically attributable to a particular cost centre. For example, the salary of the manager of the packing department can be allocated to the packing department cost centre. It is not necessary to share the salary cost over several different cost centres.

Cost *apportionment* is necessary when it is not possible to allocate a cost to a specific cost centre. In this case the cost is shared out over two or more cost centres according to the estimated benefit received by each cost centre. As far as possible the basis of apportionment is selected to reflect this benefit received. For example, the cost of rent and rates might be apportioned according to the floor space occupied by each cost centre.

The process of allocation and apportionment establishes an estimated overhead cost for each cost centre. It is now possible to calculate overhead absorption rates so that the overheads can be applied to the individual cost units.

2.3 Overhead absorption

There are several different methods which can be used to absorb overheads. You will have learned about them in your earlier studies and we will now review them and consider their relative advantages and disadvantages. The following data will be used to demonstrate their calculation.

Data for cost centre 2, year 7
Total cost centre overhead	£62,100
Production output	13,800 units
Direct labour hours	27,000 hours
Machine hours	34,500 hours
Direct wages cost	£17,250
Direct materials cost	£49,680

The overhead absorption rate for cost centre 2 could be any of the following:

Rate per unit produced $= \dfrac{£62,100}{13,800} = £4.50$ per unit

Direct labour hour rate $= \dfrac{£62,100}{27,000} = £2.30$ per direct labour hour

Machine hour rate $= \dfrac{£62,100}{34,500} = £1.80$ per machine hour

Percentage of direct wages cost $= \dfrac{£62,100}{£17,250} \times 100\% = 360\%$ of direct wages cost

Percentage of direct materials cost $= \dfrac{£62,100}{£49,680} \times 100\%$
$= 125\%$ of direct materials cost

Percentage of prime cost $= \dfrac{£62,100}{£66,930} \times 100\% = 93\%$ of prime cost

2.4 Applying the overhead absorption rate

We have demonstrated the six most common methods of calculating overhead absorption rates but only one of them would be selected for each cost centre. You should already know from your earlier studies how to apply the rates to calculate the overhead cost to be absorbed by each cost unit. However to remind you and to give some revision practice, use the following data to determine the total production cost of job number 123.

Exercise

Job 123 was manufactured solely in one cost centre. A direct labour hour rate is to be used to absorb this cost centre's overhead costs. Data relating to job 123 is as follows:

Direct material cost	£367
Direct labour cost	£405
Direct labour hours	90

Cost centre overheads are budgeted to be £2,300 with budgeted labour hour of 1,000. What is the total production cost of job 123?

 Solution

Job number 123	£
Direct material cost	367
Direct labour cost	405
Prime cost	772
Overhead absorbed (90 hours × £2.30)	207
Total production cost	979

2.5 Selecting the most appropriate absorption rate

A major factor in selecting the absorption rate to be used is a consideration of the practical applicability of the rate. This will depend on the ease of collecting the data required to use the selected rate.

It is generally accepted that a time-based method should be used wherever possible, i.e. the machine hour rate or the labour hour rate. This is because many overhead costs increase with time, for example, indirect wages, rent and rates. Therefore, it makes sense to attempt to absorb overheads according to how long a cost unit takes to produce. The longer it takes, the more overhead will have been incurred in the cost centre during that time.

In addition to these general considerations, each absorption method has its own advantages and disadvantages:

(a) *Rate per unit*. This is the easiest method to apply but it is only suitable when all cost units produced in the period are identical. Since this does not often happen in practice this method is rarely used.
(b) *Direct labour hour rate*. This is a favoured method because it is time-based. It is most appropriate in labour-intensive cost centres, which are becoming rarer nowadays and so the method is less widely used than it has been in the past.
(c) *Machine hour rate*. This is also a favoured method because it is time-based. It is most appropriate in cost centres where machine activity predominates and is therefore more widely used than the direct labour hour rate. As well as absorbing the time-based overheads mentioned earlier, it is more appropriate for absorbing the overheads related to machine activity, such as power, maintenance, repairs and depreciation.

(d) *Direct wages cost percentage.* This method may be acceptable because it is to some extent time-based. A higher direct wages cost may indicate a longer time taken and therefore a greater incidence of overheads during this time. However, the method will not produce equitable overhead charges if different wage rates are paid to individual employees in the cost centre. If this is the case then there may not be a direct relationship between the wages paid and the time taken to complete a cost unit.

(e) *Direct materials cost percentage.* This is not a very logical method because there is no reason why a higher material cost should lead to a cost unit apparently incurring more production overhead cost. The method can be used if it would be too costly and inconvenient to use a more suitable method.

(f) *Prime cost percentage.* This method is not recommended because it combines methods (d) and (e) and therefore suffers from the combined disadvantages of both.

2.6 Predetermined overhead absorption rates

Overhead absorption rates are usually predetermined, that is, they are calculated in advance of the period over which they will be used.

The main reason for this is that overhead costs are not incurred evenly throughout the period. In some months the actual expenditure may be very high and in others it may be relatively low. The actual overhead rate per hour or per unit will therefore be subject to wide fluctuations. If the actual rate was used in product costing then product costs would also fluctuate wildly. Such product costs would be very difficult to use for planning and control purposes.

Fluctuations in the actual level of production would also cause the same problem of fluctuating product costs.

To overcome this problem the absorption rate is determined in advance of the period, using estimated or budget figures for overhead and for the number of units of the absorption base (labour hours or machine hours, etc.).

A further advantage of using predetermined rates is that managers have an overhead rate permanently available which they can use in product costing, price quotations and so on. The actual overhead costs and activity levels are not known until the end of the period. It would not be desirable for managers to have to wait until after the end of the period before they had a rate of overhead that they could use on a day-to-day basis.

2.6.1 Under- or over-absorption of overheads

The problem with using predetermined overhead absorption rates is that the actual figures for overhead and for the absorption base are likely to be different from the estimates used in calculating the absorption rate.

> When this happens, the overhead will be either under- or over-absorbed. If the actual overhead incurred is higher than the overhead absorbed, then overhead is under-absorbed. If the reverse is true then the overhead is over-absorbed. The following example will demonstrate this.

Data for the latest period in two of the cost centres of XY Limited are as follows:

	Machining department	Finishing department
Estimated/budget data		
Production overhead	£340,000	£120,000
Machine hours	170,000	4,200
Direct labour hours	16,500	40,000
Actual results		
Production overhead incurred	£360,000	£129,400
Machine hours	150,000	3,900
Direct labour hours	18,290	44,100

A machine hour rate is used to absorb overhead in the machining department. The finishing department is more labour intensive therefore a labour hour rate is used. The overhead absorption rates (OARs), the overheads absorbed and the under- or over-absorbed overheads are calculated as follows:

	Machining department	Finishing department
OAR	$\dfrac{£340,000}{170,000} = £2/\text{hour}$	$\dfrac{£120,000}{40,000} = £3/\text{hour}$
O/heads absorbed	(£2 × 150,000 hours) £300,000	(£3 × 44,100 hours) £132,300
Actual overhead	£360,000	£129,400
(Under-)/over-absorption	(£60,000)	£2,900

2.6.2 The reasons for under- or over-absorption

The under- or over-absorption has arisen because the actual overhead incurred per hour was different from the predetermined rate per hour. There are two possible causes of this.

(a) The actual number of hours (machine or direct labour) was different from the number contained in the budget data. If this happens, then we would expect the variable element of the overhead to vary in direct proportion to the change in hours, so this part of the absorption rate would still be accurate. However, the fixed overhead would not alter with the hours worked and this means that the actual overhead per hour would be different from the predetermined rate.

(b) The actual production overhead incurred may be different from the estimate contained in the predetermined rate. Apart from the expected change in variable overhead referred to in (a), this would also cause an under- or over-absorption of overhead.

2.6.3 Accounting for under- or over-absorbed overheads

If overheads are under-absorbed, this effectively means that product costs have been understated. It is not usually considered necessary to adjust individual unit costs and therefore stock values are not altered. However, the cost of units sold will have been understated and therefore the under-absorption is charged to the profit and loss account for the period.

The reverse is true for any over-absorption, which is credited to the profit and loss account for the period. Some organisations do not charge or credit the under- or over-absorption to the profit and loss account every period. Instead, the amount for each period is transferred to a suspense account. At the end of the year the net balance on this account is transferred to the profit and loss account. This procedure is particularly appropriate when activity fluctuations cause under- and over-absorptions which tend to cancel each other out over the course of the year.

2.6.4 The problems caused by under- or over-absorption of overheads

If overheads are under-absorbed then managers have been working with unit rates for overheads which are too low. Prices may have been set too low and other similar decisions may have been taken based on inaccurate information. If the amount of under-absorption is significant, then this can have a dramatic effect on reported profit.

Do not make the common mistake of thinking that over-absorption is not such a bad thing because it leads to a boost in profits at the period end. If overhead rates have been unnecessarily high then managers may have set selling prices unnecessarily high, leading to lost sales. Other decisions would also have been based on inaccurate information.

Although it is almost impossible to avoid under- and over-absorption altogether, it is possible to minimise the amount of adjustment necessary at the year end. This is achieved by conducting regular reviews of the actual expenditure and activity levels which are arising. The overhead absorption rate can thus be reviewed to check that it is still appropriate to absorb the overheads sufficiently accurately by the year end. If necessary, the overhead absorption rate can be adjusted to reflect more recent estimates of activity and expenditure levels.

2.7 Illustrative example

You can use the following short example to practise the techniques which we have covered so far in this chapter.

Example

The information given below relates to the forthcoming period for a manufacturer's operation. There are four cost centres of which two are involved in production and two are service cost centres.

	Total	Production departments		Service departments	
		A	B	Canteen	Stores
	£	£	£	£	£
Allocated costs	70,022	21,328	29,928	8,437	10,329
Other costs					
Rent and rates	4,641				
Buildings insurance	3,713				
Electricity and gas	6,800				
Plant depreciation	28,390				
Plant insurance	8,517				
	122,083				
Area occupied (square metres)		7,735	6,188	1,547	3,094
Plant at cost (£000)		1,845	852	–	142
Number of employees		600	300	30	70
Machine hours		27,200	800	–	–
Direct labour hours		6,800	18,000	–	–
Number of stores requisitions		27,400	3,400	–	–

Use this information to calculate a production overhead absorption rate for department A and for department B.

Suggested solution

The first step is to prepare an overhead analysis sheet which shows the apportionment of the overheads, using the most appropriate basis for each.

Overhead item	Basis of apportionment	Total £	Dept A £	Dept B £	Canteen £	Stores £
Allocated costs	–	70,022	21,328	29,928	8,437	10,329
Rent and rates	Floorspace	4,641	1,934	1,547	387	773
Buildings insurance	Floorspace	3,713	1,547	1,238	309	619
Electricity & gas	Floorspace	6,800	2,833	2,267	567	1,133
Depreciation	Plant cost	28,390	18,450	8,520	–	1,420
Insurance	Plant cost	8,517	5,535	2,556	–	426
		122,083	51,627	46,056	9,700	14,700
Canteen	Employees	–	6,000	3,000	(9,700)	700
Stores	Requisitions	–	13,700	1,700	–	(15,400)
		122,083	71,327	50,756	–	–

The rent and rates cost is apportioned as follows:

Total floorspace = 18,564 square metres. Therefore, rent and rates cost = $\frac{£4,641}{18,564}$ = £0.25/sq m.

All of the other apportionments are calculated in the same way.

Since the canteen serves all other departments, its costs must be apportioned first, over the 970 employees in the other departments.

Once the stores have received a charge from the canteen, the total stores costs can be apportioned to the production departments.

Looking at the data for machine hours and direct labour hours in each of the departments, it appears that the most appropriate absorption base for department A is machine hours and for department B is direct labour hours. The absorption rates can now be calculated.

Production department A = £71,327/27,200 = £2.62 per machine hour
Production department B = £50,756/18,000 = £2.82 per direct labour hour

We can now extend the example a little further to practise using the calculated absorption rates.
What is the total production cost of the following job?

	Job 847
Direct material cost	£487
Direct labour cost	£317
Machine hours in department A	195 hours
Direct labour hours in department B	102 hours

The overhead absorption rates can be applied as follows:

	Job 847 £
Direct material cost	487.00
Direct labour cost	317.00
Prime cost	804.00
Production overhead	
Department A 195 hours × £2.62	510.90
Department B 102 hours × £2.82	287.64
Total production cost	1,602.54

See if you can calculate the under- or over-absorbed overhead in each of the departments using the following data:

	Department A	Department B
Actual results		
Overhead incurred	£70,483	£52,874
Direct labour hours	6,740	18,300
Machine hours	27,900	850

The first step is to calculate how much overhead would have been absorbed, based on the *actual* hours and the pre-determined overhead absorption rate for each department. This total can then be compared with the actual overhead incurred.

	Department A	Department B
Overhead absorbed	27,900 × £2.62 = £73,098	18,300 × £2.82 = £51,606
Overhead incurred	£70,483	£52,874
(Under-)/over-absorption	£2,615	(£1,268)

2.8 Recent developments in absorption costing methods

2.8.1 The criticisms of the traditional approach

Historically, the most common method of absorbing production overhead has been based on direct labour hours. This is because production tended to be labour intensive in the past and the mechanisms existed to record the labour hours attributable to particular cost units.

However, modern production methods tend to be more mechanised. This has two main effects:

(a) The nature of production overhead is changing. Costs such as power, machine maintenance and depreciation are becoming larger and more prevalent.
(b) The number of labour hours is reducing. This leads to very high figures for hourly absorption rates based on direct labour.

The use of machine hours as an absorption base can help to overcome this problem, since machine hours are more likely to reflect the incidence of machine-based overheads.

However, modern management accounting systems which use absorption costing have gone further than this and a technique called activity-based costing has been developed.

2.8.2 Activity-based costing

Activity-based costing (ABC) analyses all activities to identify what drives the costs incurred, that is, what causes the costs to increase. These cost drivers may be labour hours or machine hours but they could also be a variety of other factors.

For example, an analysis of quality control activity might identify that quality control costs are driven by the number of production runs, that is, the higher the number of production runs for a particular product, the higher are the quality control costs incurred on its behalf. The quality control costs would then be absorbed into product costs according to the number of production runs set up for that product.

The best way to see how ABC operates is to work through the following example.

Example

Information relating to the four products made and sold by a company is as follows for one period.

	Product			
	A	B	C	D
Output in units	120	100	80	120
	£ per unit	£ per unit	£ per unit	£ per unit
Direct material	40	50	30	60
Direct labour	28	21	14	21
Machine hours per unit	4	3	2	3

The four products are similar and are usually produced in production runs of 20 units and sold in batches of 10 units.

The total of the production overhead for the period has been analysed as follows:

	£
Machine department costs (rent, business rates, depreciation and supervision)	10,430
Set-up costs	5,250
Stores receiving	3,600
Inspection/quality control	2,100
Materials handling and despatch	4,620
	26,000

You have ascertained that the cost drivers to be used in an ABC exercise are as listed below for the overhead costs shown.

Cost pools	Cost driver
Set-up cost	Number of production runs
Stores receiving	Requisitions raised
Inspection/quality control	Number of production runs
Materials handling and despatch	Orders executed

The number of requisitions raised on the stores was 20 for each product, and the number of orders executed was 42, each order being for a batch of 10 of a product.

Calculate the production costs per unit, using ABC.

Solution

Cost drivers

Machine dept. cost per hour = £10,430/1,300 = £8.02
No. of prod'n runs = ouput/20
Set up and inspection/QC costs per run = (£5,250 + £2,100) ÷ 21 = £350
Stores receiving cost per requisition = £3,600/80 = £45
Materials handling cost per order = £4,620/42 = £110

Machine department costs: workings
These costs will be absorbed on the basis of machine hours

	A	B	C	D	Total
Machine hours	480	300	160	360	1,300
Overhead absorbed	£3,851	£2,407	£1,284	£2,888	£10,430

Other overhead costs: workings

	A	B	C	D	Total
Number of production runs	6	5	4	6	21
Set-up and inspection/quality control cost absorbed	£2,100	£1,750	£1,400	£2,100	£7,350
Requisitions raised	20	20	20	20	80
Stores receiving cost absorbed	£900	£900	£900	£900	£3,600
Orders executed (output/10)	12	10	8	12	42
Material handling cost absorbed	£1,320	£1,100	£880	£1,320	£4,620

The costs can now be summarised as follows:

	A £	B £	C £	D £
Direct material	4,800	5,000	2,400	7,200
Direct labour	3,360	2,100	1,120	2,520
Prime cost	8,160	7,100	3,520	9,720
Production overhead:				
Machine department	3,851	2,407	1,284	2,888
Set-up and inspection/QC	2,100	1,750	1,400	2,100
Stores receiving	900	900	900	900
Materials handling and despatch	1,320	1,100	880	1,320
Total production cost	16,331	13,257	7,984	16,928
Production cost per unit	£136.09	£132.57	£99.80	£141.07

You should now understand how cost drivers are used to absorb overheads in an ABC system. You have seen that instead of using a single measure of activity such as direct labour hours, more representative multiple measures of activity are used *(cost drivers)*. You have also seen that costs are collected into *activity cost pools* such as set-up and inspection activity, and materials handling and dispatch activity. These activities can cross the traditional departmental boundaries, that is, several departments can be involved in each activity so that the traditional method of budgeting costs for departments is not a useful basis for an ABC system.

It will be interesting to see how the unit production costs would have differed if a more traditional base had been used to absorb all of the overheads. We have the information available to use 'machine hour rate'.

$$\text{Machine hour absorption rate} = \frac{£26{,}000}{1{,}300} = £20$$

This rate can be applied to absorb all of the overheads into the product costs.

	A £	B £	C £	D £
Prime cost	8,160	7,100	3,520	9,720
Production overhead	9,600	6,000	3,200	7,200
Total production cost	17,760	13,100	6,720	16,920
Production cost per unit compared:				
Blanket machine hour rate	148.00	131.00	84.00	141.00
ABC basis	136.09	132.57	99.80	141.07
Difference	11.91	(1.57)	(15.80)	(0.07)

This comparison shows that a change in the absorption base can have a dramatic effect on the unit costs of product, particularly in the case of products A and C. If the ABC results represent a more realistic indication of the resources used by the products then the information from the ABC system would be more useful for management decisions.

Advocates of ABC argue that it results in more realistic product costs which reflect the resources used in bringing a product to its present location and condition.

2.9 The difference between marginal costing and absorption costing

So far in this text we have worked within the framework of a total costing system. With absorption costing, all stock items are valued at their full production cost. This includes fixed production overhead which has been absorbed using one of the bases which you learned about earlier.

In contrast, marginal costing values all stock items at their variable or marginal costs only. Fixed costs are treated as period costs and are written off in full against the contribution for the period.

Since the two systems value stocks differently, it follows that each will report a different profit figure for the period if stock levels alter.

2.10 Marginal costing and contribution

The terms marginal cost and variable cost tend to be used interchangeably. In marginal costing the variable costs are matched against the sales value for the period to highlight an important performance measure: contribution.

Contribution = sales value − variable costs

It is called contribution because it literally does contribute towards fixed costs and profit. Once the contribution has been calculated for the period, fixed costs are deducted to determine the profit for the period.

2.11 Preparing profit statements using marginal costing and absorption costing

The best way to demonstrate how profit statements are prepared for each of the methods is to look at a worked example.

Example

Using the information below, prepare profit statements for June and July using:

(a) marginal costing,
(b) absorption costing.

A company produces and sells one product only which sells for £50 per unit. There were no stocks at the end of May and other information is as follows.

Standard cost per unit	£
Direct material	18
Direct wages	4
Variable production overhead	3
Budgeted and actual costs per month	
Fixed production overhead	99,000
Fixed selling expenses	14,000
Fixed administration expenses	26,000
Variable selling expenses	10% of sales value

Normal capacity is 11,000 units per month.
The number of units produced and sold was:

	June units	July units
Sales	12,800	11,000
Production	14,000	10,200

2.11.1 Profit statements using marginal costing

A marginal costing system will value all units at the variable production cost of £25 per unit (£18 + £4 + £3).

Profit statements using marginal costing

	June		July	
	£000	£000	£000	£000
Sales revenue		640		550
Less variable cost of sales:				
Opening stock	–		30	
Variable production cost	(14,000 × £25) 350		(10,200 × £25) 255	
	350		285	
Closing stock (1,200 × £25)	(30)		(400 × £25) (10)	
Variable production of sales	320		275	
Variable selling expenses	64		55	
Variable cost of sales		384		330
Contribution		256		220
Less fixed overhead:				
Fixed production overhead	99		99	
Fixed selling expenses	14		14	
Fixed administration expenses	26		26	
		139		139
Profit		117		81

2.11.2 Profit statements using absorption costing

Fixed production overheads are absorbed on the basis of normal capacity which is often the same as budgeted capacity. You should recall that predetermined rates are used partly to avoid the fluctuations in unit cost rates which arise if production levels fluctuate.

$$\text{Fixed production overhead per unit} = \frac{£99,000}{11,000} = £9 \text{ per unit}$$

Full production cost per unit = £25 variable cost + £9 fixed cost = £34 per unit

This full production cost of £34 per unit will be used to value all units under absorption costing.

Since the production level is not equal to the normal capacity in either June or July there will be under- or over-absorbed fixed production overhead in both months. It is probably easier to calculate this before commencing on the profit statements.

	June	July
	£000	£000
Fixed production overhead absorbed	(14,000 units × £9) 126	(10,200 units × £9) 91.8
Fixed production overhead incurred	99	99.0
Over/(under) absorption	27	(7.2)

Profit statements using absorption costing

	June		July	
	£000	£000	£000	£000
Sales revenue		640.0		550.0
Less full production cost of sales:				
Opening stock	–		40.8	
Full production cost	(14,000 × £34) 476.0		(10,200 × £34) 346.8	
	476.0		387.6	
Closing stock	(1,200 × £34) (40.8)		(400 × £34) (13.6)	
Full production cost of sales		435.2		374.0
Gross profit		204.8		176.0
Less selling and administration expenses:				
Variable selling expenses	64.0		55.0	
Fixed selling expenses	14.0		14.0	
Fixed administration expenses	26.0		26.0	
		104.0		95.0
		100.8		81.0
Over/(under) absorbed fixed production overhead		27.0		(7.2)
Net profit		127.8		73.8

If overheads have been over-absorbed, then too much has been charged as a cost of production. This amount is therefore credited back to increase the net profit. If overheads have been under-absorbed, the amount is debited to reduce the net profit.

2.12 Reconciling the profit figures

It is important to be able to reconcile the profit figures of these alternative approaches.

2.12.1 Reconciling the profits given by the different methods

The profit differences are caused by the different valuations given to the closing stocks in each period. With absorption costing an amount of fixed production overhead is carried forward in stock to be charged against sales of later periods.

If stocks increase then absorption costing profits will be higher than marginal costing profits. This is because some of the fixed overhead is carried forward in stock instead of being written off against sales for the period.

If stocks reduce then marginal costing profits will be higher than absorption costing profits. This is because the fixed overhead which had been carried forward in stock with absorption costing is now being released to be charged against the sales for the period.

A profit reconciliation for the previous example might look like this:

	June	July
	£000	£000
Marginal costing profit	117.0	81.0
Adjust for fixed overhead in stock		
Stock increase 1,200 units × £9 per unit	10.8	
Stock decrease 800 units × £9 per unit		(7.2)
Absorption costing profit	127.8	73.8

The under- and over-absorptions of overhead are not shown in the reconciliation statements because they were written off each month. If they had been carried forward and not written off each month, they would need to be included in the reconciliation statements.

2.12.2 Reconciling the profits for different periods

You should also know how to reconcile the profits for different periods using the same method.

(a) For marginal costing, the unit rates and the amount of fixed costs charged each period are constant. Therefore, the only thing which could have caused the profit difference was the change in sales volume. The lower sales volume in July resulted in a lower contribution and therefore a lower profit (since the amount of fixed cost remained constant).

The contribution per unit is £20 as follows:

	£ per unit
Selling price	50
Variable production cost	(25)
Variable selling cost	(5)
Contribution	20

The marginal costing profit figures can be reconciled as follows:

	£000
Marginal costing profit for June	117
Decrease in sales volume for July	
1,800 units × £20 contribution	36
Marginal costing profit for July	81

(b) For absorption costing the major part of the profit difference is caused by the change in sales volume. However, a further difference is caused by the adjustments for under- and over-absorbed fixed production overhead in each of the two periods.

The profit per unit with absorption costing is £11 as follows:

	£ per unit
Selling price	50
Total production cost	(34)
Variable selling cost	(5)
Profit	11

The absorption costing profit figures can be reconciled as follows:

	£000
Absorption costing profit for June	127.8
Decrease in sales volume for July	
1,800 units × £11 profit	(19.8)
Adjustments for under/over absorption:	
June	(27.0)
July	(7.2)
Absorption costing profit for July	73.8

This may look confusing because both the under- and over-absorptions are deducted. This is because the over-absorption for June made profit for that month higher, therefore it must be deducted to arrive at July's profit. Similarly, the under-absorption in July made July's profit lower than June's, therefore it must also be deducted in the reconciliation.

2.12.3 Profit differences in the long term

The two different costing methods produce profit differences only in the short term when stocks fluctuate. If stocks remain constant then there will be no profit differences between the two methods.

In the long term, the total reported profit will be the same whichever method is used. This is because all of the costs incurred will eventually be charged against sales; it is merely the timing of the sales that causes the profit differences from period to period.

2.13 Should marginal costing or absorption costing be used?

There is no absolutely correct answer as to when marginal costing or absorption costing is preferable. However, as we shall see it is generally accepted that marginal costing statements provide the best information for the purposes of management decision-making.

Supporters of absorption costing argue that fixed production overheads are a necessary cost of production and they should therefore be included in the unit cost used for stock valuation. External financial reporting requires the use of absorption costing.

If stocks are built up for sale in a future period, for example in distilling, then absorption costing smooths out profits by carrying forward the fixed production overheads to be matched against the sales as they are made.

Supporters of marginal costing argue that management attention is concentrated on the more controllable measure of contribution. They say that the apportionment of fixed production overhead to individual units is carried out on a purely arbitrary basis, is of little use for decision-making and can be misleading.

2.14 Summary

In this chapter we have considered three alternative costing systems: absorption costing, activity-based costing and marginal costing.

We then considered the appropriateness of each of these methods for decision-making.

Breakeven Analysis

Breakeven Analysis

3

LEARNING OUTCOMES

▶ Discuss the usefulness of dividing costs into variable and fixed components in the context of short-term decision-making.

▶ Apply variable/fixed cost analysis in multiple product contexts to breakeven analysis and product mix decision-making; including circumstances where there are multiple constraints and linear programming methods are needed to reach 'optimal' solutions.

3.1 Introduction

In this chapter we will apply the principles of marginal costing and contribution analysis to breakeven analysis and simple activity change related short-term decisions.

3.2 Breakeven or cost–volume–profit analysis

Cost–volume–profit (CVP) analysis is defined in CIMA's *Official Terminology* as 'the study of the effects on future profit of changes in fixed cost, variable cost, sales price, quantity and mix'.

A more common term used for this type of analysis is *breakeven analysis*. However, this is somewhat misleading, since it implies that the focus of the analysis is the *breakeven point* – that is, the level of activity which produces neither profit nor loss. You will see in this chapter that the scope of CVP analysis is much wider than this, as indicated in the definition. However, you should be aware that the terms 'breakeven analysis' and 'CVP analysis' tend to be used interchangeably.

3.2.1 Calculating the breakeven point

Contribution is so called because it literally does contribute towards fixed costs and profit. As sales revenues grow from zero, the contribution also grows until it just covers the fixed costs. This is the breakeven point where neither profits nor losses are made.

It follows that to break even, the amount of contribution must exactly match the amount of fixed costs. If we know how much contribution is earned from each unit sold, then we can calculate the number of units required to break even as follows:

$$\text{Breakeven point in units} = \frac{\text{Fixed costs}}{\text{Contribution per unit}}$$

For example, suppose that an organisation manufactures a single product, incurring variable costs of £30 per unit and fixed costs of £20,000 per month. If the product sells for £50 per unit, then the breakeven point can be calculated as follows:

$$\text{Breakeven point in units} = \frac{£20,000}{£50 - £30} = 1,000 \text{ units per month}$$

3.3 The margin of safety

> The margin of safety is the difference between the expected level of sales and the breakeven point. The larger the margin of safety, the more likely it is that a profit will be made, i.e. if sales start to fall there is more leeway before the organisation begins to incur losses. (Obviously, this statement is made on the assumption that projected sales volumes are above the breakeven point.)

In the above example, if forecast sales are 1,700 units per month, the margin of safety can be easily calculated.

$$\begin{aligned}
\text{Margin of safety} &= \text{projected sales} - \text{breakeven point} \\
&= 1,700 \text{ units} - 1,000 \text{ units} \\
&= 700 \text{ units per month, or 41\% of sales} \left(\frac{700}{1,700} \times 100\%\right)
\end{aligned}$$

The margin of safety should be expressed as a percentage of projected sales to put it in perspective. To quote a margin of safety of 700 units without relating it to the projected sales figure is not giving the full picture.

The margin of safety might also be expressed as a percentage of the breakeven value, that is, 70 per cent of the breakeven value in this case.

The margin of safety can also be used as one route to a profit calculation. We have seen that the contribution goes towards fixed costs and profit. Once breakeven point is reached the fixed costs have been covered. After the breakeven point there are no more fixed costs to be covered and all of the contribution goes towards making profits grow.

In our example the monthly profit from sales of 1,700 units would be £14,000.

$$\begin{aligned}
\text{Margin of safety} &= 700 \text{ units per month} \\
\text{Monthly profit} &= 700 \times \text{contribution per unit} \\
&= 700 \times £20 \\
&= £14,000
\end{aligned}$$

3.4 The contribution to sales (C/S) ratio

The contribution to sales ratio is usually expressed as a percentage. It can be calculated for the product in our example as follows:

$$\text{Contribution to sales (C/S) ratio} = \frac{£20}{£50} \times 100\%$$
$$= 40\%$$

A higher contribution to sales ratio means that contribution grows more quickly as sales levels increase. Once the breakeven point has been passed, profits will accumulate more quickly than for a product with a lower contribution to sales ratio.

You might sometimes see this ratio referred to as the profit–volume (P/V) ratio.

If we can assume that a unit's variable cost and selling price remain constant then the C/S ratio will also remain constant. It can be used to calculate the breakeven point as follows (using the data from the earlier example):

$$\text{Breakeven point in sales value} = \frac{\text{Fixed costs}}{\text{C/S ratio}} = \frac{£20,000}{0.40} = £50,000$$

This can be converted to 1,000 units as before by dividing by the selling price of £50 per unit.

Exercise

A company manufactures and sells a single product that has the following cost and selling price structure:

	£/unit	£/unit
Selling price		120
Direct material	22	
Direct labour	36	
Variable overhead	14	
Fixed overhead	12	
		(84)
Profit per unit		36

The fixed-overhead absorption rate is based on the normal capacity of 2,000 units per month. Assume that the same amount is spent each month on fixed overheads.

Budgeted sales for next month are 2,200 units.

You are required to calculate:

(i) the breakeven point, in sales units per month;
(ii) the margin of safety for next month;
(iii) the budgeted profit for next month;
(iv) the sales required to achieve a profit of £96,000 in a month.

Solution

(i) The key to calculating the breakeven point is to determine the contribution per unit.

Contribution per unit = £120 − (£22 + £36 + £14) = £48

STUDY MATERIAL P2

$$\text{Breakeven point} = \frac{\text{Fixed overhead}}{\text{Contribution per unit}}$$

$$= \frac{£12 \times 2{,}000}{£48} = 500 \text{ units}$$

(ii) Margin of safety = budgeted sales − breakeven point

$$= 2{,}200 - 500$$

$$= 1{,}700 \text{ units (or } \frac{1{,}700}{2{,}200} \times 100\% = 77\% \text{ of budgeted sales)}$$

(iii) Once breakeven point has been reached, all of the contribution goes towards profits because all of the fixed costs have been covered.

Budgeted profit = 1,700 units margin of safety × £48 contribution per unit
= £81,600

(iv) To achieve the desired level of profit, sufficient units must be sold to earn a contribution that covers the fixed costs and leaves the desired profit for the month.

$$\text{Number of sales units required} = \frac{\text{Fixed overhead} + \text{desired profit}}{\text{Contribution per unit}}$$

$$= \frac{(£12 \times 2{,}000) + £96{,}000}{£48} = 2{,}500 \text{ units}$$

3.5 Drawing a basic breakeven chart

A basic breakeven chart records costs and revenues on the vertical axis and the level of activity on the horizontal axis. Lines are drawn on the chart to represent costs and sales revenue. The breakeven point can be read off where the sales revenue line cuts the total cost line.

We will use the following example to demonstrate how to draw a breakeven chart. The data is:

Selling price	£50 per unit
Variable cost	£30 per unit
Fixed costs	£20,000 per month
Forecast sales	1,700 units per month

> ❗ You must be able to prepare breakeven charts to scale using data provided. To give yourself some practice, it would be a good idea to follow the step-by-step guide that follows to produce your own chart on a piece of graph paper.

- *Step 1. Select appropriate scales for the axes and draw and label them.* Your graph should fill as much of the page as possible. This will make it clearer and easier to read. You can make sure that you do this by putting the extremes of the axes right at the end of the available space.

  The furthest point on the vertical axis will be the monthly sales revenue, that is,

  1,700 units × £50 = £85,000

The furthest point on the horizontal axis will be monthly sales volume of 1,700 units.

Make sure that you do not need to read data for volumes higher than 1,700 units before you set these extremes for your scales.

- *Step 2. Draw the fixed cost line and label it.* This will be a straight line parallel to the horizontal axis at the £20,000 level.

  The £20,000 fixed costs are incurred in the short term even with zero activity.

- *Step 3. Draw the total cost line and label it.* The best way to do this is to calculate the total costs for the maximum sales level, which is 1,700 units in our example. Mark this point on the graph and join it to the cost incurred at zero activity, that is, £20,000

	£
Variable costs for 1,700 units (1,700 × £30)	51,000
Fixed costs	20,000
Total cost for 1,700 units	71,000

- *Step 4. Draw the revenue line and label it.* Once again the best way is to plot the extreme points. The revenue at maximum activity in our example is 1,700 × £50 = £85,000. This point can be joined to the origin, since at zero activity there will be no sales revenue.
- *Step 5. Mark any required information on the chart and read off solutions as required.* Check that your chart is accurate by reading off the measures that we have already calculated in this chapter: the breakeven point, the margin of safety, the profit for sales of 1,700 units.
- *Step 6. Check the accuracy of your readings using arithmetic.* It is always good examination practice to check the accuracy of your answers and make adjustments for any errors in your chart (if you have time!)

The completed graph is shown in Figure 3.1 below:

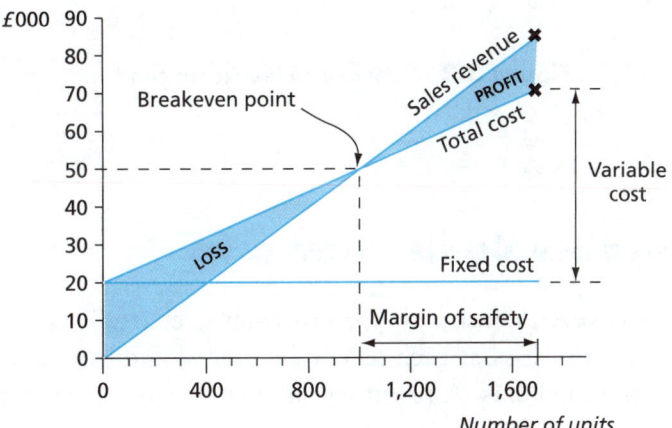

Figure 3.1 Basic breakeven chart

 Your own graph should be considerably larger than this: a full A4 graph-ruled sheet is recommended to facilitate ease of interpretation.

3.6 The contribution breakeven chart

One of the problems with the conventional or basic breakeven chart is that it is not possible to read contribution directly from the chart. A contribution breakeven chart is based on the same principles but it shows the variable cost line instead of the fixed cost line (Figure 3.2). The same lines for total cost and sales revenue are shown so the breakeven point and profit can be read off in the same way as with a conventional chart. However, it is also possible to read the contribution for any level of activity.

Using the same basic example as for the conventional chart, the total variable cost for an output of 1,700 units is 1,700 × £30 = £51,000. This point can be joined to the origin since the variable cost is nil at zero activity.

The contribution can be read as the difference between the sales revenue line and the variable cost line.

This form of presentation might be used when it is desirable to highlight the importance of contribution and to focus attention on the variable costs.

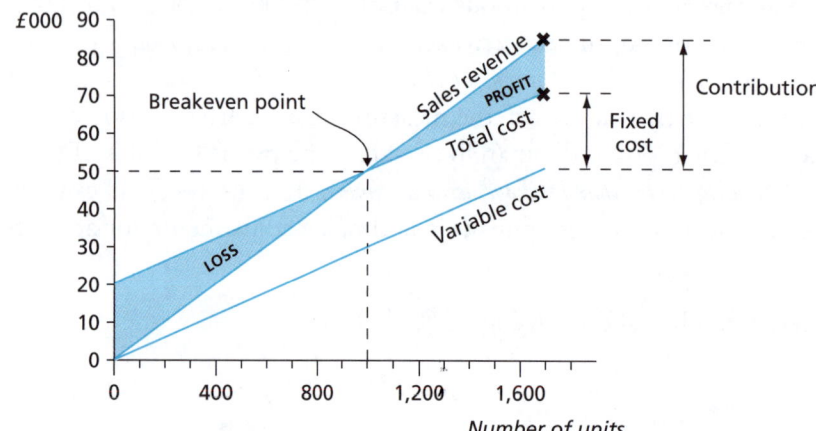

Figure 3.2 Contribution breakeven chart

3.7 The profit–volume chart

Another form of breakeven chart is the profit–volume chart. This chart plots a single line depicting the profit or loss at each level of activity. The breakeven point is where this line cuts the horizontal axis. A profit–volume chart for our example will look like Figure 3.3.

The vertical axis shows profits and losses and the horizontal axis is drawn at zero profit or loss.

At zero activity the loss is equal to £20,000, that is, the amount of fixed costs. The second point used to draw the line could be the calculated breakeven point or the calculated profit for sales of 1,700 units.

The profit–volume chart is also called a profit graph or a contribution–volume graph.

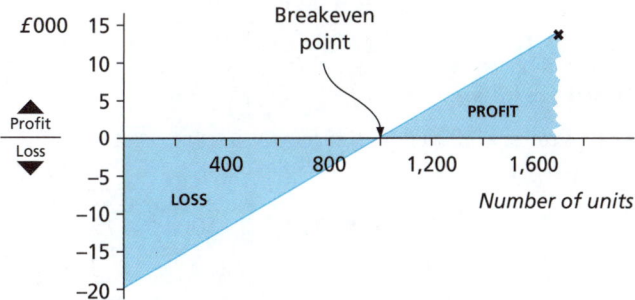

Figure 3.3 Profit–volume chart

Exercise

Make sure that you are clear about the extremes of the chart axes. Practise drawing this chart to scale on a piece of graph paper.

3.7.1 The advantage of the profit–volume chart

The main advantage of the profit–volume chart is that it is capable of depicting clearly the effect on profit and breakeven point of any changes in the variables. An example will show how this can be done.

Example

A company manufactures a single product which incurs fixed costs of £30,000 per annum. Annual sales are budgeted to be 70,000 units at a sales price of £30 per unit. Variable costs are £28.50 per unit.

(a) Draw a profit–volume chart, and use it to determine the breakeven point.
   The company is now considering improving the quality of the product and increasing the selling price to £35 per unit. Sales volume will be unaffected, but fixed costs will increase to £45,000 per annum and variable costs to £33 per unit.
(b) Draw, on the same graph as for part (a), a second profit–volume chart and comment on the results.

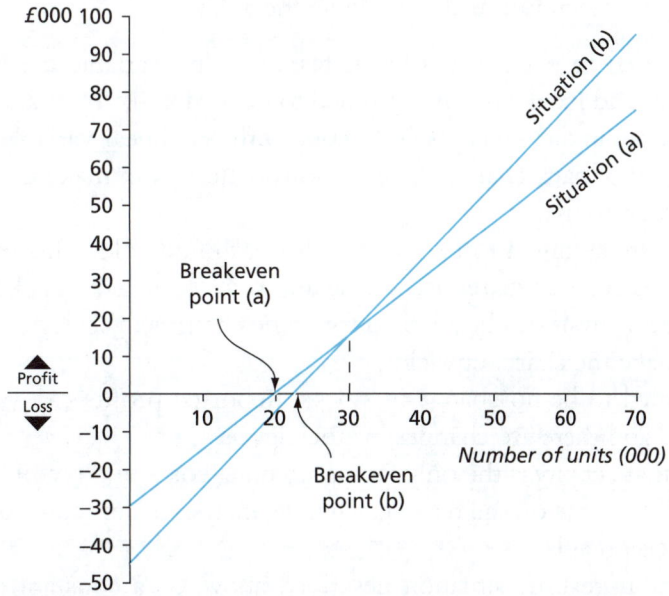

Figure 3.4 Showing changes with a profit–volume chart

Solution

The profit–volume chart is shown in Figure 3.4.
The two lines have been drawn as follows:

- *Situation (a)*. The profit for sales of 70,000 units is £75,000.

	£000
Contribution 70,000 × £(30 − 28.50)	105
Fixed costs	(30)
Profit	75

This point is joined to the loss at zero activity, £30,000, that is, the fixed costs.

- *Situation (b)*. The profit for sales of 70,000 units is £95,000.

	£000
Contribution 70,000 × £(35 − 33)	140
Fixed costs	45
Profit	95

This point is joined to the loss at zero activity, £45,000, that is, the fixed costs.

Comment on the results

The chart depicts clearly the larger profits available from option (b). It also shows that the breakeven point increases from 20,000 units to 22,500 units but that this is not a large increase when viewed in the context of the projected sales volume. It is also possible to see that for sales volumes above 30,000 units the profit achieved will be higher with option (b). For sales volumes below 30,000 units option (a) will yield higher profits (or lower losses).

The profit–volume chart is the clearest way of presenting information like this. If we attempted to draw two conventional breakeven charts on one set of axes the result would be a jumble that would be very difficult to interpret.

3.8 The limitations of breakeven (or CVP) analysis

The limitations of the practical applicability of breakeven analysis and breakeven charts stem mostly from the assumptions that underlie the analysis:

(a) Costs are assumed to behave in a linear fashion. Unit variable costs are assumed to remain constant and fixed costs are assumed to be unaffected by changes in activity levels. The charts can in fact be adjusted to cope with non-linear variable costs or steps in fixed costs, but too many changes in behaviour patterns can make the charts very cluttered and difficult to use.

(b) Sales revenues are assumed to be constant for each unit sold. This may be unrealistic because of the necessity to reduce the selling price to achieve higher sales volumes. Once again, the analysis can be adapted for some changes in selling price but too many changes can make the charts unwieldy.

(c) There is assumed to be no change in stocks. Reported profits can vary if absorption costing is used and there are changes in stock levels.

(d) It is assumed that activity is the only factor affecting costs, and factors such as inflation are ignored. This is one of the reasons why the analysis is limited to being essentially a short-term decision aid.

(e) Apart from the unrealistic situation described above of a constant product mix, the charts can only be applied to a single product or service. Not many organisations have a single product or service, and if there is more than one then the apportionment of fixed costs between them becomes arbitrary.

(f) The analysis seems to suggest that as long as the activity level is above the breakeven point, then a profit will be achieved. In reality certain changes in the cost and revenue patterns may result in a second breakeven point after which losses are made. This situation will be depicted in the next section of this chapter.

3.9 The economist's breakeven chart

An economist would probably depict a breakeven chart as shown in Figure 3.5.

The total cost line is not a straight line that climbs steadily as in the accountant's chart. Instead it begins to reduce initially as output increases because of the effect of economies of scale. Later it begins to climb upwards according to the law of diminishing returns.

The revenue line is not a straight line as in the accountant's chart. The line becomes less steep to depict the need to give discounts to achieve higher sales volumes.

However, you will see that within the middle range the economist's chart does look very similar to the accountant's breakeven chart. This area is marked as the relevant range in Figure 3.5.

For this reason it is unreliable to assume that the cost–volume–profit relationships depicted in breakeven analysis are relevant across a wide range of activity. In particular, Figure 3.5 shows that the constant cost and price assumptions are likely to be unreliable at very high or very low levels of activity. Managers should therefore ensure that they work within the relevant range for the available data, that is, within the range over which the depicted cost and revenue relationships are more reliable.

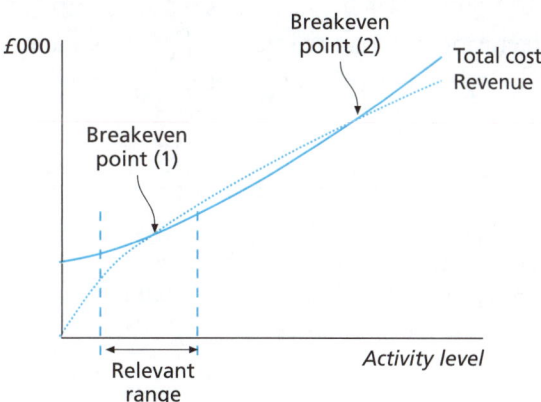

Figure 3.5 The economist's breakeven chart

3.10 Using costs for decision-making

Most management decisions involve a change in the level, method or mix of activities in order to maximise profits. The only costs that should be considered in decision-making are those that will be altered as a result of the decision. Those costs that will be affected by the decision may be referred to as *relevant costs*, while others are non-relevant and should be ignored in the analysis.

It is often the case that variable costs are relevant whereas fixed costs are not, unless the decision affects the cost structure of the organisation. Thus, information for decision-making should always be based on marginal costing principles, since marginal costing focuses on the variable costs and is not concerned with arbitrary apportionment of fixed costs that will be incurred anyway.

3.10.1 Short-term decision-making

An important point that you should appreciate for all of the decision-making techniques that you learn about in this chapter is that they are usually most relevant to short-term, one-off decisions. Furthermore, as you will see with the example of the minimum-price quotation, the analysis provides only a starting point for management decisions. The financial figures are only part of the information needed for a fully informed decision. It is also important to consider the non-financial factors which might be relevant to the decision.

> You must get into the habit of considering non-financial and qualitative factors in any decision. Many exam questions will specifically ask you to do so.

3.11 Evaluating proposals

As an introduction to using cost information to evaluate proposals, use your understanding of breakeven analysis and cost behaviour patterns to evaluate the proposals in the following exercise.

Exercise

A summary of a manufacturing company's budgeted profit statement for its next financial year, when it expects to be operating at 75 per cent of capacity, is given below.

	£	£
Sales 9,000 units at £32		288,000
Less:		
direct materials	54,000	
direct wages	72,000	
production overhead – fixed	42,000	
– variable	18,000	
		186,000
Gross profit		102,000
Less: admin., selling and dist'n costs:		
– fixed	36,000	
– varying with sales volume	27,000	
		63,000
Net profit		39,000

It has been estimated that:

(i) if the selling price per unit were reduced to £28, the increased demand would utilise 90 per cent of the company's capacity without any additional advertising expenditure;
(ii) to attract sufficient demand to utilise full capacity would require a 15 per cent reduction in the current selling price and a £5,000 special advertising campaign.

You are required to:

(a) calculate the breakeven point in units, based on the original budget;
(b) calculate the profits and breakeven points which would result from each of the two alternatives and compare them with the original budget.

Solution

(a) First calculate the current contribution per unit.

	£000	£000
Sales revenue		288
Direct materials	54	
Direct wages	72	
Variable production overhead	18	
Variable administration, etc.	27	
		171
Contribution		117
Contribution per unit (÷ 9,000 units)		£13

Now you can use the formula to calculate the breakeven point.

$$\text{Breakeven point} = \frac{\text{Fixed costs}}{\text{Contribution per unit}} = \frac{£42,000 + £36,000}{£13} = 6,000 \text{ units}$$

(b) *Alternative (i)*

Budgeted contribution per unit	£13
Reduction in selling price (£32 − £28)	£4
Revised contribution per unit	£9

$$\text{Revised breakeven point} = \frac{£78,000}{£9} \qquad 8,667 \text{ units}$$

$$\text{Revised sales volume} = 9,000 \times \frac{90}{75} \qquad 10,800 \text{ units}$$

Revised contribution = 10,800 × £9	£97,200
Less fixed costs	£78,000
Revised profit	£19,200

Alternative (ii)

Budgeted contribution per unit	£13.00
Reduction in selling price (15% × £32)	£4.80
Revised contribution per unit	£8.20

$$\text{Revised breakeven point} = \frac{£78,000 + £5,000}{£8.20} \qquad 10,122 \text{ units}$$

$$\text{Revised sales volume} = 9,000 \text{ units} \times \frac{100}{75} \qquad 12,000 \text{ units}$$

Revised contribution = 12,000 × £8.20	£98,400
Less fixed costs	£83,000
Revised profit	£15,400

Neither of the two alternative proposals is worthwhile. They both result in lower forecast profits. In addition, they will both increase the breakeven point and will therefore increase the risk associated with the company's operations. This exercise has shown you how an understanding of cost behaviour patterns and the manipulation of contribution can enable the rapid evaluation of the financial effects of a proposal. We can now expand it to demonstrate another aspect of the application of marginal costing techniques to short-term decision-making.

 Exercise

The manufacturing company decided to proceed with the original budget and has asked you to determine how many units must be sold to achieve a profit of £45,500.

 Solution

Once again, the key is the required contribution. This time the contribution must be sufficient to cover both the fixed costs and the required profit. If we then divide this amount by the contribution earned from each unit, we can determine the required sales volume.

$$\text{Required sales} = \frac{\text{Fixed costs} + \text{required profit}}{\text{Contribution per unit}}$$

$$= \frac{(£42,000 + £36,000) + £45,500}{£13} = 9,500 \text{ units}$$

3.12 Multi-product CVP analysis

The basic breakeven model can be used satisfactorily for a business operation with only one product. The model has to be adapted somewhat when one is considering a business operation with several products.

A simple example can be developed to illustrate the various model adaptations that are possible.

Example

A business operation produces three products, the X, the Y and the Z. Relevant details are:

	X	Y	Z
Normal sales mix (units)	2 :	2 :	1
	£	£	£
Selling price per unit	9	7	5
Variable cost per unit	6	5	1
Contribution per unit	3	2	4
Forecast unit sales	400	400	200

Fixed costs are £2,000 per period, not attributable to individual products.
A budget for the forecast is as follows:

	X	Y	Z	Total
	£	£	£	£
Sales revenue	3,600	2,800	1,000	7,400
Variable costs	2,400	2,000	200	4,600
Contribution	1,200	800	800	2,800
Fixed costs				2,000
Profit				800

The objective is to construct a CVP chart for the business operation. Several alternative approaches are possible and three are now considered (Figure 3.6).

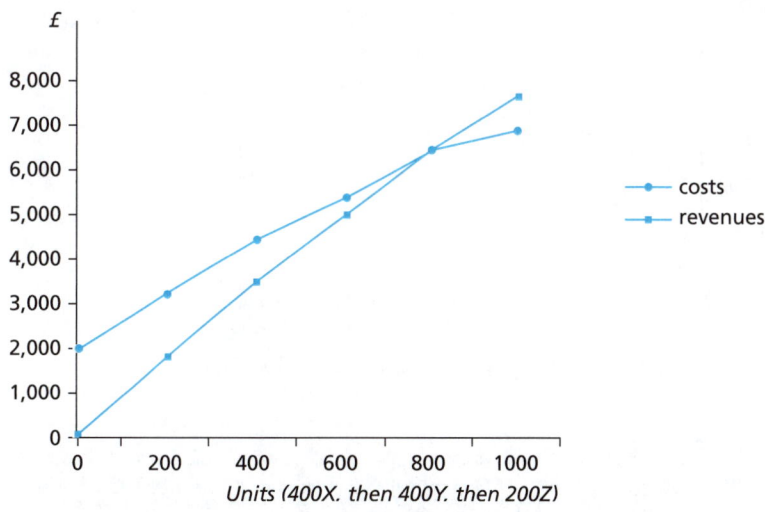

Figure 3.6 CVP chart – X, Y and Z in sequence

1. Consider the products in sequence, X then Y then Z.
   In this case it can be seen that breakeven occurs at 800 units of sales (400X plus 400Y) and the margin of safety is 200 units of Z (Figure 3.7).

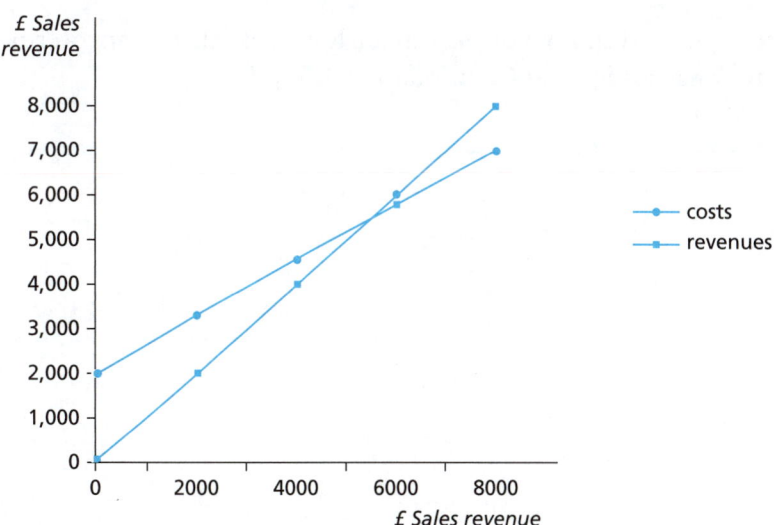

Figure 3.7 CVP chart – sales with constant product mix

2. Consider output in terms of £ sales and assume a constant product mix (2X:2Y:1Z).
   Inspection of the budget (above) shows that £1 sales is associated with £0.6216 variable costs (that is, £4,600 variable costs ÷ £7,400 sales). The contribution per £1 sales is £0.3784 (i.e. £1 − £0.6216). So, if the fixed costs are £2,000 then the breakeven point is £5,285 sales and the margin of safety is £2,115 (i.e. £7,400 forecast sales − £5,285).
3. Consider output in terms of percentage of forecast sales and a constant product mix.

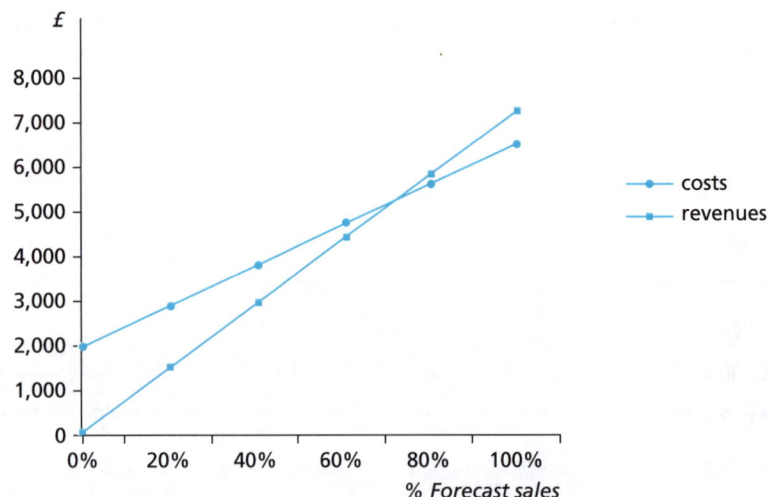

Figure 3.8 CVP chart – percentage of forecast sales

Inspection of the budget (Figure 3.8) shows that 1 per cent of forecast sales is associated with a contribution of £28.00 (i.e. £2,800 total contribution ÷ 100 per cent). So, if fixed costs are £2,000 it follows that the breakeven point is 71.43 per cent and the margin of safety is 28.57 per cent.

The general point of the foregoing discussion is that output can be viewed in several different ways. Cost–volume–profit analysis exercises can adopt any of these different ways.

3.13 Summary

In this chapter we have seen how breakeven analysis and related short-term activity decisions rely on marginal costing and Contribution analysis.

Reading 3

"Of interest to students studying papers in the Management Accounnt Pillar in helping them to recognise the relevance of Breakeven Analysis to investment decisions"

Operational Gearing
Gearing up for success?/Time to get into top gear?
G J Steven
Napier University

Many of the risks faced by a company are determined by the external environment. However, risk is also affected by internal decisions, including, decisions about how a company is to be financed and the cost structure to be adopted by a company. While financial gearing (one of the determinants of financial risk) which considers sources of long-term finance will be known to CIMA students who have studied financial accounting, operational gearing might not be so familiar. But it is important to measure and understand operational gearing to gain a full appreciation of a company's risk profile and the consequences of adopting a particular cost structure.

In simple terms, the cost structure of a company is made up of fixed and variable costs. The proportion of fixed and variable costs adopted by a company is largely a consequence of its business strategy. For example, a company that manufactures its own products or provides services using its own staff will tend to have a higher proportion of fixed costs compared to variable costs. And a company that obtains its products for resale from another manufacturer or uses contractors to provide its services will tend to have a higher proportion of variable costs.

Operational gearing (or operating leverage) is based on the mix of fixed and variable costs in a company's cost structure. Operational gearing can be determined in different ways. However, the simplest method is to consider the level of contribution earned in relation to sales i.e. the contribution to sales ratio (C/S ratio). A low C/S ratio signifies that a company has a high proportion of variable costs compared to fixed costs; and a high C/S ratio signifies that it has a low proportion of variable costs compared to fixed costs. But why is this important?

Table 1 contains data in respect of two companies that operate in the same business sector, sell similar products, are of equivalent size and have similar financial gearing ratios. The key difference between the companies is their differing cost structures. Company A has a high level of fixed costs since it since it manufactures its products. Company B has a high level of variable costs since it purchases its products from another manufacturer. The C/S ratios calculated for Company A (80%) and Company B (40%) confirm this key difference between these companies.

The data in Table 2 is based on three levels of sales and assumes that the C/S ratio and fixed costs remain constant across this range of activity. In practice, these figures may not remain constant due to the impact of economies of scale, learning effect and semi-fixed costs. The profit volume graph in Table 3, based on the data in Table B, demonstrates the significance of the differing C/S ratios for the two companies.

The profit volume graph in Table 3 illustrates that each company has a different profit profile across a range of sales. Company A has higher losses than Company B when sales are below break-even but higher profits when sales are above break-even. Why does this occur? Company A has a higher level of fixed costs than Company B and these fixed costs will be incurred irrespective of the level of sales achieved. However, when sales are above break-even, Company A reaps the reward of having a higher C/S ratio since it earns more for every product sold compared to Company B. So which company has the better operating gearing ratio? Company A, which is highly geared? Or Company B, which has a low gearing ratio?

Risk takers will prefer Company A since it offers higher levels of return if the company is successful. Risk takers are more concerned with the upside of an investment. However, the risk-averse will prefer Company B as it would produce lower losses if there is downturn in trading conditions. The risk-averse are more concerned with the downside of an investment.

Managers may also use operational gearing to influence the overall risk profile of a company. For example, managers of highly financially geared companies operating in risky business sectors may seek to reduce risk by adopting a lower level of operational gearing. Equally, companies with low levels of business and financial risks may take on higher levels of operational gearing to improve potential returns when sales are high.

There is, consequently, no right or wrong structure. It depends on business strategy, management attitude towards risk and other risks faced by a company.

The data, calculations and profit-volume graph in Tables 4, 5 and 6 for Companies C and D (that are similar in every respect with the exception of their cost structures) present a more realistic picture. Companies with different cost structures will not have the same break-even points. However, the dilemma is the same: which cost structure is best? Company C which has a lower breakeven point but offers poorer returns when sales are high? Or, Company D which offers higher returns but has a higher break-even point and will produce greater losses when sales are low? Once again, there is no simple answer.

Operational gearing is not just of interest to managers, it is also of interest to investors since it may affect their investment decisions. While investors may have a view on an appropriate level of operational gearing for a company based on their understanding of its business, they cannot confirm that view since it is not possible to calculate a reliable gearing ratio from published accounts. Interestingly, an article published in Investors Weekly in 2005 recommended that an operational gearing ratio should be included in published accounts to provide this information to investors.

Managers must be aware of the impact of operational gearing on profits and risk to make good business decisions. Investors also require information about operational risk to allow them to make informed investment decisions. It is time to understand the importance of operational gearing for business and investment decisions and appreciate that there is no simple view on what constitutes an acceptable ratio.

Further Reading

Horngren, C.T., Bhimani, A. Datar, S.M. and Foster, G., (2004) *Management and Cost Accounting (3rd Edition)*, Pearson Education Ltd.
Roy-Chaudhuri, S., (2005) The case for a new measure, *Investors Weekly*, December.
Wilkes, C. and Burke, L., (2006) *Management Accounting: Decision Management*, Elsevier.

Table 1

Company A		*Company B*	
Sales price per unit	£5.00	Sales price per unit	£5.00
Variable costs per unit	£1.00	Variable costs per unit	£3.00
Contribution per unit	£4.00	Contribution per unit	£2.00
Contribution to sales ratio	80%	Contribution to sales ratio	40%
Fixed costs	£20,000	Fixed costs	£10,000

Table 2

Company A			
Sales (£)	0	25,000	50,000
Contribution (£)	0	20,000	40,000
Fixed costs (£)	20,000	20,000	20,000
Profit/-Loss (£)	−20,000	0	20,000
Company B			
Sales (£)	0	25,000	50,000
Contribution (£)	0	10,000	20,000
Fixed costs (£)	10,000	10,000	10,000
Profit/-Loss (£)	−10,000	0	10,000

Table 3

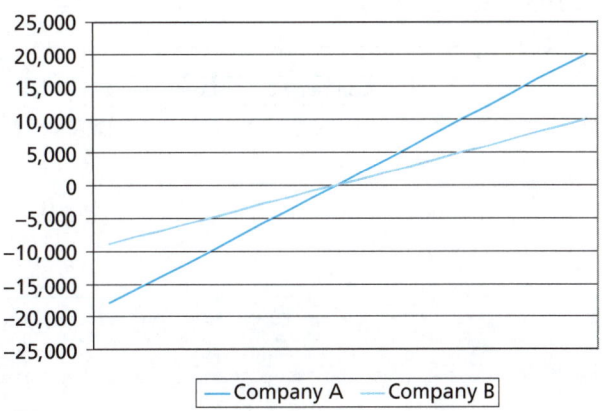

Profit-Volume Graph

Table 4

Company C		Company D	
Sales price per unit	£100	Sales price per unit	£100
Variable costs per unit	£68	Variable costs per unit	£40
Contribution per unit	£32	Contribution per unit	£60
Contribution to sales ratio	32%	Contribution to sales ratio	60%
Fixed costs	£314,000	Fixed costs	£625,000

Table 5

Company C			
Sales (£)	800,000	1,100,000	1,400,000
Contribution (£)	256,000	352,000	448,000
Fixed costs (£)	314,000	314,000	314,000
Profit/-Loss (£)	−58,000	38,000	134,000
Company D			
Sales (£)	800,000	1,100,000	1,400,000
Contribution (£)	480,000	660,000	840,000
Fixed costs (£)	625,000	625,000	625,000
Profit/-Loss (£)	−145,000	35,000	215,000

Table 6

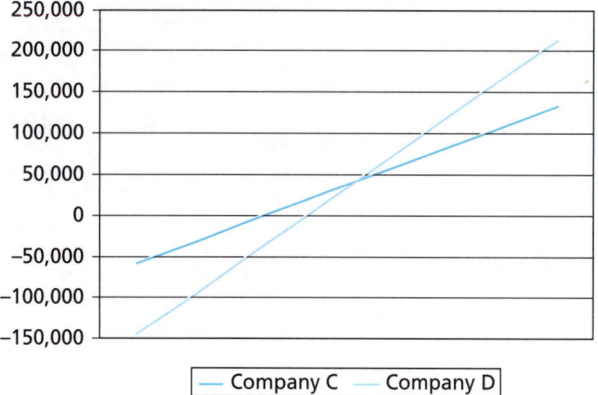

Revision Questions

Question 1 Multiple choice

1.1 A Ltd has fixed costs of £60,000 per annum. It manufactures a single product that it sells for £20 per unit. Its contribution to sales ratio is 40 per cent.

A Ltd's breakeven point in units is:

(A) 1,200
(B) 3,000
(C) 5,000
(D) 7,500.

1.2 B Ltd manufactures a single product that it sells for £9 per unit. Fixed costs are £54,000 per month and the product has a variable cost of £6 per unit.

In a period when actual sales were £180,000, B Ltd's margin of safety, in units, was:

(A) 2,000
(B) 14,000
(C) 18,000
(D) 20,000.

1.3 A company makes and sells three products: R, S and T. Extracts from the weekly profit statements are as follows:

	R	S	T	Total
	$	$	$	$
Sales	10,000	15,000	20,000	45,000
Variable cost of sales	4,000	9,000	10,000	23,000
Fixed costs*	3,000	3,000	3,000	9,000
Profit	3,000	3,000	7,000	13,000

* general fixed costs absorbed using a unit absorption rate

If the sales revenue mix of products produced and sold were to be changed to: R 20%, S 50%, T 30% then the new average contribution to sales ratio

(A) would be higher.
(B) would be lower.
(C) would remain unchanged.
(D) cannot be determined without more information. **(2 marks)**

1.4 Z Limited is a hotel that serves cakes and gateaux in its coffee shop. An analysis of its internal costs has revealed that the variable cost of preparing its own gateaux is £5.50 per gateau compared to the price of £8.00 per gateau that would be charged by an external bakery. Z Limited employs a chef to prepare the gateaux at a salary of £1,000 per month. This chef is not able to carry out any other work in the hotel and is the only employee capable of preparing the gateaux.

Calculate the minimum monthly number of sales of gateaux at which it is worthwhile preparing the gateaux in the hotel. **(2 marks)**

The following data are to be used when answering questions 1.5 to 1.7

M plc is evaluating three possible investment projects and uses a 10% discount rate to determine their net present values.

Investment	A	B	C
	£000	£000	£000
Initial Investment	400	450	350
Incremental cashflows			
Year 1	100	130	50
Year 2	120	130	110
Year 3	140	130	130
Year 4	120	130	150
Year 5*	100	150	100
Net present value	39	55	48

*includes £20,000 residual value for each investment project.

Question 2 Objective test questions

2.1 OT Ltd plans to produce and sell 4,000 units of product C each month, at a selling price of £18 per unit. The unit cost of product C is as follows:

	£ per unit
Variable cost	8
Fixed cost	4
	12

Calculate (to the nearest whole number) the monthly margin of safety, as a percentage of planned sales.

2.2 Is the following statement *true* or *false*?
The P/V ratio is the ratio of profit generated to the volume of sales.

2.3 Product J generates a contribution to sales ratio of 30 per cent. Fixed costs directly attributable to product J amount to £75,000 per month. Calculate the sales revenue required to achieve a monthly profit of £15,000.

2.4 Match the following terms with the labels **a** to **d** on the graph.

- Margin of safety
- Fixed cost
- Contribution
- Profit.

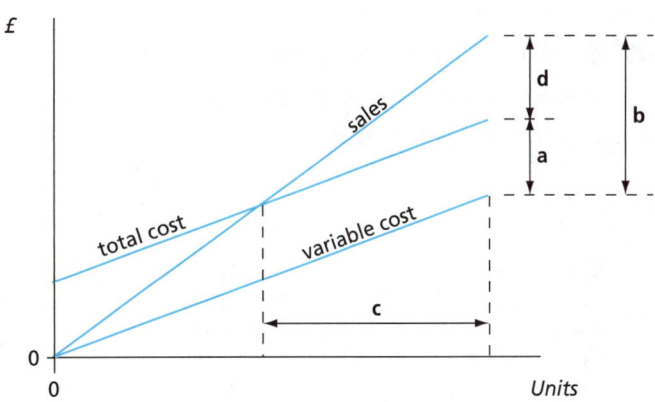

2.5 Which of the following statements about a profit–volume chart are *true*?

(a) The profit line passes through the origin.
(b) Other things being equal, the angle of the profit line becomes steeper when the selling price increases.
(c) Contribution cannot be read directly from the chart.
(d) The point where the profit line crosses the vertical axis is the breakeven point.
(e) Fixed costs are shown as a line parallel to the horizontal axis.

Question 3 Profit statements and decision-making

BSE Veterinary Services is a specialist laboratory carrying out tests on cattle to ascertain whether the cattle have any infection. At present, the laboratory carries out 12,000 tests each period but, because of current difficulties with the beef herd, demand is expected to increase to 18,000 tests a period, which would require an additional shift to be worked.

The current cost of carrying out a full test is:

	£ per test
Materials	115
Technicians' wages	30
Variable overhead	12
Fixed overhead	50

Working the additional shift would:

(i) require a shift premium of 50 per cent to be paid to the technicians on the additional shift;
(ii) enable a quantity discount of 20 per cent to be obtained for all materials if an order was placed to cover 18,000 tests;
(iii) increase fixed costs by £700,000 per period.

The current fee per test is £300.

Requirements

(a) Prepare a profit statement for the current 12,000 capacity.
(b) Prepare a profit statement if the additional shift was worked and 18,000 tests were carried out.
(c) Comment on three other factors that should be considered before any decision is taken.

Question 4 Profit–volume graphs

(a) MC Ltd manufactures one product only, and for the last accounting period has produced the simplified profit and loss statement below:

	£	£
Sales		300,000
Costs		
Direct materials	60,000	
Direct wages	40,000	
Prime cost	100,000	
Variable production overhead	10,000	
Fixed production overhead	40,000	
Fixed administration overhead	60,000	
Variable selling overhead	40,000	
Fixed selling overhead	20,000	
		270,000
Net profit		30,000

You are required to construct a profit–volume graph from which you should state the breakeven point and the margin of safety.

(b) Based on the above, draw separate profit–volume graphs to indicate the effect on profit of each of the following:

  (i) an increase in fixed cost;
  (ii) a decrease in variable cost;
  (iii) an increase in sales price;
  (iv) a decrease in sales volume.

Question 5 Breakeven charts

The following data is available concerning HF Ltd's single product Q.

	£ per unit	£ per unit
Selling price		50
Variable cost		
Direct material	7	
Direct labour	8	
Variable overhead	5	
		20
Contribution		30
Fixed overhead		15
Profit		15

A total of 1,000 units of product Q are produced and sold each month.

Requirements

(a) Using a separate piece of graph paper for each, draw the following breakeven charts and mark on each the breakeven point, the margin of safety and the monthly profit.

  (i) conventional/basic breakeven chart;
  (ii) contribution breakeven chart;
  (iii) profit–volume chart.

(b) Discuss the usefulness of each chart from a point of view of management decision-making.

Solutions to Revision Questions

✓ Solution 1

1.1 Answer: (D)

Contribution per unit = 40% of selling price = £8

$$\text{Breakeven point} = \frac{£60,000}{£8} = 7,500 \text{ units}$$

1.2 Answer: (A)

Contribution per unit = £9 − £6 = £3

$$\text{Breakeven point} = \frac{\text{Fixed costs}}{\text{Contribution per unit}} = \frac{£54,000}{£3} = 18,000 \text{ units}$$

Margin of safety = Actual sales − breakeven sales

$$= \frac{£180,000}{£9} - 18,000 = 2,000 \text{ units}$$

1.3 Answer: (B)

Contribution/Sales ratios are: R 60%, S 40%, and T 50%
Now = $22,000/$45,000 = 0.489
New = (0.6 × 0.2) + (0.4 × 0.5) + (0.5 × 0.3) = 0.47

1.4 Variable cost saving per gateaux = £2.50
Fixed cost = £1,000 per month
Minimum quantity = £1,000/£2.50 = **400 gateaux**

✓ Solution 2

2.1 Monthly fixed costs = 4,000 units × £4 = £16,000.

$$\text{Breakeven point} = \frac{\text{Fixed costs}}{\text{Contribution per unit}} = \frac{£16,000}{£18 - £8} = 1,600 \text{ units}$$

$$\text{Margin of safety \%} = \frac{\text{Planned sales} - \text{breakeven sales}}{\text{Planned sales}} \times 100\%$$

$$= \frac{4,000 - 1,600}{4,000} \times 100\% = 60\%.$$

2.2 *False.* The P/V ratio is another term for the C/S ratio. It measures the ratio of the contribution to sales.

2.3 Required sales value = $\dfrac{\text{Required contribution}}{\text{C/S ratio}} = \dfrac{£75{,}000 + £15{,}000}{0.30} = £300{,}000.$

2.4 (a) Fixed cost
  (b) Contribution
  (c) Margin of safety
  (d) Profit.

2.5 (a) *False.* The profit line passes through the breakeven point on the horizontal axis, and cuts the vertical axis at the point where the loss is equal to the fixed costs.
  (b) *True.* Profits increase at a faster rate if the selling price is higher.
  (c) *True.* A contribution breakeven chart is needed for this.
  (d) *False.* The breakeven point is where the profit line cuts the horizontal axis.
  (e) *False.* No fixed cost line is shown on a profit–volume chart.

✓ Solution 3

- In part (b) do not be tempted to use unit rates to calculate the new level of fixed costs. The current level of fixed costs is £600,000 *per period*. This will increase by £700,000.
- Also in part (b), notice that the shift premium applies only to the technicians working on the additional shift. It does not apply to all technicians' wages.
- In part (c) you may have thought of other, equally valid, factors to be considered. In an examination, if you are asked for three factors do not waste valuable time by suggesting more than three.

(a) Profit statement for current 12,000 capacity

		£000
Sales	12,000 tests @ £300/test	3,600
Direct materials	12,000 tests @ £115/test	(1,380)
Direct labour	12,000 tests @ £30/test	(360)
Variable overhead	12,000 tests @ £12/test	(144)
Contribution		1,716
Fixed costs	12,000 tests @ £50/test	(600)
Profit		1,116

(b) Profit statement for 18,000 capacity, with additional shift

		£000	£000
Sales	18,000 tests @ £300/test		5,400
Direct materials	18,000 tests @ £92/test		(1,656)
Direct labour	12,000 tests @ £30/test	(360)	
	6,000 tests @ £45/test	(270)	
			(630)
Variable overhead	18,000 tests @ £12/test		(216)
Contribution			2,898
Fixed costs			(1,300)
Profit			1,598

(c) Three other factors that should be considered are:
- Will the increase in demand continue in the long run, or is it short-lived? If it is thought that it will continue in the long run, management should consider expanding its permanent workforce so that shift premiums can be avoided.
- Will the quality of the test decrease if more tests are carried out in the same time period? Also, purchasing materials at a 20 per cent discount may indicate a decrease in the quality of the materials.
- The elasticity of demand for the test. If demand is relatively inelastic, it may be more economic to increase the price of the test.

✓ Solution 4

- Try to obtain a piece of graph paper and practise drawing your graphs to scale. Remember to use the whole of the paper – do not produce a tiny graph in the corner of the sheet.
- Remember that the graph in part (a) will cut the vertical axis at the point equal to the fixed costs, that is, the loss when no sales are made.
- Practice good exam technique: check your breakeven point arithmetically to verify that your graph is accurate.

(a)
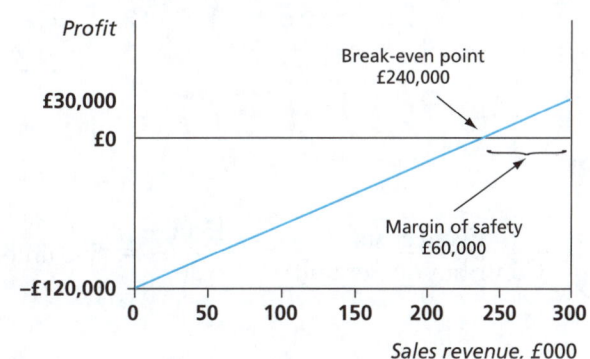

(b) These graphs show increase or decrease in profit by $+x$ or $-x$.

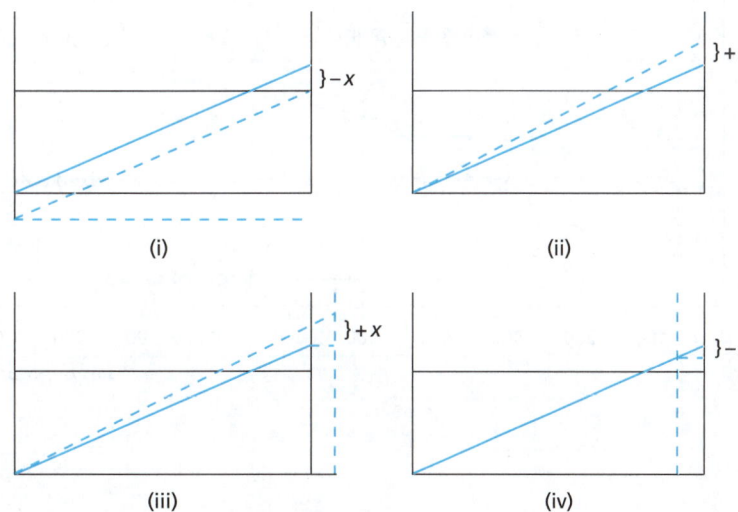

(i) An increase in fixed cost
(ii) A decrease in variable cost
(iii) An increase in sales price
(iv) A decrease in sales volume.

Solution 5

- Do not be tempted to skip this question. Use graph paper and practise drawing clear, neat breakeven charts to scale.
- To earn full marks your chart should have a title, the axes should be labelled, and the breakeven point, margin of safety and monthly profit should be clearly marked.
- Remember to take with you into the exam a ruler, a sharp pencil and an eraser.
- Choose your scales carefully to produce a large, clear chart.
- Prepare some preliminary calculations and label them clearly for the marker to see.
- Work accurately but quickly – breakeven charts can be very time-consuming to draw!
- Check the accuracy of your charts by performing a quick calculation of the breakeven point.

Preliminary calculations

	£	£
Sales value for 1,000 units 1,000 × £50		50,000
Total cost for 1,000 units:		
variable cost 1,000 × £20	20,000	
fixed cost 1,000 × £15	15,000	
		35,000
Profit for 1,000 units		15,000

Check calculation

$$\text{Breakeven point} = \frac{\text{Fixed costs}}{\text{Contribution per unit}} = \frac{£15,000}{£30} = 500 \text{ units}$$

(a) (i)

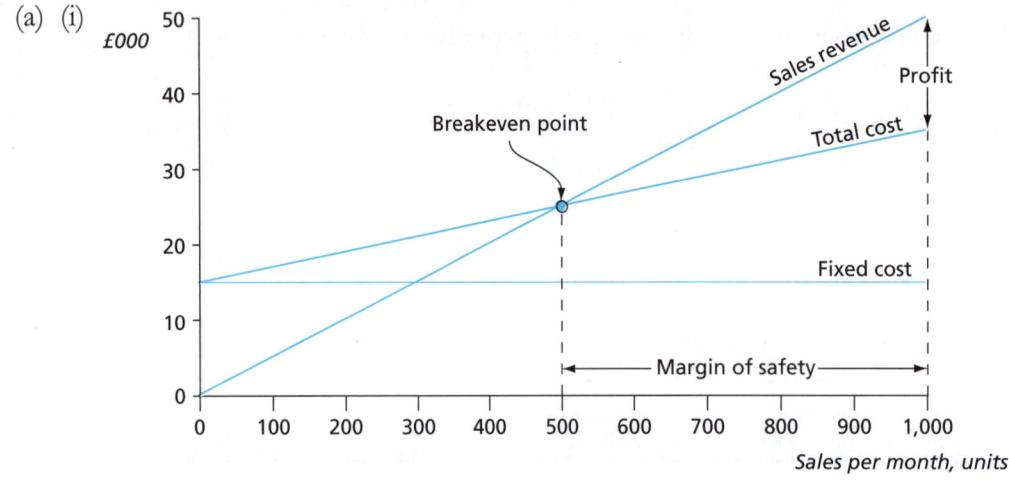

(ii)

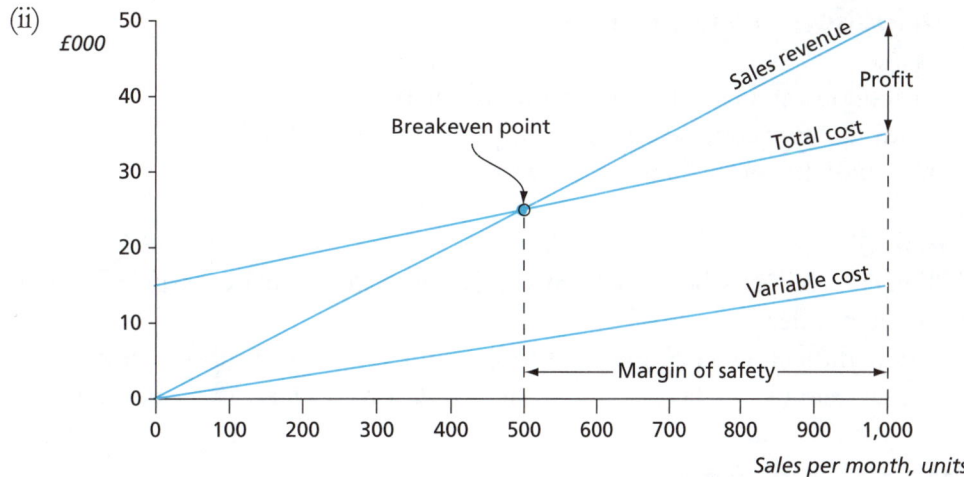

(iii)

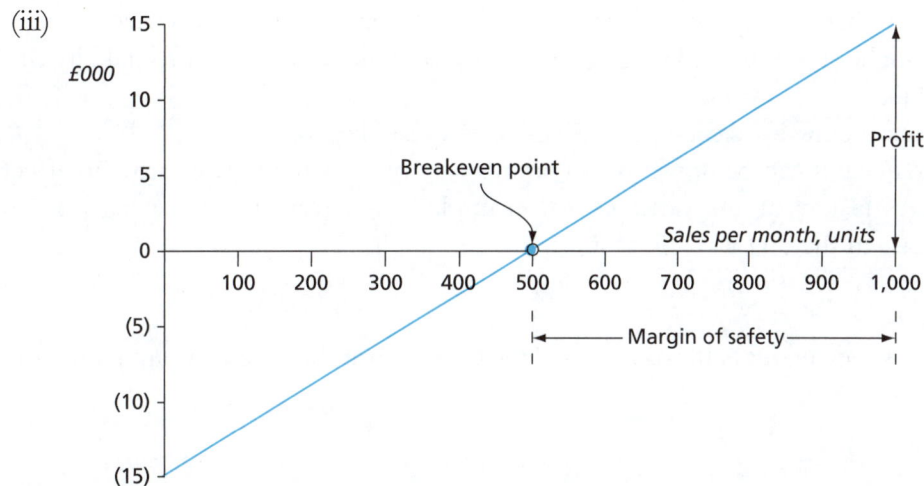

(b) Breakeven charts are useful for management decision-making because they present an easily understandable pictorial representation of the relationship between costs, volume and profit. Each of the graphs has advantages and limitations.

Conventional/basic breakeven chart

Advantages
- Shows clearly the constant nature of the fixed costs.
- The angle of the profit 'wedge' gives a visual representation of the profitability of the product: the wider the angle, the motablere rapidly profits will grow once the breakeven point has been reached. Conversely, the wider the angle the more rapidly losses will be incurred when sales volume falls below breakeven.

Disadvantages
- Although profit can be read from the chart, readings at two separate points are required in order to do so.
- It can be difficult to adapt the chart to show the effect of changes in any of the variables, for example, an increase in the selling price or a decrease in the unit variable cost.
- Contribution cannot be read directly from the chart.

Contribution breakeven chart

Advantages
- Contribution can be read directly from the chart.
- As with the conventional chart, the angle of the profit 'wedge' gives a visual representation of the profitability of the product.

Disadvantages
- Although profit can be read from the chart, readings at two separate points are required in order to do so.
- It can be difficult to adapt the chart to show the effect of changes in any of the variables, for example, an increase in the selling price or a decrease in the unit variable cost.

Profit–volume chart

Advantages
- Profit or loss for any level of activity can be read directly from the chart.
- The angle of the profit line gives a visual representation of the profitability of the product.
- The loss below breakeven point is very clearly highlighted.
- Several charts can be drawn on a common set of axes to show clearly the effect of changes in any of the variables, for example, an increase in the selling price or a decrease in the unit variable cost.

Disadvantages
- The cost behaviour patterns are not depicted, for example, the constant nature of the fixed costs.

Relevant Cost and Short-term Decisions

Relevant Cost and Short-term Decisions

4

> **LEARNING OUTCOMES**
>
> ▶ Discuss the principles of decision making including the identification of relevant cash flows and their use alongside non-quantifiable factors in making round judgements.
>
> ▶ Explain why joint costs must be allocated to final products for financial reporting purposes, but why this is unhelpful when decisions concerning process and product viability have to be taken.
>
> ▶ Discuss the usefulness of dividing costs into variable and fixed components in the context of short-term decision-making.

4.1 Introduction

In this chapter we will consider a number of short-term decision-making scenarios and how to solve them using relevant costs and revenues.

4.2 Relevant costs

> Relevant costs are those which will be affected by the decision being taken. All relevant costs should be considered in management decision-making. If a cost will remain unaltered regardless of the decision being taken, then it is called a non-relevant cost.

4.2.1 Non-relevant costs

Costs that are not usually relevant in management decisions include the following:

(a) Sunk or past costs, that is money already spent that cannot now be recovered. An example of a sunk cost is expenditure that has been incurred in developing a new product. The money cannot be recovered even if a decision is taken to abandon further development of the new product. The cost is therefore not relevant to future decisions concerning the product.

(b) Absorbed fixed overheads that will not increase or decrease as a result of the decision being taken. The amount of overhead to be absorbed by a particular cost unit might alter because of the decision; however, this is a result of the company's cost accounting procedures for overheads. If the actual amount of overhead incurred by the company will not alter, then the overhead is not a relevant cost.

(c) Expenditure that will be incurred in the future, but as a result of decisions taken in the past that cannot now be changed. These are known as committed costs. They can sometimes cause confusion because they are future costs. However, a committed cost will be incurred regardless of the decision being taken and therefore it is not relevant. An example of this type of cost could be expenditure on special packaging for a new product, where the packaging has been ordered and delivered but not yet paid for. The company is obliged to pay for the packaging even if they decide not to proceed with the product; therefore it is not a relevant cost.

(d) Historical cost depreciation that has been calculated in the conventional manner. Such depreciation calculations do not result in any future cash flows. They are merely the book entries that are designed to spread the original cost of an asset over its useful life.

(e) Notional costs such as notional rent and notional interest. These are only relevant if they represent an identified lost opportunity to use the premises or the finance for some alternative purpose.

In these circumstances, the notional costs would be opportunity costs. This explanation will become clearer when you learn more about opportunity costs later in this chapter.

 Exercise

Test your understanding of relevant and non-relevant costs by seeing if you can identify which of the following costs are relevant:

(a) The salary to be paid to a market researcher who will oversee the development of a new product. This is a new post to be created specially for the new product but the £12,000 salary will be a fixed cost. Is this cost relevant to the decision to proceed with the development of the product?

(b) The £2,500 additional monthly running costs of a new machine to be purchased to manufacture an established product. Since the new machine will save on labour time, the fixed overhead to be absorbed by the product will reduce by £100 per month. Are these costs relevant to the decision to purchase the new machine?

(c) Office cleaning expenses of £125 for next month. The office is cleaned by contractors and the contract can be cancelled by giving one month's notice. Is this cost relevant to a decision to close the office?

(d) Expenses of £75 paid to the marketing manager. This was to reimburse the manager for the cost of travelling to meet a client with whom the company is currently negotiating a major contract. Is this cost relevant to the decision to continue negotiations?

 Solution

(a) The salary is a relevant cost of £12,000. Do not be fooled by the mention of the fact that it is a fixed cost. The cost may be fixed in total but it is definitely a cost that is relevant to the decision to proceed with the future development of the new product. This is an example of a directly attributable fixed cost.

A directly attributable fixed cost may also be called a product-specific fixed cost.

(b) The £2,500 additional running costs are relevant to the decision to purchase the new machine. The saving in overhead absorption is not relevant since we are not told that the *total* overhead expenditure will be altered. The saving in labour cost would be relevant but we shall assume that this has been accounted for in determining the additional monthly running costs.

(c) This is not a relevant cost for next month since it will be incurred even if the contract is cancelled today. If a decision is being made to close the office, this cost cannot be included as a saving to be made next month. However, it will be saved in the months after that so it will become a relevant cost saving from month 2 onwards.

(d) This is not a relevant cost of the decision to continue with the contract. The £75 is sunk and cannot be recovered even if the company does not proceed with the negotiations.

Conclusion

It is essential to look to the future when deciding which costs are relevant to a decision. Costs that have already been incurred or that will not be altered in the future as a result of the decision being taken are not relevant costs.

4.3 Opportunity costs

> An opportunity cost is a special type of relevant cost. It is defined in the CIMA *Terminology* as 'the value of the benefit sacrificed when one course of action is chosen, in preference to an alternative. The opportunity cost is represented by the forgone potential benefit from the best rejected course of action.'

With opportunity costs we are concerned with identifying the value of any benefit forgone as the result of choosing one course of action in preference to another.

4.3.1 Examples of opportunity costs

The best way to demonstrate opportunity costs is to consider some examples:

(a) A company has some obsolete material in stock that it is considering using for a special contract. If the material is not used on the contract it can either be sold back to the supplier for £2 per tonne or it can be used on another contract in place of a different material that would usually cost £2.20 per tonne.

The opportunity cost of using the material on the special contract is £2.20 per tonne. This is the value of the next best alternative use for the material, or the benefit forgone by not using it for the other contract.

(b) Chris is deciding whether or not to take a skiing holiday this year. The travel agent is quoting an all-inclusive holiday cost of £675 for a week. Chris will lose the chance to earn £200 for a part-time job during the week that the holiday would be taken.

The relevant cost of taking the holiday is £875. This is made up of the out-of-pocket cost of £675, plus the £200 opportunity cost that is the part-time wages forgone.

4.3.2 Notional costs and opportunity costs

Notional costs and opportunity costs are in fact very similar. This is particularly noticeable in the case of notional rent. The notional rent could be the rental that the company is forgoing by occupying the premises itself, i.e. it could be an opportunity cost. However, it is only a true opportunity cost if the company can actually identify a forgone opportunity to rent the premises. If nobody is willing to pay the rent, then it is not an opportunity cost.

> If an examination question on relevant costs includes information about notional costs, read the question carefully and state your assumptions concerning the relevance of the notional cost.

4.4 Avoidable, differential and incremental costs

There are two other types of relevant cost that you will need to know about: avoidable costs and differential/incremental costs.

4.4.1 Avoidable costs

> CIMA defines avoidable costs as 'the specific costs of an activity or sector of a business which would be avoided if that activity or sector did not exist'.

For example, if a company is considering shutting down a department, then the avoidable costs are those that would be saved as a result of the shutdown. Such costs might include the labour costs of those employed in the department and the rental cost of the space occupied by the department. The latter is an example of an attributable or specific fixed cost. Costs such as apportioned head office costs that would not be saved as a result of the shutdown are unavoidable costs. They are not relevant to the decision.

4.4.2 Differential/incremental costs

> CIMA defines a differential/incremental cost as 'the difference in total cost between alternatives; calculated to assist decision-making'.

For example, if the relevant cost of contract X is £5,700 and the relevant cost of contract Y is £6,200 we would say that the differential or incremental cost is £500, that is, the extra cost of contract Y is £500.

4.4.3 Using incremental costs

Incremental costs can be useful if the cost accountant wishes to highlight the consequences of taking sequential steps in a decision. For example, the accountant might be providing cost information for a decision about whether to increase the number of employees in a department. Instead of quoting several different total-cost figures, it might be more useful to say 'the incremental cost per five employees will be £5,800 per month'.

Remember that only relevant costs should be used in the calculations.

4.4.4 Incremental revenues

Just as incremental costs are the differences in cost between alternatives, so incremental revenues are the differences in revenues between the alternatives. Matching the incremental costs against the incremental revenues will produce a figure for the incremental gain or loss between the alternatives.

Exercise

To consolidate the material so far on relevant costs and opportunity costs, work through the following exercise to identify the relevant costs of the decision. Try to work out the relevant cost of each item before you look at the solution.

ABC Ltd is deciding whether or not to proceed with a special order. Use the details below to determine the relevant cost of the order.

(a) Materials P and Q will be used for the contract. 100 tonnes of material P will be needed and sufficient material is in stock because the material is in common use in the company. The original cost of the material in stock is £1 per tonne but it would cost £1.20 per tonne to replace if it is used for this contract. The material Q required is in stock as a result of previous overpurchasing. This material originally cost £500 but it has no other use. The material is toxic and if it is not used on this contract, then ABC must pay £280 to have it disposed.

(b) The contract requires 200 hours of labour at £5 per hour. Employees possessing the necessary skills are currently employed by the company but they are idle at present due to a lull in the company's normal business.

(c) Overhead will be absorbed by the contract at a rate of £10 per labour hour, which consists of £7 for fixed overhead and £3 for variable.

(d) The contract will require the use of a storage unit for three months. ABC is committed to rent the unit for one year at a rental of £50 per month. The unit is not in use at present. A neighbouring business has recently approached ABC offering to rent the unit from them for £70 per month.

(e) Total fixed overheads are not expected to increase as a result of the contract.

Solution

(a) The relevant cost of a material that is used regularly is its replacement cost. This will ensure that the business profits are unaffected by the use of the material for this contract. The relevant cost of material P is therefore £1.20 per tonne.

Material Q has a 'negative' cost if used for the contract. This is the saving that will be made through not having to pay the disposal cost of £280.

(b) The relevant cost of labour is zero. The labour cost is being paid anyway and no extra cost will be incurred as a result of this contract.

(c) The fixed overhead is not relevant because we are told that fixed overheads are not expected to increase. The relevant variable overhead cost is: £3 per hour × 200 hours = £600.

Even if you are not specifically told that fixed overheads will remain unaltered, it is usual to assume that they will not increase, stating the assumption clearly.

(d) The rental cost of £50 per month is not relevant because it will not be affected by the contract. The relevant cost of using the storage unit is the forgone rental income of £70 per month.

Summary of relevant costs

	£
(i) Material P	120
Material Q	(280)
(ii) Labour	–
(iii) Variable overhead	600
(iv) Rent forgone	210
Total relevant cost	650

4.4.5 Minimum price quotations for special orders

The last example determined the relevant cost of the special order. This cost represents the minimum price that the company should charge for the order if they wish to make neither a profit nor a loss. As long as the customer pays £650 for the order the company profits will not be affected.

Obviously, this represents the absolute minimum price that could be charged. It is unlikely that ABC Ltd would actually charge this amount. They would probably wish to add a profit margin to improve the company's profits.

However, this absolute minimum value does give managers a starting point for their pricing decision. They know that the company will be worse off if the price is less than £650. If perhaps ABC Ltd is tendering for the order in competition with other suppliers they may try to obtain some information on the likely prices to be tendered by their competitors. If these prices are less than or close to £650, then ABC knows that they will not be able to offer a competitive price. On the other hand, if competitors are likely to tender a much higher price, then the managers know that they are able to price competitively.

4.5 Limiting factor decision-making

 A limiting factor is any factor that is in scarce supply and that stops the organisation from expanding its activities further, that is, it limits the organisation's activities.

The limiting factor for many trading organisations is sales volume because they cannot sell as much as they would like. However, other factors may also be limited, especially in the short term. For example, machine capacity or the supply of skilled labour may be limited for one or two periods until some action can be taken to alleviate the shortage.

4.5.1 Decisions involving a single limiting factor

If an organisation is faced with a single limiting factor, for example machine capacity, then it must ensure that a production plan is established that maximises the profit from the use of the available capacity. Assuming that fixed costs remain constant, this is the same as saying that the contribution must be maximised from the use of the available capacity. The machine capacity must be allocated to those products that earn the most contribution per machine hour.

This decision rule can be stated as 'maximising the contribution per unit of limiting factor'.

Example

LMN Ltd manufactures three products, L, M and N. The company that supplies the two raw materials that are used in all three products has informed LMN that their employees are refusing to work over-time. This means that supply of the materials is limited to the following quantities for the next period:

Material A	1,030 kg
Material B	1,220 kg

No other source of supply can be found for the next period.
Information relating to the three products manufactured by LMN Ltd is as follows:

	L	M	N
Quantity of material used per unit manufactured			
Material A (kg)	2	1	4
Material B (kg)	5	3	7
Maximum sales demand (units)	120	160	110
Contribution per unit sold	£15	£12	£17.50

Owing to the perishable nature of the products, no finished goods stocks are held.

Requirements

(a) Recommend a production mix that will maximise the profits of LMN Ltd for the forthcoming period.
(b) LMN Ltd has a valued customer to whom they wish to guarantee the supply of 50 units of each product next period. Would this alter your recommended production plan?

Solution

(a) The first step is to check whether the supply of each material is adequate or whether either or both of them represent a limiting factor.

	L	M	N	Total
Maximum sales demand (units)	120	160	110	
Material A required per unit (kg)	2	1	4	
Total material A required (kg)	240	160	440	840
Material B required per unit (kg)	5	3	7	
Total material B required (kg)	600	480	770	1,850

There will be sufficient material A to satisfy the maximum demand for the products but material B will be a limiting factor.

The next step is to rank the products in order of their contribution per unit of limiting factor. The available material B can then be allocated according to this ranking.

	L	M	N
Contribution per unit sold	£15	£12	£17.50
Material B consumed (kg)	5	3	7
Contribution per kg of material B	£3	£4	£2.50
Ranking	2	1	3

The available material B will be allocated to the products according to this ranking, to give the optimum production plan for the next period.

Product	Recommended production (units)	Material B utilised (kg)
M	160 (maximum)	480
L	120 (maximum)	600
N	20	140 (balance)
		1,220

The available material B is allocated to satisfy the maximum market demand for products M and L. The balance of available material is allocated to the last product in the ranking, product N.

(b) The recommended production plan in part (a) does not include sufficient product N to satisfy the requirement of 50 units for the valued customer. Some of the material allocated to product L (second in the ranking) must be allocated to product N. The recommended production plan will now be as follows:

Product	Recommended production (units)	Material B utilised (kg)
N	50	350
M	160	480
L	78	390
		1,220

This recommendation makes the best use of the available material B within the restriction of the market requirements for each product.

Exercise

Gill Ltd manufactures three products, E, F and G. The products are all finished on the same machine. This is the only mechanised part of the process. During the next period the production manager is planning an essential major maintenance overhaul of the machine. This will restrict the available machine hours to 1,400 hours for the next period. Data for the three products is:

	Product E £ per unit	Product F £ per unit	Product G £ per unit
Selling price	30	17	21.00
Variable cost	13	6	9.00
Fixed production cost	10	8	6.00
Other fixed cost	2	1	3.50
Profit	5	2	2.50
Maximum demand (units/period)	250	140	130

No stocks are held.

Fixed production costs are absorbed using a machine hour rate of £2 per machine hour.

You are required to determine the production plan that will maximise profit for the forthcoming period.

Solution

The first step is to calculate how many machine hours are required for each product. We can then determine whether machine hours are really a limiting factor.

	Product E	Product F	Product G	Total
Fixed production costs per unit @ £2 per hour	£10	£8	£6	
Machine hours per unit	5	4	3	
Maximum demand (units)	250	140	130	
Maximum hours required	1,250	560	390	2,200

Since 2,200 machine hours are required and only 1,400 hours are available, machine hours are a limiting factor.

The optimum production plan is the plan that maximises the *contribution* from the *limiting factor*.

Do not make the common mistake of allocating the available hours according to the profit per unit of product or according to the profit per hour.

The next step is to calculate the contribution per hour from each of the products.

	Product E	Product F	Product G
	£	£	£
Selling price per unit	30	17	21
Variable cost per unit	13	6	9
Contribution per unit	17	11	12
Machine hours per unit	5	4	3
Contribution per hour	£3.40	£2.75	£4.00
Ranking	2	3	1

The available hours can be allocated according to this ranking.

	Units to be produced	Machine hours required
Product G (maximum demand)	130	390
Product E (balance of hours)	202	1,010
		1,400

4.6 Further decision-making problems

In this last section of the chapter you will be guided through a series of exercises. These will help you to test your understanding of the use of different costs for different types of decision. Try each exercise for yourself before you read the solution.

Exercise: make or buy/outsourcing decision and accept/reject an order

A company manufactures two models of a pocket calculator. The basic model sells for £5, has a direct material cost of £1.25 and requires 0.25 hours of labour time to produce. The other model, the Scientist, sells for £7.50, has a direct material cost of £1.63 and takes 0.375 hours to produce. Labour, which is paid at the rate of £6 per hour, is currently very scarce, while demand for the company's calculators is heavy. The company is currently producing 8,000 of the basic model and 4,000 of the Scientist model per month, while fixed costs are £24,000 per month.

An overseas customer has offered the company a contract, worth £35,000, for a number of calculators made to its requirements. The estimating department has ascertained the following facts in respect of the work:

- The labour time for the contract would be 1,200 hours.
- The material cost would be £9,000 plus the cost of a particular component not normally used in the company's models.
- These components could be purchased from a supplier for £2,500 or alternatively, they could be made internally for a material cost of £1,000 and an additional labour time of 150 hours.

Requirement

Advise the management as to the action they should take.

Solution

In view of its scarcity labour is taken as the limiting factor.

The decision on whether to make or buy the component has to be made before it can be decided whether or not to accept the contract. In order to do this the contribution per labour hour for normal production must first be calculated, as the contract will replace some normal production.

Normal products	Basic		Scientist	
	£	£	£	£
Selling price		5.00		7.50
Materials	1.25		1.63	
Labour	1.50		2.25	
		2.75		3.88
Contribution		2.25		3.62
Contribution per direct labour hour		9.00		9.65

Therefore, it would be better to reduce production of the basic model, in order to accommodate the special order. An opportunity cost arises due to the lost contribution on the basic model.

Special contract	Manufacture of component
	£
Materials	1,000
Labour (£6 × 150 hours)	900
Opportunity cost (150 hours × £9.00)	1,350
	3,250

Since this is higher than the bought-in price of £2,500 the company would be advised to buy the component from the supplier if they accept the contract.

		Contract contribution
	£	£
Sales revenue		35,000
Material cost	9,000	
Component	2,500	
Labour (£6 × 1,200)	7,200	
		18,700
Contribution		16,300
Contribution per direct labour hour		£13.58

Since the contribution is higher than either of the existing products, the company should accept the contract assuming this would not prejudice the market for existing products. As the customer is overseas this seems a reasonable assumption.

Because the contribution is higher for the Scientist model it would be wise to reduce production of the basic model. However, the hours spent on producing the basic model per month are 8,000 units × 0.25 hours = 2,000, and so the contract would displace more than a fortnight's production of the basic model. The recommendation assumes that this can be done without harming long-term sales of the basic model.

Exercise: discontinuing a product

Wye plc makes and sells four products. The profit and loss statement for April is as follows:

Product	W	X	Y	Z	Total
	£	£	£	£	£
Sales	30,000	20,000	35,000	15,000	100,000
Cost of sales	16,000	8,000	22,000	10,000	56,000
Gross profit	14,000	12,000	13,000	5,000	44,000
Overhead cost:					
Selling	8,000	7,000	8,500	6,500	30,000
Administration	2,000	2,000	2,000	2,000	8,000
Net profit	4,000	3,000	2,500	(3,500)	6,000

The management team is concerned about the results, particularly those of product Z, and it has been suggested that Wye plc would be better off if it ceased production of product Z. The production manager has said that if product Z were discontinued the resources which would become available could be used to increase production of product Y by 40 per cent.

You have analysed the cost structures of each of the products and discovered the following:

Product	W	X	Y	Z	Total
	£	£	£	£	£
Variable costs	4,800	1,600	13,200	5,000	24,600
Fixed costs	11,200	6,400	8,800	5,000	31,400
	16,000	8,000	22,000	10,000	56,000

The total fixed costs figure includes £20,000 which is not specific to any one product, and which has been apportioned to each product on the basis of sales values. If the quantity of any product increases by more than 25 per cent, then the specific fixed production costs of the product will increase by 30 per cent.

The selling overhead comprises a fixed cost of £5,000 per product plus a variable cost which varies in proportion to sales value. The fixed cost is not specific to any product but the sales director believes that it should be shared equally by the four products.

The administration cost is a central overhead cost; it is not affected by the products made.

Requirements

(a) Prepare a statement which shows clearly the results of continuing to produce products W, X, Y and Z at the same volumes as were achieved in April. Present your statement in a format suitable for management decision-making.

(b) (i) Prepare a statement showing clearly the results if product Z is discontinued, and the number of units of Y is increased in accordance with the production manager's statement. (Assume that no change in selling price per unit is necessary to sell the additional units.)

(ii) Reconcile the profit calculated in (a) and (b) (i) above; advise the management team as to whether product Z should be discontinued.

(c) Explain briefly any non-financial factors which should be considered before discontinuing a product.

Solution

(a) The profit statement needs to be restated in a marginal costing format if it is to be useful for decision-making.

	W £	X £	Y £	Z £	Total £
Sales	30,000	20,000	35,000	15,000	
Variable cost of sales	4,800	1,600	13,200	5,000	
Variable selling overhead	3,000	2,000	3,500	1,500	
Contribution	22,200	16,400	18,300	8,500	
Specific fixed costs (W1)	5,200	2,400	1,800	2,000	
Net benefit	17,000	14,000	16,500	6,500	54,000
Non-specific fixed cost of sales					(20,000)
Fixed selling overhead (W2)					(20,000)
Administration costs					(8,000)
Net profit					6,000

Workings

1.

	W £	X £	Y £	Z £	Total £
Fixed costs	11,200	6,400	8,800	5,000	31,400
Non-specific fixed cost*	6,000	4,000	7,000	3,000	20,000
Specific fixed costs	5,200	2,400	1,800	2,000	11,400

* Given as £20,000 apportioned on the basis of sales values.

2. £5,000 per product × 4 = £20,000

(b) (i) Z discontinued

	£
Contribution from 40% additional sales of Y (£18,300 × 0.4)	7,320
Additional specific fixed costs (£1,800 × 0.3)	(540)
Loss of net benefit from Z	(6,500)
Net gain	280

(ii) Profit reconciliation

	£
Existing profit	6,000
Discontinuation of Z	(6,500)
Additional contribution from Y	7,320
Additional specific fixed costs	(540)
Profit if Z is discontinued and sales of Y substituted	6,280

The company should therefore discontinue product Z and substitute production and sales of product Y in the proportions given.

(c) Non-financial factors to consider include:
- possible redundancies among the workforce;
- signals which it may give to competitors, who may perceive the company as being unwilling to support its products;
- the reaction of customers, particularly those who may recently have purchased the product.

Sometimes, even when management has made the decision to discontinue a product or activity, there is still a further decision to be made: when to discontinue it. The following exercise shows how such a decision could be made.

Exercise: deciding when to close a department or factory

It is possible that some costs are avoidable in the longer term but not in the short term. For instance, it may be necessary to give notice to cease renting a space occupied by a department. If the notice required is, say, three months then the rental is an unavoidable cost until the three months' notice has expired. After that time it becomes an avoidable cost, as long as notice is given now.

The idea of costs being unavoidable in the short term adds a new dimension to our decision-making. Not only is it necessary to decide whether costs are inherently avoidable, but we may also need to determine when they will become avoidable.

In the very short term almost all costs are unavoidable. In the long term almost all costs are avoidable because the whole organisation could be shut down completely. Here we are talking about time horizons in between these two extremes.

The following exercise will give you some practice at identifying the costs which are relevant to a decision to close a department: the avoidable costs. It will also demonstrate how to decide on the correct timing for a decision.

A company is considering the closure of its internal printing department. The department prints all of the company's publicity material and it also carries out other printing jobs as required.

An external firm has offered to produce all of the company's printing requirements for a total cost of £9,000 per month. The internal printing department's costs are as follows:

(a) A total of 80,000 sheets of customised paper are used each month, at a cost of £50 per 1,000 sheets. The contract for supply of the paper requires three months' notice of cancellation. The company does not hold stocks of the paper but any excess can be sold for a net price of £20 per 1,000 sheets.

(b) A total of 400 litres of fluorescent ink are used each month, at a cost of £1.80 per litre. The contract for supply of this ink requires 1 month's notice of cancellation. No stocks of ink are held but any excess can be sold for £0.50 net per litre.

(c) Other paper and materials costs amount to £2,850 per month.

(d) The printing machinery is rented for £4,500 per month. It is operated for 120 hours each month. The rental contract can be cancelled with 2 months' notice.

(e) The two employees in the department are each paid £1,000 per month. The company has a no-redundancy policy which means that the employees are guaranteed employment even if the department closes.

(f) Overhead cost for the printing department is as follows:

  (i) Variable overhead: £4 per machine hour.
  (ii) Fixed overhead: £3 per machine hour.

Variable overhead varies in direct proportion to the machine hours operated. Fixed overhead represents an apportionment of central overheads which would not alter as a result of the printing department's closure.

Requirement

Calculate the long-term monthly saving or extra cost which will result from the closure of the printing department. If you consider that the department should be closed, you are asked to advise on the most appropriate timing for its closure.

Solution

The long-term monthly saving or cost can be calculated by identifying the relevant costs, ignoring the effect of the notice required on certain of the contracts.

The labour costs and the fixed overheads are not relevant. They would be incurred even if the department is closed.

Relevant cost of internal printing

	£ per month
Customised paper 80 × £50	4,000
Fluorescent ink 400 × £1.80	720
Other paper and material	2,850
Machine rental	4,500
Variable overhead £4 × 120	480
Total relevant cost of internal printing	12,550
Cost of external printing services	9,000
Monthly saving from closure	3,550

Therefore the offer from the external supplier should be accepted, resulting in a monthly saving of £3,550.

This saving would only be made in the 'long term', once all of the relevant notice periods have expired. In the immediate short term, some costs would still be incurred because of the need to give notice of cancellation. It is possible to demonstrate the effect of this by charting in which month each saving will be made. In the following table, 'month 1' is taken to mean 'one month from now'.

Relevant savings and revenues

	Month 1 £	Month 2 £	Month 3 £	Month 4 £
Customised paper (note 1)	–	–	–	4,000
Revenue from sale of excess paper	1,600	1,600	1,600	–
Fluorescent ink (note 2)	–	720	720	720
Revenue from sale of excess ink	200	–	–	–
Other paper and materials (note 3)	2,850	2,850	2,850	2,850
Machine rental (note 4)	–	–	4,500	4,500
Variable overhead (note 3)	480	480	480	480
Relevant savings and revenues	5,130	5,650	10,150	12,550
External cost	9,000	9,000	9,000	9,000
Saving/(excess cost) from closure	(3,870)	(3,350)	1,150	3,550

Note that the monthly saving settles down at the 'long-term' amount of £3,550 once all of the notice periods have expired.

Notes

1. The saving on customised paper will not be made until month 4, because 3 months' notice is required and the company is obliged to purchase the paper. However, if printing is ceased immediately the paper could be re-sold for £1,600 per month.
2. The saving on fluorescent ink will not be made until month 2 because the company will be obliged to purchase it for the first month. If printing is ceased immediately the ink could be re-sold for £200 for 1 month.
3. The other material costs and the variable overheads are relevant from month 1, because they can be avoided as soon as the department closes.
4. The machine rental will only be saved from month 3 onwards, because it must be paid for anyway for the next 2 months.

Recommendation

The printing department should be closed in month 3 and £1,150 will be saved in that month. From month 4 onwards the monthly saving will amount to £3,550. In the meantime, notice should be given on the relevant contracts as follows:

Customised paper: give immediate notice. Continue to use the paper for two months, then resell the supplies in month 3 when the department is closed.

Fluorescent ink: give notice at the end of month 1. The notice will then expire at the beginning of month 3 when the department is closed.

Printing machinery: give immediate notice. The notice will then expire at the beginning of month 3 when the department is closed.

Further processing decision

A joint production process results in two or more products, called joint products. The point in the production process where the joint products are identifiable as separate products is called the split-off point. The joint cost is incurred before the joint products become identifiable as separate products. When undertaking a further processing decision it must be remembered that the joint costs of the process are irrelevant as they represent sunk costs. With the further processing decision we should consider the incremental costs and incremental revenue if we further process.

The further processing decision involves the decision to:

1. sell the products at the split off point, or
2. further process to produce products with enhanced value.

In order to satisfy internal and external profit measurements and inventory valuation, it is necessary to assign all production related costs (including joint costs) to products so that costs can be allocated to inventories, and cost of goods sold.

Exercise

R Limited produces two products from a single process. During one period in which the process costs are expected to be £150,000, the following outputs are expected:

	Output	Selling Price
Product X	5,000 litres	£15 per litre
Product Y	15,000 litres	£10 per litre

Each product can be further processed using skilled labour, costing £10 per hour, to create superior products; Super X and Super Y. Further modifications will result in the following increases in labour hours and amended selling prices:

	Skilled Labour	Selling Price
Product Super X	.75 hour per litre	£25 per litre
Product Super Y	.40 hour per litre	£13 per litre

Requirement

Advise the company as to the action they should take.

Solution

	Super X	Super Y
Incremental revenue		
Super X		
(£25–£15) × 5,000	£50,000	
Super Y		
(£13–£10) × 15,000		£45,000
Incremental costs		
Super X		
.75 hour × 5,000 × £10	(£37,500)	
Super Y		
.40 hour × 15,000 × £10		(£60,000)
Incremental benefit/(cost)	£12,500	(£15,000)

Further process Product X but sell Product Y now.

4.7 Summary

This chapter has explained the concept of relevant costs and revenues including opportunity costs.

Examples of different decision-making scenarios have then been used to illustrate the application of the relevant cost concept.

Readings

4

Joint products: what process costing does, and does not, tell us

Tim Thompson, **CIMA Insider***, February 2006, Paper: P2* **Management Accounting – Decision Management**

Relevant learning outcome:
A4: 'explain why joint costs must be allocated to final products for financial reporting purposes, but why this is unhelpful when decisions concerning process and product viability have to be taken;'

Also useful to:
Paper P1 Management Accounting Performance Evaluation
Paper C1 Management Accounting Fundamentals

This article is concerned with process costing with particular emphasis on joint products and decision-making. Here are two official CIMA definitions to get us started:

Process costing
'The costing method applicable where goods or services result from a sequence of continuous or repetitive operations or processes. Costs are averaged over the units produced during the period, being initially charged to the operation or process[1]'

Joint products
'Two or more products produced by the same process and separated in processing, each having sufficiently high saleable value to merit recognition as a main product[2]'

A process is essentially a very simple concept; materials are obtained, work is done on these materials and some form of finished (or semi-finished) product emerges. As accountants, we are particularly interested in the financial aspects of this. Again, in principle, this is quite straight forward; we need to determine the costs of the input materials and the work done, and the value to be attributed to the output.

But from your earlier studies, you will recall that, in practice, the accounting for what goes on in a process can be quite complex. Here is a list of some of the key issues that may emerge in process costing and that we must be capable of dealing with:

Opening inventory in varying degrees of completion
Closing inventory in varying degrees of completion
Equivalent units
Different inventory valuation methods (e.g. FIFO, AVCO, standard costing)
Normal loss (with or without a resale value)
Abnormal loss (with or without a resale value)
Abnormal gain
Joint products
By-products
Further processing decisions
Process viability

It may be some time since you last studied, or used, process costing. How many of the above issues do you recall? How confident are you that you can deal with them?

Have a look at the following example and attempt it without referring to any notes or to the solution that follows. Once you have done this, compare your answer to the solution provided and consider what mark you might have been awarded if this had appeared in an examination. As professional accountants we would aspire to a 100% correct solution; did you achieve this? If so, then well done! If not, then do you think you earned at least the equivalent of a pass mark?

Here is the question.

A company has the worldwide monopoly on the sale of all of its products.

Part of the company's operations includes process M which receives input material from process L and converts this to make joint products A, B and C together with by-product Y.

Normal loss is 10% of the material received from process L during the month. Normal loss and any abnormal loss have no resale value. By-product Y has a resale value of £1 per kg.

The joint products may be sold immediately after process M, or further processed before being sold. Details of this, per kg, are as follows:

	Selling price after process M	Additional processing cost	Selling price after further processing
Joint product A	£15.50	£7.00	£23.00
Joint product B	£15.00	£9.00	£23.50
Joint product C	£14.50	£9.50	£24.20

For the month of October, the following data for process M is available:

Opening inventory   100 kg of material, 100% complete, value £1,000.
                                    The conversion of this was 60% complete, value £150.
Closing inventory   50 kg of material, 100% complete.
                                    The conversion of this was 40% complete.

Materials received from process L during the month was 2,000 kg, costing £21,000
Conversion costs incurred during the month were £5,200

Completed output	Joint product A,	600 kg
	Joint product B,	580 kg
	Joint product C,	540 kg
	By-product Y,	90 kg

MANAGEMENT ACCOUNTING – DECISION MANAGEMENT

The example will be considered in the context of two scenarios:

Scenario 1: Inventory is valued using FIFO (first in first out), and joint products are valued according to the weight of output.

Scenario 2: Inventory is valued using AVCO (weighted average costing), and joint products are valued according to the sales value of output at the split-off point.

Requirements

(a) Prepare the process M account for *each* of the two scenarios.
(b) Recommend, with supporting calculations, whether the joint products should be further processed.
(c) Analyse the viability of process M.

Solutions

(a) **Scenario 1**

The following items can be inserted straight away into the process M account.

Process M Account

	kg	£		kg	£
Opening inventory: material	100	1,000	Closing Inventory: material	50	
conversion		150	conversion		
Material from process L	2,000	21,000	Output: joint product A	600	
Conversion		5,200	joint product B	580	
			joint product C	540	
			by-product Y	90	
			Normal Loss	200	

The next step is to balance off the two columns of weights. We see from this that the larger total is 2,100 kg on the debit side as opposed to 2,060 kg on the credit side. The difference of 40 kg is abnormal loss and we can add this to the process account as follows.

Process M Account

	kg	£		kg	£
Opening inventory: material	100	1,000	Closing Inventory: material	50	
conversion		150	conversion		
Material from process L	2,000	21,000	Output: joint product A	600	
Conversion		5,200	joint product B	580	
			joint product C	540	
			by-product Y	90	90
			Normal Loss	200	0
			Abnormal loss	40	
	2,100	27,350		2,100	

We have also been able to insert both column totals for the debit side, the weight total on the credit side, a value of £0 for normal loss and £90 for by-product Y.

You will recall that normal loss does not bear any of the process costs since this is a "normal" feature of the production process and in this case it has no resale value. By-product Y does not bear any process costs, but the resale value of £90 relieves the process costs elsewhere.

The task now is to determine how the total of £27,350 is to be shared out between the items on the credit side. To do this, we need to prepare a statement of equivalent units ensuring, for this scenario, that we use FIFO.

Statement of equivalent units

	Process L materials	Conversion	
Opening inventory completed	0[a]	40[b]	
Started and finished in the month	1,620[c]	1,620[c]	
Abnormal loss	40[d]	40[d]	
Closing inventory	50[e]	20[f]	
Equivalent units	1,710	1,720	
Costs incurred	£20,910[g]	£5,200[h]	Total
Cost per equivalent unit	£12.22807[i]	£3.02326[j]	£15.25133[k]

Workings:

(a) The opening inventory of 100 was 100% complete in respect of process L material, therefore there was nothing to complete in this respect
(b) The opening inventory of 100 was 60% complete in respect of conversion. FIFO assumes that the remaining 40% is completed first. $100 \times 40\% = 40$.
(c) The total amount of joint product completed in the month less any of this that emerged from completing the opening inventory. This must be the same value for both materials and conversion. $600 + 580 + 540 - 100 = 1,620$.
(d) Abnormal loss of 40 units calculated earlier
(e) The closing inventory of 50 was 100% complete in respect of process L material.
(f) The closing inventory of 50 was 40% complete in respect of conversion. $50 \times 40\% = 20$.
(g) The value of material received from process L during the month, less the resale value of by-product Y. £21,000 − £90 = £20,910.
(h) The value of conversion work done during the month.
(i) £20,910/1,710 = £12.22807.
(j) £5,200/1,720 = £3.02326.
(k) £12.22807 + £3.02326 = £15.25133.

We can now calculate the value the closing inventory, the value of abnormal loss and the total value of the joint products.

Value of closing inventory
Material: $50 \times £12.22807 = £611$
Conversion: $20 \times 3.02326 = £60$
Total £671

Value of abnormal loss
$40 \times £15.25133 = £610$

Total value of the joint products

Started and finished in the month:	$1,620 \times £15.25133$	= £24,708
Opening inventory brought forward	£1,000 + £150	= £1,150
Opening inventory (conversion) completed	40×3.02326	= £121
Total		£25,979

The total value of the joints products started and finished in the month has been rounded up rather than down in order to compensate for the rounding error caused by rounding the costs per equivalent unit to only 5 decimal places of £1.

This total value of £25,979 now needs to be split between the three joint products and in scenario 1 we need to do this according to the weight of output. The total weight of output is $600 + 580 + 540 = 1,720$ kg

Joint product A £25,979 × 600/1720 = £9,063
Joint product B £25,979 × 580/1720 = £8,760
Joint product C £25,979 × 540/1720 = £8,156
Total £25,979

The value for joint product A has been rounded up rather than down for the same reason as above.

We can now enter the remaining values in the process M account.

Process M Account

	kg	£		kg	£
Opening inventory: material	100	1,000	Closing Inventory: material	50	611
conversion		150	conversion		60
Material from process L	2,000	21,000	Output: joint product A	600	9,063
Conversion		5,200	joint product B	580	8,760
			joint product C	540	8,156
			by-product Y	90	90
			Normal Loss	200	0
			Abnormal loss	40	610
	2,100	27,350		2,100	27,350

Note that the totals of the debit and credit value columns balance at £27,350. It is important that you can achieve this by calculating all of the component figures, rather than just inserting numbers to make the totals balance.

(a) *Scenario 2*

Scenario 2 involves weighted average costing and joint products being valued according to the sales value of output at the split-off point. These issues will affect the valuation of the joint products, the abnormal loss and the closing inventory. The other items on the process M account will be the same as in scenario 1 as follows.

Process M Account

	kg	£		kg	£
Opening inventory: material	100	1,000	Closing Inventory: material	50	
conversion		150	conversion		
Material from process L	2,000	21,000	Output: joint product A	600	
Conversion		5,200	joint product B	580	
			joint product C	540	
			by-product Y	90	90
			Normal Loss	200	0
			Abnormal loss	40	
	2,100	27,350		2,100	

The statement of equivalent units for scenario 2 is as follows.

Statement of equivalent units

	Process L materials	Conversion	
Completed in the month	1,720[a]	1,720[a]	
Abnormal loss	40[b]	40[b]	
Closing inventory	50[c]	20[d]	
Equivalent units	1,810	1,780	
Costs incurred	£21,910[e]	£5,350[f,g]	Total
Cost per equivalent unit	£12.10497[h]	£3.00562[i]	£15.11059[j]

Workings:

(a) Units completed in the month were 600 + 580 + 540 = 1,720.
(b) Abnormal loss of 40 units calculated earlier
(c) The closing inventory of 50 was 100% complete in respect of process L material.
(d) The closing inventory of 50 was 40% complete in respect of conversion. 50 × 40% = 20.
(e) The value of material in opening inventory plus that received from process L during the month, less the resale value of by-product Y. £1,000 + £21,000 − £90 = £21,910.
(f) The value of conversion in opening inventory plus the work done during the month.
(g) £150 + £5,200 = £5,350
(h) £21,910/1,810 = £12.10497
(i) £5,350/1,780 = £3.00562
(j) £12.10497 + £3.00562 = £15.11059

We can calculate the value of the closing inventory, the value of abnormal loss and the total value of the joint products.

Value of closing inventory

Material:	50 × £12.10497	= £605
Conversion:	20 × £3.00562	= £60
Total		£665

Value of abnormal loss
40 × £15.11059 = £604

Total value of the joint products
1,720 × £15.11059 = £25,991

The total value of the joints products has again been rounded up rather than down in order to compensate for the rounding error caused by rounding the costs per equivalent unit to only 5 decimal places of £1.

This total value of £25,991 now needs to be split between the three joint products and in scenario 2 we need to do this according to the sales value of output at the split-off point.

	Sales value		Proportion	Cost
Joint product A 600 × £15.50 =	£9,300	36.005%	£9,358	
Joint product B 580 × £15.00 =	£8,700	33.682%	£8,754	
Joint product C 540 × £14.50 =	£7,830	30.313%	£7,879	
Total	£25,830	100.000%	£25,991	

The proportion for joint product C has been rounded down rather than up to ensure that the total of the proportions is 100%.

We can now enter the remaining values in the process M account.

Process M Account

	kg	£		kg	£
Opening inventory: material	100	1,000	Closing Inventory: material	50	605
conversion		150	conversion		60
Material from process L	2,000	21,000	Output: joint product A	600	9,358
Conversion		5,200	joint product B	580	8,754
			joint product C	540	7,879
			by-product Y	90	90
			Normal Loss	200	0
			Abnormal loss	40	604
	2,100	27,350		2,100	27,350

(b) To determine whether the three joint products should be further processed or sold at the split-off point, we need to look at each product separately and consider the relevant costs. For example, joint product A yields a selling price of £15.50 at the split off point and £23.00 after further processing. To obtain this additional revenue of £7.50, further processing costs of £7.00 are needed; so further processing yields an additional relevant benefit of £0.50 per kilogram. Accordingly, joint product A should be further processed. Here are the full calculations with the associated recommendations.

	Additional relevant benefit/(cost)	Recommendation
Joint product A	£23.00 − £15.50 − £7.00 = +£0.50	Process further
Joint product B	£23.50 − £15.00 − £9.00 = (£0.50)	Sell at split-off
Joint product C	£24.20 − £14.50 − £9.50 = +£0.20	Process further

So joint products A and C should each be further processed and joint product B should be sold at the split-off point immediately after process M.

Note that this decision takes no account of the costs attributed to the joint products in process M. These costs are irrelevant as they are incurred anyway, whether or not we further process any individual joint product. The cost attributed to each joint product depended upon arbitrary decisions concerning (i) FIFO or AVCO inventory valuation and (ii) the two alternative methods of sharing the joint costs. These arbitrary decisions have no bearing on the cashflows (from customers, to suppliers and employees) or on shareholder wealth creation.

(c) We are asked to analyse the viability of process M and we can only consider the process in its entirety; we cannot meaningfully consider the viability of the individual joint products. The fundamental question is "is process M profitable in the long-run?"

To answer this, we need to make a couple of assumptions. The first assumption is that the abnormal loss is genuinely a one-off and does not reflect some long term inefficiency that should be reflected by increasing the normal loss percentage. The second assumption is that, apart from the abnormal loss, October's data is a reliable basis for the analysis.

The total cost attributed to the three joint products for October was £25,979 under FIFO and £25,991 under AVCO. The slight difference between these two figures is due to the minor changes in the cost of inputs linked with the inventory valuation method chosen; we will simply take the more cautious figure of £25,991 as the process M cost of the finished output.

The process as a whole is viable if the revenues from selling the joint products exceed the cost. However, in part (b) above we decided to further process two of the three joint products and so we must include this in the evaluation.

Revenue:	joint product A, after further processing, 600 × £23.00	= £13,800
	joint product B, at the split-off point, 580 × £15.00	= £8,700
	joint product C, after further processing, 540 × £24.20	= £13,068
	Total Revenue	£35,568
Cost:	process M	= £25,991
	additional processing, joint product A, 600 × £7.00	= £4,200
	additional processing, joint product C, 540 × £9.50	= £5,130
	Total Cost	£35,321

So process M yields a profit of £247 (£35,568 − 35,321) and can therefore be described as viable, albeit only just.

It is interesting to note here the impact that the opportunity to further process has had on the process M viability. The incremental benefit of further processing joint products A and C is (600 × £0.50) + (540 × £0.20) = £300 + £108 = £408. So we can say that without the opportunity to further process, process M would not be viable.

A further interesting perspective on this process viability issue would emerge if the company did not have the worldwide monopoly on the sale of all of its products. This would mean that it might be possible to acquire products A and C from elsewhere as an alternative to manufacturing them in process M. In this situation, given the market prices in the question, then it would be more profitable to dispense with process M and simply perform the "further" processing on these purchased materials.

What are the key messages emerging from the example?

1. Different methods of inventory valuation (FIFO, AVCO, etc.) do not affect long-run profit, cashflows or shareholder wealth. They can affect the timing of the profits and as such they can have an impact on the value of short-term financial accounting profits and inventory valuation. This should not impact on managerial decision-making.
2. Different ways of apportioning common costs between joint products (weight of output, value of output) do not affect long-run profit, cashflows or shareholder wealth. This should not impact on managerial decision-making.
3. We cannot choose to produce some joint products and not others, nor can we select the volume of each joint product. We can choose to operate the whole process or not. If we choose to operate it then we must accept whatever combination of joint products emerges.
4. Once the process is complete and the joint products have been split off, then we can make individual decisions about which joint products should be further processed and which should not.

Examination Howlers

If you want to impress the Examiner (favourably), here are a few things that you should *not* write on your examination script.

X 'The company should stop production of joint product P and increase production of joint product Q.' X

X 'The company should value inventory using the FIFO method, rather than AVCO, as this will generate more shareholder wealth.' X

X 'In a further processing decision, we can further process all joint products or none of them. We cannot further process some joint products and not others.' X

If you are still unsure why any of these three statements are erroneous, then it would be a good idea to go through this article again in detail and revisit your original earning material on process costing.

References

1. Management Accounting Official Terminology, 2000 edition, published by CIMA, ISBN 1-85971-347-5, p. 31.
2. *op cit*, p. 34.

Revision Questions

Question 1

1.1 X plc intends to use relevant costs as the basis of the selling price for a special order: the printing of a brochure. The brochure requires a particular type of paper that is not regularly used by X plc although a limited amount is in X plc's inventory which was left over from a previous job. The cost when X plc bought this paper last year was $15 per ream and there are 100 reams in inventory. The brochure requires 250 reams. The current market price of the paper is $26 per ream, and the resale value of the paper in inventory is $10 per ream.

The relevant cost of the paper to be used in printing the brochure is

(A) $2,500
(B) $4,900
(C) $5,400
(D) $6,500

(2 marks)

1.2 A farmer grows potatoes for sale to wholesalers and to individual customers. The farmer currently digs up the potatoes and sells them in 20 kg sacks. He is considering a decision to make a change to this current approach. He thinks that washing the potatoes and packaging them in 2 kg cartons might be more attractive to some of his individual customers. Which of the following is relevant to his decision?

(i) the sales value of the dug potatoes
(ii) the cost per kg of growing the potatoes
(iii) the cost of washing and packaging the potatoes
(iv) the sales value of the washed and packaged potatoes

(A) (ii), (iii) and (iv) only
(B) (i), (ii) and (iii) only
(C) (i), (ii) and (iv) only
(D) (i), (iii) and (iv) only

(2 marks)

1.3

The following details relate to ready meals that are prepared by a food processing company:

Ready meal	K $/meal	L $/meal	M $/meal
Selling price	5.00	3.00	4.40
Ingredients	2.00	1.00	1.30
Variable conversion costs	1.60	0.80	1.85
Fixed conversion costs*	0.50	0.30	0.60
Profit	0.90	0.90	0.65
Oven time (minutes per ready meal)	10	4	8

Each of the meals is prepared using a series of processes, one of which involves cooking the ingredients in a large oven. The availability of cooking time in the oven is limited and, because each of the meals requires cooking at a different oven temperature, it is not possible to cook more than one of the meals in the oven at the same time.

*The fixed conversion costs are general fixed costs that are not specific to any type of ready meal.

The most and least profitable use of the oven is

	Most profitable	Least profitable
(A)	Meal K	Meal L
(B)	Meal L	Meal M
(C)	Meal L	Meal K
(D)	Meal M	Meal L

(2 marks)

1.4

A company is preparing a quotation for a one-month consultancy project and seeks your help in determining the relevant cost of one of the members of its project team. Currently the company employs the consultant on an annual salary of £36,000. In addition, the company provides the consultant with a company car which incurs running costs of £6,000 each year. The car will continue to be provided to the consultant whether this project is undertaken by the company or not.

This consultant is fully employed on current projects and, if she were to be transferred to this new project, then an existing junior consultant would be used to cover her current work. The junior consultant would be paid a bonus of £5,000 for undertaking this additional responsibility.

Another alternative that the company is considering is hiring an external consultant who has the necessary technical knowledge to work on the new consultancy project on a one month contract at a cost of £4,500.

The relevant cost to be used in preparing the quotation is

- (A) £3,000
- (B) £3,500
- (C) £4,500
- (D) £5,000

(2 marks)

Question 2

Fudge Ltd operates at three factory sites producing a closely related product range. The 20X4 budget for Fudge Ltd's operations is as follows:

	Croydon £000	Luton £000	Southend £000
Costs:			
Variable	475	2,200	1,000
Fixed (site)	375	1,300	650
Fixed (central)	50	200	100
Sales	1,000	4,000	2,000
Profit	100	300	250

The lease of the Croydon site expires at the end of 20X4. Four alternative options have been identified for the 20X5 operations:

1. Renew the Croydon site lease at an additional annual rental of £50,000.
2. Shut the Croydon site and franchise Croydon production to another manufacturer at a 1.5 per cent commission on sales.
3. Shut the Croydon site and switch production to Luton; this would involve an additional £250,000 per year fixed costs at Luton and additional transport costs on production transferred amounting to 7.5 per cent of sales.
4. Shut down the Croydon site and switch production to Southend; this would involve additional fixed costs of £200,000 per year at Southend and additional transport costs on production transferred amounting to 10 per cent of sales.

Requirements

Evaluate the options and advise:

(a) which option is most attractive on purely financial grounds;
(b) what strategic factors are relevant which might be beyond the scope of your analysis in (a).

 ## Question 3

JP Ltd produces three joint products – A, B and C – which are then further processed. It is normal practice for the company to apportion all pre-separation costs on the basis of weight of output of each joint product.

Data for the last period is as follows:

Costs incurred up to separation point			£9,600
	Product A	Product B	Product C
Output (kg)	100	60	80
	£	£	£
Costs incurred after separation point	2,000	1,200	800
Selling price per kg			
After further processing	50	80	60
At pre-separation point (estimate)	25	70	45

Requirements

(a) Prepare a statement showing the profit or loss made by each product using the present method of apportioning pre-separation costs.

(b) Comment on the method used by JP Ltd to attribute pre-separation costs to its joint products.

(c) Advise the management of JP Ltd whether or not, on purely financial grounds, it should further process any of the three products.

Question 4

PMS plc is a large diversified organisation with several departments. It is concerned over the performance of one of its departments – department P. PMS plc is concerned that department P has not been able to meet its sales target in recent years and is considering either to reduce the level of production or to shut down the department.

The following information has been made available:

Budgeted sales and production in units	50,000
	£000
Sales	500
Less production costs	
Material A – 1 kg per unit	50
Material B – 1 litre per unit	25
Labour – 1 hour per unit	125
Variable overhead	100
Fixed overhead	50
Non-production costs	50
Total cost	400
Budgeted profit	100

The following additional information has also been made available:

(i) There are 50,000 kg of material A in stock. This originally cost £1 per kg. Material A has no other use and unless it is used by the division it will have to be disposed of at a cost of £500 for every 5,000 kg.

(ii) There are 30,000 litres of material B in stock. Any unused material can be used by another department to substitute for an equivalent amount of a material, which currently costs £1.25 per litre. The original cost of material B was £0.50 per litre and it can be replaced at a cost of £1.50 per litre.

(iii) All production labour hours are paid on an hourly basis. Rumours of the closure of the department have led to a large proportion of the department's employees leaving the organisation. Uncertainty over its closure has also resulted in management not replacing these employees. The department is therefore short of labour hours and has sufficient to produce 25,000 units. Output in excess of 25,000 units would require the department to hire contract labour at a cost of £3.75 per hour. If the department is shut down the present labour force will be deployed within the organisation.

(iv) Included in the variable overhead is the depreciation of the only machine used in the department. The original cost of the machine was £200,000 and it is estimated to have a life of 10 years. Depreciation is calculated on a straight-line basis. The machine has a current resale value of £25,000. If the machinery is used for production it is estimated that the resale value of the machinery will fall at the rate of £100 per 1,000 units produced. All other costs included in variable overhead vary with the number of units produced.

(v) Included in the fixed production overhead is the salary of the manager of department P which amounts to £20,000. If the department were to shut down the manager would be made redundant with a redundancy pay of £25,000. All other costs included in the fixed production overhead are general factory overheads and will not be affected by any decision concerning department P.

(vi) The non-production cost charged to department P is an apportionment of the total non-production costs incurred by the department.

(vii) The marketing manager suggests that either:

- a sales volume of 25,000 units can be achieved with a selling price of £9.00 per unit and an advertising campaign of £25,000; or
- a sales volume of 35,000 units can be achieved at a selling price of £7.50 with an advertising campaign costing £35,000.

Requirements

(a) As the management accountant of PMS plc you have been asked to investigate the following options available to the organisation:
   (i) reduce production to 25,000 units
   (ii) reduce production to 35,000 units
   (iii) shut down department P.
(b) Discuss the relevance of opportunity costs in decision-making.

Question 5

D runs a ceramics company that employs twenty staff. The employees work a basic 40-hour week for 48 weeks a year, and are paid on an hourly basis. The average wage per hour is £10.42. The fixed costs for the pottery total £30,000 per annum.

The company makes tableware and tiles. A set of tableware sells for £50. The costs per set are:

	£
Direct materials	10
Direct labour	10
Variable overheads	10

Tiles sell for £200 per 100 tiles and the costs per hundred are:

	£
Direct materials	20
Direct labour	50
Variable overheads	50

The normal sales mix is 600 tiles to 20 sets of tableware. In most years the company works close to normal capacity, but at present the business is operating at 60 per cent of capacity. Because of this, D has assigned two members of staff to refurbish the pottery showroom, which should take them 8 weeks to complete. He has also recently agreed to redecorate and tile the changing rooms and surround of the local swimming pool. This is a charitable work and should take three of D's staff half a year to complete. However, D has since been offered two large contracts, which he bid for a few months ago.

Fish-and-chip shops contract

The first contract is from a company that owns a chain of upmarket fish-and-chip shops. The company needs tiles for five new fish-and-chip shops that it is about to open. D has heard from a reliable source that the company plans to open a further 30 new shops over the next 2 or 3 years. The tiles for the five shops are required in 6 months' time, and each shop will require 20,000 tiles at the normal selling price less 5 per cent.

Z plc contract

The second potential contract is from a department store, Z plc, which requires 40,000 sets of pastel coloured tableware in one year's time. This may lead to further annual orders from Z plc. D has already produced designs for the product, which the company has agreed; D reckons that this took £2,500 of his time. The price agreed per set is the normal price less 15 per cent quantity discount. If he accepts the contract he will need to have the moulds made, which will cost £15,000. In order to complete this contract a considerable amount of production space is required to store and dry the moulds and to store the completed goods ready for despatch in 1 year's time.

D owns a warehouse adjacent to the pottery. This warehouse is leased to another business on an annual basis at a rental of £10,000 per annum. Fortunately, the lease is due for renewal this month and D could use the warehouse to complete the large contract for Z plc. He estimates that its use would cost him £3,000 in extra fixed operating costs per annum.

Staffing and capacity information

D has no difficulty in recruiting staff as required, but he feels that he could not absorb more than eight new employees in the coming year. Recruitment costs are £500 per employee. He also has little difficulty in getting staff to work 6 hours' overtime per week at 150 per cent of their normal rate of pay. However, they could only work at this level for half of the 48 weeks worked per annum.

If D accepted either job he could stop the two members of staff decorating the showroom and hire a contractor, which would cost £5,000. If he brought the three staff back from the work on the swimming pool he would feel obliged to make a donation of £35,000 which would pay for a contractor to finish the work. Twenty-five per cent of the pottery's output each year is made up of new one-off orders from small outlets. D feels that, if he wished to do other, more profitable, work, he could stop supplying these customers without long-term detriment to his business.

Requirements

(a) Produce calculations that show whether the contracts are feasible and profitable. Where appropriate, explain your reasoning, and the figures in your calculations.

(23 marks)

(b) Recommend, with reasons, whether D should accept either or both of the contracts. Describe the longer-term implications of the actions you recommend. (7 marks)

(Total marks = 30)

Question 6

Z manufactures three joint products (M, N and P) from the same common process. The following process account relates to the common process last month and is typical of the monthly results of operating this process:

Common Process Account

	Litres	$		Litres	$
Opening work in process	1,000	5,320	Normal loss	10,000	20,000
Materials	100,000	250,000	Output M	25,000	141,875
Conversion costs:			Output N	15,000	85,125
Variable		100,000	Output P	45,000	255,375
Fixed		180,000	Closing work in process	800	3,533
			Abnormal loss	5,200	29,412
	101,000	535,320		101,000	535,320

Each one of the products can be sold immediately after the common process, but each one of them can be further processed individually before being sold. The following further processing costs and selling prices per litre are expected:

Product	Selling price after common process $/litre	Selling price after further processing $/litre	Further variable processing cost $/litre
M	6.25	8.40	1.75
N	5.20	6.45	0.95
P	6.80	7.45	0.85

Requirement:

(a) State the method used to apportion the common costs between the products M, N and P and comment on its acceptability. Explain why it is necessary to apportion the common costs between each of the products. **(5 marks)**

(b) Evaluate the viability of the common process, and determine the optimal processing plan for each of the three products showing appropriate calculations.

(5 marks)
(Total for Question Four = 10 marks)
(Total for Section B = 30 marks)

Solutions to Revision Questions

 Solution 1

1.1 Answer: (B)

100 reams @ resale value of $10		$1,000
150 reams @ market price of $26		$3,900
		$4,900

1.2 Answer: (C)

1.3

	K	L	M
Contribution per meal	$1.40	$1.20	$1.25
Minutes	10	4	8
Contribution per minute	$0.14	$0.30	$0.16

The correct answer is C.

1.4 *The correct answer is C.*
The lowest cost option is to hire the external consultant.

 Solution 2

Tip
- Identify relevant costs and revenues associated with each of the four alternatives.

(a) Renewal of Croydon lease gives profit of £600,000
   Franchise Croydon production gives profit of £515,000
   Transfer production to Luton gives profit of £700,000
   Transfer production to Southend gives profit of £725,000*
   *Profit-maximising option.

Option 1 – Renew Croydon site lease

	£000
Renew Croydon site lease – additional rent	(50)
Revised profit (650 − 50)	600

97

Option 2 – Franchise Croydon production

If the Croydon site is shut the central fixed costs will not be saved.

Impact on sales	(1,000)
Impact on variable costs	475
Impact on fixed site costs	375
Commission income (1.5% of sales)	15
	(135)
Revised profit (650 − 135)	515

Option 3 – Shut Croydon and switch production to Luton

Again, the central fixed costs will not be saved, but the fixed site costs will be saved and are therefore relevant to the decision. The assumption is made that the sales revenue and variable cost from Croydon will be transferred to the Luton site. Therefore these two items are not affected by the decision and are not included in the calculation of revised profit.

Impact on Croydon fixed site costs	375
Additional costs – Luton	(250)
Transport costs (7.5% of sales)	(75)
	50
Revised profit (650 + 50)	700

Option 4 – Shut Croydon and switch production to Southend

Impact on Croydon fixed site costs	375
Additional costs – Southend	(200)
Additional transport costs Southend (10% of sales)	(100)
	75
Revised profit (650 + 75)	725

(b) Relevant strategic factors which are beyond the scope of analysis in (a) above include:
- impact on workforce and labour relations;
- impact on company's standing with customers;
- reduction in company's total production capacity;
- increased vulnerability to local events at remaining sites.

Solution 3

Tips
- Remember pre-separation costs are common costs and therefore irrelevant to the decision.
- When a decision on whether or not to further process is to be made, the relevant costs are incremental costs and revenue.

(a) Profit statement for the three joint products

	A £	B £	C £	Total £
Sales	5,000	4,800	4,800	14,600
Less				
Pre-sep. costs	4,000	2,400	3,200	9,600
Post-sep. costs	2,000	1,200	800	4,000
Profit/(loss)	(1,000)	1,200	800	1,000

(b) JP Ltd apportions pre-separation costs according to the physical measure – on the weight of output of each joint product. Another method available is apportioning according to market value of the joint products. Both methods are arbitrary and do not provide management with accurate apportionment of costs. It is impossible to calculate accurately the amount of pre-separation costs to be charged to individual joint products. They must therefore be looked at in total rather than on an individual product basis.

(c) The decision on whether or not to further process should be based on a comparison of incremental sales revenue and incremental costs, and not on information that includes an arbitrary apportionment of costs.

Product	Incremental revenue £	Incremental costs £	Incremental profit/(loss) £
A	2,500	2,000	500
B	600	1,200	(600)
C	1,200	800	400
			300

Therefore, further process A and C and sell B at the point of separation.

Solution 4

Tips

- A straightforward question with three decision options. Evaluate each option using relevant costs and revenue.
- Candidates frequently do not show clear workings for this type of question. A large proportion of the marks is awarded for the workings, not the final statement.

(a)

	25,000 units £	35,000 units £	Shut down £
Relevant savings and revenue			
Sales revenue	225,000	262,500	–
Material B	6,250	–	37,500
Sale of machinery	22,500	21,500	25,000
Total revenue/savings	253,750	284,000	62,500
Relevant costs			
Material A disposal	2,500	1,500	5,000
Purchase material B	–	7,500	–
Labour	62,500	100,000	–
Variable overhead (excl. depreciation)	40,000	56,000	–
Advertising campaign	25,000	35,000	–
Manager's salary	20,000	20,000	–
Redundancy pay	–	–	25,000
Total relevant costs	150,000	220,000	30,000
Net savings	103,750	64,000	32,500

	Workings		
	25,000 units	35,000 units	Shut down
1. Sales revenue			
No. of units	25,000	35,000	
Selling price	£9.00	£7.50	
Sales revenue	£225,000	£262,500	
2. Savings made on material B			
Surplus available	5,000	–	30,000
Saving per litre	£1.25		£1.25
Total saving	£6,250	–	£37,500
3. Sale of machinery			
Current market price	£25,000	£25,000	£25,000
Reduction in value	£2,500	£3,500	–
Sale proceeds	£22,500	£21,500	£25,000
4. Disposal cost of material A			
Quantity to be disposed of	25,000	15,000	50,000
Cost of disposal	£2,500	£1,500	£5,000
5. Purchase cost of material B			
Production requirement	25,000	35,000	
No. of litres to be purchased	–	5,000	
Purchase cost		£7,500	
6. Labour costs			
Normal labour costs	£62,500	£62,500	
Contract labour	–	£37,500	
	£62,500	£100,000	
7. Variable overhead			
@ £1.60 per unit*	£40,000	£56,000	

*Variable overhead/unit

	£
Total variable overhead	100,000
less depreciation	20,000
	80,000

Variable overhead/unit = $\frac{£80,000}{50,000}$

= £1.60 per unit

8. Manager's salary – relevant
9. Redundancy pay – relevant
10. General fixed overheads and non-production overheads – not relevant

(b) An opportunity cost is the value which represents the cost of the next best alternative or the benefit forgone by accepting one course of action in preference to others when allocating scarce resources.

If there is only one scarce resource, decisions can be made by ranking alternatives according to their contributions per unit of the scarce resource. However, in reality, there will be many scarce resources, and different alternatives will use alternative combinations of those scarce resources. In these situations opportunity costs are used to identify the optimum use of those resources.

Solution 5

Tip

- This answer shows different ways of calculating the answer – of course, only one is required. The answer presents only one view: some items could be treated differently, so other solutions would be acceptable in an examination.

(a) Current pottery data

	Hours
Hours worked per person per four-week month: 40 hours × 4 weeks	160
Hours worked per person per annum: 40 hours × 48 weeks	1,920
Total hours available per annum: 20 staff × 1,920 hours	38,400
Capacity currently not being used per annum – 40%	15,360
Staff working elsewhere – 25%	
Staff currently available for use per annum – 15%	5,760

Contribution from normal production:

	Tableware per set		Tiles per 100	
	£	£	£	£
Sales price		50		200
Material cost	10		20	
Labour cost	10		50	
Variable overhead	10		50	
		30		120
Contribution		20		80
No. of hours to produce: £10/£10.42		0.96		
£50/£10.42				4.80

Average contribution per hour based on standard mix:

	Hours	Contribution	Contribution per hr
		£	£
Tiles – 600	28.8	480	16.67
Tableware – 20 sets	19.2	400	20.83
Total	48.0	880	

Average contribution per hour = £880/48 = £18.33

Fish-and-chip shops contract

No. of batches = 5 shops × 20,000 tiles ÷ 100 tiles = 1,000

	Hours	Hours
Hours required = 1,000 batches × 4.8 hours		4,800
Supplied by:		
Hours currently available in next 6 months:		
5,760 × 24/48	2,880	
Plus two men decorating showroom		
(16 weeks available to work): (2 × 1,920) × 16/48	1,280	
		4,160
Hours still needed		640

The 640 hours can be found by stopping the two staff decorating the showroom (2 × (1,920 hours × 8/48 weeks) = 640 hours) and getting in a contractor, costing £5,000. The salaries of the two staff amount to 640 hours × £10.42 = £6,669. By employing a contractor D will save £1,669. (As the salaries are included in the contribution calculation that follows, only the net saving is included.)

	£
Contribution = 1,000 batches × [£80 – (5% × £200)]	70,000
Add: cost saving	1,669
Net gain	71,669

Contribution per hour = £71,669 ÷ 4,800 = £14.93
Contribution per hour in a normal year = £70,000 ÷ 4,800 = £14.58
(The other option of paying overtime is possible but this will generate an additional cost and so is not calculated.)

> *Alternative treatment:*
> Cost of 640 hours using overtime:
> Overtime possible: 15 staff × 6 hours × 24 weeks = 2,160 hours
> Overtime needed for contract for 6 months, i.e. 640 hours.
> Cost of overtime = 640 hours × overtime rate £10.42 × 150% = £10,003
> Contribution generated without the 640 hours under question:
>
> | | £ | £ |
> |---|---|---|
> | Sales revenue 1,000 batches × (£200 − 5%) | | 190,000 |
> | Less: | | |
> | Materials and variable overhead: | | |
> | 1,000 batches × £70 | 70,000 | |
> | Wages: 4,160 hours × £10.42 | 43,347 | |
> | | | 113,347 |
> | | | 76,653 |
>
> Option 1 – contractor for shop to gain extra 640 hours:
> Contribution as above less payment to contractor: £76,653 − £5,000 = £71,653
> Option 2 – work overtime to gain extra 640 hours:
> Contribution as above less overtime: £76,653 − £10,003 = £66,650

Z plc contract

Cost of work on swimming pool:

(3 staff × 40 hours × 24 weeks) × £10.42 = £30,010

This is cheaper than making a donation.

The opportunity cost of giving up small contracts is £18.33 per hour (after charging labour cost). The cost of hiring new labour is only £10.42 per hour (excluding hiring cost, which is only £500). The cost of working overtime is £15.63 per hour. Therefore hiring new staff is the cheapest option, followed by working overtime. This also helps to keep the existing products/business going.

		Hours
40,000 sets × 0.96 hours		38,400
Hours available this year if all staff		
working in pottery	15,360	
Eight new staff × 1,920 hours	15,360	
		30,720
Therefore, hours still required		7,680
Less:		
overtime − existing staff (20 × 6 hours × 24 weeks)	2,880	
new staff (8 × 6 hours × 24 weeks)	1,152	
		4,032
Remainder must be taken from small contracts		3,648

	£	£
Contribution:		
40,000 sets × (£20 − (15% × £50) = £12.50)		500,000
Add: saving on contractor for showroom		1,669
		501,669
Less additional costs:		
Rent forgone	10,000	
Extra fixed costs	3,000	
Moulds	15,000	
Contractor for swimming pool	35,000	
Recruitment costs for eight staff	4,000	
Overtime premium 4,032 hours × £10.42 × 50%	21,007	
Lost contribution on small contracts:		
£18.33 × 3,648 hours	66,868	
		154,875
Net gain		346,794

Both contracts are feasible and profitable.

(b) Z plc contract

		Hours
Maximum available hours without overtime:		
28 staff × 1,920		53,760
Less Z plc contract		38,400
Hours available for normal production – only		15,360

	£	£
Comparable contribution in a normal year		500,000
Less: fixed costs	3,000	
rent forgone	10,000	
		13,000
		487,000 ÷ 38,400 hours = £12.68

Recommendation

Assuming that D expects that normal sales will pick up in the future, and that he is comfortable with the present size of the pottery, it is suggested that he accepts the fish-and-chip shop contract. The following points need to be considered:

Tiles for fish & chip shops
- This is a profitable contract which can be met without exceeding the pottery's existing capacity. D would actually save money by getting a contractor in to decorate.
- The additional profit generated is £71,669 and the contribution per hour is £14.93, compared with an average contribution on normal production of £18.33 per hour.
- Whether D will wish to accept further contracts in future years will depend on whether there is sufficient spare capacity. The contribution per hour next year will be £14.58. This is less than the contribution on existing work and so should be pursued only if there is spare capacity.

Z plc contract
- This generates a net gain of £346,794. This is a considerable amount, but the extra amount of work that it places on D must be considered.
- There is also the possibility that D may not be able to re-let the premises immediately the contract is completed. However, the rent lost is small in comparison to the gain on the contract.
- If further contracts were available, D would be unwise to accept them – assuming that the pottery was working near capacity by this time – as the business does not have adequate capacity to meet the normal production and the contract. The contribution per hour on the contract in a normal year would be only £12.68.
- Acceptance of the very large Z plc contract would have an effect on the nature of D's business. The company would change into a manufacturer for a department store and would have little say over future designs, etc.
- There is also the worry that the pottery might become reliant on Z plc at some stage because of the large volume of work done for the company. If, in future, Z plc withdrew the contract or reduced the price it was willing to pay, D's business could be in considerable difficulty.

Solution 6

(a) The cost per litre is the same for all three joint products therefore the basis of the common cost apportionment is the number of litres output.

This is an acceptable method for the purposes of external financial reporting since it is based on the cost incurred in the common process, however its usefulness for internal reporting is limited given that there is one process that is common to all three outputs.

It is necessary to apportion the common costs between the different products so that inventory values can be derived for each form of output in order to match sales with cost of sales for the purposes of external financial reporting.

(b) The sales values of the outputs from the common process total $540,250 and the total costs attributed to the outputs from the process total $482,375 therefore the common process is viable since it generates revenues in excess of costs.

With regard to the viability of each individual product a comparison must be made between the incremental revenue from further processing and the further processing costs that are incurred. Thus:

Product	Incremental revenue per litre	Incremental cost per litre
M	$2.15	$1.75
N	$1.25	$0.95
P	$0.65	$0.85

Thus it can be seen that products M and N should be further processed whereas product P should be sold at the point of separation (i.e. after the common process). All three products are viable if this course of action is taken, however it is not viable to further process product P.

5

Linear Programming

Linear Programming

5

LEARNING OUTCOMES

▶ Apply variable/fixed cost analysis in multiple product contexts to breakeven analysis and product mix decision making; including circumstances where there are multiple constraints and linear programming methods are needed to reach 'optimal' solutions.

▶ Discuss the meaning of 'optimal' solutions and show how linear programming methods can be employed for profit maximising, revenue maximising and satisfying objectives.

5.1 Introduction

In this chapter we will see how to solve decision making problems where there is more than one scarce resource using a technique called linear programming.

We will then learn how to interpret the solution to the problem to allow managers to make better, more informed, decisions.

5.2 Basic linear programming

In the previous chapter you saw how to use basic limiting factor analysis to determine the profit-maximising sales mix for a company with a single resource constraint. The decision rule was to allocate the resource to products according to the contribution earned per unit of scarce resource, subject to any other constraints such as maximum or minimum demands for the individual products.

This technique cannot be applied when there is more than one limiting factor. In this situation a linear programming technique is used.

Linear programming is the name given to a collection of tools that are among the most widely used in management science. It is essentially a constrained optimisation technique that encompasses the general decision problem of allocating scarce resources between competing activities so as to maximise or minimise some numerical quantity such as contribution or cost. In the area of business such problems include planning production to maximise profit, mixing ingredients to minimise costs, selecting a portfolio of investments to maximise worth, transporting goods to minimise distance, assigning people to maximise efficiency and scheduling jobs to minimise time.

Linear programming involves the construction of a mathematical model to represent the decision problem where the activities of the problem constitute variables. The model then comprises a linear function that is to be optimised and a set of restrictions on the variables in the form of linear equations and inequalities. The model is then solved by an appropriate method or by the use of a computer package to obtain the optimal values for the activities.

5.2.1 Formulating the mathematical model

This is probably the most challenging part of linear programming and requires the translation of a decision problem into a system of variables, equations and inequalities. This process ultimately depends upon the skill, experience, flair and intuition of the model-builder. However, a four-step procedure can be used as an aid in the construction of the mathematical model, and the following example is used to develop this procedure.

Example

Robert Miles operates a small machine shop. Next month he plans to manufacture two new products (A and B) upon which the unit contribution is estimated to be £50 and £70, respectively.

For their manufacture both products require inputs of machine processing time, raw materials and labour. Each unit of product A requires 3 hours of machine processing time, 16 units of raw materials and 6 units of labour. The corresponding per unit requirements for product B are 10, 4 and 6. Robert forecasts that next month he can make available 330 hours of machine processing time, 400 units of raw materials and 240 units of labour. The technology of the manufacturing process is such that at least 12 units of product B must be made in any given month.

Robert Miles wishes to formulate a linear programming model so as to determine the number of units of products A and B that he should manufacture next month to maximise contribution.

The model can be formulated as follows.

Step 1 – Determining the variables

There is an *objective variable* (given the notation z) that represents the single quantity that is required to be optimised, i.e. maximised or minimised. (Profit, revenue, contribution and cost are typical such quantities.) Robert Miles desires to maximise contribution, thus the objective variable here is stated as:

Let z = total £ contribution earned next month from the manufacture of products A and B

There is a set of *decision variables* (given the notation x_1, x_2, x_3, etc.) that represent the activities of the decision problem. They are the unknown quantities whose values need to be determined to achieve the optimal value of the objective variable, which in Robert's situation is total contribution. This contribution depends upon the quantities of products A and B produced, which thus constitute the activities. Values of these quantities need to be calculated and they therefore comprise the decision variables of the model. They are defined thus:

Let x_1 = the number of units of product A manufactured next month
Let x_2 = the number of units of product B manufactured next month

It is very important to clearly define these variables; and to specify the units in which they are measured and any time period they refer to.

Step 2 – Constructing the objective function

This is a linear equation that has to be either maximised or minimised, and that contains the objective variable expressed in terms of the decision variables. It is an expression of the overall goal of the problem.

In the Robert Miles example, every product A manufactured results in a contribution of £50, and if x_1 units of this product are made then the contribution will be £50x_1. The unit contribution on product B is £70, and if x_2 of these are made a contribution of £70x_2 results. Thus, the total contribution obtained next month from the manufacture of x_1 units of A and x_2 units of B (i.e. the objective variable z) will be equal to:

£50x_1 + £70x_2

This Robert desires to maximise. Therefore, the objective function of the model is:

Maximise $z = 50x_1 + 70x_2$

Step 3 – Specifying the constraints

This is a system of linear equations and/or inequalities that restrict the values of the decision variables. They reflect, mathematically, the availability of scarce resources, technological considerations, marketing conditions, output requirements, etc.

The constraints can only be of three types – namely 'less than or equal to' (written $\leq$); 'greater than or equal to' (written $\geq$); 'strictly equal to' (written $=$).

Consider the Robert Miles case. To manufacture products A and B inputs of machine processing time, raw materials and labour are needed, and these resources are in limited supply. The quantities of the two products made (i.e. the values of x_1 and x_2) will thus be restricted in that the amount of any resource required in the manufacturing process cannot exceed its availability. Consider the case of machine processing time. Every unit of product A manufactured needs three hours of machine processing and if x_1 units are made then $3x_1$ hours of this resource are used up. Every product B made uses up ten hours and therefore if x_2 are made $10x_2$ hours are required. Thus, the total machine hours needed to manufacture x_1 units of A and x_2 units of B is $3x_1 + 10x_2$. This total requirement cannot exceed, or must be less than or equal to, the 330 hours available. Mathematically this is expressed as follows:

$$3x_1 + 10x_2 \leq 330$$

Similar arguments can be made for raw materials and labour, enabling the following two constraints to be written:

$$16x_1 + 4x_2 \leq 400$$
$$6x_1 + 6x_2 \leq 240$$

Finally, it should be noted that there is a condition that at least 12 units of product B must be manufactured. This can be translated into the constraint:

$$x_2 \geq 12$$

Step 4 – Writing out the non-negativity conditions

These are conditions imposed upon the decision variables and are expressed as $x_1 \geq 0$, $x_2 \geq 0$, etc. They must be included in the model to ensure that no negative solution values can be obtained for the decision variables. (It is worth noting that these conditions allow non-negative integer and fractional values.)

In the Robert Miles example it is not necessary to write out the non-negativity condition for x_2 as this is ensured by the constraint $x_2 \geq 12$. However, it must be stated for x_1, i.e.

$$x_1 \geq 0$$

The full linear programming model for the Robert Miles manufacturing problem can now be formally specified:

Maximise: $z = 50x_1 + 70x_2$
Subject to: $3x_1 + 10x_2 \leq 330$
$16x_1 + 4x_2 \leq 400$
$6x_1 + 6x_2 \leq 240$
$x_2 \geq 12$
$x_1 \geq 0$

5.2.2 The graphical method of solving linear programming models

This is suitable only for problems that involve two decision variables. The model constructed above will be used to develop the method.

The axes of the graph represent the two decision variables, as shown in Figure 5.1. It does not matter which variable appears on which axis. It is essential to select a scale that will eventually enable a large enough diagram to be constructed and that the axes are clearly labelled. It should also be noted that as both variables are constrained to be non-negative only the positive quadrant is drawn.

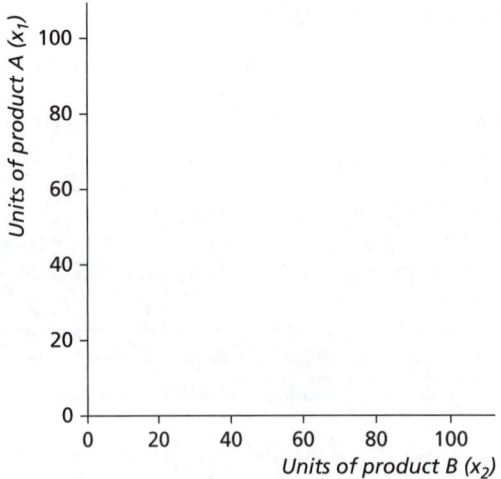

Figure 5.1

Consider the constraints of the model. The upper limit of every 'less than or equal to' constraint is a 'strict equality' and the lower limit of every 'greater than or equal to' constraint is a 'strict equality'. These limits are thus equations that, being linear, have straight-line graphs that can be plotted on Figure 5.1. The normal way of doing this is to calculate the points where the lines intersect the two axes. This is convenient and easy to do in that it is recognised that anywhere on the x_1-axis, x_2 equals zero; and on the x_2-axis, x_1 equals zero. Therefore:

$3x_1 + 10x_2 \leq 330$	$3x_1 + 10x_2 = 330$	$x_1 = 0;$	$x_2 = 33;$
		$x_1 = 110;$	$x_2 = 0;$
$16x_1 + 4x_2 \leq 400$	$16x_1 + 4x_2 = 400$	$x_1 = 0;$	$x_2 = 100;$
		$x_1 = 25;$	$x_2 = 0;$
$6x_1 + 6x_2 \leq 240$	$6x_1 + 6x_2 = 240$	$x_1 = 0;$	$x_2 = 40;$
		$x_1 = 40;$	$x_2 = 0;$
$x_2 \geq 12$		$x_2 = 12;$	
		(No interceptor on x_1 axis)	

Taking the first constraint, plot its limiting equation on Figure 5.1 to give the diagram in Figure 5.2.

Any point (i.e. values of x_1 and x_2) in or on the triangle GDH will satisfy this constraint. Such points are called feasible whereas those outside are termed infeasible.

It should be noted that points on the line GD represent the 'strict equality' whereas those below the line represent 'less than'.

Next take the second two constraints and plot their limiting equations on Figure 5.2 to give Figure 5.3. Points on or contained within the shaded area FBCDH will thus satisfy all of the first three constraints at the same time.

Finally, the equation $x_2 = 12$ is plotted on Figure 5.3 to give the diagram in Figure 5.4. This line is parallel to the x_1-axis and any point on it or to its right will satisfy the last constraint. Values of x_1 and x_2 on or within the area shaded ABCDE will satisfy all the constraints of the model. Such an area is called the *feasible region*.

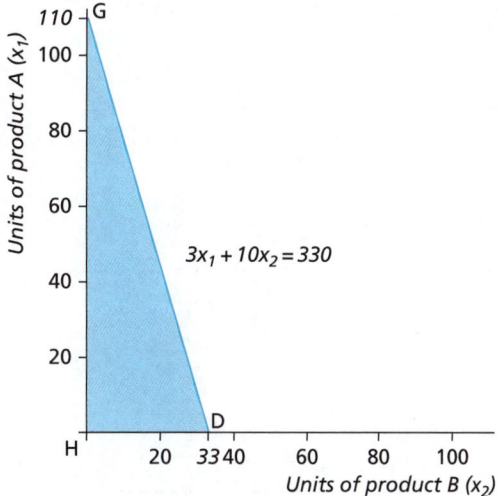

Figure 5.2

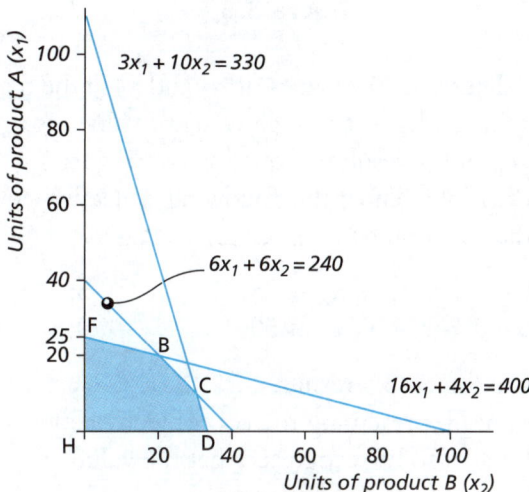

Figure 5.3

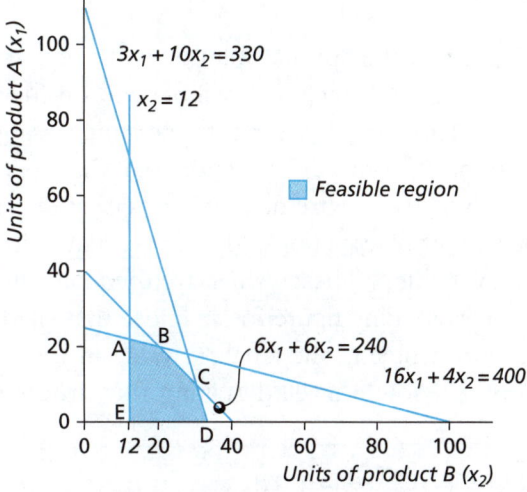

Figure 5.4

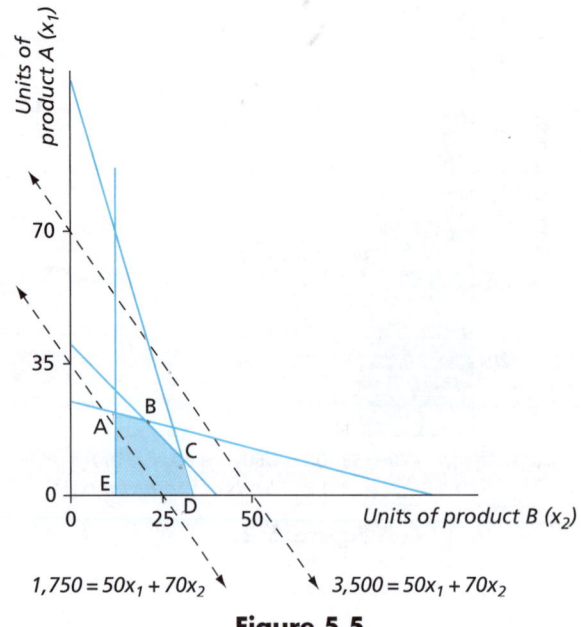

Figure 5.5

Now the objective is to determine the values of x_1 and x_2 in the feasible region that make z as large as possible. To this end select two convenient values for z, substitute them into the objective function and plot the resulting equations on Figure 5.4. In this example, 1,750 and 3,500 appear to be sensible. Thus, the following objective equations are plotted in exactly the same way as the constraints:

$1,750 = 50x_1 + 70x_2 \qquad x_1 = 0; x_2 = 25; \qquad x_1 = 35; x_2 = 0$
$3,500 = 50x_1 + 70x_2 \qquad x_1 = 0; x_2 = 50; \qquad x_1 = 70; x_2 = 0$

The information given in Figure 5.5 results.

It can be seen that the lines representing the two objective equations are parallel as they have the same slope. It should also be recognised that the value of z is constant along these lines (at 1,750 and 3,500, respectively) and that the one that is further from the origin has the larger value for z. So to find the values of x_1 and x_2 that maximise z, move parallel to these objective equations to that point within the feasible region that is the furthest from the origin, that is, point C. (Move in the opposite direction if the problem is one of minimisation.)

It can therefore be deduced that the optimal solution will occur at one of the vertices or corner points of the feasible region. Which it is will depend on the slope of the objective function and whether the problem is of a maximisation or minimisation type. Thus, it is not necessary to ever actually graph the objective function – all that is required is to determine the values of x_1 and x_2 at each of these extreme points by either reading off from the graph or by solving the appropriate pair of equations. (The latter may well be necessary to calculate the exact values of the variables.) These values are then substituted into the objective function to compute the corresponding figure for z. Those that yield the largest value for z in the case of a maximisation problem, the smallest value in the case of a minimisation problem, constitute the optimal solution. Undertaking this process for the Robert Miles case gives the following:

Point A: $\quad x_1 = 22; x_2 = 12 \quad z = 1,940$
Point B: $\quad x_1 = 20; x_2 = 20 \quad z = 2,400$

Point C: $x_1 = 10; x_2 = 30$ $z = 2,600^{**}$
Point D: $x_1 = 0; x_2 = 33$ $z = 2,310$
Point E: $x_1 = 0; x_2 = 12$ $z = 840$

** The solution is at point C.

Thus, Robert Miles should produce 10 units of product A and 30 units of product B next month to achieve maximum contribution of £2,600.

The graphical method can be summarised by the following steps:

1. Draw on a graph two axes to represent the two decision variables.
2. Plot all the constraints of the model as straight lines by evaluating where the limiting equations intersect the axes.
3. Identify the area on the graph (known as the feasible region) that satisfies all the constraints. If such an area does not exist then the model has no solution.
4. Determine the values of the decision variables at the extreme points of the feasible region, and in each case calculate the corresponding value for the objective variable.
5. If the problem is one of maximisation then the values of the decision variables computed under step 4 that yield the largest figure for the objective variable constitute the solution. In the case of a minimisation problem it is the values that give the smallest figure.

5.2.3 Further examples of the construction and graphing of constraints

Consider the Robert Miles case and the following additional requirements on the manufacture of the two products.

1. The total combined output of products A and B next month must be at least 20 units. The total number of products A and B manufactured is given by $x_1 + x_2$.

    This must be 'greater than or equal to' 20. The following constraint can be specified:

    $x_1 + x_2 \geq 20$

    The limiting equation of this constraint will intersect both the x_1 and the x_2 axes at 20. Therefore, the diagram given in Figure 5.6 results, with any point on or above the line KL satisfying the constraint, that is, being feasible.

2. The number of units of product B manufactured must be at least double the number of units of product A. This requires the value of x_2 to be at least twice the value of x_1, which can be translated into:

    $x_2 \geq 2x_1$

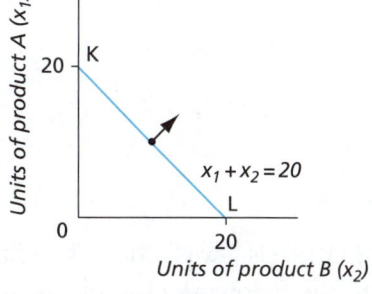

Figure 5.6

With constraints of this type it is always advisable to substitute some hypothetical values for the decision variables into the inequality to ensure that the construction has been correct. For example, letting x_1 equal 10 would mean that x_2 must be equal to at least 20, which is correct. To graph constraints such as this requires a deviation from the normal procedure as the line intersects both axes at zero. A second point can be obtained by selecting any pair of values for x_1 and x_2 (e.g. 10 and 20) that will satisfy the limiting equation.

Thus, the diagram shown in Figure 5.7 can be drawn with points on or below the line MN satisfying the constraint.

3. Products A and B must be manufactured in the ratio 2 : 7.
   This requires x_1 and x_2 to take on values such as 2 and 7; 4 and 14; 20 and 70; etc. The following equation will ensure that this is the case:

   $7x_1 = 2x_2$

   Such constraints are invariably formulated by a combination of 'trial and error', and repeated substitution of feasible values for the decision variables until the desired result is achieved.

   The procedure described in 2 above is used to graph the constraint and this is shown in Figure 5.8 As the constraint is a 'strict equality' only points on the line PQ are feasible.

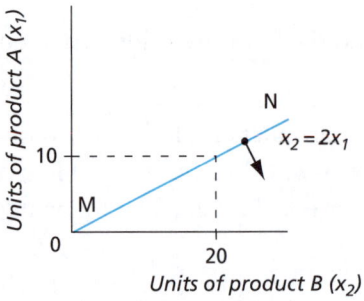

Figure 5.7

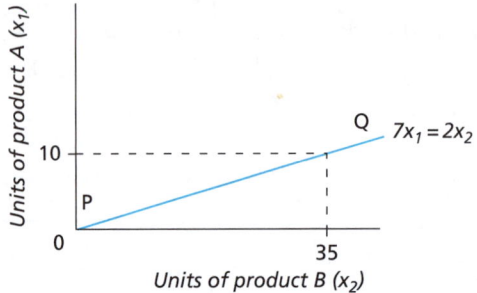

Figure 5.8

5.2.4 Multiple solutions

In a linear programming problem there is always the possibility of multiple solutions. This can be illustrated by reference to the following example, which concerns a small business called Greenfields.

Example

Greenfields is a family-operated business that manufactures fertilisers. One of its products is a liquid plant feed into which certain additives are put to improve effectiveness. Every 10,000 litres of this feed must contain at least 480 g of additive A, 800 g of additive B and 640 g of additive C. Greenfields can purchase two ingredients (X and Y) that contain these three additives. This information, together with the cost of each ingredient, is given below as follows:

	Ingredient X	Ingredient Y
Additive A	2 g	8 g
Additive B	5 g	10 g
Additive C	10 g	4 g
Cost per litre	£25	£50

Both ingredients require specialist storage facilities and as such no more than 120 litres of each can be held in stock at any one time.

Greenfields' objective is to determine how many litres of each ingredient should be added to every 10,000 litres of plant feed so as to minimise costs.

A linear programming model of this problem can be constructed by following the procedure outlined above.

- *Step 1.* As the objective is to minimise costs the objective variable can be defined as:

Let z = total cost of the additives, in pounds, for every 10,000 litres of plant feed

The quantities of the two ingredients purchased constitute the activities of the problem. Thus there are two decision variables in the model, i.e.:

Let x_1 = the number of litres of ingredient X purchased
Let x_2 = the number of litres of ingredient Y purchased

- *Step 2.* The cost of a litre of ingredient X is £25 and of ingredient Y £50. Therefore, the objective function of the model that is to be minimised is:

$$z = 25x_1 + 50x_2$$

- *Step 3.* The three additive requirements of the plant feed will constitute three constraints. Consider the case of additive A. One litre of ingredient X contains 2 g of this additive, whereas a litre of ingredient Y contains 8 g. If x_1 litres of ingredient X and x_2 litres of ingredient Y are added to every 10,000 litres of plant feed then the total number of grams of additive A thus contained will be $2x_1 + 8x_2$. This must be at least equal to the minimum requirement of 480 g. Thus the following constraint can be specified:

$$2x_1 + 8x_2 \geq 480$$

The same argument can be made for additives B and C, yielding the following two constraints:

$$5x_1 + 10x_2 \geq 800$$
$$10x_1 + 4x_2 \geq 640$$

Because of the limitations on storage, x_1 and x_2 cannot exceed 120. This can be translated into the following two constraints:

$$x_1 \leq 120$$
$$x_2 \leq 120$$

- *Step 4.* Finally, the non-negativity conditions must be stated:

$$x_1, x_2 \geq 0$$

The complete model for Greenfields' problem can now be written as:

Minimise: $z = 25x_1 + 50x_2$
Subject to:
$2x_1 + 8x_2 \geq 480$
$5x_1 + 10x_2 \geq 800$
$10x_1 + 4x_2 \geq 640$
$x_1 \leq 120$
$x_2 \leq 120$
$x_1, x_2 \geq 0$

This problem can now be solved by the graphical method as described earlier. Thus, taking the five constraints, the intercepts of their limiting equations on the x_1 and x_2 axes are calculated as follows:

$2x_1 + 8x_2 = 480$ $x_1 = 0; x_2 = 60$ $x_1 = 240; x_2 = 0$
$5x_1 + 10x_2 = 800$ $x_1 = 0; x_2 = 80$ $x_1 = 160; x_2 = 0$
$10x_1 + 4x_2 = 640$ $x_1 = 0; x_2 = 160$ $x_1 = 64; x_2 = 0$
    $x_1 = 120$ (No intercept on x_2 axis)
    $x_2 = 120$ (No intercept on x_1 axis)

Plotting each of these limiting equations gives the diagram in Figure 5.9.

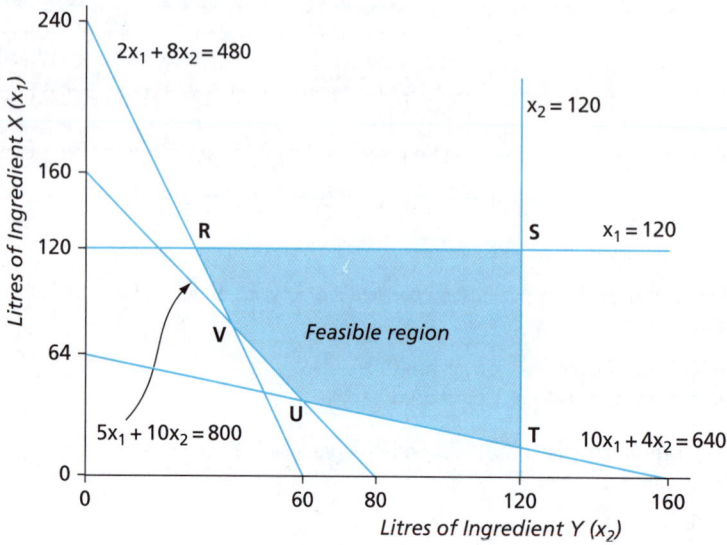

Figure 5.9

Values of x_1 and x_2 on or within the area shaded RSTUV will satisfy all the constraints of the model and thus this area constitutes the feasible region. Determining the values of the decision variables at the corner points of this region, and hence the corresponding value of the objective variable from the objective function $z = 25x_1 + 50x_2$, yields the following:

Point R: $x_1 = 120; x_2 = 30;$ $z = 4{,}500$
Point S: $x_1 = 120; x_2 = 120;$ $z = 9{,}000$
Point T: $x_1 = 16; x_2 = 120;$ $z = 6{,}400$
Point U: $x_1 = 40; x_2 = 60;$ $z = 4{,}000^{**}$
Point V: $x_1 = 80; x_2 = 40;$ $z = 4{,}000^{**}$

As the problem is one of minimisation then the optimal solution is given by the values of x_1 and x_2 that result in the smallest value of z. As can be seen there are two points that give this, namely points U and V, so therefore there is more than one solution.

If the objective function was added to Figure 5.9 then it would be parallel to the extreme edge UV of the feasible region as shown in Figure 5.10. As the problem is one of minimisation it is desired to make z as small as possible while still satisfying the constraints. This can be achieved by moving the objective function as close to the origin as possible while remaining within the feasible region. Any point along the line UV satisfies this condition and thus any values of x_1 and x_2 between U and V constitute a solution.

Thus, when the objective function does not move to an extreme corner of the feasible region but to an extreme edge, *multiple solutions* exist. (In fact, there are an infinite number of solutions as there are an infinite number of points along any line such as UV.) The normal practice in such situations is to report the two sets of values of the decision variables at the ends of the line, that is, at points U and V.

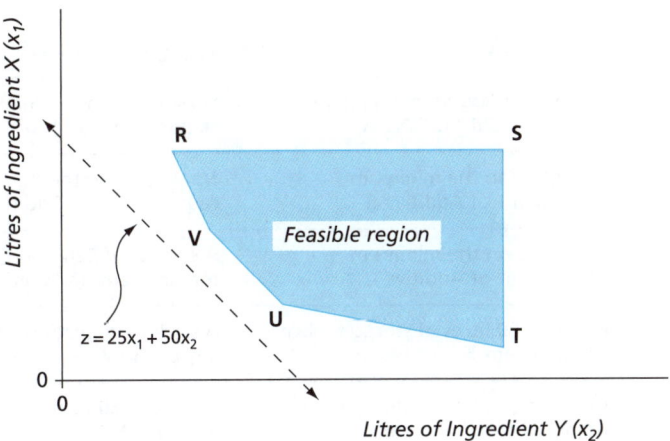

Figure 5.10

Therefore, Greenfields should purchase either 40 litres of ingredient X and 60 litres of ingredient Y, or 80 litres of ingredient X and 40 litres of ingredient Y to achieve a minimum cost of £4,000.

5.2.5 Slack and surplus

In a linear programming model, if the optimal values of the decision variables are substituted into the left-hand side of the constraints then important information concerning unused scarce resources, over-production, etc., can be obtained. Also, it will be revealed which of the constraints are of crucial importance or what is termed *binding*.

If this is done for the model in the Robert Miles case, where the optimal solution was $x_1 = 10$ and $x_2 = 30$, then the following is obtained:

Machine Time: $\quad 3x_1 + 10x_2 \leq 330: \quad 3(10) + 10(30) \leq 330: \quad 330 = 330$

This shows that the total amount of machine processing time required to manufacture the optimal product mix (i.e. 10 units of product A and 30 units of product B) equals the total amount available. There is therefore no spare capacity of this resource or no *slack*.

Raw materials: $\quad 16x_1 + 4x_2 \leq 400: \quad 16(10) + 4(30) \leq 400: \quad 280 < 400$

The left-hand side is 120 less than the right-hand side. Thus to produce the optimal product mix results in 120 unused units of this resource, i.e. a slack of 120 units of raw materials.

Labour: $\quad 6x_1 + 6x_2 \leq 240: \quad 6(10) + 6(30) \leq 240: \quad 240 = 240$

The left-hand side equals the right-hand. So there is no slack labour in the manufacture of the optimal product mix.

$x_2 \geq 12$, but in the optimal solution $x_2 = 30$. Thus, there is a surplus on the minimum production requirement for product B of 18 units.

From the above it can be seen that the concept of slack is concerned with 'less than or equal to' constraints, whereas surplus is associated with 'greater than or equal to' constraints. Further, the analysis reveals that the machine processing and labour constraints are the ones of crucial importance in that both of these resources have been used to their full capacity, that is, there is no slack. It may be (correctly) deduced that obtaining more of these resources would enable more of the two products to be produced, and hence contribution to be increased.

	Point U $x_1 = 40; x_2 = 60$	Point V $x_1 = 80; x_2 = 40$
$2x_1 + 8x_2 \geq 480$	A surplus of 80g on the minimum requirement of Additive A	No surplus on the minimum requirement of Additive A
$5x_1 + 10x_2 \geq 800$	No surplus on the minimum requirement of Additive B	No surplus on the minimum requirement of Additive B
$10x_1 + 4x_2 \geq 640$	No surplus on the minimum requirement of Additive C	A surplus of 320g on the minimum requirement of Additive C
$x_1 \leq 120$	A slack of 80 litres of storage space for Ingredient X	A slack of 40 litres of storage space for Ingredient X
$x_2 \leq 120$	A slack of 60 litres of storage space for Ingredient Y	A slack of 80 litres of storage space for Ingredient Y

Figure 5.11 Slack and Surplus values for Greenfields

The values of the slacks and surpluses for the Greenfields case can be calculated in a fashion similar to that described above. However, it must be remembered that this problem had multiple solutions so there will be more than one set of such values. Figure 5.11 provides the slack and surplus values for the two extreme solutions, i.e. points U and V in Figure 5.9. These are obtained by substituting the x_1 and x_2 values for U and V into the constraints.

It should be noted that in the case of more than one optimal solution, the values of any slack and/or surplus are one of the factors that should be taken into account when ascertaining which of the solutions might be preferable.

5.2.6 Shadow prices and opportunity costs

In the Miles case, in the last section we saw that obtaining more of those resources which were used to their full capacity would enable more of the two products to be produced, and hence contribution to be increased.

> A shadow price is defined in CIMA's *Official Terminology* as 'an increase in value which would be created by having available one additional unit of a limiting resource at its original cost. This represents the *opportunity cost* of not having the use of the one extra unit.'

In the Miles case, where machine time and the availability of labour were binding constraints, the shadow price of each resource would help managers to decide, for example, whether it is worth renting extra machine capacity at a given cost.

Example: calculating the shadow price

To demonstrate the calculation of the shadow price let us assume that one more unit of labour can be made available. This would alter the constraint for labour to:

$6x_1 = 6x_2 \leq 241$

The coordinates of point C would then alter to:

Point C: $x_1 = 10.23; x_2 = 29.93$ and so $z = 2,606.6$

The maximum achievable contribution has increased by £6.60 and this is the shadow price of a unit of labour.

This indicates the premium it is worth paying, above the basic rate, in order to obtain another unit of labour. Thus management can make better informed decisions concerning the payment of overtime premiums or bonuses, for example.

Note, however, that the calculated shadow price applies only for small changes in the availability of a binding constraint. If large changes occur then this may change the shape of the feasible region to such an extent that the optimal solution is altered.

The shadow price is also the amount by which contribution would be reduced if one fewer unit of labour was available. Thus, management can identify the *opportunity cost* of deciding to put the labour to an alternative use.

A small factory makes two components, C_1 and C_2, and has the following constraints on weekly production:

Operative time	240 staff hours
Raw material A	500 kg
Raw material B	400 litres

C_1 uses two staff hours, 5 kg of A and 5 litres of B to make each unit.
C_2 uses three staff hours, 5 kg of A and 4 litres of B to make each unit.
The contributions to profit from each unit of C_1 and C_2 are £150 and £100, respectively. It is known that all production can be sold.

Requirement

Represent the above situation as a linear programming model, if the object is to maximise total weekly profit. (Denote the units of C_1 and C_2 produced each week by X_1 and X_2, respectively.)

Solution

Maximise weekly profit: $Z = 150X_1 + 100X_2 (£)$
Subject to:
$2X_1 + 3X_2 \le 240$
$5X_1 + 5X_2 \le 500$
$5X_1 + 4X_2 \le 400$
$X_1, X_2 \ge 0$

The last constraint is called the non-negativity constraint. It ensures that no negative solution can be obtained for X_1 and LX_2.

5.3 The Simplex method

A linear programming problem with more than two decision variables (e.g. more than two products) cannot be plotted on the two axes of a graph. Therefore, we need a different method of solving the problem: the Simplex method. The Simplex method begins in the same way, by setting up equations for the objective function and the constraints.

Example: Simplex method

Woodhurst is a furniture company that specialises in high-quality products. The company can manufacture four different types of coffee table (small, medium, large and ornate). Each type of table requires time for the cutting of the component parts, for assembly and for finishing. The data in the table below has been collected for the year now being planned.

Table	Hours required per table			Contribution on each table, £
	Cutting	Assembly	Finishing	
Small	2	5	1	60
Medium	2	4	4	123
Large	1	3	5	135
Ornate	6	2	3	90
Capacity in hours	3,000	9,000	4,950	

Owing to other commitments, no more than a total of 1,800 coffee tables can be made in any given year. Also, market analysis reveals that the annual demand for the company's small coffee table is at least 800.

The company wishes to determine how many of each type of coffee table it should produce in the coming year to maximise contribution.

Woodhurst's production problem can be formulated as a linear programme.

The objective variable is stated as:

Let z = total contribution earned in the coming year, in pounds, from the production of the coffee tables

The quantities of the four types of coffee table to be produced are the activities of the problem. Thus there are four decision variables in the model, defined as:

Let x_1, x_2, x_3, x_4 = the number of small, medium, large and ornate coffee tables to be produced in the coming year

The company wishes to maximise contribution, so the objective function is:

Maximise $z = 60x_1 + 123x_2 + 135x_3 + 90x_4$

The quantities of the four types of coffee table made will be restricted by the limited availability of cutting, assembly and finishing time. Thus there will be three constraints specifying, respectively, that the amount of cutting, assembly and finishing time used up in production cannot exceed that which is available. These are written as:

$$2x_1 + 2x_2 + 1x_3 + 6x_4 \leq 3{,}000$$
$$5x_1 + 4x_2 + 3x_3 + 2x_4 \leq 9{,}000$$
$$1x_1 + 4x_2 + 5x_3 + 3x_4 \leq 4{,}950$$

The sum of the four decision variables cannot exceed 1,800 as there is a ceiling on the total number of coffee tables to be manufactured. Thus the following constraint must be included in the model:

$$x_1 + x_2 + x_3 + x_4 \leq 1{,}800$$

The requirement that at least 800 small coffee tables must be produced can be expressed mathematically as:

$$x_1 \geq 800$$

Finally, non-negativity conditions must be stated for the other three decision variables, that is,

$$x_2, x_3, x_4 \geq 0$$

The complete model for Woodhurst's problem is therefore:

Maximise: $z = 60x_1 + 123x_2 + 135x_3 + 90x_4$
Subject to: $2x_1 + 2x_2 + 1x_3 + 6x_4 \leq 3{,}000$
$5x_1 + 4x_2 + 3x_3 + 2x_4 \leq 9{,}000$
$1x_1 + 4x_2 + 5x_3 + 3x_4 \leq 4{,}950$
$x_1 + x_2 + x_3 + x_4 \leq 1{,}800$
$x_1 \geq 800$
$x_2, x_3, x_4 \geq 0$

This model cannot be solved graphically as there are more than two decision variables. A general algebraic method of solving linear programming problems, based on the fundamental concept that the optimal solution occurs at a corner point of the feasible region, could be used. This is called the Simplex method. A computer package that embodies this method has been used, and this will typically yield the information as given in Figure 5.12.

Objective function variable (z): 168,780.0000

Variable	Value	Relative loss
x_1	950.0000	0.0000
x_2	250.0000	0.0000
x_3	600.0000	0.0000
x_4	0.0000	48.0000

Constraint	Slack/surplus	Worth
1	0.0000	9.0000
2	1,450.0000	0.0000
3	0.0000	21.0000
4	0.0000	21.0000
5	150.0000	0.0000

Figure 5.12

1. The *variable* and *value* columns mean that $x_1 = 950$; $x_2 = 250$; $x_3 = 600$; $x_4 = 0$. Therefore to maximise contribution in the coming year, Woodhurst should manufacture 950 small coffee tables, 250 medium ones and 600 large ones. None of the ornate coffee tables should be made.
2. $z = 168{,}750$ which shows that the total contribution that will be earned from the above production of coffee tables in the coming year is £168,750.
3. The *constraint* and *slack/surplus* columns provide information concerning the slack values for the 'less than or equal to' constraints and the surplus values for any 'greater than or equal to' constraints.

From your earlier studies of linear programming you should recall that a slack variable is the amount of resource which will be unused in a specific linear programming solution. A surplus is the extra that is produced above the minimum requirement in a 'greater than or equal to' constraint.

- Constraint 1 is $\leq$ and refers to cutting time. Its slack is zero, showing that all available cutting time will be used.
- Constraint 2 is $\leq$ and refers to assembly time. The slack here equals 1,450 and thus there will be 1,450 unused hours of assembly time. Thus, assembly time is not a binding constraint.
- Constraint 3 is $\leq$ and refers to finishing time. Its slack is zero, indicating that all of this resource will be used.
- Constraint 4 is $\leq$ and refers to the ceiling on the total number of coffee tables produced of 1,800. The slack is zero, showing that this ceiling has been met exactly.
- Constraint 5 is $\geq$ and specifies that at least 800 small coffee tables are made. It has a surplus equal to 150, indicating that production is 150 above the minimum requirement, so 950 of these tables are made. (This is borne out by the fact that $x_1 = 950$.)

5.4 Worth and relative loss

Figure 5.12 provides two other columns: *worth* and *relative* loss. Taking worth initially, consider the first and third constraints, which refer to the availability of cutting and finishing time respectively. Both of these have slacks equal to zero, showing that these resources have been fully utilised. If more of these resources could be obtained then more coffee tables could be made and hence contribution would be increased. Thus these resources have a positive worth, or what is known as a positive *shadow price*, and the figures in the worth column provide this information, i.e. the amount by which contribution (or generally z) would alter if the availability of the resource was changed by one unit. Thus one extra hour of cutting time would increase contribution by £9 and one extra hour of finishing time would increase it by £21.

The worth figure of 21 corresponding to the fourth constraint indicates the change in contribution, in pounds, that would occur if the ceiling on total production alters by one.

The second constraint, which deals with assembly time, has a worth of zero. This is because there are 1,450 hours of this resource left unused and clearly any increase will leave contribution unaltered.

Thus, it can be stated that any constraint having a slack of zero will have a positive worth figure. Any constraint having a positive slack will have a worth value of zero.

In the case of the relative loss column consider the value of 48. This corresponds to the decision variable x_4 which refers to ornate coffee tables. No ornate coffee tables are to be manufactured. However, if one was to be manufactured then the value of total contribution (or generally z) would be reduced by £48. Thus, a relative loss of £48 would be incurred for every one of these products made. It would only be worth while to make ornate coffee tables if its unit contribution increases from its current figure of £90 to £138.

The relative loss figures for the other decision variables and hence the other coffee tables all equal zero. This indicates that these products should be made as no relative loss would be incurred.

Therefore, it can be concluded that only those decision variables having a relative loss of zero will have a positive value in the optimal solution.

5.5 Summary

In this chapter we have seen how we can solve multiple resource constraint problems using Linear Programming and interpret the results.

Reading 5

The article which follows shows how a computer modelling technique (known as Simplex) can be used to carry out the linear programming technique when there are more than two decisions variables.

Straight thinking

Grahame Steven, *CIMA Insider*, **December 2001 © CIMA. Reproduced with permission**

While demand usually determines an organisation's level of activity, most companies will sometimes have to determine how best to allocate scarce resources among competing claims – in other words, decide which customer gets which, if any, of a company's products.

This can be difficult since there may be internal constraints – shortage of material, labour, machine time – and the company may need to take account of commercial considerations, including contracts, multiple purchasing by customers and meeting the needs of major customers.

Limiting factor analysis and linear programming are the two most common techniques used by management accountants to allocate scarce resources, but when should these techniques be used?

As a general guide, they can be applied to the following situations:

- limiting factor analysis: mutiple products, one constraint;
- linear programming (graphical): two products, multiple constraints;
- linear programming (simplex): multiple products, multiple constraints;
- linear programming (computer model): multiple products, multiple constraints.

CIMA's syllabus requires students to undertake limiting factor analysis and use the graphical and computer methodologies for linear programming. They must be able to formulate the Simplex model and interpret the results.

Using Solver, part of Microsoft Excel, the model approach to linear programming can create a linear programming model that can be used to solve a business problem. The model produces data that tests student understanding of the information contained in output reports.

For example, Woodhurst Ltd, which manufactures coffee tables, has produced data for the next budget period (see Table A).

You need to find out what is Woodhurst's profit-maximising sales mix.

Table A Woodhurst: data for budget

Table type	Cutting time per table	Assembly time per table	Finishing time per table	Contribution per table
Small	2 hours	5 hours	1 hour	£60
Medium	2 hours	4 hours	4 hours	£123
Large	1 hour	3 hours	5 hours	£135
Ornate	6 hours	2 hours	3 hours	£90
Capacity	3,000 hours	9,000 hours	4,950 hours	

Manufacturing capacity: 1,800 tables p.a.
Contract: 800 small coffee tables for a major high street retailer.

Step 1: basic model

	A	B	C	D	E	F	G	H
1	Woodhurst	Small	Medium	Large	Ornate	Total		
2		per unit	per unit	per unit	per unit			
3								
4	Contribution	£60	£123	£135	£90			
5								
6	Cutting	2	2	1	6		<=	3,000
7	Assembly	5	4	3	2		<=	9,000
8	Finishing	1	4	5	3		<=	4,950
9	Capacity						<=	1,800
10	Demand: small						>=	800
11	Demand: medium						>=	0
12	Demand: large						>=	0
13	Demand: ornate						>=	0
14		Small	Medium	Large	Ornate			
15	Product mix	0	0	0	0			

Step 2: formulae

Profit-maximising contribution	F4 = +B4 * B15 + C4 * C15 + D4 * D15 + E4 * E15
Total use of cutting time	F6 = +B6 * B15 + C6 * C15 + D6 * D15 + E6 * E15
Total use of assembly time	F7 = +B7 * B15 + C7 * C15 + D7 * D15 + E7 * E15
Total use of finishing time	F8 = +B8 * B15 + C8 * C15 + D8 * D15 + E8 * E15
Manufacturing capacity	F9 = +B15 + C15 + D15 + E15
Minimum demand: small tables	F10 = +B15
Minimum demand: medium tables	F11 = +C15
Minimum demand: large tables	F12 = +D15
Minimum demand: ornate tables	F13 = +E15

Step 3: Solver parameters

Click cell F4, click tools, then click Solver to set up the parameters for this problem:

- Set target cell: click F4
- By changing cells: highlight B15:E15
- Subject to the constraints
- Click add
- Cell reference: highlight F6:F9
- Constraint: highlight H6:H9

- Click OK
- Click add
- Cell reference: highlight F10 : F13
- Change sign to >=
- Constraint: H10 : H13
- Click OK
- Click options
- Tick assume linear model
- Tick assume non-negative
- Click OK
- Click solve
- Click on the following reports: answer, sensitivity
- Click OK

The first step is to set up the basic model for Woodhurst on Excel exactly as shown in the step 1. The next step is to input the formulae into the model – as in steps 2 and 3. Don't forget that Excel contains comprehensive help for Solver.

Successful completion of steps 1 to 3 will produce the report shown in step 4, which shows that the profit-maximising sales mix is 950 small tables, 250 medium tables, 600 large tables, and 0 ornate tables. Any other combination of products will generate a lower contribution.

Given that students are required to interpret output from a linear programming model, what does the answer report (step 5) indicate? It shows that the profit-maximising sales mix will generate a contribution of £168,750. The report then highlights which of the constraints are binding (fully utilised) and those which are not – in other words, where there is spare capacity.

Step 4: solution

	A	B	C	D	E	F	G	H
		Small	Medium	Large	Ornate	Total		
1	Woodhurst	per unit	per unit	per unit	per unit			
2								
3								
4	Contribution	£60	£123	£135	£90	£168,750		
5								
6	Cutting	2	2	1	6	3,000	<=	3,000
7	Assembly	5	4	3	2	7,550	<=	9,000
8	Finishing	1	4	5	3	4,950	<=	4,950
9	Capacity					1,800	<=	1,800
10	Demand: small					950	>=	800
11	Demand: medium					250	>=	0
12	Demand: large					600	>=	0
13	Demand: ornate					0	>=	0
14		Small	Medium	Large	Ornate			
15	Product mix	950	250	600	0			

Step 5: answer report

Click on answer report 1 to obtain the following report:

Target cell (max)

Cell	Name	Original value	Final value
G5	Contribution total	£168,750	£168,750

Adjustable cells

Cell	Name	Original value	Final value
C16	Product mix small	950	950
D16	Product mix medium	250	250
E16	Product mix large	600	600
F16	Product mix ornate	0	0

Constraints

Cell	Name	Cell value	Formula	Status	Slack
G7	Cutting total	3,000	G7 <= I7	Binding	0
G8	Assembly total	7,550	G8 <= I8	Not binding	1,450
G9	Finishing total	4,950	G9 <= I9	Binding	0
G10	Capacity total	1,800	G10 <= I10	Binding	0
G11	Demand: small total	950	G11 >= I11	Not binding	150
G12	Demand: medium total	250	G12 >= I12	Not binding	250
G13	Demand: large total	600	G13 >= I13	Not binding	600
G14	Demand: ornate total	0	G14 >= I$14	Binding	0

Step 6: sensitivity report

Click on sensitivity report 1 to obtain the following report:

Adjustable cells

Cell	Name	Final value	Reduced cost	Objective coefficient	Allowable increase	Allowable decrease
C16	Product mix small	950	0	60	27	10
D16	Product mix medium	250	0	123	7	7
E16	Product mix large	600	0	135	9	10
F16	Product mix ornate	0	0	90	48	1.E + 30

Constraints

Cell	Name	Final value	Shadow price	Constraint RH side	Allowable increase	Allowable decrease
G7	Cutting total	3,000	9	3,000	450	188
G8	Assembly total	7,550	0	9,000	1.E + 30	1,450
G9	Finishing total	4,950	21	4,950	450	750
G10	Capacity total	1,800	21	1,800	83	75
G11	Demand: small total	950	0	800	150	1.E + 30
G12	Demand: medium total	250	0	0	250	1.E + 30
G13	Demand: large total	600	0	0	600	1.E + 30
G14	Demand: ornate total	0	−48	0	42	0

Step 7: test data 1

Input 3001 into cell H6, click tools, click solver, click solve

	A	B	C	D	E	F	G	H
1	Woodhurst	Small	Medium	Large	Ornate	Total		
2		per unit	per unit	per unit	per unit			
3								
4	Contribution	£60	£123	£135	£90	£168,759		
5								
6	Cutting	2	2	1	6	3,001	<=	3,001
7	Assembly	5	4	3	2	7,551	<=	9,000
8	Finishing	1	4	5	3	4,950	<=	4,950
9	Capacity					1,800	<=	1,800
10	Demand: small					950	>=	800
11	Demand: medium					251	>=	0
12	Demand: large					599	>=	0
13	Demand: ornate					0	>=	0
14		Small	Medium	Large	Ornate			
15	Product mix	950	251	599	0			

Step 8: simulation 2

Input 1 into cell H13, click tools, click solver, click solve

	A	B	C	D	E	F	G	H
1	Woodhurst	Small	Medium	Large	Ornate	Total		
2		per unit	per unit	per unit	per unit			
3								
4	Contribution	£60	£123	£135	£90	£168,702		
5								
6	Cutting	2	2	1	6	3,000	<=	3,000
7	Assembly	5	4	3	2	7,545	<=	9,000
8	Finishing	1	4	5	3	4,950	<=	4,950
9	Capacity					1,800	<=	1,800
10	Demand: small					951	>=	800
11	Demand: medium					244	>=	0
12	Demand: large					604	>=	0
13	Demand: ornate					1	>=	1
14		Small	Medium	Large	Ornate			
15	Product mix	951	244	604	1			

Allowable increase/decrease indicates the points at which a different range of products will be made and when a constraint will become non-binding or binding.

The key information contained in this report (step 6) is shadow price, since this indicates what will happen if more scarce (binding) resources are made available, or if resources are allocated to produce a product which is not included in the profit-maximising sales mix. No shadow price is indicated for assembly since it is not a binding resource; it is under-utilised.

The report shows that contribution will increase by £9 for every extra hour of cutting time that is made available, £21 for every extra hour of finishing time and £21 for every one unit increase in capacity. The report also shows that contribution will decrease by £48 for every ornate table that is made. If resources are allocated to make ornate tables, then this means that fewer other tables can be made.

The best way, however, of demonstrating the predicted impact on contribution by making more scarce resources available, or by diverting resources to make another product is to input revised data into the model.

The report shown in step 7 confirms that contribution will increase by £9 if one extra hour of cutting time is made available. This model confirms the predicted impact of making more of the other binding and non-binding resources (assembly time) available.

Step 8 confirms that contribution will decrease by £48 if scarce resources are used to make one ornate table.

Limiting factor analysis and linear programming are valuable tools that can be used to determine the optimum use of resources for complex business problems. While students are not expected to solve Simplex in CIMA exams, they are required to set up computer models and interpret the output. Excel Solver can help students to understand this approach since it makes it relatively simple to set up models for business problems and input amended data to test shadow price information contained in output reports.

Detailed knowledge of Excel or any other computer package is not required to answer exam questions on this topic.

Postscript

There is no substitute for the practical application of the model you have just read about. Try to obtain access to a linear programming computer model and input the data for yourself. Experiment, as in the article, with different combinations of output to ensure, for example, that you understand the meaning of the shadow price information.

Revision Questions

Question 1

Show each of the following constraints on a separate (X_1, X_2) graph:

(a) $5X_1 + 10X_2 \leq 150$ (5 marks)
(b) $4X_1 + 8X_2 \geq 160$ (5 marks)
(c) $X_1 \leq 15$ (5 marks)
(d) $X_2 \geq 20$ (5 marks)
(e) $6X_1 \geq X_2$ (5 marks)

(Total marks = 25)

Question 2

A small factory makes two components, C_1 and C_2, and has the following constraints on weekly production:

Operative time	240 staff hours
Raw material A	500 kg
Raw material B	400 litres

C_1 uses two staff hours, 5 kg of A and 5 litres of B to make each unit.
C_2 uses three staff hours, 5 kg of A and 4 litres of B to make each unit.
The contributions to profit from each unit of C_1 and C_2 are £150 and £100, respectively. It is known that all production can be sold.

(a) Represent the above situation as a linear programming model, if the object is to maximise total weekly profit. (Denote the units of C_1 and C_2 produced each week by X_1 and X_2 respectively.) (5 marks)
(b) Show the constraints from (a) above on a graph and indicate the feasible region. (5 marks)
(c) Determine the product mix which will maximise weekly profit, and the maximum weekly profit, in (a) above. (5 marks)
(d) What slack is there on the constraints in (a)? (5 marks)
(e) In the situation above, selling prices and the costs of materials are expected to change, with the effect that the profit contributions on C_1 and C_2 become £120 and £180 respectively. How will this change the above answers? (5 marks)

(Total marks = 25)

Question 3

Farmer Giles owns a remote 100-hectare (ha) farm in Cumbria. The only available labour is that of Giles himself (35 hours per week) and Mrs Giles (15 hours per week). The farm is suitable for both arable and dairy farming.

The financial implications (£/ha per year) of the alternative forms of cultivation are:

	Arable	Dairy
Sales proceeds (Grain/milk)	210	400
Variable costs	20	190
Contribution	190	210

The labour requirements (minutes per week per ha) are:

Arable	Dairy
10	35

Requirements

(a) Construct a diagram to illustrate the impact of the constraints on the possible alternative forms of land use. **(15 marks)**

(b) Calculate the combination of hectares devoted to each of arable and dairy use that maximizes contribution from the farm. **(10 marks)**

(Total marks = 25)

Question 4

RAB Consulting Ltd specialises in two types of consultancy project.

- Each type A project requires twenty hours of work from qualified researchers and eight hours of work from junior researchers.
- Each type B project requires twelve hours of work from qualified researchers and fifteen hours of work from junior researchers.

Researchers are paid on an hourly basis at the following rates:

Qualified researchers	£30/hour
Junior researchers	£14/hour

Other data relating to the projects:

Project type	A	B
	£	£
Revenue per project	1,700	1,500
Direct project expenses	408	310
Administration*	280	270

* Administration costs are attributed to projects using a rate per project hour. Total administration costs are £28,000 per 4-week period.

During the 4-week period ending on 30 June 2000, owing to holidays and other staffing difficulties, the number of working hours available are:

Qualified researchers	1,344
Junior researchers	1,120

An agreement has already been made for twenty type A projects with XYZ group. RAB Consulting Ltd must start and complete these projects in the 4-week period ending 30 June 2000.

A maximum of 60 type B projects may be undertaken during the 4-week period ending 30 June 2000.

RAB Consulting Ltd is preparing its detailed budget for the 4-week period ending 30 June 2000 and needs to identify the most profitable use of the resources it has available.

Requirements

(a) (i) Calculate the contribution from each type of project. **(4 marks)**
 (ii) Formulate the linear programming model for the 4-week period ending 30 June 2000. **(4 marks)**
 (iii) Calculate, using a graph, the mix of projects that will maximize profit for RAB Consulting Ltd for the 4-week period ending 30 June 2000.
  (Note: projects are not divisible.) **(9 marks)**
(b) Calculate the profit that RAB Consulting Ltd would earn from the optimal plan. **(3 marks)**
(c) Explain the importance of identifying scarce resources when preparing budgets and the use of linear programming to determine the optimum use of resources. **(5 marks)**
(Total marks = 25)

Question 5

A linear programming model is concerned with maximizing profit in a situation with three variables and four constraints on resources. The printout from a computer program used to solve the model shows:

Objectives function variable (z) 16,300

Variable	Value	Relative loss
x_1	400	0.00
x_2	0	8.00
x_3	180	0.00

Constraint	Slack/surplus	Worth
1	0	4.00
2	0	3.50
3	100	0.00
4	125	0.00

Requirement

Explain what is indicated by the printout.

Solutions to Revision Questions 5

Solution 1

- This is an exercise in basic algebra and geometry. You should draw on your basic mathematics to answer it.
- CIMA management accounting examinations frequently involve constructing graphs and you should make sure you know how to do this. It is wise to take a sharp pencil and a ruler into the examination room with you.

(a)
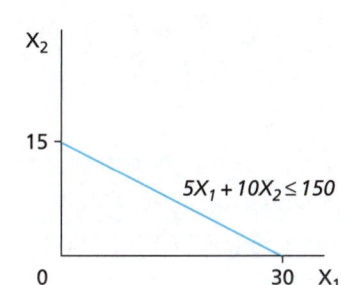

(b)
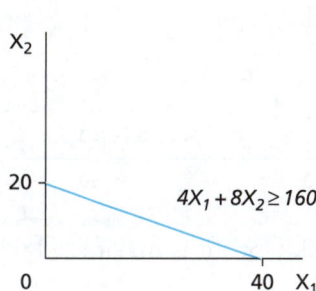

(c)
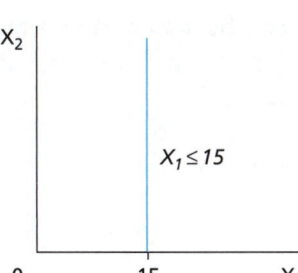

(d)
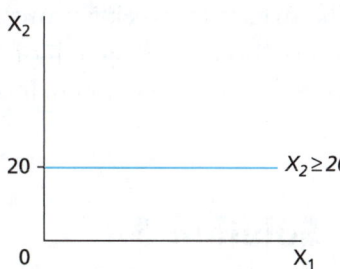

(e)
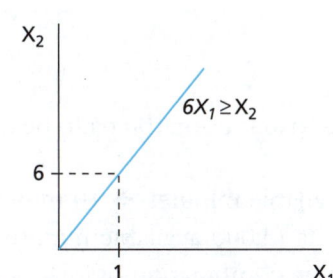

Solution 2

- A graphical representation often helps you understand the nature of the problem. You may therefore find it helpful to start with requirements (b).
- The feasibility limit in a linear programming problem is often represented by a 'dog's leg' and the optimum solution is frequently found to be at one of the discontinuities thereon. Consider why this might be so.
- The question invites the use of graph paper, but if you have time you may care to answer it using a spreadsheet model.

(a) Maximise weekly profit: $Z = 150X_1 + 100X_2$ (£)
    Subject to: $2X_1 + 3X_2 \leq 240$
                            $5X_1 + 5X_2 \leq 500$
                            $5X_1 + 4X_2 \leq 400$
                            $X_1, X_2 \geq 0$

(b)
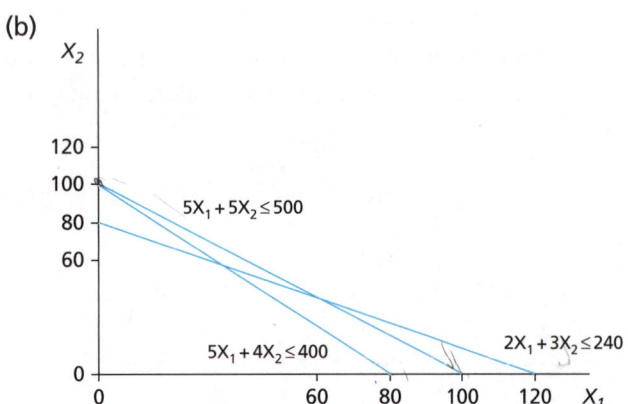

(c) Weekly profit is maximised when $X_1 = 80$ and $X_2 = 0$, at a level of £12,000.

(d) Eighty staff hours are unused. 100 kg of raw material A are unused. Raw material B is full utilised.

(e) The maximum weekly profit becomes £14,400. This can be achieved at a number of points (because the graph of the objective function is parallel to a constraint) between $X_1 = 34, X_2 = 57$ (approximately) and $X_1 = 0, X_2 = 80$.

 ## Solution 3

- The question is pitched at an elementary level for those comfortable with basic algebra and/or graphic skills.
- It can be answered using either algebra or graph paper.

(a) The two constraints are land and labour.

    The impact of land is to allow 100 ha to be devoted to arable, or 100 ha to be devoted to dairying, or some combination of the two.

    The impact of labour is to allow 300 ha (3,000 available minutes ÷ 10 minutes per hectare) to be devoted to arable farming, or 85.714 ha (3,000 available minutes ÷ 35 minutes per hectare) to be devoted to dairying, or some combination of the two.

This position may be illustrated graphically as follows:

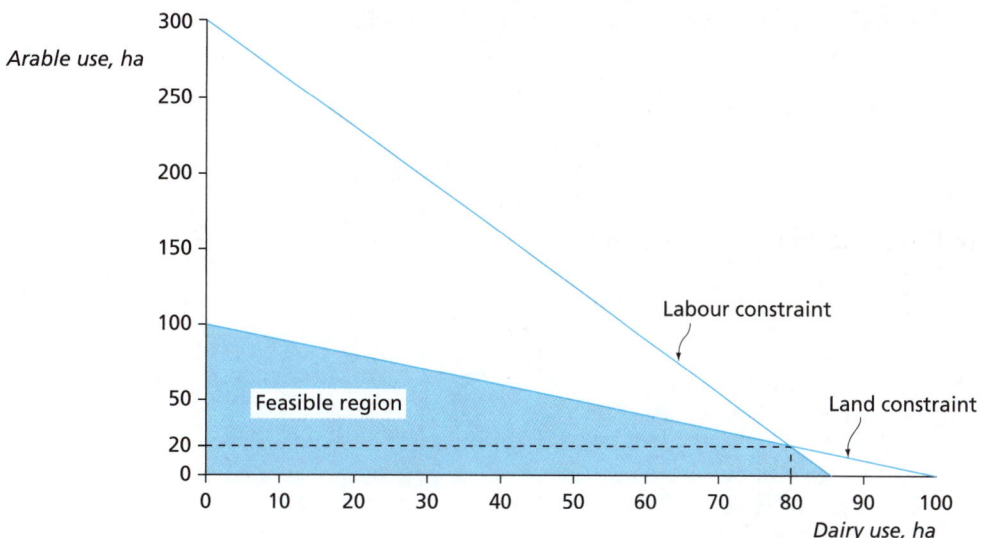

(b) The feasible area lies within both constraints (see diagram) and the only points worth considering are the three 'discontinuities':
1. arable 100, dairying nil;
2. arable nil, dairying 85.714;
3. arable 20, dairying 80. (This last point can be determined from inspection of the diagram or algebraically by determining the values for x and y where the two equations $y = 300 - 3.5x$ (labour) and $y = 100 - x$ (land) intersect.)

The contributions generated at the three points are:

1. £19,000 that is, 100 ha arable × £190;
2. £18,000, that is, 85.714 ha dairy × £210;
3. £20,600, that is, (20 ha arable × £190) + (80 ha dairy × £210).

Clearly, combination 3 offers maximum contribution.

✓ Solution 4

- The critical point to appreciate is that the situation involves two variables (A and B projects) and a number of constraints.
- The linear programming model must therefore be based on A and B output as the two axes, and the constraints being represented by lines.
- Note that the question invites comment on the use of linear programming in the context of the budgeting exercise.

(a) (i) The contributions per project are as follows.

	A £	B £
Fee	1,700	1,500
Researchers:		
Qualified	600	360
Junior	112	210
Expenses	408	310
	1,120	880
Contribution	580	620

The iso-contribution line is $580A + 620B$.

(ii) Constraints used in the linear programming model:

$20A + 12B \leq 1{,}344$ (Qualified researchers)
$8A + 15B \leq 1{,}120$ (Junior researchers)
$B \leq 60$ (Maximum type-B projects)
$A \geq 20$ (Minimum type-A projects)

(iii) Profit-maximising product mix

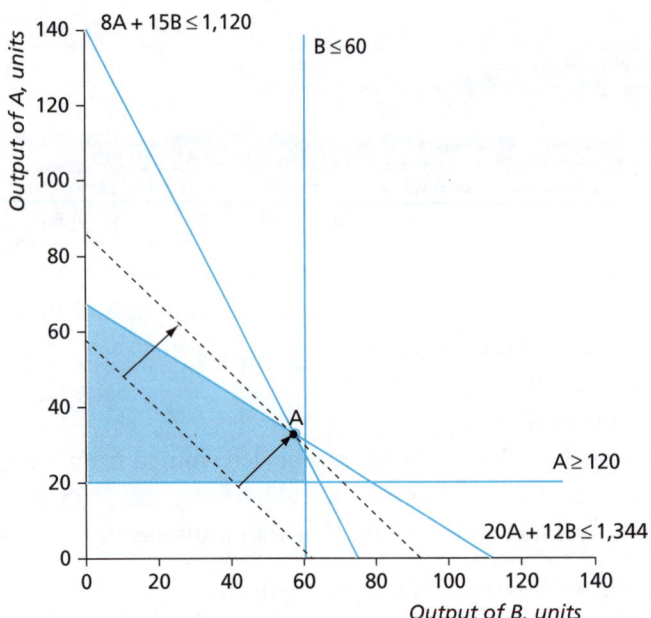

> You must use graph paper so that you can accurately read off the values on each axis.

The area constrained is the feasible region. Add the iso-constribution line, shown as the dotted rule (the easiest method in this case is to divide through the iso-contribution equation by 10, so that $580A + 620B$ becomes $58A + 62B$). Shifting the iso-contribution line outwards indicates that the most profitable point of the feasible region is at point A, which relates to production of 33 units of A and 57 units of B.

(b) Project contributions

	£
A: 33 @ £580	19,140
B: 57 @ £620	35,340
Total contribution	54,480
Less: fixed costs	28,000
Profit	26,480

(c) It is important to identify scarce resources when preparing budgets because they restrict the activity level of the organisation. If they are ignored, the budget is unattainable and is of little relevance for planning and control.

If there is only one scarce resource its optimum use can be determined by ranking in relation to the contribution generated by each product/service per unit of the scarce resource consumed. When there is more than one scarce resource, linear programming is used to identify the most profitable use of resources.

Linear programming is a technique that considers the resources available and thus identifies the possible combinations of those resources. It assumes that all costs can be classified as either fixed or variable in relation to a single activity measure (commonly, units of output). Based on this assumption, linear programming maximises the total contribution in respect of the resources available. The solution may be found graphically by using all of the coordinates of the corners of the feasible region, in each case calculating the contribution that would result from such an output combination. An alternative is to use an iso-contributin line to select the output combination which has the greatest contribution. Where there are more than two types of output a graphical solution is not possible: instead, the Simplex method is used.

Solution 5

Tips

- Without access to a PC and a suitable linear programming system in the examination room, it is not practical to set really searching linear programming questions involving more than two variables. This question indicates the kind of thing that is possible in the circumstances.
- The question is inviting you to describe a solution rather than calculate that solution.

Profit can be maximised at £16,300, when $X_1 = 400$, $X_2 = 0$ and $X_3 = 180$. At the profit-maximising point, the resources relating to constraints 1 and 2 are fully utilised, while there is slack on resources 3 and 4 of 100 and 125, respectively.

For it to be worthwhile producing any units of X_2, its unit profit would have to be increased by 8.00.

If an extra unit of resource relating to constraint 1 became available, maximum profits would increase by 4.00. For constraint 2, an extra unit would enable maximum profits to increase by 3.50.

Pricing

Pricing

6

LEARNING OUTCOMES

▶ Explain the particular issues that arise in pricing decisions and the conflict between 'marginal cost' principles and the need for full recovery of all costs incurred.

▶ Apply an approach to pricing based on profit maximisation in imperfect markets and evaluate the financial consequences of alternative pricing strategies.

6.1 Introduction

In this chapter we will learn the alternative pricing strategies that an organisation may adopt in the pricing of its products or services.

The price to be charged to customers for the business's products or services is often one of the most important decisions to be made by managers. Not all businesses are free to determine their own selling prices: for example some are unable to influence the external price and are obliged to accept the prevailing market price for their goods. For these businesses cost control is an important factor in maintaining profitability.

Other businesses are in a position to select their selling price. The objectives that they pursue in their pricing policy will affect the price to be charged for each product or service. For example the business may be concerned with profit maximisation: in this chapter you will see how managers can use cost and demand analysis to determine the theoretical profit-maximising price.

Other objectives may also affect a company's pricing policy. For example the company may be seeking to maximise revenue, to gain the largest share of the market, to utilise spare capacity or merely to survive. In this chapter we will be looking at many of the different aspects which influence a company's pricing strategy, beginning with the price elasticity of demand.

6.2 Demand and the product life cycle

6.2.1 Price elasticity of demand

Businesses make a profit by selling goods and services at a price that is higher than their cost. Profit is the result of the interaction between cost, volume and price (see Figure 6.1).

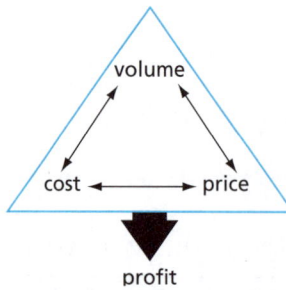

Figure 6.1 The cost, volume, price triangle

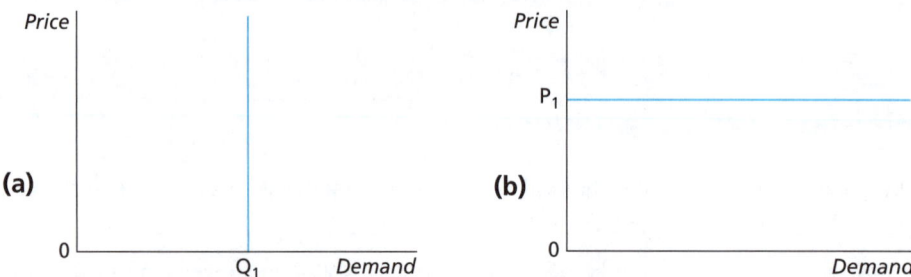

Figure 6.2 Extremes of price/demand trade-off

For instance, the volume of goods sold affects the cost per unit. If the volume increases, the fixed overheads are spread over more units and so the cost per unit decreases. Cost is also influenced by price. This is discussed in target costing later in this text; the aim is to be able to produce at a target cost which is less than the target selling price. This chapter, however, concentrates on the link between price and volume and its resulting effect on profit. Pricing decisions are very important because they have a major effect on volume sold and, as a consequence, on profit generated.

One of the major considerations of a pricing decision is the effect a change in price will have on volume sold. If price is reduced, by how much will demand increase? If price is increased will a large or small decrease in demand occur? A complete answer to these questions, if such an answer does indeed exist, will involve a number of different factors in the total marketing mix, but the basic microeconomic analysis of demand is the fundamental starting point. There are two extremes of the price/demand trade-off, represented graphically in Figure 6.2.

In (a), the same quantity, Q_1, will be sold regardless of the selling price, as demand is completely unresponsive to changes in price. Demand is, therefore, completely inelastic, and the supplier would (theoretically) have unlimited scope, and considerable incentive, to increase price. In (b), demand is limitless at a particular price, P_1, but it would vanish at prices above P_1, that is demand is completely elastic. Under these circumstances there is obviously no point in reducing price below P_1, as this will cause existing profits to fall. Needless to say, these two extremes are rarely seen in practice, and the more normal situation is represented by one of the charts in Figure 6.3.

In both (c) and (d) the supplier is faced with a downward-sloping demand curve, in which reductions in price will result in increased demand and vice versa. This is a negative relationship, or negative correlation, as a decrease in price implies an increase in demand, and vice versa.

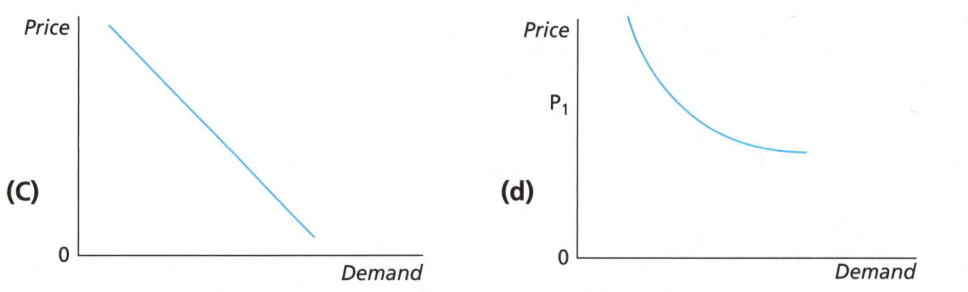

Figure 6.3 Typical price/demand trade-off curves

The slope of the line is the critical factor for a pricing decision, and is expressed by the following formula:

$$\pi \quad \text{Elasticity of demand} = \frac{-\text{\% change in quantity demanded}}{\text{\% change in price}}$$

The numerator and denominator are expressed in terms of percentage change rather than in any absolute amount, in order to avoid distortions caused by the use of different units of measurement. Given the slope of the curve, the negative sign in the numerator has the effect of making the outcome positive, which is generally considered a more convenient representation. Note that the formula measures movement between two discrete points on the curve, and that even though the slope itself is constant, elasticity will differ between different points on the curve. If point elasticity is greater than 1, demand is considered elastic. This means that a fall in price increases demand considerably so that total revenue increases, but an increase in price decreases demand substantially so that total revenue falls. On the other hand, if point elasticity is less than 1 (i.e. it is inelastic) a fall in price will increase demand, but not by a sufficient amount to maintain the previous revenue level, yet a rise in price will increase total revenue.

This is important information for an organisation. For example, when price elasticity is high (i.e. more than 1) the organisation will have difficulty in situations where cost inflation is higher than price inflation, because putting up prices in line with costs will cause a disproportionately large reduction in demand, and total revenues will decline. In times of inflation it is better to put up prices frequently by a small amount each time, as customers do not appear to notice the increases – or certainly do not react to them. If prices are held and then substantially increased in a single price rise, demand is likely to fall off sharply. In practice the prices of many products (e.g. consumer durable products) need to fall over time in order to increase demand. It is vital, therefore, to make costs fall by the same percentage if margins are to be maintained.

Different point elasticity can be seen in practice, as customers do not tend to react evenly to price increases. For example, £1 or £2 may be a psychological barrier and if price is increased over this level demand drops quite rapidly. If the product is sold in a supermarket the organisation needs to know how customers react to different prices in order to determine which price points are crucial. In Figure 6.4, the rise between 38p and 40p triggers a large reduction in demand. To complicate the issue an organisation does not decrease price with the aim of increasing volume in isolation. The effect on volume will depend on how competitors react to the price change, and on the price elasticity of the products.

Different products in the same industry have different price elasticity because they are sold in slightly different markets due to product differentiation. This means that two or

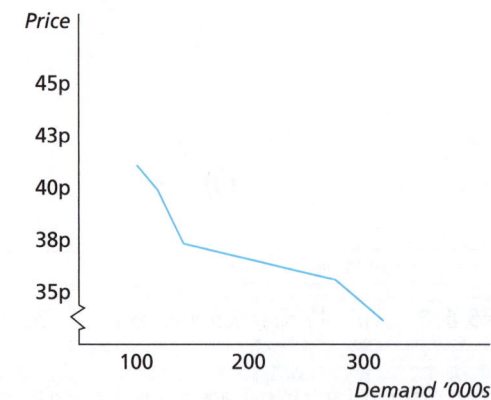

Figure 6.4 Graph showing customer reaction to price increases

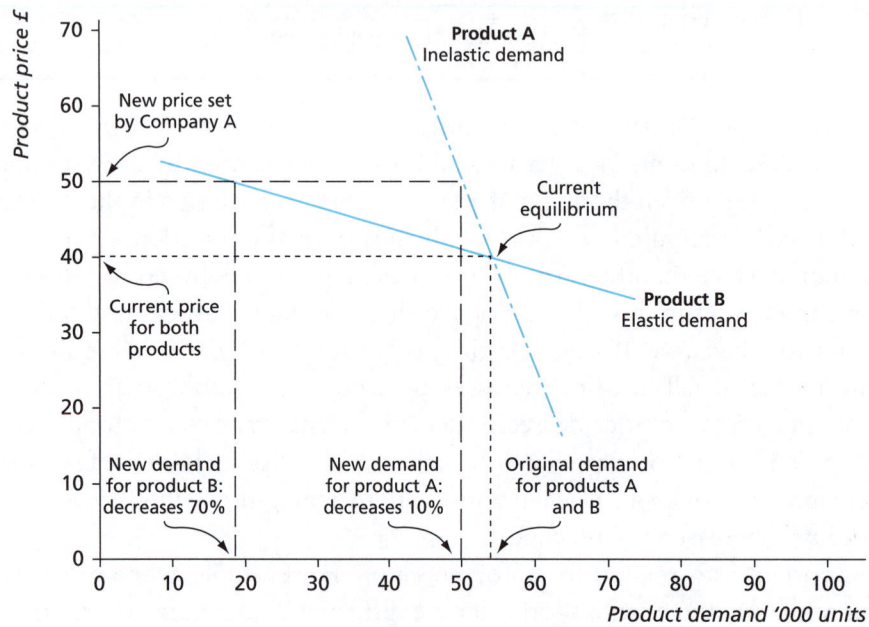

Figure 6.5 Price elasticity of demand: product price rises

more products are sold that have different features, quality, sizes and so on. For example, a Volkswagen Golf GTI (the high-performance model) may enjoy lower price elasticity than the standard Golf 1.4E, so that the price of the former can be increased more safely than can that of the latter.

Figure 6.5 shows two companies. Company A's product A has a highly inelastic demand, while company B's product B has relatively elastic price elasticity.

In an industry in which costs of production are rising, the responsiveness of demand is an essential factor when deciding on price levels. In Figure 6.5 the company producing product A could increase price by 25 per cent, from £40 to £50, with only a 10 per cent effect on volume (from about 54,000 down to 50,000 units). If the company that produces product B attempts to follow the price rise, its volume will fall from about 54,000 units to approximately 18,000 – the result of very elastic demand. In an industry where prices are falling, then the greater the price elasticity the greater the potential for increasing sales volume.

It is also important for an organisation to take account of expected competitors' reactions to any price increases the organisation makes. This is represented in one form by the kinked demand curve, which is discussed in an article in the 'Reading' section. The article compares economists' view on pricing with that of accountants.

Factors affecting price elasticity

When making decisions on products, markets and competitors, other factors, including the following, should be considered:

- *Scope of the market.* The larger the defined market, the more inelastic is the demand for the broader definition of product. For example, the total market for transport is relatively inelastic, whereas the market for 21-speed pedal cycles is comparatively elastic.
- *Information within the market.* Consumers may not know of the competing products in sufficient time to reassess their purchasing behaviour.
- *Availability of substitutes.* The less the differentiation between competing products, the greater the price elasticity of those products. Differentiated products benefit from customer awareness and preference, so their demand patterns tend to be more inelastic.
- *Complementary products.* The inter-dependency of products results in price inelasticity, because the volume sales of the dependent good rely on sales of the primary good. The consumer will make a purchase of the complementary product in order to achieve satisfaction from the primary good. For example, the purchase of a radio, remote control toy car or a torch, etc., all require the purchase of the complementary product – batteries.
- *Disposable income.* The relative wealth of the consumers over time affects the total demand in the economy. Luxury goods tend to have a high price elasticity, while necessities are usually inelastic.
- *Necessities.* Demand for basic items such as milk, bread, toilet rolls, etc., tend to be very price inelastic.
- *Habit.* When consumers act automatically, the products are usually price inelastic.

In practice few organisations attempt to set prices by calculating demand and elasticity. This is probably because it is exceptionally hard to determine demand under different circumstances with any certainty. However, most organisations will have some idea of the elasticity of their products and this will consciously or unconsciously have some bearing on the way prices are set. There are a number of different techniques for setting prices that depend on the type of market and product.

6.2.2 The product life cycle

Products and services, like human beings, have a life cycle. This is represented by the generic curve shown in Figure 6.6. The length of the life cycle varies considerably from a year or so, for some children's toys, to hundreds of years, as in the case of binoculars, for example. The product life cycle is divided into four basic stages as shown in Figure 6.6; each stage has different aims and expectations.

Price is a major variable over the product life cycle. Depending on market structure and demand, different pricing strategies will be appropriate for different stages in the cycle. The four stages in the life cycle and appropriate price strategies are described below.

(i) Introductory phase

Demand will be low when a product is first launched onto the market, and heavy advertising expenditure will usually be required to bring it to consumers' attention. The aim is to

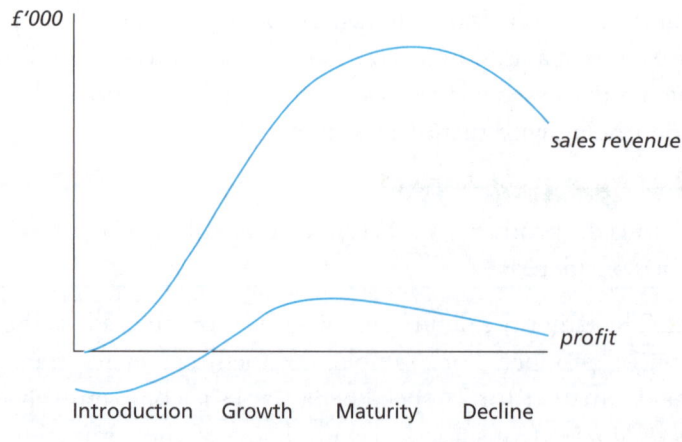

Figure 6.6 The product life cycle

establish the product in the market, which means achieving a certain critical mass within a certain period of time. The critical mass is the sales volume that must be achieved in order to make the product viable in the medium term. Depending on the nature of the product, a price penetration (low entry price) policy may be adopted in order to reach the critical mass quickly. On the other hand the market may be skimmed and so a high introductory price may be set.

(ii) Growth
Once the hurdle of the introductory stage has been successfully negotiated, the product enters the growth stage, where demand shows a steady and often rapid increase. The cost per unit falls because of economies of scale with the greater level of production. The aim at this stage is to establish a large market share and to perhaps become the market leader. Market share is easier to obtain during the growth stage because the market is growing and increased market share does not have to be gained by taking sales from another company. In a more mature market, market share has to be poached from competitors and their reaction may be unpleasant as they try to hold on to their market share. During the growth stage competitors will enter the market, some of which will not survive into the maturity stage. Despite the fact that competing products will be launched into the growing market and pricing is often keen in order to gain market share, it is usually the most profitable stage for the initial supplier.

(iii) Maturity
The increase in demand slows down in this stage, as the product reaches the mass market. The sales curve flattens out and eventually begins to fall. As market maturity is reached the organisation becomes more interested in minimising elasticity. Products have to be differentiated in order to maintain their position in the market and new users for mature products need to be found to keep demand high. Generally, profits will be lower than during the growth stage.

(iv) Decline
When the market reaches saturation point, the product's sales curve begins to decline. When the market declines price wars erupt as organisations with products which have elastic demand seek to maintain full utilisation of their production capacity.

Profits can still be made during the early part of this stage, and the products will be managed to generate cash for newer products. This will determine how prices are set. Eventually rapidly falling sales inevitably result in losses for all suppliers who stay in the market. This particular product has effectively come to the end of its life cycle, and alternative investment opportunities must be pursued.

Despite the recent general tendency to shorter life cycles, the length of any particular stage within the cycle and the total length of the life cycle itself will depend on the type of product or service being marketed. Although the curve will be characterised by a sustained rise, followed by levelling out and falling away, the precise shape of the curve can vary considerably. Life cycles are discussed further later in this text.

6.2.3 The profit-maximisation model

A mathematical model can be used to determine an optimal selling price. The model is based on the economic theory that profit is maximised at the output level where marginal cost is equal to marginal revenue.

Full use of the model requires a knowledge of calculus, which is outside the scope of your syllabus. However, you may be asked to provide answers to questions such as the two examples which follow.

Example

Maximum demand for a company's product M is 100,000 units per annum. The demand will be reduced by 40 units for every increase of £1 in the selling price. The company has determined that profit is maximised at a sales volume of 42,000 units per annum.

What is the profit maximising selling price for product M?

Solution

In the demand equation $p = a - bx$
where p = price
x = quantity demanded
a, b = constants

Maximum demand is achieved when the product is free, that is, when $p = 0$

When price = 0, demand, $x = 100,000$ $0 = a - 100,000b$ (i)
When price = 1, demand, $x = 99,960$ $1 = a - 99,960b$ (ii)
Subtract $1 = 40b$
   $b = 0.025$
Substitute in (i) $a = 100,000 \times 0.025$
   $= 2,500$

The demand equation for product M is therefore $p = 2,500 - 0.025x$

When $x = 42,000$ units, $p = 2,500 - (0.025 \times 42,000)$
   $= 1,450$

Therefore, the profit-maximising selling price is £1,450 per unit.

Example

Another product, K, incurs a total cost of £10 per unit sold, as follows.

	£ per unit
Variable production cost	4
Variable selling cost	2
Fixed production cost	3
Fixed selling and administration cost	1
Total cost	10

The marginal revenue (MR) and demand functions for product K are:

$$MR = 200 - 0.4x$$
$$p = 200 - 0.2x$$

Where p = price, x = quantity demanded per period

What is the profit-maximising selling price of product K and what quantity will be sold per period at this price?

Solution

Marginal cost per unit of product K = variable cost per unit = £6

Profit is maximised when marginal cost = marginal revenue
i.e. when $6 = 200 - 0.4x$
$x = 485$

When $x = 485$, $p = 200 - (0.2 \times 485) = 103$

Therefore the profit-maximising selling price is £103 per unit, at which price 485 units will be sold per period.

6.2.4 Limitations of the profit-maximisation model

The profit-maximisation model is of limited practical use because of the following limitations:

- It is unlikely that organisations will be able to determine the demand function for their products or services with any degree of accuracy.
- The majority of organisations tend to aim to achieve a target profit, rather than the theoretical maximum profit.
- Determining an accurate and reliable figure for marginal or variable cost poses difficulties for the management accountant.
- Unit marginal costs are likely to vary depending on the quantity sold. For example bulk discounts may reduce the unit materials cost for higher output volumes.
- Other factors, in addition to price, will affect the demand, for example, the level of advertising or changes in the income of customers.

Nonetheless, the profit-maximisation model does make some attempt to take account of the relationship between the price of a product and the resulting demand.

6.3 Pricing strategies based on cost

6.3.1 Total cost-plus pricing

There are many different pricing strategies, and it may come as a surprise to would-be accountants that cost is only one of many methods and is certainly not universally used as the key method for pricing.

Cost-plus pricing involves adding a mark-up to the total cost of the product, in order to arrive at the selling price. Unfortunately, because of fixed costs, the full cost of a product will be a function of the number of units produced, which in turn will be a function of the number of units sold. Yet sales quantity will be a function of the price charged for the product, and so the argument is circular.

Where an order is placed with a jobbing company (a company that makes products to order) for a specific quantity of a product made to the customer's specification, cost-plus may be an acceptable pricing method. But for the majority of organisations this is not the case. Other factors will influence the decision, such as competition and product differentiation.

Nevertheless it is reassuring to have some knowledge of cost and price at particular volumes, even if the knowledge is not perfect.

If an organisation does use cost as the basis for pricing it has to decide whether to employ a standard mark-up or whether to vary the mark-up according to the market conditions, type of customer, etc. A standard mark-up is used by some organisations, such as government contractors and some job costing companies, but the majority of companies vary the percentage to reflect differing market conditions for their products. The example below demonstrates total cost pricing, using varying cost assumptions of total cost.

Example

A company is replacing product A with an updated version, B, and must calculate a base cost, to which will be added a mark-up in order to arrive at a selling price. The following variable costs have been established by reference to the company's experience with product A, although they may be subject to an error margin of ±10 per cent under production conditions for B:

	£
Direct material	4
Direct labour (1/4 hr @ £16/hr)	4
Variable manufacturing overheads (1/4 hr of machine time @ £8/hr)	2
Total variable cost per unit	10

As the machine time for each B would be the same as for A, the company estimates that it will be able to produce the same total quantity of B as its current production of A, which is 20,000 units. 50,000 machine hours may be regarded as the relevant capacity for the purposes of absorbing fixed manufacturing overheads. Current fixed costs are £240,000 for the production facilities, £200,000 for selling and distribution, and £180,000 for administration. For costing purposes, the 20,000 units of B can be assumed to consume 10 per cent of the total selling, distribution and administration costs.

Alternative 1, using conventional absorption costing principles and building in the conservative error margin

	£
Variable production costs (as above)	10.0
add: allowance for underestimate 10%	1.0
	11.0
add: fixed manufacturing cost	
1/4 hour of machine time @ £4.8/hour (£240,000/50,000 hours)	1.2
Base cost	12.2

Alternative 2, as 1 but including administrative costs

	£
Base cost as under 1 above	12.2
add: fixed administrative costs:	
(£180,000 × 10% = £18,000 ÷ 20,000 units)	0.9
Base cost	13.1

Alternative 3, as 2 but including selling and distribution costs

	£
Base cost as under 2 above	13.1
add: fixed selling and distribution costs:	
(£200,000 × 10% = £20,000 ÷ 20,000 units)	1.0
Base cost	14.1

Depending on the analysis adopted, the base cost varies from £12.2 to £14.1. The base cost rises with each alternative, as an increasing proportion of the total costs is recovered. The profit mark-up built into the pricing formula is therefore likely to fall with each alternative from 1 to 3.

The profit mark-up needs to be based on some assumption. Normally it is fixed so that the company makes a particular return on capital based on a particular capacity utilisation.

A number of advantages are claimed for cost-plus pricing:

(i) The required profit will be made if budgeted sales volumes are achieved.
(ii) It is a particularly useful method in contract costing industries such as building, where a few large individual contracts can consume the majority of the annual fixed costs and the fixed costs are low in relation to the variable costs.
(iii) Assuming the organisation knows its cost structures, cost-plus is quick and cheap to employ. Its routine nature lends itself to delegation, thus saving management time.
(iv) Cost-plus pricing can be useful in justifying selling prices to customers; if costs can be shown to have increased, this strengthens the case for an increase in the selling price.

However, there are a number of problems with cost-plus pricing:

(i) There will always be problems associated with the selection of a 'suitable' basis on which to charge fixed costs to individual products or services. Selling prices can show great variation, depending on the apportionment basis chosen. This can lead to over- or under-pricing relative to competitors and unprofitable business can be won by mistake and profit can decline.
(ii) If prices are set on the basis of normal volume, and actual volume turns out to be considerably lower, for whatever reason, cost-plus can give management a false sense of security. Management may not fully understand that projected profits can be more than offset by under-absorbed overheads.
(iii) Cost-plus pricing takes no account of factors such as competitor activity.
(iv) Cost-plus overlooks the need for flexibility in the different stages of a product's life cycle. It takes no account of the price customers are willing to pay and price elasticity of demand. The following example illustrates this point.

Example

The variable cost of product A is £10. Fixed manufacturing costs of £1m are spread over an estimated production and sales volume of 200,000 units, i.e. £5 per unit. This gives a total cost of £15 per unit. The cost-plus approach used by the manufacturer of A, based on a standard mark-up of 40 per cent on the product's total cost, dictates a selling price of £21. Assuming all costs were as anticipated, and the company managed to sell 200,000 units at the fixed price of £21, a gross profit of £1.2m (£6 × 200,000) would be earned. Suppose, however, that a market survey had indicated the price elasticity of demand for the product shown in Table 6.1.

Table 6.1

Price (£)	Demand (units)
19	250,000
20	240,000
21	200,000
22	190,000
23	160,000

A more correct analysis of the pricing problem would have concentrated on maximising total contribution, and therefore total profitability as shown in Table 6.2.

Table 6.2

Selling price £	Variable cost £	Cont'n £	Demand	Total cont'n. £m	Profit £m
19	10	9	250,000	2.25	1.25
20	10	10	240,000	2.40	1.40
21	10	11	200,000	2.20	1.20
22	10	12	190,000	2.28	1.28
23	10	13	160,000	2.08	1.08

The decision to use a full cost-plus price of £21 has an associated opportunity cost. In failing to take into consideration the market conditions the organisation has forgone an extra profit of £200,000 and its market share is lower than it could have been.

6.3.2 Marginal cost-plus pricing

To the accountant, marginal cost is the same as variable cost. Some of the reasons for using it in preference to total cost are as follows:

- It is just as accurate as total cost-plus pricing. A larger mark-up percentage is added because both fixed costs and profit must be covered, but the uncertainty over the fixed costs per unit remains in both pricing methods.
- Knowledge of marginal cost allows the possibility of pricing below total cost when times are bad, in order to fill capacity.
- It can be used very successfully to price specific contracts because it can be used to recognise relevant costs and opportunity costs as well as sunk costs.
- It also recognises the existence of scarce or limiting resources, the use of which by competing products and services needs to be reflected in the selling price if profit is to be maximised. If there is a scarce or bottleneck resource the aim must be to maximise the total contribution from the limiting factor. The contribution that each alternative product or service makes from each unit of the scarce resource must be calculated and a suitable profit margin added.

Example

A company has been producing A successfully for a number of years, and demand appears to be static into the foreseeable future at a market price of £15 per unit. A market has just developed in product B, which the company could produce without additional investment in plant, and without increasing or retraining the existing labour force. Unfortunately, however, B uses the same basic direct material as product A, that is, units of material C – which is in short supply. The company must determine a minimum selling price for B, below which it would not be worthwhile to divert resources from A. Costs for the two products are given in Table 6.3.

Table 6.3

Product	A £		B £
Direct material:			
6 units of C @ £0.60	3.60	5 units of C @ £0.60	3.00
Direct labour:			
1/2 hour @ £6.00	3.00	1/2 hour @ £6.00	3.00
Variable overhead	2.40		1.00
	9.00		7.00
Selling price	15.00		
Contribution	6.00		

Contribution per unit of material C = £6 ÷ 6 units = £1

> A produces a contribution of £6 using 6 units of C, that is, a contribution per unit of C, the limiting factor, of £1. B uses five units of C. The company must therefore seek a contribution of £5 (5 units of material C × £1). So the price must be at least £7 + £5 = £12.

Marginal costing as a basis for pricing has always had its sceptics. The main criticism is based on the following type of scenario. There are two companies A and B competing with similar products in a market. The market is in recession and sales have decreased. Company A assesses its costs and lowers its price to below total cost, but well above marginal cost, in order to gain more market share. This tactic works; demand is elastic and so company A gains market share at the expense of company B. In order to get back its market share company B reduces its price below that of company A. Both companies now have their original market share but their margins are reduced. Company A then lowers the price again, etc. This continues, until one company is forced out of business. The remaining company now has to increase prices to the original level, which may well be difficult and can incur customer resistance.

The article by Mike Lucas, in the 'Reading' section, discusses the issues involved in pricing on cost further.

6.4 Other pricing strategies

6.4.1 Premium pricing

Premium pricing is pricing above competition on a permanent basis. This can only be done if the product appears 'different' and superior to competition, which normally means establishing a brand name based on one of the following:

- Quality
- Image/style
- Reliability/robustness
- Durability
- After-sales service
- Extended warranties.

In order to establish a brand, heavy initial promotion is required and the name must be constantly advertised or promoted thereafter. Brand names, such as, Levi, Mars, Coca-Cola, etc., require many millions of pounds spent on them each year. The benefit is a higher selling price generating a larger profit per unit and customer loyalty, making the product relatively price inelastic. These benefits must, of course, outweigh the cost of keeping the brand name in front of the customers.

6.4.2 Market skimming

Skimming is a technique where a high price is set for the product initially, so that only those who are desperately keen on the product will buy it. Then the price is lowered, making the product more accessible. When the next group of customers have had a chance to buy at that price, the price is lowered again, and so on. The aim of this strategy is usually to maximise revenue. But, on occasions, it is also used to prolong the life of older products.

Consumer durable companies tend to skim the market. This is done, to a certain extent, to recover large research and development costs quite quickly. But the products also lend themselves to this treatment as trend-setters are willing to pay a high price to own the latest gismo, and the rest of the population follow their example in later years. Books are also sold this way, with new novels published in hardback at a high price. The hard cover costs little more than a soft cover. Avid readers of that author will buy the hardback book at the high price. A year or so later the book is reissued with a soft cover at a much cheaper price in order to reach a wider audience.

Price skimming was probably first employed at the end of the eighteenth century by Josiah Wedgwood, the famous ceramics manufacturer. He made classical-shaped vases decorated with sprigs of decoration, which he sold to the rich and well-to-do. Naturally he priced his products accordingly. As the designs became old and well known he reduced the price on those lines and introduced new designs at the high price. Thus, he created different tiers of markets for his products, and people who were not so well off could afford a piece which had been in production for some years. This marketing technique helps to prolong a product's life and extracts the maximum profit from it.

If demand for a new or innovative product is relatively inelastic the supplier has the chance of adopting a market skimming price strategy. It is usually much easier to reduce prices than increase them, so it is better to begin with a high price, and lower it if demand appears more elastic than anticipated. If profitable skimming is to be sustained beyond the introductory phase, there must be significant barriers to entry to the market, in order to deter too many potential competitors entering attracted by the high prices and returns. In the case of books only one company own the rights to publish. Wedgwood had created an image/brand among the rich and famous which others could not copy, especially if they wished to undercut his prices. Consumer durable products have high manufacturing costs that deter too many companies entering the industry.

6.4.3 Penetration pricing

Penetration pricing occurs when a company sets a very low price for the new product initially. The price will usually be below total cost. The aim of the low price is to establish a large market share quickly by encouraging customers to try the product and then to repeat buy. This type of tactic is used, therefore, where barriers to entry are low. It is hoped to establish a dominant market position, which will prevent new entrants coming into the market because they could not establish a critical mass easily with prices so low.

In the past, companies used penetration pricing when they introduced a new product, such as a new spray polish, through supermarkets. The price would be, say, between 60 per cent and 80 per cent of the ultimate price. Customers would buy the new product largely because of its price and, it was hoped, repeat buy either because they did not notice the price increase or because they did not mind paying for a good product. If customers do notice the price increase they are likely to be put off further purchases if the increase is too large. If a company succeeds with this type of pricing it wins a large market share very quickly which competitors will find hard to break into.

6.4.4 Price differentiation

If the market can be split into different segments, each quite separate from the others and with its own individual demand function, it is possible to sell the same product to different customers at different prices. Marketing techniques can be employed to create market segmentation, if natural demarcation lines are not already in existence. Segmentation will usually be on the basis of one or more of the following:

- time (e.g. rail travel is cheaper off-peak, hotel accommodation, telecommunications);
- quantity (e.g. small orders at a premium, bulk orders at a discount);
- outlet/function (e.g. different prices for wholesaler, retailer, end consumer);
- geographical location (e.g. urban and rural sites, wealthy and poor districts, different countries);
- product content (e.g. sporty versions of a small car).

6.4.5 Loss leader pricing

When a product range consists of one or more main products and a series of related optional 'extras', which the customer can 'add on' to the main product, the supplier can set a relatively low price for the main product and a high one for the 'extras'. Obviously, the aim is to stimulate sufficient demand for the former to ensure the target return from sales of the latter. The strategy has been used successfully by aircraft engine manufacturers, who win an order with a very competitively priced main product that can only be serviced by their own, highly priced spare parts.

Gillette did not invent the safety razor but the market strategy Gillette adopted helped to build market share. Gillette razors were sold at 1/5 of the cost to manufacture them but only Gillette blades fitted and these were sold at a price of 5 cents. The blades cost only 1 cent to manufacture and so Gillette made large profits once it had captured the customer.

6.4.6 Product bundling

Bundling is putting a package of products together to make, for example, a complete kit for customers, which can then be sold at a temptingly low price. It is a way of creating value for customers and increasing company profits. It is a strategy that is often adopted in times of recession when organisations are particularly keen to maintain sales volume. One industry where this tactic started in the recession of the early 1990s is the computer industry. A manufacturer might decide to substantially reduce the profit margin on some hardware, such as printers. If, for example, only half its PC purchasers would also buy the company's model of printer, a bundled package which includes the PC and the printer for a lower combined price may well prove very successful. On the other hand, some customers will be put off by product bundling as they do not want the complete package; they will resent the increased price, however small it is.

Bundling can be extremely successful, especially when tried on mature products for the first time. For instance, Amstrad had considerable success when it entered the hi-fi market and demystified the technology by being the first company to sell a complete package of amplifier, deck and speakers. This was more than just a pricing strategy: it was a complete marketing strategy.

Whether a bundling strategy will succeed depends on the predicted increase in sales volume and the changes in margin. There are likely to be other cost changes such as savings in product handling, packaging and invoicing costs. Longer-term implications and competitors' reactions must not be ignored. For example, how will customers react when products are 'unbundled'? Will this result in a marked decline in sales? Will bundling be seen as an inferior product strategy which will have long-term implications for the brand's image? Will competitors retaliate by bundling their products? If they do this, will the strategy be successful?

Example

Bundling is profitable in situations in which some buyers value one of the items in a bundle relatively highly, but the remainder slightly above or below cost price. Other buyers place a relatively high valuation on both or all of the items in the bundle. Four film exhibitors, A to D, are willing to pay the following prices for two films X and Y:

A values X at £16,000 and Y at £5,000
B values X at £14,000 and Y at £6,000
C values X at £11,000 and Y at £10,000
D values X at £10,000 and Y at £11,000

The distributor's marginal cost of supplying each film is £8,000.

The distributor offers X and Y separately at £14,000 and £8,000 respectively, or the pair as a package for £21,000. The result is that A, C and D hire the package and B hires film X only, as the cost of both the bundle and film Y exceed his particular valuations. The distributor's profit would be (£21,000 × 3) + (£14,000) − (£8,000 × 7) = £21,000.

However, A might also prefer to hire film X for £14,000, instead of taking the package, as the extra cost of the bundle exceeds his valuation of Y by £2,000. If A did choose this option, the distributor's profit would rise to £22,000, as he does not have to supply either A or B with film Y, which has a supply cost in excess of their valuations: (£21,000 × 2) × (£14,000 × 2) − (£8,000 × 6) = £22,000.

Bundling is a particularly efficient means of exploiting price differentiation. Buyers are offered a pricing structure in which they are charged higher prices for buying the items separately (X + Y = £22,000) than in a package (X + Y = £21,000). Bundling works as a discriminatory device by:

- Using the package to extract the most from those customers who value it most. (In our example C and D, who placed relatively high valuations on both films.)
- Charging a relatively high separate price for the item in the package that is valued very highly by some particular buyers. (In our example film X, which was valued very highly by both A and B.)

If the distributor did not bundle he would make a profit of £19,000, as A and B would purchase product X and C and D would purchase product Y.

6.4.7 Pricing with additional features

The decision to add extra features to a product is a similar decision to bundling products. Most people prefer to have extra features incorporated into the product but they may not be prepared to pay the extra price. Others do not require the extra features and view them as a definite disadvantage. This is likely to be the case with older customers and electrical or electronic equipment. Older people find mastering the equipment quite difficult and they do not want extra features that make operation even more difficult. The following exercise considers an extra feature, the resulting price and its effect on market share.

 Exercise

Epsilon Electronics is about to launch a replacement for its popular CD and tape recorder and needs to decide what features to incorporate in the new model. One suggestion is to include a radio timer that would allow pre-set radio recordings to be made. The following information is known:

Cost to manufacture CD, tape and radio recorder (called product A) £60.

Cost to manufacture the same product with an addition of a pre-set timer for radio recording (called product B) £67.

Administration costs are £20 per unit.

Sales price for product A: wholesale £90, retail £180.
Sales price for product B: wholesale £99, retail £198.

The additional feature in product B is not rated by 95 per cent of existing CD recorder purchasers, but the other 5 per cent would consider it to be an advantage and would definitely buy such a model. The feature would attract some new customers to the CD recorder market, increasing the total market by 5 per cent.

The manufacturer has a 40 per cent share of the existing market and would expect to maintain that if it introduced product A.

If product B was introduced at a price of £198 (rather than the proposed £180 without the timer) 30 per cent of those not requiring the additional feature would switch to competitors' products.

The product, either A or B, would have a life of one year before needing updating. The estimated CD recorder market size for the coming year is 5 million units.

Requirement

Which product should Epsilon produce?

 Solution

If product A is produced:

Market share = 40% of 5m = 2m
Margin per unit = £90 − £60 = £30
Admin. Costs = £20 × 2m = £40m

	£m
Therefore, total margin = 2m × £30	= 60
Less: admin. Costs	40
Net gain	20

If product B is produced:

Market share:	£m
CD recorder buyers = 70% × 95% of 2m	= 1.33
Radio timer buyers = 5% of 2m	= 0.10
New customers = 5% of 5m	= 0.25
Total	1.68

Margin per unit = £99 − £67 = £32
Admin. costs (if variable) = £20 × 1.68m = £33.6m

	£m
Therefore, total margin = 1.68m × £32	= 53.76
Less: admin. costs	33.60
Net gain	20.16

If admin. costs are fixed:	£m
Total margin	53.76
Less: admin. costs (if fixed)	40.00
Net gain	13.76

The decision will therefore rest on the behaviour pattern of the administration costs, but the difference in the forecast net gain is not large.

6.4.8 Using discounts in pricing

There are a number of reasons for using discounts to adjust prices:

- To get cash in quickly.
- To differentiate between different types of customer, wholesale, retail, etc.

- To increase sales volume during a poor sales period without dropping the price permanently.
- Some industries give discounts as normal practice, for example the antique trade, and some retail shops seem to have semi-permanent sales.
- Perishable goods are often discounted towards the end of their life or the end of the day, or seconds are often sold off cheaply. This may not be a good strategy as it does not improve the company image, and some customers may get wise and delay their purchase until the end of the day when prices are cheaper.

6.4.9 Controlled pricing

A significant proportion of the previously nationalised industries in the UK have been 'privatised' into the private sector, with a constraining influence usually called the industry 'regulator'. Examples of these regulating bodies are Oftel (telecommunications) and Ofwat (water).

Many of these companies are in a largely monopolistic situation and so regulation of these industries was perceived as desirable. Regulation largely takes the form of controlling price so that the monopolistic companies cannot exploit their unique position. The regulators use selling price as the means of controlling the volume of supply in the industry. They may also decide to specify the quality of the product or level of service that must be achieved or to prohibit the company operating in certain sectors.

When an industry is regulated on selling price, the elasticity is zero. No price change is allowed. Not only does this mean that 'small' customers pay less than they otherwise would, but large customers pay more than one might expect under more competitive positions. Over recent years all of the monopolistic industries have introduced some kind of discounted price for very large customers, which is beginning to allow genuine competition to enter the market. Gradually other billing companies have been allowed to enter the market and so price has become more flexible.

6.5 Summary

In this chapter we have learned about the alternative pricing theories and techniques that may be used by an organisation.

Reading 6

This article discusses the conflicting accounts in economics and management accounting literature on how cost information is used in pricing and product mix decisions.

The pricing decision – economists versus accountants

Mike Lucas, *Management Accounting*, June 1999 © CIMA. Reproduced with permission

Much concern has been expressed in the management accounting literature in recent years about the use of full cost in pricing and output decisions. Shim and Sudit[1], for example, found that 70 per cent of companies surveyed used full cost-based pricing, 12 per cent used variable cost-based pricing and only 18 per cent used market-based pricing. Similar results have been uncovered by, among others, Cooper[2] and Drury et al.[3]

The concern has been tempered slightly by the findings of Drury et al. that cost information is used 'flexibly'. They cite two primary pieces of evidence to support this contention. First, many respondents to their questionnaire survey used both full costing and marginal costing when appropriate. Second, a majority of respondents stated that, while full cost price was important, it was sometimes changed. The impression remains, however, that full costs still play an important role in many pricing and output decisions.

The use of full cost-plus pricing is, of course, at variance with the economist's prescription for maximisation – setting price at a level which equates marginal cost (MC) and marginal revenue (MR). If the accounting research findings are indeed correct, the implications for economic efficiency (and microeconomic theory) are profound.

Economics research findings

The consternation expressed in the accounting literature parallels a debate which took place among economists many years ago. In 1939 Hall and Hitch[4] uncovered evidence that firms did not adhere to marginalist, profit-maximising principles by expanding output to the point where MR = MC. Rather they found that price was set by adding a (fairly constant) mark-up to full cost.

Hall and Hitch gave as reasons for this apparent non-conformity with profit maximising behaviour, the following:

1. Producers don't know their demand or marginal revenue curves, and this for two reasons:
   (a) they don't know consumers' preferences;
   (b) many producers, as oligopolists, do not know what the reaction of their competitors would be to a change of price.
   (Admittedly, this research was before the development of econometrics, which now makes possible the statistical estimation of demand curves. However, for many

products – and especially new products – sufficient empirical data is unlikely to be available.)

2. Firms fear that if they cut prices, competitors would also cut. On the other hand, if they increased prices, it is typically believed, competitors would not match the increase. This accounts for the price 'stickiness' depicted by the famous 'kinked demand curve' (see Figure 1).

3. Changes in price can be costly to implement, a nuisance to salesmen and are disliked by distributors and consumers. Consequently, frequent price changes will be resisted, whereas profit maximising behaviour implies prices changing whenever there is a change in demand or cost.

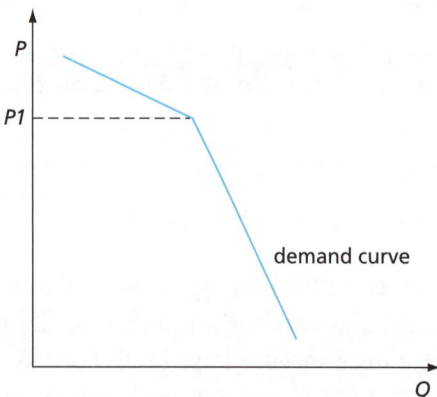

Figure 1 The kinked demand curve

The firm believes its demand curve to be as shown in Figure 1. If price is increased above the current price, P1, competitors will not follow suit; consequently, above P1, the demand curve is very elastic. This implies that the increase in profit per unit will not compensate for the reduction in the number of units sold and so total profit will fall. If price is reduced below P1, competitors will follow suit, consequently, the firm's demand curve is inelastic below this point, implying that the (small) increase in the number of units sold will not compensate for the reduction in price per unit and total profit will fall.

Consequently, the firm will be reluctant to change price from its current level in response to minor changes in cost or market conditions. This is held to explain the apparent 'price stickiness' observed in practice.

The findings of Hall and Hitch[4] were described by Barback[5] as 'the first blast in the offensive against orthodox (marginalist) analysis'. + Not surprisingly, the orthodox economists fought back vigorously in defence of their marginalist model of behaviour. Edwards,[6] for example, contended, *'those who argue that the automatic basing of prices on conventional cost statements is the rule ... have not taken adequate account of the informal and unrecorded stages in the price fixing process. Before the preparation of the cost estimate and between its preparation and the actual determination of the price, discussion usually takes place ... about the assumptions underlying the cost figures and about the market situation'*. Since Hall and Hitch's attack on marginalist theory, economics researchers (e.g. Machlup[7]) claim to have uncovered substantial evidence of 'implicit marginalism'. This phrase describes the situation where, although firms may not consciously think in terms of equating MR and MC, they nevertheless act as though they were doing so. In the same way, while a snooker player may not be consciously aware of the theorems of trigonometry, he nevertheless acts in accordance with them.[8]

Among the evidence of implicit marginalism summarised by Dorward[9] are: shading the full-cost price and discounting for different and changing market circumstances; selecting a lower profit margin when competition becomes more intense; and reducing the overhead charge to reflect short-term fixity of certain costs (the first two examples are equivalent to estimating a MR function; the last to estimating a short-run MC function).

The reconciliation of full cost pricing and marginalist theory

Economists have attempted to demonstrate that full cost-plus pricing is compatible with marginalist theory. A typical exposition is that of Koutsoylannis.[10] According to this representation, the full cost price is constituted as follows:

$$P = AVC + \text{costing margin}$$

where P is price, AVC is average variable cost and the costing margin = AFC + NP (where AFC = fixed cost divided by the expected number of units, and NP = normal profit mark up based on historical or industry norm).

The firm, it is suggested, looks at its long-run position and aims at long-run profit maximisation. However, given the uncertainty about the future, the firm bases its price on the short-run average variable cost. This is believed by businessmen to be a good approximation to the long-run marginal cost.

Full cost pricing is then reconciled to marginalist theory by taking AVC to be the firm's best estimate of long-run marginal cost, and adjustments to the costing margin in response to competitive conditions to be the firm testing out its demand curve and by implication its unknown marginal revenue function.

Not all economists concur with this argument – see, for example Barback and Gordon[11]. However since the neoclassical marginalist paradigm still dominates much of economics education, it would appear that the majority of (academic) economists accept the view articulated by Dorward: 'the general pricing behaviour is implicitly marginalist, with both explicit marginalism and rigid full cost pricing being minority practices'.

Accounting research methodology

The foregoing suggests that accounting researchers may have missed the evidence of implicit marginalism by asking the wrong questions. As Edwards observes: '*In discussions, so many businessmen, and especially accountants, repeat the conventions described by the costing textbooks, little realising how important it is that researchers should be told about the adjustments that they are constantly making … in order to meet the market situation*'. In similar vein, Pearce[12] showed that in one firm, whose managers firmly believed they worked on cost-plus, job prices found by cost-plus became the actual prices in only a minority of sales (quoted from Baxter and Oxenfeldt[13]).

It may well be that questionnaire surveys (on which much of the accounting research evidence is based) are inappropriate for researching pricing decisions, in-depth interviews being necessary for a fuller understanding (see Kaplan and Johnson[14]). On the other hand, there is the danger that in-depth interviews involve subconscious prompting which will induce the answer the interviewer wants to hear. Also, the results are more open to subjective interpretation; the interviewer is, in effect, asking us to accept his or her reading of the situation. This could, conceivably, explain the findings of economics researchers anxious to preserve the neoclassical paradigm.

ABC and long-run marginal cost

Activity-based costing (ABC) is, of course, based on the concept of long-run avoidable (marginal) cost; to the extent that ABC product costs give a good representation of this, marginalist theory is vindicated for the firms concerned. It is, however, still only a minority of firms that use ABC and, even where used, the conditions that would produce a good proxy for long-run avoidable cost are not necessarily being fulfilled – in particular with regard to the treatment of 'indivisibilities'.

'Indivisibilities' refers to the phenomenon whereby reductions in the level of output may not permit proportionate reductions in the level of inputs (this occurs because, while it is usually possible to duplicate a process, it may not be possible to halve it).

The cost of indivisible resources should not be attributed to individual products since, by definition (to the extent that they are indivisible), they will be incurred regardless of activity level and are therefore unavoidable with regard to a particular product.

The assignment of indivisible costs to particular products is particularly a danger where multistage allocations are performed as, for example, described by Woods.[15] Woods describes how ABC often takes place within a system of multi-stage allocations which hide the indivisibility (and hence longer-term fixity) of certain costs – which nevertheless end up being assigned to particular products. He explains the process as follows:

> All costs incurred within an organisational unit, along with costs assigned from other units whose cost drivers it uses, are further assigned to the unit's services or products, with its cost drivers as a base. If the producing unit is a production department, the recipient of its costs will be its physical product ... (thus) ABC mixes fixed and variable costs before assigning them to outputs, a circumstance that can lead to suboptimal decisions.

Attribution to indivisible resource costs renders cost accounting, including ABC, open to the charge made against it in 1938 by Coase:[16] 'Any claim that modern cost accounting ... enables unprofitable products to be discovered and eliminated is misleading. It is only possible to discover whether or not a particular activity is profitable by comparing the avoidable costs with the receipts – and this is a task which modern cost accounting methods do not enable one to perform.'

Conclusion

Economic theory postulates that profit is maximised by setting price at a level which equates MR and MC. With most cost accounting systems geared to providing information for financial reporting purposes, identification of marginal cost (short-run or long-run) would require a considerable amount of sophisticated analysis by management. Even ABC costs often do not provide a good representation of long-run marginal cost (as discussed above).

Do managers really perform such an analysis or do they simply take full cost as supplied by the cost accounting system and use it directly for pricing and output decisions (especially long-run decisions for which conventional marginal costing may be considered inappropriate)? It could be that accounting research methodology has been flawed; on the other hand, economists could be finding what they want to find!

It seems that Robertson's[17] conclusion of 1956, that the debate over the theory of pricing could not be regarded as closed, remains valid today!

References

1. Shim, T and Sudit, T F: 'How manufacturers price products', *Management Accounting* (USA), February 1994, pp. 37–39.
2. Cooper, R: 'Explicating the logic of ABC', *Management Accounting* (UK), November 1990, pp. 58–60.
3. Drury, C, Braund, S, Osborne, P and Tayles, M: *A Survey of Management Accounting Practices in UK Manufacturing Companies*, ACCA Publications, London 1993.
4. Hall, R I and Hitch, C I: 'Price theory and business behaviour', *Oxford Economic Papers* No 2, 1939, pp. 12–45.

5. Barback, R H: *The Pricing of Manufactures*, Macmillan, London, 1964.
6. Edwards, R: 'The pricing of manufactured products', *Economica*, Vol 19, 1952, pp. 298–307.
7. Machlup, F: 'Marginal analysis and empirical research', *American Economic Review*, Vol 36, No 4, part 1, September 1946, pp. 519–554.
8. Friedman, M: *Essays in Positive Economics*, University of Chicago Press, 1953.
9. Dorward, N: *The Pricing Decision*, Harper and Row, London, 1987.
10. Koutsoylannis, A: *Modern Microeconomics*, Macmillan, London, 1979.
11. Barback, R H and Gordon, B A: 'Short period price determination in theory and practice', *American Economic Review*, Vol 38, No 3, June 1948.
12. Pearce, H I: 'A study in price policy', *Economica*, Vol 23, 1956, pp. 114–127.
13. Baxter, W I: 'Approaches to pricing: economist versus accountant', *Business Horizons*, Vol 4, 1961, pp. 77–90.
14. Kaplan, R S and Johnson, H I: *Relevance Lost: The Rise and Fall of Management Accounting*. Harvard Business School Press, 1987.
15. Woods, M D: 'Completing the picture: economic choices with ABC', *Management Accounting* (USA), Vol 74, No 6, 1992, pp. 53–57.
16. Coase, R H: 'Business organisation and the accountant' (1938), In Solomons, D. (ed): *Studies in Costing*. Sweet and Maxwell, London, 1952.
17. Robertson, D H: *Economic Commentaries*, p. 40, Staples, London, 1956.

Revision Questions

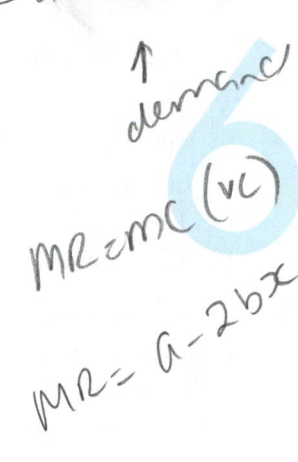

Question 1

1.1 ABC plc is about to launch a new product. Facilities will allow the company to produce up to 20 units per week. The marketing department has estimated that at a price of £8,000 no units will be sold, but for each £150 reduction in price one additional unit per week will be sold.

Fixed costs associated with manufacture are expected to be £12,000 per week.

Variable costs are expected to be £4,000 per unit for each of the first 10 units; thereafter each unit will cost £400 more than the preceding one.

The most profitable level of output per week for the new product is

(A) 10 units
(B) 11 units
(C) 13 units
(D) 14 units
(E) 20 units

1.2 Market research by Company A has revealed that the maximum demand for product R is 50,000 units each year, and that demand will reduce by 50 units for every £1 that the selling price is increased. Based on this information, Company A has calculated that the profit-maximising level of sales for product R for the coming year is 35,000 units.

This price at which these units will be sold is:

(A) £100
(B) £300
(C) £500
(D) £700
(E) £900

1.3 Another product manufactured by company A is product M. At a price of £700 for product M there would be zero demand, and for every £40 reduction in the selling price the demand would increase by 100 units. The variable cost of producing a unit of product M is £60.

Company A knows that if the demand equation for product M is represented by $p = a - bx$, where p is the selling price and x is the quantity demanded at price p, then the marginal revenue (MR) for product M can be represented by $MR = a - 2bx$.

The profit-maximising output of product M is:

(A) 100 units
(B) 700 units
(C) 800 units
(D) 1,600 units
(E) 1,750 units

1.4 A company is considering the pricing of one of its products. It has already carried out some market research with the following results:
  The quantity demanded at a price of $100 will be 1,000 units
  The quantity demanded will increase/decrease by 100 units for every $50 decrease/increase in the selling price
  The marginal cost of each unit is $35
  Note that if Selling Price (P) = a – bx then Marginal Revenue = a – 2bx
  Calculate the selling price that maximises company profit. **(4 marks)**

Question 2

B Ltd manufactures blodgets. It has been ascertained that the market for blodgets is as follows:

- at unit price £20, no blodgets are demanded or sold;
- at unit price nil, 5,000 blodgets are demanded;
- for price levels intermediate between £20 and nil there is a linear relationship between price and demand.

The variable cost of manufacturing a blodget is £5 at all levels of output.

Requirements
Calculate the unit selling prices which will:

(a) maximise revenue; and
(b) maximise profit.

Question 3

W has recently completed the development and testing of a new product which has cost $400,000. It has also bought a machine to produce the new product costing $150,000. The production machine is capable of producing 1,000 units of the product per month and is not expected to have a residual value due to its specialised nature.

The company has decided that the unit selling prices it will charge will change with the cumulative numbers of units sold as follows:

Cumulative sales units	Selling price $ per unit in this band
0 to 2,000	100
2,001 to 7,000	80
7,001 to 14,500	70
14,501 to 54,500	60
54,501 and above	40

Based on these selling prices, it is expected that sales demand will be as shown below:

Months	Sales demand per month (units)
1–10	200
11–20	500
21–30	750
31–70	1,000
71–80	800
81–90	600
91–100	400
101–110	200
Thereafter	NIL

Unit variable costs are expected to be as follows:

	$ per unit
First 2,000 units	50
Next 12,500 units	40
Next 20,000 units	30
Next 20,000 units	25
Thereafter	30

W operates a Just in Time (JIT) purchasing and production system and operates its business on a cash basis.

A columnar cash flow statement showing the cumulative cash flow of the product after its Introduction and Growth stages has already been completed and this is set out below:

	Introduction	Growth	
Months	1–10	11–30	
Number of units produced and sold	2,000	5,000	7,500
Selling price per unit	$100	$80	$70
Unit variable cost	$50	$40	$40
Unit contribution	$50	$40	$30
Total contribution	$100,000	$425,000	
Cumulative cash flow	($450,000)	($25,000)	

Requirements:

(a) Complete the cash flow statement for each of the remaining two stages of the product's life cycle. **Do not copy the Introduction and Growth stages in your answer.** Ignore the time value of money. (5 marks)

(b) Explain, using your answer to (a) above and the data provided, the possible reasons for the changes in costs and selling prices during the life cycle of the product.

(5 marks)

(Total for Question Three = 10 marks)

Solutions to Revision Questions

Solution 1

Tip
- In question 1.1 the best approach is to calculate the profit for a range of outputs from 10 units upwards, then select the output with the highest profit.

1.1 Answer: (B)

Units	Total variable costs £	Selling price per unit £	Total sales revenue £	Total contribution £
10	40,000	6,500	65,000	25,000
11	44,400	6,350	69,850	25,450
12	49,200	6,200	74,400	25,200
13	54,400	6,050	78,650	24,250

1.2 Answer: (B)

In the demand equation $p = a - bx$
When price $= 0$, demand, $x = 50,000$ $\therefore 0 = a - 50,000b$ (i)
When price $= 1$, demand, $x = 49,950$ $\therefore 1 = a - 49,950b$ (ii)
Subtract $1 = 50b$
                                        $b = 0.02$
Substitute in (i) $a = (50,000 \times 0.02)$
                                        $= 1,000$
The demand equation for product R is $p = 1,000 - 0.02x$
When $x = 35,000$ units, $p = 1,000 - (0.02 \times 35,000) = 300$

1.3 Answer: (C)

In the demand equation $p = a - bx$
When price $= £700$, demand $= 0$ $\therefore 700 = a$
When price $= £660$, demand $= 100$ $\therefore 660 = a - 100b$
Substitute for a $660 = 700 - 100b$
                                     $b = 0.4$
The demand equation for product M is $p = 700 - 0.4x$
The marginal revenue equation is given by $MR = 700 - 0.8x$
Profit is maximised when marginal cost = marginal revenue

169

2007.1

i.e. when $60 = 700 - 0.8x$
$x = 800.$

1.4 Price at which demand = zero

$$= \$100 + \left(\frac{1000}{100} \times \$50\right) = \$600$$

$P = \$600 - 0.5x$
$MR = \$600 - x$
$MC = \$35$
$MC = MR$
$\$35 = \$600 - x$
$x = \$565$
$p = \$600 - \$(0.5 \times 565)$
$= \$317.50$

✓ Solution 2

Tips
- This is a simple example of a topic which features in many pricing questions. Read Section 3.2.3 again if you are unsure of this.
- Two methods could be used as a solution to this question:
  (i) by calculating the total sales revenue and costs for various levels of activity and determining the optimum activity level;
  (ii) or using calculus, which is by far a much quicker and more straightforward method.

The use of calculus is outside the scope of your *Management Accounting – Decision Making* syllabus, therefore we have shown only the first method.

For every £1 reduction in selling price demand will reduce by:

$$\frac{5,000 - 0}{20} = 250 \text{ units}$$

Demand	Selling price £	Sales revenue £	Variable cost @ £5 per unit £	Contribution £
0	20	0	0	0
1,000	16	16,000	5,000	11,000
2,000	12	24,000	10,000	14,000
3,000	8	24,000	15,000	9,000
4,000	4	16,000	20,000	4,000
5,000	0	0	25,000	(25,000)

From the above table it can be seen that revenue is maximised between 2,000 and 3,000 units. A more accurate figure can be determined by drawing a graph.

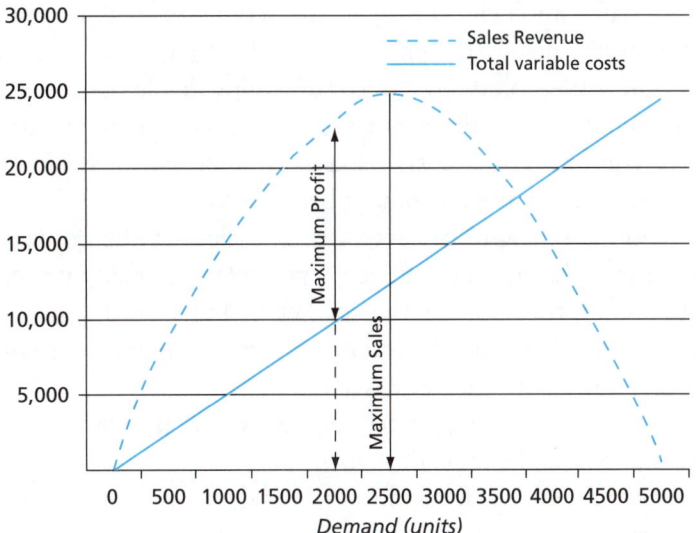

Sales revenue is maximised at approximately 2,500 units and profit is maximised at approximately 1,900 units.

To calculate the selling price for these two levels of output, we can insert the number of units into the equation for the demand function:

Demand function: $q = 5{,}000 - 250p$
$p = 20 - 0.004q$

where p = selling price
q = level of output

(a) when $q = 2{,}500$:
$2{,}500 = 5{,}000 - 250p$
$p = 10$

∴ Revenue is maximised when the selling price is £10

(b) when $q = 1{,}900$:
$1{,}900 = 5{,}000 - 250p$
$p = 12.4$

∴ Profit is maximised when the selling price is £12.40

✓ Solution 3

(a)

Weeks	Introduction* 1–10	Growth* 11–30		Maturity 31–70		Decline 71–110
Number of units produced and sold	2,000	5,000	7,500	20,000	20,000	20,000
Selling price per unit	$100	$80	$70	$60	$60	$40
Unit variable cost	$50	$40	$40	$30	$25	$30
Unit contribution	$50	$40	$30	$30	$35	$10
Total contribution	$100,000	$425,000		$1,300,000		$200,000
Cumulative cash flow	($450,000)	($25,000)		$1,275,000		$1,475,000

* Note: The Introduction and Growth stages are shown here for completeness. Candidates were not required to include these in their answer.

(b) Economies of scale are likely to explain the reduction in unit costs over time. More specifically this could include the impact of the learning curve and the benefits of bulk purchase discounts. It is noted though that the unit variable cost rises in the decline stage and this is consistent with the diseconomy of scale, say in material purchase price, caused by the reduced volumes. Other costs also start to increase, possibly as a consequence of the reducing efficiency of the equipment being used,

The reduction in selling prices over time is typical of the product life cycle. Market skimming in the introduction stage reflects high unit prices paid by a select few customers. The company's competitors enter the market in the growth phase and selling prices reduce (a) to stimulate demand, (b) to compete with new market entrants, and (c) to reflect the effect of economies of scale on costs.

At the maturity stage, selling prices stabilise at $60 per unit. This reflects what may be an established oligopolistic market price.

In the decline stage prices fall to attract what demand is still available as newer, better products emerge.

Risk and Uncertainty

Risk and Uncertainty 7

> **LEARNING OUTCOMES**
>
> ▸ Evaluate the impact of uncertainty and risk on decision models that may be based on CVP analysis, relevant cash flows, learning curves, discounting techniques, etc.
>
> ▸ Apply sensitivity analysis on both short- and long-run decision models to identify variables that might have significant impacts on project outcomes.
>
> ▸ Analyse risk and uncertainty by calculating expected value tables and standard deviations togethet with probability tables and histograms.
>
> ▸ Prepare expected value tables and ascertain the value of information.
>
> ▸ Prepare and apply decision trees.

7.1 Introduction

In this chapter we will recognise the uncertainty that exists when costs and revenues are estimated and how the risk associated with such uncertainty can be evaluated.

7.2 Probability

7.2.1 The probabilistic model and expected value

It would be rare for the outcome of a business decision to be known in advance, as a measure of risk or uncertainty is present in almost all situations. Risk and uncertainty have different specific meanings in decision theory. Risk exists where the decision-maker has knowledge, probably due to previous experience, that several alternative outcomes are possible. Previous experience enables the decision-maker to ascribe a probability to the likely occurrence of each alternative. On the other hand uncertainty exists where the future is unknown and so the decision-maker has no previous experience and no statistical evidence on which to base predictions. For the purposes of this syllabus the difference between risk and uncertainty is not important, as their treatment will be the same. But in most circumstances uncertainty is the problem rather than risk and so it will be referred to this way.

Uncertainty can be incorporated into the forecasting by using a probabilistic model, which incorporates an allowance for uncertainty measured in terms of probabilities.

A number of decision criteria have been developed to assist decision-makers in choosing between various options. By far the most commonly used criterion is that of selecting the option with the greatest expected value (EV), when dealing with profit or revenue, or with lowest EV, when dealing with costs. The EV is calculated by weighting the possible outcomes by their probabilities and then summing the result.

Example: calculating the expected value

An organisation is considering launching a new product. It will do so if the expected value of the total revenue is in excess of £1,000. It is decided to set the selling price at £10. After some investigation a number of probabilities for different levels of sales revenue are predicted; these are shown in Table 7.1.

Table 7.1 Situation I

Units sold	Revenue £	Probability	Pay-off £
80	800	0.15	120
100	1,000	0.50	500
120	1,200	0.35	420
		1.00	EV 1,040

The expected sales revenue at a selling price of £10 per unit is £1,040, that is [800 × 0.15] + [1,000 × 0.50] + [1,200 × 0.35]. In preparing forecasts and making decisions management may proceed on the assumption that it can expect sales revenue of £1,040 if it sets a selling price of £10 per unit. The actual outcome of adopting this selling price may be sales revenue that is higher or lower than £1,040. And £1,040 is not even the most likely outcome; the most likely outcome is £1,000, since this has the highest probability.

The single figure of the expected value of revenue can hide a wide range of possible actual results.

Furthermore, not all decision-makers will have the same attitude towards risk. There are three main types of decision maker.

- *Risk neutral* decision-makers ignore the possible variations in outcome and are concerned only with the most likely outcome.
- *Risk seekers* are concerned only with the best possible outcome, no matter how unlikely it is to occur.
- *Risk averse* decision-makers prefer the alternative with the least variation associated with it.

Utility is another important aspect of risk and uncertainty that is described in detail later. The basis of the theory is that an individual's attitude to certain risk profiles will depend on the amount of money involved. For example, most people would accept a bet on the toss of a coin, if the outcome were that they would win £6 if it came down heads and if it came down tails they would pay £4. The average person would be happy to play secure in the knowledge that they would win if the game were repeated over a long enough period; if not it would still be a good bet. But if the stakes were raised so that the win was £6,000 on a single toss coming down heads and a loss of £4,000 if it came down tails, the average person might think twice and reject the bet as being too risky. Utility theory attaches weights to the sums of money involved; these are tailor-made to the individual's attitude towards winning and losing certain sums of money.

Therefore, considering a proposed option solely on the basis of its expected value ignores the range of possible outcomes. For instance, after the investigation in the previous example the predicted revenues might have been different. They might have been as shown in Table 7.2.

Table 7.2 Situation II

Units sold	Revenue £	Probability	Pay-off £
40	400	0.15	60.0
100	1,000	0.50	500.0
137	1,370	0.35	479.5
		1.00	EV 1,039.5

Both situations give rise to the same expected sales revenue of £1,040 (to the nearest £), but the two situations are not the same. The second involves a wider dispersal of possible outcomes; hence it involves higher risk. If the decision-makers are risk averse they will judge the range of possible outcomes described in the second situation to be worse than the first. If the decision-makers are risk seekers they may prefer the second situation, because of the higher outcome in the best possible situation. However, in this case, the dire downside of £400 may put them off. Whatever the case it can be seen that the evaluation of the options solely on the basis of their expected value may not always be appropriate.

7.2.2 Examples of expected value calculations

Two simple exercises of uncertainty follow. Try them yourself before looking at the answers.

Exercise

A company buys in sub-assemblies in order to manufacture a product. It is reviewing its policy of putting each sub-assembly through a detailed inspection process on delivery, and is considering not inspecting at all. Experience has shown that the quality of the sub-assembly is of acceptable standard 90 per cent of the time. It costs £10 to inspect a sub-assembly and another £10 to put right any defect found at that stage. If the sub-assembly is not inspected and is then found to be faulty at the finished goods stage the cost of rework is £40.

Requirement

Advise the company whether or not they should change their policy.

Solution

Four outcomes are possible:

(i) Inspect and find no problems – cost £10.
(ii) Inspect and find problems – cost £20.
(iii) Do not inspect and no problems exist – no cost.
(iv) Do not inspect and problems do exist – cost £40.

If sub-assemblies achieve the required standard 90 per cent of the time then there is a 10 per cent chance that they will be faulty.

The expected value of the cost of each policy is as follows:

Inspect   [0.9 × £10] + [0.1 × £20] = £11
Do not inspect   [0.9 × £0] + [0.1 × £40] = £4

Taken over a long enough period of time, a policy of not carrying out an inspection would lead to a saving in cost of £7 per sub-assembly. On a purely quantitative analysis, therefore, this is the correct policy to adopt.

However, in the real world such a high level of failures is incompatible with a requirement for a 'quality product', and the concept of continuous improvement. It would be more useful to ask the supplier some basic questions regarding his quality management, in order to bring about a fundamental shift towards outcome (iii), rather than simply implementing a policy on the basis of such an uncritical analysis of the situation.

Exercise

An individual is considering backing the production of a new musical in the West End. It would cost £100,000 to stage for the first month. If it is well received by the critics, it will be kept on at the end of the first month for a further 6 months, in which case a profit of £350,000 would be made. If the critics dislike it, it will close at the end of the first month. There is a 50:50 chance of a favourable review.

Requirement
Should the individual invest in the musical?

 Solution

The expected value of backing the musical is:

$$[0.5 \times £250{,}000] - [0.5 \times £100{,}000] = £75{,}000$$

As this provides a positive return it would be accepted on the basis of expected values as the alternative yields zero. However, the expected value can be misleading here as it is a one-off situation and the expected profit of £75,000 is not a feasible outcome. The only feasible outcomes of this project are a profit of £250,000 or a loss of £100,000.

While almost everybody would welcome a profit of £250,000, not many individuals could afford to sustain a loss of £100,000 and they would place a high utility on such a loss. Many investors would be risk averse in such a situation because they would not consider that a 50 per cent chance of making £250,000 was worth an equal 50 per cent risk of losing £100,000; the loss might bankrupt them. On the other hand, if the individual were a multi-millionaire the return of 250 per cent would be very appealing and the loss of a mere £100,000 would have a low utility attached to it.

The two exercises have only had single-point outcomes, that is conformity or otherwise with a pre-set quality standard and a successful show or a flop. It is obvious that the two outcomes of the first exercise represent the only possible alternatives and so quantification of the related pay-offs along the lines of the example appears reasonable. It is also obvious that the profit of £250,000 predicted for a successful show in the case of the second exercise is far too precise a figure. It would be more realistic to assume a range of possible successful pay-offs, as they will vary, according to the number of seats sold and the price of the seats. If probabilities are attached to each estimate, the expected value of a successful outcome will take account of the range of possible outcomes, by weighting each of them by its associated probability. The range of possible outcomes might be as in Table 7.3.

Table 7.3

Outcome Profit £	Probability	Expected Value £
(100,000)	0.50	(50,000)
200,000	0.175	35,000
250,000	0.20	50,000
300,000	0.075	22,500
350,000	0.05	17,500
	1.00	75,000

The statement of a range of possible outcomes and their associated probabilities is known as a probability distribution. Presenting the distribution to management allows two further useful inferences to be drawn:

- *The most likely successful outcome.* That is the successful outcome with the highest probability (a profit of £250,000 in Table 7.3).
- *The probability of an outcome being above or below a particular figure.* The particular figure will either be the expected value or a figure of consequence, such as zero profit, where a lesser outcome might have dire consequences. By summing the probabilities for pay-offs of £200,000 and £250,000, it can be concluded that there is a 37.5 per cent probability that profits will be £250,000 or less if the musical is successful. By summing those for £300,000 and £350,000 it can be determined that the probability of a profit of £300,000 or more in the event of success is only 12.5 per cent.

So far only a very small number of alternatives have been considered in the examples. In practice a greater number of alternative courses of action may exist, uncertainty may be associated with more than one variable and the values of variables may be interdependent, giving rise to many different outcomes.

The following exercise looks at the expected value of a manufacturing decision, where there are three alternative sales volumes, two alternative contributions, and three alternative levels of fixed cost. The number of possible outcomes will be $3 \times 2 \times 3 = 18$.

Example

A company is assessing the desirability of producing a souvenir to celebrate a royal jubilee. The marketing life of the souvenir will be 6 months only. Uncertainty surrounds the likely sales volume and contribution, as well as the fixed costs of the venture. Estimated outcomes and probabilities are shown in Table 7.4.

Table 7.4

Sales units	Probablity	Contn. per unit £	Probablity	Fixed cost £	Probablity
100,000	0.3	7	0.5	400,000	0.2
80,000	0.6	5	0.5	450,000	0.5
60,000	0.1			500,000	0.3
	1.0		1.0		1.0

Table 7.5 shows the expected value of the contribution to be £49,000. Totalling up the joint probabilities for each set of sales shows the project has a 56.5 per cent chance of making a net contribution, a 33 per cent chance of making a loss, and a 10.5 per cent chance of making neither a net contribution nor a loss.

This can be quite hard to visualize and it may be more useful to use a decision tree to express the situation, as shown in the next section.

Table 7.5

Sales units	Contn. per unit a £	Total contn. a £	Fixed cost b £	Probability	Joint prob. c	Expected value of net contn. (a−b) ×c £
100,000	7	700,000	400,000	0.3 × 0.5 × 0.2	0.030	9,000
	7	700,000	450,000	0.3 × 0.5 × 0.5	0.075	18,750
	7	700,000	500,000	0.3 × 0.5 × 0.3	0.045	9,000
	5	500,000	400,000	0.3 × 0.5 × 0.2	0.030	3,000
	5	500,000	450,000	0.3 × 0.5 × 0.5	0.075	3,750
	5	500,000	500,000	0.3 × 0.5 × 0.3	0.045	0
80,000	7	560,000	400,000	0.6 × 0.5 × 0.2	0.060	9,600
	7	560,000	450,000	0.6 × 0.5 × 0.5	0.150	16,500
	7	560,000	500,000	0.6 × 0.5 × 0.3	0.090	5,400
	5	400,000	400,000	0.6 × 0.5 × 0.2	0.060	0
	5	400,000	450,000	0.6 × 0.5 × 0.5	0.150	(7,500)
	5	400,000	500,000	0.6 × 0.5 × 0.3	0.090	(9,000)
60,000	7	420,000	400,000	0.1 × 0.5 × 0.2	0.010	200
	7	420,000	450,000	0.1 × 0.5 × 0.5	0.025	(750)
	7	420,000	500,000	0.1 × 0.5 × 0.3	0.015	(1,200)
	5	300,000	400,000	0.1 × 0.5 × 0.2	0.010	(1,000)
	5	300,000	450,000	0.1 × 0.5 × 0.5	0.025	(3,750)
	5	300,000	500,000	0.1 × 0.5 × 0.3	0.015	(3,000)
					1.000	49,000

7.3 Decision trees

7.3.1 Method and applications

A decision tree is another way of analysing risk and uncertainty. The decision tree model is only as good as the information it contains. The main difficulty is of course, as always, accurately predicting the probabilities that determine the uncertainty. However, a decision tree is a simple and visual way of presenting probabilistic information to management and as such can be quite a useful tool.

The options that management are seeking to evaluate may be very simple. For example, two alternative business plans, A and B, may be under consideration, both of uncertain outcome. Table 7.6 shows the likely possible outcomes of plans A and B.

When the expected profit is calculated it appears that plan B would be the best option. However plan B has a 0.3 chance of a loss of £10,000 whereas plan A will always generate a profit of some sort.

The information can be portrayed in a decision tree as shown in Figure 7.1. The squares and circles are symbols that have a special meaning. The square represents a point at which

Table 7.6

	Plan A		Plan B	
	Profit £	Probability	Profit £	Probability
Adverse	20,000	0.5	(10,000)	0.3
Favourable	60,000	0.5	90,000	0.7
Expected profit	40,000		60,000	

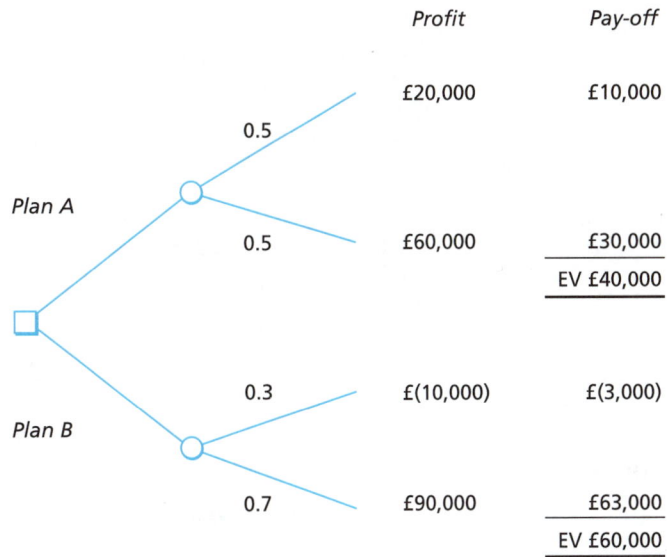

Figure 7.1 Decision tree: plans A and B

a decision is made; in this case there is only one decision to be made – the choice between plan A and plan B at the outset. A circle represents a point at which a chance event takes place. The lines, the branches of the tree, represent the logical sequence between the nodes to the different possible outcomes. The values under the heading 'Profit' in Figure 7.1 represent the possible outcomes. The 'Pay-off' figures are calculated by multiplying the possible outcomes by their probabilities as in the earlier examples.

This basic approach holds good for all decision trees but most decisions are more complicated and require decision trees with more complex features. For example, there may be two or more uncertainties within a business situation, as in the following exercise:

Exercise

The management of a business has to decide whether to launch a new product or not. If the product is launched there are two elements of uncertainty:

- There is a 0.7 probability that sales will be 8,000 units per month but a 0.3 probability that sales will be 5,000 units per month.
- If sales are 8,000 units per month, there is a 0.5 probability that the contribution per unit will be £2 and a 0.5 probability that it will be negative – £(1). If sales are 5,000 units per month there is a 0.6 probability that the contribution per unit will be £3 and a 0.4 probability that it will be £1.

Requirement
Draw a decision tree and advise management as to their best course of action.

Solution

Figure 7.2 shows the decision tree for the product launch.

The sales units on each path are multiplied by the contribution per unit to give the total contribution. This is then multiplied by the probability of occurrence to give the pay-off. The pay-off on the first pathway is £16,000 × 0.7 × 0.5 = £5,600. All paths are summed

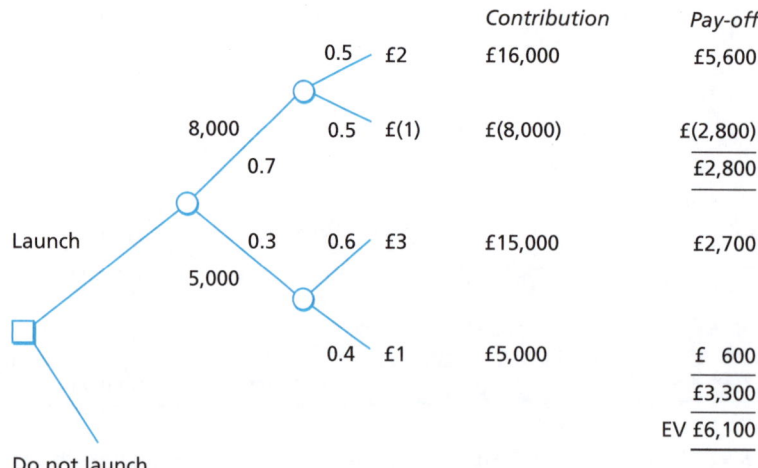

Figure 7.2 Decisions tree: product launch

to give an expected value of £6,100 if the product is launched and, obviously, if the product is not launched the return is zero. So in the absence of other considerations the decision-maker would decide to launch the new product.

Sometimes there are two or more decision points as in the following exercise.

 Exercise

A company has prepared the design for a new product. It can either sell the design, for £100,000, or attempt to develop the design into a marketable product at a cost of £150,000. If the company decides to develop the product, the chances of success are 0.7. If the attempt fails the design can only be sold for £20,000. If the attempt succeeds the business has the choice of either selling the design and developed product for £180,000 or marketing the product. If the product is marketed then there is a 0.6 probability that the product will generate a cash inflow of £800,000 and a 0.4 probability that it will generate a cash outflow of £(100,000). Both figures exclude items previously mentioned.

Requirement

Draw a decision tree and advise management as to their best course of action.

 Solution

The situation is shown in the form of a decision tree in Figure 7.3. For purposes of clarity the two decision points are labelled A and B.

Although in practice decision A precedes decision B, for the purposes of calculation decision B has to be decided first.

Decision B

The expected cash flow on the first path is £800,000 − £150,000 = £650,000. This is then multiplied by the probability of occurrence once the decision to market has been made, that is, by 0.6 to give £390,000. The expected value of marketing is £290,000 and that of selling the designs and product just £30,000 [£180,000 − £150,000]. Therefore, it will pay to market the product if development goes ahead.

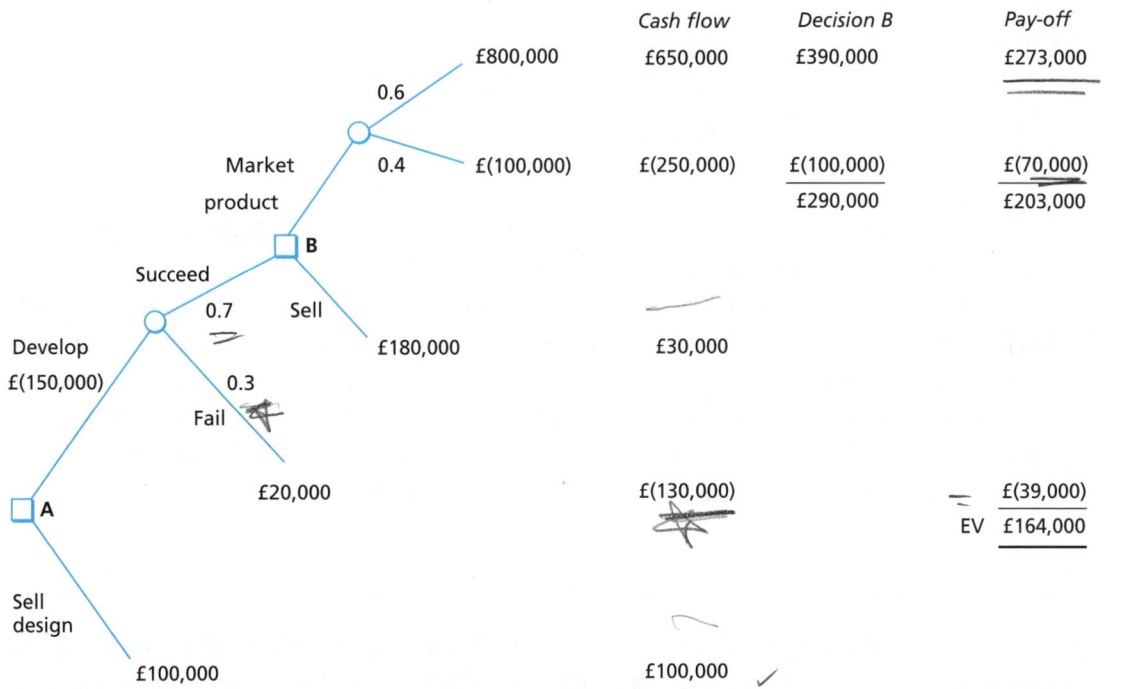

Figure 7.3 Decision tree: develop or not?

Decision A

The expected value of marketing and of failure are summed and compared with the £100,000 if the designs are sold. The £390,000 on the first path is multiplied by the probability of success, 0.7, etc. as shown under the 'Pay-off' column. The expected value is £164,000. This is greater than £100,000 and so the product should be developed and marketed.

A number of other factors arise from this exercise which should be taken into account when considering decision tree-type problems:

- *Time value of money.* The rejected option (the sale of the design) would bring an immediate income whereas the cash flow generated by product development is spread over time. If the span of time under consideration is in excess of a year or so, the time value of money should be incorporated in the calculations. The time value of money is discussed in detail later in this text, and we will return to this example at that stage.
- *Assumes risk neutrality.* As mentioned under probability, some decision-makers do not choose options which give the greatest expected value, because they are either risk seekers or risk averse. In the exercise, for instance, there is a 0.3 probability of losing £130,000 and the recommended course of action offers a 0.28 [0.7 × 0.4] probability of losing £250,000 if the product development is successful. The safe option of selling the design, with its guaranteed inflow of £100,000, could be the more attractive.
- *Sensitivity analysis.* The analysis depends very much on the values of the probabilities in the tree. The values are usually the subjective estimates of the decision-makers, and, no matter how experienced the people involved are, the values must be open to question. In the exercise, a small change in the estimated probabilities of success and failure in the product development phase from 0.7 : 0.3 to 0.6 : 0.4 would change the expected value from £164,000 to £122,000, which is much closer to the sell option.

		£
£650,000 × 0.6 × 0.6	=	234,000
£(250,000) × 0.6 × 0.4	=	(60,000)
		174,000
Less: (130,000) × 0.4		(52,000)
		122,000

The decision is therefore very sensitive to changes in the predicted probabilities. Sensitivity analysis is discussed further later in this text.

- *Oversimplification.* In order to make the tree manageable, the situation has often to be greatly simplified. This makes it appear far more discrete than it really is. In reality the product in the exercise is unlikely to have just two possible values following successful development and marketing. In practice, it is much more likely that the outcomes would form a near continuous range of inflows and outflows. This cannot be shown on a decision tree, and so any decision tree usually represents a simplified situation.

7.3.2 The value of perfect information

One feature of uncertainty in business situations is that it is often possible to reduce it or even eliminate it. For example, market research can be used to determine with a reasonable degree of accuracy what the demand for a new product will be. However, market research costs money and the decision-maker has to decide whether it is worth paying for the research in order to reduce or eliminate the uncertainty of product demand.

The following exercise shows this.

 Exercise

The launch of a new product is being considered. There is a 0.6 chance that demand for the product will be strong and a 0.4 chance that demand will be weak. Two strategies for the launch are possible. Strategy 1 involves high promotion costs and will generate a net cash inflow of £120,000 if demand proves to be strong. However, if demand proves to be weak then a net cash outflow of £(30,000) will result. Strategy 2 involves low promotion costs. If demand proves to be strong then this will generate a net cash inflow of only £80,000 but if demand proves weak then a net cash inflow of £20,000 is still generated.

Requirement
(a) Draw a decision tree and advise which course of action generates the greatest expected profit.
(b) What is the maximum amount that should be paid for market research to determine with certainty whether demand will be strong or weak?

 Solution

(a) The required decision tree shown in Figure 7.4.
   The decision tree model suggests that Strategy 1 should be adopted since it generates the higher expected value. That is £60,000 as opposed to the £56,000 generated by Strategy 2. The problem with this is that if demand turns out to be weak Strategy 1 gives

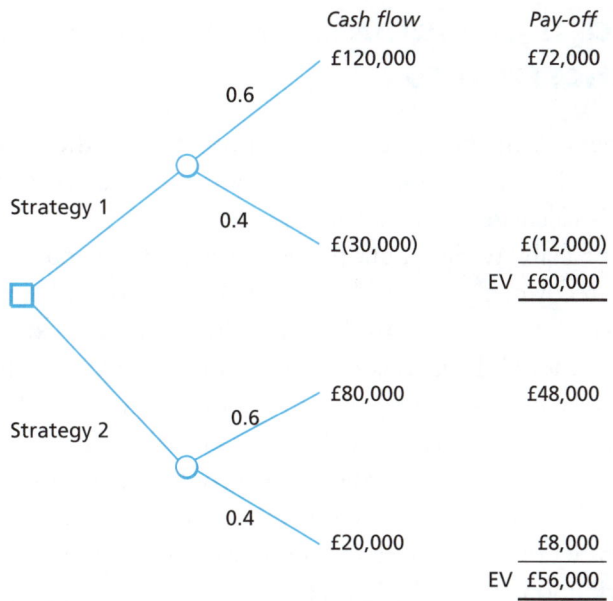

Figure 7.4 Decision tree: promotion cost strategies 1 and 2

a negative cash flow of £30,000 compared with a positive cash flow of £20,000 from Strategy 2. In the case of weak demand Strategy 1 will turn out to have been the wrong choice.

(b) If the research predicted that demand would be strong then Strategy 1 would be adopted giving a cash inflow of £120,000. If the research predicted that demand would be weak then Strategy 2 would be adopted giving a cash flow of £20,000.

Hence the expected cash flow outcome, with the research, will be £80,000, that is [£120,000 × 0.6] + [£20,000 × 0.4].

The expected cash inflow outcome without the research is £60,000.

Hence the value of the research and perfect information is £20,000, that is [£80,000 − £60,000].

The maximum amount that the decision-maker should pay for the research is £20,000.

7.4 Uncertainty in investment appraisal

Later in this text you will be studying investment appraisal in detail. Investment appraisal involves the forecasting of cash flows associated with a project and clearly there will be some uncertainty attached to such forecasts.

The techniques for dealing with uncertainty that you have learned about in this chapter, using probabilities and sensitivity analysis, are useful for dealing with uncertainty in investment appraisal. However, these are not the only methods available to the management accountant.

You will see that it also possible to allow for uncertainty by other methods, including the following:

- Adjusting the required rate of return to allow for the perceived degree of risk; the cash flows from a more risky project might be discounted using a higher discount rate.
- Adjusting the payback time required; for a project that is perceived to be more risky, a shorter payback period might be required.

7.5 Standard deviations to measure risk and uncertainty

The conventional measure of the dispersion of a probability is the standard deviation. The standard deviation is the square root of the mean of the squared deviations from the expected value and is calculated using a formula.

If we have two probability distributions with different expected values their standard deviations are not directly comparable. We can overcome this problem by using the coefficient of variation, which is the standard deviation divided by the expected value.

Expected values, standard deviations or coefficient of variations are used to summarise alternative courses of action however it must be remembered that they do not provide all the relevant information to the decision maker. The probability distribution will provide the decision maker with all of the information they require. It would be appropriate to use expected values, standard deviations or coefficient of variations for decision making when there are a large number of alternatives to consider i.e. where it is not practical to consider the probability distributions for each alternative.

Example

A company is considering whether to make product X or product Y. They cannot make both products. The estimated sales demand for each product is uncertain and the following probability distribution of the profits for each product has been identified:

Product X

Profit Outcome (£)	Estimated Probability	Weighted Amount (£)
£3,000	0.10	£300
£3,500	0.20	£700
£4,000	0.40	£1,600
£4,500	0.20	£900
£5,000	0.10	£500
	Expected Value	£4,000

Product Y

Profit Outcome (£)	Estimated Probability	Weighted Amount (£)
£2,000	0.05	£ 100
£3,000	0.10	£ 300
£4,000	0.40	£1,600
£5,000	0.25	£1,250
£6,000	0.20	£1,200
	Expected Value	£4,450

Using an expected value approach the company's decision would be to produce product X. However, lets consider the standard deviation calculations for each product:

Product X

Profit Deviatioin from Expected Value	Squared Deviatioin (£)	Probability	Weighted Amount (£)
£3000 − £1,000	1,000,000	0.10	100,000
£3500 − £ 500	250,000	0.20	50,000
£4000 − £ 0	0	0.40	0
£4,500 + £ 500	250,000	0.20	50,000
£5000 + £1,000	1,000,000	0.10	100,000
	Sum of squared deviation		300,000
	Standard deviation		547.72
	Expected value		4,000

Product Y

Profit Deviatioin from Expected Value	Squared Deviatioin (£)	Probability	Weighted Amount (£)
£2000 − £2,450	£ 6,002,500	0.05	£ 300,125
£3000 − £1,450	£ 2,102,500	0.10	£ 210,250
£4000 − £ 450	£ 202,500	0.40	£ 81,000
£5,000 + £ 550	£ 302,500	0.25	£ 75,625
£6000 + £1,550	£ 2,402,500	0.20	£ 480,500
	Sum of squared deviation		£1,147,500
	Standard deviation		£1,071.21
	Expected value		£4,450

The expected net present value for each product gives us an average value based upon the probability associated with each possible profit outcome. If net present value is used for decision making, then on that basis Product Y would be produced as it yields the highest return.

However, the net present value for each product does not indicate the range of profits that may result. By calculating the standard deviation, this allows us to identify a range of values that could occur for the profit for each product. Product Y has a higher standard deviation than Product X and is therefore more risky. There is not a significant difference in net present value for each of the products. However, Product X is less risky than Product Y and therefore the final selection will depend on the risk attitude of the company.

7.6 Maximin, Maximax and Regret Criteria

Sometimes it is not always possible to assign probabilities to possible outcomes. When this situation exists, the manager might use the following criteria to make decisions: maximin, maximax or the criterion of regret.

The maximin criterion suggests that a decision maker should select the alternative that offers the least unattractive worst outcome. The decision maker assumes that the worst possible outcome will always occur and therefore he/she should select the largest payoff under these circumstances. This means that the decision maker would choose the alternative that maximises the minimum profit.

On the other hand, the maximax criterion looks at the best possible results and therefore the decision maker assumes that the best payoff will occur, i.e. maximise the maximum profit.

Once a decision maker selects a criteria that turns out not to be the best he/she will regret the selection of not having chosen another alternative when he/she had the opportunity. This is known as the 'regret criterion'.

Example

A company needs to decide which one of the three products to launch. Each of the products could lead to varying levels of profit and these have been constructed in the following payoff table:

Products	Worst	Profits £'000s Most Likely	Best
X	10	12	22
Y	15	18	20
Z	8	11	15

Requirements
(a) Which product should be launched using the maximin decision rule?
(b) Which product should be launched using the maximax decision rule?

 Solution

(a) Maximin decision rule

The maximin criterion suggests that a decision maker should select the alternative that offers the least unattractive worst outcome, i.e. the manager will go for the product which gives the highest minimum profit. The highest minimum profit in this case is Product Y as this offers £15,000 as against £10,000 for Product X and £8,000 for Product Z.

(b) Maximax decision rule

The maximax criterion looks at the best possible results and therefore the decision maker assumes that the best payoff will occur, i.e. maximise the maximum profit.

Applying the maximax decision rule, Product X would be chosen as this maximises the maximum profit possible.

7.7 Summary

In this chapter we have learned how risk and uncertainty arise and how they affect decisions according to the risk attitude of the decision-maker.

Readings

7

Utility

It has been implied in the main text that expected value has limitations for a single decision because only one outcome will occur – not the weighted average. The monetary consequences of a loss could be disastrous, and the size of the investment and the resulting loss may matter to a greater or lesser extent to different individuals. Utility theory was first put forward by Bernoulli. He suggested the following hypothesis:

The decision of an individual on whether or not to accept a particular gamble depends on the utility which he attaches to the sums of money involved and not just on the sums themselves.

He, therefore, proposed that sums of money be converted to their utility values by utilising a diminishing marginal utility curve. Probabilities could then be multiplied by the utility of the monetary consequences obtained from the curve to arrive at an expected utility value (EUV). The unit of measure of utility is the utile. Figure 1 shows a utility curve. The money

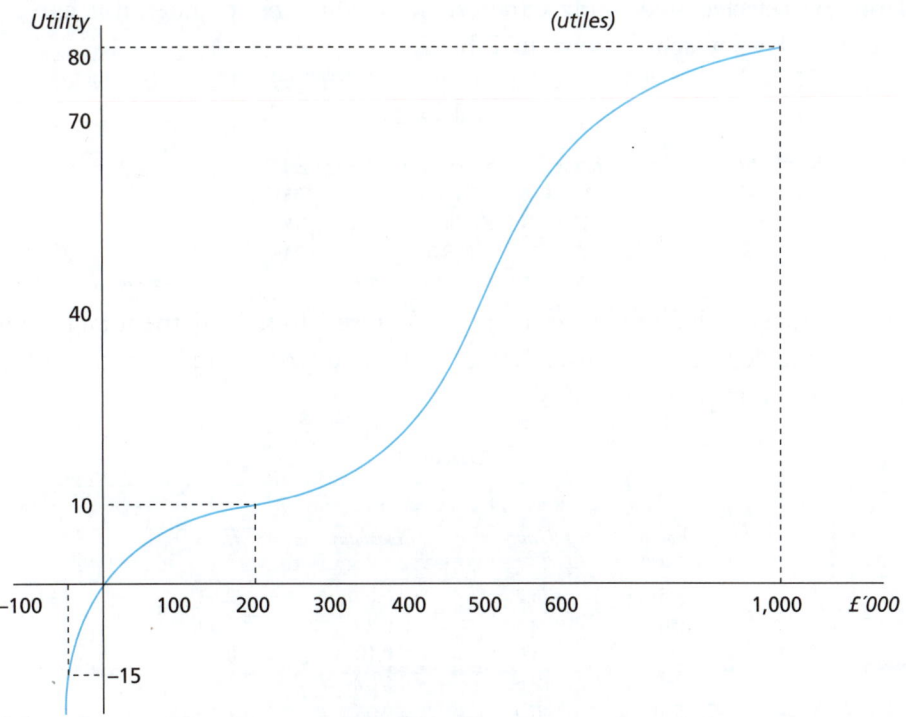

Figure 1 Utility curve

value is turned into utiles by reading from the curve, so £1,000,000 is equal to 80 utiles and £200,000 to 10 utiles.

An individual has to choose between the three ventures shown in Table 1. Which should he choose using the utility curve in Figure 1?

Table 1

Venture 1 Investment £50,000		Venture 2 Investment £20,000		Venture 3 Investment £30,000	
Benefit £K	Prob.	Benefit £K	Prob.	Benefit £K	Prob.
(50)	0.60	(20)	0.30	(30)	0.70
100	0.20	100	0.40	300	0.20
200	0.10	240	0.30	500	0.05
500	0.07			600	0.05
1,000	0.03				

Answer

The benefits are converted into utiles and then multiplied by the probabilities.

Venture 1			Venture 2			Venture 3		
U	P	EUV	U	P	EUV	U	P	EUV
(14)	0.6	(8.4)	(4)	0.3	(1.2)	(5)	0.7	(3.5)
5	0.2	1.0	5	0.4	2.0	15	0.2	3.0
10	0.1	1.0	12	0.3	3.6	40	0.05	2.0
40	0.07	2.8			4.4	70	0.05	3.5
80	0.03	2.4						5.0
		(1.2)						

Venture 3 is marginally better than Venture 2 and should therefore be selected. Venture 1 should not be selected under any circumstances. This answer does not agree with the expected value (EV), which is shown in Table 2.

Table 2

Venture	EUV	EV
1	(1.2)	£75K
2	4.4	£106K
3	5.0	£94K

If it was possible to limit the investment in Venture 1 to half of the total the investment becomes acceptable with a positive EUV as Table 3 shows. Therefore reducing the size of the investment can improve the EUV.

Table 3

Half Venture 1

Money £K	Utility	Probability	EUV
(25)	(4.2)	0.60	(2.52)
50	2.5	0.20	0.50
100	5.0	0.10	0.50
250	12.5	0.07	0.875
500	40.0	0.03	1.20
			0.555

Simulation and Monte Carlo technique

The term simulation is commonly used to refer to the Monte Carlo method. This involves the use of random number tables or some other method of generating random numbers. This is demonstrated in the following example.

A company has a machine which processes units which arrive for processing at an uneven rate. At times, long intervals between arrivals might result in the machine standing idle and at other times short intervals might result in queues of units waiting to be processed. Each unit takes 5 minutes to be processed.

In this situation the capacity of the machine depends on its operating characteristics (technical capacity) and, in addition, the typical pattern of arrivals of units for processing. Knowledge of the actual capacity is important for a range of reasons: production planning, budgeting, investment appraisal, etc. A Monte Carlo simulation can be carried out to analyse the processing of units by the machine. This is done as follows.

The first step is to determine the frequency distribution of the arrival times of the units at the machine. The probability of arrival time intervals (that is, the time between successive arrivals) is shown in Table 4. A frequency distribution can be allotted once the relative frequency has been determined. Numbers between 0 and 99 are allocated starting with 2 minutes where the relative frequency is 0.02 and so the two numbers 0 and 1 are allocated to this frequency. The numbers 2–6 are allocated to the 3-minute interval where the frequency is 0.05, 11 numbers are allocated to the 4-minute interval, etc. See Table 5.

Table 4

Minutes between arrivals	Probability
2	0.02
3	0.05
4	0.11
5	0.20
6	0.22
7	0.31
8	0.09
Total	1.00

Table 5

Arrival interval	Probability	Frequency Distribution	Random number
2	0.02	00–01	
3	0.05	02–06	05
4	0.11	07–17	
5	0.20	18–37	23
6	0.22	38–59	
7	0.31	60–90	
8	0.09	91–99	

To determine the average total waiting time per hour and the actual (as opposed to technical) capacity of the machine to process units in that hour, a typical pattern of arrivals for a 1-hour period must be determined. This is done using a random number table or using spreadsheet or other software. Table 6 is a random number table.

Table 6

23	15	75	48	59	01	83	72	59	93	76	24	97	08	96	95	23	03	67	44
05	54	55	50	43	10	53	74	35	08	90	61	18	37	44	10	96	22	13	43
14	87	16	03	50	32	40	43	62	23	50	05	10	03	22	11	54	38	08	34
38	97	67	49	51	94	05	17	58	53	78	80	59	01	94	32	42	87	16	95
97	31	26	17	18	99	75	53	08	70	94	25	12	58	41	54	88	21	05	13
11	74	26	93	81	44	33	93	08	72	32	79	73	31	18	22	64	70	68	50
43	36	12	88	59	11	01	64	56	23	93	00	90	04	99	43	64	07	40	36
93	80	62	04	78	38	26	80	44	91	55	75	11	89	32	58	47	55	25	71
49	54	01	31	81	08	42	98	41	87	69	53	82	96	61	77	73	80	95	27
36	76	87	26	33	37	94	82	15	69	41	95	96	86	70	45	27	48	38	80
07	09	25	23	92	24	62	71	26	07	06	55	84	53	44	67	33	84	53	20
43	31	00	10	81	44	86	38	03	07	52	55	51	61	48	89	74	29	46	47
61	57	00	63	60	06	17	36	37	75	63	14	89	51	23	35	01	74	69	93
31	35	28	37	99	10	77	91	89	41	31	57	97	64	48	62	58	48	69	19
57	04	88	65	26	27	79	59	36	82	90	52	95	65	46	35	06	53	22	54
09	24	34	42	00	68	72	10	71	37	30	72	97	57	56	09	29	82	76	50
97	95	53	50	18	40	89	48	83	29	52	23	08	25	21	22	53	26	15	87
93	73	25	95	70	43	78	19	88	85	56	67	16	68	26	95	99	64	45	69
72	62	11	12	25	00	92	26	82	64	35	66	65	94	34	71	68	75	18	67
61	02	07	44	18	45	37	12	07	94	95	91	73	78	66	99	53	61	93	78
97	83	98	54	74	33	05	59	17	18	45	47	35	41	44	22	03	42	30	00
89	16	09	71	92	22	23	29	06	37	35	05	54	54	89	88	43	81	63	61
25	96	68	82	20	62	87	17	92	65	02	82	35	28	62	84	91	95	48	83
81	44	33	17	19	05	04	95	48	06	74	69	00	75	67	65	01	71	65	45
11	32	25	439	31	42	36	23	43	86	08	62	49	76	67	42	24	52	32	45

One random number is allocated to each .01 frequency. This is done by randomly selecting a number from the table. If the first number selected is the first number in the table, that is 23, it is matched with the frequency distribution where it can be seen that it corresponds with the 5-minute interval. This means that the first unit arrives after five minutes. The next number in the table is then selected, say, 05 moving down the column, this corresponds with a 3-minute interval and so the process continues. Eventually the results in Table 7 will be produced for the typical 1-hour period.

Table 7

Unit number	Random number	Time in minutes Interval	Arrival	Departure	Queuing/ (idle time)
1	23	5	5	10	0
2	05	3	8	15	2
3	14	4	12	20	3
4	38	6	18	25	2
5	97	8	26	31	(1)
6	11	4	30	36	1
7	43	6	36	41	0
8	93	8	44	49	(3)
9	49	6	50	55	(1)
10	36	5	55	60	0
11	07	4	59	65	1

Idle time occurs where a unit does not arrive for processing until at least one minute after its predecessor has left. For example, processing of unit 4 starts at minute 20 and ends at minute 25. Since unit 5 does not arrive until minute 26 there will be one minute of down time before processing on unit 5 can start.

Careful consideration of the figures in Table 7 reveals that the typical processing hour runs from minute 5 to minute 65. The period minute 0 to minute 5 waiting for the first unit to arrive is an initial start up which will not repeat itself if the machine is in continuous operation and so the typical hour will be taken from minute 5 to minute 65.

During the hour eleven units are fully processed, there is a total of nine minutes of queuing and five minutes of down time. The critical point is that although the technical capacity of the machine is 12 units per hour (i.e., 60 minutes @ 5 minutes per unit) its actual capacity is eleven units per hour because of the conditions under which it is being operated. Therefore any production plan or budget will have to be based on the assumption that the machine can only process eleven units per hour.

One common application for this technique is in estimating counter queues in shops, banks, post offices and building societies. The length of waiting time predicted will determine the number of staff required. This scenario presents another difficulty, in that there are two uncertainties: firstly, customers do not arrive at an even rate and secondly, some customers require more and some require less than the average service time. Thus two sets of frequency probabilities are used and two different random numbers.

Stock holding systems are another area where simulation models can be used to good effect in order to minimise stock holdings without an undue risk of a stock-out. Alternatively random numbers can be used to predict pay-off values for any probability distribution.

The impact of risk and uncertainty on managerial decision-making

Tim Thompson, *CIMA Insider*, September 2005, Paper: P2 *Management Accounting – Decision Management*

Relevant learning outcome:
C1: 'evaluate the impact of uncertainty and risk on decision models that may be based on CVP analysis, relevant cash flows, learning curves, discounting techniques etc.;'

Introduction
What effect do risk and uncertainty have on managerial decision-making? In this context, we will be looking at some of the techniques that can be used to evaluate an opportunity that has presented itself and that requires a decision.

Underpinning our discussion is human behaviour and we will be focussing on how the attitudes and perceptions of managers can affect the decisions that they make. We all have our expectations, aspirations and fears; some of us have an optimistic view of life, whereas others are pessimists. It follows that two people, when faced with the same opportunity, might very well come up with two different decisions about it based upon their different outlooks.

Risk and uncertainty defined
Both risk and uncertainty are based on the recognition that there are multiple possible outcomes that can emerge from a decision. The wider the range of these outcomes, the more risky, or uncertain, is the situation. The difference between risk and uncertainty is

the extent to which the number, value and likelihood of these outcomes can be confidently quantified.

An example of risk can be derived from a pack of playing cards. If we are presented with a full pack and draw one card at random, we can calculate with confidence the probability of this card being the ace of spades. We know that there are 52 possible outcomes (there are 52 cards in the pack) and we know exactly what these outcomes are (each card is unique and identifiable). Thus, using the law of proportions, we can state with confidence that the probability of drawing the ace of spades is 1/52 (or 0.1923 or 19.23%).

But the analogy of playing cards does not really correspond with the reality of business decision-making. Unlike the repetitive and predictable nature of playing cards, business decisions are characterized by a high degree of uniqueness. Accordingly, it is difficult to identify every possible outcome that might emerge and yet more difficulty to establish the likelihood of each of these outcomes; we call this uncertainty.

Despite this clear distinction between risk and uncertainty, there is a paradox; for decision-making purposes managers tend to ignore (or at least work around) this distinction. To evaluate a business decision involving uncertainty, managers will use judgement (or educated guesswork), to predict as best they can all of the possible outcomes and their associated probabilities. Having done this, they then treat an uncertain situation as if it was characterised by risk. In practice, therefore, management accounting techniques usually treat risk and uncertainty as one and the same thing. For the remainder of this article, we will use 'risk' as the blanket term to cover both risk and uncertainty.

Attitudes to risk

One of the models used to describe different individuals' attitudes to risk identifies three classifications as follows.

Risk-seeking

This term does not mean that the individual seek risks as an end itself, but rather as a means to an end. Recognising the established linkage between risk and return, the individual seeks a very high return and accepts the high level of risk that normally accompanies this. This attitude is often to be found in an entrepreneurial individual who plans to set up a new business and hopes to become a millionaire. In order to achieve this, the entrepreneur may need to take out a substantial loan and he will willingly risk all of his personal assets as security for this borrowing.

Risk-averse

This attitude is concerned with limiting risk. At an extreme level, the interpretation of this is that the individual adopts an ultra-cautious approach and eliminates as much risk as possible. In so doing the individual must accept the very low returns that normally accompany this very low risk.

In practice, though, the term risk averse is not usually perceived in this extreme way. An alternative, less radical, interpretation is that risk aversion describes the way that rational individuals are expected to deal with risk. For a given rate of return, rational decision makers will seek the highest level of return that will achieve this. Alternatively, for a given level of return, they will seek the lowest level of associated risk.

Risk-neutral

A risk-neutral individual pays no attention to the range of the outcomes that may emerge from a decision, but focuses on a single value that represents the situation facing him. For this purpose, statistical averages are often used, although simply focussing on the most likely outcome would also fall under this classification.

A practical example

A fruit trader plans to travel to market tomorrow. He has a small stall at the market and only a limited amount of cash available to buy stock to sell. Accordingly, he can select only one type of fruit to buy from the wholesaler today ready for tomorrow's market. There are four types of fruit from which the trader can make his selection; apples, pears, oranges and strawberries. From past experience, our trader expects that trading conditions tomorrow will fall into one of four headings; bad, poor, fair or good and each of these trading conditions has the same likelihood of occurring. Again using past experience, the trader has quantified the profit [+£] or loss [(£)] that he thinks he will earn tomorrow depending upon his choice of fruit and the trading conditions that emerge. These are as follows.

Fruit:	*Apples*	*Pears*	*Oranges*	*Strawberries*
Trading Condition				
Bad	(£1,000)	(£1,200)	(£300)	(£600)
Poor	(£200)	(£400)	(£100)	(£300)
Fair	+£600	+£700	+£200	+£100
Good	+£1,000	+£1,200	+£400	+£440

Let us now consider some of the alternative approaches that our trader might take to determine which type of fruit he will purchase and take to tomorrow's market, depending on the attitude to risk that is to prevail.

The maximin approach

This approach involves looking at the worst possible outcome only for each of the four types of fruit. That is to say we will focus on bad trading conditions only. We need to look for the best outcome amongst the four types of fruit in these conditions, although it might be more accurate to say that since all of these are loss-making we are looking for the least worst. In so doing, we completely ignore the outcomes that might emerge if trading conditions are other than bad. Clearly, the maximin choice will be oranges, since the anticipated loss of £300 is the least worst of the four types of fruit. This ultra-cautious approach indicates an aversion to risk that may be based upon some deep-rooted fear of failure.

The maximax approach

Here, we are looking to select the opportunity that offers the highest possible return. We will consider only good trading conditions, completely ignoring what might happen under fair, poor and bad. This would lead us to select pears with the highest possible profit of £1,200. In hoping that good trading conditions will emerge, we are taking an optimistic outlook on the situation and not worrying about the fact that, if trading conditions are bad, then pears will lead to the largest loss of £1,200.

The minimax regret approach

Sometimes known simply as "Regret", this approach makes a decision today based upon how our trader might feel at the end of tomorrow's market. Having made his choice of the type of fruit he will sell, his success at the market will depend on the trading conditions that emerge and the trader has no control over this. His choice may turn out to be the best for the trading conditions that emerge and if so the trader will be happy. Alternatively, the trader may get to the end of tomorrow's market and have a feeling of regret, since he had not selected the type of fruit that would have been best under the trading conditions that emerged.

If for example, the trader selects oranges and trading conditions prove to be bad, then he will feel no regret as this type of fruit will have yielded the least worst loss of £300. But if, trading conditions turn out to be good, then the trader will regret having chosen oranges rather than pears which would have provided a much higher profit of £1,200 in this situation. Not only can we identify that this regret will exist, but we can also quantify it. Having earned a profit of £400 instead of £1,200, then the amount of regret will be £800.

For each trading condition, one of the types of fruit will yield no regret as it would represent the best choice as follows:

Trading Condition	Best choice
Bad	Oranges
Poor	Oranges
Fair	Pears
Good	Pears

From this, we can derive the following table that quantifies the regret that the trader would retrospectively feel for each combination of type of fruit and trading condition.

Fruit:	Apples	Pears	Oranges	Strawberries
Trading Condition				
Bad	£700	**£900**	NIL	£300
Poor	£100	£300	NIL	£200
Fair	£100	NIL	£500	£600
Good	£200	NIL	**£800**	**£760**

In the above table, we have used bold figures to identify the maximum possible regret that the trader could feel for each of the four types of fruit. The key point here is that, although regret is a retrospective feeling, these figures are known in advance and the trader can use this information to select the type of fruit for tomorrow's market. The trader will select the type of fruit whose maximum potential regret is the lowest of the four. He will therefore choose apples with a maximum regret of £700.

There is evidence of aversion to risk here. The trader does not make profit/loss the prime focus of his decision-making but focuses on how badly he might feel tomorrow if things do not work out.

The expected value approach

For each type of fruit, the trader will calculate a single figure that represents all of the possible outcomes for that fruit and their respective probabilities. In other words, the expected value (or EV) is the weighted average of the probability distribution.

The formula for this is

Expected value = Σpx

where x is the value of each outcome, and p is the associated probability
Here are the calculations:

Fruit:	Apples			Pears		
Trading Condition	x	p	px	x	p	px
Bad	(£1,000)	0.25	(£250)	(£1,200)	0.25	(£300)
Poor	(£200)	0.25	(£50)	(£400)	0.25	(£100)
Fair	+£600	0.25	+£150	+£700	0.25	+£175
Good	+£1,000	0.25	+£250	+£1,200	0.25	+£300
		Σpx	+£100		Σpx	+£75

Fruit:	Oranges			Strawberries		
Trading Condition	x	p	px	x	p	px
Bad	(£300)	0.25	(£75)	(£600)	0.25	(£150)
Poor	(£100)	0.25	(£25)	(£300)	0.25	(£75)
Fair	+£200	0.25	+£50	+£100	0.25	+£25
Good	+£400	0.25	+£100	+£440	0.25	+£110
		Σpx	+£50		Σpx	(£90)

The trader will select the type of fruit with the highest expected value, this is apples with an EV of +£100. Although this is called the expected value, one thing that the trader will not expect tomorrow is a profit of £100, since this is not one of the four possible outcomes that apples offer on a single day of trading. What this means is that if the trader went regularly to market, and chose apples every day, then over time his average profit would be expected to be £100 (or thereabouts).

In focussing solely on the weighted average of the outcomes, the trader ignores the danger of losing £1,000 on any one day. He also ignores the attractiveness of making a £1,000 profit on any one day. For this reason, the EV approach is described as risk neutral. The EV tells us that selecting apples is the best long-term decision. This is also recommended if we choose to use the EV approach for our short-term decision about tomorrow's market.

Concluding remarks

Commercial organisations exist to make profits for their owners and it is the responsibility of managers to make decisions that will yield these profits. But managers are human beings and they are subject to the fears, hopes and expectations that affect us all. The way that managers react to these pressures helps to determine their view of risk and this can influence the decisions that they make.

The maximin and minimax regret approaches both reflect aversion to risk, whereas the Maximax approach is clearly risk-seeking. The expected value approach is seen as risk-neutral; it does not actively seek risk, but it does imply at least a tacit willingness to accept it.

Here is a summary of the decision that would emerge from each of the approaches that we have discussed.

Maximin	Oranges
Maximax	Pears
Minimax Regret	Apples
Expected Value	Apples

In our practical example, there is a consensus that strawberries will not be selected. Otherwise, any of the remaining three types of fruit could be chosen depending on the attitude of the trader.

Revision Questions

Question 1

1.1 A processing company operates a common process from which three different products emerge. Each of the three products can then either be sold in a market that has many buyers and sellers or further processed independently of each other in three other processes. After further processing each of the products can be sold in the same market for a higher unit selling price. Which of the following is required to determine whether or not any of the products should be further processed?

(i) Total cost of the common process
(ii) The basis of sharing the common process cost between the three products
(iii) The total cost of each of the three additional processes
(iv) The unit selling price of each product after further processing
(v) The unit selling price of each product before further processing
(vi) The percentage normal loss of each further process
(vii) The actual units of output of each product from the common process.

(A) (iii), (iv), (vi) and (vii) only
(B) (i), (ii), (iii), (iv), (vi) and (vii) only
(C) (i), (ii), (v) and (vii) only
(D) (iii), (iv), (v), (vi) and (vii) only   (3 marks)

1.2 Z plc is preparing a quotation for a one off contract to manufacture an item for a potential customer. The item is to be made of steel and the contract would require 300 kgs of steel. The steel is in regular use by Z plc and, as a consequence, the company maintains an inventory of this steel and currently has 200 kgs in inventory. The company operates a LIFO basis of inventory valuation and its most recent purchases were as follows:

   20 November 2006   150 kgs costing £600
   3 November 2006   250 kgs costing £1,100

The steel is easily available in the market where its current purchase price is £4.25 per kg. If the steel currently held in inventory was to be sold it could be sold for £3.50 per kg.

The relevant cost of the steel to be included in the cost estimate is

(A) £1,050
(B) £1,260
(C) £1,275
(D) £1,300

(2 marks)

1.3 X is considering the following five investments:

Investment	J	K	L	M	N
	$000	$000	$000	$000	$000
Initial investment	400	350	450	500	600
Net Present Value	125	105	140	160	190

Investments J and L are mutually exclusive, all of the investments are divisible and none of them may be invested in more than once. The optimum investment plan for X assuming that the funding available is limited to $1 m is

(A) $400,000 in J plus $600,000 in N.
(B) $400,000 in M plus $600,000 in N.
(C) $500,000 in M plus $500,000 in N.
(D) $350,000 in K plus $600,000 in N plus $50,000 in M.

(2 marks)

1.4 A company has estimated the selling prices and variable costs of one of its products as follows:

Selling price per unit		Variable cost per unit	
$	Probability	$	Probability
40	0.30	20	0.55
50	0.45	30	0.25
60	0.25	40	0.20

Given that the company will be able to supply 1,000 units of its product each week irrespective of the selling price, and that selling price and variable cost per unit are independent of each other, calculate the probability that the weekly contribution will exceed $20,000.

(3 marks)

1.5 A company sells three different levels of TV maintenance contract to its customers: Basic, Standard and Advanced. Selling prices, unit costs and monthly sales are as follows:

	Basic	Standard	Advanced
	£	£	£
Selling price	50	100	135
Variable cost	30	50	65
Monthly contracts sold	750	450	300

Calculate the average contribution to sales ratio of the company

(i) based on the sales mix stated above; and
(ii) if the total number of monthly contracts sold remains the same, but equal numbers of each contract are sold.

(4 marks)

 Question 2

FRS Ltd is considering undertaking a project, the cash flow outcome of which depends on whether market demand proves to be weak (probability 0.25) or strong (probability 0.75).

Weak market demand will result in a negative cash flow of £180,000, while strong market demand will give rise to a positive cash flow of £500,000.

A market research consultant has offered to prepare a forecast on whether the market will be weak or strong for a fee of £80,000. Past experience with this firm indicates that it has a 0.8 chance of correctly forecasting strong market demand and a 0.6 chance of correctly forecasting weak market demand.

Requirements
(a) Advise FRS Ltd on whether or not the project is viable without the forecast.
(b) Advise FRS Ltd on whether or not the value of the forecast to FRS Ltd is greater or less than the fee requested by the consultant.

Question 3

For the past 20 years a charity organisation has held an annual dinner and dance with the primary intention of raising funds.

This year there is concern that an economic recession may adversely affect both the number of persons attending the function and the advertising space that will be sold in the programme published for the occasion.

Based on past experience and current prices and quotations, it is expected that the following costs and revenues will apply for the function:

			£
Cost:	Dinner and dance:	Hire of premises	700
		Band and entertainers	2,800
		Raffle prizes	800
		Photographer	200
		Food at £12 per person (with a guarantee of 400 persons minimum)	
	Programme:	A fixed cost of £2,000 plus £5 per page.	
Revenues:	Dinner and dance	Price of tickets	£20 per person
		Average revenue from:	
		Raffle	£5 per person
		Photographs	£1 per person
	Programme:	Average revenue from:	
		Advertising	£70 per page

A sub-committee, formed to examine more closely the likely outcome of the function, discovered the following from previous records and accounts:

No. of tickets sold	No. of past occasions
250–349	4
350–449	6
450–549	8
550–649	2
	20

No. of programme pages sold	No. of past occasions
24	4
32	8
40	6
48	2
	20

Several members of the sub-committee are in favour of using a market research consultant to carry out a quick enquiry into the likely number of pages of advertising space that would be sold for this year's dinner and dance.

Requirements

(a) Calculate the expected value of the profit to be earned from the dinner and dance this year.
(b) Recommend, with relevant supporting financial and cost data, whether or not the charity should spend £500 on the market research enquiry and indicate the possible benefits the enquiry could provide.

NB: All workings for tickets should be in steps of 100 tickets and for advertising in steps of 8 pages.

Question 4

The managing director of XYZ plc has devolved some decision making to the operating divisions of the firm. He is anxious to extend this process but first wishes to be assured that decisions are being taken properly in accordance with group policy.

As a check on existing practice he has asked for an investigation to be made into a recent decision to increase the price of the sole product of Z division to £14.50 per unit due to rising costs.

The following information and estimates were available for the management of Z division.

(1) Last year 75,000 units were sold at £12 each with a total unit cost of £9 of which £6 were variable costs.
(2) For the year ahead the following cost and demand estimates have been made.

Unit variable costs

Pessimistic	Probability	0.15	£7.00 per unit
Most likely	Probability	0.65	£6.50 per unit
Optimistic	Probability	0.20	£6.20 per unit

Total fixed costs

Pessimistic	Probability	0.3	Increase by 50%
Most likely	Probability	0.5	Increase by 25%
Optimistic	Probability	0.2	Increase by 10%

Demand estimates at various prices (units)

			£13.50	£14.50
	Price per unit			
Pessimistic	Probability	0.3	45,000	35,000
Most likely	Probability	0.5	60,000	55,000
Optimistic	Probability	0.2	70,000	68,000

(Unit variable costs, fixed costs and demand estimates are statistically independent.)

For this type of decision the group has decided that the option should be chosen which has the highest expected outcome with at least an 80 per cent chance of breaking even.

Requirements

(a) Assess whether the decision was made in accordance with group guidelines.
(b) Comment on the estimates for the decision and describe what other factors might have been considered.

Solutions to Revision Questions

✓ Solution 1

1.1 Answer: (D)
Statements (iii), (iv), (v), (vi) and (vii) are correct.

1.2 Answer: (C)
300 kgs @ £4.25 = £1,275.

1.3 Answer: (C)
Calculate the profitability index values of each of the investments and rank them:

Investment	Profitability Index	Rank
J	0.3125	3rd
K	0.3000	5th
L	0.3111	4th
M	0.3200	1st
N	0.3166	2nd

Invest in:

M	$500,000	yielding $160,000
N	$500,000	yielding $158,333
Total	$1,000,000	yielding $318,333

1.4 Weekly contribution of $20,000 if sales demand = 1,000 units equals a contribution of $20 per unit.

The following combinations of selling price and variable cost per unit yield a contribution of more than $20 per unit:

Selling Price	Variable Cost	Probability
$50	$20	0.45 × 0.55 = 0.2475
$60	$30	0.25 × 0.25 = 0.0625
$60	$20	0.25 × 0.55 = 0.1375
		0.4475

Answer = 44.75%

1.5

Previous ratio:	Basic £'000	Standard £'000	Advanced £'000	Total £'000
Sales	37.5	45	40.5	123
Contribution	15	22.5	21	58.5
C/S ratio = 47.6%				
New ratio:				
Sales	25	50	67.5	142.5
Contribution	10	25	35	70
C/S ratio = 49.1%				

Solution 2

Tips

- A straightforward question on the value of information.
- Drawing a decision tree is a simple and visual way of presenting information and will help you in answering this question.

The position may be represented by the following decision tree diagram:

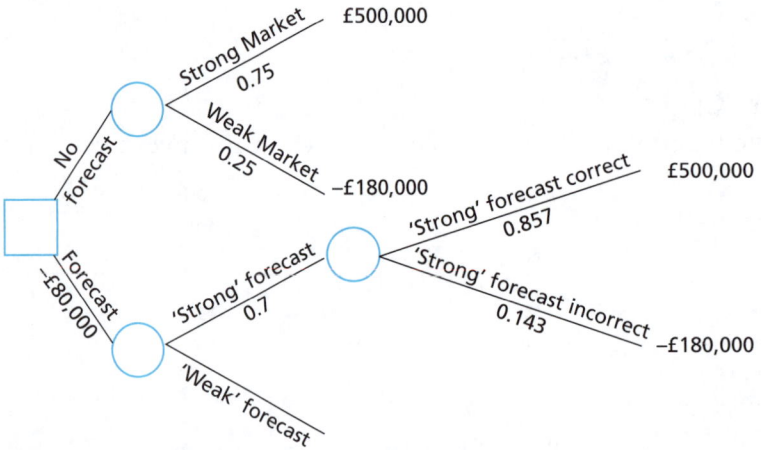

If a weak market is forecast then we may assume that it will be believed and the project will be abandoned at once – since there would be no point in proceeding with a project considered certain to result in a negative cash flow. The probability of the consultant forecasting strong market demand is 0.7, comprising two components, each with a separate outcome, as follows:

Probability of a correct forecast	0.8 × 0.75 = 0.6
Probability of an incorrect forecast	0.4 × 0.25 = 0.1
	0.7

It follows that the probability of a strong market demand forecast being correct is 0.857 (i.e. 0.6/0.7) and the probability of a strong market demand forecast being incorrect is 0.143 (i.e. 0.1/0.7).

The expected cash flow generated by proceeding without a forecast is £330,000 (i.e. (£500,000 × 0.75) + (−£180,000 × 0.25)). Hence the project is viable without a forecast.

The expected cash flow generated by proceeding with a forecast is:

$$0.7[(£500,000 \times .857) + (-£180,000 \times 0.143)] - £80,000 = £201,932$$

The value of the forecast does not justify the fee. The forecast should not be commissioned.

Solution 3

(a) The probability of ticket sales based on past experience is:

Number of tickets sold	Probability	
250–349	0.2	(4 out of 20)
350–449	0.3	(6 out of 20)
450–549	0.4	(8 out of 20)
550–649	0.1	(2 out of 20)
	1.0	

Average revenue per person

	£
Price of ticket	20
Raffle	5
Photograph	1
	26

Fixed costs for the event

	£
Hire of premises	700
Band and entertainers	2,800
Raffle prizes	800
Photographer	200
	4,500

Expected profit from the dinner and dance

Ticket sales (midpoint)	Income	Food	Fixed costs	Profit	Prob.	Expected profit
	£	£	£	£		£
300	7,800	4,800	4,500	(1,500)	0.2	(300)
400	10,400	4,800	4,500	1,100	0.3	330
500	13,000	6,000	4,500	2,500	0.4	1,000
600	15,600	7,200	4,500	3,900	0.1	390
					Expected profit	1,420

The probability of the number of programme pages sold based on past experience is:

Programme pages sold	Probability	
24	0.2	(4 out of 20)
32	0.4	(8 out of 20)
40	0.3	(6 out of 20)
48	0.1	(2 out of 20)
	1.0	

Expected profit on programme advertising

Programme pages sold	Income	Costs	Profit/ (loss)	Prob.	Expected profit
	£	£	£		£
24	1,680	2,120	(440)	0.2	(88)
32	2,240	2,160	80	0.4	32
40	2,800	2,200	600	0.3	180
48	3,360	2,240	1,120	0.1	112
				Expected profit	236

Total expected profit from the dinner and dance and programme advertising is = £1,420 + £236
= £1,656

(b) If the policy is to hold a dinner and dance each year and to accept losses in some years and profits in others, there is no advantage in spending £500 on the market research enquiry. Market research is justifiable only if it affects action taken – a decision on whether or not to hold a dinner and dance and thus avoid any losses.

From the workings in (a) above, it can be seen that an overall loss will be incurred only when 300 tickets are sold. The expected loss that will be incurred if 300 tickets are sold is calculated as:

Loss from sale of 300 tickets £	Profit/(loss) on programmes £	Total loss £	Joint prob.	Expected value £
(1,500)	(440)	(1,940)	0.04	(77.6)
(1,500)	80	(1,420)	0.08	(113.6)
(1,500)	600	(900)	0.06	(54.0)
(1,500)	1,120	(380)	0.02	(7.6)
			Expected loss	(252.8)

The expected value of the market research is £252.80 and the cost of the research is £500. The expenditure on market research is not justified.

Solution 4

Tips

- It is important to be clear on the group guidelines and to identify the various options available to the decision-makers before you begin your calculations.
- This is a question with three variables each of which can take three values. It is therefore important to plan your answer and work systematically.

(a) The group guidelines are to choose the option with the highest expected outcome and at least an 80 per cent chance of breaking even.

Expected contribution = Expected demand × expected contribution per unit.
Expected variable cost per unit = £7 × 0.15 + £6.50 × 0.65 + £6.20 × 0.20
= £6.515

Selling price = £13.50

Expected contribution per unit = £13.50 − £6.515
= £6.985
Expected demand = 45,000 × 0.3 + 60,000 × 0.5 + 70,000 × 0.2
= 57,500 units
Expected contribution = 57,500 × £6.985
= £401,637.50

Selling price = £14.50

Expected contribution per unit = £14.50 − £6.515
= £7.985
Expected demand = 35,000 × 0.3 + 55,000 × 0.5 + 68,000 × 0.2
= 51,600 units
Expected contribution = 51,600 × £7.985
= £412,026

Expected outcome is maximised at a selling price of £14.50.
Consider the probability of at least breaking even is 80% at a selling price of £14.50.

Selling price £14.50

	Prob.	Demand Probability	35,000 0.3	55,000 0.5	68,000 0.2
Contribution per unit					
£7.50 Joint prob.	0.15		£262,500 0.045	£412,500 0.075	£510,000 0.03
£8.00 Joint prob.	0.65		£280,000 0.195	£440,000 0.325	£544,000 0.13
£8.30 Joint prob.	0.20		£290,500 0.06	£456,500 0.10	£564,400 0.04

Last year's fixed cost = 75,000 × (£9 − £6) = £225,000

Expected fixed costs for this year are:

Increase	Fixed costs	Probability
50%	£337,500	0.3
25%	£281,250	0.5
10%	£247,500	0.2

Losses are incurred when contribution is less than fixed costs and the probability of these occurring is as follows:

Contribution	Fixed costs	Probability
£262,500	£337,500	0.045 × 0.3 = 0.0135
£262,500	£281,250	0.045 × 0.5 = 0.0225
£280,000	£337,500	0.195 × 0.3 = 0.0585
£280,000	£281,250	0.195 × 0.5 = 0.0975
£290,500	£337,500	0.060 × 0.3 = 0.0180
		0.2100

Probability of a loss = 0.21
Therefore probability of at least breaking even = 1 − 0.21
= 0.79

The guideline that the option chosen should have at least an 80 per cent chance of breaking even has not been met.

(b) Comments on the estimates for the decision:

- All estimates of costs are likely to be subjective, based on past costs and estimates concerning inflation.
- The probabilities will be subjective, since it is unlikely that sufficient past data is available to produce reliable data.
- The demand estimates are subjective, although it is possible that they were supported by market research.
- The three variables – variable costs, fixed costs and demand – may not be independent.

The main additional factors to take into account, apart from possible interdependence, are other selling prices, both outside this range and within it. Continuous probability distributions may be considered instead of discrete probabilities.

Investment Appraisal

Investment Appraisal

Learning Outcomes

- Explain the process involved in making long-term decisions.
- Apply the principles of relevant cash flow analysis to long-run projects that continue for several years.
- Calculate project cash flows, accounting for tax inflation, and apply perpetuities to derive 'end of project' value where appropriate.
- Apply activity-based costing techniques to derive approximate 'long run' product or service costs appropriate for use in strategic decision making.
- Explain the financial consequences of dealing with long-run projects, in particular the importance of accounting for the 'time value of money'.
- Evaluate project proposals using the techniques of investment appraisal.
- Compare, contrast and evaluate the alternative techniques of investment appraisal.
- Evaluate and rank projects that might be mutually exclusive, involve unequal lives and/or be subject to capital rationing.
- Apply sensitivity analysis to cash flow parameters to identify those to which net present value is particularly sensitive.
- Produce decision support information for management, integrating financial and non-financial considerations.

8.1 Introduction

In this chapter you will learn how the principles of decision-making and the effects of risk and uncertainty are applied to long-term decision-making which is often referred to as investment appraisal.

8.2 The different appraisal methods

8.2.1 Introduction

This chapter deals with the various techniques of investment appraisal used in capital budgeting decisions.

Capital budgeting addresses two problems:

- How much should be spent on projects/assets?
- Which projects should be undertaken and which assets should be acquired?

This includes decisions on whether to:

- Invest in a new product line;
- Acquire new premises or plant;
- Enter a new market;
- Undertake research and development;
- Launch an advertising campaign;
- Launch a new product;
- In the case of the public sector – build a new school, new hospital or new road.

It is important to make sound capital budgeting decisions because:

- the decisions often involve large amounts of money;
- the commitment may be for a long period of time;
- it may not be easy to reverse a decision once implemented;
- once a project is undertaken it may preclude other strategic choices being made.

The techniques discussed in this chapter are methods used to assess the *financial merits* of particular investments but there are other aspects to consider before making an investment decision. These include:

- The identification of all possible options/projects.
- The strategic direction of the organisation and whether the project under consideration will complement this.
- Whether the organisation has the skills to implement the project successfully.
- What will happen if the project is rejected – will the organisation be able to maintain its present status *vis-à-vis* its competitors, etc., without new investments? (Profitability will not be maintained over the years without new investment.)

The financial analysis of investment decisions must be seen as being subservient to strategic analysis and this should be borne in mind throughout this chapter.

The main evaluation methods are:

- Net present value (NPV).
- Payback (PB).
- Discounted payback (DPB).
- Internal rate of return (IRR).
- Accounting rate of return (ARR).

Each of these evaluation techniques will be discussed in turn. It is important to realise that the evaluation techniques are not mutually exclusive and most organisations today use more than one method. This is a trend that is increasing, according to Pike and Wolfe (1988). The most popular method used by organisations is payback; almost all organisations use it. This can be seen in Table 8.1. The majority of firms now also use either net present value and/or internal rate of return. By using these methods in conjunction with payback they are able to bring into consideration several different aspects of the investment decision.

8.2.2 Net present value (NPV)

Shareholder value will be maximised by accepting those projects that offer a positive NPV and rejecting all others, under the normally assumed (but incorrect) investment conditions of perfect information, perfect capital markets and no risk. The other evaluation techniques do not necessarily produce results that maximise shareholder value, but as Figure 8.1 demonstrates they are widely used.

	Total %	Rarely %	Positive responses Often %	Mostly %	Always %
Firms using					
Payback	92	5	16	24	47
Accounting rate of return	56	13	15	10	18
Internal rate of return	75	9	11	13	42
Net present value	68	16	15	14	23

Source: Pike and Wolfe (1988)

Figure 8.1 Methods of investment appraisal

The NPV technique recognises that cash received in the future is less valuable than cash received today. This is because of the time value of money. If, for example, you inherited £10,000 today and did not wish to spend it immediately you might deposit the money in a bank or building society. By the end of the first year it would be worth more than £10,000. If the interest rate was 5 per cent, it would be worth £10,500.

The formula for this calculation is:

£1 invested today at 5% in 1 year's time is worth £1 + 0.05 = 1.05
£1 invested today at 5% in 2 years' time is worth £$(1 + 0.05)^2$ = £1.103
£1 invested today at 5% in 3 years' time is worth £$(1 + 0.05)^3$ = £1.158

This is compound interest and expresses what a £ invested today is worth at a particular moment in the future.

The management of an organisation do not wish to know this when making investment decisions. Instead they want to know what a £ received in the future is worth in terms of today's values. This is what NPV calculations do. The formula is:

£1 receivable in 1 year's time at 5% is worth $\dfrac{£1}{1.05}$ = £0.952 today

£1 receivable in 2 year's time at 5% is worth $\dfrac{£1}{(1.05)^2}$ = £0.909 today

£1 receivable in 3 year's time at 5% is worth $\dfrac{£1}{(1.05)^3}$ = £0.864 today

The figures 0.952, 0.907 and 0.864 represent the present value of £1 received in 1, 2 and 3 years, respectively, at a cost of capital of 5 per cent. These figures are also known as discount factors.

If the present value of the future cash inflows exceeds that of the outflows, a positive NPV will result and the project should be accepted. If it does not, the NPV is negative and the project should be rejected.

		Project			
		A	B	C	D
Cash flows		£	£	£	£
Year					
0		(2,000)	(2,000)	(1,000)	(1,000)
1		1,000	20	640	0
2		1,000	20	640	0
3		50	1,600	20	0
4		50	1,600	20	1,800

Figure 8.2

Year	Discount factor 5%	A £		B £	C £	D £
0	1	(2,000)		(2,000)	(1,000)	(1,000)
1	0.952	952	(1,000 × 0.952)	19	609	0
2	0.907	907	(1,000 × 0.907)	18	580	0
3	0.864	43	(50 × 0.864)	1,382	17	0
4	0.823	41	(50 × 0.823)	1,317	16	1,481
	NPV =	(57)		736	222	481

Figure 8.3

The mathematical formula for calculating the discount factor is:

$$\text{Discount factor} = \frac{1}{(1+r)^n}$$

where r is the discount rate/opportunity cost of capital and n is the number of the time period.

The discount factors can also be obtained from tables, which are included at the end of this *Study System*. These tables will be supplied in the examinations.

Figure 8.2 gives information on four projects and Figure 8.3 uses the NPV technique to assess them. The layout is the generally accepted one and should always be used. It is important to remember that Year 0 is a day – the first day of the project. Year 1 is the last day of the first year and Year 2 is the last day of the second year, etc. It is generally assumed that all cash inflows received during a year are received on the last day of the year, even if in reality they are received earlier or throughout the year. It is possible in practice to use monthly or quarterly discount rates if this assumption could distort the result, but this is only done very rarely and will not be required in the examination. The discount rate is usually assumed to be the organisation's cost of capital. Further discussion and calculation of this is beyond the scope of this syllabus.

Project A has a negative NPV and should be rejected because it provides a return that is less than the cost of capital, 5 per cent. But projects B, C and D show positive NPVs and they should all be accepted if the organisation has adequate funds.

 Exercise: calculating the NPV without using present value tables

You might come across an examination question which requires you to calculate the NPV using a discount rate which does not feature on the present value table.

To deal with this you will need to calculate your own discount factors using the formula given earlier. To get some practise at doing this, try calculating the NPV for project B in the last example, using a cost of capital of 7.5 per cent.

 Solution

Year		Discount factor	Cash flow £	Present value £
0		1.000	(2,000)	(2,000)
1	$1/(1 + 0.075)^1$	0.930	20	19
2	$1/(1 + 0.075)^2$	0.865	20	17
3	$1/(1 + 0.075)^3$	0.805	1,600	1,288
4	$1/(1 + 0.075)^4$	0.749	1,600	1,198
NPV =				522

Limitations of the NPV method

Although the NPV method provides managers with a simple decision rule: accept projects with a positive NPV, it does suffer from a number of disadvantages.

- The speed of repayment of the original investment is not highlighted.
- The cash flow figures are estimates and may turn out to be incorrect.
- Non-financial managers may have difficulty understanding the concept.
- Determination of the correct discount rate can be difficult.

Some of these limitations are not present in the payback method and as we have seen many organisations combine an assessment of the payback period with discounted cash flow in their appraisal.

8.2.3 Payback (PB)

Payback offers a different view of the investment decision and to some extent copes with an uncertain future by concentrating on early cash inflows. Payback is simply the time it takes for the cash inflows from a project to equal the cash outflows so that the project has paid back its initial investment. The payback period for the four projects is given in Figure 8.4 where the payback year is underlined.

Project	Initial outlay £	Year 1 £	Cumulative cash flows Year 2 £	Year 3 £	Year 4 £	Payback
A	2,000	1,000	2,000	2,050	2,100	2 years
B	2,000	20	40	1,640	3,240	4 years
C	1,000	640	1,280	1,300	1,320	2 years
D	1,000	0	0	0	1,800	4 years

Figure 8.4

If you look carefully at the data you will see that, whereas project A pays back in exactly 2 years, project C would actually achieve payback some time during year 2, if we can ignore the end-of-year assumption concerning cash flows.

Occasionally, the payback period might be calculated assuming that cash flows occur evenly throughout the year. In this case the payback period for project C would be calculated as follows:

$$\text{Payback period for project C} = 1 \text{ year} + \frac{£(1{,}000 - 640)}{£640}$$

$$= 1.6 \text{ years}$$

Similarly, the payback period for project B would be 3.2 years, and project D would be 3.6 years.

$$\text{Payback period for project B} = 3 \text{ years} + \frac{£(2{,}000 - 1{,}640)}{£1{,}600}$$

$$= 3.2 \text{ years}$$

$$\text{Payback period for project D} = 3 \text{ years} + \frac{£1{,}000}{£1{,}800}$$

$$= 3.6 \text{ years}$$

However, the assumption of even cash flows during the year may be somewhat inaccurate; therefore the payback periods stated in Table 8.4 are likely to be expressed with sufficient precision.

Management usually specifies a standard payback time for all investment decisions; this is normally quite short, say, 3 years. If the project pays back within this period it will be accepted, otherwise it will be rejected. If the project is not rejected on the payback criterion it is likely to be subjected to further analysis, probably using discounting techniques, before it is finally accepted.

In the previous example, assuming that the required payback is three years, projects A and C would be accepted, but using the NPV method projects B, C and D would be accepted. If the management judge projects by requiring them to meet both payback and NPV criteria, only project C would be accepted. This may seem to be prudent but it must be remembered that if no investments are made the organisation will decline relative to its competitors, as it will not be able to maintain its profitability in the long term. So care must be taken to make sure that the two hurdles, the discount rate and the payback period, are realistic ones and not overstated – the cost of capital must not be set unrealistically high or the payback period too short.

The advantages of using payback are as follows:

- It is the simplest evaluation method and is very easy to understand.
- It keeps organisations liquid by favouring projects with early cash inflows. NPV, of course, also does this by discounting, but not to such an extent. An organisation that is liquid tends to remain in business. The cash released by early inflows can also be re-invested in other profitable projects sooner.
- It helps to eliminate time risk. Using NPV an organisation might accept a long-term project with, perhaps, a 10-year payback. If predictions of market and costs beyond say, year 3 prove wrong, as they might in an uncertain world, the project could prove disastrous. Payback minimises this by selecting projects that recover their costs quickly.

However, academics criticise payback because:

- No weighting is given to the timing of the cash inflows, that is, an inflow received in year 2 is considered the same in terms of value as an inflow in year 1. In the example, the £1,000 received in year 2 in project A is accorded the same value as the £1,000 received in Year 1.
- Cash flows received after the cut-off point are ignored. This is the reason why projects B and D have been rejected.

The first criticism can easily be remedied by discounting the cash flows, thus creating discounted payback as described below. The second criticism, while true, is rather unnecessary as it is the counter to the key strengths of the payback technique which are the second and third advantages given above. The criticism can be overcome, however, by using a discounted payback index.

8.2.4 Discounted payback (DPB)

Discounted payback is simply the payback cash flows discounted by the cost of capital. Inspection of Figure 8.3 above reveals the DPBs for each of the four projects shown in Figure 8.5.

Project	Initial outlay	Cumulative discounted cash flows				Payback
		Year 1	Year 2	Year 3	Year 4	
	£	£	£	£	£	
A	2,000	952	1,859	1,902	1,943	No payback
B	2,000	19	37	1,419	2,736	4 years
C	1,000	609	1,189	1,206	1,222	2 years
D	1,000	0	0	0	1,481	4 years

Figure 8.5

Until very recently, most research did not differentiate between PB and DPB. But a recent survey carried out by Lefley and Sarkis found that 54 per cent of UK and 65 per cent of US manufacturing companies made use of DPB, and that 25 per cent of UK and 33 per cent of US companies stated it was the most 'important' investment appraisal method they used.

It has been argued by some that the DPB approach is just a truncated version of NPV, but this is not necessarily true. In practice the discount rates often differ. The discount rate used by companies in NPV calculations is often adjusted to take account of project risk and uncertainty and so the rate will be higher (this is dealt with later), whereas the discount rate used in DPB is the unadjusted cost of capital, as the decision-maker's function is to judge the payback period of the project against that required to deal with the uncertainty.

If DPB is used, the projects chosen will be those that maximise shareholder value modified by the payback so that the organisation remains liquid and flexible. By combining these two techniques management should be able to make the best possible decisions with the available information.

8.2.5 Discounted payback index (DPBI) or profitability index

One of the questions that decision-makers often ask, apart from how quickly does the project pay for itself, is how many times does it recover the funds invested. This is particularly important if funds are scarce.

The DPBI provides one measure of this as follows:

$$\text{DPBI} = \frac{\text{Present value of net cash inflows}}{\text{Initial cash outlay}}$$

The DPBIs for the previous example are calculated in Figure 8.6.

	A	B	C	D
Present value of net cash inflows (£)	1,943	2,736	1,222	1,481
Initial outlay (£)	2,000	2,000	1,000	1,000
DPBI	0.97	1.37	1.22	1.48

Figure 8.6

The higher the figure for DPBI, the greater the return. A figure for DPBI below 1.0 indicates, as in the case of project A, that the net cash inflows are lower than the initial cash outlay.

You might come across the index expressed in a slightly different way, in which case it might be referred to as the profitability index:

$$\text{Profitability index} = \frac{\text{Net present value of project}}{\text{Initial outlay}}$$

This index would be calculated as in Figure 8.7.

	A	B	C	D
Net present value (£)	(57)	736	222	481
Initial outlay (£)	2,000	2,000	1,000	1,000
Profitability index	–	0.37	0.22	0.48

Figure 8.7

This index provides similar information, but it shows the net present value per £1 invested in a project. This measure can be more meaningful than the simple + or − result presented by an NPV calculation, particularly, as stated earlier, if funds for investment are limited.

8.2.6 Internal rate of return (IRR)

The IRR is a variation of the NPV method. One of the main problems with using the NPV method is deciding on the correct discount rate. Judging the correct discount rate is not easy as it depends on interest rates, inflation, etc., and these factors can vary considerably from year to year, making it difficult to decide in year 0 what the correct discount rate to use in year 4 may be. IRR avoids this difficulty by not specifying a rate in advance.

IRR is the discount rate at which the sum of the discounted cash inflows equals the discounted cash outflow(s), so that the NPV is zero.

The IRR can be determined by trial and error. In the following example (Figure 8.8) for project C the trial discount rates used are 5 and 25 per cent.

Year	Cash flow	Discount rate 5%	Discounted cash flow	Discount rate 25%	Discounted cash flow
	£		£		£
0	(1,000)	1.000	(1,000)	1.000	(1,000)
1	640	0.952	609	0.800	512
2	640	0.907	580	0.640	410
3	20	0.864	17	0.512	10
4	20	0.823	16	0.410	8
			222		(60)

Figure 8.8

Interpolation is used to determine the discount rate, between 5 per cent and 25 per cent, at which the NPV is zero.

$$IRR = DR_1 + \left[\frac{NPV_1}{(NPV_1 - NPV_2)} \times (DR_2 - DR_1) \right]$$

where DR = discount rate

For project C:

$$\text{IRR} = 5\% + \left[\frac{222}{222 + 60} \times (25 - 5)\right]$$

$$= 5\% + \frac{(222 \times 20\%)}{282}$$

$$= 5\% + 15.74\%$$

$$= 20.74\%$$

The IRR of project C would then be compared to the organisation's cost of capital and accepted if the IRR was greater. This will always lead to the selection of an identical set of projects as the NPV method.

Often, however, an organisation has to choose between projects rather than just selecting all those that meet the required hurdle rate. This will occur when the organisation's choice is limited for financial reasons or where there are different investment options within the same overall project.

Examples of the latter are: whether to build a hotel or a block of flats on a piece of land, or which of two types of manufacturing machinery to purchase for a new product. When making this type of decision, the decision-maker should be very wary of using IRR.

To illustrate this, suppose projects B and CC, whose cash flows are given in Figure 8.9, are mutually exclusive, that is, the decision-maker can only choose one of them. Figure 8.10 gives the IRR and two NPVs for the two projects. Use the cash flows from Figure 8.9 to check these for yourself.

Year	B	CC
	£	£
0	(2,000)	(2,000)
1	20	1,280
2	20	1,280
3	1,600	40
4	1,600	40

Figure 8.9

	B	CC
IRR	15%	20%
NPV at 5%	£726	£448
NPV at 16 %	£(59)	£102

Figure 8.10

The NPV and IRR contradict one another if a discount rate of 5 per cent is used, but agree if a discount rate of 16 per cent is used. Only by using NPV will the organisation always make decisions that maximise shareholder value. The reason the two methods do not always agree is due to the timing of the cash inflows between the two projects. The cash inflows are relatively greater for project B, but because they come in the later years they are not so valuable if a high cost of capital is used. This can be seen when the 16 per cent discount rate is used. The graph in Figure 8.11 shows that the preference between the two projects changes between 11 per cent and 12 per cent. If the cost of capital is below 11 per cent B is better, if it is more than 12 per cent CC is preferred, until the NPV becomes negative at 20 per cent.

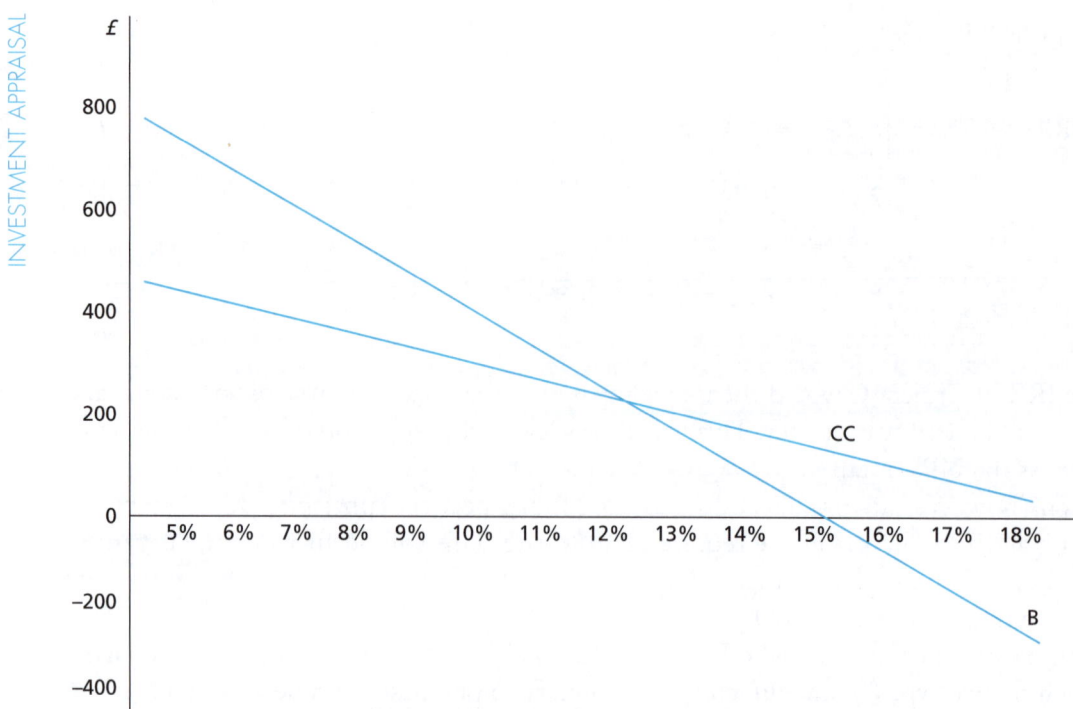

Figure 8.11   Net present values of Projects B and CC

8.2.7 Multiple IRRs

A single figure for IRR will result only when the cash flows follow the normal pattern of an initial out-flow followed by a series of inflows over the years. Where the cash flow signs change between positive and negative a number of times over the years, it is likely that a number of real solutions may exist. This is illustrated in the following example.

M is contemplating building a prototype machine, the cost of which will be paid for in two stages. Income can be expected from its demonstration. The machine will be expensive to break up and dispose of at the end of its life. The predicted cash flows are given in Figure 8.12, and Figure 8.13 shows the calculations at discount rates of 6 and 30 per cent, both of which give a NPV close to zero.

Year	Cash flow £
0	(3,910)
1	(10,000)
2	40,000
3	(26,510)

Figure 8.12

Year	Cash flow £	Discount rate 6 %	NPV £	Discount rate 30 %	NPV £
0	(3,910)	1.000	(3,910)	1.000	(3,910)
1	(10,000)	0.943	(9,434)	0.769	(7,692)
2	40,000	0.890	35,600	0.592	23,668
3	(26,510)	0.840	(22,258)	0.455	(12,067)
		NPV	(2)		(1)

Figure 8.13

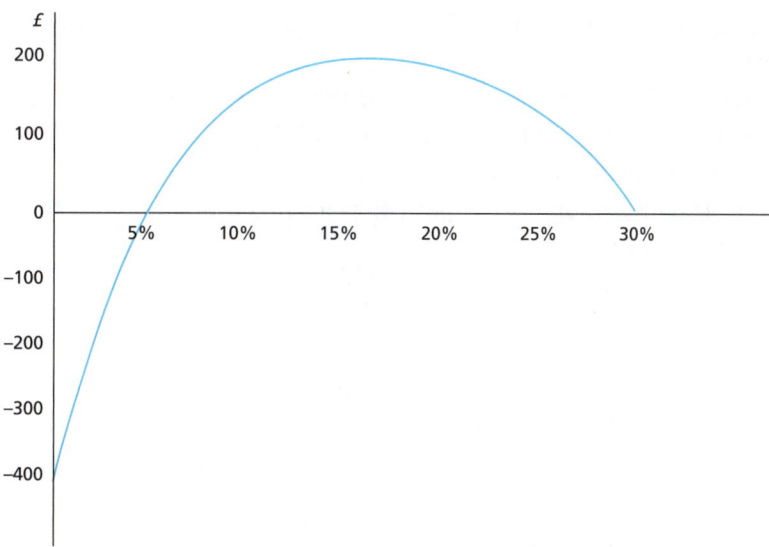

Figure 8.14 The net present value of the cash flows given in Figure 8.12

As both IRRs are equally valid, the decision whether or not to accept the project needs to be made using NPV. As seen in Figure 8.14, the discount rates between 6 and 30 per cent give positive NPVs and so if the organisation's cost of capital is in this range, the project should be accepted.

While projects with multiple sign changes are rare, care should also be taken if two projects are being compared, and if rather than discounting the cash flows of two projects separately one project is deducted from the other to give a single stream of cash flows prior to discounting. This method is likely to produce cash flows whose signs change from year to year and this can again give multiple IRRs.

Given the problems with the use of IRR, you may wonder why it is such a popular technique. Explanations for its popularity are:

- Users are familiar with using percentage rates, such as return on capital (ROC), mortgage rates, bank rates, etc. The yield of an investment is directly comparable to these and is easier to understand as a consequence.
- It avoids specifying a discount rate in advance. It can be a difficult matter predicting the cost of capital some years into the future.
- It allows the decision-maker to make a judgement. Malcolm Smith (1999) suggests that the + sign of the NPV method means that no judgement is required to make the decision. IRR, on the other hand, does require some judgement and is therefore preferred by managers. With NPV, the judgement of the required discount rate is made at a prior stage and is often a rate common to all projects. With IRR, managers can mentally adjust the required rate for a project according to the perceived risk involved.

8.2.8 Modified internal rate of return (MIRR)

Apart from the problem of multiple rates of return, the main criticism of the IRR method is its basic assumption that all interim cash inflows are reinvested elsewhere at the IRR of the project under consideration. If the IRR is considerably higher than the cost of capital this will be an unlikely assumption. If the assumption is not valid the IRR method overestimates the real return. Another criticism of IRR is that it cannot cope with variations in the cost of capital over the life of the project.

A relatively recent development that overcomes these shortcomings is the modified internal rate of return (MIRR) (Lefley and Morgan, 1997). The data for project CC given in Figure 8.9 is used to calculate the MIRR in Figure 8.15, assuming the cost of capital is now 10 per cent. The resulting figure of 13 per cent can be compared with the previous IRR calculated in Figure 8.10 of 20 per cent.

Year	Cash flow £	10 %	Reinvestment £
1	1,280	1.331	1,704
2	1,280	1.210	1,549
3	40	1.100	44
4	40	1.000	40
			3,337

Year 0 outflow
Year 4 inflow

$$\frac{£2,000}{£3,337} = 0.599$$

In the tables for year 4:

$$0.599 = 13.5\%$$

Figure 8.15

The calculations in Table 8.13 are worked out as follows: compound interest is used to determine a total inflow figure at the end of year 4 assuming that all cash inflows are immediately reinvested at 10 per cent (cost of capital). So the £1,280 that is released at the end of year 1 is reinvested for 3 years, hence the rate of 1.331 ($1.1 \times 1.1 \times 1.1$). The total cash outflow in year 0 is compared with the inflow from year 4; the resulting figure, 0.599, is the discount factor in year 4. This is then checked along the year 4 row in the DCF tables to give a return of 13.5 per cent. This means that £3,337 received in year 4 is equivalent to £2,000 in year 0 if the discount rate is 13.5 per cent.

The MIRR of 13.5 per cent is thought by many to be a more appropriate measure than the traditional IRR, which can overstate the return if it is impossible to reinvest the cash inflows at the IRR. However, there is still a certain amount of controversy over this issue and time will tell whether it will be used widely in practice and replace IRR itself.

8.2.9 Accounting rate of return (ARR)

This method is not recommended because it can produce incorrect results, but as it is still quite widely used in practice it is discussed here. The ARR is the project's return on investment or ROI, but in this context it is known as the accounting rate of return. The ARR will tend to vary from year to year over the life of the project. This is because the cash inflows change, affecting profit, and the capital/investment gradually decreases as the assets are depreciated.

Annual ARRs/ROIs are not usually calculated; instead the average annual profit is normally expressed as a percentage of the average, or mid-point, investment:

$$\text{ARR} = \frac{\text{Average annual profit from the project}}{\text{Average investment}} \times 100$$

It is the only investment appraisal method that uses annual profit rather than annual net cash flow, and so depreciation must be deducted from annual net cash inflow to arrive at a figure that approximates to profit. If the initial investment has a residual or sales value at the end of the project's life this must be brought into the calculation of the average investment figure.

Using the previous data for projects A, B, C and D given in Figure 8.2, and making the following assumptions, the ARRs are as shown in Figure 8.16.

Assumptions

- The initial outflow in year 0 represents the purchase of a fixed asset.
- Depreciation is the only difference between cash flow and profit.
- The asset will be depreciated to zero value over the life of the project.

	A £	B £	C £	D £
Total cash inflow (A = 1000 + 1000 + 50 + 50)	2,100	3,240	1,320	1,800
Less depreciation	2,000	2,000	1,000	1,000
Accounting profit	100	1,240	320	800
Project life – years	4	4	4	4
Ave. accounting profit	25	310	80	200
Ave. investment (mid-point figure)	1,000	1,000	500	500
ARR	$\frac{25}{1,000} \times 100$	$\frac{310}{1,000} \times 100$	$\frac{80}{500} \times 100$	$\frac{200}{500} \times 100$
	2.5 %	31 %	16 %	40 %

Note: if the assets in project A had a disposal value at the end of Year 4 of, say, £500, the average investment would be:

$$\frac{£2,000 + £500}{2} = £1,250$$

Figure 8.16

Figure 8.14 shows that project D is the best project in terms of return but this must be compared with the organisation's required rate of return. If the required rate is the same as the rate used in the earlier NPV calculation, that is, 5 per cent, only A would be rejected and both methods would give the same results. But this is not always the case. If, on the other hand, the required rate of return was 16 per cent, the ARR would select projects B and D as being acceptable. The results of using a discount rate of 16 per cent in a NPV calculation are shown in Figure 8.17.

Year	Discount factor 16 %	A £	B £	C £	D £
0	1.000	(2,000)	(2,000)	(1,000)	(1,000)
1	0.862	862	17	552	0
2	0.743	743	15	476	0
3	0.641	32	1,025	13	0
4	0.552	28	884	11	994
	NPV =	(335)	(59)	52	(6)

Figure 8.17

This shows that only project C would be accepted with a discount rate of 16 per cent. (From the previous IRR calculations it is known that project C has an IRR of about 20 per cent.)

This difference between ARR and NPV is of concern because managers are often judged by the return on capital of their division or business unit. They will only wish to invest in projects that increase the ROI of their division and at times this will clash with good decision-making which requires the use of NPV.

On the other hand, ARR is still used by companies to assess projects – why is this if it can give misleading results? It may be due to:

- a familiarity with the use of profit as a measure;
- the desire to maintain a strong balance sheet – if this is so a project like D which is perfectly acceptable on a NPV basis would not be considered;
- the need for judgement, as discussed earlier.

8.2.10 Example comparing ARR and NPV

Example

It is 2 January 20X1 and the management of G Ltd, a subsidiary of GER Group, has estimated the following results for the coming year ending 31 December 20X1:

	£000
Profit before depreciation	500
Fixed assets:	
Original cost	1,500
Accumulated depn at yr end	720
Net current assets (average for yr)	375

GER group assesses new projects using discounted cash flow and a cost of capital of 15 per cent. But it assesses the performance of its subsidiaries and their managers using ROI, based on the following:

(i) *Profit*: Depreciation of fixed assets is calculated on a straight-line basis on a presumed life of 5 years.
Profit/loss on sale is included in the profit for the year.

(ii) *Capital employed*: Fixed assets are valued at original cost less depreciation as at the end of the year.
Net current assets are valued at the average value for the year.

In addition to the normal transactions the management of G Ltd is considering submitting the following proposals to GER:

(i) At the start of the year it could sell for £35,000 a fixed asset which originally cost £300,000 and which has been depreciated by 4/5 of its expected life. If it is not sold the asset will generate a profit before depreciation of £45,000 during the coming year.
(ii) At the start of the year it could buy for £180,000 plant that would achieve reductions of £57,000 per annum in production costs. The plant would have a life of 5 years after which it would have no resale value.

Requirement

Evaluate the two proposals from the point of view of: (a) G Ltd's chief executive officer (CEO), and (b) GER group's chief accountant.

Solution

G Ltd's CEO will be interested in the ROI/ARR as the subsidiary's performance is judged on that basis, while GER's accountant will be concerned about the NPV for sound investment purposes.

Profit less depreciation = £500,000 − (£1,500,000 × 1/5) = £200,000
Capital employed = £1,500,000 − £720,000 + £375,000 = £1,155,000

$$\text{Current expected ROI} = \frac{£200,000}{£1,155,000} \times 100\% = 17.3\%$$

(i) (a)

The current book value of the asset = £300,000 − (4 × £60,000) = £60,000
Loss on sale = £60,000 − £35,000 = £25,000
Depreciation for the coming year (included in the estimated profit figure) = £60,000

To calculate the new ROI:

Revised profit = original profit + depreciation added back − loss on sale − profit forgone
Revised capital = original capital − book value of asset

$$\text{Revised ROI} = \frac{£(200{,}000 + 60{,}000 - 25{,}000 - 45{,}000)}{£(1{,}155{,}500 - 60{,}000)} \times 100\%$$

$$= 17.35\%$$

This ROI is marginally better than the current expected one and so the asset should be sold from the CEO of G Ltd's point of view.

(i) (b)
Using NPV

	Cash flow £	15% factor	Present value £
Year 0	35,000	1.000	35,000
Year 1	(45,000)	0.870	(39,100)
Net present value			(4,100)

This shows a negative NPV and so the asset should be retained.

(ii) (a)

$$\text{Revised ROI} = \frac{£(200{,}000 - 36{,}000\ \text{depreciation} + 57{,}000)}{£(1{,}55{,}000 + 1{,}44{,}000\ \text{year} - \text{end net book value})} \times 100\%$$

$$= 17.01\%$$

As this is lower than the current expected ROI the new asset should not be purchased from the CEO of G Ltd's point of view.

(ii) (b)

	Cash flow £	15% factor	Present value £
Year 0	(180,000)	1.000	(180,000)
Years 1-5	57,000	3.352*	191,064
			11,064

* Notice that, instead of multiplying 57,000 separately by each of the discount factors for years 1–5, we have used the cumulative total of the five discount factors. We will return to look at this in more detail in the next section.

As this is a positive NPV the asset should be purchased.
For the two projects in question the two methods give different answers. This will not always be the case but if a manager's performance is measured in terms of ROI the manager will assess all projects using ARR. If projects need a positive NPV in order to be accepted by head office the manager will only put forward proposals that give an increased ROI and a positive NPV. This will exclude some acceptable projects with positive NPVs but which have unacceptable ROI/ARRs.

8.2.11 Summary of the four investment appraisal methods

- The techniques which do not use discounting, that is straightforward payback and ARR, are still widely used in practice despite being theoretically inconsistent with the objective of maximising shareholder value.
- DPB is a widely used technique.
- IRR does not always select the best project where a choice has to be made between projects. This usually happens when the projects' IRR are many percentage points away from the organisation's cost of capital.
- Where cash flow signs change from year to year the IRR cannot be relied upon to give the correct answer.

- NPV is the only technique to always give a result that will maximise shareholder value.
- NPV is not used universally. For example, Japanese companies usually rely on payback techniques. Table 8.16 gives an indication of the use of the four main methods.

8.3 Making the cash flows and NPV model more realistic

8.3.1 Using the annuity rate

This is just a calculation short cut. It can be very time consuming to calculate the NPV of a project by hand if the project runs for a number of years. If the project has the same cash inflow every year, as many do, rather than discounting each year separately the annuity rate can be used. The annuity rate is the sum of the discount rates; see Figure 8.18.

Year	Discount rate – 5%	Annuity 5%
1	0.952	0.952
2	0.907	1.859
3	0.864	2.723
4	0.823	3.546

Figure 8.18

These tables are given in the back of this *Study System*.

For a project with an outflow of £30,000 in year 0 and inflows of £20,000 in years 1 and 2 the calculation of net present value is shown in Figure 8.19.

	Cash flow £	Annuity 5%	Net present value £
Year 0	(30,000)	1	(30,000)
Years 1–2	20,000	1.859	37,180
			7,180

Figure 8.19

8.3.2 Unequal lives

Two mutually exclusive projects with different life spans cannot be compared adequately without making an adjustment for the difference in their lives. Projects X and Y are two such projects; their cash flows are given in Figure 8.20.

Year	X £	Y £
0	(30,000)	(30,000)
1	20,000	37,500
2	20,000	

Figure 8.20

In order to cope with this problem the projects' cash flows must be repeated for enough years until both projects finish in the same year. For example, if one project has a life of

4 years and the other a life of 3 years, year 12 would be the first time the projects both finish together. So the cash flows for the first would be repeated three times and for the second four times and the discounted cash flow would be carried out over 12 years. Projects X and Y fortunately have simpler cash flows and Y needs only to be repeated once as shown in Figure 8.21.

Year	X £	Y £
0	(30,000)	(30,000)
1	20,000	37,500 + (30,000)
2	20,000	37,500

Figure 8.21

These cash flows can now be discounted and the NPVs will be comparable. However, this method is rather time-consuming and a simpler method exists. It is to discount the projects once only and to divide the NPV by the annuity rate, that is the sum of the discount rates over the life of the project. This produces an average annual figure, known as an annualised equivalent, that allows the project returns to be compared fairly. This is done in Figure 8.22.

Year	Discount rate 5%	NPV X £	NPV Y £
0	1	(30,000)	(30,000)
1	0.952	19,040	35,700
2	0.907	18,140	
	1.859	7,180	5,700
		÷ 1.859	÷ 0.952
Annualised equivalent =		£3,862	£5,987

Handwritten notes: 1) W/out NPV 2) Divide by DF 3) Annualised equivalent; ΣDiscount; ΣNPV

Figure 8.22

Figure 8.22 shows that project Y is the better investment when the difference in lives is removed.

It is not possible to stipulate that mutually exclusive investments should always be considered over the same period of time. Each case must be judged on its merits. The choice depends on the degree of freedom of action the organisation has when the shorter-lived project ends. If the organisation is forced to reinvest in similar assets at this point the projects should be compared over equal time periods. This situation will arise if the assets are manufacturing equipment and the organisation knows that the product will be made for many years ahead – longer than the life of the assets. Another example of this is when an organisation chooses between different types and sizes of vehicles for product distribution.

On the other hand, if the organisation is not going to invest in similar assets when the assets' productive lives end, the method described above should not be used. An example of this is if the two projects are marketing strategies for the launch of a novelty product. Under these circumstances it clearly makes no sense to repeat the cash flows as the product can only be launched once.

8.3.3 Asset replacement cycles

This is when a company has to make a decision to replace assets. The decision involves what to replace the asset with and when to replace.

If we are replacing assets we may be replacing them with a choice of more than one other asset, these assets may have different lifespans and therefore using NPV will not necessarily give us the right answer. To overcome this problem we have two methods available to us:

1. Lowest Common Multiple Method
2. Annualised Equivalent

Lowest common multiple method

This is where we find the smallest number, which we can divide into by each of a set of numbers. For example, if we have two projects, one with a life of 2 years and one with a life of 3 years the common multiple is 6 years. We then calculate the NPV of the two options over 6 years and compare the results.

Annualised equivalent

This is where the NPV is calculated and converted into an annual equivalent cost to allow comparisons of cost year on year.

Steps:

1. Calculate the NPV of the asset costs.
2. Based on the cost of capital and life of the assets find the cumulative discount factor from the cumulative discount tables.
3. Divide the NPV by the cumulative discount factor to find the annual equivalent cost for each asset.
4. Make your selection based on the least amount of annual cost.

Example

C Ltd. is considering replacing an asset with one of two possible machines.

Machine X	–	Initial Cost	£120,000
		Life	3 years
		Running Cost	£20,000 per annum
Machine Y	–	Initial Cost	£60,000
		Life	2 years
		Running Cost	£35,000 per annum

Cost of capital is 10%

Requirements

(a) Calculate the NPV of each machine and on this basis make a decision.

(b) Considering the different lifespans of the machines, determine which machine should be purchased using:
   (i) Lowest Common Multiple Method
   (ii) Equivalent Annual Cost Method.

Solution

(a)

NPV – Machine X

Years	Description	Cashflow	Discount Factor	Present Value
0	Outlay	£120,000	1.00	£120,000
1–3	Running Cost	£ 20,000	2.487	£ 49,740
			NPV	£169,740

NPV – Machine Y

Years	Description	Cashflow	Discount Factor	Present Value
0	Outlay	£60,000	1.00	£ 60,000
1–2	Running Cost	£35,000	1.736	£ 60,760
			NPV	£120,760

On the basis of the NPV calculation Machine Y should be selected as it has the lowest NPV cost.

(b)

(i) **Lowest common multiple method**

The lowest common multiple is 6 years and therefore each machine is evaluated on this timescale.

NPV – Machine X

Years	Description	Cashflow	Discount Factor	Present Value
0	Outlay	£120,000	1.00	£120,000
1–3	Running Cost	£ 20,000	2.487	£ 49,740
3	Replace	£120,000	0.751	£ 90,120
4–6	Running Cost	£ 20,000	1.868	£ 37,360
			NPV	£297,220

NPV – Machine Y

Years	Description	Cashflow	Discount Factor	Present Value
0	Outlay	£60,000	1.00	£ 60,000
1–2	Running Cost	£35,000	1.736	£ 60,760
2	Replace	£60,000	0.826	£ 49,560
3–4	Running Cost	£35,000	1.434	£ 50,190
4	Replace	£60,000	0.683	£ 40,980
5–6	Running Cost	£35,000	1.185	£ 41,475
			NPV	£302,965

Machine X should be purchased as it is the least cost option.

(ii) **Equivalent annual cost method**

	Machine X	Machine Y
NPV (from a)	£169,740	£120,760
Cumulative discount factor	2.487	1.736
Annual equivalent Cost	£68,251	£69,562

Machine X should be purchased as it is the least cost option.

When to replace

The concept of annualised equivalents can be used in determining the optimum replacement cycle for an asset. This decision involves how long to continue operating the existing asset before it is replaced with an identical one. As the asset gets older, it may become less efficient, its operating costs may increase and the resale value will reduce.

In deciding on the replacement cycle, each project must be tested this is achieved by:

1. Calculating the present value of the total costs incurred if the asset is kept for 1, 2 or 3 years.
2. Calculating the annual equivalent cost for each replacement cycle.
3. The lowest annual equivalent cost will then be the replacement cycle selected.

Example

JP Ltd operates a delivery vehicle, which cost £20,000 and has a useful life of 3 years. JP Ltd has a cost of capital of 5 per cent. The details of the vehicle's cash operating costs for each year and the resale value at the end of each year are as follows.

	Year 1 £	Year 2 £	Year 3 £
Cash operating costs	9,000	10,500	11,900
End of year resale value	14,000	11,500	8,400

Requirement

Determine how frequently the vehicle should be replaced.

Solution

The first step is to calculate the present value of the total costs incurred if the vehicle is kept for 1, 2 or 3 years.

		Keep for 1 year		Keep for 2 years		Keep for 3 years	
Year	5% discount factor	Cash flow £	Present value £	Cash flow £	Present value £	Cash flow £	Present value £
0	1.000	(20,000)	(20,000)	(20,000)	(20,000)	(20,000)	(20,000)
1	0.952	5,000	4,760	(9,000)	(8,568)	(9,000)	(8,568)
2	0.907			1,000	907	(10,500)	(9,524)
3	0.864					(3,500)	(3,024)
Total present value			(15,240)		(27,661)		(41,116)

These present value figures are not comparable because they relate to different time periods. To render them comparable they must be converted to average annual figures, or annualised equivalents, by dividing by the cumulative discount factors as before:

	Keep for 1 year	Keep for 2 years	Keep for 3 years
Total present value of cost	£15,240	£27,661	£41,116
Cumulative 5% factor	0.952	1.859	2.723
Annualised equivalent	£16,008	£14,880	£15,100

The lowest annualised equivalent cost occurs if the vehicle is kept for 2 years. Therefore, the optimum replacement cycle is to replace the vehicle every 2 years.

Inflation and asset replacement cycles

If you are given inflation in an asset replacement cycle question it is not appropriate to use the annualised cost method. You must take account of the inflation and its impact on the individual cash flows and follow the lowest common multiple method. An example of how inflation impacts on this type of situation is Question 2 of the November 2005 exam paper on page 571.

8.3.4 Capital rationing

Sometimes the amount of capital that an organisation can invest in long-term projects is limited and so a choice must be made between a number of different projects. Management will obviously wish to select those projects that will give the greatest return per £ invested, provided the projects are compatible with the long-term strategic objectives of the organisation.

Year	M	N	O	P	Q
	£	£	£	£	£
0	(100,000)	–	(60,000)	(120,000)	(80,000)
1	20,000	(160,000)	(40,000)	60,000	(100,000)
2	50,000	80,000	40,000	45,000	100,000
3	70,000	100,000	80,000	45,000	110,000

Figure 8.23

The decision becomes more difficult if the time horizon is a long one and investments do not start at the same time. Figure 8.23 contains cash flow figures for five different projects.

If it is assumed that the organisation's cost of capital is 5 per cent and that the funds available in year 0 are £200,000, it is clear that even if the net present values are positive the organisation cannot invest in all four projects. N is irrelevant to the calculations if the capital rationing is in Year 0, but a choice must be made between the others.

The profitability index discussed earlier in this chapter can be used to rank the projects. The first step is to calculate the net present values of the projects and then express them as a percentage of the initial outflow so that comparable returns are obtained. This is done in Figure 8.24.

Year	Discount rate 5%	M £	O £	P £	Q £
0	1.000	(100,000)	(60,000)	(120,000)	(80,000)
1	0.952	19,040	(38,080)	57,120	(95,200)
2	0.907	45,350	36,280	40,815	90,700
3	0.864	60,480	69,120	38,880	95,040
Net present value		24,870	7,320	16,815	10,540
		÷	÷	÷	÷
		100,000	60,000	120,000	80,000
		24.87%	12.20%	14.02%	13.18%
Ranking		1st	4th	2nd	3rd

Figure 8.24

Project N has been omitted because it is not relevant to the current decision – which is simply what funds to invest next year. All four projects have positive NPVs and so would be accepted if funds allowed. With £200,000 to invest project M would be chosen and five-sixths of project P assuming that the project allows partial investment. In many situations this would not be possible and so a decision would have to be made on the basis of NPVs. Investing in projects P and Q would give a gross NPV of £27,355. No other feasible combination could better this.

Capital rationing is not really a practical approach for the majority of organisations. It works well if the company is an investment company but for the majority of organisations providing a service or manufacturing products its solution will not be helpful. This simple view of capital rationing also takes no account of outflows in year 1 (which O and Q require) and whether there will be funds available in that year and in following years.

8.3.5 The discount rate

In all the examples considered so far a constant discount rate has been used, on the assumption that the cost of capital will remain the same over the life of the project. As the factors which influence the cost of capital, such as interest rates and inflation, can change considerably over a short period of time an organisation may wish to use different rates over the life of the project. NPV and DPB allow this but IRR and ARR present a uniform rate of return. Using NPV, for example, a different discount factor can be used for each year if so desired.

Perhaps one of the major problems in using a discounted cash flow method is deciding on the correct discount rate to use. It is difficult enough in year 1 but deciding on the rate for, say, year 4 may be very difficult because of changes in the economy, etc. If a very low rate is chosen almost all projects will be accepted, whereas if a very high discount rate is chosen very few projects will be accepted.

Looking back over the years it would appear that the majority of managers have probably used too high a discount rate and have, as a consequence, not invested in projects that would have helped their organisation to grow in relation to their competitors. There are no prizes for being too conservative; it is just as much a failing as being too optimistic. Porter (1992) and Baldwin and Clark (1994) have blamed this tendency on the perceived need for short-term share price appreciation. But it may be that Kaplan and Atkinson (1989) are closer to the mark when they suggest that it is because discount rates are based on accounting rates and incorrectly include an inflationary element.

If there is any doubt over the correct discount rate to use, sensitivity analysis – described below – can help.

8.3.6 Sensitivity analysis

So far in this chapter it has been assumed that all the quantitative factors in the investment decision – the cash inflows and outflows, the discount rate and the life of the project – are known with certainty. In reality this is very rarely the case. Sensitivity analysis recognises this fact. The CIMA *Terminology* defines *sensitivity analysis* as:

> A modelling and risk assessment procedure in which changes are made to significant variables in order to determine the effect of these changes on the planned outcome. Particular attention is thereafter paid to variables identified as being of special significance.

As the definition indicates, sensitivity analysis can be applied to a variety of planning activities and not just to investment decisions. For example it can be used in conjunction with breakeven analysis to ascertain by how much a particular factor can change before the project ceases to make a profit.

In sensitivity analysis a single input factor is changed at a time, while all other factors remain at their original estimates. There are two basic approaches:

- An analysis can be made of all the key input factors to ascertain by how much each factor must change before the NPV reaches zero, the indifference point.
- Alternatively specific changes can be calculated, such as the sales decreasing by 5 per cent, in order to determine the effect on NPV. The latter approach might generate results such as those in Figure 8.25, while the former approach is illustrated in the example that follows.

Variable	Adverse variation	Revised NPV	% change in NPV
Project life	– overestimated by		
	1 year	£50	83%
	2 years	(£550)	192%
Cost of labour	– underestimated by		
	5%	£300	50%
	10%	(£150)	125%
Sales volume	– overestimated by		
	2%	£150	25%
	5%	(£650)	208%

Figure 8.25

 ## Exercise

The initial outlay for equipment is £100,000. It is estimated that this will generate sales of 10,000 units per annum for four years. The contribution per unit is expected to be £6 and the fixed costs are expected to be £26,000 per annum. The cost of capital is 5 per cent.

Requirements
(i) Calculate the NPV.
(ii) By how much can each factor change before the company becomes indifferent to the project?

 ## Solution

(i)

		£
Contribution = £6 × 10,000 =		60,000
Less: fixed costs		26,000
Cash inflow per annum		34,000

		Cash flow £	Discount rate 5%	NPV £
Year 0	Outlay	(100,000)	1	(100,000)
Years 1-4	Annual cash inflow	34,000	3.546	120,564
				20,564

(ii) NPV can fall by £20,564 before the indifference point is reached.
This means that the annual cash flows can change by

$$X \times 3.546 = £20,564$$
$$X = £5,800$$

Therefore, the fixed costs can rise by £5,800 to £20,200 – this is a change of 22 per cent.
The contribution can fall by £5,800 to £54,200 – this is a change of 9 per cent. This is the variation caused by price changes, volume changes and efficiency changes in costs.

Without more detailed knowledge of the project, it can probably be safely assumed that the project is not sensitive to a change in fixed costs as a change of 22 per cent seems very unlikely. This project is not particularly sensitive to changes in any of the factors calculated. On the other hand it is very difficult to predict future sales of some projects and an error of 10 per cent may be expected. The contribution is made up of many factors (the individual variable costs and the selling price) and without more detailed knowledge it is not possible to comment further.

Sensitivity analysis is very simple to carry out using a spreadsheet model and as a consequence has become very popular in recent years. Once the model has been built a single cell can be altered by trial and error to determine the change needed to make the NPV zero.

As sensitivity analysis is carried out without the specification of the precise probability of a particular event occurring, it is easy to apply. Any outcome that appears critical as a result of the analysis can then be examined in more detail before a final decision is made. Its usefulness therefore lies in its role as an attention-directing technique as it directs attention to those factors that have the most significant impact on the outcome of the project. Armed with this knowledge management can take action to make sure that the events that are within their control stay within acceptable parameters.

In the example in Figure 8.24, wage rates may be critical. So management may seek to obtain a wage agreement that will limit rates of pay in the future so as to prevent the danger of even higher rates.

In the example in Figure 8.24, the life of the project and the sales volume are likely to be outside the control of management. If, after sensitivity analysis, the decision-makers are still unsure about a particular factor, such as sales volume, they may seek a full risk assessment based on a probability distribution for this particular factor and assess the resulting NPVs.

It is important that the output from a sensitivity analysis is not misinterpreted. Sensitivity analysis looks at the change in one factor in isolation but in the real world it is likely that several factors would move together and so the actual outcome of the project might depend on the combined performance of several or all of the variables. Figure 8.26 shows the probability of the occurrence of the 'most likely' figure for each of the factors given in Figure 8.25.

Variable	Probability of 'most likely' outcome
Project life	0.9
Cost of labour	0.7
Sales volume	0.5

Figure 8.26

The figures in Figure 8.26 indicate a high degree of confidence in the estimate of the project life while there is less confidence in the other two factors. If it is assumed that the outcomes of each of the variables are independent, the probability of all three most likely outcomes occurring together is obtained by the multiplication of the probabilities, that is,

$0.9 \times 0.7 \times 0.5 = 0.315$

This shows that there is a 32 per cent probability that the most likely NPV will occur.

 Exercise

Here is another exercise involving sensitivity analysis. Try it for yourself before looking at the solution.

A company is about to enter a new product market and has to determine which of two options it should select for its distribution strategy. The net present value for the project with each option has been calculated for two possible annual demand figures.

Sales demand outcome	Option X NPV £000	Option Y NPV £000
Lowest expected – 20,000 units	2.0	3.0
Highest expected – 55,000 units	15.5	10.0

The directors wish to compare the sensitivities of the two options to changes in forecast annual sales demand.

Solution

The range of possible NPVs can be depicted on a graph. Although the NPV will not alter in a strictly linear fashion in response to changes in sales demand we can assume that the relationship will be approximately linear.

The graph helps the directors to assess the sensitivity of the options to variations in sales demand as follows.

- Above a sales demand of 25,000 units per annum, option X results in the highest NPV. If there is an equal chance of any demand within the given range occurring, option X will be preferable for approximately 86 per cent of the possible outcomes.
- However, if a low sales volume is more likely then option Y would be preferable.
- Sales volume can reduce to as low as 5,000 units each year before option Y ceases to earn a positive NPV.

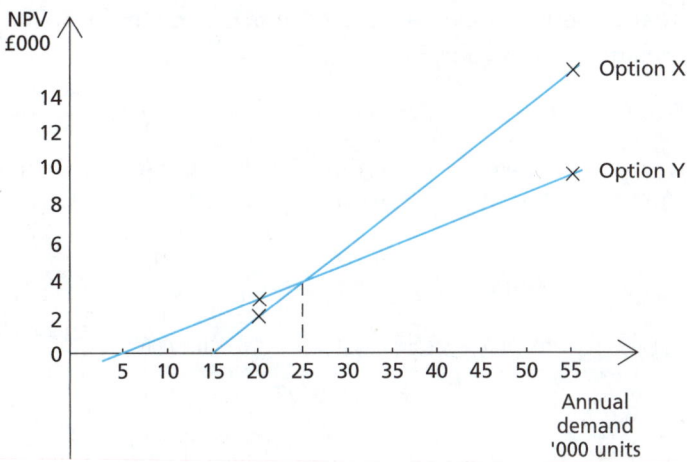

8.3.7 Risk

Risk in this context is business risk, that is the risk arising from the project rather than financing or financial risk. Rather obviously, the higher the risk the higher the required rate of return will be. There are many different ways of dealing with the perceived risk implicit in the project. They are:

- Sensitivity analysis, as previously discussed.
- The use of probability distributions, as previously mentioned briefly.
- Adjustment of the required rate of return/cost of capital. This is a popular method in the UK. Individual projects are not normally assessed using individual rates specific to that project. Instead, say, three categories of risk are used (high, medium and low risk) and each has its own discount rate. Updating an existing manufacturing system will probably be considered low risk and be given a low discount factor, whereas bringing out an entirely new product concept may be considered high risk and be given a high discount factor.
- Adjustment of the payback time required; for a project perceived to be more risky, a shorter payback period would be required.

- Reduce cash inflows by, say, 20 per cent for a high-risk project.
- The use of decision tree analysis.

It is important that two methods are not used together otherwise there is a chance that double counting will take place and sound investments will not be made.

Organisations in different countries tend to use different methods. In the UK sensitivity analysis is the most popular method. In the USA the managers prefer to make their own subjective assessments, and many do not incorporate any of the above methods into the analysis itself. In Japan, Taiwan and Poland, a shortened payback time is widely used (Horngren et al., 1999).

Exercise

To give yourself some practice in taking account of the time value of money in decision tree analysis, it would be useful to return now to the example in Figure 7.3 of Chapter 7.

The time value of money can be incorporated quite simply, by multiplying the figures in the cash flow column by the relevant discount factor before multiplying by the probabilities.

Using the example data and assuming that it took one year to develop the designs and a further year before the contribution was received, and assuming the cost of capital is 10 per cent, the revised position is shown in Figure 8.27.

Outcome £	Cash flow £	Discount factor 10%	Net present value £	Pay-off £
800,000	650,000	0.826	536,900	225,498
(100,000)	(250,000)	0.826	(206,500)	(57,820)
			330,400	167,678
180,000	30,000	0.909	27,270	
20,000	(130,000)	0.909	118,170	(35,451)
				EV 132,227
100,000	100,000	1.000	100,000	

Figure 8.27

Taking account of the time value of money did not alter the final decision, but it did reduce the differential between the two expected value figures.

> The incorporation of risk and uncertainty into project appraisal is a popular exam topic, so make sure that you try the relevant practice questions.

8.3.8 Inflation

Inflation, which is the decline in purchasing power of the monetary unit, means that £1 received in 1 year's time is not as valuable in real terms as £1 received today. When inflation is low it is not a very important factor in the investment appraisal decision but when it rises above, say, 10 per cent it can become a major factor. During the 1960s and 1970s, several countries had inflation rates in excess of 100 per cent and this makes forward planning virtually impossible because of the unpredictability of future costs and revenues.

The cost of capital that a company uses is known as the monetary cost of capital and it includes an element that is due to inflation. That is, part of the rate includes a factor for the anticipated decline in the general purchasing power of the cash that the investment generates. If this element is stripped from the monetary rate the real rate of return is left.

The real rate of return is the return required to cover the investment risk and will of course vary from industry to industry.

There are two approaches for dealing with inflation in investment appraisal:

- *The real approach.* This uses the real rate of return rather than the monetary cost of capital. If this is done all cash flows must be predicted in terms of today's £. This method requires the discount rate to be adjusted but normally no adjustments are needed to future predicted cash flows because it is normal to predict them in terms of today's £. Thus it is a relatively simple method in terms of calculations.
- *The monetary approach.* This uses the monetary cost of capital. As a consequence future cash flows must be predicted in terms of their monetary value in years to come, which means adjusting the values by the predicted inflation rates. This is a lengthier calculation but is to be preferred as it allows for different inflation rates to be used for different types of cash flow. For example, materials may have a different inflation rate to direct labour.

The real rate of return can be found by using the following formula:

$$RR = \frac{(1 + MR)}{(1 + IR)} - 1$$

If the monetary rate (MR) = 13.4%

and the inflation rate (IR) = 5%, then

$$\text{the real rate (RR)} = \frac{(1 + 0.134)}{(1 + 0.05)} - 1$$
$$= 8\%$$

Conversely, the monetary rate is found using the formula:

$$MR = (1 + RR)(1 + IR) - 1$$
$$= (1 + 0.8)(1 + 0.05) - 1$$
$$= 13.4\%$$

Exercise

A company is considering investing in a project which requires an initial investment of £150,000. The cash inflows during years 1–3 are expected to be £55,000 per annum. The company's monetary cost of capital is 10 per cent and inflation is expected to be 6 per cent during the life of the project.

Requirements
(i) Calculate the NPV of the project using the real rate of return as the discount rate.
(ii) Calculate the NPV of the project using the monetary cost of capital as the discount rate.

Solution
(i)

$$\text{The real rate (RR)} = \frac{1.10}{1.06} - 1$$
$$= 3.8\%$$

We cannot look up discount factors for 3.8 per cent because they are not shown in the tables. Therefore, we will need to calculate the discount factors for ourselves.

Using the formula that we learned earlier in the chapter, the discount factor for each year is $1/(1 + r)^n$

Year		Discount factor 3.8%
1	$1 \times 1/(1 + 0.038)$	0.963
2	$0.963 \times 1/1.038$	0.928
3	$0.928 \times 1/1.038$	0.894

These discount factors can now be applied to the real cash flows.

Year	Cash flow £	Discount factor 3.8%	NPV £
0	(150,000)	1.000	(150,000)
1	55,000	0.963	52,965
2	55,000	0.928	51,040
3	55,000	0.894	49,170
			3,175

(ii) Inflation of cash flows:

Year	
1	$55,000 \times 1.06 = 58,300$
2	$58,300 \times 1.06 = 61,798$
3	$61,798 \times 1.06 = 65,506$

Year	Cash flow £	Discount factor 10%	NPV £
0	(150,000)	1.000	(150,000)
1	58,300	0.909	52,995
2	61,798	0.826	51,045
3	65,506	0.751	49,195
			3,235

The difference in final net present values is due to rounding up the real rate of return. Therefore, the same NPV results from both approaches; the real approach and the monetary approach.

8.3.9 Incorporating the effect of taxation

The effect of taxation can have a major impact on the viability of a capital investment project. The explanation of taxation given below is simplified because a detailed knowledge of tax is not required for this examination. Thus, it is assumed that tax is payable on profit without adjustment and that profit is the same as net cash inflow.

Corporation tax must be paid on annual profits thus creating cash outflows that reduce the annual net cash inflows. If the company's profit is £10,000 and the corporation tax rate is 30 per cent, the corporation tax liability is £3,000. On the other hand, a writing-down allowance is given if an asset is purchased; this reduces the cost of the purchase because the allowance can be set against annual profits thus reducing the tax liability.

Writing-down allowances (WDA) are expressed as a percentage, say 25 per cent. This percentage is applied to the cost of the asset, and any installation costs, etc., which are an integral part of the asset's use, on a reducing balance basis. Note that installation costs include preparing the site for the new asset and may include removing an old machine or knocking down old buildings and structures. So if the asset cost £950 and it cost £50 to install, the total cost would be £1,000. If the WDA is 25 per cent the allowance would be £250 in the first year. In year 2 it would be £1,000 − £250 = £750 × 25 per cent = £187.5.

In the year in which the asset is sold there will be a balancing allowance or charge depending on whether the sale price is higher or lower than the initial cost less the total WDA given to date. In the previous example, if the asset were sold at the end of year 3 for £500 the balancing allowance would be £62.50. (The asset's value for taxation purposes in year 3 is £750 − £187.5 = 562.50; deduct the sales price of £500 to leave £62.50.)

The writing-down allowances are set against the profit for the year and so they reduce a company's liability for corporation tax. For example, if the company made a profit of £10,000 during Year 1 and the rate of corporation tax is 30 per cent, its corporation tax payment will be £10,000 − £250 = £9,750 × 30 per cent = £2,925.

The effect of taxation will not necessarily occur in the same year as the relevant cash flow that causes it. Under the new taxation regime of corporation tax self-assessment the tax on the annual profit becomes due in four instalments. If it is assumed the organization has the standard 12-month accounting period the instalments are due in the 7th, 10th, 13th and 16th months from the start of the accounting period. This means that two instalments fall due within the same year as the causal profit/cash inflow, and the remaining two instalments fall due in the following year.

Example

The management of a company are making a decision on whether or not to purchase a new piece of plant and machinery which costs £100,000. The new machine will generate a net cash flow of £30,000 each year for 4 years. At the end of the fourth year it will be sold for £20,000. The company's cost of capital is 5 per cent. Writing-down allowances are 25 per cent reducing balance and corporation tax is 30 per cent.

Calculation of writing-down allowances:

Year	Asset cost £	30% Tax saved £	Year 1 £	Year 2 £	Year 3 £	Year 4 £	Year 5 £
	100,000						
Year 1 WDA (25%)	25,000	7,500	3,750	3,750			
	75,000						
Year 2 WDA (25%)	18,750	5,625		2,813	2,812		
	56,250			6,563			
Year 3 WDA (25%)	14,063	4,219			2,110	2,109	
	42,187				4,922		
Disposal proceeds	20,000						
Year 4 WDA	22,187	6,656				3,328	3,328
						5,437	

Calculation of corporation tax on profit:

Year 1 profit £30,000 − tax 30% = £9,000 − payable   Year 1 £4,500
                                                                                   Year 2 £4,500
Year 2 profit £30,000 − tax 30% = £9,000 − payable   Year 2 £4,500
                                                                                    Year 3 £4,500, etc.

The net present value of the project can now be calculated.

Year	Asset £	WDA tax saved £	Profit £	Profit tax £	Total £	Disc. Factor 5%	PV £
0	(100,000)				(100,000)	1.000	(100,000)
1		3,750	30,000	(4,500)	29,250	0.952	27,846
2		6,563	30,000	(9,000)	27,563	0.907	25,000
3		4,922	30,000	(9,000)	25,922	0.864	22,397
4	20,000	5,437	30,000	(9,000)	46,437	0.823	38,218
5		3,328		(4,500)	(1,172)	0.784	(919)
NPV							12,542

Example

Using the data in the previous example, assume in addition that the company had to pay £5,000 to remove and dispose of an old machine before the new machine costing £100,000, which makes the same product, could be installed. The removal is treated as part of the cost of the new machine and the WDAs and the new calculation would be:

Calculation of writing-down allowances:

Year	Asset cost £	Tax saved £	Year 1 £	Year 2 £	Year 3 £	Year 4 £	Year 5 £
	105,000						
Year 1 WDA (25%)	26,250	7,875	3,938	3,937			
	78,750						
Year 2 WDA (25%)	19,688	5,906		2,953	2,953		
	59,062			6,890			
Year 3 WDA (25%)	14,766	4,430			2,215	2,215	
	44,296				5,168		
Disposal proceeds	20,000						
Year 4 WDA	24,296	7,289				3,645	3,644
						5,860	

Calculation of corporation tax on profit:

Year 1 profit £30,000 − tax 30% = £9,000 − payable   Year 1 £4,500
                                                                                      Year 2 £4,500
Year 2 profit £30,000 − tax 30% = £9,000 − payable   Year 2 £4,500
                                                                                      Year 3 £4,500, etc.

Year	Asset £	WDA tax saved £	Profit £	Profit tax £	Total £	Disc. Factor 5%	PV £
0	(105,000)				(105,000)	1.000	(105,000)
1		3,938	30,000	(4,500)	29,438	0.952	28,025
2		6,890	30,000	(9,000)	27,890	0.907	25,296
3		5,168	30,000	(9,000)	26,168	0.864	22,609
4	20,000	5,860	30,000	(9,000)	46,860	0.823	38,566
5		3,644		(4,500)	(856)	0.784	(671)
NPV							8,825

> ❗ If questions requiring taxation calculations are included in the examination the rate of corporation tax and the percentage writing-down allowance will be given in the question. This is because in reality they may change from year to year.

Now try this example. It incorporates tax and inflation and will demonstrate again the two possible ways of dealing with inflation in NPV calculations.

Either:
- discount real cash flows at the real rate of return;

or:
- discount money cash flows at the monetary (nominal) rate of return.

Example

The management of a company are making a decision on whether or not to purchase a new piece of office equipment, which costs £75,000. The equipment will generate a net cash flow of £35,000 per annum. At the end of the fourth year the equipment can be sold for £25,000. The equipment does not qualify for writing-down allowances. The corporation tax rate is 30 per cent.

Requirement

Assume that all cash flows are given in real terms, that 5 per cent is the real cost of capital and that annual inflation will be 4 per cent.

Calculate the NPV for this project using:

(a) the real cost of capital;
  and then
(b) the nominal (money) cost of capital.

Solution

(a) *Real cost of capital 5%*

Year	Asset £	Profit £	Corp. tax £	Total £	Discount factor 5%	Present value £
0	(75,000)			(75,000)	1.000	(75,000)
1		35,000	(5,250)	29,750	0.952	28,322
2		35,000	(10,500)	24,500	0.907	22,222
3		35,000	(10,500)	24,500	0.864	21,168
4	25,000	35,000	(10,500)	49,500	0.823	40,739
5			(5,250)	(5,250)	0.784	(4,116)
					NPV	33,335

(b) *Monetary (nominal) cost of capital*

$$(1 + m) = (1 + r)(1 + i)$$
$$(1 + m) = (1 + 0.05)(1 + 0.04)$$
$$m = 9.2\%$$

The required discount factors are:

Year		9.2% Discount factor
1	1 × 1/1.092	0.916
2	0.916 × 1/1.092	0.839
3	0.839 × 1/1.092	0.768
4	0.768 × 1/1.092	0.703
5	0.703 × 1/1.092	0.644

The monetary or nominal discount rates will be applied to the actual money cash flows.
Disposal proceeds allowing for inflation

$$£25,000 \times (1.04)^4 \times £29,246$$

The corporation tax calculation

	Profit £	30% tax £	Payable Year 1 £	Payable Year 2 £	Payable Year 3 £	Payable Year 4 £	Payable Year 5 £
Year 1 £35,000 × $(1.04)^1$	36,400	10,920	5,460	5,460			
Year 2 £35,000 × $(1.04)^2$	37,856	11,357		5,678	5,679		
Year 3 £35,000 × $(1.04)^3$	39,370	11,811			5,906	5,905	
Year 4 £35,000 × $(1.04)^4$	40,945	12,284				6,142	6,142
			(5,460)	(11,138)	(11,585)	(12,047)	(6,142)

The project money cash flows can now be displayed.

Year	Asset £	Profit £	Corporation tax £	Total £	Discount factor 9.2%	Present value £
0	(75,000)			(75,000)	1.000	(75,000)
1		36,400	(5,460)	30,940	0.916	28,341
2		37,856	(11,138)	26,718	0.839	22,416
3		39,370	(11,585)	27,785	0.768	21,339
4	29,246	40,945	(12,047)	58,144	0.703	40,875
5			(6,142)	(6,142)	0.644	(3,955)
					NPV	34,016

You will note that both approaches give the same answer. The small difference between the two figures is simply due to rounding.

8.4 Post-completion appraisal

8.4.1 The investment cycle

As stated at the beginning of the chapter, the financial evaluation of projects is only part of the investment process. The full process is represented in Figure 8.3. This shows that the investment process is a cycle, rather than a discrete event.

The post-completion appraisal of projects provides a mechanism whereby experience gained from past projects can be fed into the organisation's decision-making processes to aid decisions on future projects. In other words, it aids organisational learning. A post-completion appraisal reviews all aspects of a completed project in order to assess whether it has lived up to initial expectations. This is a forward-looking rather than backward-looking technique. The task is often carried out by a small team, which typically consists of an accountant and an engineer who have had some involvement in the project. Surprisingly, it is rare to find that post-completion appraisal is the responsibility of the internal audit department. This is because it is not considered an audit of past events but a means of improving future decisions.

For many years, post-completion appraisals were neglected in academic literature and rarely used in practice. By the end of the 1980s this had begun to change as surveys carried out at this time showed, so that today it is practised by around 80 per cent of large companies.

8.4.2 Benefits of post-completion appraisal

None of the surveys explain why post-completion audit became more popular during the 1980s. It has been suggested that it may be the result of a time lag. Discounted cash flow techniques were very rarely used before the mid-1960s. When the technique was introduced managers may have been shocked to find that projects assessed by this method often failed to live up to their expectations. As a consequence, by the 1980s managers began to take other steps to make project appraisal more accurate, and this included instigating a post-completion appraisal process. There are other explanations. For example, over the years the constitution of the average organisation's costs has changed from variable to fixed, i.e. more overheads have been incurred, and under these circumstances it becomes even more important to make the correct investment decisions. When this is coupled with a fast-changing world, wrong decisions can prove disastrous, and so any technique which helps avoid 'bad' investments and improves future assessment is to be welcomed.

The following benefits may be gained from a post-completion appraisal; the benefits are split into three types as classified by Mills and Kennedy (1993).

A – Benefits relating to the performance of the current project
- It enables speedy modification of under-performing/over-performing projects, by identifying the reasons for the under-/over-performance.
- It makes it more likely that 'bad' projects are:
  (i) terminated; and
  (ii) terminated at an earlier stage.

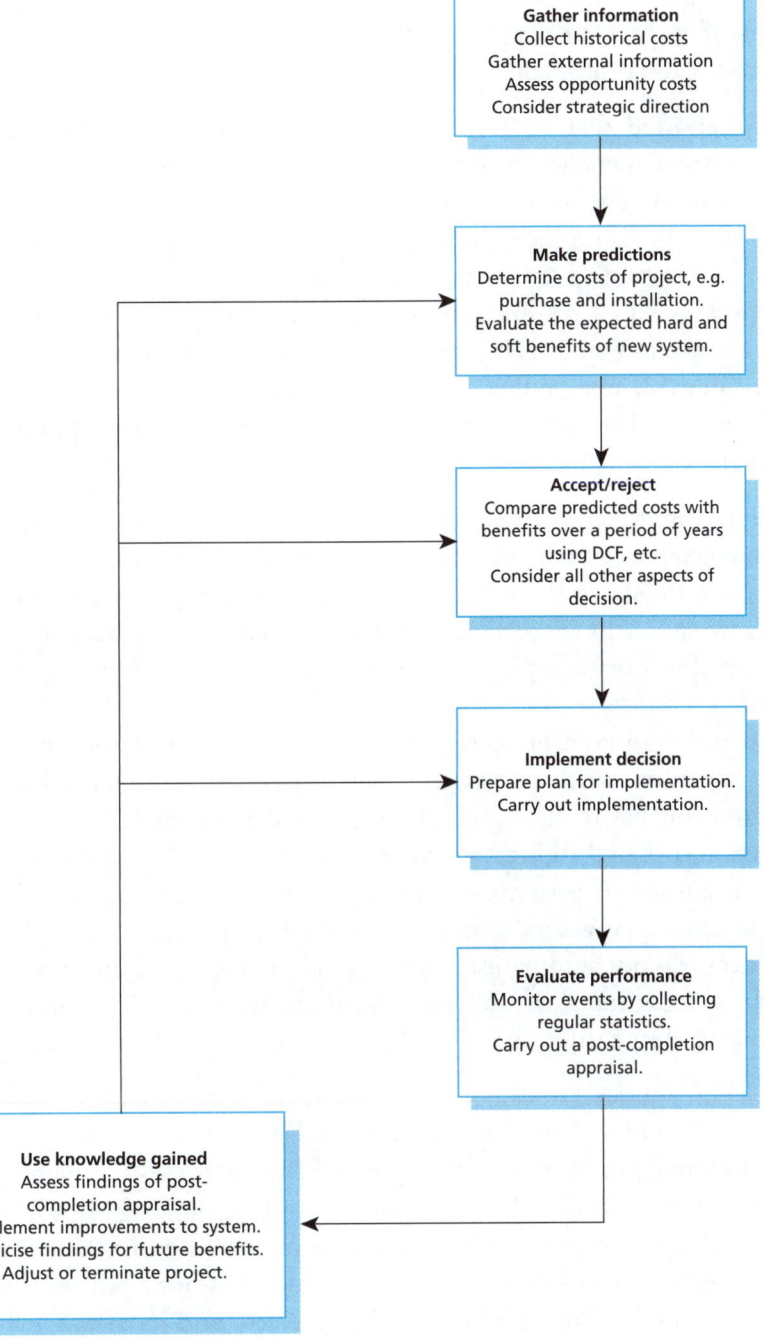

Figure 8.28 The Investment cycle

B — Benefits which relate to the selection and performance of future projects
- It improves the quality of decision making by providing a mechanism whereby past experience can be made available to future decision-makers.
- It encourages greater realism in project appraisal as past inaccuracies in forecasts are made public. It tends to stop managers looking at their pet projects in a favourable light and ensures a more realistic approach to predicting future outcomes.
- It highlights reasons for successful projects. This may be important in achieving greater benefits from future projects.

C – Benefit to the investment appraisal system itself
- It provides a means of improving control mechanisms, by formally highlighting areas where weaknesses have caused problems.

Mills and Kennedy reported that at the time of their research the companies they surveyed had all gained type C benefits from their post-completion appraisals and that 40 per cent hoped to gain type B benefits. However, only 20 per cent sought type A benefits. This might seem surprising, but is probably because projects can be monitored more effectively by other means. For example, regular and routine monitoring of weekly sales or the time taken to complete stages in a research and development project would prove more effective than a post-completion audit. Thus post-completion appraisal is a management tool to assist in better future planning rather than a control technique.

F R Gulliver (1987) reported on BP's experience with post-completion appraisal. Four main benefits had arisen:

- Before post-completion appraisal existed BP's management approved unrealistically low budgets because planners inaccurately predicted the scope of the project when they submitted the budget. Now BP approves budgets in phases, and each phase becomes more accurate as planners work out the project's details. Because managers know that the projects are to be subjected to post-completion appraisal the plans they draw up are more accurate and realistic.
- The knowledge that rushing into a project, such as a company acquisition, in order to forestall action by competitors is often unwise. If there is any doubt about the soundness of the project the company has rarely regretted not going ahead with it.
- Before post-completion appraisal BP's management made some bad decisions on which contractors to use. As a result of post-completion appraisal a contractor evaluation unit was set up which monitors contractors' performance and aids future choice.
- BP found that engineers do not automatically make good managers. As a result of post-completion appraisal a department was set up to help engineers develop control techniques and procedures and to ensure that the right person manages the right project.

A good post-completion appraisal does not set out to identify the costs and benefits of a project in precise detail. (As pointed out above, this particular task will normally have been carried out as part of a routine project monitoring system.) Instead it seeks to identify general lessons to be learned from a project. It is not intended to be a policing exercise and, if it is to be effective, should not be seen as such. Thus the term post-completion appraisal is a more accurate term than post-completion audit. Even though it is not a policing exercise any attempts to hide or ignore realities are likely to be revealed, and its effect will be to encourage honesty in facing problems at all levels of the organisation.

The article by Mathijs Brantjes (the controller at Heineken) et al. in the Readings section illustrates how a post-project appraisal may be carried out in practice and discusses some of the practical issues involved.

8.4.3 Project abandonment

During a post-completion appraisal it may be realised that the project is not likely to be so profitable as first thought and the possibility of abandoning it or terminating it early should be considered. Past cash flows are, of course, irrelevant to the decision – only future cash flows need to be considered. Abandoning the project is only necessary when the net discounted expected future cash flow of the project becomes negative.

Example

Case I

A project, P, has expected cash flows as shown in Figure 8.29.

Year	Expected cash flow £	Discount rate 10%	Discounted cash flow £
0	(3,500)	1.000	(3,500)
1	2,000	0.909	1,818
2	2,000	0.826	1,653
3	2,000	0.751	1,503
		Expected net present value	1,474

Figure 8.29

The initial investment of £3,500 in project P represents the purchase of a customised machine, the price of which is known with certainty. Because it is a customised machine its resale value is low; it can only be sold for £1,000 immediately after purchase. Once the machine is bought, therefore, the expected value of abandoning the project would be £1,000 (1.0 × £1,000). This must be compared with the expected value of continuing with the project, which is £4,974 (£1,818 + £1,653 + £1,503). In this case the expected benefits of continuing with the project far outweigh the returns from abandoning it immediately.

Case II

The decision to abandon a project will usually be made as a result of revised expectations of future revenues and costs. These revisions may be consistent with the data on which the original investment decision was based, or represent an alteration to earlier expectations. If the decision is consistent with the original data, the possibility, but not the certainty, that the project might have to be abandoned would have been known when the project was accepted. In these circumstances, project abandonment is one of a known range of possible outcomes arising from accepting the project. The cash flows in Table 8.29 were the expected ones, based on the probabilities given in Figure 8.30.

Year 0		Year 1		Year 2		Year 3	
£	p	£	p	£	p	£	
(3,500)	0.33	3,000	0.33	3,000	0.33	3,000	
	0.33	2,000	0.33	2,000	0.33	2,000	
	0.33	1,000	0.33	1,000	0.33	1,000	
Expected value		2,000		2,000		2,000	

Figure 8.30

In year 0, the expected net cash inflow in each year of project P's 3-year life is £2,000. The actual outcome of any of the 3 years is unknown at this point, and each of the three possible outcomes is equally likely. The factors that will cause any one of these results to occur may differ each year, or they may be the same each year. In some instances, a particular outcome in the first year may determine the outcome of years 2 and 3 with certainty. For example, the outcome of £3,000 in year 1 may mean that this same outcome will follow with certainty in years 2 and 3. Similarly outcomes of £2,000 and £1,000 in year 1 may be certain to be repeated in years 2 and 3. In year 0, the investor can only calculate the expected net cash flow in years 2 and 3, but with perfect correlation of flows between years these future flows are known with certainty at the end of year 1. If the year 1 inflow is either £3,000 or £2,000, perfect correlation between years will ensure that the actual NPV of the project will be positive. But if the first year's outcome is £1,000, the investment will have a negative NPV of £1,014, that is (£[3,500] + £1,000 × 2.486). Should the project be abandoned? The information is now certain and so the decision on whether to abandon should be made using a risk-free interest rate and not the company's normal cost of capital. If we assume that the risk-free rate is 5 per cent, the present value of continuing at the end of year 1 will be:

Year	Cash flow £	Discount rate 5%	Discounted cash flow £
0	(1,000)	1.000	(1,000)
1	1,000	0.952	952
2	1,000	0.907	907
			859

Clearly, the project should not be abandoned.

Case III

Suppose a buy-back clause had been part of the sale agreement for the machine, which requires the supplier to repurchase the machine on demand for £2,000 at any time up to and including the first anniversary of the sale. The abandonment value of the project at the end of year 1 will be £2,000. When this is compared with the £1,859 present value of continuation, it is clear that the company should plan to terminate the project at the end of year 1, if the actual outcome of that year proves to be £1,000. When the buy-back option is included, the possible outcomes will change as shown in Figure 8.31.

Year 0 £	p	Year 1 £	p	Year 2 £	p	Year 3 £
(3,500)	0.33	3,000	0.33	3,000	0.33	3,000
	0.33	2,000	0.33	2,000	0.33	2,000
	0.33	1,000	0.33	0	0.33	0
		2,000 ⎫				
Expected value		2,667 ⎭		1,667		1,667

Figure 8.31

Including abandonment in the plan increases the expected NPV of the project by £80:

Year	Cash flow £	Discount rate 10%	Discounted cash flow £
0	(3,500)	1.000	(3,500)
1	2,667	0.909	2,424
2	1,667	0.826	1,378
3	1,667	0.751	1,252
			1,554

This type of problem can be analysed using a decision tree. Figure 8.32 sets out the data in this format.

The method outlined below can be utilised even where the correlation of cash flows between years is less than perfect. The correlation can range from perfectly positive (as in our example) to perfectly negative. Where the correlation is zero, that is total independence of cash flows between years, the method cannot be used. But in all other instances the knowledge gained in Year 1 will enable the forecast for later years to be refined to a greater or lesser extent. This in turn will allow the expected present value of continuing with the project to be compared with the present value of termination.

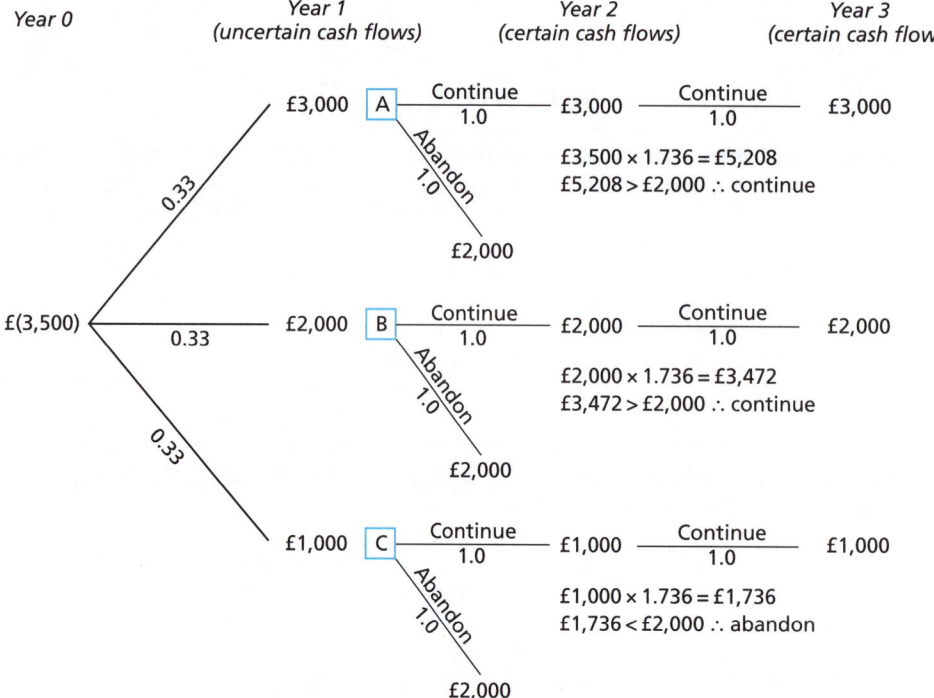

Figure 8.32 Decision tree for the cash flows in Figure 8.31

Case IV

During a project's life, events that were unforeseen at the time of the original decision may occur and have an impact on the expected cash flows of the project. Such events will require a revision of future predictions.

In the previous example the announcement of a new tax charged on revenues during the course of year 1 would necessitate a review of the project's profitability. If the effect of the new tax would be to reduce the project's revenues after year 1 by 50 per cent, the position would be as shown in Figure 8.33.

The introduction of the new tax means that a cash flow of £2,000 in year 1 will now be followed by only £1,000 in years 2 and 3. This will mean that the project should be abandoned in year 1. At the time the project was being considered, this situation was not, and could not have been, foreseen by the decision-maker.

Under these circumstances it would be surprising if there was any resistance to the idea of terminating the project, as external events, for which no one could be held responsible, had made it necessary. But when a revision in future expectations arising from errors in the original forecasts, or due to problems in project implementation, indicate that abandonment is necessary, it can be much more difficult to acknowledge and accept. The post-completion audit team will play a significant role in identifying and highlighting the changed circumstances in such situations.

Year 0		Year 1		Year 2		Year 3
£	p	£	p	£	p	£
(3,500)	0.33	3,000	0.33	1,500	0.33	1,500
	0.33	2,000	0.33	1,000	0.33	1,000
	0.33	1,000	0.33	500	0.33	500
Expected value		2,000		1,000		1,000

Figure 8.33

Example

Project X had the following expected cash-flow pattern at the time of its approval:

Year	Discounted cash flow
	£m
1	(8)
2	(16)
3	(24)
4	55
Net present value	7

The company experienced great difficulty in implementing the project in year 1, and the actual costs incurred during that year were £16m. The company must then ask itself whether the actual outcome in year 1 necessitates any revision in the expected outcomes of later years. If no revision is required, further costs of £40m (year 0 values) must be incurred to secure inflows of £55m (year 0 values). The expected net present value of continuing with project X beyond year 1 will thus be £15m (year 0 values). (Note that adjusting the figures to year 1 values would increase the expected NPV slightly, strengthening the case for continuation.)

The overall result of the investment would, of course, be negative by £1m, if years 2–4 costs and revenues are as forecast. The excess spend of £8m in year 1 is greater than the £7m net present value originally predicted. However, at the end of year 1 the £16m is a sunk cost and does not influence a decision on termination made at that time.

8.4.4 Role of post-appraisal in project abandonment

Those intimately involved with a project may be reluctant to admit, even to themselves, that early problems with a project are likely to continue. When problems are being experienced in project implementation, those involved may be tempted to try to resolve the situation in one of two ways. They can make a change in the original plans and/or incur further expenditure in order to meet the original objective.

Whether either of these responses is appropriate will depend on the particular circumstances of the project but any significant changes or deviations should not be undertaken without the formal approval of higher management. The control systems in place will normally require changes of scope to be documented and approved before they are undertaken. It is usually the responsibility of the engineers associated with the project to ensure that this is done. Expected project cost overruns should be highlighted by the routine monitoring of project expenditure by accounting staff, and formal approval should be obtained for the anticipated overspend. A prerequisite of approval by top management will often be the provision of the same level of detailed justification as was required when the initial funds were sanctioned. These controls ensure that significant changes to the character of a project cannot be made without top management's approval. However, they do not, of themselves, ensure that the option to terminate a project is considered, although it would be unlikely that management would fail to consider this possibility.

Some companies require an audit to be carried out on all projects that need additional funds. The request for further funding would then be considered alongside the audit report. Routine monitoring of projects tends to focus almost exclusively on costs. An audit will review both costs and revenues, and, most importantly, focuses on the future. By checking the continuing validity of both forecast costs and revenues, the post-audit team is in a position to prepare a report to advise management on the wisdom of continuing with the project.

8.5 Summary

This chapter has dealt with the methods for determining whether to invest in a particular long-term project and has considered measures for assessing an investment centre's performance. Key points are as follows:

- The net present value (NPV) method of investment appraisal always produces the correct investment decision if the aim is to maximise shareholder value.
- The internal rate of return (IRR) of a project is the discount rate at which the NPV is zero.
- IRR can give multiple rates of return if cash flows are unusual.
- Payback is widely used in practice and has a number of advantages and disadvantages. It is the time taken for the cumulative cash inflows from a project to equal the initial outflow.
- Accounting rate of return is based on the accounting profit after depreciation. Its use has a number of limitations.
- Discounted payback may also be used to appraise projects.
- Calculation of a discounted payback index or profitability index can be useful if funds are scarce.
- Annuity rates can be used to simplify calculations when annual cash flows are equal.
- When projects with lives of unequal lengths are being considered they can be adjusted to a comparable basis through the use of annualised equivalents.
- Sensitivity analysis is a useful technique for assessing risk in a project.
- Inflation may be incorporated into discounted cash flow analysis in two ways: discount monetary cash flows at the monetary cost of capital, or discount real cash flows at the real cost of capital.
- Taxation affects the cash flows associated with a project, often also in the year following that in which the taxable profit is earned.
- Writing-down allowances are spread over the life of a capital asset, affecting cash flows throughout the life of a project.
- A post-completion appraisal has a number of benefits, many of which relate to future investment decisions and to the investment appraisal system itself.
- The project abandonment decision is based on relevant, future costs and revenues.

Readings

Gain Sharing Arrangements

Tim Thompson Paper: P2 *Management Accounting* **– Decision Management**

Primary relevant learning outcome:
D9: 'Discuss gain sharing arrangements whereby contractors and customers benefit if contract targets for cost, delivery etc. are beaten'

Other relevant learning outcome(s):
B1: 'Explain the processes involved in making long-term decisions'
B6: 'Evaluate project proposals using the techniques of investment appraisal'
B7: 'Compare, contrast and evaluate alternative techniques of investment appraisal'
B8: 'Evaluate and rank projects that might be mutually exclusive, involve unequal lives and/or be subject to capital rationing'

Synopsis
The main theme of this article is gain sharing arrangements and how they may be of benefit both to customers and to suppliers/contractors. A practical example is included that links gain sharing with the use of net present value and profitability index within an environment where capital rationing is in force.

The Possibilities and Practicalities of Gain Sharing Arrangements

Any discussion of gain sharing arrangements in the context of learning outcome D9 requires an understanding of what constitutes a business contract. A contract is an agreement whereby two parties commit to some form of exchange. This exchange may include any combination of the supply of physical goods, the provision of services and the payment of money. Once a contract is made, it is legally enforceable and if one of the parties fails to fully perform its share of the bargain, then the law will protect the other party.

We encounter contracts in many aspects of our lives. For example, when an employee starts a new job, he or she enters into a contract with the employer. The exchange here is the work performed by the employee in return for the salary paid by the employer. Another example would be where a supplier agrees to provide some materials in return for the payment that will be made by the customer.

These two examples are relatively straightforward forms of contract and the obligations entered into by the two parties are very clear. Some contracts, though, relate to substantial, long-term projects, examples of which might include the installation of a major new computer system or substantial public works such as the building of a new motorway. This type of contract is fraught with risk and the actual amount of work needed to be carried out can be very difficult to ascertain with any degree of certainty; for example, extreme weather conditions can adversely affect the completion of a motorway project.

But who should bear the responsibility for this type of risk? If a new computer system is late in being implemented, then there may be substantial consequential costs to the customer, for example in continuing to run an expensive paper-based system. It follows that the customer will be keen to ensure that the system is implemented on time and may wish to include clauses that penalise the supplier in the event of lateness. The supplier would prefer not to be faced with the possibility of paying such penalties, but may have to accept these clauses in order to gain the business. This being the case, then the supplier will probably attempt to incorporate some contingencies in the timings and price of the contract in order to protect the planned profit on the deal. Another approach, though, would be for both parties to recognise the possibility of delays that are caused by external factors beyond their control and agree to some arrangement whereby this risk is shared.

It is fair to say that much attention is paid in contract negotiations to the various types of downside risk such as late delivery, cost over-runs and under-performance after delivery. But what about the upside possibilities? What if there is potential for delivery to be ahead of target, or for costs to be less than those anticipated, or for performance to exceed the specified requirement?

If delivery of a new computer system can be made early, then the customer can begin to reap the benefits that much sooner. If costs are lower, then the supplier's profit should be enhanced. If performance is above that specified, then this may enable the customer to make additional efficiency savings elsewhere in the organisation.

Exploiting this upside potential clearly makes sense and what is needed is a contractual arrangement whereby both parties will actively seek this. It is in this aspect of contracts that we encounter gain sharing and the principle is startlingly simple; both parties agree to share any benefits that are achieved over and above those specified in the baseline terms of the contract.

This is by no means a new idea; executive bonuses based on company profits and productivity bonuses for employees have been around for a long time. In fact, some of these schemes fall within the wider definition of gain sharing. However, these types of bonus are based upon contracts between parties within the organisation. Learning outcome, D9, indicates that in Paper P2, we are concerned with gain sharing in the context of contracts between separate organisations, i.e. contractors (or suppliers) and customers.

A radical form of gain sharing is where a supplier agrees to perform its side of the contract with no guarantee of receiving a payment. Instead, any payment received is based upon the benefits that emerge to the customer as a result of the successful completion of the supplier's side of the bargain. This is clearly a very risky stance for the supplier to take; it could spend a small fortune and walk away with nothing. Alternatively, if the benefits to the customer are substantial then the supplier could find itself rewarded with a large return. In this situation, the supplier could almost be described as taking an equity stake in the customer rather than entering into a contract with it.

This all sounds very appealing; if it works well then a gain sharing contract passes the test of providing a 'win-win' deal and both parties are happy. But how can this be made to work in practice? A key feature must be the provision of information by both parties to one another and this may be easier said than done. For decades, business has been carried out within an atmosphere of secrecy with companies grudgingly releasing as little information as they possibly can whilst meeting the disclosure requirements of the Companies Act, Financial Reporting Standards and the Stock Market. It would represent a major culture shift for many organisations to release commercially sensitive financial information to a supplier or customer even if this was done under a strict confidentiality agreement. There would certainly need to be a high degree of trust between the two parties and this type of relationship can take time to develop.

This is not to say that gain sharing is a bad idea. It has potential to provide significant gains to both parties and even to the economy as a whole. But to be successful, organisations must ensure that they deal with the practicalities and information sharing is a key issue here. Furthermore, in negotiating the treatment of upside potential, the organisations must not forget that contractual arrangements still need to be clear about who bears the downside risk.

A practical example

A company has a maximum of £10 million to spend on capital projects in the forthcoming year and there are four projects that it would like to implement. After careful analysis of the relevant cashflows and discounting at the appropriate cost of capital, the following summary of these four independent capital projects has emerged:

	Initial Outlay	Net Present Value (NPV)
Project A	£2 million	+£500,000
Project B	£4 million	+£1,200,000
Project C	£3 million	+£600,000
Project D	£3 million	+£550,000

None of the projects are divisible, and none will yield substantial positive cashflows during the first year of operation.

All of the projects offer a positive NPV and are therefore attractive. However, to implement all of these projects would need a total of £12 million initial investment and this is greater than the funds that are available. Accordingly, the company must choose how to use the £10 million and this decision will be based upon maximising the total NPV of the projects that are selected.

The company can calculate the Profitability Index (PI) for each of the projects as follows:

Project A	500,000/2,000,000 = 0.250
Project B	1,200,000/4,000,000 = 0.300
Project C	600,000/3,000,000 = 0.200
Project D	550,000/3,000,000 = 0.183

Thus the initial ranking of the four projects, based upon PI and in descending order, is B, A, C and D. But we know that these four projects cannot all be implemented due to the £10 million investment maximum. If the company prioritised based upon the PI rankings, then it would select projects B, A and C only and would disregard project D. This would yield a total NPV of £2,300,000 and would use £9 million of the available funds. Since project D is not divisible, there is no possibility of implementing part of it and so the remaining £1 million of investment funds would remain unused. (This unused investment is deemed to have a NPV of zero, since it will either be invested at the cost of capital or, perhaps, returned to the investor.)

But is this selection of B, A and C really the most effective use of the available funds? The problem here is that, since we have a solution that does not use all of the available investment funds, we may not have found the optimal solution by simply using the PIs.

Let's take a more detailed look at every feasible combination of the four projects, starting with the B, A and C combination suggested by PI.

	Initial Outlay	Net Present Value (NPV)
Project A	£2 million	+£500,000
Project B	£4 million	+£1,200,000
Project C	£3 million	+£600,000
Totals	£9 million	+£2,300,000

	Initial Outlay	Net Present Value (NPV)
Project A	£2 million	+£500,000
Project B	£4 million	+£1,200,000
Project D	£3 million	+£550,000
Totals	£9 million	+£2,250,000

	Initial Outlay	Net Present Value (NPV)
Project B	£4 million	+£1,200,000
Project C	£3 million	+£600,000
Project D	£3 million	+£550,000
Totals	£10 million	+£2,350,000

	Initial Outlay	Net Present Value (NPV)
Project A	£2 million	+£500,000
Project C	£3 million	+£600,000
Project D	£3 million	+£550,000
Totals	£8 million	+£1,650,000

From this, we see that the best combination is actually B, C and D. This provides £2,350,000 of aggregate NPV compared with only £2,300,000 if we had selected B, A and C. This indicates that we should exclude project A from our plans and instead include project D, despite the fact that project A has the higher PI.

Does this make sense? In this case it does. Despite project D having a lower PI than project A, it enables the company to use (profitably) the remaining £1 million of funding available for investment. The extra £50,000 of NPV can be reconciled as follows:

	NPV Generated	
Investment	Project A	Project D
First £2 million	2 × 0.25 = £500,000	2 × 0.183 = £366,667
Next £1 million	NIL	1 × 0.183 = £183,333
Total	£500,000	£550,000

Having finally decided that the company should invest in projects B, C and D, the company will still be disappointed if it cannot exploit the additional wealth creating opportunity of project A. Is there anything that it can do about this?

One alternative might be to delay the project for a while and use positive cashflows generated from the other projects to provide the investment funds. However, we were told above that 'none will yield substantial positive cashflows in the first year of operation' and so this approach would not appear to be open to the company.

Perhaps a more fundamental question would be to ask why there is a limit of £10 million on the funds available for investment. Such a restriction is known as 'capital rationing' and this can exist in two forms. The first of these is 'hard capital rationing' and this exists when external finance providers (shareholders and lenders) refuse to provide the additional finance. In this case, if the company cannot persuade them to change their minds, then little more can be done. By comparison, 'soft capital rationing' exists where the restriction on funding is imposed by the managers of the company and where it would be within their power to ease this restriction. Why might the managers impose such a restriction? One reason might be that there is no additional equity finance available and the managers are reluctant to increase the company's gearing by taking on further borrowing. Sometimes, though, the reason may be rather less rational; if the argument is simply that the company always invests £10 million per year then this would be indicative of inertia rather than meaningful decision-making.

But if the company really cannot find the extra £2 million to invest in project A, might gain sharing offer a possible solution? Let's take a more detailed look at what project A actually involves. This project would be an investment in up-to-date computer software that should, in time, dramatically improve the planning of service requests from customers and the associated response times. The benefits of this should include a substantial reduction in the overtime worked and more customer orders received due to more competitive quotations and a stronger quality image.

Might the company and the software supplier both be interested in a gain sharing arrangement here? If so, how might the deal be structured?

By calculating of NPV, we provide a simplified view of a complex range of forecast future cashflows; a single, notional figure expressed in today's terms. More specifically, it is the present value of all relevant cash benefits minus the present value of all relevant cash expenses. However, the company is not in a position to make any immediate payment to the supplier. Suppose that, instead, the company offered to pay to the supplier all relevant cash benefits as they arise up to the point that their present value equals the £2 million capital cost of the deal. (Since the supplier would receive these payments over time, he would receive more than £2 million in cash; this would compensate him for the time value of money.) Once this threshold has been reached, then the remaining relevant cash benefits could be split between the company and the supplier, perhaps on a 50/50 basis.

To the company, even though the total net cash benefits (with NPV of +£500,000) are to be shared with the supplier, this should still be a wealth creating investment and one that otherwise might not be feasible. To the supplier, this gain sharing arrangement may be the only way that this potentially profitable deal can proceed. To the supplier, this also represents an opportunity to make a return on the deal greater than that available through a fixed price contract. At the same time, though, the supplier must also take on board the additional risk that his revenues from the deal may be lower than that offered through a fixed price contract. As discussed earlier, this transfer of risk from the customer (the company) to the supplier or contractor is a key characteristic of gain sharing arrangements.

Note:
Readers wishing to learn more about gain sharing, when this term is used to describe types of incentive bonus plan for employees, may be interested in the following source:
Armstrong, M. and Murlis, H., '*Reward Management: A Handbook of Remuneration Strategy and Practice*', 3rd edition, 1994, Kogan Page, ISBN 0749410094, Chapter 23.

Post-completion auditing with Heineken

Mathijs Brantjes, Henk von Eije, Frans Eusman and Wout Prins, *Management Accounting*, April 1999 © CIMA. Reproduced with permission

Until recently, many continental European companies hardly gave any attention to the ex-post evaluation of capital investment projects. But the concept of the learning organisation has triggered renewed interest in the post-completion audit (PCA). This renewed attention now gives us the opportunity to discuss the steps which are considered to be relevant for the application of a PCA, using experience gained within the Heineken corporation.

Objectives and advantages

A post-completion audit can be defined as 'an objective and independent appraisal of all phases of the capital expenditure process as it relates to a specific project'.[1] From the writings of various authors four main reasons for a PCA can be distilled:

1. It enables a check to be made on whether the actual results correspond with the expected results. If this is not the case, the reason can be sought. This could form the basis for improvements in projects that are not functioning as expected or can cause projects to be abandoned.
2. It generates information which allows an appraisal to be made of the managers who took the investment decision. Managers will therefore tend to arrive in advance at more realistic estimates of the advantages and disadvantages of their proposed investments.
3. It can produce lessons for the decision-making process. If these lessons are actually learned, people will be able to make a better evaluation of the significance and the profitability of future projects.
4. Finally, it can provide for better project planning. If in the evaluation it is found that the planning of the investment programme was poor, provision can be made to ensure that it is better for future investments.

Ranked in order of importance, Neale and Homes[2] found that managers see advantage in the fact that a PCA:

- improves the quality of decision-making;
- encourages more realism in decision-making on new investment projects;
- is a means for improving control and guidance;
- improves a company's performance;
- helps in identifying key variables (critical success factors);
- allows changes to be made more swiftly in projects which are not doing very well;
- increases the frequency with which projects are terminated.

In view of these advantages it is not surprising that large companies now regularly want to evaluate investments using PCAs. However, to implement a PCA successfully, certain requirements have to be met.

Requirements of a PCA

A very important requirement is to clarify the question of why a PCA is wanted. This is because there is an area of tension between current ideas on (i) performance appraisal and the reward linked to it and (ii) the ideas circulating these days in regard to the 'learning organisation'. The people who have to work together on a PCA will tend to present the facts in a more favourable light if that will increase their reward, but it does not automatically result in a clearer understanding of the strengths and weaknesses of the investment and of the investment process. The introduction of a PCA procedure can thus arouse suspicion. Is it really a management tool for improvement or are scores being settled as well?

At Heineken the Executive Board of Heineken NV (the corporate head office) encourages the conducting of PCAs in the context of a philosophy of 'best practices'. It is made clear that a PCA is something that can help everyone. The term used in this context, therefore, is not 'settling' but 'rendering' account. There's a big difference.

Another major requirement is that the objectives of the investment project must be clear from the start, as a PCA is impossible without an adequate investment proposal. Included in that proposal there should be a statement of the concrete goals of the investment. The PCA can then be conducted on the basis of those goals. In that respect the prospect of a PCA immediately heightens awareness when drawing up an investment proposal. If the goals have to be clearly stated, people will think more about the reasons and motives for the investment.

Lessons taught by a concrete PCA

We shall now describe the content of the PCA report of one of the first PCAs carried out at Heineken Nederland, which is the Dutch regional division of Heineken NV. The PCA relates to the replacement of an old bottling line dating from 1976 at the Den Bosch brewery. The PCA report starts with project information like the approval dates and planned investment expenditures. These are followed by a summary of the goals of the capital investment and the experience and problems in implementing the investment programme. Next, the 'outcomes' of the project, e.g. efficiency achieved, number of people employed, maintenance time, the quality of filling and working conditions, are described. The audit report then looks at the financial results and the departures from the planned expenditures. The results of the new bottling line are then compared with the planned objectives. Table 1 gives a brief overview of the planned and actual outcomes in this PCA. The audit report concludes with what could be learned from the investment project.

Table 1 Comparison of the plan with the actual situation at the time of PCA

Objectives	Plan	Actual
Efficiency	Increase from 65% to 80%	No increase yet
Staff savings	From 13 to 7 per shift	Achieved
Forklift savings	1 vehicle less	1 and possibly 2 vehicles less
Savings on overhaul of old bottling line	1.3 million guilders of savings	Savings achieved, but as a result of reusing part of the old bottling line another 1.8 million guilders is spent in additional overhaul costs
Savings on maintenance	Savings of 0.4 million guilders annually	Savings estimated at 0.3 million guilders annually
Quality	50% reduction in damage	Achieved
Working conditions	Level of noise Accessibility Safety Attainability	All much improved, but not quantified

One of the lessons learned from this PCA within Heineken Nederland was that the variables which are less easily quantified (e.g. working conditions) must be defined as far as is possible in a quantifiable form.

This means that not only must the objectives be stated in the investment proposal, but they should also be stated, wherever possible, in terms which are measurable.

Another lesson learned was related to the fact that some of the planned investments were not undertaken because it was discovered that the old machinery could still be put to good use. This resulted in a lack of clarity over the planned savings on maintenance and to unforeseen modifications and modification costs. These additional costs – which were made visible as a result of the PCA – taught managers of Heineken Nederland not to depart so quickly from the original plans.

The impression might then be gained, however, that the learning process originating from a PCA encourages ossification during the implementation phase. But if, in general, the PCA procedure does indeed result in better thought-out investment proposals, there should be no objection to extra robustness in the implementation of these proposals. Improvements during implementation are still possible but they need to be justified and fully documented.

The design of a PCA procedure

Since the PCA described in the preceding paragraph, further PCAs have been performed, using a PCA procedure designed for Heineken Nederland. In order to give this procedure concrete shape, a number of questions were answered. The principal questions are given below.

What projects will be subjected to a PCA?

A clear picture is required of projects which are to be subjected to a PCA. Are only investments in buildings and/or machinery being looked at, or are commercial investments and acquisitions also to be examined? Often, financial criteria are set for the projects to be subjected to a PCA. But qualitative criteria can also be important.

It is quite conceivable, for example, that new trial projects will not be excessively expensive. However, according to what is known as the real option theory[3] value is frequently created in these projects.

Wrong ideas in this area could therefore cost an organisation dear (or result in a considerable loss of profits). It is therefore desirable – in spite of modest capital expenditures – to conduct PCAs for projects of this kind as well.

At Heineken NV all capital investments above a certain expenditure threshold together with smaller but innovative projects can now be subject to a PCA.

When should a PCA be carried out?

Mills and Kennedy[4] indicate that PCAs can be classified as being oriented to:

(a) project control;
(b) improving the investment system;
(c) the performance of future projects.

A PCA of type (a) is used to control current investment project outlays and thus must take place during the implementation phase. However, this is similar to normal project monitoring procedures. At Heineken Nederland, as such procedures are already available, the new PCA-procedure was primarily aimed at learning from the outcomes of past projects in order to improve the selection and performance of future projects (type (c)). But in addition, improvements in the investment system (type (b)) also emerged.

At Heineken Nederland a PCA is conducted some months after the end of the implementation phase of the investment project. Frequently, in this time it has been possible to operate on a trial basis and to make any necessary adjustments: most teething troubles will be over and the investment should be functioning normally. Naturally, it is still impossible to evaluate whether all the cash flow projections are actually working out; this often depends on various external circumstances. What, however, can be evaluated is whether the project budget was properly estimated, what can be improved in the implementation phase of subsequent investments, how the installation is functioning at that time and whether the expected savings and improvements seem realistic.

Under whose responsibility does a PCA fall?

Contrary to what the textbooks would have us believe, it will never be possible to evaluate an investment completely objectively. There are many elements that interfere with the investment. This leaves room for personal interpretation and perhaps portraying the results in a better light. It is therefore better to separate responsibility for the investment decision from that of the PCA. This means that the line management involved will not conduct the PCA. In order to avoid conflicts of interest and corporate blindness, experts from outside the company could even be used.

Nevertheless, Heineken Nederland opted not to do the latter. It is those who are most involved in the investment that have the knowledge needed to undertake a good PCA. For this reason the staff of the Planning and Control departments have been called in. This could be the Planning and Control department of Heineken Nederland or that of the business unit concerned, depending on which department prepared the original investment proposal. So, the Planning and Control departments not only help to decide on whether or not to make the investment, but are also responsible for the PCA. The justification for this internal audit is based on the notion that a professional controller works autonomously and an attempt is made to establish quantifiable objectives which limit the necessary qualitative evaluations. Moreover, the Planning and Control departments keep the files which contain all the information on an investment. It follows that the PCA can be recorded in the same file as all the other information. In this way information is always readily available and there is a complete file on every investment.

Who provides the information?

The knowledge and experience of those directly responsible for the implementation of the project will be used in carrying out the PCA. But in addition, information concerning the specific objectives of the investment will be discussed with specialists. For example, if an investment is intended to reduce energy consumption, the head of the energy department will be consulted. In the case of microbiological objectives, the technical department will be consulted, and in the case of health and safety objectives the health and safety officer.

Who is given access to the PCA reports?

With PCAs it is important that not only the top management gains insight into the consequences of investments. Those involved in the project and those likely to be involved in future projects should also learn from the experiences. In this way the PCA is related to the concept of the 'learning organisation'. The relevant information must therefore be widely available to many and in Heineken Nederland a separate file is compiled consisting of all PCAs carried out up to date. For the time being this file is kept in the Planning and Control department in question, but it is intended that the information will be made more widely available throughout the corporation via groupware (e.g. Lotus Notes).

What actions are induced by a PCA?

Conducting a PCA has to mean more than simply accumulating information. Only action taken on the basis of that information will produce results. At Heineken Nederland this means that the management of each of the five business units is invited to present a PCA carried out in their unit at the quarterly meetings with the senior management of Heineken Nederland. The managers of the business units and the managers of Heineken Nederland discuss each PCA and the lessons learnt. This creates a knowledge base which makes it likely that during discussions of future capital projects knowledge of past PCAs will be used. Moreover, in the future others will be able to access the information on past PCAs and managers may then be asked to indicate how they have used past experience from PCAs in their current investment proposals.

The procedure implies that all capital investments are not necessarily subject to a PCA and that business unit managers can be selective. Self-selection bias is, however, reduced because senior management can also ask for a PCA of a specific investment.

Costs and usefulness

In the preceding sections we have shown what has been learnt within Heineken Nederland from a concrete PCA and how a new PCA procedure has been institutionalised. One might wonder, however, whether the advantages outweigh the cost involved in carrying out PCAs.

Within Heineken Nederland the cost of individual PCAs turned out to be a pleasant surprise. A PCA took between two days and a week of direct work time for one person. This may be caused by the fact that these were mainly PCAs of traditional projects: less tangible marketing projects were not subjected to a PCA. More recently, two PCAs of foreign acquisitions of Heineken NV took on average one week for two persons. Such small time costs are in line with the research of Kennedy and Mills,[5] who found that it is unusual to have anyone working full-time generating PCA reports.

However, the indirect time has to be added to the direct time costs; e.g. the time required for improving the original investment proposal, for gathering the PCA information, and for administering, analysing and discussing the PCAs. In Heineken most of this indirect time is charged to the Planning and Control departments.

On the other hand, the employees of these Planning and Control departments are now able to communicate more easily about new investment projects. Discussing project proposals and PCA reports produces a 'prospective visualisation' on the part of all those involved and everyone is enthusiastic about this.

Finally, we may mention that as a result of the experiences described in this article, the Executive Board of Heineken NV has, in the context of promoting 'best practices', called for PCAs to be conducted within the entire group worldwide.

Conclusions

Summarising, we can say that for relatively large companies it is useful to conduct PCAs on a regular basis. Lessons can be learnt and the quality of the investment system and of future investment decisions can be improved. In designing a PCA procedure at Heineken

Nederland, questions emerged that will probably be asked within every organisation. Contrary to what is often thought, conducting a PCA does not appear to be an expensive business. A PCA procedure seems even to have hidden benefits as communications about new capital investments are improved.

1. Gadella, J and J Jones: 'Post completion review', Management Accounting, Vol 74, September 1996, pp 38–39.
2. Neale, CW and DEA Holmes: 'Post-auditing capital projects', *Long Range Planning*, Vol 23 (4), 1990, pp 88–96.
3. Bushby, JS and CGC Pitts: *Real options in practice. An exploratory survey of how finance officers deal with flexibility in capital appraisal*, Cranfield University and Warwick Business School, October 1996.
4. Mills, R and JA Kennedy: 'Experiences in operating a post-audit system,' *Management Accounting*, Vol 71 (10), November 1993, pp 26–28.
5. Kennedy, JA and R Mills: 'Post completion auditing in practice', *Management Accounting*, Vol 71 (9), October 1993, pp 22–25.

Postscript

This article contains a lot of useful information that could help you to answer an examination question about post-completion appraisal. If you have fallen into the trap of simply skimming through it, go back and read it again more thoroughly.

This time make notes as you go, to help you to answer questions such as:

- What benefits might be gained from a post-completion audit (PCA)?
- Who should be responsible for carrying out a PCA?
- Which projects should be subjected to a PCA?
- What type of objectives might be monitored with a PCA? (see Table 1)

You have seen the application of sensitivity analysis to give a feel for how a project's results might be affected by changes in the values of critical variables.

The following article uses a simple example to demonstrate the technique in more detail.

The gentle touch

Bob Scarlett, *CIMA Insider*, February 2003 © CIMA. Reproduced with permission

According to the 2000 edition of CIMA *Official Terminology*, sensitivity analysis is a 'modelling and risk assessment procedure in which changes are made to significant variables in order to determine the effect of these changes on the planned outcome'.

Sensitivity analysis is a more general approach than its more specific, quantitative equivalents, and it can be used in many areas of business decision-making with varying levels of refinement. Consider the following simple example of a project proposal to make and sell units over three years:

Initial capital cost	£4,000
Annual unit sales	100
Selling price per unit	£60
Variable cost per unit	£35
Fixed cost per year	£900

You would normally evaluate this project using an appropriate discount rate – say, 6 per cent – which gives the following result:

Year	Cash flow	Discount	PV
0	−4,000	1.000	−4,000
1	1,600	0.943	1,509
2	1,600	0.890	1,424
3	1,600	0.840	1,344
Net present value (NPV):			277

The positive NPV gives the appearance of a viable project; but in most practical situations there are uncertainties. You often find that the various elements aren't sure figures. Instead, they represent the mean or most likely outcomes from a range of possibilities.

For example, the figure of 100 unit sales per year is a forecast. Actual sales in any one year could be above or below that number. A sensitivity analysis would seek to give an impression of what the overall outcome of the project might be with a range of alternative annual unit sales results. For example, it might be judged that a worst-case scenario would be annual sales of 90 units and a best-case scenario would be 110 units. The three alternative outcomes would therefore be:

Case	Unit sales	NPV
Worst	90	−391
Forecast	100	277
Best	110	945

The sensitivity of the project to annual unit sales can be represented graphically (see Figure 1). The graph provides the following insights:

- Around 70 per cent of possible outcomes in the range of 90 to 110 annual unit sales give a positive NPV.
- Annual sales of 96 units or greater are required to give a positive NPV.

Presenting the sensitivity analysis in this way gives an impression of the dynamics of the situation, but it's still an imperfect one. For one thing, it's likely that results outside the range

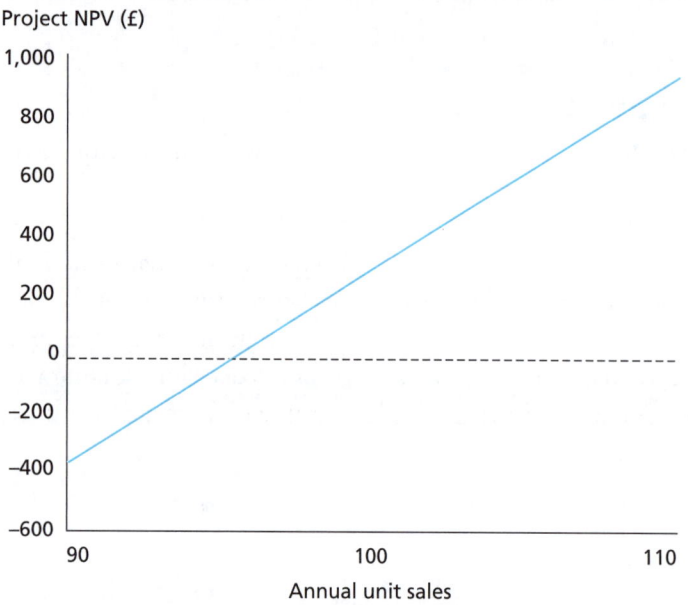

Figure 1 Sensitivity to unit sales

		NPV (£)	% change
Base case		277	–
With 2.5% adverse variances			
Initial capital cost	£4,100.00	177	−36.10
Selling price per unit	£58.50	−124	−144.77
Variable cost per unit	£35.88	43	−84.48
Fixed cost per year	£922.50	217	−21.66
Units sold per year	97.50	110	−60.29

Figure 2 The impact of 2.5 per cent adverse variances in each project element

of 90 to 110 unit sales are possible. For another, it's unlikely that annual unit sales are the only uncertain element.

It is possible that all elements are uncertain. You might conduct a sensitivity analysis to get an idea of which of them gives rise to the greatest uncertainty in the overall outcome. For example, you could consider the impact on the project's NPV of a 2.5 per cent adverse variance in each element in turn. So NPV is recalculated with an initial capital cost of £4,100 (i.e. £4,000 × 1.025) with all other factors held constant and so on. The resultant NPVs can be seen in Figure 2.

This process gives the following insights:

- A relatively small proportional change in any one of the elements produces a much larger change in the overall outcome.
- The viability of the project is more vulnerable to some key variables than it is to others. The NPV of this project seems particularly sensitive to unit selling price, given that a 2.5 per cent adverse variance in this element causes a 144 per cent adverse variance in NPV.

It may be possible to re-engineer a project in some way to alter its risk/return profile. For example, customers might be prepared at the outset to contract for £59.50 as a fixed selling price, but guarantee to buy the units. In this scenario the expected project NPV would drop from £277 to £143. The expected return would fall, but a major source of uncertainty affecting its viability would be eliminated.

You may also be faced with a choice between alternative methods of achieving given objectives. Where there are key variables, sensitivity analysis can help here as well. For example, say you need to provide a given standard of service for a five-year period and there are two ways of achieving this:

- A high-capital approach involving the purchase of equipment that cost £14,000 and has a residual value of £1,400. This methods uses 200 resource units annually.
- A low-capital approach involving the purchase of equipment that costs £2,800 and has a disposal cost of £1,200. This uses 360 resource units.

The cost of capital is 10 per cent. There is uncertainty surrounding the likely average cost of a resource unit over the term, but it will lie somewhere between £10 and £30.

A sensitivity analysis will offer useful insights in this case. You can project the NPV of costs at alternative resource unit prices as follows:

£ per unit	High cap	Low cap
10	20,712	17,192
15	24,503	24,015
20	28,294	30,839
25	32,085	37,662
30	35,875	44,486

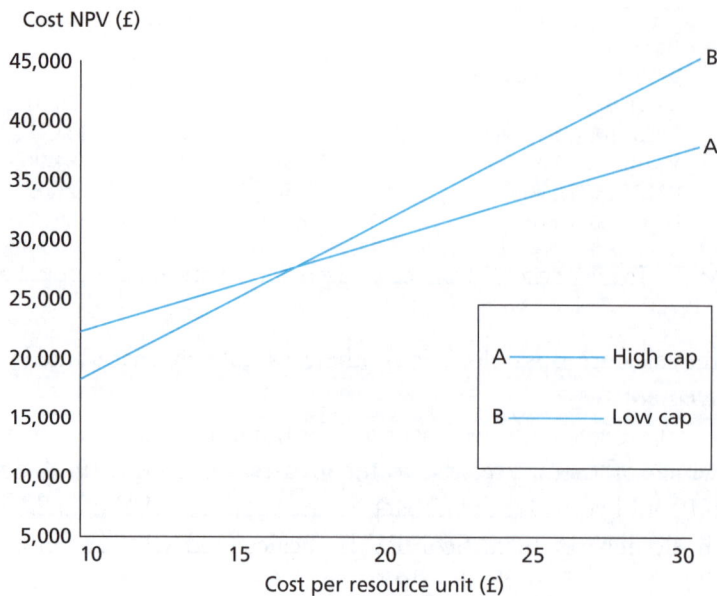

Figure 3 Sensitivity to resource costs

The sensitivity of the project to resource costs can also be represented graphically (see Figure 3). The insights revealed by this analysis include:

- The high-capital approach offers a cheaper solution in about 70 per cent of the possible unit price outcomes, including the mean figure of £20 per unit.
- The low-capital approach offers a cheaper solution only if the unit price is below £16. Even in the case of the lowest price (£10 per unit) the difference between the two approaches is only around £3,500.

Purely on the basis of the information given, you would probably choose the high capital approach, but the process of using sensitivity analysis may distort decision-making. When considering issues related to risk and uncertainty, decision-makers commonly make certain working assumptions. One of these is that, in conditions of uncertainty, the probability distribution of possible project outcomes is grouped symmetrically around a mean and most likely outcome. Indeed, many business projects are like that. The sensitivity analysis in this case uses a unit price of £20 as the median position, so you may be inclined to assume this is the expected result, and that outcomes close to this figure are more likely than ones remote from it. If you run projects often enough, you might expect the median to be the average outcome.

Sensitivity analysis tends to focus on ranges of possible outcomes without considering the probabilities of different results within them. It may be that outcomes at one extreme of the range are actually more likely than ones in the centre. In this case, the low-capital approach may be preferable if there is a high probability that resource unit prices will be at the lower end of the range.

Business decision-making is an art form. Sensitivity analysis is a general approach that can give decision-makers powerful insights into the problem they are confronting, but it is not a technique that can provide the solution to that problem.

Postscript

Now you should have a sound understanding of how sensitivity analysis helps managers to focus on the critical variables in a project appraisal.

The following article takes the analysis of uncertainty a step further. It considers the possibility that the rate of return on a project can vary from year to year *within* the life of a project, i.e. the annual rate of return does not remain constant for the whole duration of a project.

The article demonstrates the Monte Carlo distribution that you met earlier in this text, which helps with the analysis of risk.

Tools for dealing with uncertainty

Excerpted with permission from Management Accounting published by the Institute of Management Accounts, Montvale, NJ. For more information about reprints contact PARS International Corp. at +1-212-221-9595.

Sophisticated spreadsheet software incorporating probability functions can help you forecast more accurately.

Aside from the proverbial death and taxes, there is little in life that is certain. As management accountants, we recognise that one of our most crucial uncertainties involves capital investments. Why, then, are so many of us still using analysis tools designed for fixed numbers?

Let's take a simple example. Your company is considering a $1 million capital investment. The project is expected to return 12 per cent per year, with the annual profits reinvested annually.

What will be your final compounded return at the end of 20 years?

If you are like most management accountants, you will use the traditional compounding formula (multiplying your initial investment times one plus the rate of return raised to the 20th power). This time-honored analysis approach tells you that your final compounded return should be $9,646,293. But is this the best answer?

Unfortunately, it is not – at least for most capital investment projects. The compounding formula works well for investments in which the annual rate of return is fixed. But this is not the situation with most capital investments. While the initial outlay may be a fairly firm number, the annual rate of return most likely will vary from year to year. Thus, this project might yield a 25 per cent (or higher) return in a good year and a 0 per cent return (or even a loss) in another year. Even a relatively safe capital investment (say, a market rate financial instrument) can involve variable rates of return.

But the compounding formula operates as though the rate of return is exactly 12 per cent for all 20 years, with no variability. Because the formula has no way of recognising the uncertainty in the annual rates of return, it may not be providing the best answer.

The most popular capital budgeting tools (the compounding formula, the internal rate of return, and net present value calculations) are simple to use and can be handled with little more than a pocket calculator. But they all suffer from a major drawback: they provide a single-number answer by assuming that their input is a set of fixed or known numbers, with no provision for variability.

A popular way of dealing with uncertainty: sensitivity analyses

One way of providing for uncertainty is to rerun the calculations several times using different fixed values. Today's computerised spreadsheets make it easy to play 'what-if' games. By changing the numbers and re-performing the calculations, we can generate various possible outcomes. Comparing these different outcomes generally provides a better analysis than merely looking at a single point estimate.

Continuing our example above, a modern analyst would use the compounding formula to arrive at the $9,646,293 figure and also to provide alternative possibilities from the what-if analyses, showing the effect of changing the estimated rate of return from 12 per cent to, say, 10 per cent or 14 per cent. By reporting multiple possible final values, the analyst is providing more and better information than by reporting a single point estimate. The name for this technique is 'sensitivity analysis.' This approach provides a much more realistic means of analysing uncertain situations than simply using the compounding formula alone, but it still uses analysis tools that operate on only one set of numbers at a time. The fact remains that no matter how many times we rerun the calculations, the formula still operates as though the rate of return is constant throughout all 20 years of the project's life. Ideally, our analysis should employ a tool that incorporates the possible changes from year to year in the annual rate of return. Even more important, we need to know the probability of earning different amounts from our project, not just a list of some possible amounts.

A better way: probability distribution

Statisticians tell us that the law of large numbers applies to most situations involving uncertainty and that variable numbers tend to cluster around a central value or mean. Financial research has shown that annual rates of return on most modern investments do indeed form a 'normal distribution' around a mean. Values close to the mean occur with greater frequency than values farther away from the mean. If you can establish a reasonable estimate of the mean and have some idea of the range of possible realistic values, you generally can get by with handling your uncertainty as a probability distribution.

Traditional analysis tools (the compounding formula in our example) yield a single point estimate of the project's final value (see Figure 1). If we were to use the formula by itself, our analysis would show that the project will return exactly $9,646,293. Most management accountants, however, recognise the uncertainty and report several different possible outcomes, assuming that the most likely final values will centre around $9,646,293. Values far away from this figure will be unlikely, while values close to it will be more likely. The analyst even may illustrate the relative likelihood of the different outcomes with such a probability distribution as that in Figure 2.

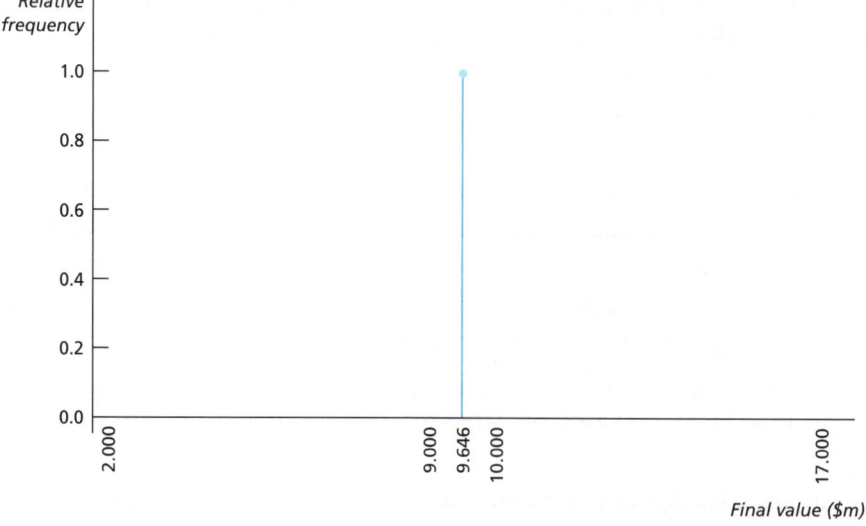

Figure 1 Formula estimate

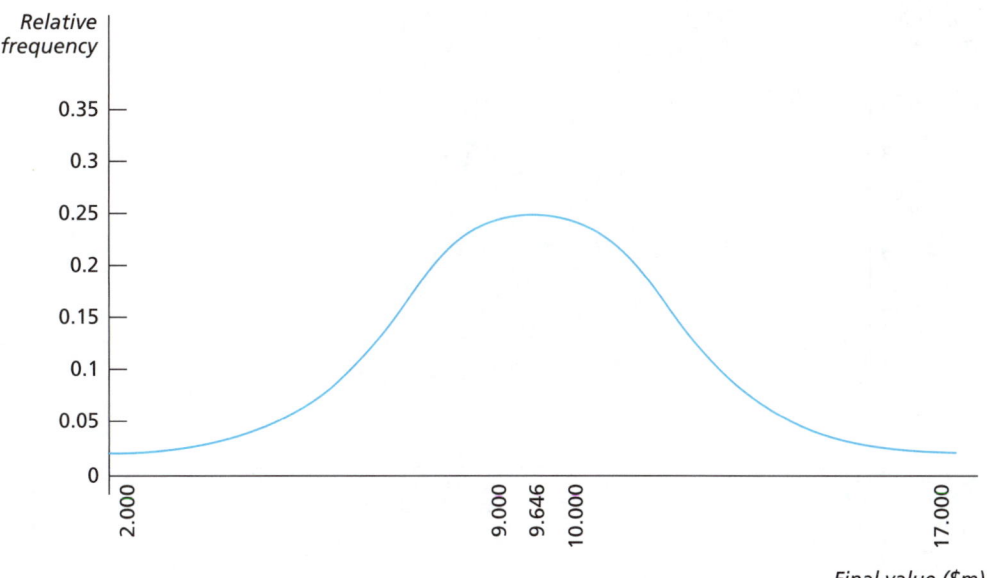

Figure 2 Normal distribution

Figure 2 is superior to Figure 1 in that it shows relative likelihood of many possible final values ranging from a very unlikely $2 million figure all the way up to an equally unlikely $17 million. The most likely values, however, are close to $9,646,293. And most analysts assume that the probability curve is symmetric, as shown in Figure 2. In other words, they assume the chances of earning slightly less than the projected amount are about the same as the chances of earning slightly more than the projected amount.

But is this the case? Assuming the rate of return does average 12 per cent over the life of the project, are the chances of slightly underperforming the estimate the same as the chances of slightly outperforming it? It might surprise you to learn that Figure 3 is actually a more accurate illustration of the likely final values of our project!

Surprises from modern analysis tools

Figure 3 reveals some startling new information about our project. First, the most probable final value (represented by the peak of the probability curve) is not the $9,646,293 predicted by the traditional analysis formula! Rather, it is somewhat less. From looking at Figure 3, you see that it is more likely that our project's final value will be approximately $9 million rather than the approximately $9.6 million reported by the traditional analysis approach.

Management accountants and financial analysts who have for years relied on the formulae are astounded to see this increase in the likelihood of underperforming the formula estimate. But even more surprising is the fact that the probability distribution is not symmetric. For example, the chances of the project yielding half a million dollars less than the $9,646,293 are actually much greater (perhaps two or three times as great) than the chances of earning half a million dollars more than that amount. In other words, while the chance of slightly underperforming the formula's prediction has increased, the chance of outperforming the formula's prediction by the same amount has gone down quite dramatically. Also, the probability of 'losing one's shirt' has diminished somewhat, while the probability of making much more than the formula estimate has increased.

What causes these surprising results? The answer lies in the fact that the rate of return can vary from year to year. Each year's earnings are dependent not only on that single year's

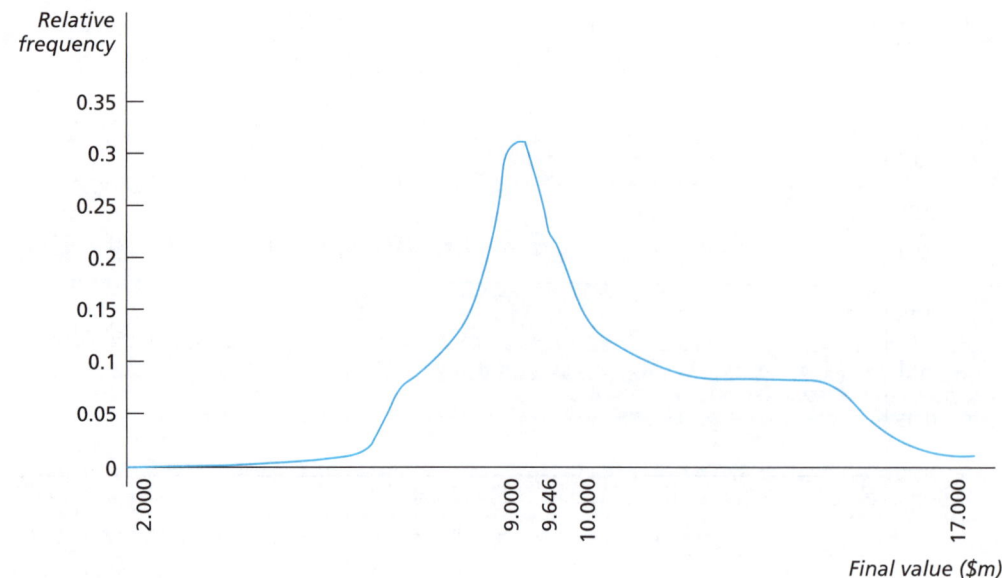

Figure 3 Monte Carlo distribution

rate of return, but also on all previous years' rates, because the project involves compounding reinvestment. Thus, if you assume that the rate of return averages 12 per cent annually over the course of the 20-year project, and you assume that the changes occur in accordance with the law of large numbers (specifically, in accordance with a normal probability distribution from year to year), you still come up with the skewed probability curve for the final value of the project shown in Figure 3 because of the changing rates of return. (For an explanation of this phenomenon, see 'Some Surprising Statistics', below.)

SOME SURPRISING STATISTICS

When using analysis models that approximate reality, surprising results sometimes emerge. Take the probability distribution of our compound investment's final value. Most people, including many financial analysts, would assume that if the annual rate of return varies in a normal (and symmetric) fashion across the 20-year life of the project, then the possible final values also should vary in a symmetric pattern. This makes intuitive sense. But it isn't what actually happens.

Consider closely the value of the investment at the end of the first year. The exact rate of return during that year is unknown, but it will vary around a 12 per cent expected value. If we expect the rate of return to vary in a normal fashion, at the end of the first year we will have a range of possible final values that will be centered around $1.12 million (for our $1 million original investment). This probability distribution is symmetric because it is the product of a fixed amount (the original investment) multiplied by a normal probability distribution (the rate of return).

Most things change in the second year, though. This time, we are not multiplying a constant by a normal distribution. We are multiplying one normal distribution (the final value at the end of the first year) by another normal distribution. It yields a skewed, asymmetric distribution known in statistical circles as a log-normal distribution.

The skewness of the probability distribution becomes even more pronounced in the third year, and the symmetry continues to degrade as more and more compounding periods are added. By the 20th year, you have the noticeably asymmetric distribution shown in Figure 3. The unusual shape of the distribution curve and the probabilities associated with each of the possible outcomes of the project derive directly from the compounding of the investment. Once the initial investment is made, all future values are unknown figures. Using probability distributions to illustrate these unknown values is a more accurate approach than simply treating them as fixed estimates. Therefore, the asymmetric probability of the project's final value is a better predictor of the project's performance than a perfectly symmetric curve fitted around the traditional financial formula's output.

Sophisticated tools, but easy to use

Probability curves such as Figure 3 can give a much more accurate picture of the likely outcome of projects under uncertainty. These analyses can be generated by a little-used analysis tool that is included in most of today's modern spreadsheet software. This tool enables us to create mathematical models that more closely approximate real-life situations involving uncertainty.

As our capital budgeting problem involves an uncertain annual rate of return that varies from year to year, we must develop an analysis model with a rate of return that varies from year to year. In addition, we need to analyse many different combinations of these varying annual rates of return.

Until a few years ago, creating such a model required extensive computer programming, weeks of effort, and significant time on a large mainframe or minicomputer. Today, though, with the recent advances in personal computers, including larger memory capacities, faster and more powerful numerical processors, and advanced software, we now have the ability to build such mathematical models on our desktops in a matter of minutes.

The tools necessary to construct probability distributions can be found on all of the popular Windows-based spreadsheets – Lotus 1-2-3, Excel, Supercalc, and Quattro-Pro. Specific instructions vary from package to package, but they are contained in the On-Line Help features. Look for Help topics involving random number generators, probability distributions, and statistical tools.

To analyse our sample problem properly, we begin by constructing a spreadsheet showing how the project's returns will be reinvested (Figure 4). But instead of the 12 per cent

Year	Rate of return	Final value
1	12.00%	$1,120,000
2	12.00%	$1,254,000
3	12.00%	$1,404,928
4	12.00%	$1,573,519
5	12.00%	$1,762,342
6	12.00%	$1,973,823
7	12.00%	$2,210,681
8	12.00%	$2,475,963
9	12.00%	$2,773,079
10	12.00%	$3,105,848
11	12.00%	$3,478,550
12	12.00%	$3,895,976
13	12.00%	$4,363,493
14	12.00%	$4,887,112
15	12.00%	$5,473,566
16	12.00%	$6,130,394
17	12.00%	$6,866,041
18	12.00%	$7,689,966
19	12.00%	$8,612,762
20	12.00%	$9,646,293

Figure 4

Year	Rate of return	Final value
1	11.30%	$1,113,000
2	12.10%	$1,247,673
3	13.30%	$1,413,614
4	14.10%	$1,612,933
5	9.00%	$1,758,097
6	10.00%	$1,933,907
7	13.00%	$2,185,315
8	15.50%	$2,524,038
9	16.50%	$2,940,505
10	14.00%	$3,352,175
11	14.50%	$3,838,241
12	8.00%	$4,145,300
13	11.00%	$4,601,283
14	7.00%	$4,923,373
15	10.30%	$5,430,480
16	13.10%	$6,141,873
17	11.50%	$6,848,188
18	9.50%	$7,498,766
19	14.20%	$8,563,591
20	12.05%	$9,595,504

Figure 5

annual rate of return for all 20 years, we want to substitute a variable rate of return, one that is expected to average 12 per cent over the 20 years. Because we assume the rates of return will average 12 per cent and might vary between 0 per cent and 25 per cent, we can say that, in any one year, the rate of return will come from a normal distribution with a mean of 12 per cent and a standard deviation of about 6 per cent. We use the computer's random number generator to draw 20 values from a distribution with a mean of 12 and a standard deviation of 6. Then we incorporate these values as the assumed rate of return for each of our 20 years. This approach gives us one possible outcome of our capital project. In other words, if it just so happens that the annual rates of return come out as shown in Figure 5, then our project's final value will be $9,595,504.

The particular combination of annual rates of return shown in Figure 5 is only one of many possible combinations. We also must look at others. In fact, we need to duplicate the scenario many times (a technique known as Monte Carlo analysis) to represent the many different combinations of annual rates of return. By constructing hundreds, or even thousands, of possible combinations and then displaying a histogram of the final outcomes, we begin to get a feel for the likely performance of our project.

There are numerous add-in products on the market that enhance the major spreadsheet packages, making it easy to perform thousands of Monte Carlo scenarios. These software products are surprisingly easy to learn and operate, especially for users already familiar with the Windows point-and-click system. One such package, known as @RISK, is able to perform 1,000 iterations of the above scenario with only a few keystrokes. Therefore, the calculation of 2,000 scenarios of our capital budgeting problem can be performed in less than three minutes on a 486 computer. Furthermore, most of the packages automatically display the histogram upon completion of their calculations, giving you an instant picture of the likely outcomes of your investment.

More problem solving

This same technique (drawing numbers from a probability distribution and constructing a histogram of the final outcomes) can be used to simulate the uncertainty of discount rates for net present value analysis. It also can be used to simulate the uncertainty surrounding cash flow amounts, future revenues, and expenses. Yet another use for it might involve modeling possible changes in tax rates or inflation rates – or almost any uncertain figure. All that is needed is some idea (or assumption) about the possible behaviour of the uncertain value, such as its expected average and likely variability. Often the assumption can be simply the one that would have been used in the formula analysis, coupled with the estimated rate of variability over time.

By constructing a model that resembles the real situation more closely, you can see that the likely outcome of a capital project may be very different from what you normally would expect, based on the traditional analysis output. The likelihood of doing very poorly, fairly well, or extremely well on a given project may surprise you and other decision makers. A realistic probability distribution requires additional information, which cannot be provided by the traditional analysis tools. This information even may affect management's decision in some situations (see 'Good News, Bad News', below.) Regardless, it always is better to provide management with the best information possible.

GOOD NEWS, BAD NEWS: WHAT THE PICTURE TELLS US

Figure 3 is a much more accurate portrayal of our project's expected performance. Most important, it presents some new information that might make a difference in the decision as to whether to accept or reject the project. Let's take a close look at exactly what this new tool is telling us that we didn't know before. To make the comparison, we will use the compounding formula's predicted value ($9,646,293) as a base because it is the figure that most analysts would have presented to management.

First, as mentioned in the text, the probability of the project's value coming in slightly under the base is much higher than the probability of hitting the base or of hitting any other possible value. Some managers may consider it misleading to say that the project likely will return $9,646,293 when, in fact, the most probable return is less than this amount.

More significant, the chance of slightly outperforming the base by a given amount is much less than the probability of slightly underperforming the base by the same amount. Again, managers may consider it misleading to quote the $9,646,293 figure when the chances of making a million less than this figure may be two or three times the likelihood of making a million more than the figure.

The bad news, then, is that the project probably will slightly underperform the base estimate and probably will not slightly overperform the base estimate. But wait! There is some good news, too.

Look at the ends of the curve

The possibility of losing your shirt on the investment has almost disappeared compared with the chance of making a killing. In other words, the possibility of coming out far under the base prediction is extremely low, compared with the chance of outperforming the base by the same large amount. Managers who don't mind the risk of slightly underperforming the base prediction but who want to avoid an extremely low final value – especially if it means a chance at yielding an extremely high final value – might be more inclined to accept the project if they had access to this probability distribution. In short, decision makers find the probability distribution analysis a much richer source of information than the traditional sensitivity analysis using common capital budgeting techniques.

There is still uncertainty

Of course, any time we try to predict the future, we are dealing with unknown information. Modern analysis tools are only as good as the input with which they are provided. We will continue to encounter problems trying to estimate future returns' means and their variability. But for a given set of input information, these sophisticated tools can greatly expand the richness of information provided as output.

Remember: the traditional capital budgeting tools may be providing your decision makers with misleading figures regarding the likely performance of your investment projects. A much better tool would be one that enables you to construct a mathematical model that depicts the actual situation more accurately, including year-to-year variations.

With the advent of powerful spreadsheet software incorporating statistical probability functions, it now is feasible to perform analyses that portray the real situation more accurately. By using these more sophisticated models, you can do a much better job of forecasting the likelihood of possible outcomes, which can lead to your making better decisions for your company.

1. Note that the annual rates of return in Figure 5 do indeed average 12 per cent across the 20-year life of the project and that the final value is less than the $9,646,293 predicted by the formula. This is in line with the probability curve shown in Figure 3, which predicts that final values slightly less than the $9,646,293 will occur with greater frequency than amounts slightly above it.

Postscript

If you can, try to obtain access to a spreadsheet package and use it to construct probability distributions like the ones in this article. This will help you to gain a more practical understanding of how random number generators, probability distributions and the various statistical tools can improve the quality and usefulness of the information presented to management.

P2 Management Accounting Decision Management

Learning Outcomes (for the two articles): A1, B10, C4, D3

Synopsis

In this article, Tim Thompson introduces an imaginary case of a company that has a tricky short-term quality problem. At the end of this article, students are invited to prepare their own answers to a requirement based upon the case. In a second article, to be published shortly, Tim will offer his solution to this requirement. A key message is that, when dealing with a short-term problem, we should be mindful of our organisation's longer term objectives.

The AGJ Case: Bayes's Theorem and the Issue of Quality (1)

AGJ supplies a product called the 'Pool Heater' and sells it to local authorities, country clubs and private householders. As the name suggests, this product is used to heat the water in swimming pools that are owned by these customers. AGJ buys various components from suppliers and assembles these into the finished product. A key stated policy within AGJ is its commitment to quality.

Each pool heater contains a critical component named 'Component Y'. It is company policy source all critical components from two separate suppliers and, when the company was formed, AGJ began obtaining Component Y from both HKP and PQR.

Unfortunately, 6 months after AGJ was formed, HKP went out of business and immediately ceased to supply Component Y. However, AGJ managed to obtain additional supplies from PQR and, as a result, was able to meet all of its customer demand. Subsequently, AGJ found a new supplier (XYZ) to ensure that its dual sourcing policy was continued.

Some 6 months after HKP failed, there was a board meeting at AGJ and the directors spent much time complimenting each other on how well they had managed the switch to the new supplier. They were particularly pleased that all of the stock originally supplied by HKP had been used in assembly and that the associated Pool Heaters had all been sold.

A week later, however, AGJ was in turmoil. A former employee of HKP had 'blown the whistle' and notified AGJ as follows:

1. For the year prior to going out of business, HKP had failed to inspect any of the Component Y that it had manufactured and shipped to its customers. This was a cost-cutting measure taken when it was clear that HKP was in financial difficulty.
2. Before this cost-cutting exercise, HKP had inspected all such components and scrapped any that were found to be faulty. On average, 3 per cent of these components were found to be faulty by this inspection process.
3. The inspection was an industry-standard process, but it did not detect all faulty components. In common with the rest of the industry, 0.5 per cent of the components that were sent to customers still subsequently failed.

A further AGJ board meeting was immediately convened and the following extracts were recorded in the verbatim minutes:

Managing Director

'This is a nightmare. If any of the products that we have sold include a faulty Component Y then we know that this will eventually cause the Pool Heater to fail. We give a 5 year guarantee on these products and we are committed to rectifying any faults that occur.

I cannot imagine what will be the cost to us in terms of our damaged reputation, but we need to begin by knowing something about the costs of putting any failed Pool Heaters back into operation.'

Technical Director

'We already knew about the industry-standard failure rate of 0.5 per cent and were expecting this to arise for both the PQR and the HKP supplied components. We have not yet had any Component Y failures in the Pool Heaters that we have sold but we anticipate that any failures that do occur will begin to arise in about 3 months' time.'

Production Director

'We certainly do not inspect these components ourselves. This would be a non value-added activity and, anyway, we do not have the technology needed to carry out such inspection. A 0.5% failure rate is very low and we should be able to live with the consequences of any failures that do occur at this level.'

Technical Director

'If a Component Y does fail, then it will need to be replaced with a new one costing $100. But to do this would require an emergency visit by a service engineer. It would take an average of three hours to travel to and from the customer and to carry out the repair. As you will recall, we have previously established that the opportunity cost of these service engineers is $50 per hour.

But the problem is not that simple; when a failure occurs, it is not just a matter of replacing the faulty Component Y. These pool heaters have water running through them and if the component fails, then water will leak out and create all sorts of damage to our customers' premises or homes. We have previously researched this in some detail and we estimate that, on average, we would have to pay a further $500 for each Component Y failure to clear up this mess and rectify the damage.

We already have in place detailed plans to deal with any such failures. The service engineer will identify whether it was HKP or PQR that supplied the faulty component and we will keep detailed records of all of the costs that we incur. With the guarantees provided by the suppliers, we expected to recharge these costs in full to the supplier. So, although we guarantee the product, at the end of the day it is the supplier, not us, that should pay for the fault and its consequences. The problem that we now have, of course, is that we cannot make such a recharge to HKP since it has gone out of business. We will have to bear that cost ourselves and I am very worried that I will be held accountable in the future for some significant adverse cost variances.'

Sales and Marketing Director

'If the number of failed components is to be as great as we are now expecting, then I agree that this will cost us even more in terms of our reputation; we could lose future sales as the result of this. I think that we should look at ways of eliminating, or at least minimising, this danger. All of our customers will be visited within the next 3 months by our service engineers for routine maintenance of the Pool Heaters. At these visits, could we inspect the Component Y in all of the Pool Heaters concerned? If we did this, then we could replace all of the ones found to be faulty. With luck, we might complete this before any of the components actually do fail.'

Production Director

'The greater risk is clearly with the components supplied by HKP. Unfortunately, we don't keep records of which supplier's components were assembled into which pool heater – this is information that we have never been asked to provide. What we do know is that we have assembled and sold a total of 4,000 pool heaters since we started the business. Our purchasing records show that, of the 4,000 Component Y that we purchased, 2,500 were obtained from HKP and 1,500 from PQR.'

Finance Director

'Carrying out this inspection during the routine maintenance visits would mean that there would be no additional travelling costs. The only relevant costs would be a) the purchase of replacement components for each one found to be faulty, b) the extra time that the service engineers would need to spend on the inspection and replacement activities, and c) the cost of providing any testing equipment.'

Technical Director

'I already have some figures here. Replacing a Component Y is one of the standard operations for which the service engineers are trained; each one should take 30 minutes.

However, if we are going to carry out this inspection, then we do need some special testing equipment. For a cost of $20,000 (in total, not per engineer), we can equip all of our engineers with a device that can be taken on site to test the Component Y. If the component proves to be faulty, then it can be replaced. This testing will take about 15 minutes for each Pool Heater. These testing devices are 100% reliable and will detect all faulty components. This testing would also detect those faulty components that we were planning to accept within the 0.5% normal failure rate. It would also ensure that any components that we use as on-site replacements are not faulty.'

Finance Director

'I think that we are in a position to evaluate the alternatives that we face. We seem to have three choices here.

We could take the 'passive' approach. This would involve waiting for any failures to occur and dealing with them as they happen.

Alternatively, there are two possible 'active' approaches and both of these involve the service engineers inspecting all of the Pool Heaters concerned and making replacements as required. The first of these would be to launch an immediate programme of special visits by the engineers and the second would be to carry out this activity at the routine maintenance visits.

I think that the first key issue here is to determine how many Component Y we might reasonably expect to fail. We also need to determine the likelihood that, if a Component Y is found to be faulty, it was supplied by HKP as opposed to PQR. This is important as the financial consequences to us for each of these suppliers' components is radically different. I recall from my CIMA studies that Bayes's Theorem may be of help here. Using this, I should be able to calculate some expected values to determine the estimated costs of the alternatives and this should help us to make our decision.'

Managing Director

'I don't think that the first of your 'active' approaches is feasible. We simply do not have enough service engineers to commit to such an extensive additional exercise. You had better focus your attention on a comparison of your 'passive' approach with the second of your 'active' approaches.

Please get to work on this straight away and let me know when you have prepared your figures. We will reconvene this board meeting tomorrow and make a decision as to what we will do about this.'

At that point, the board meeting was adjourned and the Finance Director returned to his office. He prepared himself for a long night's work, but by the early evening he had prepared some draft notes ready to edit into his formal paper for the board.

Requirement

Imagine that you are the Finance Director of AGJ and prepare draft notes to address the following:

1. Evaluate the numerical data in this case and, based upon this alone, recommend whether the company should adopt the 'active' or the 'passive' approach to solve the problem.
2. Demonstrate how Bayes's Theorem may be useful in evaluating the data in the case.
3. Discuss the longer term issues of quality that the company should consider and comment on whether this might affect the recommendation that you made in 1. above.

A specimen solution to this case will be published in a forthcoming article.

Synopsis

In his previous article, Tim Thompson introduced an imaginary case of a company that had a tricky short-term quality problem. At the end of that article, students were invited to assume the role of the Finance Director of AGJ and to prepare draft notes to address the following:

1. Evaluate the numerical data in this case and, based upon this alone, recommend whether the company should adopt the 'active' or the 'passive' approach to solve the problem.
2. Demonstrate how Bayes's Theorem may be useful in evaluating the data in the case.
3. Discuss the longer-term issues of quality that the company should consider and comment on whether this might affect the recommendation that you made in 1. above.

In this second article, Tim offers his solution to this requirement. A key message is that, when dealing with a short-term problem, we should be mindful of our organisation's longer term objectives.

The AGJ Case: Bayes's Theorem and the Issue of Quality (2)

In the previous article, we introduced an imaginary company called AGJ that makes Pool Heaters for supply to local authorities, country clubs and private householders. AGJ was faced with a serious quality problem resulting from potentially faulty components in its installed products and this was compounded by the recent corporate failure of one of its suppliers of these components. We left the case with a fraught board meeting having been adjourned and the Finance Director returning to his office to prepare a paper to be considered by the board when it convened the following day.

Here are the draft notes that the Finance Director prepared.

Draft Notes

We do not currently know, for any one of our customers, whether the Component Y was originally supplied by HKP or PQR. What we do know is that for any one customer:

P(Component Y was sourced from HKP) = 2,500/4,000 = 0.625 = 62.5%
P(Component Y was sourced from PQR) = 1,500/4,000 = 0.375 = 37.5%

We are all familiar with the multiplication rule (otherwise known as the 'and' rule) in probability. This states that to calculate the probability of two events both occurring, we multiply their respective probabilities. (This assumes, of course, that the two events are not mutually exclusive.)

With this theoretical insight, we can apply Bayes's Theorem to AGJ's Pool Heater component problem. There is an expectation that 0.5% of the components will fail anyway.

Over and above this, we can expect that 3% of the remaining components that have been supplied by HKP will also be faulty.

Of course, we do not know for certain how many faulty components have been supplied to AGJ. If we were really lucky, then this could be zero; with all of the faulty components being supplied to HKP's and PQR's other customers. If we were really unlucky, though, then we might have received all of these suppliers' faulty components. The first thing to do is to calculate an expected value (EV) of the number of these faulty components that will have found their way into our Pool Heaters. Once we have analysed this 'most likely' figure for the total faulty components, then we should also consider one optimistic scenario and one that is pessimistic. Let's use $+/-$ 20% for these two alternative scenarios.

Of the components supplied by PQR, then we expect that 0.5% will prove to be faulty.

We would originally have expected that this would also be the case for components supplied by HKP. But now we know that we should also expect 3% of the remaining HKP components to be faulty too. So the probability of an HKP component being faulty is

$$0.5\% + (99.5\% \times 3\%) = 0.5\% + 2.985\% = 3.485\%$$

There are four possible circumstances in respect of each installed Pool Heater and these can be represented diagrammatically as follows.

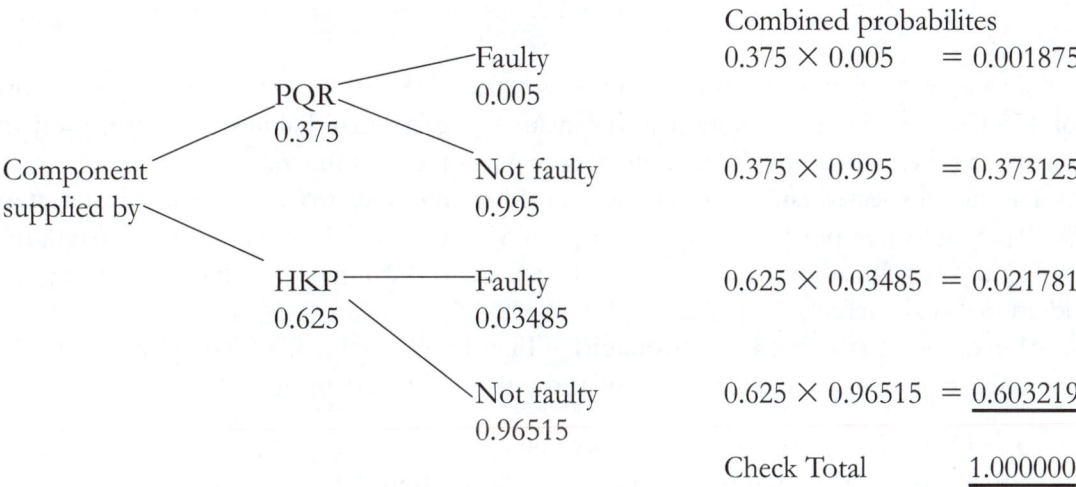

Using Bayes's Theorem, we can ask the following question:

'If a component is found to be faulty, what is the likelihood that it was originally sourced from HKP and what is the probability that it was sourced from PQR?'

To answer this, we can construct the following diagram. This simply reverses the sequence from the above 'supplier then whether faulty', to 'whether faulty then supplier'.

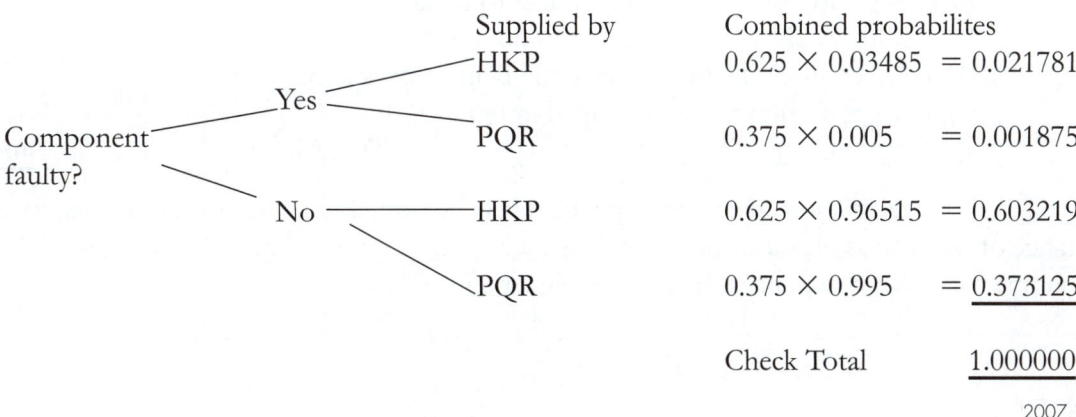

From this, we can deduce that the probability of a component being faulty is 0.021781 + 0.001875 = 0.023656 i.e. 2.3656% (and the probability that it is not faulty is 97.6344%).

Furthermore, if we find that a component is faulty, then the probability that it was supplied by HKP is 0.021781 / 0.023656 = 92.0739% (and the probability that it was supplied by PQR is 7.9261%).

Thus, from the total of 4,000 components Y that have been installed, we can estimate that 2.3656% will be faulty i.e. 95 to the nearest whole number. Of this 95, we estimate that 87 (i.e. 92.0739% of them) will have been supplied by HKP and 8 (i.e. 7.9261%) will have been supplied by PQR.

Alternative Courses of Action and their Costs

Alternative 1 (the 'passive' approach) – do nothing now, wait for any faults to arise and deal with them at that time

Each fault in a HKP sourced component will result in the following costs all of which are irrecoverable:

Purchase replacement component	$100
Service engineer's time (3 hours at $50)	$150
Cost of damage to customer's premises	$500
Total	$750

Since we are expecting 87 faulty components from HKP, this would result in a total cost of $750 × 87 = $65,250. (Note that this includes the 'normal' failures; there is no way of recharging these costs and they are an integral part of our problem.)

The eight expected faults in the PQR-sourced components would also result in a cost of $750 per faulty component. However, this would be dealt with by recharging the cost in full to PQR. Thus, ignoring the wider issue of damage to our reputation, there will be no net additional costs here.

Alternative 2 (the 'active' approach) – Inspect all of the 4,000 components during routine servicing visits and replace all of those that are found to be faulty

a) One-off cost to obtain the testing equipment	$20,000
b) Labour cost of testing each of the 4,000 components during planned maintenance: 0.25 hours × $50 per hour × 4,000 components =	$50,000
c) Labour cost of replacing faulty components supplied by HKP: 0.5 hours × $50 per hour × 87 components =	$2,175
d) Purchase 87 new components at $100 each =	$8,700
e) Labour cost of testing these 87 new components (for simplicity, assume that none prove to be faulty) 0.25 hours × $50 per hour × 87 components =	$1,088
f) All costs connected with replacing the faulty components supplied by PQR; assume recharged in full to PQR	NIL
TOTAL	$81,963

The above calculations represent the most likely outcome. It is also useful to consider a range of other possible outcomes. As discussed earlier, let's look at the consequences of the number of failed components being 20% higher and 20% lower.

For the passive approach, the total costs could be as low as $65,250 − 20% = $52,200 or as high as $65,250 + 20% = $78,300.

For the active approach, only the labour and material costs of replacing the faulty HKP components and the testing of the replacements are variable. The cost of the testing equipment and the labour costs of testing the installed components are fixed. These variable costs total $2,175 + $8,700 + $1,088 = $11,963 and could vary by +/− 20% i.e. by +/− $2,393.

Thus the total cost of the active approach could be as low as $81,963 − $2,393 = $79,570 or as high as $81,963 + $2,393 = $84,356.

The potential costs can be tabulated as follows:

	Passive Approach ($)	Active Approach ($)
Best case	52,200	79,570
Most likely case	65,250	81,963
Worst case	78,300	84,356

The Finance Director presented the above information to the board members when they reconvened the next morning. He pointed out that, in each scenario, the expected costs of the two alternatives was clearly in favour of the 'passive' approach. Despite this, the Finance Director recommended that the 'active' approach should be taken and the rest of the board eventually agreed with him.

Why was this apparently more expensive decision taken? And what further action did the board take in respect of quality at AGJ?

With both the 'passive' and 'active' approaches described above, the company would be reacting to a quality fault that was present within products that had been made and sold. However, there is a distinction between the two approaches. The 'passive' approach represents a willingness to accept an **external failure** whereby when the fault comes to light the customer is fully aware of it. In terms of the company's reputation, this is the most damaging type of problem.

By comparison, the 'active' approach can be classified as an **appraisal**. Although the Pool Heaters concerned had been sold and were installed at customers' premises, the identification and correction of the problem products hopefully would (and, happily, did) take place without the customer witnessing a failure.

The board debated this issue at some length and decided that dealing with the problem via appraisal would be better than letting it become an external failure. They looked at the costs involved and decided that the additional short-term expenditure on the 'active' approach was worthwhile. They preferred to accept this rather than suffer the long-term damage to reputation and profits that would surely emerge if the failures were allowed to occur.

The board continued to meet regularly and made some significant decisions about quality within the company. An early decision was to make the step up from simply having a policy of 'commitment to quality' to actually doing something about it. They formed the view that any form of failure (whether internal or external) was unacceptable and they did not want the company to be involved with any costs of non-conformance. They determined that the best way to solve a problem is to prevent it happening in the first place. The next step was, therefore, to ensure that AGJ tested every Component Y that was delivered from its suppliers. This increased labour costs in the production department (but there was no need to buy any more test equipment; the devices that had been bought for the service engineers were used here). Any faulty Component Y detected at this inspection was returned to the supplier who sent a free replacement by return. Thus the company had focussed firmly on conformance rather than dealing with non-conformance.

As time went by, though, some doubts began to emerge about whether this type of 100% inspection was truly the best approach to quality. More and more, the directors became irritated that, within the industry, a 0.5% failure rate in these components was somehow perceived to be acceptable. They developed the view that the only acceptable level of quality should be 'zero defects'. They determined that all supplies of Component Y should be 100% error-free on delivery and that AGJ's own inspection of these incoming components should be abolished. AGJ approached its two suppliers of Component Y to discuss this and indicated that it was prepared to pay a premium price for this quality guarantee. In so doing, AGJ recognised that true quality only exists when there is conformance throughout the supply chain.

PQR, one of AGJ's two suppliers of Component Y, agreed to the principle of zero-defect supply and within 6 months had achieved this. XYZ, the other supplier, argued that it was achieving the industry benchmark of a 0.5% failure rate and that there was no need to discuss any improvement on this.

Only one of these two suppliers is still doing business with AGJ.

Revision Questions

Question 1

1.1 A company is evaluating a new product proposal. The proposed product selling price is £180 per unit and the variable costs are £60 per unit. The incremental cash fixed costs for the product will be £160,000 per annum. The discounted cash flow calculation results in a positive NPV:

		Cash flow	Discount rate	Present value
		£	£	£
Year 0	Initial outlay	(1,000,000)	1.000	(1,000,000)
Years 1–5	Annual cash flow	320,000	3.791	1,213,120
Year 5	Working capital released	50,000	0.621	31,050
Net present value				244,170

What is the percentage change in selling price that would result in the project having a net present value of zero?

(A) 6.7 per cent
(B) 7.5 per cent
(C) 8.9 per cent
(D) 9.6 per cent
(E) 10.5 per cent

1.2 A company has determined that the net present value of an investment project is $12,304 when using a 10% discount rate and $(3,216) when using a discount rate of 15%.

Calculate the Internal Rate of Return of the project to the nearest 1%.

(2 marks)

1.3 A company has a nominal (money) cost of capital of 18% per annum. If inflation is 6% each year, calculate the company's real cost of capital to the nearest 0.01%.

(2 marks)

Data for questions 1.4 and 1.5

A company is considering investing in a manufacturing project that would have a 3-year life span. The investment would involve an immediate cash outflow of £50,000 and have a zero residual value. In each of the 3 years, 4,000 units would be produced and sold. The contribution per unit, based on current prices, is £5. The company has an annual cost of capital of 8 per cent. It is expected that the inflation rate will be 3 per cent in each of the next 3 years.

1.4 The net present value of the project (to the nearest £500) is

- (A) £4,500
- (B) £5,000
- (C) £5,500
- (D) £6,000
- (E) £6,500

1.5 Calculate the payback period of investment A.

(2 marks)

1.6 Calculate the discounted payback period of investment B.

(3 marks)

1.7 Calculate the Internal Rate of Return (IRR) of investment C.

(3 marks)

1.8 An investment company is considering the purchase of a commercial building at a cost of £0.85m. The property would be rented immediately to tenants at an annual rent of £80,000 payable in arrears in perpetuity.

Calculate the net present value of the investment assuming that the investment company's cost of capital is 8% per annum.

Ignore taxation and inflation.

(2 marks)

1.9 A bakery produces three different sized fruit pies for sale in its shops. The pies all use the same basic ingredients. Details of the selling prices and unit costs of each pie are as follows:

	Small $ per pie	Medium $ per pie	Large $ per pie
Selling price	3.00	5.00	9.00
Ingredients	1.80	2.40	4.60
Direct labour	0.40	0.50	0.60
Variable overhead	0.30	0.50	0.80
Weekly demand (pies)	200	500	300
Fruit (kgs per pie)	0.2	0.3	0.6

The fruit used in making the pies is imported and the bakery has been told that the amount of fruit that they will be able to buy for next week is limited to 300 kgs. The bakery has established its good name by baking its pies daily using fresh fruit, so it is not possible to buy the fruit in advance.

Determine the mix of pies to be made and sold in order to maximise the bakery's contribution for next week.

(3 marks)

Question 2

A manager is evaluating a three-year project which has the following relevant pre-tax operating cashflows:

Year	1	2	3
	$'000	$'000	$'000
Sales	4,200	4,900	5,300
Costs	2,850	3,100	4,150

The project requires an investment of $2 m at the start of year 1 and has no residual value.

The company pays corporation tax on its net relevant operating cashflows at the rate of 20%. Corporation tax is payable in the same year as the net relevant pre-tax operating cashflows arise. There is no tax depreciation available on the investment.

The manager has discounted the net relevant post-tax operating cashflows using the company's post-tax cost of capital of 7% and this results in a post-tax net present value of the project of $1.018 m.

Requirements

(a) Briefly explain sensitivity analysis and how the manager may use it in the evaluation of this project. **(4 marks)**

(b) Calculate the sensitivity of the project to independent changes in
   (i) the selling price;
   (ii) the cost of capital.

(6 marks)
(Total for Question Two = 10 marks)

 ## Question 3

AVN designs and assembles electronic devices to allow transmission of audio/visual communications between the original source and various other locations within the same building. Many of these devices require a wired solution but the company is currently developing a wireless alternative. The company produces a number of different devices depending on the number of input sources and the number of output locations, but the technology used within each device is identical. AVN is constantly developing new devices which improve the quality of the audio/visual communications that are received at the output locations.

The Managing Director recently attended a conference on world class manufacturing entitled 'The extension of the value chain to include suppliers and customers' and seeks your help.

Requirements

Explain
(i) the components of the extended value chain; and

(3 marks)

(ii) how each of the components may be applied by AVN.

(7 marks)
(Total for Question Three = 10 marks)

Question 4

A group consists of three operating divisions. Divisions A and B are long established and situated at the main site using old plant and equipment. The two divisions make much use of shared facilities. Division C is recently established at an independent site using its own new equipment. The three divisions are treated as profit centres with performance assessed on the basis of 'divisional return on capital employed', calculated as follows:

$$\frac{\text{Divisional net income before tax and interest, less share of HO costs}}{\text{Share of fixed assets at book value plus share of current assets}}$$

In the case of assets or head office costs not clearly attributable to any one division, the relevant figures are apportioned between divisions on a turnover basis. The divisions are currently generating a ROCE of about 10 per cent each.

In order to improve profitability a new system of investment appraisal has been introduced requiring that all new investments should be able to show an independent ROCE (judged on the above criteria) of at least 15 per cent.

Division B proposes a new project, detailed as follows:

Cost of new dedicated equipment	£75,000 (assumed to have a 5-year life)
Working capital	£75,000
Share of old equipment	£20,000 (assumed to have an indefinite life)
Life of project	5 years
Sales per year	140 units at £390 each
Variable costs	£150 per unit
Fixed costs per year	£17,000 including depreciation

Requirements
(a) Comment on the present methods of performance appraisal and investment analysis.
(b) Comment on the viability of B's proposal in the light of the foregoing.

Question 5

A company is considering which of two mutually exclusive projects it should undertake. The finance director thinks that the project with the higher NPV should be chosen whereas the managing director thinks that the one with the higher IRR should be undertaken especially as both projects have the same initial outlay and length of life. The company anticipates a cost of capital of 10 per cent and the net cash flows of the projects are as follows:

Year	Project X £000	Project Y £000
0	(200)	(200)
1	35	218
2	80	10
3	90	10
4	75	4
5	20	3

Requirements
(a) Calculate the NPV and IRR of each project.
(b) Recommend, with reasons, which project you would undertake (if either).

(c) Explain the inconsistency in ranking of the two projects in view of the remarks of the directors.
(d) Identify the cost of capital at which your recommendation in (b) would be reversed.

Note: You might find it interesting to answer this question using a computer spreadsheet.

Question 6

You are considering the purchase of a new truck which will be required to travel 50,000 miles per year. Two suitable models are available, details of which are as follows:

- the Kam, having a life of 4 years and a price of £20,000; the running cost is initially 20p per mile but this figure will rise by 5p per mile for each year the truck is in service; a new engine will need to be fitted at a cost of £5,000 after the truck has been in service for 3 years;
- the Tru, having a life of 6 years and a price of £35,000; the running cost is initially 15p per mile but this will rise by 3p per mile for each year the truck is in service.

The cost of capital is 12 per cent.

Requirement
Explain which truck (the Kam or the Tru) should be purchased.

Question 7

Camp plc has produced and marketed sleeping bags for several years. The sleeping bags are much heavier than some of the modern sleeping bags being introduced to the market. The company is concerned about the effect this will have on its sales. Camp plc are considering investing in new technology that would enable them to produce a much lighter and more compact sleeping bag. The new machine will cost £250,000 and is expected to have a life of four years with a scrap value of £10,000. In addition an investment of £35,000 in working capital will be required initially.

The following forecast annual trading account has been prepared for the project:

	£
Sales	200,000
Materials	(40,000)
Labour	(30,000)
Variable overheads	(10,000)
Depreciation	(20,000)
Annual profit	(100,000)

The company's cost of capital is 10 per cent. Corporation tax is charged at 30 per cent and is payable quarterly, in the 7th and 10th months of the year in which the profit is earned and the 1st and 4th month of the following year. A writing-down allowance of 25 per cent on reducing balance is available on capital expenditure.

Requirement
Advise the management of Camp plc on whether they should invest in the new technology. Your recommendation should be supported with relevant calculations.

Question 8

Apex Ltd has just completed the development of a new personal alarm device. Development costs totalled £50,000 and marketing costs to date total £5,000. A market survey suggests that the optimum price for the personal alarm is £49.90, at which price 2,000 units would be sold each month.

The personal alarm market changes rapidly and the market survey indicated that the probability of demand being maintained for:

> 2 years is 0.1
> 3 years is 0.5
> 4 years is 0.4

In order to start commercial production of the new device Apex Ltd must install a new automated assembly line at a cost of £1.2 million. The assembly line can produce the required quantity of the product but cannot be used for any other purpose and has nil disposal value. Because nobody has used this type of assembly line before, its life expectancy is uncertain. The best estimate available suggests that there is a 50 per cent chance that it will last for 4 years and an equal chance that it will last for only 3 years.

The unit variable cost of the personal alarm is £20.00 and attributable fixed costs totalling £100,000, excluding depreciation, will be incurred each year the personal alarm is produced.

The cost of capital is 14 per cent per annum.

Requirements

(a) Calculate the expected net present value of going ahead with the production of the new personal alarm device.
(b) Advise the management on the viability of the project. You should:
   (i) refer to your calculations in (a) above
   (ii) include details of any assumptions made
   (iii) discuss any other factors you consider should be taken into account when making the final decision on whether to begin commercial production or not.

 Question 9

MN plc has a rolling programme of investment decisions. One of these investment decisions is to consider mutually exclusive investments A, B, and C. The following information has been produced by the investment manager.

	Investment decision A £	Investment decision B £	Investment decision C £
Initial investment	105,000	187,000	245,000
Cash inflow for A: years 1–3	48,000		
Cash inflow for B: years 1–6		48,000	
Cash inflow for C: years 1–9			48,000
Net present value (NPV) at 10 % each year	14,376	22,040	31,432
Ranking	3rd	2nd	1st
Internal rate of return (IRR)	17.5 %	14 %	13 %
Ranking	1st	2nd	3rd

Requirements

(a) Prepare a report for the management of MN plc which includes:
- a graph showing the sensitivity of the three investments to changes in the cost of capital;
- an explanation of the reasons for differences between NPV and IRR rankings – use investment A to illustrate the points you make;
- a brief summary which gives MN plc's management advice on which project should be selected.

(b) One of the directors has suggested using payback to assess the investments. Explain to him the advantages and disadvantages of using payback methods over IRR and NPV. Use the figures above to illustrate your answer.

Question 10

A company is considering the replacement of its delivery vehicle. It has chosen the vehicle that it will acquire but it now needs to decide whether the vehicle should be purchased or leased.

The cost of the vehicle is £15,000. If the company purchases the vehicle it will be entitled to claim tax depreciation at the rate of 25% per year on a reducing balance basis. The vehicle is expected to have a trade-in value of £5,000 at the end of three years.

If the company leases the vehicle, it will make an initial payment of £1,250 plus annual payments of £4,992 at the end of each of three years. The full value of each lease payment will be an allowable cost in the computation of the company's taxable profits of the year in which the payments are made.

The company pays corporation tax at the rate of 30% of its profits.

50% of the company's corporation tax is payable in the year in which profits are made and 50% in the following year. Assume that the company has sufficient profits to obtain tax relief on its acquisition of the vehicle in accordance with the information provided above.

The company's after tax cost of capital is 15% per year.

Note: Tax depreciation is not a cash cost but is allowed as a deduction in the calculation of taxable profits.

Requirement

Calculate whether the company should purchase or lease the vehicle and clearly state your recommendation to the company. **(10 marks)**

Question 11

A printing company is considering investing in new equipment which has a capital cost of £3 million. The machine qualifies for tax depreciation at the rate of 25% per year on a reducing balance basis and has an expected life of five years. The residual value of the machine is expected to be £300,000 at the end of five years.

An existing machine would be sold immediately for £400,000 if the new machine were to be bought. This existing machine has a tax written down value of £250,000.

The existing machine generates annual revenues of £4 million and earns a contribution of 40% of sales. The new machine would reduce unit variable costs to 80% of their former value and increase output capacity by 20%. There is sufficient sales demand at the existing prices to make full use of this additional capacity.

The printing company pays corporation tax on its profits at the rate of 30%, with half of the tax being payable in the year that the profit is earned and half in the following year.

The company's after tax cost of capital is 14% per year.

Requirement

(a) Evaluate the proposed purchase of the new printing machine from a financial perspective using appropriate calculations, and advise the company as to whether the investment is worthwhile.

(15 marks)

(b) Explain sensitivity analysis and prepare calculations to show the sensitivity of the decision to independent changes in each of the following:
  (i) annual contribution;
  (ii) rate of corporation tax on profits.

(10 marks)
(Total for Question Five = 25 marks)

Solutions to Revision Questions

Solution 1

Tip
- You will need to use some accurate workings for Question 1.6. Although your workings will not receive any marks, if you keep them neat you will reduce the likelihood of errors.

1.1 Answer: (C)

To find the number of units:

Contribution per unit: £180 − £60 = £120

	£
Annual cash flow	320,000
Fixed costs	160,000
Total contribution	480,000 ÷ £120 = 4,000 units

The net present value of the project is £244,170. Therefore, the net present value of the revenue can fall by £244,170.

Current net present value of the revenue: £180 × 4,000 × 3.791 = £2,729,520
Therefore the fall in selling price: £244,170 ÷ £2,729,520 = 8.9 %

1.2 The internal rate of return of the project is 10% + [($12,304 / $15,520) × 5%] = 14%

1.3 1.18/1.06 = 1.1132
Real cost of capital = 11.32%

1.4 Answer: (A)

Annual inflow = £5 × 4,000 = £20,000

Real rate = $\dfrac{1 + 0.08}{1 + 0.03} - 1 = 0.0485$

Discount factors: Year 1 $\dfrac{1}{1.0485}$ 0.954

Year 2 $\dfrac{1}{1.0485^2}$ 0.910

Year 3 $\dfrac{1}{1.0485^3}$ 0.868

                                                  2.732   × £ 20,000 = £54,640

NPV = £4,500 (to the nearest £500)

Alternative method:

	Annual cash inflow inflated		8%	Present value
	£	£		£
Year 1	20,000 × 1.03	20,600	0.926	19,076
Year 2	20,000 × 1.03²	21,218	0.857	18,184
Year 3	20,000 × 1.03³	21,855	0.794	17,353
				54,613

1.5

Year	£000	£000 to date
1	100	
2	120	220
3	140	360
4	120	480

Payback period = 3 years + 40/120ths of year 4 = **3.33 years**

1.6 Discounted cashflows are

Year	£000	£000	£000
1	130 × 0.909	118.17	
2	130 × 0.826	107.38	
3	130 × 0.751	97.63	
4	130 × 0.683	88.79	411.97
5	130 × 0.621		80.73

Discounted payback occurs in year 5 and can be estimated as:
4 years plus (450 − 411.97) / 80.73 of year five = **4.47 years**

1.7 Discount using 20% cost of capital

Year	Cashflow	Discount Factor	Present Value
	£000		£000
0	(350)	1.000	(350)
1	50	0.833	42
2	110	0.694	76
3	130	0.579	75
4	150	0.482	72
5	100	0.402	40
NPV			(45)

	Discount Factor	NPV £000
	10%	(48)
	20%	(45)
Change	10%	(93)

IRR = 10% + (48/93 × 10%) = **15% (approx)**

1.8

£80,000 × 1/0.08 = £1m therefore NPV = **£0.15m**

1.9

	Small	Medium	Large
Contribution/pie	$0.50	$1.60	$3.00
Contribution/kg	$2.50	$5.33	$5.00
Ranking	3rd	1st	2nd
Make (pies)	NIL	500	250
Uses (kgs)	NIL	150	150

Solution 2

(a) Sensitivity analysis identifies the most critical elements of a decision by measuring the extent to which each individual element must change before it causes the decision maker to change their decision.

The manager may use this technique to identify whether the acceptability of the project is more sensitive to changes in sales, costs, rate of taxation, or cost of capital. If more information were available the manager could consider the effects of changes to individual items of cost.

(b)

(i) The NPV of sales must reduce by $1.018 m before the manager's decision changes.
The post tax present value of sales is:

Year		
1	$4.2 m × 80% × 0.935 =	$ 3.142 m
2	$4.9 m × 80% × 0.873 =	$ 3.422 m
3	$5.3 m × 80% × 0.816 =	$ 3.460 m
		$10.024 m

The % change required (i.e. sensitivity) = $1.018 m/$10.024 m = 10%

(ii) The sensitivity of the cost of capital is found by determining the discount % that causes the NPV to equal zero (i.e. the IRR).
Discount using 20%:

Year		
1	($4.2 m − $2.85 m) × 0.8 × 0.833 =	$0.900 m
2	($4.9 m − $3.10 m) × 0.8 × 0.694 =	$0.999 m
3	($5.3 m − $4.15 m) × 0.8 × 0.579 =	$0.533 m
		$2.432 m
Less: Initial Investment		$2.000 m
NPV		$0.432 m

	Discount Factor	NPV $
	7%	1.018 m
	20%	0.432 m
Change	13%	0.586 m

IRR = 7% + (1.018/0.586 × 13%) = 29.6%
The % change required is 22.6/7 = 323%

 Solution 3

(a)

The Extended Value Chain includes both internal and external factors, whereas the Value Chain includes only the internal factors. The value chain is the sequence of business factors that add value to the organisation's products and services and comprises the following:

R&D   Design   Production   Marketing   Distribution   Customer Service
The Extended Value Chain adds Suppliers to the left hand side and Customers to the right hand side and recognises the importance of the relationships that the organisation has with these external parties in the overall process of adding value.

(b)

AVN is operating in a market that is constantly changing as a result of new technology being developed. As a consequence AVN needs to ensure that their organisation is as efficient and flexible as possible. By building a relationship with a small number of suppliers, AVN can benefit by being assured of receiving quality components without the need for excessive inspection of deliveries. This relationship also benefits the supplier as they are guaranteed continuity of demand and can plan to meet AVN's production schedules.

Each of the internal factors can be applied to AVN as follows:

R&D
The generation of, and experimentation with, ideas for new devices and processes;

Design
The detailed planning and engineering of devices and processes;

Production
The coordination and assembly of resources to produce a product;

Distribution
The mechanism by which AVN's products are delivered to their customers;

Customer Services
The support activities provided to customers before and after the devices are installed.

Customers are the other important external factor within the extended value chain. AVN must meet the demands of customers both present and future. In a highly competitive market such as that found today, it is essential that AVN understands the needs of its customers and seeks to organise itself to meet those needs in the most efficient and effective way possible if it is to survive.

Solution 4

(a) This general approach to project appraisal is open to criticism on a number of grounds, including the following:

- ROCE is a moving target which will rise as the life of the project proceeds due to the depreciation of fixed assets; it is difficult to see any logic behind basing project appraisal on performance in year 1 only;
- accounting profit is a subjective concept which is vulnerable to choice of accounting methods;
- there is no automatic reason why the use of existing facilities and equipment should be brought into consideration; these represent sunk costs which need not be considered (on the principle of marginality) unless there is some special reason to do so;
- the cost of new equipment and working capital receive exactly the same treatment; this is not appropriate since the working capital is fully recovered at the end of the project's life.

(b) An approach which avoids these problems is DCF analysis.

The annual income from the project is [(140 units × £(390 − 150)) − £17,000] = £16,600. Based on an annual income of £16,600 and capital employed of £170,000 the project yields an independent ROCE of 9.8 per cent. As such, it falls well below the Group's threshold of 15 per cent and is unlikely to be approved.

The project has a cash flow profile as follows:

Year	£
0	−150,000
1–4	31,600*
5	106,600**

* £33,600 contribution less £2,000 fixed cost cash flow (depreciation = £75,000/5 = £15,000)
** includes £75,000 recovery of working capital

DCF analysis of the above figures gives an IRR of around 14 per cent. This could be viable – depending on the risk inherent in the project and the IRR of alternatives.

Solution 5

Tip
- The key to this question is in understanding the reinvestment assumptions implicit in NPV and IRR calculations.

(a)

Factor 10%	Factor 20%	Project X £000	PV 10% £000	PV 20% £000	Project Y £000	PV 10% £000	PV 20% £000
1.000	1.000	(200)	(200.00)	(200.00)	(200)	(200.00)	(200.00)
0.909	0.833	35	31.82	29.16	218	198.16	181.59
0.826	0.694	80	66.08	55.52	10	8.26	6.94
0.751	0.579	90	67.59	52.11	10	7.51	5.79
0.683	0.482	75	51.23	36.15	4	2.73	1.93
0.621	0.402	20	12.42	8.04	3	1.86	1.21
		NPV	29.14	(19.02)	NPV	18.52	(2.54)

@ 10%   NPV Project X = £29,140
@ 10%   NPV Project Y = £18,520
@ 20%   NPV Project X = (£19,020)
@ 20%   NPV Project Y = (£2,540)

IRR Project X = 16%
IRR Project Y = 18%

(b) Undertake Project X:
- it has a positive NPV, indicating that it exceeds the company's cost of capital;
- assuming that the company's objective is to maximise the present value of future cash flows X offers the higher NPV.

X offers a higher NPV, whereas Y offers a high IRR. Where such conflicting indications appear it is generally appropriate to accept the NPV result, NPV being regarded as technically more sound than IRR.

(c) The two projects have radically different time profiles. X's cash inflows are grouped in the three middle years of the project, while nearly 90 per cent of Y's inflows come in the first year of the project. This leads to Y showing a higher IRR.

Risk, uncertainty and timing of cash flows may be considered by the directors in making the final investment decisions.

(d) Mutually exclusive project

The recommendation would be reversed at a cost of capital of approximately 14 per cent.

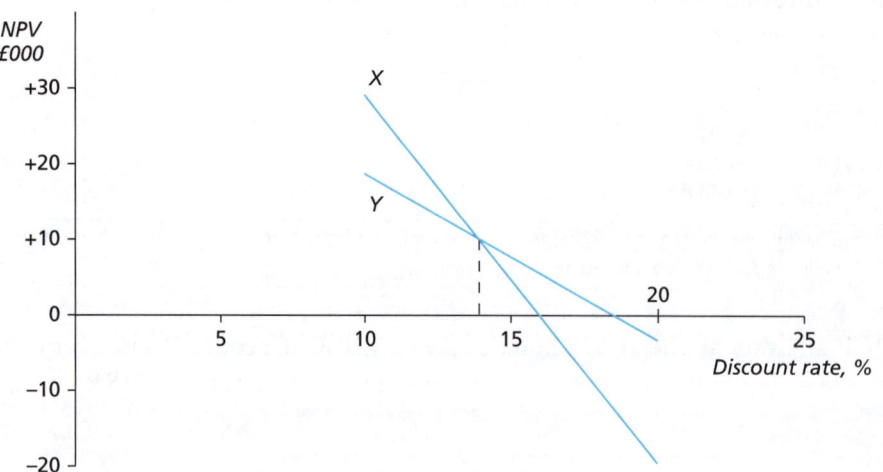

Note: You should appreciate that the true relationship between NPV and discount rate is a curvilinear one. A straight-line assumption is made to simplify calculations.

Solution 6

Tips

- Comparison of the two projects is complicated by their unequal lives.
- Use annualised costs to compare the two projects.

The annualised cost of the Kam is £21,160.

Workings

Year	Costs £	12% DCF	PV £
0	20,000	1.000	20,000
1	10,000	0.893	8,930
2	12,500	0.797	9,963
3	20,000	0.712	14,240
4	17,500	0.636	11,130
		3.037	64,263

The annualised equivalent of £64,263 is £21,160 (£64,263/3.037). This is determined by calculating the NPV of acquiring and operating a Kam over four years and converting it to an equal annual equivalent cost by dividing the NPV by 3.037, the cumulative discount factor for four years at 12 per cent.

The annualised cost of the Tru is £19,270.

Workings

Year	Costs £	12% DCF	PV £
0	35,000	1.000	35,000
1	7,500	0.893	6,698
2	9,000	0.797	7,123
3	10,500	0.712	7,476
4	12,000	0.636	7,632
5	13,500	0.567	7,655
6	15,000	0.507	7,605
		4.112	79,239

The annualised equivalent of £79,239 is £19,270 (£79,239/4.112).
It follows that the Tru is the best option as it has a lower annualised cost.

Solution 7

Tips

- This question incorporates taxation in capital investment appraisal.
- Begin by calculating the writing-down allowance (WDA) for the new investment and the tax relief.
- Calculate the net cash flow by working systematically in columns taking account of initial investment, working capital, scrap value, contribution, tax relief on WDA and tax on contribution, before calculating the present value.
- Remember that the working capital will be recovered at the end of the project.

Writing-down allowance

Year	Asset value £	30% Tax saved £	Year 1 £	Year 2 £	Year 3 £	Year 4 £	Year 5 £
	250,000						
Year 1 25% WDA	62,500	18,750	9,375	9,375			
	187,500						
Year 2 25% WDA	46,875	14,062		7,031	7,031		
	140,625						
Year 3 25% WDA	35,156	10,546			5,273	5,273	
	105,469						
Year 4 scrap value	10,000						
Year 4 bal. adj.	95,469	28,640				14,320	14,320
			9,375	16,406	12,304	19,593	14,320

NPV calculation for new investment

Year	Machine/ W/capital £	Tax relief on WDA £	Contribution £	Tax on contribution £	Net cash flow £	DCF 10%	PV £
0	(250,000)						
	(35,000)				(285,000)	1	(285,000)
1		9,375	120,000*	(18,000)	111,375	0.909	101,240
2		16,406	120,000	(36,000)	100,406	0.826	82,935
3		12,304	120,000	(36,000)	96,304	0.751	72,324
4	10,000	19,593	120,000	(36,000)	148,593	0.683	101,489
	35,000						
5		14,320		(18,000)	(3,680)	0.621	(2,285)
				Net present value of new investment			70,703

* Contribution = Annual profit + Depreciation (100,000 + 20,000)

As the net present value of the new investment is positive the advice to management should be to invest in the new technology.

Solution 8

Tips

- A question that combines the time value of money, and decision trees which you encountered in Chapter 2.
- The marketing and development costs already incurred are sunk costs that are not relevant to the decision.

(a)

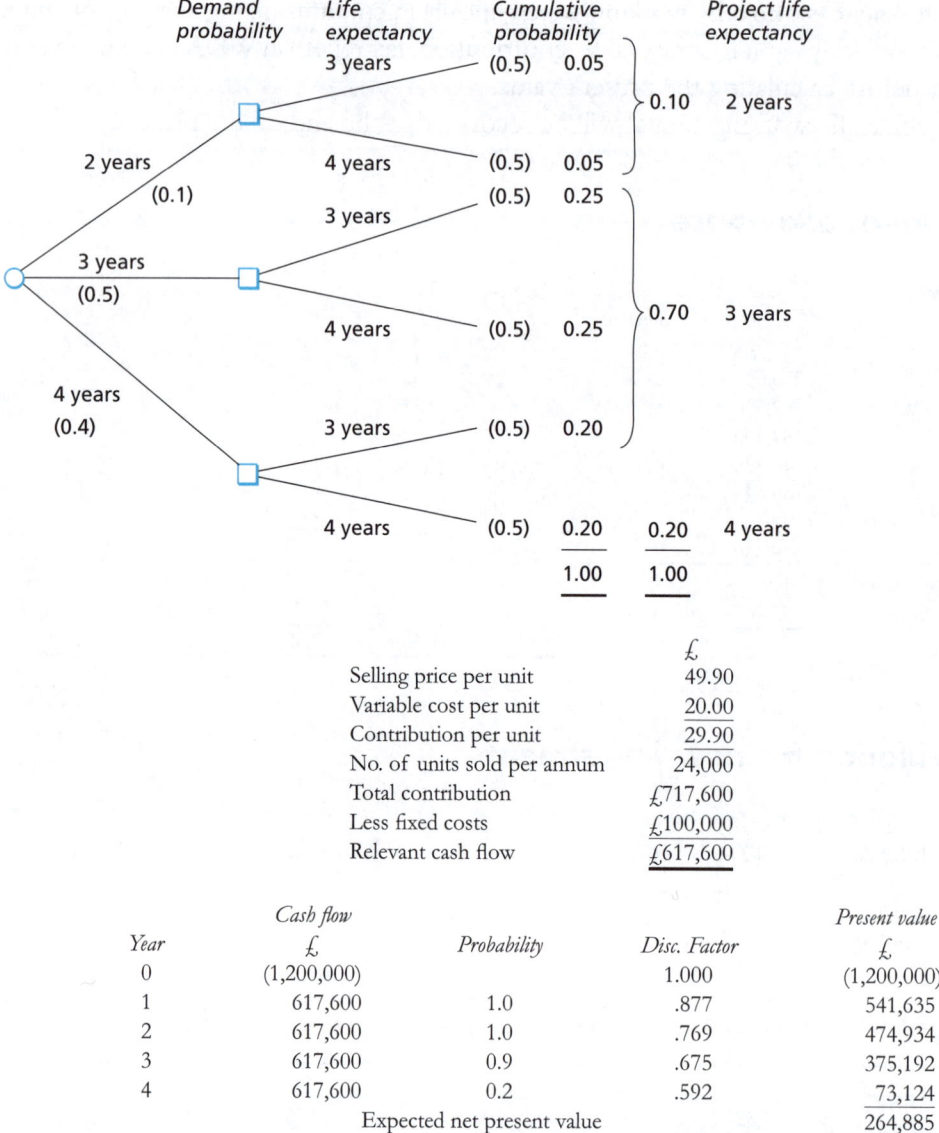

		£
Selling price per unit		49.90
Variable cost per unit		20.00
Contribution per unit		29.90
No. of units sold per annum		24,000
Total contribution		£717,600
Less fixed costs		£100,000
Relevant cash flow		£617,600

Year	Cash flow £	Probability	Disc. Factor	Present value £
0	(1,200,000)		1.000	(1,200,000)
1	617,600	1.0	.877	541,635
2	617,600	1.0	.769	474,934
3	617,600	0.9	.675	375,192
4	617,600	0.2	.592	73,124
			Expected net present value	264,885

(b) (i) The financial analysis in (a) above shows that the production and sale of the new personal alarm will result in a positive expected net present value of £264,885. As it is a large positive value the project will not be sensitive to slight errors in the estimation, for example of probabilities. The maximum NPV the project could earn is:

$$£617,600 \times 2.914 - £1,200,000 = £599,686$$

and there is a 0.2 probability of this occurring.

The minimum NPV the project could earn is, if the demand lasts for only 2 years

£617,600 × 1.647 − £1,200,000 = − £182,810

and there is 0.1 probability of this occurring.

(ii) The assumptions made include the following:
- Forecasts made are reasonably accurate.
- Taxation and inflation are ignored.
- The capital investment required is available.
- The cost of capital of 14 per cent is a reasonable estimate.

(iii) Other factors Apex Ltd should consider before making a decision are as follows:
- The availability of space, raw materials, etc.
- The reliability of the assembly line.
- Labour skills required - is additional training required?
- Threat of competitors and substitutes.
- Could the additional investment in this project be put to better use elsewhere?

Solution 9

(a) **Report**

To: The Management of MN plc
From: Management Accountant
Re: Investment opportunities A, B & C
Date: 21 November 20X1

Introduction
The three projects have different investment and return profiles as can be seen from the graph below. This graph can be used to select the best project for a particular cost of capital/discount rate. It shows that project C is better at 10 per cent discount rate, followed by B and then A, as shown by the NPV result. At 15 per cent, A is the only project yielding a positive NPV.

Differences between the NPV and IRR ranking
Normally, the NPV method provides the correct answer and maximises shareholder value, but in this instance other factors need to be considered. The three projects have two factors that differ. First, the length of the project, and second, the size of the initial sum of money invested. These two factors cause the difference in the results given in the question.

The length of the project
Project A only lasts for 3 years, whereas the others last for 6 and 9 years. The NPV method assumes that at the end of year 3 no further investment is made in a project of a similar nature and funds earn the cost of capital/discount rate. This is the reason why Project A is ranked in third place. In reality, funds could probably be reinvested in a similar project earning 17.5 per cent or at least in another project of a different nature earning above 10 per cent, the cost of capital.

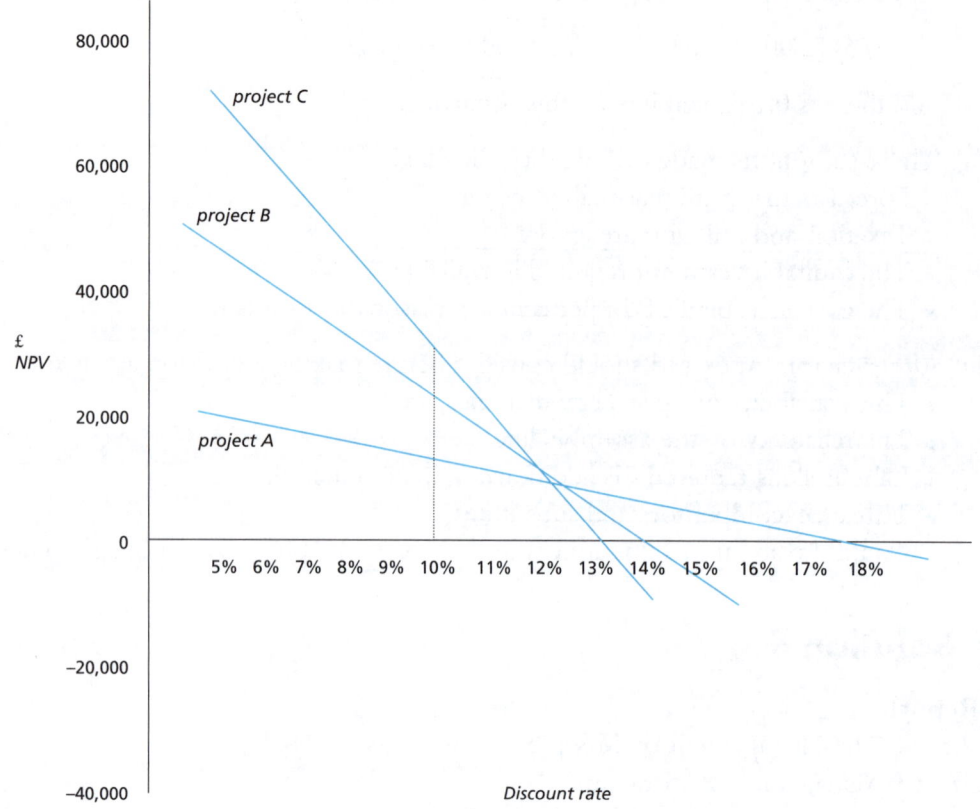

The calculation below shows the present value earned each year.

	Project A	Project B	Project C
Net present value at 10% a year	£14,376	£22,040	£31,432
Cumulative discount rate	2.487	4.355	5.759
	= £5,780	£5,061	£5,458
Ranking	1st	3rd	2nd

If funds could be reinvested in a project equal to A at the start of year 4 and again in year 7, the investment flow would generate an annual present value of £5,780 for 9 years and would be ranked first.

It could also be argued that where projects have similar returns, the one with the shorter life (Project A) should always be undertaken, because of the difficulty in predicting the future correctly. A fairly certain short term project may be better than a much longer term project generating a similar return. This is because the longer term project ties up funds that might not be as profitably used as originally predicted because of a change in circumstances, for example a rise in inflation.

The size of the investment

The other point to bear in mind is the size of the initial investment. If the NPV is expressed as a percentage of the initial investment, the following rankings are obtained:

	Project A	Project B	Project C
Net present value	£14,376	£22,040	£31,432
Initial investment	105,000	187,000	245,000
	= 13.69%	11.79%	12.83%
Ranking	1st	3rd	2nd

Project A gives a marginally better return, but if the money is not invested in Project C what will be done with it? The question implies that other investment opportunities exist which would allow for the additional investment of £140,000. If these do not exist, Project C may well be better. As can be seen in the following table, project C gives an additional positive net cash flow of £17,056 on the additional investment. This represents a return of 13 per cent each year on the excess investment. 48,000 × (5.132 − 2.361) = £133,008. Therefore, Project C is a better investment if the company has no alternative investment and can only reinvest at the time value of money during years 4–9.

	Project A	*Present value 10%* *Project C*	*Additional cash flow*
	£	£	£
Year 0	(105,000)	(245,000)	(140,000)
Year 1–3	119,376	119,376	–
Year 4–9	–	157,056	157,056
			17,056

Summary

- Project A is the best project if similar investment opportunities can be made in years 4 and 7. If this is not the case, Project C should be selected.
- Adopting Project A has the added advantage of keeping future options open and keeping the company liquid by returning the capital outlay quickly.

Signed: Management Accountant.

(b) Payback is a very simple method for assessing projects, which can be easily understood and calculated. Its main virtue is that it keeps the business liquid by returning funds quickly. This is obviously an advantage when the future is uncertain. However, by concentrating on the short term, projects with good returns after the payback date may be turned down and the longer-term strategic position of the company may be jeopardised. This is because investments in new technology, for example, may not be made at an early stage.

Payback is a traditional assessment method, but today discounted payback is more widely used.

If a payback method is to be used discounted payback is preferable. As can be seen from the calculations below, discounted payback alters the return time considerably and with a 10% cost of capital Project C's payback is in excess of 7 years when the returns are discounted.

	Project A	*Project B*	*Project C*
Payback	2.2 years	3.9 years	5.1 years
Discounted payback	2.6 years	5.2 years	7.5 years

Many companies use several investment appraisal methods – often NPV and payback. Perhaps MN plc should consider replacing IRR with discounted payback.

Solution 10

Purchase

Tax Depreciation

			Tax relief @ 30%
			£
Cost		15,000	
Yr 1 WDA		(3,750)	
		11,250	1,125
Yr 2 WDA		(2,812)	
		8,437	844
Yr 3 Disp Bal All'ce		(5,000)	
		3,437	1,031

Cashflow

Year	0	1	2	3	4
	£	£	£	£	£
Investment	(15,000)			5,000	
Tax savings:					
Current Year		563	422	516	
Previous Year			563	422	515
	(15,000)	563	985	5,938	515
DF @ 15%	1.000	0.870	0.756	0.658	0.572
PV	(15,000)	490	745	3,907	295
	NPV = £(9,563)				

Lease

Cashflows

		£	Tax relief @ 30% £
Year 0		1,250	375
Years 1–3		4,992	1,498

NPV Calculation

		£	£
Yr 0	Lease	(1,250) × 1.000	(1,250)
	Tax saving	188 × 1.000	188
Yr 1	Tax saving	187 × 0.870	163
Yrs 1–3	Lease	(4,992) × 2.284	(11,402)
Yrs 1–3	Tax saving	749 × 2.284	1,711
Yrs 2–4	Tax saving	749 × 1.986	1,488
			(9,102)

Leasing is the preferred option.

 ## Solution 11

(a) New sales = £4.0 m × 1.20 = £4.8 m

Variable costs are 60% of sales now but will reduce by 20% to 48% of sales (60% × 80%).

Thus contribution will be 52% of sales:

New contribution = £2.496 m/year
Old contribution = £1.600 m/year
Increase in contribution = £0.896 m/year

Cashflows

Year	0	1	2	3	4	5	6
	£m	£m	£m	£m	£m	£m	£m
Investment	(3.000)					0.300	
Old m/c	0.400						
Contribution		0.896	0.896	0.896	0.896	0.896	
	(2.600)	0.896	0.896	0.896	0.896	1.196	–
DF @ 14%	1.000	0.877	0.769	0.675	0.592	0.519	
PV	(2.600)	0.786	0.689	0.605	0.530	0.621	

Pre Tax NPV = 0.631
Tax NPV   = (0.368)
Post Tax NPV = 0.263   Worthwhile

Tax Depreciation

	Old	New	
Year 1	£	£	£
WDV b/f	250,000		
Disposal	400,000		
	(150,000)		
Bal chg	150,000		(150,000)
	NIL		
Addition		3,000,000	
WDA @ 25%		(750,000)	750,000
			600,000
		2,250,000	
Year 2			
WDA @ 25%		(562,500)	562,500
		1,687,500	
Year 3			
WDA @ 25%		(421,875)	421,875
		1,265,625	
Year 4			
WDA @ 25%		(316,406)	316,406
		949,219	
Year 5			
Disposal		(300,000)	
		649,219	
Ball All'ce		(649,219)	649,219
		NIL	

Tax

Year	Contribution	CA's	Taxable
	£m	£m	£m
1	0.896	0.600	0.296
2	0.896	0.563	0.333
3	0.896	0.422	0.474
4	0.896	0.316	0.580
5	0.896	0.649	0.247

Tax payable

Year		Payable 1 £m	2 £m	3 £m	4 £m	5 £m	6 £m
1	0.296 × 30% = 0.088	0.044	0.044				
2	0.333 × 30% = 0.100		0.050	0.050			
3	0.474 × 30% = 0.142			0.071	0.071		
4	0.580 × 30% = 0.174				0.087	0.087	
5	0.247 × 30% = 0.074					0.037	0.037
		0.044	0.094	0.121	0.158	0.124	0.037
DF @ 14%		0.877	0.769	0.675	0.592	0.519	0.456
PV		0.039	0.072	0.082	0.094	0.064	0.017

NPV of tax = £0.368 million

(b) *Sensitivity Analysis* is carried out before a decision is finally made. It is used to test how sensitive a potential decision is to a change or inaccuracy in the variables that have been used to reach the initial decision. Each variable is tested independently. The smaller the change required to change the initial decision then the more sensitive is that variable and the more justified is a manager in taking more care over the value of that variable. A key issue is the extent to which each variable is controllable by management. These factors enable management to decide whether or not to proceed with the initial decision.

In the context of this question sensitivity analysis

- measures the effect on NPV of changes in input variables.
- identifies the most critical input variable to the decision.

Contribution
The PV of contribution can reduce by £0.263 million before the proposal has a zero NPV.

Presently
Pre tax contribution has a PV of   £m
2.496 × 3.433   8.569

Tax on contribution has a PV of
2.496 × 30% × 50% (yrs 1–5) = 0.3744

0.3744 × 3.433 =   (1.285)

plus

2.496 × 30% × 50% (yrs 2–6) = 0.3744
0.3744 × 3.012 =   (1.128)
                                           6.156

Thus a reduction of $\frac{0.263}{6.156}$ = 4.3% is needed before NPV = zero.

Tax rate
The PV of the tax payable = £0.368 million
This would have to increase by £0.263 million before the proposal has an NPV of zero.
That is to say, tax rates would have to increase by $\frac{0.263}{0.368}$ = 71.5%

Thus the solution is more sensitive to changes in contribution than it is to changes in the rate of tax.

The Value Chain – TQM

The Value Chain – TQM

> **LEARNING OUTCOMES**
>
> ▸ Explain the concepts of continuous improvement and Kaizen costing that are central to total quality management and prepare cost of quality reports.
>
> ▸ Compare and contrast value analysis and functional analysis.
>
> ▸ Explain the concept of the value chain and discuss the management of contribution/profit generated throughout the chain.
>
> ▸ Evaluate the impacts of just-in-time production, the theory of constraints and total quality management on efficiency, inventory and cost.

9.1 Introduction

In this chapter we will consider the impact of the modern environment working practices and management accounting systems.

In particular, we will consider the effects of continuous improvement, Kaizen costing, value analysis, functional analysis, the value chain, total quality management and just-in-time. As part of the value chain we will also consider supply chain management which encompasses the co-ordination of order generation, order taking, order fulfilment and distribution of products and services.

9.2 Continuous improvement

Continuous improvement involves a constant effort to eliminate waste, reduce response time, simplify the design of both products and processes, and improve the quality and performance of activities that in turn will result in an increase in customer satisfaction.

The traditional approach that organisations took was to use historical data to establish standards and to work to these standards and compare actual results with predetermined standards. This resulted in an approach which focused on achieving and maintaining standards rather than a policy to strive for continuous improvement.

Japanese manufacturers identified two approaches to continuous improvement called target costing (discussed later) and Kaizen costing.

9.3 Kaizen costing

 'A Japanese term for continuous improvement in all aspects of a company's performance, at every level.'

Kaizen is the Japanese term for making improvements to a process through small incremental amounts, rather than through large innovations.

Kaizen costing is applied during the manufacturing stage of the products life cycle whereas target costing is applied during the design stage. Kaizen costing therefore focuses on achieving cost reductions through the increased efficiency of the production process. Improvement is the aim and responsibility of every worker in every activity, at all times. Through continual efforts significant reductions in cost can be achieved over time. In order to strive to continually achieve cost reductions an annual (or monthly) Kaizen cost goal is established. Actual results are then compared with the Kaizen goal and then the current actual cost becomes the base line for setting the new Kaizen goal the following year that is continually striving to achieve cost reduction. It should be noted however that as the products are already at the production stage the cost savings under Kaizen costing are smaller than target costing. Cost reductions under target costing are achieved at the design stage and therefore more significant savings can be made as it is at this stage that 80–90% of the product costs are locked in.

9.4 Value analysis

'A systematic interdisciplinary examination of the factors affecting the cost of a product or service, in order to devise means of achieving the specified purpose most economically at the required standard of quality and reliability.'

Value analysis is a form of cost reduction and also a process improvement technique that uses information which has been collected about a product's design and production process and examines various elements of the design and production process to identify any improvement efforts required. The overall aim of value analysis is to improve profitability by reducing costs without necessarily increasing prices, compromising the quality or usefulness of the product.

Many manufacturers and suppliers noticed that they were incorporating features into their products which their customers did not require. Value analysis is therefore concerned with the company taking a critical look at each feature of a product, questioning its use and eliminating any unjustifiable features.

Value analysis is carried out by companies in the following way:

1. The company establishes the exact requirement of their customers. This way they can ensure that the product they produce satisfies these requirements and that all elements incorporated into the product contribute some value to it. A team consisting of engineering, technical and production staff together with an accountant will work together to design the product which meets the essential design objectives at minimum costs i.e. eliminating inessential and unnecessary costs.
2. The company will then investigate whether or not there are alternative ways of achieving the customers requirements. For example, in car manufacturing it may be possible to

use standard components rather than specific components. All alternatives will then be considered and costed.
3. A selection process will then take place based on the best alternative and authorisation will be sought before implementing the new alternative.
4. The new proposal will be implemented.
5. The new proposal will then be evaluated to establish whether the expected benefits from the change have taken place.

Value analysis has many benefits to a company, the obvious one the elimination of inessential and unnecessary costs. Other benefits include a potential increase in sales as customers' requirements will be met due to the interest shown in them. Also staff will be motivated by the fact that value analysis encourages them to put forward their ideas for cost reduction.

Value analysis requires the use of functional analysis.

9.5 Functional analysis

'An analysis of the relationships between product functions, their perceived value to the customer and their cost of provision'

With functional analysis the company will breakdown the product into its many functions and place a price or value on each of these functions which reflects the amount the customer is willing to pay. The sum of the values for each function will then make up the price of the product from which a target profit is deducted to arrive at a target cost. The next step will then be to compare the target cost of each function of the product to the price the customer is willing to pay and if the cost of the function exceeds the benefit then the function should be either, modified, re-evaluated and an alternative found or eliminated.

9.6 The value chain

The driving force behind the adoption of Automated Manufacturing Technologies (AMTs) is the knowledge that excellence in manufacturing is a *sine qua non* for success in the globally competitive market in which most major producers operate. However, while excellence in manufacturing is a *necessary* condition, it is not of itself *sufficient* to ensure success. It must be accompanied by a thorough appreciation of the relationship between *all* the factors within the value chain – the sequence of business factors by which *value* is added to the organisation's products and services. The value chain is illustrated in Figure 9.1.

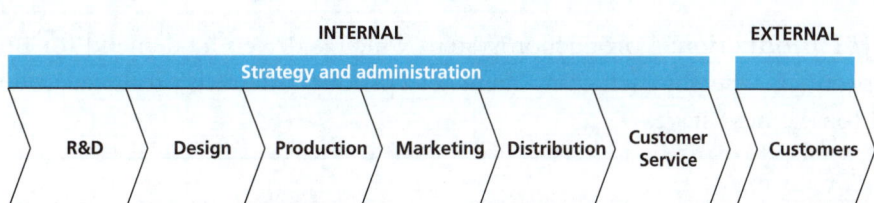

Figure 9.1 The value chain

- *Research and development*. The generation of, and experimentation with, ideas for new products, services or processes.
- *Design*. The detailed planning and engineering of products, services or processes.
- *Production*. The coordination and assembly of resources to produce a product or deliver a service.
- *Marketing*. The process by which potential customers learn about and value the attributes of the organisation's products or services, and are persuaded to buy them.
- *Distribution*. The mechanism by which the organisation's products or services are delivered to the customer.
- *Customer service*. The support activities provided to customers.

Functions within the value chain are not necessarily sequential; the organisation can gain important competitive advantages by activating individual parts of the chain concurrently. The major consideration is their smooth *coordination* within the framework of the organisation as a whole.

World-class manufacturing (WCM) describes the ability of those players in the market who 'get the value chain right', and are able to manufacture innovative products of a uniformly high quality at a low cost. Implicit in WCM – indeed, built into the performance measurement system – is a desire for continuous improvement: the world-class manufacturer will not stand still, but will constantly strive to increase innovation, reduce total costs and improve product quality, while maintaining a first-class customer service. In this sense, WCM can be seen as a philosophy, in much the same way, and for much the same reasons, as several of the production operations systems and management strategies, to which we now turn.

9.7 Just-in-time concept

There can be few students of business-related topics who have not heard of just-in-time (JIT) production methods, and their major contribution to the Japanese 'economic miracle'. The CIMA *Official Terminology* defines JIT as:

> **JIT**: A system whose objective is to produce or procure products or components as they are required by a customer or for use, rather than for stock. A just-in-time system is a 'pull' system, which responds to demand, in contrast to a 'push' system, in which stocks act as buffers between the different elements of the system, such as purchasing, production and sales.

JIT production is defined as:

> **JIT production**: a production system which is driven by demand for finished products whereby each component on a production line is produced only when needed for the next stage.

And, JIT purchasing as:

> **JIT purchasing:** a purchasing system in which material purchases are contracted so that the receipt and usage of material, to the maximum extent possible, coincide.

These *Official Terminology* definitions give JIT the appearance of being merely an alternative production management system, with similar characteristics and objectives to techniques such as MRP. However, JIT is better described as a *philosophy*, or approach to management, as it encompasses a commitment to continuous improvement and the pursuit of excellence in the design and operation of the production management system.

The JIT approach is results-driven, with the aim being the elimination of all non-value-added costs. It is surprising how little of what traditionally happens in a manufacturing system actually adds *value* to the product. The lead time to produce and sell a good consists not only of processing it, but also inspecting it for quality, moving it from machine to machine, having it 'queue' at each machine as it waits for further processing, and finally storing it as a finished good prior to sale. It will be apparent that value is only added to the product during the actual *processing* stages. These have been estimated to represent as little as 10 per cent of the total manufacturing lead time in many companies, and thus up to 90 per cent of production time adds costs but no *value*.

The aim of JIT is to see the *manufacturing lead time* equal to the *processing time*. Although this objective is unlikely ever to be achieved in practice, it nevertheless creates the correct climate for the commitment to continuous improvement and excellence referred to above. Impressive gains have been recorded – Japanese companies that have used JIT for five years or more have reported a 30 per cent increase in labour productivity, a 90 per cent reduction in quality rejection rates, a 60 per cent drop in stock levels, and a 15 per cent reduction in the factory space required to carry out the manufacturing activity.

These gains can be seen to stem from JIT's search for continuous improvement, which exposes problems that were previously hidden. An analogy with a boat sailing along a river is often used to explain this result, as seen in Figure 9.2.

The production process in a multi-product plant represents the boat, and the levels of stocks that a company holds are the determinants of the water level of the river. A high level of raw material and component stocks, work in progress and finished goods would indicate that the river is extremely deep. As these stocks are reduced, the water level reduces. The bed of the river may contain rocks, the height and quantity being determined by the number of problems that a company faces in its production. The 'rocks' may be caused by

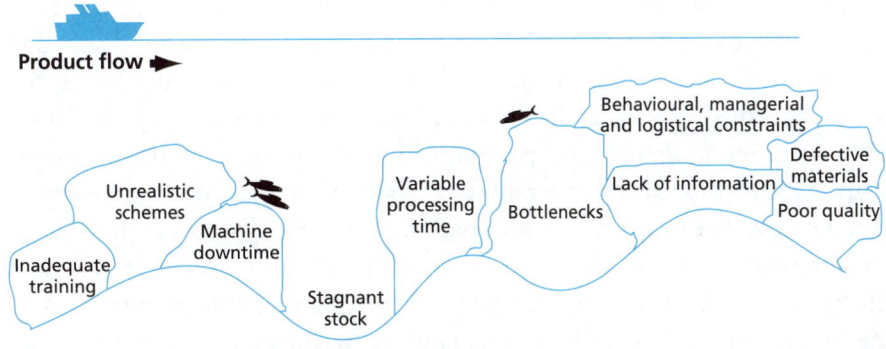

Figure 9.2 The just-in-time concept

poor production scheduling, machine breakdown, absenteeism, inefficient plant layout, excessive rework, schedule interruption through order expediting, etc. However, these rocks do not cause a problem to the boat on the surface, provided that the water depth – the level of inventory – is sufficient to cover them. As the water level – the inventory – goes down, the rocks – the problems within the company – will be exposed. The inevitable consequence of this is that the boat will crash into the rocks and be damaged.

This damage can be avoided in one of two ways. The first, the traditional Western way, is to keep the water level deep – maintain high levels of stocks. An alternative way, and the way consistent with the JIT philosophy, is to remove the *rocks*, so that the boat can sail quite safely in a much *lower* level of water. The difficulty faced by management is that, when the rocks are under the water, the problems remain buried and do not receive attention. However, as the water level starts to reduce, it becomes imperative that action is taken to eliminate the problems exposed. This happens in a JIT environment.

Applying this to the real manufacturing situation, there can be no doubt that high levels of work in progress do provide a measure of localised flexibility: for example, if an operative is working at a particular workstation that is capable of producing a number of different products, he has the flexibility to move *between* products; if his schedule dictates that he should be producing a batch of product A on a particular day, but the components to enable this to be done are missing, if work in progress is available for product B, the worker can turn his attention to the production of B instead of A. At a *local* level, this appears to be 'efficient': both the worker and the machine are busy producing output. However, the effect of operating for *localised* 'efficiency' is that *global* plant efficiency is usually reduced. Production of B will *only* be useful to the company if the batch can complete its progress through the plant and be sold without further delay. If product B is being produced off schedule, it is actually highly unlikely that such an outcome will occur. Product B will pass on to the next process, where it is highly likely to 'queue' before its production can be continued. The output of the worker has therefore not increased the profitability of the company at all – it has merely increased work in progress inventory, which *reduces*, rather than *increases*, profitability.

9.7.1 JIT systems

In a JIT system, lack of components to complete a batch of product A would simply stop the worker manufacturing at all. However, and more importantly, it would also focus minds on solving the problem as to *why* components were not available. Once the system is operating smoothly again, this situation should not recur. JIT can thus be seen to expose problems within a plant, and force management to address problems and rectify them, rather than simply bury them by holding excess inventory. Excess inventory is seen as the *result* of problems, rather than a *solution* to problems. However, JIT should not be regarded as a technique to be employed in reducing stockholdings; it is a philosophy whose application has reduced stock levels as one of its outcomes. It is within JIT firms that one sees the alternative costing system known as 'backflush costing', which relies on minimal levels of stock for its rationale.

In a JIT environment, 'family groups' of products – products with similar production requirements – are manufactured in separate cells along production-line principles. That is, all the machines needed to carry out the manufacture of a particular product family are arranged in the form of a discrete 'mini' assembly line. The machines are grouped closely together in the sequential order required by processing, and products move from machine to machine in a constant flow, without 'queuing' by machines or returning to stores, thus minimising lead times and work in progress.

The traditional manufacturing environment operates on a 'push-through' basis, in which one process supplies parts to the next process without regard to the latter's immediate ability to continue work on those parts. Work in progress is an unavoidable feature of such a system. In contrast, the JIT system works on a 'pull' principle, whereby one workstation 'pulls' the part from the previous station; work will not begin in any workstation until the signal to produce the part has been received from the next station in the process. The bin, or container, that is passed to the previous workstation to give the 'pull' signal, is known in Japanese as the 'kanban', hence the use of this word to describe JIT systems. As production only commences once the 'pull' signal has been received, this has the obvious consequence of keeping work in progress at a low level – indeed, as we saw earlier, a build-up of stock would be considered to be a sign of problems in such a system. A certain amount of idle time can result from this, but, the JIT philosophy regards it as less detrimental to the organisation as a whole than a build-up of stock. A more important consequence of the 'pull' system, however, is that problems in any part of the system will immediately halt the production line, as earlier workstations will not receive the 'pull' signal and later stations will not have their own 'pull' signals answered. As noted above, this would have the powerful effect of concentrating all minds on finding a long-term solution to the problem.

Workers in a JIT cell are trained to operate all the machines within it, and perform routine preventive maintenance on them. This level of flexibility is reflected in the high level of trust and responsibility placed on workers – the JIT approach assumes that they will perform better when they are given a large degree of authority over the activities of their workstations. Thus, any JIT worker can stop the production line if he or she is falling behind, or if he or she identifies a problem. The philosophy assumes that other workers will rally round to solve the problem. In this context, quality circles – voluntary groupings of people of the same level with similar duties, who meet to discuss and solve work-related problems – are frequently seen in conjunction with JIT. Members of each circle only discuss their own problems in their *own* work area, so that conflicts do not arise through inter-circle criticisms.

The analogy of the boat and the river emphasised the role of buffer stocks in protecting the traditional manufacturing system against shortages caused by innate problems such as poor-quality production or machine breakdowns. JIT operates with minimal stock levels; its approach is to 'get it right first time', and the aim is 'zero defects'. In the absence of the attainment of this 'ideal' situation, JIT is still able to cut scrap and rework. If transfer batches are small, product is quickly manufactured and quality checked – any problems are quickly found and only a small amount of work in progress will need to be reworked.

Defects cause breakdowns in the value chain: they stop the flow of production, create expensive rework and lead to late deliveries to customers. Many JIT firms have reduced their level of defects substantially – a figure of 90 per cent was mentioned earlier – by adopting quality awareness and total quality management (TQM) programmes (see later in this chapter). This approach is consistent with JIT's policy of continuous improvement.

9.7.2 JIT and supplier relationships

The JIT approach to purchasing also emphasises the quality aspects that we have just noted. The CIMA definition of JIT purchasing, quoted earlier, is somewhat narrow, and fails to capture the essence of the relationship between the JIT firm and its suppliers. In this relationship, we see a holistic backward extension of the value chain illustrated earlier in this chapter. This is shown in Figure 9.3.

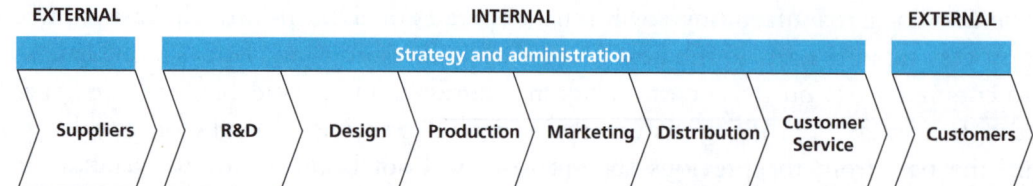

Figure 9.3 The value chain extended

Underlying the CIMA definition is the well-known stock facet of JIT purchasing, whereby more frequent deliveries of materials and parts, timed to coincide with their use in the production process, lead to minimum levels of inventory. However, of equal importance is JIT's insistence that suppliers take responsibility for the quality of their goods; the onus is on the *supplier* to inspect the parts or materials before delivery and guarantee their quality. The not inconsiderable savings in inspection costs go happily with the benefits of increased quality to achieve cost reduction – another facet of continuous improvement. This enhanced level of service (in the absence of WCM) is obtained by reducing the number of suppliers and increasing the business given to each of them. Longer-term commitments are entered into, assuring the supplier of continuity of demand, and enabling the supplier to plan to meet customers' production schedules.

9.8 Total quality management (TQM)

9.8.1 Quality as a concept

CAD allows quality to be *designed* into products; CAM provides the *means* to produce goods of consistently high quality; and new approaches, such as JIT, with its search for continuous improvement and strategy of 'zero defects', furnish the philosophical background for the current *focus* on quality. It will be obvious from these discussions that a commitment to quality is a sign of a world-class manufacturer; furthermore, product reliability – in all its senses – is becoming an increasingly important competitive weapon in the market place. We shall now turn to a brief consideration of the place of quality in the modern business environment, and its use as a management strategy.

Quality has many dimensions, but can perhaps best and most simply be defined as 'conformity with requirements'. From a customer's point of view – and customers can be internal as well as external – a product that meets their requirements is a 'quality product'. There is clearly a relationship between *time* and *quality*: having the product or service delivered at the time it is required is a major requirement of most consumers. There is clearly also a relationship between *performance* and *quality*: being able to rely on the product or service to perform consistently to the required standard is another major requirement of most customers. It is increasingly the case that a firm that cannot meet the external customer's quality requirements will go out of business, so that the *need* to do so becomes a prerequisite for staying *in* business. It can be difficult to quantify the opportunity cost of not obtaining business, but there are several *measurable* costs of external failure to deliver a quality product. These include the marketing costs associated with failed products, the manufacturing or process engineering costs relating to failed products, the cost of returned products, repair costs, travel costs to visit sites with faulty products, and liability claims.

The cost of failing to deliver a quality product *internally* can be categorised under three headings: *internal failure* costs, *appraisal* costs and *prevention* costs. Examples of internal failure costs would be the costs of scrap, rework and manufacturing and process engineering required to correct the failed process. As we saw under JIT, it is the aim of *total quality management* (TQM) *programmes* to completely eliminate these internal failure costs by working towards a goal of zero defects. It is contended that, in many companies, the costs of internal failure are so great that a total quality programme can be financed entirely from the savings that are made from it – hence the expression 'quality is free'.

Appraisal costs are connected with measuring conformity with requirements. They would include the costs of incoming inspections and set-up inspections, and the costs of acquiring and operating the process control and measuring equipment. As we noted under the previous section, if suppliers adopt a total quality approach, the cost of incoming inspections can be eliminated.

Prevention costs are the costs of ensuring that defects do not occur in the first place. They would include routine preventive repairs and maintenance to equipment, and quality training for operatives, as well as the building of quality into the design and manufacturing processes. As the resources devoted to prevention – and hence the costs of prevention – increase, the other two costs of quality can be expected to decline.

We must reiterate that, in the early 2000s, the acquisition of a competitive advantage is less a precursor of excessive profits than a prerequisite for survival. The market for manufactured goods is now a global one, so that manufacturers cannot rely on domestic markets to protect them from overseas competition. The catchphrase for successful businesses in the late 1990s and beyond, has been continuous improvement. Whatever a company has achieved today, in quality as in all other dimensions of competition, will need to be surpassed tomorrow, if it is to retain its market share and current level of success.

As mentioned above, one of the inputs to a product is the skills and efficiency of the employees. Training can improve these employee skills and efficiencies provided the employee also perceives the benefits of such training.

Training can occur both inside and outside the workplace. Internal training could be in the ideas of team working and quality discussion groups, which are known as quality circles. Quality attitudes are important, for no amount of discussion or training are likely to have the desired effect unless employees understand and accept the benefits of quality.

When a product is designed, its specification should consider factors that will minimise future rectification costs. Production methods should be as simple as possible and use the skills and resources existing within the sphere of knowledge of the organisation and its employees. It is significant that, in the modern environment, it is often found that 90 per cent of the production costs of a given product are determined in its design phase. Effective performance management therefore involves monitoring costs and results over the whole life cycle of a product. Just considering production costs over a one-month period (in the form of traditional standard costing and variance analysis) may therefore be of marginal relevance. Ensuring that quality factors have been correctly engineered into the design of products may therefore only be apparent when costs are reported on a 'life cycle' basis.

An information system is needed to provide feedback on the success or otherwise of quality procedures. Such systems should attempt to measure both monetary and non-monetary factors.

Quality can be measured in terms of its effect on profit via costs and revenues, and also in non-monetary terms. An example of a monetary measure would be the costs of rectification, whereas non-monetary measures may include the percentage of wastage or the number of customer complaints.

Care must be taken with regard to traditional performance reports such as variance analysis, which can operate in opposition to quality. For example, favourable price variances can arise because of using poorer-quality resources. These poorer quality inputs may lead to a reduction in the quality of outputs.

9.8.2 TQM in practice

TQM may be defined as the continuous improvement in quality, productivity and effectiveness obtained by establishing responsibility for process as well as output. In this, every process has an identified process owner within the organisation and every person in an organisation operates within a process and contributes to its improvement. The idea is that quality is the key strategic variable in achieving strategic advantage. When a customer considers buying a product he or she is influenced in his or her choice of supplier by factors other than the technical specification of the product – such as speed of delivery, customisation, reliability, ease of placing an order and attractiveness of design. All these are quality-related factors. The TQM movement argues that ability to deliver these quality-related factors is a function of process, that is, it is a function of how the organisation works.

There are two recurring themes that run through much of the literature on TQM. These are 'teams' and 'empowerment'. Employee empowerment is considered to liberate talents and facilitate the deployment of skills. Teams are considered to improve the coordination of functions and skills within the organisation. The cooperative ethic lies at the heart of what TQM is all about.

TQM is a philosophy and a movement rather than a body of techniques. There are many alternative definitions and models of TQM. However, the central idea is that quality is the key strategic variable in business and it is a variable that is amenable to organisational culture. The idea is that quality should be a feature that is rooted in the structure of the organisation. Quality should impact on the way that the organisation is run and on the way that staff are recruited, assessed, promoted and rewarded. The view that quality is something imposed on staff by inspectors is anathema to the TQ movement. W. Edwards Deming, widely accepted as the founder of the TQM movement, argued that mass inspection of goods ties up resources and does not improve quality. Quality has to come from within the process rather than being imposed on it from without.

The main features of a TQM-oriented organisation include:

- Top priority is given to satisfying customers and the organisation is structured in a way that ensures interest convergence of owners, employees, suppliers and management in achieving this. Managers should act as facilitators rather than controllers.
- People are considered to be the key internal guarantors of success. Decision-making processes are participative. Management is both visible and accessible.
- Constant change is considered a way of life and the organisation is structured in a manner that readily embraces change. The organisation structure is flat, requiring employees to use initiative and communicate directly with customers and suppliers.
- The organisation pursues continuous improvement and not static optimisation. The concept of 'an optimum defects level' rooted in traditional cost accounting is entirely alien to TQM. Performance is measured against an external benchmark and not against an internal standard, in order to emphasise the possibility of improvement.
- The emphasis is on prevention of problems and faults rather than detection. Employees have a wide span of activity but a short span of control.

Achieving and improving quality is the central theme that runs through all of these features. This is particularly relevant in the era of flexible manufacturing when products are highly customised and product life cycles are short. Customer service and product innovation have become major elements in the quality of products that are being offered.

One feature of traditional management accounting is that it may not report the cost of quality failure and quality assurance. Poor-quality work results in costs, but those costs may be 'buried' at several points in the management accounting system and thus not be specifically reported. For example, the costs of quality failure may include:

- internally rejected and test-failed units;
- compensation/replacement for units rejected and returned by customers;
- rectification costs;
- compensation for units failed in service with customers;
- loss of customer goodwill and market reputation.

It is notable that some of these things are opportunity costs that have no immediate impact on accounting costs and are not therefore reported through a conventional management accounting system.

The adoption of a TQM approach is likely to require the provision of comprehensive cost of quality reports that are supplied on a frequent basis to all levels in the organisation. This involves identifying the costs of quality control, quality failure and quality assurance – and collecting them together for management information and reporting purposes. It is only when the costs of quality are known that the measures needed to achieve and maintain high quality can be justified.

TQM is a cultural thing and over the years it has attracted critics as well as followers. The debate between the two groups is explored in the article titled 'Quality streak' in the Reading section of this chapter.

9.9 Business process re-engineering

A business process consists of a collection of activities that are linked together in a co-ordinated manner to achieve a specific objective. Business process re-engineering involves examining business processes and radically redesigning these processes to achieve cost reduction, improved quality and customer satisfaction. BPR is all about major changes to how business processes operate.

Material handling is an example of a business process and may consist of the following separate activities; material requisitioning, purchase requisitioning, processing purchase orders, inspecting materials, storing materials and paying suppliers. This process could be re-engineered by sending the material requisitions directly to an approved supplier and entering into an agreement which entails delivering high quality material in accordance with the production requirements. This change in business process could result in cost reduction by the elimination of; the administration involved in placing orders, the need for material inspection and storage. By re-engineering the material handling business process the company will reduce costs without compromising the quality of the products delivered to customers.

9.10 Summary

In this chapter we have discussed continuous improvement, Kaizen costing, value analysis, functional analysis, total quality management and just-in-time.

Reading 9

Quality Streak

Bob Scarlett, *CIMA Insider*, 9 September 2001, (pp. 22–23)

The Cost of Total Quality

Over the last 20 years, total quality management (TQM) has become a ubiquitous organisational phenomenon. It is encountered in sectors ranging from manufacturing to healthcare and education. The total quality 'movement' has captured the imagination of business managers, writers, consultants and academics. The design and operation of total quality programmes has generated a minor business consulting industry in its own right.

Background

The idea that quality is a key success factor in business is an old one. Producing products may be far easier than producing products which give acceptable value to the customer. The value that a customer derives from a product depends heavily on its quality as well as its technical specification. If a customer is considering buying a product (which can be a component, a service or a finished good) then he will be influenced in his decision by how quickly it can be delivered, how far it can be customised to meet his precise requirements, how reliable it will be in service and how pleasing its appearance is. All these last issues pertain to quality.

The traditional cost accounting view of quality is that it has a cost. That cost is composed of two main elements:

- Compliance costs – the organisational costs of ensuring that quality is achieved. These include quality inspection, quality training and product sampling.
- Conformance costs – the costs of failing to achieve perfect quality. These include re-working costs, replacement costs and customer rejection costs.

There is a trade-off between the two. This trade-off may be illustrated by the diagram overleaf.

This diagram illustrates the quality cost structure of a manufacturing operation. In order to achieve 0 per cent defects, compliance costs must be high (£10,000) but these can be reduced as higher levels of defects are accepted. At 0 per cent defects, conformance costs are nil but these rise as higher levels of defects are accepted. In theory, there is an optimum level of acceptable defects – which in this case is at 2 per cent. This occurs at the point where total quality costs (compliance and conformance) are minimised.

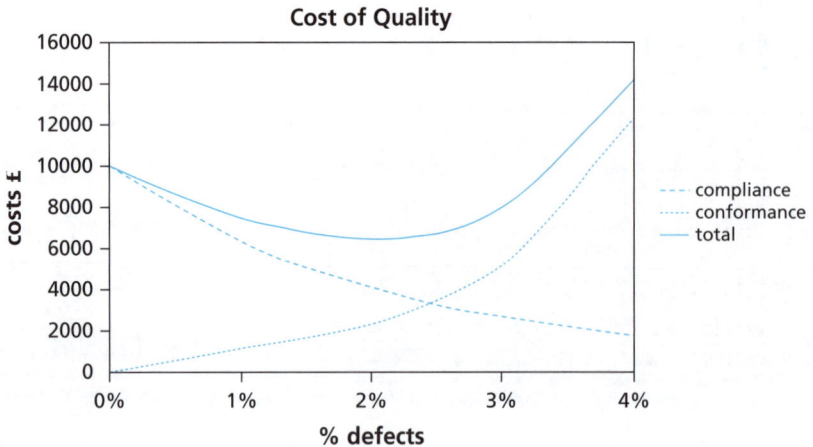

The main thinking that arises from this traditional view is that quality costs are important and may be the subject of management decisions. They should be specifically identified and reported on by the management accounting system. Quality costs are not always easy to identify and may be dispersed through the costing system of the whole operation. Their total may not be apparent. Furthermore, the long-term implications of poor quality on terms of customer response may not be immediately quantifiable.

One modern innovation is the Cost of Quality Report. This seeks to identify all the costs associated with maintaining quality and the costs of failing to maintain quality. These costs can be matched against targets and benchmarks to provide performance measure. Measures taken to maintain quality may extend to locating technical specialists at the factory site of suppliers.

The TQM concept

The TQM concept came to the fore in the 1980s although it is generally considered to originate in the post-war reconstruction of Japanese industry. The TQM name itself was a brand name used by PA Consultants.

It is a philosophy and a movement that attracts followers. It is not just a body of techniques. There are many alternative definitions of TQM. However, the central concept is that quality is the key strategic variable in business and it is a variable that is amenable to organisational culture. The idea is that quality should be a feature that is rooted in the structure of the organisation. Quality should impact on the way that the organisation is run and on the way that staff are recruited, assessed, promoted and rewarded. The view that quality is something imposed on staff by inspectors is anathema to the TQ movement.

A recent management seminar was given in Newcastle by a firm of consultants promoting a TQM model called 'Six Sigma'. The presenter was asked how TQM related to the Cost of Quality diagram shown above. He replied that TQM does not recognise the idea of compliance costs. The activities that those costs relate to should be immersed in the normal functioning of the organisation. Hence it is only conformance costs that need be considered – resulting in 0 per cent defects being optimum.

One advocate of TQM described it as follows:

> TQM focuses on customer delight, error removal, training and involvement of all employees, visible leadership and the continuous improvement process
>
> David Luther, V-P Corning Industries, 1992

The main features of a TQM oriented organisation include:

- Top priority is given to satisfying customers and the organisation is structured in a way that ensures interest convergence of owners, employees, suppliers and management in achieving this. Managers should act as facilitators rather than controllers.
- People are considered to be the key internal guarantors of success. Decision-making processes are participative. Management is both visible and accessible.
- Constant change is considered a way of life and the organisation is structured in a manner that readily embraces change. The organisation structure is flat, requiring employees to use initiative and communicate directly with customers and suppliers.
- The organisation pursues continuous improvement and not static optimisation. The concept of 'an optimum defects level' illustrated above is entirely alien to TQM. Performance is measured against an external benchmark and not against an internal standard.
- The emphasis is on prevention of problems and faults rather than detection. Employees have a wide span of activity but a short span of control.

Achieving and improving quality is the central theme that runs through all of these features. This is particularly relevant in the era of flexible manufacturing when products are highly customised and product life cycles are short. Customer service and product innovation have become major elements in the quality of products that are being offered.

TQM is far more than just a body of quality control techniques. It cuts right across the more traditional aspects of management rooted in Taylorism and Scientific Management. It has found wide acceptance throughout all sectors of industry and there are many organisations that claim to have derived substantial benefits from it.

When Japanese companies came to the UK in the 1980s they brought TQM with them. At the Nissan plant in Sunderland, staff at all levels wore the same company uniform and shared the same dining facilities. Almost all administrative and management staff shared an open plan office. Many of the British workers, coming from traditional engineering companies, found the approachability of Japanese managers to be refreshing. This made a profound impact on local people and businesses at the time.

The problems with TQM

There are two recurring themes that run through much of the literature on TQM. These are 'teams' and 'empowerment'. Employee empowerment is considered to liberate talents and facilitate the deployment of skills. Teams are considered to improve the coordination of functions and skills within the organisation. The cooperative ethic lies at the heart of what TQM is all about.

However, 20 years' experience of TQM has raised awkward questions.

Do employees and management really find 'empowerment' to be liberating? Empirical studies suggest that 'empowerment' often amounts to the delegation of additional duties to employees. Limits have to be placed on what employees can do, so empowerment is often associated with rules, bureaucracy and form-filling. That apart, many employees find most satisfaction from outside work activities and are quite happy to confine themselves to doing what they are told while at work. The proponents of TQM are often very work-centred people themselves and tend to judge others by their own standards.

Do teams contribute to organisational effectiveness? Just calling a group of people who work in the same office 'a team' does not make it a team. A team requires a high level of cooperation and consensus. Many competitive and motivated people find working in a team environment to be uncongenial. It means that every time you want to do anything you have to communicate with and seek approval from fellow team members. In practice, this is likely to involve bureaucracy and form-filling.

Is quality really a function of system? TQM tends to proceed from the assumption that variations in quality can be explained by features in the organisational system. The idea is that by changing the system you can improve quality. However, it can be argued that TQM merely moves empowerment from management to employees. It has been argued that the latter cannot be expected to succeed where the former have failed.

Experience with TQM

Management literature offers many examples of the success of TQM and the benefits that some organisations have obtained from it.

However, experience is not all good. Many organisations that have attempted TQM have found that it involves a great deal of additional bureaucracy. When the attempt is anything less than fully committed, then the results can be unfortunate. Some organisations have found themselves with two parallel structures. A new TQM structure is set up complete with committees and teams – but the old hierarchical structure remains in existence which actually amounts to 'the real organisation'.

One UK study (A.T. Kearney) reported found that only 20 per cent of organisations who had tried TQM reported positive results from it. A US study (Arthur D. Little) put the figure somewhat higher at 30 per cent. Celebrated failures include:

- Florida Power and Light Company discontinued its TQ programme after extensive employee complaints concerning excessive paperwork. This decision was taken in spite of the company having won Japan's 'Deming Prize' for quality management in 1989.
- British Telecom launched a TQ programme in the late 1980s but was reported (*The Economist*, 18 April 1992) to have abandoned most of it after three years. It was claimed that BT became bogged down in TQ related bureaucracy and took some time to recover from it.

Conclusion

In appraising TQM one has to appreciate that it is not a well-defined technique that can offer a 'quick fix' solution to specific perceived problems. Rather, it is an organisational philosophy that embraces a wide variety of different techniques and ideas. For example, JIT and benchmarking are closely associated with TQM.

The general theme of TQM is the need to move away from a traditional hierarchic organisation structure in order to respond to the demands of an increasingly customer service oriented business environment where quality is the key strategic variable. Those organisations which have made a success of TQM are ones which understand its limitations and are prepared to take the long view.

Revision Questions

 Question 1

Japanese companies that have used just-in-time (JIT) for five or more years are reporting close to a 30 per cent increase in labour productivity, a 60 per cent reduction in inventories, a 90 per cent reduction in quality rejection rates, and a 15 per cent reduction in necessary plant space. However, implementing a just-in-time system does not occur overnight. It took Toyota over twenty years to develop its system and realise significant benefits from it.

Source: Sumer C. Aggrawal, *Harvard Business Review*

Requirements

(a) Explain how the benefits claimed for JIT in the above quotation are achieved and why it takes so long to achieve those benefits. **(15 marks)**
(b) Explain how management information systems in general (and management accounting systems in particular) should be developed in order to facilitate and make best use of JIT. **(10 marks)**
(Total marks = 25)

 Question 2

The X group is a well-established manufacturing group that operates a number of companies using similar production and inventory holding policies. All of the companies are in the same country though there are considerable distances between them.

The group has traditionally operated a constant production system whereby the same volume of output is produced each week, even though the demand for the group's products is subject to seasonal fluctuations. As a result there is always finished goods inventory in the group's warehouses waiting for customer orders. This inventory will include a safety inventory equal to two weeks' production.

Raw material inventories are ordered from suppliers using the Economic Order Quantity (EOQ) model in conjunction with a computerised inventory control system which identifies the need to place an order when the re-order level is reached. The purchasing department is centralised for the group. On receiving a notification from the computerised inventory control system that an order is to be placed, a series of quotation enquiries are issued to prospective suppliers so that the best price and delivery terms are obtained for each order. This practice has resulted in there being a large number of suppliers to the X group. Each supplier delivers directly to the company that requires the material.

The Managing Director of the X group has recently returned from a conference on World Class Manufacturing and was particularly interested in the possible use of Just In Time (JIT) within the X group.

Requirement

Write a report, addressed to the Managing Director of the X group, that explains how the adoption of JIT might affect its profitability. **(10 marks)**

Question 3

A firm of financial advisors has established itself by providing high quality, personalised, financial strategy advice. The firm promotes itself by sponsoring local events, advertising, client newsletters, having a flexible attitude towards the times and locations of meetings with clients and seeking new and innovative ideas to discuss with its clients.

The senior manager of the firm has recently noticed that the firm's profitability has declined, with fewer clients being interested in the firm's new investment ideas. Indeed, many clients have admitted to not reading the firm's newsletters.

The senior manager seeks your help in restoring the firm's profitability to its former level and believes that the techniques of *Value Analysis* and *Functional Analysis* may be appropriate.

Requirements

(a) Explain the meanings of, and the differences between, Value Analysis and Functional Analysis. **(4 marks)**

(b) Briefly explain the series of steps that you would take to implement Value Analysis for this organisation. **(6 marks)**

(Total for Question Three = 10 marks)

Question 4

The Managing Director of a manufacturing company based in Eastern Europe has recently returned from a conference on modern manufacturing. One of the speakers at the conference presented a paper entitled 'Compliance versus Conformance – the quality control issue'. The Managing Director would like you to explain to her some of the concepts that she heard about at the conference.

Requirement

Prepare a report, addressed to the Managing Director, that discusses quality costs and their significance for the company. Your report should include examples of the different quality costs and their classification within a manufacturing environment. **(10 marks)**

Note: 2 marks are available for report format

(Total for Section B = 30 marks)

Solutions to Revision Questions

✅ Solution 1

- In answering this question, it is important to appreciate that JIT is not merely a stock management technique. Rather, it is a management philosophy.

(a) The benefits of JIT, as described by Aggrawal, are gained by a revolutionary change in work practices, company culture and external relationships. JIT is not just about running a production facility with less inventory, it is a way of working that reduces traditional practices which do not add value to the product. Such 'non-value-adding' practices include warehousing and stock movement within the factory, testing for quality control, running machinery merely to accumulate large stocks of WIP at a bottleneck down the line and setting-up machinery to run a batch of different specification or product.

The new company culture gives workers the power to manage the production process by moving to where they are needed on the production line or by solving their own problems (quality circles). This requires co-operation between workers and a new approach to management. Furthermore, the workers self-test their work (to ensure quality assurance) and must feel free to halt production if there is a problem. Workers need to be multi-skilled, i.e. there can be no demarcation across traditional skill boundaries, so that set-up times and maintenance down-time may be minimised. These new working practices coupled with new technology reduce inefficiencies in the production process and result in new working patterns.

New external relationships must be developed, especially with the suppliers of materials and components. The supplies must be defect-free, on time and delivered more frequently in smaller lots. There should be no inspection of goods received. Therefore, new standards need to be established with tighter tolerances, warranties and changed packaging requirements. In return, the supplier will become the sole supplier, but will take on board the responsibility for R&D for the items supplied.

All of the above changes are quite radical and involve everyone concerned with the production process. The JIT philosophy will work only when workers are empowered, that is, free to make decisions and own up to mistakes; this cultural change for both workers and management requires much training and much practice. Thus, the benefits of JIT do not appear overnight.

(b) The introduction of a JIT production process will result in smaller batch sizes, that is, smaller production runs and more changeovers, lower inventory levels and more frequent deliveries, fewer direct labour and machine hours, but more indirect labour for quality assurance, software development, R&D, etc.

Thus, we see a need for faster gathering, grouping and analysis of performance for control purposes. Fortunately, computer-controlled processes capture much of the information required, such as what was done, when it was done, how long it took and what was produced. This enables traceable costs to be collected and monitored for each cost centre. This process must start at the component level, and for every stage in the production process the number of set-ups, orders, inspections, labour and machine time, etc., must be built into the product cost-control exercise.

Electronic data interchange will enable the system to match the pace of frequent deliveries on to the shop floor, and as a Kanban system will be used the day-to-day variation in inventory will be small. A complete production scheduling system will be required such as MRP2. This will allow for management accounting exercises such as capacity utilisation to be carried out.

The empowered workers will not require variance analysis, but motivational control will be more important and will use physical performance indicators, such as average set-up time or number of defects. Standard costing will still be required, but mainly as a foundation in preparing the financial accounting reports. To control the rising indirect costs, budget control will become more important. Cost planning will need to cater for blueprints for new products or production methods and for cost reduction as an ongoing process.

Thus, the development in management information systems is more of evolution and change in emphasis, as opposed to the revolution on the shop floor when JIT is introduced.

Solution 2

REPORT

To: Managing Director
From: Management Accountant
Subject: The effect on profitability of adopting a JIT system
Date: 25 May 2005

Introduction

This report explains the meaning of JIT purchasing and JIT production and the effect of its introduction on the profitability of the X group.

JIT purchasing

JIT (just in time) purchasing is a system whereby materials are ordered from suppliers to be delivered just as they are needed by the production processes. There are a number of features of a JIT purchasing system. These include the development of a reliable communication system between the production and purchasing departments and external suppliers. The number of suppliers is often small, and they need to be flexible enough to be able to react to the demands of the X group. The basic principle of JIT purchasing is that the X group would not hold inventory of raw materials and therefore it is essential that the suppliers are reliable both in terms of delivery times and the quality of the materials supplied.

JIT production

JIT (just in time) production is a system whereby items are manufactured so that they may be delivered to the customers just as they require them. Where there is a series of manufacturing processes this principle extends to the completion of items at each stage of the production process just as the next process requires them. As a consequence of adopting this manufacturing methodology the X group would not hold inventories of finished goods nor any significant levels of work in progress.

The effect on profitability

The introduction of a JIT purchasing and a JIT production system can be expected to affect profit as follows:

- There will be a reduction in inventory holding costs since inventories of raw materials and finished goods will be eliminated.
- There will probably be an increase in the price paid for raw materials to compensate the supplier for the additional flexibility that they are required to offer.
- There may be cost increases as a result of peaks and troughs of demand which cause fluctuating production levels and result in higher labour costs through overtime.
- There may be additional costs incurred in ensuring that the quality of the materials delivered and the quality of the items manufactured are acceptable to the customer.
- More management time may be spent on planning the resource utilisation rather than on making strategic decisions to improve the profitability of the X group.

Solution 3

(a) Value analysis is an examination of the factors affecting the cost of a product or service with the objective of achieving the specified purpose most economically at the required level of quality and reliability.

Functional analysis is an analysis of the relationships between product functions, the cost of their provision and their perceived value to the customer.

Value analysis is thus a form of cost reduction which is based upon investigating the processes involved in providing a product or service whereas functional analysis focuses on the value to the customer of each function of the product or service and from this determines whether it is necessary to reduce the cost of providing each function.

(b) There are a series of steps that the firm of financial advisors need to use to implement Value Analysis into the organisation:

1. The firm needs to identify the requirements of their clients so that they can ensure that the services they provide give value to their clients. It has been stated that many clients do not read the firm's newsletters, clearly then the newsletters have no value to these clients in their present form. Perhaps the newsletters should be abandoned and their cost saved; or perhaps the form or content of the newsletter could be changed to make it more valuable from a client perspective.

2. Once the firm has identified the services that are valued by their clients they can then consider alternative ways of providing those services. Each of these alternatives is then costed.
3. A choice is made between the alternatives.
4. Implement the changes.
5. Evaluate the effect of the changes to determine whether the expected benefits have arisen.

Solution 4

REPORT

To: Managing Director
From: Management Accountant
Subject: Quality
Date: May 2006

Introduction

This report provides the basis for discussion at the company's next board meeting. It outlines the approaches to quality that may be adopted by the company, in particular the conflict between 'Conformance' and 'Non-Conformance' in terms of costs and the perceptions of our customers.

Quality Costs

There are two broad approaches to the quality issue which each have their own costs, some of which are easier to identify and measure than others.

Quality costs can be analysed into two categories:

1. Costs of conformance; and
2. Costs of non-conformance.

Costs of conformance are the costs that are incurred in order to try to ensure that the quality of the final products or services meets the customers' expectations. This category can be sub-analysed into two further groups:

1. Appraisal costs – which are the costs incurred in testing/measuring and checking the product or service to ensure that it meets the quality targets that have been set, examples include the operating costs of test equipment; and
2. Prevention costs – which are costs that are incurred in order to prevent poor quality products or services from being produced; examples include training costs and routine maintenance of production equipment.

Costs of non-conformance are the costs that arise as a consequence of failing to meet the quality target. This category can also be sub-analysed into two further groups:

1. Internal failure costs – which are costs of reworking and correcting items of poor quality that have been discovered prior to despatch to customers; and
2. External failure costs – which are costs associated with poor quality products or services being delivered to the customer such as the cost of customer complaints.

Significance of quality costs

In the modern environment, with increased levels of competition and increasingly demanding customers who expect the products and services being provided to them to be of the highest quality, an organisation is required to carefully consider its target market and the price/quality relationship that its customers will demand.

The decision to incur inspection and appraisal costs is often seen as an attempt to minimise the costs of failure as there is clearly a relationship between incurring conformance costs and avoiding non-conformance costs. It is necessary to determine the level of failure that would be acceptable to customers given the specific price/quality relationship referred to above.

It is possible to achieve 100% quality in respect of all items delivered to customers but this would require that every item would have to be checked individually prior to its despatch. Clearly this would be time consuming and costly.

An alternative approach would be to test a sample of the items to be delivered to customers and rely on that sample being representative of the entire consignment. Clearly this would be less time consuming and therefore less costly but there is an increased risk that one or more of the items delivered would not be of the appropriate quality, thus increasing non-conformance costs.

Conclusion

This report has provided a basis of discussion at our next board meeting.

Activity-based Approaches

Activity-based Approaches

10

LEARNING OUTCOMES

- Evaluate the impacts of just-in-time production, the theory of constraints and total quality management on efficiency, inventory and cost.
- Apply the techniques of activity-based management in identifying cost drivers/activities and explain how process re-engineering can be used to eliminate non-value adding activities and reduce activity costs.
- Apply activity-based costing ideas to analyse direct customer profitability and extend this analysis to distribution channel profitability.
- Apply Pareto analysis as a convenient technique for identifying key elements of data and in presenting the results of other analysis, such as activity-based profitability calculations.

10.1 Introduction

In this chapter we will compare activity-based costing (ABC) with absorption costing and see how the use of ABC can improve management decision-making.

10.2 The overhead problem

10.2.1 Cost behaviour

One of the core accounting activities is the recording and analysis of costs. Costing systems first accumulate costs by broad classifications such as material, labour, power, etc., and then further analyse them by assigning them to cost objects. A cost object is defined as anything for which a separate measure of costs is desired. Thus the range of possible cost objects is considerable and includes products, customers, services, brands, departments, etc. An organisation's cost accounting system will routinely collect information about some, but by no means all, possible cost objects. The system will have been designed with the organisation's needs in mind and will assign costs to the cost objects that are important to that particular organisation. All cost accounting systems must take account of, and cope with, why costs occur and how they behave. Basically there are three main categories of cost behaviour:

- Purely variable costs – for example, direct materials.
- Variable costs which are fixed in the short term – for example, direct labour.
- Fixed costs that become variable in the longer term – for example, rent and business rates.

The costs which are purely variable present few problems as they can easily be attributed to products, services, customers, etc., and are therefore straightforward to deal with. The second category of costs, those that are fixed in the short term, cannot be directly attributed to products, services, customers, etc. Yet the costs would not exist without the products, services, etc., as they are incurred in order to create them. Decisions about the level of expenditure on these costs cannot be made on a daily basis and may be made on an annual basis when the annual budget is set and activity levels determined. Costs incurred by the purchasing department are examples of this, that is labour costs and other costs that are incurred in placing and chasing orders. Staff in the purchasing department cannot be employed or dismissed on a daily basis and so predetermining the correct level of activity is vital to good cost management. It is the accurate analysis of this type of cost that is crucial to a good costing system. These costs are attached to products by the use of an absorption rate, which traditionally has been based on labour hours or machine hours depending on the degree of mechanisation on the factory floor. Where there is a causal link between time and the variable overhead being incurred this is quite an acceptable method but if there is no causal link the calculation will not be accurate. (For example, there is no direct causal relationship between the cost of procuring materials and the time taken to make products.)

Fixed costs also become variable if the time horizon under consideration is long enough, or if the activity level changes by a significant amount. They are rather different from other categories as they tend to be incurred by strategic decisions rather than being triggered by particular products, customers, services, etc. As a consequence their provision is reviewed less frequently and this is normally done by a specific, one-off cost analysis. These costs are excluded in short-run decisions that require a marginal costing approach, because they do not change in the short term so they are not relevant. But they are relevant to long-term decisions where long-run average costs, which incorporate them, are needed. They are also relevant because they may be avoidable in the long term if different product decisions are made. Traditional absorption costing uses the same method to attach costs to products for both sets of overheads, i.e. labour hours or machine hours.

10.2.2 Absorption costing

Traditional absorption costing evolved in the early 1900s. In 1901 the British Federation of Master Printers set out to find a solution to the cost/price problem. Twelve years later, in 1913, they issued The Printer's Cost Finding System, which was an absorption costing system. Absorption costing was not unknown at the time but was as revolutionary as activity-based costing has been in more recent years. The printers' federation helped to institutionalise absorption costing, as the printing industry was a leading high-tech industry at the time using state of the art technology, which other industries looked up to. Because traditional overhead absorption was designed for production companies it dealt with production costs only and, as a consequence, it is less suitable for service or retail organisations.

Also because stock had to be valued at full production cost only in the published accounts, other costs such as R&D, administration, and marketing have not been related to products.

When traditional absorption costing evolved early this century overheads were only a small part, say, 10 per cent of the cost of production for the average company. Direct labour costs were much higher, say, 50 per cent of the cost of the product. This meant that the absorption method spread 10 per cent of costs on the basis of 50 per cent of costs. Because overheads were such a small part of total costs any inaccuracies in the absorption process were small and insignificant and did not distort product costs. A few organisations may have this cost structure today, and in such cases traditional absorption costing is perfectly adequate. Most companies, however, now have those percentages reversed and it creates a considerable degree of inaccuracy if 50 per cent of the costs are spread on the behaviour of 10 per cent of the costs. Yet it is vital that an organisation's costing system spreads overheads accurately.

Traditional absorption costing was not designed to make decisions of a short-term nature, and can never be used for this purpose. Marginal costing (variable costing) should be used when short-term decisions on matters such as product/service profitability are required. But if long-term decisions need to be made, long-run average costs are required which an absorption costing system provides. However, the system must be accurate and for all the reasons outlined above, total absorption costing is unlikely to produce the required accuracy.

10.2.3 Direct product profitability (DPP)

As traditional absorption costing, which normally uses labour hours as a basis for absorption, is rarely suitable for service and retail organisations, other methods had to be devised. One relatively new way of spreading overheads in retail organisations, which is used in the grocery trade in particular, is direct product profitability (DPP). DPP started in the US in the 1960s at General Electric, and was then taken up and used by Procter & Gamble in the 1980s. In 1985 the Food Marketing Institute in the US laid down a standard approach to the system and two years later DPP was taken up by the Institute of Grocery Distribution in the UK. The system described below was introduced in the late 1980s and has since undergone transformation as activity-based costing, described later in this chapter, has developed.

Retail organisations traditionally deducted the bought-in cost of the good from the selling price to give a gross margin. The gross margin is of little use for controlling the costs of the organisation itself or making decisions about the profitability of the different products. This is because none of the costs generated by the retail organisation itself are included in its calculation. For example, it does not include the storage costs of the different goods and these costs vary considerably from one good to another. A method was needed which related the indirect costs to the goods according to the way the goods used or created these costs.

Table 10.1 shows the DPP for good A. Directly attributable costs have been grouped into three categories and are deducted from the gross margin to determine the good's DPP.

Warehouse and store costs will include items such as labour, space and insurance costs, while transport costs will include labour, fuel and vehicle maintenance costs. The usual way to spread these costs across the different goods sold is in relation to volume or area occupied, as most costs increase in direct proportion to the volume of the good or the space it occupies. However, there are some exceptions to this; for example, insurance costs may be

Table 10.1 Direct product profit for good A

	£	£
Selling price		1.50
Less: bought-in price		0.80
Gross margin		0.70
Less: Direct product costs:		
Warehouse costs	0.16	
Transport costs	0.18	
Store costs	0.22	
		0.56
Direct product profit		0.14

Table 10.2

Product	Gross margin %	DPP %
Ice cream	20.4	4.6
Baby food	11.0	5.5
Toothpaste	31.2	18.8
Wine	45.3	17.2
Paper tissues	15.7	0

better spread on value or on a risk index. Risk is greater with refrigerated or perishable goods. Refrigeration costs must only be related to those products that need to be stored in the refrigerator. Handling costs can also be treated in a different manner as they tend to vary with the number of pallets handled rather than the volume of the good itself. The labour involved in shelf stacking may also need to be spread on a different basis.

The result of this type of DPP cost analysis may give information such as that given in Table 10.2.

Table 10.2 shows that for ice cream there is a considerable drop between the gross margin and the DPP because its refrigerated storage is expensive. It also shows that paper tissues, which had quite a healthy gross margin, are just breaking even with DPP; this is because they are very bulky relative to their price. While the supermarket or other retailer does not have the luxury of stopping selling paper tissues, because obviously it would lose considerable trade if it did not stock a complete range of goods, it does have other choices. The choices are merchandising ones, such as where to display the stock and in what position on the shelves. Stock at eye level sells more quickly than that above or below eye level. The brand with the greatest margin should be placed at eye level. Goods at the front of the store tend to sell faster than goods at the back. This explains why tissues are rarely found close to the entrance or the cash till.

With manufactured products a cost per unit for the different products is often calculated and the products ranked. For a retail organisation DPP per unit may not be the best measure to use. DPP per unit of time adds another dimension to the measurement and DPP per unit of time per measure of space adds a third. This is automatically built in when overheads are spread if a cost per cubic metre, centimetre per day, or per week, is calculated as a basic overhead rate and each product uses this rate multiplied by the volume and the number of days or weeks in the system. In the example in Table 10.1 the store costs would be based on a rate per cubic centimetre or metre per day and the product can be costed according to its size and the time it takes to flow through the system. For example, if the store cost per cubic cm is £0.0073 per day and good A is 10 cubic cm and the average stay in the store is three days, the store cost per item is £0.0073 × 10 × 3 = £0.22.

Table 10.3 DPP values by product group. From Doherty et al. (1993)

Product group	Sales as a % of total sales	DPP as a % of total DPP
A1	3.20	3.40
A2	3.07	3.31
B1	2.84	2.89
B2	3.05	2.85
C1	2.75	2.66
A3	2.26	2.48

According to Doherty et al. (1993) the single most valuable aspect of DPP lies in its diagnostic capabilities, allowing managers to ask questions, such as why did a product group over- or under-perform. Table 10.3 shows that product group A2 accounts for 3.07 per cent of sales but for 3.31 per cent of DPP. Upon investigation it emerged that stock-turn was managed particularly well in this group. Product B2 has 3.05 per cent of sales but accounts for only 2.85 per cent of DPP. An investigation of the warehouse costs might explain this or the opportunity of offering multi-packs might reduce costs.

Because it spreads costs across products which are normally classified as indirect, such as space costs, as well as direct costs, readers may be surprised that the word 'direct' is used in the title. According to Efficient Consumer Response, ECR Europe, direct product costs include direct costs as well as the costs of handling, space and inventory which are the indirect cost that can be allocated directly to the product based on one or more product characteristics.

The benefits of DPP may be summarised as:

- better cost analysis;
- better pricing decisions;
- better management of store and warehouse space;
- the rationalisation of product ranges;
- better merchandising decisions.

In recent years DPP has developed considerably in parallel with activity-based costing. DPP has become much more sophisticated and is now very similar to activity-based costing. One of the reasons for its development during the 1990s has been the development of EPOS and EFTPOS (electronic point of sale and electronic funds transfer) systems that have enabled access to the detailed data needed for direct product cost and profitability calculations. Even in 1993 Doherty et al. said that:

> DPP in retailing is not and cannot be a fully-fledged costing system, where every last penny of expense has to be recovered. The level of cost information available to retailers is generally not detailed enough to allow for that.

Since then technology has improved and it is quite possible to cost product lines with reasonable accuracy.

Indirect costs may be analysed into basic cost categories as follows. These are very similar to those discussed later for activity-based costing.

- *Overhead cost*. This is incurred through an activity that is not directly linked to a particular product.
- *Volume-related cost*. Products incur this cost in relation to the space they occupy. This is the cost described previously and includes storage and transport costs.

- *Product batch cost.* This is often a time-based cost. If product items (i.e. a number of identical products which are handled together as a batch) are stacked on shelves, a labour time cost is incurred. If shipping documents have to be prepared for an order or batch, this again is a labour time cost.
- *Inventory financing costs.* This is the cost of tying up money in stock and is the cost of the product multiplied by the interest rate per day or per week.

Each of the categories above will contain a number of individual activities, such as:

- check incoming goods;
- repack or pack out for storing;
- inspect products;
- refill store shelf.

DPP software systems can be purchased to model costs in practice. They require a number of key variables to be input in order to analyse different situations. The variables are:

- *Buying and selling prices.* The retailer has the option to adjust the selling price. A price increase from a supplier can always be used to increase the gross margin, but the higher the selling price relative to other retailers the slower stock movement is likely to be.
- *Rate of sale.* This is critical and needs to be as fast as possible in order to minimise space costs at the warehouse and the store, and to avoid loss of interest on money tied up in stock.
- *Stock-holding size.* The aim is to hold as little stock as possible in keeping with JIT principles without running out of stock.
- *Product size.* This is the cubic area that the product occupies and is important because space costs per item will be incurred according to size.
- *Pallet configuration.* The larger the number of cases on the pallet the cheaper handling costs per unit will be.
- *Ordering costs.* Obviously fewer orders will be cheaper but fewer orders will mean holding more stock.
- *Distribution routes.* Are the goods transported direct to the store or is a central warehouse used? Transporting goods direct to the store is a high cost activity for the supplier and it is usually better to use a central warehouse, even for goods with a short shelf life.

10.3 Activity-based costing (ABC)

10.3.1 Introduction

Contrary to what might be imagined, many organisations do not particularly wish to know how much it costs to make a product with precise accuracy. This is because pricing is based on what the market will bear, competitors' moves, etc. Others however do price on cost and need to be able to determine it with reasonable accuracy. The latter organisations have greatly benefited from the development of ABC, which is a more modern absorption costing method, which evolved between the 1960s and the 1980s to produce more accurate product costs.

It should not be assumed that all traditional absorption costing systems are not accurate enough to give adequate information for pricing purposes or other, long-run management decision purposes. Some traditional systems treat overheads in a detailed way and relate them to service cost centres as well as direct cost centres. The service centre overheads are then spread over the direct cost centres before absorption rates are calculated.

The main cause of inaccuracy is in the calculation of the absorption rate itself, which, as we saw earlier, is usually based on direct labour hours or machine hours. These rates assume that products that take longer to make generate more overheads. This is not correct by any means as the majority of overheads do not vary directly with hours. We have also seen that traditional systems which use labour cost as an overhead absorption basis have reduced in accuracy as the ratio of overheads to labour costs has increased dramatically.

Furthermore, traditional absorption costing systems are limited in the information they provide. More is needed than a system which attempts to cost products and ABC provides this.

The first part of this section will look at ABC in its traditional role as a system to spread overheads but this is not the main benefit of using the system. Its advantages as a cost management system, etc., will be discussed later.

In order to understand how ABC operates it is necessary to understand the meaning of several terms:

 Definitions

> A *cost object* is any item for which cost measurement is required, for example, a product or a customer.
>
> A *cost driver* is any factor that causes a change in the cost of an activity. There are two categories of cost driver:
>
> (1) A *resource cost driver* is a measure of the quantity of resources consumed by an activity. It is used to assign the cost of a resource to an activity or cost pool.
> (2) An *activity cost driver* is a measure of the frequency and intensity of demand placed on activities by cost objects. It is used to assign activity costs to cost objects.

In traditional absorption costing, overheads are first related to cost centres and then to cost objects, that is, products. In ABC, overheads are related to activities or grouped into cost pools (depending on the terminology preferred). Then they are related to the cost objects, for example, products. (Unlike traditional absorption costing ABC has other cost objects such as customers – this will be discussed later.) The two processes are, therefore, very similar, but the first stage is different as ABC uses activities instead of functional departments (cost centres).

The problem with using functional departments is that they tend to include a series of different activities, which incur a number of different costs that behave in different ways. Activities also tend to run across functions; for instance, procurement of materials often includes raising a requisition note in a manufacturing department or stores. It is not raised in the purchasing department where most procurement costs are incurred. Activity costs tend to behave in a similar way to each other, that is, they have the same cost driver. Therefore, ABC gives a more realistic picture of the way in which costs behave.

As with traditional absorption costing, ABC rates are calculated in advance, normally for a year ahead, and so the same rates are used for a year at a time. The advantage of this is that any seasonal variations will be spread, giving an average cost. If this was not done and actual rates were used the absorption rates would vary monthly. This would mean that when output was high the overhead rate would be low and vice versa; if pricing were based on cost the prices quoted would be higher when the business was slack.

The different stages in ABC calculations are listed below and are shown in Figure 10.1.

(1) *Identify the different activities within the organisation.* Usually the number of cost centres that a traditional overhead system uses is quite small, say up to fifteen. In ABC the number of activities will be much more, say 200; the number will depend on how the management subdivides the organisation's activities. It is possible to break the organisation down into many very small activities. But if ABC is to be an acceptable and practical system it is necessary to use larger groupings, so that, say, 40 activities may be used in practice. The additional number of activities over cost centres means that ABC should be more accurate than the traditional method regardless of anything else.

(2) *Relate the overheads to the activities*, both support and primary, that caused them. This creates 'cost pools' or 'cost buckets'. This will be done using resource cost drivers that reflect causality.

(3) *Support activities are then spread across the primary activities* on some suitable base, which reflects the use of the support activity. The base is the cost driver that is the measure of how the support activities are used.

(4) *Determine the activity cost drivers* that will be used to relate the overheads collected in the cost pools to the cost objects/products. This is based on the factor that drives the consumption of the activity. The question to ask is – what causes the activity to incur costs? In production scheduling, for example, the driver will probably be the number of batches ordered.

(5) *Calculate activity cost driver rates* for each activity, just as an overhead absorption rate would be calculated in the traditional system:

$$\text{Activity cost driver rate} = \frac{\text{Total cost of activity}}{\text{Activity driver}}.$$

The activity driver rate can be used to cost products, as in traditional absorption costing, but it can also cost other cost objects such as customers/customer segments and distribution channels. The possibility of costing objects other than products is part of the benefit of ABC. The activity cost driver rates will be multiplied by the different amounts of each activity that each product/other cost object consumes.

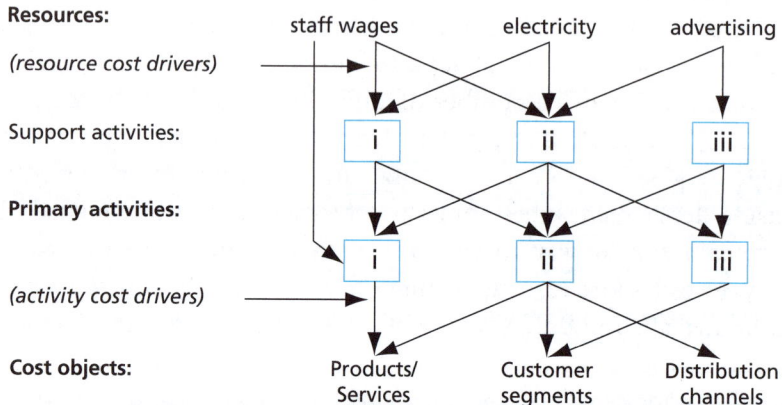

Figure 10.1 Cost flow in activity-based costing

Activities basically fall into four different categories, known as the manufacturing cost hierarchy. These categories are generally accepted today but were first identified by Cooper (1990). The categories help to determine the type of activity cost driver required. The categories are:

- *Unit level activities.* The costs of some activities (mainly primary activities) are strongly correlated to the number of units produced. For example, the use of indirect materials/consumables tends to increase in proportion to the number of units produced. Another example of a unit level activity is the inspection or testing of every item produced, if this was deemed necessary or, perhaps more likely, every 100th item produced.
- *Batch level activities.* The costs of some activities (mainly manufacturing support activities) are driven by the number of batches of units produced. Examples of this are:
  - Material ordering – where an order is placed for every batch of production
  - Machine set-up costs – where machines need resetting between each different batch of production
  - Inspection of products – where the first item in every batch is inspected rather than every 100th item quoted above.
- *Product level activities.* The costs of some activities (often once only activities) are driven by the creation of a new product line and its maintenance, for example, designing the product, producing parts specifications and keeping technical drawings of products up to date. Advertising costs fall into this category if individual products are advertised rather than the company's name.
- *Facility level activities.* Some costs cannot be related to a particular product line, instead they are related to maintaining the buildings and facilities. Examples are the maintenance of buildings, plant security, business rates, etc. Also included in this category are salaries, such as the production manager's. Advertising campaigns that promote the organisation would also be included.

The first and last categories above are the same as those in traditional absorption costing and so if an organisation's costs are mainly made up of these two categories ABC will not improve the overhead analysis greatly. But if the organisation's costs fall mainly in the second and third categories an ABC analysis will provide a different and more accurate analysis.

Although non-manufacturing costs have been included in the examples above, some organisations only use ABC for production costs. This is because traditional overhead absorption dealt with production costs only for stock valuation purposes in the financial accounts. As a consequence, the organisation may not have split up administration and marketing costs and related them to products in the past and they may continue with this policy. However, if the best is to be obtained from ABC all costs need to be split into activities.

10.3.2 Simple example of traditional absorption costing and ABC

As a simple introduction to ABC, work through the following example. The number of departments and activities is coincidental and is used just for simplicity in this demonstration.

A company produces three products for which the standard costs and quantities per unit are as follows:

	A	B	C
Quantity produced	10,000	20,000	30,000
Direct material £ per unit	50	40	30
Direct labour £ per unit	30	40	50
Labour hours per unit – dept. 1	3	4	5
Machine hours per unit – dept. 2	4	4	7
No. of purchase requisitions	1,200	1,800	2,000
No. of set ups	240	260	300

Production overhead analysed by department
– Department 1 = £1,100,000
– Department 2 = £1,500,000
£2,600,000

Department 1 is labour intensive and Department 2 is machine intensive.

Total labour hours in Department 1 = 183,333
Total machine hours in Department 2 = 500,000

Production overhead analysed by activity
– Receiving/inspecting £1,400,000
– Production scheduling/machine setup £1,200,000
£2,600,000

Number of batches received/inspected = 5,000
Number of batches for scheduling and set-up = 800

Traditional absorption costing

Absorption rates:

$$\text{Dept 1} = \frac{£1,100,000}{183,333} = £6 \text{ per labour hour}$$

$$\text{Dept 2} = \frac{£1,500,000}{500,000} = £3 \text{ per machine hour}$$

Product cost statement

	A £	B £	C £
Direct materials	50	40	30
Direct labour	30	40	50
Overhead:			
Dept 1 (3 hours × £6, etc.)	18	24	30
Dept 2 (4 hours × £3, etc.)	12	12	21
	110	116	131

Activity-based costing

Cost driver rates:

$$\text{Receiving/inspecting} = \frac{£1,400,000}{5,000} = £280 \text{ per requisition}$$

$$\text{Production scheduling/machine set ups} = \frac{£1,200,000}{800} = £1,500 \text{ per set-up}$$

Product cost statement

	A £	B £	C £
Direct materials	50	40	30
Direct labour	30	40	50
Overhead:			
Receiving[1]	34	25	19
Prod. scheduling[2]	36	20	15
	150	125	114

[1] $34 = £280 \times 1{,}200 \div 10{,}000$ units; $25 = £280 \times 1{,}800 \div 20{,}000$ units; $19 = £280 \times 2{,}000 \div 30{,}000$ units

[2] $36 = £1{,}500 \times 240 \div 10{,}000$ units; $20 = £1{,}500 \times 260 \div 20{,}000$ units; $15 = £1{,}500 \times 300 \div 30{,}000$ units

The two absorption methods produce different results. Product C appears to be much more expensive using the traditional method than it does with ABC, while product A is the opposite. This is because product C incurs more labour and machine hours per unit. Therefore product C absorbs more overhead when the traditional method is used.

A study of the information concerning purchase requisitions and set ups shows that product C involves fewer requisitions and set ups per unit than product A. Therefore an ABC analysis of overheads assigns relatively fewer overheads to product C. If it is assumed that ABC is more accurate, which it may or may not be, then product C would be overpriced on the traditional method and sales would presumably be poor as a consequence – assuming competitors supply more cheaply. Product A would be the opposite: sales would be high and it is possible that the company would unknowingly make a loss per unit on product A. If the company wanted to improve profit it might well initiate an advertising campaign for product A and find that, although it is successful in raising the volume of A, the overall profit has decreased.

10.3.3 Activity-based management

Initially companies switched from traditional absorption costing to ABC in order to produce more accurate cost information for products, as shown above. The managers in some of these companies were surprised by the information revealed, because it gave them a different perspective of the build-up of costs. This led them to adjust their pricing policies and to develop different product strategies, as they found that previously high volume, long production run products had been over-costed and low volume, short production run products under-costed. (Total absorption costing averages batch costs, such as set-up, over all products rather than relating them to the batch.)

To summarise, ABC is particularly needed by organisations for product costing where:

- production overheads are high in relation to direct costs;
- there is a great diversity in the product range;
- products use very different amounts of the overhead resources;
- consumption of overhead resources is not primarily driven by volume.

But if ABC is only considered to be a more detailed and accurate overhead absorption costing system many organisations may decide to do without it. On the continent, in France, Germany, the Netherlands and Spain many organisations use a sophisticated 'full cost' absorption method and so they have not found it necessary to change to an ABC system.

In these organisations overheads are usually charged to auxiliary cost centres as well as main cost centres. The auxiliary cost centres are in turn charged to the main cost centres. From the main cost centres the overheads are charged to products.

This is not dissimilar to a full traditional absorption costing system used in the UK which uses service or indirect cost centres (such as maintenance) that are then charged in their turn to the direct cost centres. Advocates of using ABC for accurate overhead apportionment usually compare the ABC technique with the most basic traditional absorption costing system where one blanket overhead rate is applied. They then argue that ABC provides more accurate results which, under those circumstances, it is bound to do. Using a blanket rate is not normal even in the UK and so the benefits of ABC will not be as great as they make out. Indeed there may be no benefit at all as far as product costing is concerned.

However, organisations that have switched to ABC have found other benefits that fall under the heading of activity-based management (ABM), and it is in this area that the real benefit of ABC often lies. It produces another way of viewing the organisation and is like looking at the organisation from another perspective.

> CIMA's *Official Terminology* defines ABM as a 'system of management which uses activity-based cost information for a variety of purposes including cost reduction, cost modelling and customer profitability analysis'. ABM uses the basic information provided by an ABC analysis to help managers to ensure that customer needs are satisfied with the minimum use of organisational resources.

ABM measures the effectiveness of key activities by identifying how activity costs can be reduced and value to customers can be increased. It also focuses management's attention on key value-adding activities, key customers and key products in order to maintain or increase competitive advantage.

There are three main benefits that will be discussed in detail in the following sections:

- Cost management of activities.
- The ability to cost objects other than products, for example, customers.
- Strategic activity management.

10.3.4 Activity-based management: cost management of activities

Empirical studies of ABC implementation have frequently shown that the greatest benefit derived from its adoption is in cost management, rather than in the provision of more accurate product costs. When companies use ABC information for cost management it can be said that they have moved beyond ABC to ABM. In carrying out the analysis necessary to establish an ABC product cost it may become clear, for example, that the current organisation of activities leads to duplication, and hence waste. The organisation and flow of processes can therefore be changed to eliminate duplication and achieve cost savings.

ABC also provides information that can be used to regularly monitor activities and so it aids continuous cost management or cost control. In order to appreciate the cost management insights which ABC can routinely provide it is important to understand the meaning of 'activity or resource consumption'.

An activity may be viewed as being a collection of resources, which provide an organisation with service potential. When that potential is used, resource consumption takes place. For example, raw material is a resource that may be incorporated into products; consumption takes place when it is incorporated into the product.

The amount of resource consumed (or activity demanded) in a period by cost objects, such as products, need not equal the amount of resource available. In the case of raw materials it rarely does, as most organisations keep a stock of raw materials. The same principle can be applied to overheads. The provision of indirect or support activities provides service potential. ABC assigns these costs to cost objects, such as products, on the basis of their demand for the activity or consumption of that resource.

For example, providing a quality inspection department requires the provision of many resources, such as personnel, office accommodation, etc. If the quality control team is fully occupied in carrying out inspections, the resources provided for quality inspection will be exactly the same as the resources consumed. And if this is the case the whole cost of the activities will be recovered or assigned, via a cost driver rate based on the number of inspections, to the products inspected. Unlike material stock, however, unused capacity in the quality inspection department cannot be kept for a later date. So it is important that the management of an organisation control the provision of an activity and its resources if costs are to be minimised.

A change in the level of demand for an activity does not necessarily lead to an immediate change in the level of provision of that activity. It may be possible to meet a short-term increase in demand without an increase in the provision and hence no additional expense is incurred.

For example, if the demand for quality inspections increases, the existing staff may be able to meet the demand by working extra hours, but if the extra demand for inspections continues, additional people will have to be employed. Most activities cannot be increased immediately because it takes time to hire and fire staff, etc., and so usually there is a delay between the increase or decrease in the use of the activity and the change in the level of provision.

If activity/resource consumption decreases, the employees providing the resource are unlikely to bring the fact that they now have some slack in their working week to the attention of the managers. A traditional absorption costing system will not bring this matter to the attention of the managers either, and so the situation may continue for some considerable time. On the other hand, an ABC system will immediately highlight the drop in demand for the resource as the cost driver rate would be applied to fewer inspections/units.

Thus, ABC gives managers the power to turn what have hitherto been considered fixed costs into variable costs. This is because what makes a cost (or resource) variable is not its inherent nature. Instead the variability is a function of managers' decisions about how much to spend and how quickly to adjust the supply of resources as requirements change.

Cooper and Kaplan (1988) insist that cost drivers must be based on *possible* activity measures. This is because the standard activity cost drivers that the system uses must reflect the underlying efficiency of the activities, as measured by the cost and quantity of resources supplied to perform each activity. This must be how much work can be done rather than how much work the organisation expects to do or has done in the past for a particular activity. If the predetermined standard is say £25 per customer order and 100 orders are handled this month, the cost of the activity allocated to the orders is £25 × 100 = £2,500. But if the budgeted expenses for the activity for the month are £3,000, the cost of unused capacity is £500. This differentiates the ABC process from traditional overhead absorption where the aim is to recover costs incurred rather than highlighting inefficiencies. With traditional overhead absorption costing overhead rates are usually based on the expected activity level for the coming period, which may be, say, 85 per cent of the possible level.

When Sanyo introduced ABM in 1994 (Sakurai, 1997), they found the biggest benefit gained was the identification of many causes of non-value-added expenditure. Many of these were attributed to the 'superfluous flesh' which the company had gained in the bubble period of the late 1980s. There were many under-used resources in the company and without the use of ABM they would not have been identified.

ABM showed that more than 25 per cent of one division's human resources were not adding value. 252 employees of the 1,000 employed in this division were identified as unnecessary. They were not laid-off but were moved to new value-added businesses. This was an important factor in getting employee involvement in the continuing use of the technique. In addition ABM helped Sanyo identify three problems which needed to be corrected:

- the existence of barriers between departments;
- human resource management was backward and not operating successfully;
- there was no firm business policy for developing new businesses.

10.3.5 Costing objects other than products

In pre-computer times the costing department was limited in the information that it could provide, as all calculations had to be done by hand. Modern databases have made it possible to store large amounts of data rather than aggregated data, that is, information. This raw data can be used to provide different sets of information such as product cost information. By using ABC organisations create the basic building blocks of information – that is, costs accumulated by activities which are then expressed in the form of activity cost drivers. The cost drivers can be used to provide a number of different sets of information.

The most important set may be information on customers or groups of customers, which is discussed in the next section. However, organisations often want more than just information on products and customers. Other business aspects include research, market development, improving organisational learning, etc.; each one of these makes demands on the different activities of the business and can be costed by using the basic building blocks of activity costs and their drivers. These other cost objects fall into two main categories:

- *Business development*, which includes new product, market/technology development.
- *Organisation infrastructure*, which includes new IT systems and physical or organisational structures.

It is usually important for management to pay attention to both these areas, first to make sure that adequate investment is made to secure the organisation's future and then to control costs. Being able to cost these two categories is therefore very useful.

10.3.6 Activity-based management: customer profitability analysis

In many organisations, it is just as important to cost customers as it is to cost products. Different customers or groups of customers differ in their profitability. This is a relatively new ABM technique that ABC information makes possible because it creates cost pools for activities. Customers use some activities but not all, and different groups of customers have different 'activity profiles'.

Service organisations, such as a bank or a hotel, in particular need to cost customers. A bank's services for a customer will include the following types of activities:

- withdrawal of cash;
- unauthorised overdraft;
- request for a statement;
- stopping a cheque;
- returning a cheque because of insufficient funds.

Different customers or categories of customers will each use different amounts of these activities and so customer profitability profiles can be built up, and customers can be charged according to the cost to serve them. A hotel may have activities that are provided for specific types of customers, such as well laid-out gardens, a swimming pool and a bar. Older guests may appreciate and use the garden, families the swimming pool and business guests the bar. If the activities are charged to the relevant guests a correct cost per room-night can be calculated for this type of category. This will show the relative profitability and lead to strategies for encouraging the more profitable guests.

Even a manufacturing organisation can benefit from costing its customers. Not all customers cost the same to serve even if they require the same products. Some customers may be located a long way from the factory and transport may cost more. Other customers may be disruptive and place rush orders that interrupt production scheduling and require immediate, special transport. Some customers need after-sales service and help with technical matters, etc. Table 10.4 contains information on four different customers, A, B, C and D in a manufacturing organisation. A single product is sold but the selling price differs because of trade discounts offered. Table 10.5 contains the cost per unit of each business activity and Table 10.6 shows the results of the customer profitability analysis.

In this example all four customers are profitable, but C and D are not particularly so when compared with A and B. When an organisation analyses the profitability of its customers it is not unusual to find that a Pareto curve exists (see Figure 10.2). That is, 20 per cent of customers provide 80 per cent of the profit. In Figure 10.2 it can be seen that in this case the last 80 per cent of customers do not all generate profit. The last 50 per cent actually reduce the total profit. There is no point in serving these customers as the situation stands but it may be foolish just to refuse to serve them. Instead it may be better to turn them into profitable customers if this is possible.

Table 10.4 Information on four customers

	A	B	C	D
No. of units sold	60,000	80,000	100,000	70,000
Selling price net of discount	25p	23p	21p	22p
No. of sales visits	2	4	6	3
No. of purchase orders	30	20	40	20
No. of deliveries	10	15	25	14
Kilometres per journey	20	30	10	50
No. of rush deliveries	–	–	1	2

Table 10.5 Costs of each activity

Sales visit	£210 per visit
Order placing	£60 per order
Product handling	£0.10 per item
Normal delivery cost	£2 per kilometre
Rushed delivery cost	£200 per delivery

Table 10.6 Customer profitability analysis

	A £	B £	C £	D £
Revenue net of discount	15,000	18,400	21,000	14,400
Costs:				
Sales visits (£210 × 2, etc.)	420	840	1,260	630
Order processing (£60 × 30, etc.)	1,800	1,200	2,400	1,200
Product handling (£0.10 × 60,000, etc.)	6,000	8,000	10,000	7,000
Delivery (£2 × 20 × 10, etc.)	400	900	500	1,400
Rush deliveries (£200 × 1, etc.)	–	–	200	400
	8,620	10,940	14,360	10,630
Operating profit	6,380	7,460	6,640	3,770
Percentage profitability	43%	41%	32%	26%

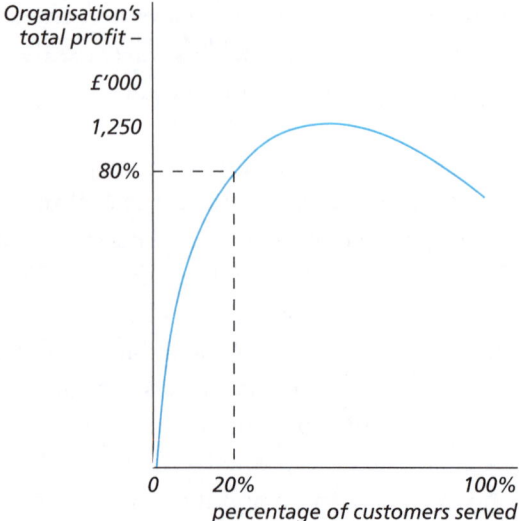

Figure 10.2 Customer profitability curve

A multifunctional team should be set up to find ways of making these customers profitable. Usually it is the small volume/order customers who are unprofitable because of high production batch costs and order processing, etc. One organisation introduced a third-party wholesaler into the supply chain and significantly reduced the cost of serving the small order customers. At the same time the organisation found that the product-range and service to the small customers improved, and so the company saved costs and the customer received an improved service.

More detail on customer profitability analysis will be found in an article in the 'Readings' section for this chapter.

10.3.7 Distribution channel profitability

Distribution channels are in simple terms the means of transacting with customers. The channel is the point of purchase which may or may not be the point of communication, payment, delivery and after sales support. Companies may transact with their customers through direct channels e.g. sales teams, telephone, shops, Internet or through indirect channels e.g. retailers, wholesalers, resellers, agents.

Regardless of whether a company's channels are direct or indirect they should always consider the ultimate needs of the customer and therefore use the channels to ensure that those needs are satisfied. Customers will look for ease of access to the supplier, reciprocal communication, products and services which satisfy their needs, prompt delivery, after sales support to name but a few.

The channel a company selects is therefore a critical driver to business profitability. A company should not only aim to satisfy the needs of the customer but must also ensure that the products and services that they are providing are profitable. The method of channel distribution chosen can account for a significant proportion of total cost and choosing the wrong channel can result in significant losses for that particular product or service. Key aspects that the company needs to consider in relation to their distribution channels include; access to the customer base, brand awareness, competitiveness, achieving sales and market targets, speed of payment, customer retention rates and most importantly of all profitability.

In companies it is just as important to cost channels as it is to cost products and customers. Different channels will differ in profitability. Activity based costing information makes this possible because it creates cost pools for activities. Channels will use some activities but not all, and different channels will have different 'activity profiles'. This makes channel profitability analysis possible and allows company's to build up distribution channel profitability profiles. It can be possible therefore for a company to identify costly distribution channels for perhaps low margin products or services which they are supplying through direct channels which may best be offered through indirect channels thus resulting in reduced channel distribution costs and a better profitability profile for the product or service.

10.3.8 Activity-based management: strategic activity management

Strategic activity management recognises that individual activities are part of a wider process. Activities are grouped to form a total process or service. For example, serving a particular customer involves a number of discrete activities that form the total service. Strategic activity management attempts to classify each activity within the whole as a value-added or non-value-added activity. Non-value-added activities are unnecessary and should be eliminated.

Bellis-Jones (1992) noted that typically prior to the introduction of ABM 35 per cent of staff time was spent on diversionary (non-value-added) activities. After the introduction of ABM, total staff time declined and the percentage of time spent on diversionary activities fell to 20 per cent of the reduced time.

Non-value-added activities are often caused by inadequacies within the existing processes and cannot be eliminated unless the inadequacy is addressed. For example, dealing with customer complaints is a diversionary activity, but it cannot be eliminated unless the source of the complaints is eliminated. Another example of a non-value-added activity that is caused to a certain extent by inadequacies in the existing processes is machine set-up time. Better product design so that fewer components are used or the use of more standard components will reduce the set-up time between component runs. So management must concentrate on eliminating non-value-added activities.

But strategic activity management is more than just eliminating non-value-added activities, important though this is.

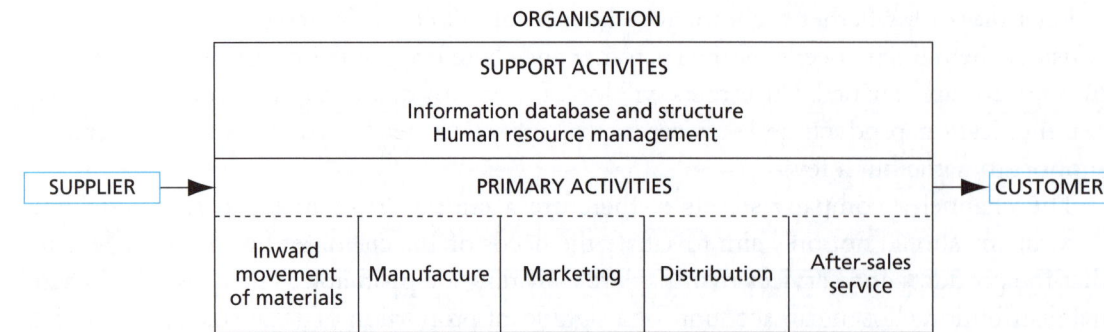

Figure 10.3 The value chain for a single organisation

ABC information can be used in an ABM system to assist strategic decisions, such as:

- Whether to continue with a particular activity.
- The effect on cost structure of a change in strategy, e.g. from mass production to smaller lots.
- How changes in activities and components affect the suppliers and the value chain.

The value chain is simply a large activity map for the organisation and its position in the industry chain. The chart in Figure 10.3 is a modified version of Porter's generic value chain. It consists of the main activities both primary (which should add value) and support (potentially non-value-adding unless they aid the primary activities to created more value-added). The organisation's value chain can be linked with other organisations' value chains to form an industry value chain.

10.3.9 Using ABC in service industries and activities

Despite the concentration on manufacturing organisations so far in this chapter, ABC can be used by all types of organisation, such as retail, service, nationalised, etc., and in all areas of the business. Three brief examples are considered below, mainly to identify the different types of activities and cost drivers.

- AT&T, the US telephone and telecommunications company, first used ABC in the early 1990s as a pilot project in its sales invoicing department according to Hobdy et al. (1994). It used the following types of activities to collect costs:
  – Monitoring billing records
  – Editing checks
  – Validating data
  – Correcting errors
  – Printing, sorting and dispatching invoices.
  It then spread the activity cost pools on cost drivers that included the following:
  – No. of customers tested
  – Change requests
  – Service orders
  – Customer locations
  – Printer hours
  – Pages printed.

AT&T found that ABC not only helped managers to manage the costs, but it also helped them improve operating processes and supplier relationships and to raise customer satisfaction.

This shows another role for ABC, namely its use as a one-off attention-directing technique to assess an activity and its impact on the business. Whether it continues to be used as a one-off technique or becomes an integral part of the costing systems is up to management.

- ABC is also used in a wide range of service industries, from hospitals to credit card companies. Research into hospital costs and activities by Huang and Kirby (1994) has identified two main cost drivers for a hospital:
  - The number of days spent in hospital. Costs included in this category were routine nursing care, meals and laundry.
  - The number of admissions. Costs included in this category were obtaining and using the patient's medical history, preparation for surgery, after-surgery care and invoicing insurers and collecting funds.

This particular piece of research found that Medicare (i.e. the government reimbursement scheme) had been considerably over-charged because it dealt with older patients who stayed longer in hospital than others on private insurance. As a consequence the absorption rate used prior to ABC, which was a single day rate, gave a charge which was too high for long-stay patients.

10.3.10 Problems with implementing ABC

Much has been written in academic journals of the benefits of using ABC and ABM. The majority of organisations still do not use either. Why, if the majority of academics consider it to be so useful, do practitioners not employ ABC? The obvious reason is that they do not agree on its usefulness or cost effectiveness in terms of costs and benefits. For ABC to be effective an accurate system is required with as many as 50 different activities identified and costs attributed to them. This requires considerable time and effort.

A certain amount of research has focused on the problems of implementing the system. These have suggested reasons why some organisations have pilot schemes that are then not proceeded with. Friedman and Lyne (1999) provide some clues as to why it has not been taken up with more enthusiasm from case study research they carried out. Some reasons they draw attention to are:

- Where it was devised for a single project that was not taken up the system got dropped as well. As communication between business units in a large organisation is often not very good, the work was not developed further by other units.
- Finance department opposed its implementation. Often finance staff appear less than dynamic and unable to perceive the needs of the production staff.
- General ledger information too poor to provide reliable ABC information. The resulting figures would have been no better than traditional absorption methods.

Of course, if organisations do not have reliable ABC information then they also forgo the cost management advantages of an ABM system. Since ABC provides the basic building blocks of activities, without ABC there can be no ABM.

10.4 Pareto analysis

10.4.1 The rule

Pareto analysis is based on the 80:20 rule that was a phenomenon first observed by Vilfredo Pareto, a nineteenth century Italian economist. He noticed that 80 per cent of the wealth of Milan was owned by 20 per cent of its citizens (see Figure 10.4). This phenomenon, or some kind of approximation of it (70:30, etc.), can be observed in many different business situations. The management accountant can use it in a number of different circumstances to help direct management's attention to the key control mechanisms or planning aspects.

The Pareto phenomenon often shows itself in relation to profitability. It is often the case that around 80 per cent of an organisation's contribution is generated by 20 per cent of the revenue. A situation similar to this can be seen in Figure 10.5 where the contributions of five products are plotted on a cumulative basis. Twenty per cent of the sales revenue generates 80 per cent of the contribution.

It is not always advisable to delete products from the range if they are not very profitable or their price cannot be increased, without carrying out careful analysis. The poor

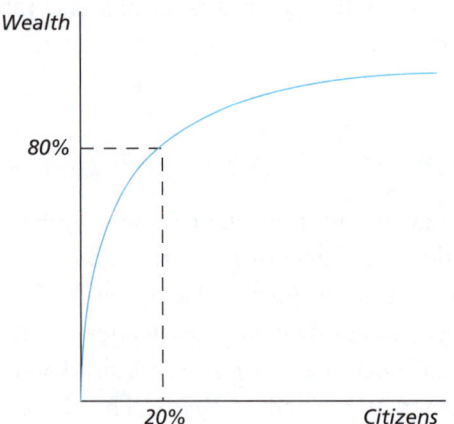

Figure 10.4 Pareto chart of wealth distribution in Milan

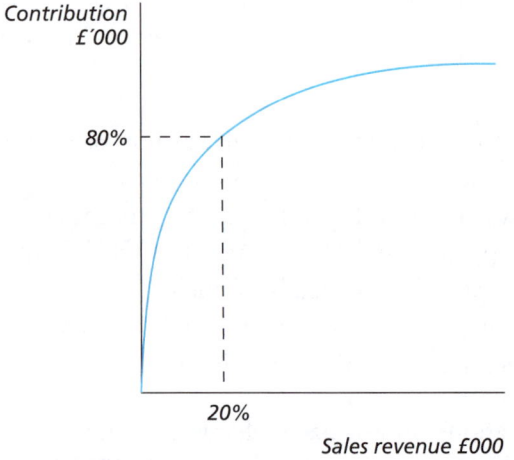

Figure 10.5 Product profitability chart

performers may be new products establishing themselves in the market and they may have a profitable future. The imbalance is almost inherent and cannot normally be removed. However, the products that generate the largest proportion of the contribution need to be looked after, so that they can continue to generate at this level. One reason for their profitability may be a high degree of branding which has the effect of increasing the contribution margin per unit. The company must continue to spend money promoting the brand so as to keep it in front of the public.

10.4.2 Uses of Pareto analysis

Pareto analysis has a number of different uses in business; some of these are described below.

Instead of analysing products, customers can be analysed for their relative profitability to the organisation. Again, it is often found that approximately 20 per cent of customers generate 80 per cent of the profit. There will always be some customers who are less profitable than others, just as some products are less profitable than others. The key with customers is to make sure that the overall profile does not degenerate and the aim should be to improve the profile. This can be seen in Figure 10.6 where the solid line represents the present position and the two dotted lines represent a change in performance for the better and worse. Line (ii) shows improved performance in the sense that customers are contributing more evenly to the profit, thus stabilising the position of the organisation. With the 'worse profile', the loss of, say, two of the best customers might seriously jeopardise the organisation's future.

Another use for Pareto analysis is in stock control where it may be found that only a few of the goods in stock make up most of the value. A typical analysis of stock may reveal the situation shown in Table 10.7.

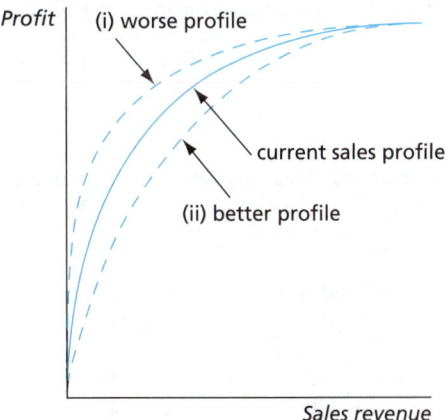

Figure 10.6 Pareto chart showing customer profitability

Table 10.7

Product	Value	% of value	% of volume	Action
A	High value	70	10	Control carefully
B	Medium value	20	20	Medium control
C	Little value	10	70	No control

The outcome of this type of analysis may be to increase control and safeguards on the 10 per cent of the stock that is of a particularly high value and to remove or reduce the controls on the stock that is of little value. Alternatively it may be found that a few items take up most of the storage space and therefore storage costs are unduly high for these items. It may be possible to move towards a just-in-time system for these items only, thus saving money and space.

Another study might relate to activity-based costing and overheads. It may show that 20 per cent of an organisation's cost drivers are responsible for 80 per cent of the total cost. By analysing, monitoring and controlling those cost drivers that cause most cost, a better control and understanding of overheads will be obtained.

Exercise

ABC Limited manufactures and sells seven products. The following data relates to the latest period.

Product	Contribution £000
P	96
Q	36
R	720
S	240
T	12
U	60
V	24
	1,188

Requirement

Prepare a Pareto chart of product contribution and comment on the results.

Solution

The first step is to rearrange the products in descending order of contribution and calculate the cumulative contribution:

Product	Contribution £000	Cumulative contribution £000	Cumulative %
R	720	720	61
S	240	960	81
P	96	1,056	89
U	60	1,116	94
Q	36	1,152	97
V	24	1,176	99
T	12	1,188	100
	1,188		

The cumulative data can now be used to produce the required Pareto chart showing product contribution:

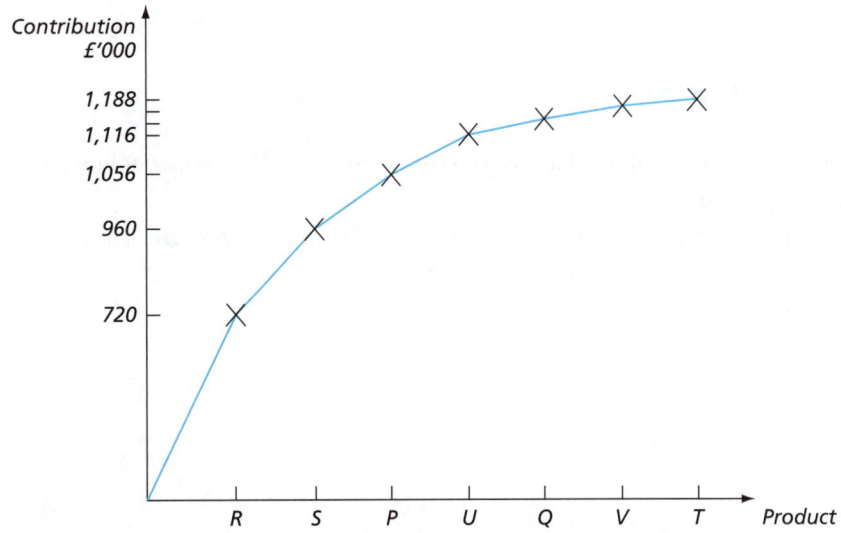

The analysis shows that more than 80 per cent of the total contribution is earned by two products: R and S. The position of these products needs protecting, perhaps through careful attention to branding and promotion. The other products require investigation to see whether their contribution can be improved through increased prices, reduced costs or increased volumes.

The term 'Pareto diagram' usually refers to a histogram or frequency chart on product quality (see Figure 10.7). In the 1950s Juran observed that a few causes of poor quality usually accounted for most of the quality problems – hence the name Pareto. Figure 10.7 shows a frequency chart for poor quality in boxed cakes, and it can easily be imagined how it could be turned into a Pareto chart. The purpose of the analysis, in this case, is to direct attention to the area where the best returns can be achieved by solving most of the quality problems,

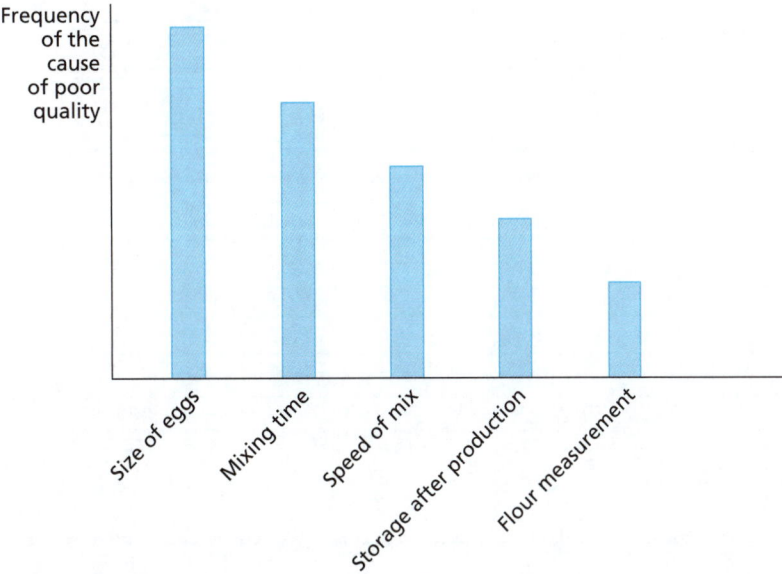

Figure 10.7 Pareto diagram showing the causes of quality problems in boxed cakes

perhaps just with a single action. In this case more accurate grading of eggs by volume by the supplier may solve about 40 per cent of the total quality problem and if the mixing time is made more accurate at least 75 per cent of the problems will be removed.

10.5 Summary

In this chapter we have compared activity-based costing (ABC) approaches to those of traditional absorption costing.

In making this comparison we have seen how the use of ABC often develops into activity-based management approach to controlling the organisation.

Readings

A comprehensive example of ABC

This example builds on the simpler example in the text and presents a more detailed, and therefore realistic, calculation. Section I illustrates the calculation of the traditional method – try the calculation yourself before looking at the answer. Section II illustrates the calculation using ABC – again try the calculation yourself before you read on. Section III deals with the problem of genuine fixed costs, that is facility level costs.

Section I – Traditional analysis

A company manufactures three products – X, Y and Z, whose direct costs are given in Table 1.

Table 1

	X	Y	Z
	£	£	£
Direct material	67.92	63.27	56.79
Direct labour (@ £3/hr):			
Machining	13.08	14.73	17.01
Assembly	24.00	27.00	31.20
	105.00	105.00	105.00

The data in Table 2 was used in calculating the direct labour costs above, and will be used to determine the production overhead charged to each product under the 'traditional' costing method.

Table 2

	X	Y	Z	Total
Machine time (hours)	10.00	9.00	8.00	
Direct labour (hours):				
Machining	4.36	4.91	5.67	
Assembly	8.00	9.00	10.40	
Production (units)	50,000	30,000	16,250	
Total machine hours	500,000	270,000	130,000	900,000
Total labour hours:				
Machining	218,000	147,300	92,137	457,437
Assembly	400,000	270,000	169,000	839,000
				1,296,437

Table 3 contains information on the company's overheads.

Table 3

	£000	Total £000
Production overhead		
Indirect labour:		
Machining	900	
Assembly	600	
Purchasing/order processing	600	
Factory management	100	2,200
Power:		
Machining	400	
Assembly	100	500
Indirect materials:		
Machining	200	
Assembly	200	
Purchasing	100	
Factory management	100	600
Depreciation:		
Machining	600	
Assembly	300	
Purchasing	200	
Building	400	1,500
Security		100
Grounds maintenance		100
Total production overhead		5,000

Requirement

Prepare a traditional overhead analysis and calculate product costs for the three products. Assume that the machining department uses a machine hour absorption rate and the assembly department a labour hour rate.

Solution

Step 1 – Assign production overhead to cost centres

	£000	Total £000
Machining:		
Indirect labour	900	
Power	400	
Indirect materials	200	
Depreciation	600	2,100
Assembly:		
Indirect labour	600	
Power	100	
Indirect materials	200	
Depreciation	300	1,200
Purchasing/order processing:		
Indirect labour	600	
Indirect materials	100	
Depreciation	200	900
Factory management:		
Indirect labour	100	
Indirect materials	100	
Depreciation	400	
Security	100	
Grounds maintenance	100	800
Total production overhead		5,000

Step 2 – Reallocate services department costs to production departments on a suitable basis

	£000	Total £000
Machining:		
Indirect costs (from step 1)	2,100	
Reallocation of service centre costs*	600	2,700
Assembly:		
Indirect costs (from step 1)	1,200	
Reallocation of service centre costs*	1,100	2,300
Purchasing/order processing:		
Indirect costs (from step 1)	900	
Reallocate on basis of direct labour cost	(900)	0
Factory management:		
Indirect costs (from step 1)	800	
Reallocate on basis of direct labour cost	(800)	0
Total production overhead		5,000

* Service centre costs are to be reallocated on the basis of direct labour cost. Since all labour hours are paid at the same rate per hour, this is the same as using direct labour hours. The reallocations, in £000, are:
Machining = $457{,}437/1{,}296{,}437 \times £(900 + 800) = £600$
Assembly = $839{,}000/1{,}296{,}437 \times £(900 + 800) = £1{,}100$

Step 3 – Calculate absorption rate
Machining: based on total machine hours

$$\frac{\text{Total overhead costs}}{\text{Total machine hours}} = \frac{£2{,}700{,}000}{900{,}000} = £3 \text{ per machine hour}$$

Assembly: based on total assembly labour hours

$$\frac{\text{Total overhead costs}}{\text{Total labour hours}} = \frac{£2{,}300{,}000}{839{,}000} = £2.74 \text{ per labour hour}$$

Step 4 – Calculate full product cost

	X £	Y £	Z £
Direct costs (as before)	105.00	105.00	105.00
Production overhead:			
Machining	30.00	27.00	24.00
Assembly	21.92	24.66	28.50
	156.92	156.66	157.50

Section II – ABC analysis. Allocating all costs to products

The information and data in Tables 4, 5 and 6 will be used to determine cost drivers and calculate overheads.

Table 4

Product information

X	Y	Z
High volume	Medium volume	Low volume
Large batches	Medium batches	Small batches
Few purchase orders placed	Medium purchase orders placed	Many purchase orders placed
	Medium components	Many components
Few customer orders placed	Medium customer orders placed	Many customer orders placed

Table 5

Product information

	X	Y	Z	Total
Typical batch size	2,000	600	325	
No. of production runs	25	50	50	125
No. of inspections	25	50	50	125
Purchase orders placed	25	100	200	325
Customer orders received	10	100	200	310

Table 6

Analysis of indirect labour

	£000	Total £000
Machining:		
Supervision	100	
Set-up	400	
Quality control	400	900
Assembly:		
Supervision	200	
Quality control	400	600
Purchasing/order processing:		
Resource procurement	300	
Customer liaison/expediting	300	600
Factory management:		
General administration		100
		2,200

Requirement

Prepare an ABC analysis and calculate product costs.

Solution

Step 1 – Identify production-related activities

Activities

(1) Machining
(2) Machine set-up
(3) Machining quality control
(4) Assembly
(5) Assembly quality control

(6) Resource procurement
(7) Customer liaison/expediting
(8) Factory management

	Step 2 – Identify the cost of activities	Step 3 – Identify cost driver	Step 4 – Reallocate factory management costs pro rata to other costs	Total
Total	£000		£000	£000
(1) Machining:				
Supervision	100			
Power	400	Machine running		
Indirect materials	100	time		
Depreciation	600		230	1,430
	1,200			
(2) Machine set-up:		No. of set-ups		
Indirect labour	400	(batch size)		
Indirect materials	50		85	535
	450			
(3) Machining quality control:		No. of inspections		
Indirect labour	400	(batch size)		
Indirect materials	50		85	535
	450			
(4) Assembly:				
Supervision	200	Direct labour		
Power	100	hours worked		
Indirect materials	100			
Depreciation	300		135	835
	700			
(5) Assembly quality control:		No. of inspections		
Indirect labour	400	(batch size)		
Indirect materials	100		95	595
	500			
(6) Resource procurement:		No. of orders		
Indirect labour	300	placed (product/batch size)		
Indirect materials	50			
Depreciation	100		85	535
	450			
(7) Customer liaison/expediting:		No. of orders		
Indirect labour	300	received (product)		
Indirect materials	50			
Depreciation	100		85	535
	450			
(8) Factory management (see note below):				
Indirect labour	100	No obvious driver		
Indirect materials	100	(size of business?)		
Depreciation	400			
Security	100			
Grounds maint.	100			
	800		(800)	0
	5,000		0	5,000

There is no obvious driver for the common costs collected under the heading 'factory management' so they have been reallocated to other activity cost pools on the basis of their total costs.

Step 5 – Calculate overhead from cost drivers

Rate per machine hour:

$$\frac{\text{Total overhead costs}}{\text{Total machine hours}} = \frac{£1,430,000}{900,000} = £1.59 \text{ per machine hour}$$

Rate per set-up:

$$\frac{\text{Total overhead costs}}{\text{Total set-ups}} = \frac{£535,000}{125} = £4,280 \text{ per batch}$$

Rate per machining inspection:

$$\frac{\text{Total overhead costs}}{\text{Total inspections}} = \frac{£535,000}{125} = £4,280 \text{ per batch}$$

Assembly rate per direct labour hour:

$$\frac{\text{Total overhead costs}}{\text{Total assembly hours}} = \frac{£835,000}{839,000} = £1.00 \text{ per labour hour}$$

Rate per assembly inspection:

$$\frac{\text{Total overhead costs}}{\text{Total inspections}} = \frac{£595,000}{125} = £4,760 \text{ per batch}$$

Rate per order placed:

$$\frac{\text{Total overhead costs}}{\text{Total orders placed}} = \frac{£535,000}{325} = £1,646 \text{ per batch}$$

Rate per order received:

$$\frac{\text{Total overhead costs}}{\text{Total orders received}} = \frac{£535,000}{310} = £1,726 \text{ per batch}$$

Step 6 – Calculate full product cost

	X			Y			Z		
		£	£		£	£		£	£
Direct costs (as before)			105.00			105.00			105.00
Overhead									
per machine hour:			15.90			14.31			12.72
per set-up:	$\frac{£4,280}{2,000}$	=	2.14	$\frac{£4,280}{600}$	=	7.13	$\frac{£4,280}{325}$	=	13.17
per machine inspection:	$\frac{£4,280}{2,000}$	=	2.14	$\frac{£4,280}{600}$	=	7.13	$\frac{£4,280}{325}$	=	13.17
Assembly rate @ £1 per dlh			8.00			9.00			10.40
per assembly inspection:	$\frac{£4,760}{2,000}$	=	2.38	$\frac{£4,760}{600}$	=	7.93	$\frac{£4,760}{325}$	=	14.65
per order placed:	$\frac{£1,646 \times 25}{50,000}$	=	0.82	$\frac{£1,646 \times 100}{30,000}$	=	5.49	$\frac{£1,646 \times 200}{16,250}$	=	20.26
per order received:	$\frac{£1,726 \times 10}{50,000}$	=	0.35	$\frac{£1,726 \times 100}{30,000}$	=	5.75	$\frac{£1,726 \times 200}{16,250}$	=	21.24
Overhead sub-total			31.73			56.74			105.61
Direct costs + overheads			136.73			161.74			210.61

Rationalisation of overhead charged:

Product	Overhead (£)	Production	Total £000
X	31.73	50,000	1,585
Y	56.74	30,000	1,700
Z	105.61	16,250	1,715
			5,000

Comparison of product costs under each method

	X £	Y £	Z £
'Traditional'	156.92	156.66	157.50
Activity-based costing	136.73	161.74	210.61

Product Z – with a low total production volume, many purchase and customer orders, and frequent small production runs – has a significantly higher cost under ABC than under the 'traditional' method. The opposite is the case with product X, which has a high total production volume, relatively few orders and large production runs.

Section III – ABC analysis. Excluding facility level costs

In the calculation in Section II the ABC costs, like traditional costs, contain an allocation of the factory management costs within each cost driver – or absorption – rate. Factory management costs were allocated to other activities simply because of the lack of an identifiable driver with which to associate them with products. Factory management is a 'facility level' activity and, as such, cannot be identified directly with another activity, and certainly not with a particular product.

Despite the lack of an identifiable driver, it can be argued that this cost should not be identified arbitrarily with the other activities, but should be left within its own cost pool.

If this is done, Step 4 in the ABC analysis above would be omitted, and the calculation would proceed as follows:

ABC analysis when factory management costs are not reallocated to other activities

The production-related activities have already been identified in Step 1

		Step 2 – Identify the cost of activities £000	Step 3 – Identify cost driver
(1)	Machining	1,200	Machine running time
(2)	Machine set-up	450	No. of set-ups (batch size)
(3)	Machining quality control	450	No. of inspections (batch size)
(4)	Assembly	700	Direct labour hours worked
(5)	Assembly quality control	500	No. of inspections (batch size)
(6)	Resource procurement	450	No. of orders placed (product/batch size)
(7)	Customer liaison/expediting	450	No. of orders received (product)
(8)	Factory management	800	No obvious driver (size of business)
		5,000	

(Step 4 – Omitted)

Step 5 – Calculate overhead from cost drivers

Rate per machine hour:

$$\frac{\text{Total overhead costs}}{\text{Total machine hours}} = \frac{£1,200,000}{900,000} = £1.333 \text{ per machine hour}$$

Rate per set-up:

$$\frac{\text{Total overhead costs}}{\text{Total set-ups}} = \frac{£450,000}{125} = £3,600 \text{ per batch}$$

Rate per machining inspection:

$$\frac{\text{Total overhead costs}}{\text{Total inspections}} = \frac{£450,000}{125} = £3,600 \text{ per batch}$$

Assembly rate per direct labour hour:

$$\frac{\text{Total overhead costs}}{\text{Total assembly hours}} = \frac{£700,000}{839,000} = £0.834 \text{ per labour hour}$$

Rate per assembly inspection:

$$\frac{\text{Total overhead costs}}{\text{Total inspections}} = \frac{£500,000}{125} = £4,000 \text{ per batch}$$

Rate per order placed:

$$\frac{\text{Total overhead costs}}{\text{Total order's placed}} = \frac{£450,000}{325} = £1,385 \text{ per order}$$

Rate per order received:

$$\frac{\text{Total overhead costs}}{\text{Total order's received}} = \frac{£450,000}{310} = £1,452 \text{ per order}$$

Factory management costs of £800,000 have no obvious driver, and are not included in the costs above.

Step 6 – Calculate full product cost

	X			Y			Z	
	£	£	£	£	£	£	£	£
Direct costs (as before)		105.00			105.00			105.00
Overhead								
per machine hour:		13.33			12.00			10.67
per set-up:	$\frac{£3,600}{2,000}$ =	1.80	$\frac{£3,600}{600}$	=	6.00	$\frac{£3,600}{325}$	=	11.08
per machine inspection:	$\frac{£3,600}{2,000}$ =	1.80	$\frac{£3,600}{600}$	=	6.00	$\frac{£3,600}{325}$	=	11.08
Assembly rate @ £0.834 per dlh		6.67			7.51			8.67
per assembly inspection:	$\frac{£4,000}{2,000}$ =	2.00	$\frac{£4,000}{600}$	=	6.67	$\frac{£4,000}{325}$	=	12.31
per order placed:	$\frac{£1,385 \times 25}{50,000}$ =	0.69	$\frac{£1,385 \times 100}{30,000}$	=	4.62	$\frac{£1,385 \times 200}{16,250}$	=	17.05
per order received:	$\frac{£1,452 \times 10}{50,000}$ =	0.29	$\frac{£1,452 \times 100}{30,000}$	=	4.84	$\frac{£1,452 \times 200}{16,250}$	=	17.87
Overhead sub-total		26.78			47.64			88.73
Direct costs + overheads		131.58			152.64			193.73

Rationalisation of overhead charged:

Product	Overhead (£)	Production	Total £000
X	26.58	50,000	1,329
Y	47.64	30,000	1,429
Z	88.73	16,250	1,442
			4,200

In this second approach, the £800,000 factory management costs have been left unallocated. Obviously, for stock valuation purposes, it would be necessary to allocate them to products, albeit on an arbitrary basis. They could be allocated to products in proportion to the allocation of other overhead costs, as shown below:

Overhead charged:

Product	Total overhead (1) £000	Factory management cost (2) £000	Total production overhead allocated (1) + (2) £000
X	1,329	253	1,582
Y	1,429	272	1,701
Z	1,442	275	1,717
	4,200	800	5,000

Apart from minor rounding differences, the total allocation as shown in the final column above is identical to that in the same column in Section II, and thus the total overhead charged to the three products is identical under both approaches. However, the second approach may be much more helpful to management by directing attention to the resource implications of manufacturing particular products. For example, Table 7 shows product Y's comparative costs.

Table 7

ABC cost of product Y:	Factory management costs allocated to other activities £	Factory management treated as a separate activity £
Direct costs (as before)	105.00	105.00
Overhead		
Unit level activity cost:		
Per machine hour	14.31	12.00
Assembly rate	9.00	7.51
Batch level activity cost:		
Per set-up	7.13	6.00
Per machine inspection	7.13	6.00
Per assembly inspection	7.93	6.67
Per order placed	5.49	4.62
Product level activity cost:		
Per order received	5.75	4.84
Overhead sub-total	56.74	47.64
Facility level activity cost		
Factory management costs:	–	9.08*
Total production overhead	56.74	56.72
Direct costs + overheads	161.74	161.72

*$\dfrac{£272,000}{30,000}$

In the first analysis, the cost driver rates do not give an accurate reflection of the resource consumption implications of performing particular activities, as they contain an arbitrary allocation of factory management costs. The second analysis provides cost driver rates that do reflect truly the long-run costs of performing particular activities. This information may be useful to management in identifying cost reduction opportunities, as well as for product costing purposes.

In addition to identifying 'factory management' as a separate cost pool, Table 6 has also grouped costs in accordance with the hierarchy outlined in Section 10.3.1. This provides management with a clear view of the resource consumption that will result in the long run, if production of Y is maintained at 30,000 units and the organisation of production remains the same. If the volume of production of Y were to change, both ABC analyses draw management's attention to the fact that the change in overhead resource consumption brought about by the change in volume would not be proportionate to the change in the number of units produced. In the first analysis even the resource consumption of unit level activities would not change proportionately to the change in production volume, as there is no reason to expect the facility level costs of factory management, included therein via the allocation process, to change proportionately with changes in volume. In the second analysis, where there are no arbitrary cost allocations, the resource consumption of unit level activities would change proportionately with the change in volume. However, the change in the consumption of the other overhead resources would depend on precisely how the change in volume was achieved, e.g. were there more batches. For example, volume could be expanded by increasing the size of each batch of Y, in which case the consumption of batch level resources would remain constant, despite the rise in volume. ABC analyses thus provide a clearer insight into the way in which resource consumption, and ultimately cost, will change as a result of the specific changes in activities that accompany a particular change in volume.

The following Reading looks at the experiences of a company that has implemented activity-based management effectively. The article offers a number of tips for ABM and warns of the need for careful planning and a radical rethink of company culture.

Tool of the trade

Stephanie Gourdie, *Financial Management*, November 2001

> **Tips for ABM**
> - Get the support of senior management
> - Recognise that ABM requires a major investment in time and resources
> - Know what ABM can achieve and what information you want from the system
> - Decide which model to use
> - Choose the model approach that emphasises the operational understanding of all activities in the business
> - Involve people in the field
> - Transfer ownership of cost management from the accounts department to the departments and processes where costs are incurred
> - Don't underestimate the need to manage the change process
> - Link ABM to corporate objectives in the form of increased product profitability and added value for customers

Since professors Robin Cooper and Robert Kaplan codified and developed activity-based costing (ABC)[1], many organisations have implemented it, but few are using it for cost management. The original emphasis of ABC was on developing more accurate product costs. It was based on the principle that resource-consuming activities caused costs, not volume of products, as assumed by traditional cost-allocation methods. Overhead costs were allocated and traced back to activities that consumed resources, such as purchasing, set-ups and material handling.

A cost driver was then selected for each activity centre. The choice of driver was based on two things: it had to measure the resources a product used for a particular set of activities; and it had to be linked to the changes of costs in the activity centre (a cause–effect relationship).

Cost drivers can include the number of purchase orders, material movements or set-up hours. The overhead rate for each activity was worked out by dividing the activity cost by the capacity of the cost driver. The costs of products were determined by multiplying the number of the cost driver of the activity used by the product, by the overhead rate for that activity, for all activities used by that product.

ABC systems could then be applied to cost management. This was labelled activity-based management (ABM), defined by Don Hansen and Maryanne Mowen[2] as 'a system-wide, integrated approach that focuses management's attention on activities with the objective of improving customer value and the profit achieved by providing this value'.

The progress to ABM involved a shift in focus from the original ABC system – producing information on activity-based product costs – to producing information to improve management of processes. The idea is to analyse the activities that make up a company's processes and the cost drivers of those activities, then question why the activities are being carried out and how well they are being performed. ABM provides the activity information and the costs of inefficient activities, and quantifies the benefits of continuous improvements.

Companies can then improve operations by re-engineering (complete redesign of processes), redesigning plant layouts, using common parts, outsourcing or strengthening supplier and customer relationships and developing alternative product designs.

Research on the implementation of ABC in Europe[3] shows that adoption of ABM remains low. One organisation in New Zealand has used ABM to improve the way it manages some of its processes, to get rid of non-value-added activities and to reduce costs substantially through efficiencies. It has achieved this by following certain 'dos and don'ts' in implementing accounting systems.

The organisation provides information services, record-keeping, testing, research and advisory services for New Zealand's agriculture sector. Its mission is to lead the world with its research and create wealth for its stakeholders, and its profit objective is to have enough resources to fund research and development. It has been through the same changes, including restructuring, that many New Zealand public-sector organisations went through in the 1980s.

The drive to implement ABM began with calls for more efficiency and accountability and a need to be seen to have efficient business practices and be more customer-orientated. The emphasis was on efficiency, total quality and effectiveness – all of which were in the firm's mission statements and business plans.

The board constantly requested more information and ABM offered the management accounting team a way of providing better quality service. But ABM was a major undertaking and the team had to proceed carefully.

ABM required a major investment in time and resources. Apart from the cost of the software, staff had to be taken away from their existing jobs and trained to set up and use the system. The activity analysis stage, for example, was long and sometimes arduous: it took three people nine months to implement.

Since ABM's introduction, the models have been reviewed annually for budgets and actuals and updated for budgets, forecasts and actuals. This process takes three people between five and ten weeks depending on the number and complexity of process changes.

Managers had to be clear about the potential benefits of ABM and what information the organisation wanted. Members of the management accounting team attended seminars and investigated several packages. They knew they wanted more than just an ABC package. They needed to establish product profitability, improve distribution of overheads, activities and costs of processes and find out how to improve these.

The organisation's clients, who were also its shareholders, believed they had the right to query prices. So the system had to provide information about the relationship between prices and costs. It also needed an integrated decision support system that could carry out business process efficiency simulations.

There are plans to extend the system to include calculations of customer profitability, activity-based budgeting, and the balanced scorecard. The balanced scorecard 'translates an organisation's mission and strategy into operational objectives and performance measures for four different perspectives: the financial perspective; the customer perspective; the internal business process perspective; and the learning and growth perspective'[2]. In other words, activities carried out in an organisation should be linked to its strategic objectives.

The next step was to decide which model to use. Some organisations operate standalone ABM systems using either spreadsheets or third-party packaged software. Others integrate the system in their wider information systems. The maximum business advantage cannot be achieved until ABM is an integral part of an organisation's reporting system.

The New Zealand organisation chose a software package that could map the process. This approach would suit any organisation with inputs, demands, processes and constrained resources. It already had a mainframe database of activity data and a separate accounting system. The use of data warehousing allowed summary information from its two systems to be stored and accessed for multidimensional modelling, including accounting models for budgeting ABC costs, ABM information, simulations and forecasting.

It is important to pick a model that emphasises the operational understanding of all activities in the business. Instead of going down the financial decomposition analysis route – which analyses the accounting records of the organisation – the organisation chose the process model approach. This analyses the operations, identifying the key activities and resources consumed, by asking what people do, what resources are consumed and how. From the answers, appropriate activity drivers can be established, as can the inputs and outputs to each activity and the relationship between activities.

Managers gathered data from both operational and financial sources and carried out interviews to find out about processes. Some costs were allocated on traditional cost drivers, such as area, others on transactional cost drivers, such as number of visits by truck or technician. For each cost driver, costs were divided into fixed and variable. Some were more obvious than others and work was done to find an approximate division.

A pilot project was recommended in order to achieve results in six to eight weeks, develop a team of experts and convince managers of the benefits. The pilot chosen had defined inputs and outputs and was contained with simple and clear process flows. There was also clear output from each activity.

First, the project mapped the process showing different activities outside the ABM software. This procedure was useful as it helped the 'mapper' to understand the components of the process and how they interacted. The pilot study initially involved high-level mapping but, with hindsight, it would have been easier if it had been less detailed.

A key point is to involve people other than just the management accounting team. The model approach enables this because much of the original information must be obtained from people in the field. So the organisation used the management accounting team to implement the system, but seconded members from the field to use local expertise.

As part of the new system, ownership of cost management had to be transferred from the accounting department to the departments and processes where costs were incurred. Some units were not happy about this, but since there was a shift in performance criteria so divisional managers' salaries depended on results, they were motivated to make it work.

Perceptions of how different departments in the company worked had not changed, so staff did not feel threatened. People were keen to contribute, perhaps because of the good relationship between management accounts and other staff.

Agreement was obtained on criteria for measuring overheads and it turned out to be pretty straightforward to put numbers to activities and capacity levels. Tests showed that figures were generally reasonable and it is unlikely that investing far more time and resources would have made them significantly more accurate. Reports and graphs were prepared for each division so they could monitor their progress.

Implementing ABM meant a change in the culture of the whole organisation. It had to change from a public-sector-style company into a commercial enterprise (there is still ambivalence about how much profit it should make). The firm also had to worry about budgets and costs for the first time – it had never before had management accounting systems for cost management and budgeting.

Transition to the ABM system had to be gradual. First, the firm developed a cash objective budget system. From this, it built a simple ABC system model. Few products were dropped and the firm still expected to make a profit or break even. Economic conditions and other external factors were taken into account since there was a high proportion of fixed costs, but the new ABM philosophy made it clear to managers that the size of the 'cake' was fixed.

The information from the ABM system was used to show managers where divisions were unprofitable. It was left to them to cut costs and become more efficient. At the moment, part of the general divisional managers' salaries is performance-related, but the aim is to extend this to more layers of management. Managers and staff are more aware of their portfolios.

Reports are made to the board twice a year, so the accounting system is particularly important. The first report is for the budget, detailed forecast and product profitability, and the second for actual compared with previous. The forecasting and budgeting processes both take two months. In January, managers are asked for their capital budgeting requirements and forecasts for the year until the end of May. Departments meet the following February to finalise their budgets. Budgets are completed by mid-April and the dollars are fed into the ABM model.

Senior managers have also had to change focus. The new system gives them more information about what is going on in divisions and they have had to adjust their management practices accordingly. The systems did create some concern about how big a slice of cake people would have, and operational divisions now question expenditure on overheads.

The organisation needed to link ABM to corporate objectives in the form of increased product profitability and improved value for customers. Performance measures for divisional managers included ABM improvements. Introducing ABM was not seen as a cost-cutting exercise and the processes were seen to be important and effective at meeting the needs of customers.

Overall, ABM was used to ensure the organisation was doing the thing right. The introduction of the balanced scorecard will ensure it is also doing the right thing.

References

1. R Kaplan, D Norton, 'The Balanced Scorecard – Measures That Drive Performance', *Harvard Business Review*, January/February 1992.
2. D Hansen, M Mowen, *Cost Management Accounting and Control*, South Western College Publishing, 2000.
3. M Fahy, G O'Brien, 'As Easy as ABC? It Seems Not', *Accountancy Ireland*, February 2000.

The following Reading looks at areas that are not revealed by conventional accounting techniques. It recognises that the transaction is the common denominator between product and customer and that customers vary considerably in their use of resources. Within an ABM system, an ABC analysis allows an organisation to measure and analyse customer account profitability.

Customer profitability analysis

Robin Bellis-Jones, *Management Accounting*, February 1989 © CIMA. Reproduced with permission

Fuelled by pressure from the City, the post-war retail sector has merged, acquired and rationalised to the point where a limited number of major retailers can wield great purchasing power at the expense of their suppliers. The latter, in terms of their commercial clout, remain relatively fragmented and powerless except where a particularly strong brand name exists. In this increasingly competitive environment, customer service has become a key element in the battle for both volume and margin.

Suppliers have often responded by either increasing discounts or increasing the level of service available to their retailers, hoping that the additional volume generated will protect their profits. However, the additional volumes or services often create extra activity – and cost – which more than offsets the additional margins generated.

Confusion in this key area has led to a certain amount of conflict between accounting and marketing staff and has led to a proliferation of courses such as 'Marketing for Accountants' and 'Finance for Non-Financial Managers'. But although such courses increase understanding, they do not address the fundamental commercial issues.

In fact many companies have resigned themselves to low, decreasing profitability on the grounds that the trading environment is 'becoming more difficult'. But the reality is that they squander otherwise profitable parts of their business by supplying service at below true cost.

Sophisticated analysis of all costs and revenues generated by outlet, rather than simply the gross margin less trade discount, is the solution.

Companies need to be able to quantify and present the implications of the trading relationship so that it can add real value to commercial decisions. Such an approach should answer key questions which conventional accounting fails to address – questions such as:

- Does market sector X meet our profitability criteria? Has it ever? Can it ever? If so, how?
- Which account generates the greatest profit contribution and how best can we protect it?
- What are the maximum discount/service packages we can afford in the next round of negotiations with our largest customers while still meeting our profit objectives?

- What type of account should we focus our new business effort on for maximum profitability?
- Do our large accounts really make money? Under what conditions are we prepared to walk away from that volume and what will we have to do as a consequence?
- Does this product contribute sufficiently to profitability to justify retaining it in the range?
- Should we stay in this market?

If these questions cannot be answered accurately then the success of related decisions will be minimal. Crucially, competitors who do understand how their costs are driven can significantly enhance their profitability against the sector trend.

The barriers to measuring account profitability

Although most companies recognise the need to answer such questions, most are constrained by the following factors:

- Conventional accounting philosophy is inappropriate to this type of analysis.
- Most companies are organised along functional lines, where the operations being quantified cross several functional boundaries. Often, some functions won't support such analysis, thereby devaluing the effort of others – a kind of 'functional myopia'.
- Some companies feel it is inappropriate to allocate the cost of providing a service to those who receive it.
- Many companies place strong emphasis on the measurement of profit centre performance. Although this orientation is valuable in measuring overall performances, it is also introverted in that it does not focus on customer performance at the individual level – the level at which many commercial decisions are made.

As a result of these constraints few companies get beyond measuring account profitability at the level of gross margin net of trade discount; they prefer to focus on easy rather than valuable measurements. In other words most companies understand the issues but do not know how to resolve them.

This article describes a solution which provides an immensely powerful and flexible means of quantifying and understanding the trading relationship, as well as a means of supporting key commercial decisions.

We describe the technique as customer profitability analysis (CPA).

Customer profitability analysis

CPA demands that all costs relevant to the trading relationship with any particular customer outlet are taken into account. This is necessary because gross margin net of trade discount is not an accurate measure of profitability. This approach is illustrated in Figure 1.

The CTN (confectioner/tobacconist/newsagent) outlet shown in the diagram provides a graphic example. At face value it generates a high level of contribution but, once all of the variable costs of each service aspect are taken into account, it is in fact marginally unprofitable. Some outlets suffer a much more severe reduction in profitability than others. Whatever the effect, however, reduced profit is caused by those overhead costs which vary with both activity, timescale and customer type and which could and should touch on most functions within the business. The following list is a sample cross-section:

- Quality control
- Merchandising

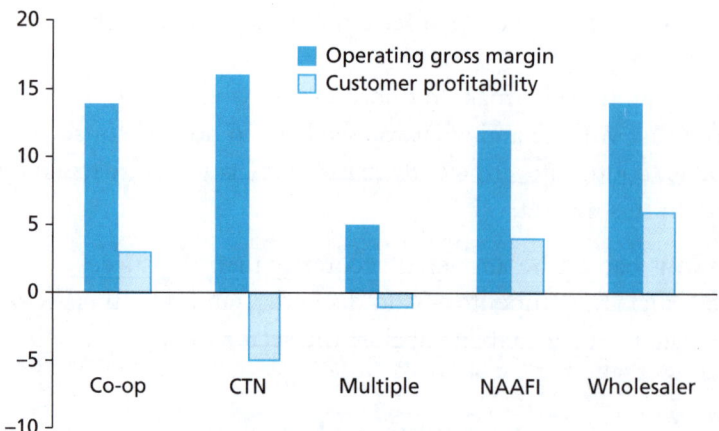

Figure 1 Profitability as a percentage of sales

- Sales force
- Retrospective discounts
- Distribution
- Purchasing
- Promotions
- Financing costs
- Enquiries.

The fundamental question which needs to be asked of each overhead element is, 'What aspect of the relationship with the customer does this support and how does it vary with activity levels and customer?'

For example, the cost of full-pallet transactions is quite different to that of break bulk; telesales is more time-efficient than a field sales force; merchandising is required by some outlets but not others; some customers demand pre-priced goods whereas others do not. These questions become particularly important when it is recognised that:

- activity-related costs which support the relationship with the customer independently of product costs can account for up to 60 per cent of sales value;
- when expressed as a percentage of sales value, these costs can vary widely depending on both the type of customer and the level of activity.

As no two customers are the same, profitability can vary enormously from one customer to another. None of these variations are revealed by conventional accounting techniques and their extent is illustrated in Figure 2.

Importance of the transaction

Relating these variations to the customers responsible is the problem. Conventional accounting has failed to recognise that the transaction is the common denominator between product and customer outlet and is therefore the ultimate profit centre. Exchange of goods as recorded against a single product line item on a sales invoice is the most refined level of identifiable transaction.

Undertaking analysis at this level of detail means that the undesirable necessity to use 'averages' is removed, so the results are far more credible. This change in accounting philosophy means the overall profit and loss account can be re-analysed to produce an individual

Total sales	Customer-driven variations in cost as a percentage of sales
Discounts and adjustments	0 – 25
Selling and order-taking	2 – 20
Storage and distribution	2 – 35
Production and purchasing	20 – 70
Marketing and advertising	1 – 20
Gen. admin. and fixed costs	10 – 30
Profit	← Scope for massive profit variations

Figure 2 Variability of costs

profit statement for each customer outlet. Subsequently these may be re-analysed to examine entire multiples as single entities or, further still, to look at an entire market sector, such as all multiples, as a whole.

CPA integrates the cost effect of all functions into the customer base and highlights the relationship between individual actions and policies – and their impact on each customer account.

CPA can require a significant mainframe 'number crushing' resource – PCs are still too small. However, once this stage is complete customers have a flexible profitability database capable of analysis in a wide range of ways, each dependent on the nature of the question being asked.

Analysis of the customer profitability database

A full CPA will cover all products sold to all outlets over a defined period of time. The profitability database therefore tends to be large and requires analytical techniques to help focus management attention on the most urgent issues.

A particularly powerful technique is decision grid analysis (DGA). This plots each account on a graph of profitability against volume of business (see Figure 3).

It highlights all outlets against four key categories, each of which will require a different managerial response. It is also the first step in defining what characterises a profitable or unprofitable customer, so providing the sales and marketing effort with a stronger focus on attractive accounts. Other techniques, such as cumulative outlet contribution analysis (COCA), also highlight how major resources (and assets) frequently stand behind those accounts that only generate marginal or negative contributions.

However, although such analyses make interesting reading, they are of no value unless they lead to action. The four main ways of achieving this are:

- productivity improvements;
- account engineering;
- commercial strategy;
- competitor modelling.

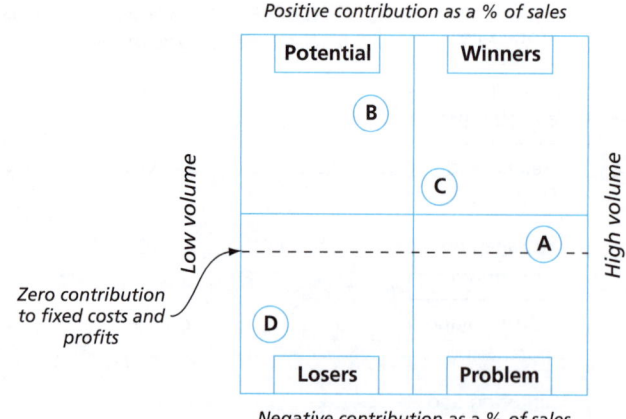

Figure 3 Decision grid analysis

Productivity improvements

Before embarking on a CPA exercise it is essential to make sure that the company's overall operations are as cost-effective as possible.

Many achieve a competitive level of productivity by undertaking reviews of technology, utilisation, performance and planning in each function. But, although yielding some benefits, such reviews are generally limited because they are function-based; they cannot take account of inefficiencies within the web of interfunctional relationships on which every company depends for its day-to-day operations.

The quickest, most effective way of fully understanding all overhead activities – and the costs which they drive – is to undertake a thorough review of overhead effectiveness.

The total quality approach we have developed at Develin and Partners aims to ensure that resource is focused on the key objectives of the business and the needs of the customer and not on discretionary, unnecessary activities.

As a methodology it has proved outstandingly successful; it can typically save between 10 and 20 per cent of all overhead costs and enhance customer service.

Account engineering

Account engineering asks critical questions and compares and evaluates answers. Its purpose is to enhance the profitability of the supplier to an acceptable level for each outlet.

For example:

- What will be the impact of distributing to major customers via their national distribution centres rather than through our own network?
- What is the implication of serving small accounts through third-party wholesalers?
- Which are the least profitable accounts and how can their profitability be most easily improved?

Four factors key to successful account engineering are understanding that:

1. Customer expectations of service, in all its forms, can be managed.
2. Internal cost structure must be modified to reflect any changes resulting from account engineering.

3. The implementation of account engineering decisions must be carefully planned and the results clearly monitored.
4. Top management commitment is essential, especially in view of the cross-functional nature of the effect of some decisions.

The adoption of account engineering is the equivalent of exchanging a shotgun for a sniper's rifle. It is the supplier's equivalent of the retailer's use of direct product profitability in supporting commercial decisions.

Commercial strategy

A clear view of customer profitability is essential for evaluating and developing a sound commercial strategy; it is the only way of linking the company's external trading relationship at customer level to its internal cost structure. This is not an end in itself but merely a base for developing more credible and focused strategy. It complements the supplier's understanding of the market, the players within it and the company's competitive positioning.

Competitor modelling

Competitor modelling is a natural extension of CPA. The supplier achieves this by establishing an understanding of the customer profitability profile of his own company and the differences between himself and a target competitor. By evaluating these differences it is possible to assess which customers, segments and activities of the target competitor are most vulnerable to competitive action. Such evaluation is a valuable supplement to both market intelligence and intuitive feel for the right decision.

Currently CPA is an exception in a few of the more advanced companies. Five years from now CPA will be a routine part of the planning and control process for many companies in the retail sector. In ten years its extension into competitor modelling will be a frequent occurrence.

Summary

Customer profitability analysis fills a crucial gap in the range of analytical and management accounting tools available to management:

- It puts the customer first – at the centre of the analysis.
- It quantifies the trading relationship and measures account profitability.
- It is a powerful analytical tool.
- It emphasises the concepts of 'right first time' and 'total quality'.
- It replaces the shotgun with the sniper's rifle and allows the supplier to identify precisely which accounts are eroding overall profitability – and those which are contributing to it.
- It enables senior management to make major decisions relating to the shape of the customer base with a much greater degree of confidence than has been possible so far.
- It integrates the effort of the company across functional boundaries in pursuit of customer satisfaction.
- It can provide a basis for constructive dialogue between buyer and seller to improve margins.

References

Booth, R (1994), 'Life Cycle Costing', *Management Accounting*, June.
Cooper, R and Kaplan, R (1988), 'The Promise – and Peril – of Integrated Cost Systems', *Harvard Business Review*, July–August.

Cooper, R (1990), 'Cost Classification in Unit-based and Activity-based Manufacturing Cost Systems', *Journal of Cost Management*, Fall.

Doherty, C, Maier, J and Simkin, L (1993), 'DPP Decision Support in Retail Merchandising', *Omega, International Journal of Management Science*, vol. 1.

Friedman, A and Lyne, S (1999), *Success and Failure of Activity-based Techniques; A Long-term Perspective*, CIMA.

Hobdy, T, Thompson, J and Sharman, P (1994), 'Activity-based Management at AT&T', *Management Accounting USA*, April.

Hiromoto, T (1988), 'Another Hidden Edge, Japanese Management Accounting', *Harvard Business Review*, July–August.

Huang, Y and Kirby, A (1994), 'Distorted Medicare Reimbursements: The Effect of Cost Accounting Choices', *Journal of Accounting Research*, Fall.

Johnson, H T (1992), *Relevance Regained*, Free Press.

Johnson H T and Kaplan, R (1987), *Relevance Lost: The Rise and Fall of Management Accounting*, Harvard University Press.

Jones, J and Wright, M (1987), 'Material Burdening: Management Accounting Can Support Competitive Strategy', *Management Accounting USA*, August.

Mertz, M and Hardy, A (1993), 'ABC puts Accountants on the Design Team at Hewlett-Packard', *Management Accounting USA*, September.

Morgan, M and Weerakoon, P (1989), 'Japanese Management Accounting: Its Contribution to the Japanese Economic Miracle', *Management Accounting*, June.

Puxty, A (1993), *The Social and Organisational Context of Management Accounting*, CIMA.

Raffish, N and Turney, P (1991), 'Glossary of Activity-Based Management', *Journal of Cost Management*, Fall.

Sakurai, M (1997), 'The Historical Development and Present Status of Management Accounting in Japan', paper presented at London University.

Swierings, R J and Weick, K E (1987), 'Management Accounting for Action', *Organisations and Society*, vol. 12, no. 3.

Yoshikawa, T, Innes, J, Mitchell, F and Tanake, M (1993), *Contemporary Cost Management*, Chapman Hall, London.

For all its professed benefits, activity-based costing is not an easy system to implement. In the following article, the author draws on his experiences of establishing ABC in a shipping company to describe the key decisions to be made – and the major pitfalls to be avoided.

Voyage of discovery

Selvan Naidoo, *Financial Manager*, **May 2002**

Activity-based costing (ABC) is often viewed as a daunting task, perhaps quite rightly so. The processes of data accumulation and cleansing demand a lot of effort, but following a few basic principles from the start can help to sharpen your focus and improve results.

Many ABC projects set out in search of costing information, but this can be an extremely broad area and can mean different things at different levels of management. It is therefore critical that you establish at the outset exactly what you want to achieve from the exercise.

First, you need to decide whether or not the results will be used at a strategic level. This will significantly influence the extent of your activity analysis. If only a high-level review is required, then the amount of analysis could be aggregated to a much more manageable level. Conversely, if strategic cost management is the key objective, then it may be necessary to go down to the level of individual tasks. It must be noted that the law of diminishing returns is very much applicable when comparing the objectives of the project with the effort, cost and accuracy of its outputs.

Second, you need to establish whether you want to focus on certain areas – e.g. operations, regional support costs and head-office costs. When I participated in a recent ABC implementation in a shipping company, the project team took a phased approach. We first analysed the total cost composition of the business, which then indicated the areas on which we needed to focus.

At this stage it is also important to agree with management the level of accuracy (e.g. 80 per cent) that would be acceptable. It is hard, if not impossible, to achieve everything with the first model – ABC modelling is often a repetitive process. Targeting the significant cost pools and producing meaningful information early on should create a tremendous amount of goodwill and credibility for the process, which should help you to tackle the more difficult areas with confidence.

Third, you need to decide which products or services you want to cost. Often you will find that 20 per cent of your products bring in 80 per cent of the revenues. I am in no way advocating that you shouldn't pay attention to the rest of your products, but you must take careful account of the time, resources, supporting information and maintenance work required to do so.

All these decisions, together with your project plan and key aims, are critical and should be agreed and signed off by the key stakeholders. The involvement of operational staff from the start of the project can also prove extremely valuable, because it lends credibility to what the project team is doing. If these conditions are not in place, you may well be forced to make frequent changes even when the project is at an advanced stage. The main concern is not one of change itself, but of the amount of change that may be required. With the shipping project, all too often we found that we had to rework the entire process owing to a dearth of data, changes in attitude and a lack of initial involvement from the senior management team.

Because ABC, like business process re-engineering, is a 'top-down' strategy, support from the very top of the organisation is critical. It is important that senior managers not only preach it; they must 'live it' to ensure the project's credibility. Their full support is essential for building commitment, ensuring that enough resources are allocated, removing any barriers and ratifying the results.

A note of caution: you do need to manage the expectations of the project's sponsor, the executive committee and the senior management team. Often their hopes are so high that they believe ABC will solve all their business problems. This added pressure may affect the project team and compromise its performance, so a failure to set them straight is likely to put the entire project at risk.

Dedicated resources are a must. When using consultants, it is important that they also put enough of their time and effort into the project. There is a direct relationship between the level of dedicated full-time resources and the quality of the results. Don't fool yourself: a part-time role will not yield the desired outcome.

Project management is another vital area. If you are using consultants, I suggest that they be managed internally. It is also important to set up following forums to ensure effective management and communication:

- **Steering committee** (sponsor, programme manager, project managers and consultants) – to make decisions, allocate resources and remove obstacles.

- **Working forum** (programme manager, project managers and consultants) – to focus on the operational aspects, including project aims.
- **Technical committee** (project managers, consultants and operational staff) – to foster participation, information exchange and validation at operational level.
- **Workshops** (consultants and staff).

ABC does not lend itself to ongoing information-sharing. Although there is a fair amount of data analysis and model-building to do before any meaningful results can be shared, it is important that the management team is given regular progress reports. In too many cases managers see the first results of their involvement only towards the end of the project. This can be overwhelming for them and cause them to take a sceptical view of the findings. Even if the figures seem correct, the recipients will tend to doubt what they are told.

While information systems may have an abundance of data, it is not usually in the structure or level of detail that is required. I cannot stress enough how critical it is to have systems that track the correct type of data. Out biggest problem lay in extracting cost-driver data. In fact, after several attempts, we had to settle for a number of surrogate drivers in the absence of the correct data. Even with enterprise resource planning solutions in place, data extraction is rarely easy, because these systems are often not based on the company's business model. Never underestimate the effort it takes to obtain the information you need in the correct format.

If you are implementing ABC across a number of sites, it is advisable to take a gradual approach, especially if it's the first time you have attempted the process. This will enable you to carry what you have learnt across business units. A pilot implementation could help you to put the task into perspective.

If a business unit is the subject of more than one major project, there is always the chance that there will be clashes of objectives, competition for resources and added pressure on operational staff. Given the demands of ABC, it is advisable not to contaminate it with other projects that have similar deadlines and demands on resources.

Lastly it's worth noting that an effective ABC implementation can be a double-edged sword. While people learn and develop hugely valuable skills when working on such projects the experience also makes them highly sought-after commodities on the jobs market. Unless your company has effective retention and succession planning strategies in place, there is a distinct risk that they will be lured away to work for competitors. After our ABC implementation, for example, the entire project team left the shipping company. Now the firm has to go back and start the process all over again with a completely new team.

Postscript

Did you notice the application of Pareto analysis? Many of the articles in this Study System provide you with such practical applications of the techniques you are learning. Remember – an exam question might ask you for practical examples of how a specific technique may be applied. Examples such as the application in this article would give you useful material as the basis for your answer.

Revision Questions

Question 1

1.1 Which of the following is a correct definition of activity-based management?

(A) An approach to the costing and monitoring of activities which involves tracing resource consumption and costing final outputs. Resources are assigned to activities and activities to cost objects based on consumption estimates. The latter utilise cost drivers to attach activity costs to outputs.

(B) The identification and evaluation of the activity drivers used to trace the cost of activities to cost objects. It may also involve selecting activity drivers with potential to contribute to the cost management function with particular reference to cost reduction.

(C) A method of budgeting based on an activity framework and utilising cost driver data in the budget-setting and variance feedback processes.

(D) A system of management which uses activity-based cost information for a variety of purposes including cost reduction, cost modelling and customer profitability analysis.

(E) A grouping of all cost elements associated with an activity.

1.2 In an ABC system, which of the following is likely to be classified as a batch level activity?

(A) Machine set-up
(B) Product design
(C) Inspection of every item produced
(D) Production manager's work
(E) Advertising.

1.3 XY Ltd manufactures two products, the X and the Y. Data for last period were as follows:

	X	Y
Production output (units)	450	11,550
Batch size (units)	30	35

Set-up costs incurred = £24,150.

Using an activity-based costing approach, the set-up costs allocated to products X and Y would be:

	Product X	Product Y
(A)	£780	£23,370
(B)	£906	£23,244
(C)	£1,050	£23,100
(D)	£11,146	£13,004
(E)	£12,075	£12,075

1.4 AB plc is a supermarket group which incurs the following costs:
   (i) the bought-in price of the good;
   (ii) inventory financing costs;
   (iii) shelf refilling costs;
   (iv) costs of repacking or 'pack out' prior to storage before sale.
   AB plc's calculation of direct product profit (DPP) would include

   (A) all of the above costs
   (B) all of the above costs except (ii)
   (C) all of the above costs except (iv)
   (D) costs (i) and (iii) only
   (E) cost (i) only.

1.5 When building up the cost of a product or service using activity-based costing, which of the following would NOT be used as levels of classification?
   (i) unit;
   (ii) batch;
   (iii) value added;
   (iv) product;
   (v) non-value added;
   (vi) facility.

   (A) (ii) and (iii)
   (B) (iii) and (iv)
   (C) (iii) and (v)
   (D) (iii), (iv) and (vi)
   (E) (v) and (vi)

? Question 2

ABC Ltd produces a large number of products including A and B. A is a complex product of which 1,000 are made and sold in each period. B is a simple product of which 25,000 are made and sold in each period. A requires one direct labour hour to produce and B requires 0.6 direct labour hours to produce.

ABC Ltd employs twelve salaried support staff and a direct labour force that works 400,000 direct labour hours per period. Overhead costs are £500,000 per period.

The support staff are engaged in three activities – six staff engaged in receiving 25,000 consignments of components per period, three staff engaged in receiving 10,000 consignments of raw materials per period and three staff engaged in disbursing kits of components and materials for 5,000 production runs per period.

Product A requires 200 component consignments, 50 raw material consignments and ten production runs per period. Product B requires 100 component consignments, eight raw material consignments and five production runs per period.

Requirements

(a) Calculate the overhead cost of A and B using a traditional system of overhead absorption based on direct labour hours;
(b) Identify appropriate cost drivers and calculate the overhead cost of A and B using an activity-based costing system;
(c) Compare your answers to (a) and (b) and explain which gives the most meaningful impression of product costs.

Question 3

Bean Products Ltd manufactures two types of beanbags – Standard and Deluxe. Both beanbags are produced on the same equipment and use similar processes. The following budgeted data has been obtained for the year ended 31 December 20X1.

Product	Standard	Deluxe
Production quantity	25,000	2,500
Number of purchase orders	400	200
Number of set-ups	150	100
Resources required per unit		
Direct material (£)	25	62.5
Direct labour (hours)	10	10
Machine time (hours)	5	5

Budgeted production overheads for the year have been analysed as follows:

	£
Volume related overheads	275,000
Purchases related overheads	300,000
Set-up related overheads	525,000

The budgeted wage rate is £20.00 per hour.

The company's present system is to absorb overheads by product units using rates per labour hour.

However, the company is considering implementing a system of activity-based costing. An activity-based investigation revealed that the cost drivers for the overhead costs are as follows:

Volume related overheads:	Machine hours
Purchases related overheads:	Number of purchase orders
Set-up related overheads:	Number of set-ups

Requirements

(a) Calculate the unit costs for each type of beanbag using:
   (i) the current absorption costing method.
   (ii) the proposed activity-based costing approach.
(b) Compare your results in (i) and (ii) above and briefly comment on your findings.

Question 4

Companies operating in an advanced manufacturing environment are finding that about 90 per cent of a product's life cycle cost is determined by decisions made early in the cycle. Management accounting systems should therefore be developed that aid the planning and control of product life cycle costs and monitor spending at the early stages of the life cycle. (Statement paraphrased from a well-known accounting text)

Requirements

Having regard to the above statement:

(a) explain the nature of the product life cycle concept and its impact on businesses operating in an advanced manufacturing environment;
(b) explain life cycle costing and state what distinguishes it from more traditional management accounting practices;
(c) compare and contrast life cycle budgeting with activity-based management; identify and comment on any themes that the two practices have in common.

Question 5

Explain your answers to (a) and (b) with figures/calculations where appropriate.

(a) Many manufacturing companies in different countries throughout the world have sought to influence managers' behaviour by the method(s) they employ to charge overheads to products.

Requirement

Discuss how overhead systems may be used to:
 (i) direct or manipulate decisions made by departmental managers;
 (ii) influence product design decisions that affect costs occurring during the product's life cycle.

(b) Certain types of costing system encourage operational managers to produce in excess of both budget and demand.

Requirement

Discuss the statement made above. Your answer should cover the following areas:

- the types of costing system that encourage this behaviour;
- how these costing systems encourage over-production;
- what can be done to overcome the problem of over-production created by a costing system.

Question 6

Garden Wizard Ltd manufactures a variety of garden tools for many markets including one item, the EC Trimmer, a hedge trimmer, that is only sold through Garden Centres and DIY chain shops. Currently three large DIY chains (X, Y and Z) and several smaller garden centres purchase this item. Garden Wizard sells this hedge trimmer at £40 per unit and the standard product cost is £20 per unit. Assume 40 per cent of the standard product cost represents fixed overheads.

Delivery costs vary according to the distance travelled and costs £5 per kilometre. In addition when a customer's stocks are very low, Garden Wizard makes the occasional emergency delivery which is outside its normal delivery schedule. These cost £500 per delivery. Each customer also negotiates discounts on sales prices. Order taking costs are £200 per order. Publicity costs are specific to each customer as all publicity occurs in the shops and garden centres. Data relating to each of the customers are as follows:

	X	Y	Z	Other Garden Centres
Sales in units	10,000	5,000	3,000	6,000
Kilometres travelled	1,000	500	1,200	7,500
Number of emergency deliveries made	0	0	2	0
Number of orders taken	5	3	7	10
Discounts*	20%	15%	20%	6%
Sales commission*	10%	10%	10%	10%
Publicity costs	£27,000	£39,000	£45,000	£57,000

* Discounts and sales commission are calculated as a percentage of the sales value.

Requirements

(a) Comment on the profitability of each of Garden Wizard Ltd's existing customers and what action it should take. Your response should be supported with suitable financial calculations.

(b) What factors should Garden Wizard Ltd consider before deciding to drop a customer?

Question 7

RS plc is a retail organisation. It has fifteen supermarkets, all of which are the same size. Goods are transported to RS plc's central warehouse by suppliers' vehicles, and are stored at the warehouse until needed at the supermarkets – at which point they are transported by RS plc's lorries.

RS plc's costs are:

	£000
Warehouse costs, per week	
Labour costs	220
Refrigeration costs	160
Other direct product costs	340
	720

	£000
Head-office costs, per week	80
Labour costs	76
Other costs	156

	£000
Supermarket costs, per shop per week	
Labour costs	16
Refrigeration costs	24
Other direct product costs	28
	68

	£
Transport costs per trip	
Standard vehicles	3,750
Refrigerated vehicles	4,950

The company has always used retail sales revenue less bought-in price to calculate the relative profitability of the different products. However, the chief executive is not happy with this method and has asked for three products – baked beans, ice cream and South African white wine – to be costed on a direct product profit basis. The accountant has determined the following information for the supermarket chain:

	Baked beans	Ice cream	White wine
No. of cases per cubic metre (m³)	28	24	42
No. of items per case	80	18	12
Sales per week – items	15,000	2,000	500
Time in warehouse – weeks	1	2	4
Time in supermarket – weeks	1	2	2
Retail selling price per item	£0.32	£1.60	£3.45
Bought-in price per item	£0.24	£0.95	£2.85

Additional information:

Total volume of all goods sold per week	20,000 m³
Total volume of refrigerated goods sold per week	5,000 m³
Carrying volume of each vehicle	90 m³
Total sales revenue per week	£5m
Total sales revenue of refrigerated goods per week	£650,000

Requirements

(a) Calculate the profit per item using the direct product profitability method.
(b) Discuss the differences in profitability between the company's current method and the results of your calculations in (a), and suggest ways in which profitability could be improved.
(c) Explain how the direct product profit method differs from traditional overhead absorption.

? Question 8

S & P Products plc purchases a range of good quality gift and household products from around the world; it then sells these products through 'mail order' or retail outlets. The company receives 'mail orders' by post, telephone and Internet. Retail outlets are either department stores or S & P Products plc's own small shops. The company started to set up its own shops after a recession in the early 1990s and regards them as the flagship of its business; sales revenue has gradually built up over the last 10 years. There are now 50 department stores and 10 shops.

The company has made good profits over the last few years but recently trading has been difficult. As a consequence, the management team has decided that a fundamental reappraisal of the business is now necessary if the company is to continue trading.

Meanwhile the budgeting process for the coming year is proceeding. S & P Products plc uses an activity-based costing (ABC) system and the following estimated cost information for the coming year is available:

Retail outlet costs:

Activity	Cost driver	Rate per cost driver	Number each year for Department store	Own shop
		£		
Telephone queries and request to S & P	Calls	15	40	350
Sales visits to shops and stores by S & P sales staff	Visits	250	2	4
Shop orders	Orders	20	25	150
Packaging	Deliveries	100	28	150
Delivery to shops	Deliveries	150	28	150

Staffing, rental and service costs for each of S & P Products plc's own shops cost on average £300,000 a year.

Mail order costs:

Activity	Cost driver	Rate per cost driver		
		Post	Telephone	Internet
		£	£	£
Processing 'mail orders'	Orders	5	6	3
Dealing with 'mail order' queries	Orders	4	4	1
		Number of packages per order		
Packaging and deliveries for 'mail orders' – cost per package £10	Packages	2	2	1

The total number of orders through the whole 'mail order' business for the coming year is expected to be 80,000. The maintenance of the Internet link is estimated to cost £80,000 for the coming year.

The following additional information for the coming year has been prepared:

	Department store	Own shop	Post	Telephone	Internet
Sales revenue per outlet	£50,000	£1,000,000			
Sales revenue per order			£150	£300	£100
Gross margin: mark-up on purchase cost	30%	40%	40%	40%	40%
Number of outlets	50	10			
Percentage of 'mail orders'			30%	60%	10%

Expected Head Office and warehousing costs for the coming year:

	£
Warehouse	2,750,000
IT	550,000
Administration	750,000
Personnel	300,000
	4,350,000

Requirements

(a) (i) Prepare calculations that will show the expected profitability of the different types of sales outlet for the coming year.

  (ii) Comment briefly on the results of the figures you have prepared.

(b) In relation to the company's fundamental reappraisal of its business,

  (i) discuss how helpful the information you have prepared in (a) is for this purpose and how it might be revised or expanded so that it is of more assistance;

  (ii) advise what other information is needed in order to make a more informed judgement.

Solutions to Revision Questions

Solution 1

1.1 Answer: (D)

ABM uses the information provided by an ABC analysis to improve organisational profitability.

Option (A) defines ABC
Option (B) defines activity driver analysis
Option (C) defines activity-based budgeting
Option (E) defines an activity cost pool.

1.2 Answer: (A)

Machine set-up costs are likely to be driven by the number of batches produced; therefore this is a batch level activity.

Product design (B) is a product level activity.

The inspection of every item produced (C) is a unit level activity.

The production manager's work cannot be related to a particular product line; therefore this is a facility level activity.

Advertising of individual products would be a product level activity. If the advertising is concerned with promoting the company's name then this would be a facility level activity.

1.3 Answer: (C)

Number of batches produced = number of machine set-ups:

Product X 450 ÷ 30	15
Product Y 11,550 ÷ 35	330
Total no. of set-ups	345

Cost per set-up = £24,150/345 = £70
Allocated as follows:

	£
Product X £70 × 15	1,050
Product Y £70 × 330	23,100

1.4 Answer: (A)

All of the costs described can be identified with specific goods and would be deducted from the selling price to determine the direct product profit.

1.5 Answer: (C)

The four generally accepted categories of activity are unit level activities, batch level activities, product level activities and facility level activities.

 Solution 2

Tip

- This question illustrates the simple concept that underpins activity-based costing.

(a) Overhead costs of £500,000 and direct labour hours of 400,000 give an overhead absorption rate of £1.25 per hour.

Applied to the two products this OAR gives overhead costs as follows:

		Per unit
A (1 hour × £1.25)		£1.25
B (0.6 hour × £1.25)		£0.75

(b) Three appropriate cost drivers are:
- Receiving components;
- Receiving raw materials;
- Disbursing kits of components and raw materials.

Relating overhead costs to these drivers using the number of indirect staff engaged in each activity as the basis gives the following results:
- Receiving components – £250,000; £10 per receipt;
- Receiving raw materials – £125,000; £12.50 per receipt;
- Disbursing kits – £125,000; £25 per issue.

The products therefore attract overheads as follows:

		Product A £		Product B £
Receiving components	(200 × £10)	2,000	(100 × £10)	1,000
Receiving raw materials	(50 × £12.50)	625	(8 × £12.50)	100
Disbursing kits	(10 × £25)	250	(5 × £25)	125
Total		2,875		1,225
Overhead cost per unit		£2.88		£0.05

(c) Advocates of ABC would argue that the product costs shown in (b) are more meaningful than those shown in (a) because those in (b) are based on a more sensitive analysis of the activities giving rise to overhead costs.

It is clear that the relative cost impact of the activities involved in producing the two products appears much more clearly when ABC is used.

 Solution 3

Tips

- The first step is to determine the overhead absorption rate/cost driver rates for each activity.
- These rates can then be applied to the data given for each product.

	Standard	Deluxe	Total
Production quantity	25,000	2,500	
Direct labour hours required	250,000	25,000	275,000
Total production overhead			£1,100,000
Overhead absorption rate per lab. hour			£4.00
Machine hours required	125,000	12,500	137,500
Total purchase orders	400	200	600
Total set-ups	150	100	250
Cost per cost driver			
Volume related overheads			£275,000
Machine hours required			137,500
Volume related overheads/machine hour			£2.00
Purchases related overheads			£300,000
Total purchase orders			600
Purchases related overheads/order			£500.00
Set-ups related overheads			£525,000
Total set-ups			250
Set-up related overheads per set-up			£2,100.00

(a) (i) Unit costs using existing overhead absorption rate

Product	Standard	Deluxe
	£	£
D. Material	25.00	62.50
D. Labour costs	200.00	200.00
Overheads (10 labour hours × £4)	40.00	40.00
Total cost per unit	265.00	302.50

(a) (ii) Unit costs using ABC

Product	Standard	Deluxe	
	£	£	
D. Material	25.00	62.50	
D. Labour costs	200.00	200.00	
Overheads:			
Volume related (£2 × 5 machine hr)	10.00	10.00	
Purchases related (£500 × 400 orders ÷ 25,000)	8.00	40.00	(£500 × 200 orders ÷ 2,500)
Set-up related (£2,100 × 150 set-ups ÷ 25,000)	12.60	84.00	(£2,100 × 100 set-ups ÷ 2,500)
Total cost per unit	255.60	396.50	

(b)

	Standard	Deluxe
Cost per unit traditional method	£265.00	£302.50
Cost per unit ABC	£255.60	£396.50
Difference	£9.40	£−94.00
% change	3.55%	−31.07%

A significant difference in the costing of the Deluxe beanbag. The ABC approach attributes the cost of resources to each product which those resources on a more appropriate basis than the traditional absorption costing method. The price of the Deluxe should be reviewed in the light of the new unit cost.

Solution 4

Tip

- Part (c) asks you to compare and contrast life cycle budgeting with activity-based management. You will earn fewer marks if you simply describe the two systems, without attempting to draw any comparisons between them.

(a) The product life cycle (PLC) is shown in the diagram below:

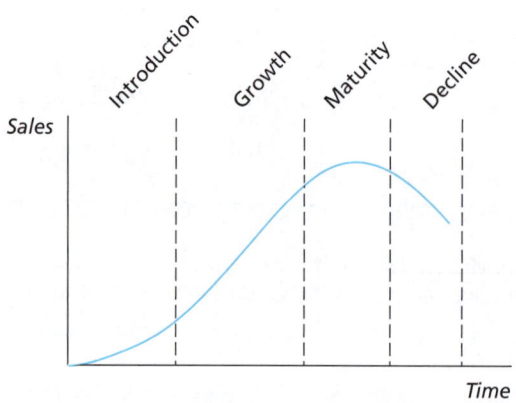

When a product is first successfully introduced to the market, supported by an expensive advertising campaign, it will only achieve a relatively low sales volume. In an Advanced Manufacturing Technology (AMT) environment, a very large amount of fixed cost will already have been incurred in R&D, designing the product and building or re-equipping the production line.

In the growth stage, sales increase and unit costs fall as the high fixed costs per unit decrease. Although new entrants may start to compete at this stage, this is the most profitable stage of the PLC.

The product is said to be mature when sales demand levels off. In a static market, price competition will reduce the profitability of each firm. Firms will seek to differentiate their product at this stage.

Eventually, the product will become obsolete and falling sales will ensue. This is the decline phase of the PLC. Firms will begin to pull out of the market or focus on promotional marketing strategies and reduce selling price. Before this stage is reached, the firm must have developed a replacement product, thereby incurring further large fixed costs for R&D, design and new production facilities.

In AMT environments, the time period for the product life cycle is decreasing. For example, the longest life cycle for a mass-produced motor car has reduced from over four decades for both the VW Beetle and the Morris Minor to less than 25 years for the Renault 5, which ceased production in 1996. However, most models must be renewed in much shorter timeframes. Vauxhall is setting up new production facilities for manufacturing a revamped Corsa in the UK. The Corsa was launched only a few years ago. The PLC concept enables clear strategic planning regarding the development of new products, cash flows and marketing activities.

(b) Life cycle costing (LCC) involves collecting cost data for each product from inception, through its useful life and including any end costs. These data are compared with the life cycle budgeted costs for the product. This comparison will show if the expected savings from using new technology or production methods, etc., have been realised.

The recognition of the total support required over the life of the product should lead to a more effective allocation of resources and is therefore an improvement on traditional budgeting which focuses on financial years, rather than product life span.

There is also a change in cost focus. LCC gathers costs for each product, whereas traditional costing methods follow costs by function, for example, R&D, production, marketing and so on. Thus, for manufacturers, LCC makes explicit the relationship between design choice and production and marketing costs. The insights gained from comparing budgeted and actual life cycle costs may be used to refine future decisions.

LCC may be used by consumers as well as producers. A recent analysis has shown that the life cycle cost of purchasing a personal computer (PC) is around six times the purchase cost. Staff training and extra software will cost three times the cost of the PC and maintenance will cost twice the purchase cost over the life of the PC.

It has been recognised in AMT environments that up to 90 per cent of the costs incurred throughout a product's life cycle will be determined before the product reaches the market. Thus, the early decisions regarding product design and production method are paramount and LCC attempts to recognise this situation.

The high fixed cost of introducing a new product coupled with reduced life cycle periods is a major challenge to profitability in AMT environments. LCC is a technique that may be used to improve management decision making in such conditions.

(c) Activity-based management (ABM) uses the understanding of cost drivers found from activitybased costing (ABC) to make more informed decisions. In particular, this approach yields a better understanding of overhead costs in AMT environments compared to traditional absorption methods. ABM aims to improve performance by:
- eliminating waste;
- minimising cost drivers;
- emulating best practice; and
- considering how the use of resources supports both operational and strategic decisions.

Thus, ABM seeks to consider all the activities performed by the organisation in order to serve a customer or produce a product.

Results of ABM in an AMT environment include:
- increased production efficiency;
- reduced production costs;
- increased throughput; and
- increased quality assurance.

These gains may be realised by:
- simplified product designs;
- more use of common sub-assemblies;
- reduced set-up times;
- reduced material handling; and
- better use of the workforce, for example, multi-skilling.

Thus, ABM is very similar to LCC in some respects – for example:
- both attempt to increase management understanding of overhead costs;
- both consider how the use of resources supports strategic decisions, that is, both look at how resource inputs are used to obtain the required organisational outputs.

In an AMT environment, both methods focus management attention on the need to produce simplified products using common components and common sub-assemblies and to maximise the output from expensive capital investments.

LCC leads to major reviews at the end of the major stages in a product life cycle, whereas ABM is a continuous system that strives to drive down both short-term and long-term costs.

Solution 5

Tips

- There are some useful practical examples in Chapter 7 that you can use to illustrate your answer.
- Even if the question does not specifically invite you to use figures to explain your answer, it is a good idea to do so for improved clarity.

(a) (i) In some countries and organisations where costs are controlled through absorption costing, the behaviour of staff is manipulated through the amount of cost charged to a cost centre or activity. For example, in the UK during the 1970s, manufacturing direct labour was often viewed as a nuisance and the direct labour cost was thought to be too high. Similarly, in Japan, some manufacturing companies, such as *Hitachi*, have considered that the way forward is by 'aggressive automation' – replacing men with machines at all costs. So if overheads were absorbed on direct labour hours, the departmental cost of employing extra staff would be much higher than just the immediately perceived costs of salaries and associated employment costs. As a result of the overhead charge, a manager would think very carefully before employing more staff.

For example, if the overhead absorption rate was 300% of direct labour cost, a new employee being paid £20,000 a year would cost the department £80,000 in total. Whether it is ethically acceptable to manipulate behaviour patterns like this is open to question. It produces a costing system that does not cost products correctly and treats managers in rather a juvenile manner. Should they not be told the company's strategy and/or the true cost of employment in terms of space and so on? Space costs themselves can be high and managers can be profligate with their use of space if they are not made aware of its cost. If managers are told the cost per square metre per annum, they may well redesign their departments (where space is limited), thus saving out-of-pocket costs.

(ii) Some companies in the USA and Japan, such as '*Textronix*' and *Hitachi*, have tried to influence and control the design of products through the absorption rate. Product life cycle costs are largely controlled at the design stage; the number of parts used and percentage of standard parts in a product influence cost. So, for example, if the overhead charge is based on the number of component parts in a product, there is an incentive to reduce the number of components used.

This can be taken a stage further so that designers prefer to use standard parts, that is, parts already in use on other products in the company rather than new components. At '*Textronix*', the accountants devised an ABC system that channelled all material-related costs through one cost driver, so that components that were not used in large numbers were penalised – thus penalising non-standard components. It was done in this way:

$$\frac{\text{Material overhead}}{\text{Total no. of different components used}} = \frac{\pounds 10\text{m}}{5,000} = \pounds 2,000$$

£2,000 carrying cost per different component

High usage component (40,000 units used per annum):

$$\text{Material overhead cost per unit} = \frac{\pounds 2,000}{40,000 \text{ units}} = \pounds 0.05$$

Low usage component (400 units used per annum):

$$\text{Material overhead cost per unit} = \frac{£2,000}{400 \text{ units}} = £5$$

Life cycle costs also include disposing of waste and recycling materials, and companies are increasingly being held responsible for these costs. Companies can use the overhead method outlined above to reduce the costs of disposing of products. This can be done by ensuring that all the plastic used within a car is of the same type and, therefore, is easy to dispose of. Designers would be encouraged to do this by a financial penalty for introducing a part made of a different type of plastic.

(b) Absorption costing systems encourage over-production. This is because all manufacturing costs are absorbed into the manufacturing cost per unit. The problem is created because of the nature of costs: variable and fixed. If another unit is produced, variable costs will be incurred and can be directly related to the additional unit, but additional fixed costs will not normally be incurred and must be spread amongst the units produced, if a total cost per unit is required. So the fixed costs are spread across more units reducing the cost per unit. Thus, profit can be increased not only by selling more, but also by producing units for stock, that is, by increasing stock over the period. The effect of this can be seen on the profit and loss account:

Production	1,000 units	1,200 units	1,400 units
	£	£	£
Sales units (1,000 units @ £10)	10,000	10,000	10,000
Opening stock	–	–	–
Production costs:			
Variable £4 per unit			
Fixed costs £3 per unit			
(based on £3,000/1,000 units)			
Total cost £7	7,000	8,400	9,800
Less: Over-absorption of fixed costs (200 units × £3, etc)		(600)	(1,200)
Less: Closing stock	–	(1,400)	(2,800)
Profit	3,000	3,600	4,200

It can be seen that the greater the stock, the greater the profit. If manager's rewards are based on profit, they will be keen to produce for stock. (The profit does not increase in this way with marginal costing where profit reflects sales made.) If staff are paid overtime or bonuses on high levels of production, the additional cost per unit could mitigate this effect. However, if it does not do so totally, the position could be even worse as managers incur additional costs per unit in order to build for stock.

Ways of overcoming the problem

(i) Over production can be prevented if stockholding costs are charged against profit, or a maximum stock level is set and the payment of bonuses is made only if stock is below this level.

(ii) If residual income is used as a performance measurement instead of profit, managers will be deterred from producing for stock. This is because a cost of capital charge is made against profit before residual income is calculated, and the higher the stock level, the more financial resources are tied up in the business segment and the higher the cost of capital charge.

(iii) Some production methods and their costing systems prevent the build up of stock, in particular JIT. The theory of constraints/throughput accounting also does this, because a balance is sought in production and only stock prior to the bottleneck is held.

Solution 6

Tips

- A straightforward question on customer account profitability.
- Calculate the contribution per unit before attempting to calculate the profitability of each customer.
- Calculate the C/S and profit/sales ratios and comment on your findings.

(a) Contribution per unit of the EC Trimmer

	£
Total product cost	20
Fixed overhead (40%)	8
Variable cost per unit	12
Selling price	40
Contribution per unit	28

Customer account profitability statement

	X	Y	Z	Other Garden Centres
No. of units sold	10,000	5,000	3,000	6,000
	£'000	£'000	£'000	£'000
Sales	400.0	200.0	120.0	240.0
Variable prod. cost	(120.0)	(60.0)	(36.0)	(72.0)
Contribution	280.0	140.0	84.01	168.0
Delivery cost	(5.0)	(2.5)	(6.0)	(37.5)
Emergency delivery	–	–	(1.0)	–
Order costs	(1.0)	(0.6)	(1.4)	(2.0)
Discounts	(80.0)	(30.0)	(24.0)	(14.4)
Sales commission	(40.0)	(20.0)	(12.0)	(24.0)
Publicity costs	(27.0)	(39.0)	(45.0)	(57.0)
Profit before fixed overheads	127.0	47.9	(5.4)	33.1
C/S %	70%	70%	70%	70%
Profit/Sales %	32%	24%	(5)%	14%

The C/S ratio for all outlets is a constant 70 per cent. However the net profit to sales ratio varies from 32 per cent for X to −5 per cent for Z. There are several reasons for this range in profitability. Z, though a small customer compared to the others, has managed to negotiate very favourable terms – a 20 per cent trade discount and high publicity costs. It also places several small orders and is the only outlet in need of emergency deliveries.

Customer X on the other hand (Garden Wizard's largest customer) is prudent in the number of orders it places and publicity expenses are relatively low, making it the most profitable of all the customers. The profitability of 'Other Garden Centres' is 14 per cent as delivery costs are high. This could be due to several deliveries being made to various garden centres rather than to one central warehouse.

A customer profitability analysis highlights loss-making customers such as Z and enables organisations to have the necessary information when negotiating new contracts.

(b) From the financial analysis above, Garden Wizard may decide to drop customer Z as it makes a loss. It should however consider other qualitative factors before such a decision is made. Can it renegotiate its discount policy? Will it be able to reduce its publicity costs? Should it start charging for emergency deliveries outside its normal delivery schedule? Can the spare capacity made available be put to better use? Garden Wizard should also consider the impact this decision will have on the sale of its other products and its long-term relationship with customer Z.

Solution 7

Tips

- You may have used a different basis for setting out your calculations. As long as the final answer is the same you will earn full marks.
- The first step is to calculate unit rates for all the costs – remember to analyse the refrigeration costs separately.

(a) Warehouse costs (excluding refrigeration) = £560,000 ÷ 20,000 m³   £28 per cubic metre per week
Warehouse refrigeration costs = £160,000 ÷ 5,000 m³   £32 per cubic metre per week
Standard vehicle cost = £3,750 ÷ 90 c.m   £41.67 per cubic metre per week
Refrigerated vehicle costs = £4,950 ÷ 90 c.m   £55 per cubic metre per week
Supermarket costs (excluding refrigeration) = £44,000 ×15 ÷ 20,000 m³   £33 per cubic metre per week
Supermarket refrigeration costs = £24,000 ×15 ÷ 5,000 m³   £72 per cubic metre per week

	Baked beans £	Ice cream £	White wine £
Selling price	0.320	1.600	3.450
Bought-in price	0.240	0.950	2.850
Gross margin	0.080	0.650	0.600
Warehouse cost (excluding refrigeration):			
£28 ÷ 28 ÷ 80 × 1 week	0.013		
£28 ÷ 24 ÷ 18 × 2 weeks		0.130	
£28 ÷ 42 ÷ 12 × 4 weeks			0.222
Warehouse – refrigeration:			
£32 ÷ 24 ÷ 18 × 2 weeks		0.148	
Standard vehicle costs:			
£41.67 ÷ 28 ÷ 80	0.019		
£41.67 ÷ 42 ÷ 12			0.083
Refrigerated vehicle costs:			
£55 ÷ 24 ÷ 18		0.127	
Supermarket costs (excluding refrigeration):			
£33 ÷ 28 ÷ 80 × 1 week	0.015		
£33 ÷ 24 ÷ 18 × 2 weeks		0.153	
£33 ÷ 42 ÷ 12 × 2 weeks			0.131
Supermarket cost – refrigeration:			
£72 ÷ 24 ÷ 18 × 2 weeks		0.333	
	0.047	0.891	0.436
Direct product profit	0.033	(0.241)	0.164
Profit/sales ratio	10.3%	–	4.8%

(b)
Gross margin/sales	25.00%	40.63%	17.39%
Gross margin per m³	£179	£281	£302
DPP per m³	£74	(£104)	£83

Using the company's normal costing method, ice cream appears to be very profitable with a gross margin/sales ratio of 41 per cent. The other two products are not quite so profitable.

Under the direct product profit (DPP) method (which attempts to relate the other costs to the products on a realistic basis), the position is reversed: baked beans and white wine are much more profitable, while ice cream now shows a loss.

The loss of profitability of ice cream is caused by:

- refrigeration costs. With DPP, the refrigeration costs are charged only to those products that use the refrigerators. The current system does not highlight this, as refrigeration costs are treated as fixed costs and are not charged to any products;
- the time it takes to move through the system. If deliveries were more frequent, so that only one week's stock was held at both the warehouse and the supermarket, then 24p (8p + 16p) per carton would be saved on refrigeration. This would eliminate the loss.

The loss of profitability of baked beans relative to the wine is due to the product's physical volume, which is relatively large in comparison to the contribution it generates.

(c) The traditional full-cost method relates all costs, including administrative and head-office costs, to the product, whereas DPP relates only those costs to the product that the product directly helps to cause (both fixed and variable). This excludes administrative and head-office costs, which in traditional overhead analysis are often apportioned on some arbitrary basis such as units or sales revenue. This arbitrary apportionment does little to help management understand costs and the way in which they are incurred.

DPP is very similar to activity-based costing in that costs are related to causal activities, such as shelf stacking, preparing import documentation and transportation. Traditional absorption costing rarely does this as costs are related to cost centres, which tend to be departments. As a result:

- cost control is therefore regarded as a departmental concern and is the job of the departmental manager. DPP and ABC take an organisation-wide view of cost control;
- traditional absorption costing is unlikely to produce an analysis of costs which reflects the true cost of the product, whereas DPP is used for this purpose. This means that decisions such as efficient replenishment, product pricing and promotion, assortment and shelving and product line development can be made with confidence.

Solution 8

Tip

- The volume of data in this question on direct product profitability can appear a bit daunting at first. The key is to adopt a systematic approach to allocating the costs to each type of outlet.

(a) (i) *Calculation of net margin per type of outlet:*

	Department store £	Own shop £	Mail order Post £	Mail order Telephone £	Mail order Internet £
Sales revenue	50,000	1,000,000	150.00	300.00	100.00
Gross margin[1] (50,000 + 1.30, etc)	11,538	285,714	42.86	85.71	28.57
Less: Staffing etc.		300,000			
Telephone queries (£15 × 40, etc)	600	5,250			
Sales visits (£250 × 2, etc)	500	1,000			
Orders (£20 × 25, etc)	500	3,000			
Packaging (£100 × 28, etc)	2,800	15,000			
Delivery (£150 × 28, etc)	4,200	22,500			
Order cost			5.00	6.00	3.00
Queries			4.00	4.00	1.00
Packing & delivery (£10 × 2, etc)			20.00	20.00	10.00
Internet cost[2]					10.00
	8,600	346,750	29.00	30.00	24.00
Net margin	2,938	(61,036)	13.86	55.71	4.57
Net margin/sales	5.9%		9.2%	18.6%	4.6%
	4th	5th	2nd	1st	3rd

Calculation of total margin for each type of outlet:

	Department stores £000	Own shops £000	Mail order Post £000	Mail order Telephone £000	Mail order Internet £000	Total £000
Total revenue[3]	2,500	10,000	3,600	14,400	800	31,300
Total net margin	146.90	(610.36)	332.64	2,674.08	36.56	2,579.82

Notes:

1. Gross margin calculation for 30% of purchase cost:
    $100 = 0.3X + X$
    $X = 76.92\%$
    $0.3X = 23.076\%$
    £50,000 × 23.076% = £11,538

2. Total number of mail orders = 80,000

    ∴ Number of Internet orders = 80,000 × 10% = 8,000
    Internet link cost per order = £80,000 ÷ 8,000 orders = £10

3. Calculation of total revenues and net margins.

		Total revenue £000		Total net margin £000
Department stores				
50 outlets	(× £50,000)	2,500	(× £2,938)	146.9
Own shops				
10 outlets	(× £1,000,000)	10,000	(× (£61,036))	(610.36)
Mail order – post				
80,000 × 30% = 24,000 orders	(× £150)	3,600	(× £13.86)	332.64
Mail order – telephone				
80,000 × 60% = 48,000 orders	(× £300)	14,400	(× £55.71)	2,674.08
Mail order – internet				
80,000 × 10% = 8,000 orders	(× £100)	800	(× £4.57)	36.56

(ii) The calculations on the previous page show the following:
- S & P's own shops will make a considerable 'loss'.
- The department store sales will not generate as good a profit as the 'mail order' side.
- The telephone mail order, that is 46% of the business, will generate 104% of the current total profit.
- The Internet business is not particularly profitable in the coming year, but it will presumably grow quite quickly. If this happens, the charge for maintaining the Internet, which is expressed by each order, will presumably decline as it is likely to be a semi-fixed cost.

(b) (i) The calculations show the profitability of the different types of outlet for the coming year only, which is of some use. For example, it shows that S & P's own shops make a considerable loss and it would appear, on the surface, that the company would be better off without them, perhaps transferring the business to franchises within department stores. It also indicates that the emphasis of the business should be switched to the mail order side, as it is more profitable and, in particular, to the telephone section.

However, the latter shows how dangerous this kind of assumption can be because the telephone section may have peaked and, in future, growth in the Internet section may be at the expense of the telephone section. Therefore, decisions about future strategies cannot be made on predicted short-term costs and revenues. Any attempt to do so could prove disastrous. Growth in the market, competitors' moves, customers' needs and requirements must be the basis for any decisions.

The ABC costs could, however, be used to highlight areas for cost reduction and procedural changes which could assist longer-term profitability. ABC is a method for apportioning costs and it suffers from the same defects as every absorption method. In S & P's case, the analysis does not look very detailed/accurate and so may be little better than a traditional absorption system.

The head office and warehousing costs need to be examined in detail to determine which type of outlet incurs what part of the cost, as these costs may be caused and used more by some types of outlets than others. If this is so, what would happen to cost if one type of outlet was abandoned and others increased in size?

(ii) Other information needed to make a more informed judgement is likely to be:
- Customers' changing purchasing habits;
- Same customer purchases across outlet types, that is, do customers buy from shops and order by telephone;
- Competitors' moves;
- New entrants into the market – especially in the Internet business;
- Future economic conditions;
- Exchange rate movements – as some goods are imported;
- Increase in disposable income;
- The image created by the different types of outlet, that is do their own shops create the brand or company name;
- Past data to establish trends.

Then specific information will need to be collected for the fundamental reappraisal of the business. For example, if the decision to close S & P's own shops was being considered, a detailed study of the interrelationship between outlets should be carried out, as having the products on display in shops might be necessary in order to maintain the high level of telephone orders. For instance, potential customers may visit to see colours, quality, and so on. Products on display are also a form of advertising for the company and this would be lost if the shops were closed.

Learning and Experience Curves

Learning and Experience Curves 11

> **LEARNING OUTCOME**
>
> ▶ Explain and apply learning and experience curves to estimate time and cost for new products and services.

11.1 Introduction

In this chapter learning and experience curves will be explained together with their application to decision-making.

11.2 The learning curve

11.2.1 Introduction

In practice, it is often found that the resources required to produce given amounts of a product tend to decline as output accumulates. It costs more to produce the first unit of a product than it does to produce the one thousandth unit. Various factors contribute to this relating to labour, material and overhead costs. One significant element in this is the learning curve effect.

The learning curve relates to the observed tendency for workers to become more adept at a task the more times they perform it.

11.2.2 The nature of the learning curve

According to the *Official Terminology*:

> *Learning curve*: The mathematical expression of the phenomenon that, when complex and labour-intensive procedures are repeated, unit labour times tend to decrease at a constant rate. The learning curve models mathematically this reduction in unit production time.

The recognition of the so-called learning curve phenomenon stems from the experience of aircraft manufacturers, such as Boeing, during the Second World War. They observed that the time taken to assemble an individual aircraft declined as the number of aircraft assembled increased: as workers gained experience of the process, their proficiency, and hence speed of working, increased. The 'learning' gained on the assembly of one plane was translated into the faster assembly of the next. The actual time taken by the assembly workers was monitored, and it was discovered that the rate at which the learning took place was not random, but rather was *predictable*. It was found that the *cumulative* average time *per unit* decreased by a fixed percentage each time the *cumulative* production *doubled*. In the aircraft industry, the percentage by which the cumulative average time per unit declined was typically 80 per cent. For other industries, other rates may be appropriate. Further, the unit of measurement may more sensibly be taken as a *batch* of product, rather than as an individual unit. This does not, of course, affect the underlying principle.

Let us take as an example a learning rate of 90 per cent. In this case, if the first batch of a product is produced in 100 hours, the *cumulative average* time taken to produce two batches (a doubling of the *cumulative* production) would be 90 hours, giving a total production time of $2 \times 90 = 180$ hours. The actual time taken to produce the second batch (the batch being the unit of measure in this case) would thus be 80 hours, the *cumulative total* time taken to produce two batches – 180 hours – less the time taken to produce the first batch – 100 hours. As a doubling of *cumulative* production is required, in order to observe the benefits of learning in the form of reduced average labour hours per unit of cumulative production, it will be appreciated that the effects of the learning rate on labour time will become much *less* significant as production increases. Table 11.1 shows this.

The graphs in Figure 11.1 show the data from Table 11.1 plotted both on an ordinary and on a double logarithmic scale. It will be noted that the double logarithmic form is linear; the ordinary form is not.

The learning percentage is usually somewhere between 70 per cent and 85 per cent. The more complicated the product the steeper the learning curve will be. For example, research on Japanese motorbikes found that the small 50cc bikes had a learning curve of 88 per cent, the 50–125cc bikes, one of 80 per cent and the 250cc bikes, one of 76 per cent.

Table 11.2 illustrates how an 80 per cent learning curve works, as units are doubled from 1 to 2, to 4, to 8.

In constructing Tables 11.1 and 11.2, it was assumed that we already knew the learning rate that applied to this particular situation. However, it must be appreciated that, in the real

Table 11.1 Cumulative average time learning rate: 0.90

Batches	Cumulative average time per batch (hours)	Cumulative total (hours)
1	100.00	100
2	90.00	180
4	81.00	324
8	72.90	583
16	65.61	1,050
32	59.05	1,890
64	53.14	3,401
128	47.83	6,122
256	43.05	11,021
512	38.74	19,835

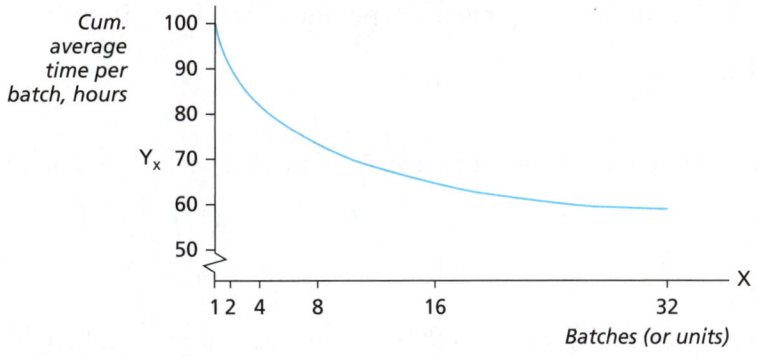

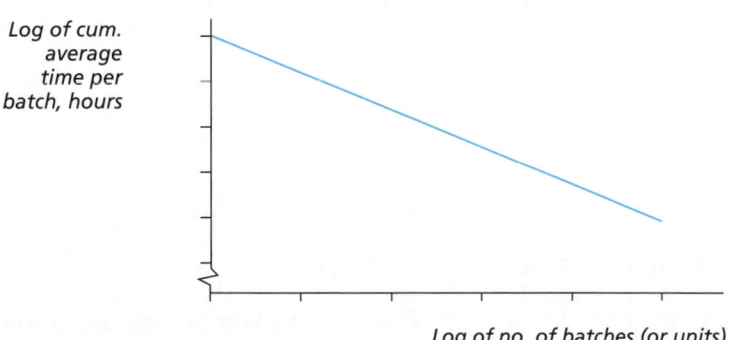

Figure 11.1 Cumulative data graphs

Table 11.2 An 80 per cent learning curve

No. of units	Average time per unit	Total time in hours	Additional units	Additional time	Time per unit
1	10	10			
2	8 (10 × 80%)	16	1	6 hours	6 hours
4	6.4 (8 × 80%)	25.6	2	9.6	4.8 (6 × 80%)
8	5.12 (6.4 × 80%)	40.96	4	15.36	3.8 (4.8 × 80%)

world, this rate can only be established by observation. Records must be kept of the number of units/batches produced and the associated time taken, in order to construct the equivalent of Table 11.1 (although it is likely that fewer observations would actually be taken). It is then the job of the engineer or accountant to deduce the learning rate from these observations, which will require the specification of an equation to fit the data. For example, the observations in Table 11.1 are plotted in Figure 11.1, and can be described by the equation:

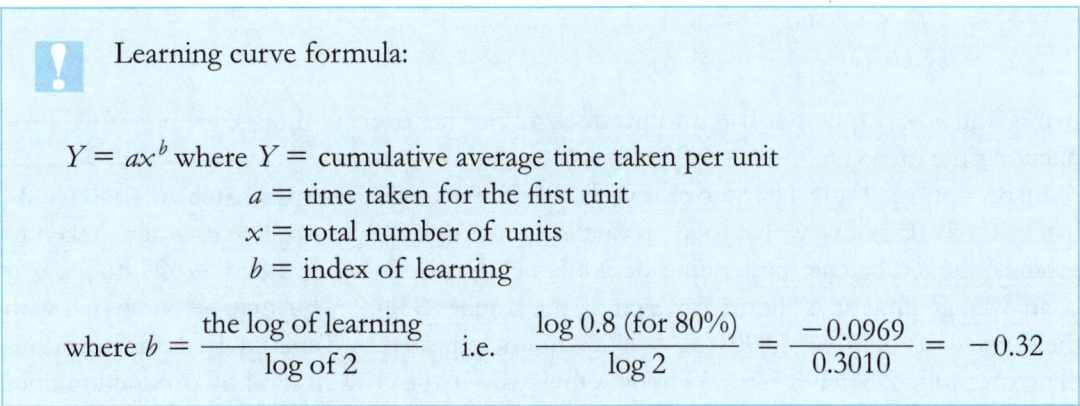

Thus, in Table 11.2, the average time taken per unit, for 8 units, is given by:

$$Y = 10 \times 8^{-0.32}$$
$$= 5.14$$

which, allowing for rounding, is the same average time that was derived in Table 11.2.

Exercise

Derive the learning curve formula for a 90 per cent learning rate, and apply it to confirm the cumulative average time per unit for 64 units, as shown in Table 11.1.

Solution

$Y = ax^b$

b, the index of learning $= \dfrac{\log 0.9}{\log 2} = -0.152*$

*This is calculated using a scientific calculator, but you can use log tables if you prefer. Inserting the relevant data into the formula, we get:

Average time taken per unit $= 100 \times 64^{-0.152}$
$= 53.14$

This agrees with Table 11.1 above.

The learning curve equation is not normally used to check earlier calculations in the way that we have just done, but is rather used to assess the time that will be required for an output level that does *not* represent a doubling of the cumulative production total, and thus cannot be determined by simply creating a table such as the one used earlier. For example, let us assume that the manufacturer above has the opportunity to bid for a contract to produce ten batches of his product, and wishes to estimate the time it will take to complete the contract, in order to help set the tender price. If the cumulative total production of his product to date is 32 batches, the learning curve equation can be employed to calculate the cumulative average time per batch to produce 42 batches: the 32 already produced, plus the ten under consideration:

$Y_x = ax^b$
$Y_x = 100 \times 42^{-0.152}$
$Y_x = 100 \times 0.5666$
$Y_x = 56.66$

that is, the *average* time per batch to produce 42 batches is 56.66 hours, giving a total production time of $56.66 \times 42 = 2{,}380$ hours.

Inspection of Table 11.1 above reveals that the average time per batch to produce 32 batches is 59.05 hours, with a total production time of 1,890 hours. The total time taken to produce the ten batches under consideration will thus be $2{,}380 - 1{,}890 = 490$ hours, that is, an average time of 49 hours for each of the batches 33–42. This may be compared with the average of $(3{,}401 - 1{,}890)/32 = 47.20$ hours indicated by Table 11.1 for the next doubling of a full 32 batches from 33 to 64. Obviously, if the current level of production does not lie on a table such as Table 11.1, that particular average time, and the corresponding cumulative hours to date, will need to be calculated from the same formula.

11.2.3 Uses of the learning curve

(i) In circumstances where the learning curve is likely to operate, that is, in complex assembly operations, knowledge of the rate of learning can help in price setting.
(ii) When setting budgets, the effects of the learning curve should be taken into account. Standard costs should reflect the point that has been reached on the learning curve, so that those set on the basis of the 'steady state' (i.e. that point at which learning has become insignificant) will be lower than those set during the learning period. This is necessary if variances arising during the learning period are to be meaningful.
(iii) The learning curve has been found to be particularly useful in determining the likely costs to be incurred in fulfilling government contracts. This provides a rational basis for price negotiation and cost control.

A number of points about learning curves must be stressed:

(i) Learning curves chart the reduction in *time* per unit as experience is gained; they do not measure a reduction in cost *per se*. However, if hourly wages are constant, the labour cost *per unit* will decline as a result of the learning curve phenomenon.
(ii) In addition to direct labour costs, only those costs that are *directly* related to direct labour time, that is, any overheads that vary directly with those hours, can be expected to decline as a result of the learning curve.
(iii) Learning is likely to be greatest in complex assembly environments, of which aircraft assembly is a prime example. If labour is working in a *machine-paced* environment, there is no significant opportunity to alter the *rate* of working, and thus the learning phenomenon in terms of direct labour time cannot exist. However, the experience that plant managers gain in scheduling work in such an environment may result in a reduction in the direct labour hours required for a given level of production.
(iv) The learning rate, which is a function of workers' learning, is *not* something which can be positively fostered as a cost-reduction technique.

11.2.4 Learned behaviour

Learning is often assumed to be automatic and just volume related, but it is not that simple. Learning is not a matter of law, it is achieved by focusing attention on, and striving for, improved performance. Two organisations with identical staff and resources would not necessarily achieve the same amount of learning, as management's attitude and the organisation's culture create learning.

Why do all employees achieve the same level of performance? Why does all learning stop at the same point? It seems it is all to do with the expectations of the company. Cyert and March (1963) said that 'the behaviour of an organisation is created through routines and routines stabilise an individual's behaviour making all workers' behaviour similar and routines are developed and maintained through interpretation of the past'. By routines Cyert and March meant habits, that is paperwork, weekly meetings, rules, roles who does what, etc. Levitt and March (1988) argued that organisations learn by '*encoding inferences from history into routines that guide behaviour*'. So routines, roles, habits, conventions, etc., have beliefs embedded in them. In this way routines can be made sufficiently independent of individuals and survive personnel turnover.

11.2.5 Experience curves

Experience curves are very similar to learning curves. Learning curves deal only with labour hours and therefore labour cost reducing by a set percentage. But experience curves cover all costs and yet they are very similar in percentage terms to learning curves. All costs reduce with experience to some extent. Material costs may decrease slightly with quantity discounts, etc., but will not decrease by a large amount. Variable overheads often follow the pattern of direct labour and so may decrease in a similar way. Fixed overheads will decrease per unit as more units are made and can also decrease by a substantial amount per unit.

Knowledge of the experience curve for a new product can be very useful indeed. For example it can be used to enter a new market and for achieving a critical mass within a certain period of time. If only a few units are made and sold, cost per unit will be high. But the organisation can plan to sell at a price that is less than the initial cost per unit because the managers know that if they set the price at that level by the end of the first year they will have sold a particular volume. If this volume is achieved the average cost per unit will have fallen considerably and the first year's trading will have generated an overall profit (even though the first units made a loss) as well as having established a viable market share.

This comes close to dumping products on the market in some people's eyes. The following exercise demonstrates this type of pricing.

Exercise

CLE is a small company wishing to enter the lower end of the PC market. It has a product that has been well tested and proved reliable. To date 2,000 have been made at an average cost per unit of £650. However, the product was aimed originally at the cheaper end of the market and management wanted to launch at a retail price of £399 to compete satisfactorily and to achieve adequate volume. The retailer traditionally receives a 50 per cent mark-up in this product area. A market survey has already been carried out showing the share of the cheap PC computer market (estimated total next year, 500,000 computers) that CLE might achieve during the first year with a launch retail price of £399.

Market share %	Probability
2.5	0.05
5	0.1
7.5	0.25
10	0.35
12.5	0.15
15	0.1

Feelings among the directors are strong. The accountant says that the product cannot be launched at so low a price and that a price of £600 is much more realistic. The marketing director disagrees and says that the new product will not get any worthwhile market share at that price. The production manager says capacity is available for only 20,000 units a year unless £250,000 is spent on additional equipment, which would in effect double capacity. Further capacity can be obtained by contracting out manufacture to one of several firms whose costs are relatively low. It has been estimated that this type of product has an 80 per cent experience curve. The company has £0.5 m available in cash and bank overdraft.

Requirements
(a) Should the company launch the product at a price of £399?
(b) Provide calculations which help to assess the risk involved.

Solution

(a) With a retail sales price at £399 and 50 per cent mark-up on purchase price required by the retailer, CLE's cost must be £266 or less.

Expected market share in units

2.5% of 500,000	= 12,500 × 0.05 =	625
5% " "	= 25,000 × 0.10 =	2,500
7.5% " "	= 37,500 × 0.25 =	9,375
10% " "	= 50,000 × 0.35 =	17,500
12.5% " "	= 62,500 × 0.15 =	9,375
15% " "	= 75,000 × 0.10 =	7,500
		46,875

Experience curve

Cumulative volume	Ave. cost p.u. (× 80%)	Total cost
(a)	(b)	(a × b)
	£	£m
2,000	650	1.3
4,000	520	2.08
8,000	416	3.33
16,000	332.8	5.32
32,000	266.3	8.52
64,000	213	13.64

Sales of 32,000 units virtually meet the cost criterion of £266. The additional expenditure of £250,000 to increase the capacity above the 20,000 unit level is very small in relation to the total cost of £8.52 m but does increase the average unit cost to £274 at the 32,000 unit level.

To find the cost of 40,000 units (maximum capacity) using the experience curve formula:

$$Y = ax^b$$

The cost for the first unit is unknown but we know that 2,000 units cost £650 per unit, therefore:

$$650 = a \times 2{,}000^{\log 0.8/2}$$
$$650 = a \times 2{,}000^{(-0.32193)}$$
$$a = £7{,}510$$

For 40,000 units to be produced in the coming year:
Obtain the cumulative average for 42,000 units as 2,000 have already been produced:

$$\begin{aligned} Y &= 7{,}510 \times 42{,}000^{(-0.32193)} \\ &= 7{,}510 \times 0.0324816 \\ &= £243.94 \text{ (say £244)} \end{aligned}$$

The cost for 40,000 units will then be:

$$(42{,}000 \times £244 - (2{,}000 \times £650))$$
$$= £8{,}948{,}000 \text{ or £224 per unit}$$

CLE's total margin for 40,000 units	=	40,000 × (266 − 224)
	=	£1.68 m
Less: equipment cost		0.25 m
Net gain		1.43 m

Further units can be bought in for resale assuming the price is satisfactory, thus a larger profit can be made.

(b) If only 12,500 units are sold average unit costs are:

$$Y = 7{,}510 \times 14{,}500^{(-0.32193)}$$
$$= 7{,}510 \times 0.0457436$$
$$= £344$$

The cost for 12,500 units will be:

		£
14,500 units × £344 =		4,988,000
Less: 2,000 units × £650 =		1,300,000
		3,688,000 or £295 per unit

So at the minimum volume a unit loss of £29 (£266 − £295) will be made. To this must be added the wasted investment of £250,000 in additional capacity if the cost was incurred in advance. Breakeven is at approximately 23,500 units.

$$Y = 7{,}510 \times 25{,}500^{(-0.32193)}$$
$$= 7{,}510 \times 0.0381419$$
$$= £286$$

The cost for 23,500 will be:

		£
25,500 units × £286 =		7,293,000
Less: 2,000 units × £650 =		1,300,000
		5,993,000 or £255 per unit

This gives a contribution of £11 per unit (£266 − £255), sufficient to just cover the equipment cost of £250,000.

Recommendation

Proceed but obtain additional funds. The £500,000 available at present will only finance a stock level of about 2,200 units (£500,000 ÷ £224). This is sufficient for just over two weeks sales if the expected volume of 47,000 units per annum is achieved. As the sales estimates are rather uncertain it would be easy to run out of stock. Not only current sales would be lost but also potential sales due to unreliability. In addition, £250,000 will be required for the equipment needed to increase capacity to 40,000 units per annum.

11.3 Summary

In this chapter we have learned about learning and experience curves and their implication for decision-making.

Reading 11

Further insights into learning curves can be obtained by reading the following article. In particular, the article considers limitations in the application of the learning curve effect.

Learning curves
Bob Scarlett, *CIMA Student*, **August 1994**

Learning curve theory is essentially a mathematical model that seeks to relate the labour time (and thereby the labour-related costs) of production to the volume of production. It recognises the fact that in a manufacturing environment the labour time required to perform a task declines with the number of times that the task is performed.

Implicit in learning curve theory is a representation of the relationships between production volume and technical, financial and behavioural variables. In practice such relationships are complex and any mathematical model seeking to represent them has to be an approximation. The accountant has to have a firm grasp of learning curve theory and its limitations in order to make it an effective tool for management purposes.

The basic ideas behind learning curve theory are common sense. Let us start by looking at a very simple example of how labour time is likely to respond to production volume.

A simple manufacturing task is the assembly of a printed circuit board (PCB). Where limited output of a particular PCB is required then this is likely to be a manual task carried out by an operative. The operative has to assemble the various components and solder them on to the board using a circuit diagram for guidance. Assembling the first PCB might require 30 minutes, involving frequent reference to the diagram and checks to ensure that the components are being fitted correctly. However, assembling subsequent PCBs will become a progressively less time-consuming task as the operative becomes more familiar with, and adept at, the task. The position concerning assembly of the first five PCBs might be as follows:

PCB	Time taken Minutes	Total time Minutes	Cumulative ave. time/unit Minutes
1	30	30	30.0
2	18	48	24.0
3	10	58	19.3
4	5	63	15.7
5	4	67	13.4

The key observations to note here are that:

- the cumulative average time per unit (i.e. total time/cumulative output) declines as output increases;

- the decline in cumulative average time per unit becomes less as progressively higher levels of output are considered.

The above observations are just common sense. Moving from the first to the second unit of output is likely to have a more substantial effect on average labour time per unit than moving from the nineteenth to the twentieth unit.

The figures shown above may be represented graphically to illustrate the key observations. The following diagrams are not drawn to scale.

First, the total time taken may be plotted against the total units produced. This gives a curve rising but with its slope diminishing as we move to the right:

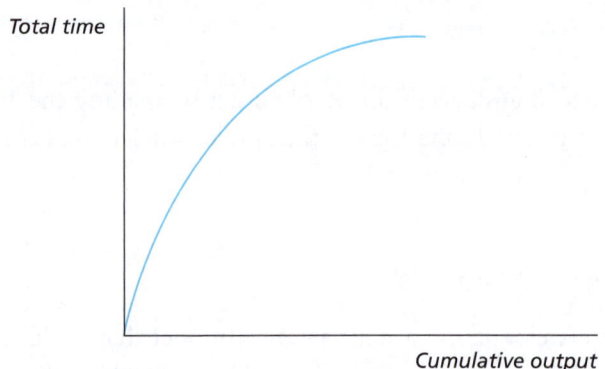

Second, the cumulative average time per unit can be plotted against the total units produced. This gives a curve dropping from a point (let us call it *a*) and with its slope diminishing as we move to the right:

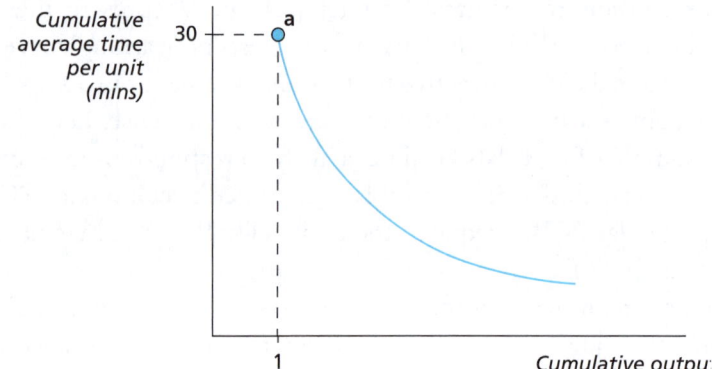

Consideration of the second diagram will show that *a* is the time taken to produce the first unit of output. It is the second diagram that is of most interest for present purposes. The tendency of labour time per unit to decline as output increases is known as a learning curve effect.

The manager is often confronted with the problem of seeking to predict what labour time is required to produce a given level of output. To do this when learning curve effects are known to exist requires that those effects are expressed in a form suitable for incorporation in a mathematical model.

By convention, that form is the impact on cumulative average hours per unit of doubling output – i.e. moving from a level of output of 1 unit to a level of output of 2 units, or from a level of output of 4 units to a level of output of 8 units. So, if we say that production involves 'an 80 per cent learning curve effect' what we mean is that by doubling the postulated output we will reduce the cumulative average hours per unit to 80 per cent of what it was previously.

This may be illustrated by a simple example. Let us say that we are producing units and that the time taken to produce one unit on its own (and not as part of a batch) is 100 hours. Experience has shown that production involves an 80 per cent learning curve effect. The labour hours associated with alternative batch sizes of 1, 2, 4 and 8 units may be determined as follows:

Batch size (units produced)	Cumulative ave. hours per unit	Total hours
1	100.0	100.0
2	80.0	160.0
4	64.0	256.0
8	51.2	409.6

It can be seen that by moving from 1 to 2 units the cumulative average hours per unit is reduced from 100 hours to 80 hours (i.e. $100 \times 80\%$) and so on. The data can be plotted on a graph as follows:

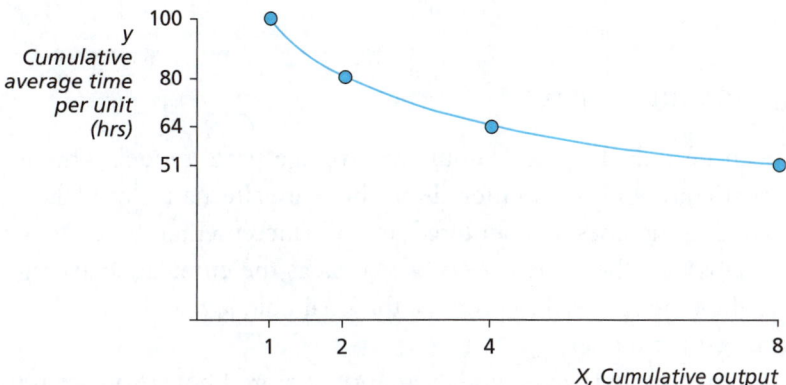

The general shape of this curve and the pattern of cost behaviour that it illustrates corresponds broadly to the 'common sense' appraisal of PCB assembly explored above.

If the graph is drawn accurately to scale it is possible to read from it the cumulative average hours per unit associated with batch sizes (e.g. six units) intermediate between those postulated. The reader should not hesitate to adopt such a graphical methodology if that is all he/she is comfortable with; however, this requires technical drawing skills of some order to produce accurate results.

An alternative approach is to derive the mathematical formula for a particular learning curve.

The standard formula for a curve of the kind in the above diagram is:

$$y = ax^n$$

where a and n are constants. It is known that a is 100 since this is the cumulative average hours per unit at a batch size of one unit – if x is 1 then x^n is 1 regardless of what n is.

On an 80 per cent learning curve n may be determined from:

$$\frac{\log 0.8}{\log 2}$$

i.e.

$$\frac{-0.0969}{0.3010} = -0.322$$

So the relevant formula is:

$$y = 100x^{-0.322}$$

or

$$y = 100 \div x^{0.322}$$

We can determine the cumulative average hours per unit at a batch size of six by substituting into the equation, thus:

$$\begin{aligned} y &= 100 \div 6^{0.322} \\ &= 56.2 \end{aligned}$$

It follows that the total hours required to produce a batch of six units is 337.2 (i.e. 56.2 × 6).

Were we operating on a 90 per cent learning curve then n in the above equation would be determined as follows:

$$\log 0.9 \div \log 2$$

i.e.

$$-0.0458 \div 0.3010 = -0.152$$

What has been described is the 'cumulative average-time' model. This is the learning curve model most commonly encountered but there are alternative models.

One alternative sometimes encountered is the 'incremental time' (or 'marginal' or 'direct') model. This uses the same $y = ax^n$ formula as the cumulative average-time model but y is taken as the time required to produce the final unit; a, x and n are the same as in the cumulative average-time model.

The relative merits of alternative models are not explored here. You are reminded, however, that any mathematical model only serves to give an approximation of a complex reality. The management accountant has to use his/her judgment on the applicability of particular models to particular circumstances.

When learning curve theory is incorporated in future CIMA examination questions candidates may assume that the cumulative average-time model is applicable unless explicit instructions are given to the contrary.

Careful thought is sometimes required in the application of learning curve theory. Two particular points of difficulty are:

(a) *The choice of average or incremental hours as being the most relevant measure of time taken to produce a given set of units*

   In the preceding example it was seen that it should take 409.6 hours to produce a batch of eight units and 337.2 hours to produce a batch of six units. If you are required to undertake a variance analysis of the costs of producing the final two units of an eight-unit batch then you have to identify the standard hours required to produce those final two units.

   There are two possibilities here. You could adopt 72.4 incremental hours (i.e. 409.6 − 337.2 hours) as the standard or alternatively you could adopt 102.4 average hours (i.e. 51.2 hours × 2). Careful consideration suggests that a standard hours requirement of 72.4 would probably give the most meaningful results in a variance analysis exercise. But the relative merits of the two alternative possibilities depend on circumstances.

(b) *The point at which learning curve effects begin and end*

If production takes the form of a series of intermittent batches then the problem arises of deciding how far learning curve effects achieved in one batch are carried forward to subsequent batches.

At one extreme they may be fully carried forward. In this case total production is accumulated in order to determine average hours per unit. This is likely to arise when successive batches are produced by the same operatives with short time intervals between batches.

At the other extreme there may be a complete discontinuity between batches. Learning curve effects are achieved as output increases within a batch but those effects are lost by the time the next batch is started. This is likely to arise when there is a considerable time interval between successive batches and there is a high rate of labour turnover.

In conclusion, the learning curve is a simple mathematical model but its application to management accounting problems requires careful thought. CIMA's examiners will take care to ensure that questions set in examinations do not cross the border between 'requiring careful thought' and 'creating ambiguity'. In approaching learning curve problems candidates should pay close attention to the instructions given, which should be interpreted in a strict and literal way.

Exercise

Accounting students often have difficulty with the mathematics involved in the learning curve and in similar modelling technique. Management accounting students should be able to manipulate algebraic equations involving the use of powers. This involves understanding how to use traditional logarithm tables and/or use of relevant functions in a scientific calculator.

Test your mathematical skills by carrying out the following exercise.

1. $24{,}000 = K \dfrac{1m \times 6.2m}{9{,}000^n}$

2. $20{,}000 = K \dfrac{0.5m \times 2.5m}{4{,}000^n}$

You are required to calculate the values of K and n.

Workings

1. $24{,}000 = \dfrac{6.2bnK}{9{,}000^n}$ or $K = 24{,}000 \times \dfrac{9{,}000^n}{6.2bn}$

2. $20{,}000 = \dfrac{1.25bnK}{4{,}000^n}$ or $K = 20{,}000 \times \dfrac{4{,}000^n}{1.25bn}$

Therefore:

$$24{,}000 \times \dfrac{9{,}000^n}{6.2bn} = 20{,}000 \times \dfrac{4{,}000^n}{1.25bn}$$

or $\dfrac{4{,}000^n}{9{,}000^n} = \dfrac{24 \times 1.25}{20 \times 6.2}$

or $n \log 4{,}000 - n \log 9{,}000 = \log 0.2419354$
or $3.60206n - 3.95424n = -0.61630$
$n = 1.75$
Therefore:

$$24{,}000 = \frac{6.2 \text{bn} K}{9{,}000^{1.75}}$$

$$K = 24{,}000 \times \frac{8.316189}{6.2\text{m}} = 0.03219$$

Revision Questions

Question 1

1.1 R Ltd has been investigating the time taken to produce one of its products, and found that a 90 per cent learning curve appears to be applicable. If the time taken for the first unit is 4.000 hours, the *total* time taken for units 5–8 *only* is:

(A) 10.368 hours
(B) 11.664 hours
(C) 12.960 hours
(D) 23.328 hours
(E) 36.000 hours.

1.2 A production operation operates on an 85 per cent learning curve. It takes 100 hours to produce the first unit in a batch. To produce a 14-unit batch takes:

(A) 1,400 hours
(B) 962 hours
(C) 114 hours
(D) 754 hours
(E) 521 hours.

1.3 Data relating to the production of the first twelve units of a new product are as follows.

Time taken to produce the first unit	15 hours
Cumulative time taken to produce first 12 units	81 hours

The percentage learning effect is closest to

(A) 45%
(B) 55%
(C) 70%
(D) 80%
(E) 90%.

1.4 A hospital is considering investing $80,000 in a new computer system that will reduce the amount of time taken to process a patient's records when making an appointment. It is estimated that the cash benefit of the time saved will be $20,000 in the first year,

$30,000 in the second year and $50,000 in each of the next three years. At the end of five years the computer system will be obsolete and will need to be replaced. It is not expected to have any residual value.

Calculate the payback period to one decimal place of one year. **(2 marks)**

1.5 A company is preparing a quotation for a new product. The time taken for the first unit of the product was 30 minutes and the company expects an 85% learning curve. The quotation is to be based on the time taken for the final unit within the learning period which is expected to end after the company has produced 200 units.

Calculate the time per unit to be used for the quotation.

Note: The learning index for an 85% learning curve is − 0.2345 **(4 marks)**

1.6 H is launching a new product which it expects to incur a variable cost of $14 per unit. The company has completed some market research to try to determine the optimum selling price with the following results. If the price charged was to be $25 per unit then the demand would be 1,000 units each period. For every $1 increase in the selling price, demand would reduce by 100 units each period. For every $1 reduction in the selling price, the demand would increase by 100 units each period.

Calculate the optimum selling price.

Note: If Price (P) = a − bx; then Marginal Revenue = a − 2bx **(3 marks)**

Question 2

'The learning curve is a simple mathematical model but its application to management accounting problems requires careful thought.'

Requirements

Having regard to the above statement:

(a) explain the 'cumulative average-time' model commonly used to represent learning curve effects.
(b) sketch two diagrams to illustrate, in regard to a new product, the relative impacts of 70, 80 and 90 per cent learning curves on:
   - cumulative average hours per unit,
   - cumulative hours taken.
(c) explain the use of learning curve theory in budgeting and budgetary control; explain the difficulties that the management accountant may encounter in such use.
(d) compare and contrast the learning curve with the experience curve; explain the circumstances when each may be most relevant.

Solutions to Revision Questions

Solution 1

1.1 Answer: (A)

No. of units	Average time per unit hours	Total time hours	Incremental time hours
1	4.000	4.000	
2	3.600	7.200	
4	3.240	12.960 }	10.368
8	2.916	23.328 }	

1.2 Answer: (D)

In the learning curve formula $Y = ax^b$

b, the learning index, is given by $b = \dfrac{\log 0.85}{\log 2} = \dfrac{-0.0706}{0.3010}$

$$= -0.2345$$

∴ average time per unit for 14 units $= 100 \times 14^{-0.2345}$
$$= 53.856$$
∴ time for a batch of 14 units $= 53.856 \times 14 = 753.984$ hours

1.3 Answer: (D)

Cumulative average time taken per unit $= \dfrac{81}{12} = 6.75$ hours

Using the learning curve formula, $Y = ax^b$

$$6.75 = 15(12)^b$$
$$(12)^b = 0.45$$

Taking logs, $b \log 12 = \log 0.45$

$$b = \dfrac{\log 0.45}{\log 12}$$
$$= \dfrac{-0.3468}{1.0792}$$
$$= -0.3213$$

418 SOLUTIONS TO REVISION QUESTIONS P2

Since $b = \dfrac{\log \text{of learning}}{\log 2}$

$-0.3213 = \dfrac{\log \text{of learning}}{0.3010}$

$\therefore \log \text{of learning} = -0.0967$

Using tables, or the log 10^x button on a scientific calculator, the log of the learning rate converts back to 0.8.

1.4 After 2 years the total inflows = $50,000
After 3 years the total inflows = $100,000

Therefore payback occurs after **2.6 years**

1.5 $y = ax^b$
At 200 units: $y = 30 \times 200^{-0.2345} = 8.660$
Total time = $8.660 \times 200 = 1,732.00$ minutes

At 199 units: $y = 30 \times 199^{-0.2345} = 8.670$
Total time = $8.670 \times 199 = 1,725.33$ minutes

The time for the 200th unit to be used for the quotation is **6.67 minutes**

1.6 Marginal cost (MC) = $14
Price (P) = $35 − 0.01q
Marginal Revenue (MR) = $35 − 0.02q
So if MC = MR then:
14 = 35 − 0.02q
0.02q = 21
q = 1,050
Price = $35 − (0.01 × 1,050) = $24.50

Solution 2

- Explaining anything usually requires that it be set in context. In the present situation, the CAT model is most fully explained when compared with alternatives such as the 'incremental' model.
- It is critical to appreciate that the cumulative average hours per unit declines more rapidly with output if the learning curve effect is greater. It should be understood that a 70 per cent learning curve effect is 'greater' than a 90 per cent effect.
- Similarly, it is critical to appreciate that cumulative hours taken increases less rapidly with output if the learning curve effect is greater. There is a simple logic behind the mathematics that you must understand.

(a) The 'cumulative average time' model commonly used to represent the learning curve effects is demonstrated below for a 70 per cent learning curve:

Number of units produced	Cumulative average time required per unit	Total time required	Incremental time required for additional units
1	100.0	100.0	0.0
2	70.0	140.0	40.0
4	49.0	196.0	56.0
8	34.3	274.4	78.4

In this model, the cumulative average time required to produce a unit of production is reduced by a constant proportion of the previous cumulative average time, every time the cumulative output doubles.

In the above example, unit 1 requires 100 hours, but units 1 and 2 require only 140 hours, unit 2 being produced in 40 hours due to labour having learned how to perform more efficiently. Units 3 and 4 require only a further 56 hours' work, etc.

This may be modelled mathematically by the equation

$$Y = ax^n$$

where Y = cumulative average hours per unit, x = cumulative demand, and a and n are constants.

This is only one of the several models that may be used to predict the relationship between output and labour requirements.

(b)

> The question required only a sketch of the general shape of the curves, no calculations were required. However, the following calculations might have been made by candidates unsure of the general shape of the curves.

80 per cent learning curve

Number of units produced	Cumulative average time required per unit	Total time required
1	100.0	100
2	80.0	160
4	64.0	256
8	51.2	410

90 per cent learning curve

Number of units produced	Cumulative average time required per unit	Total time required
1	100.0	100
2	90.0	180
4	81.0	324
8	72.9	583

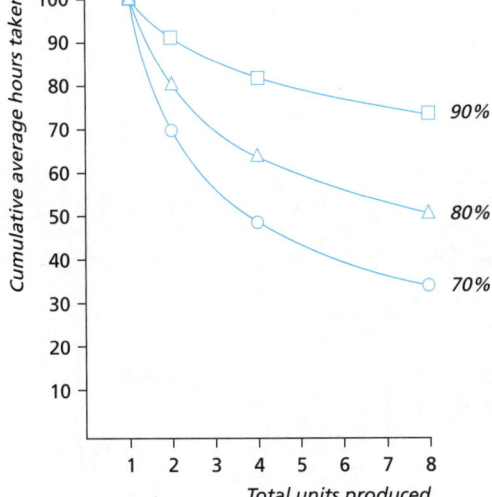

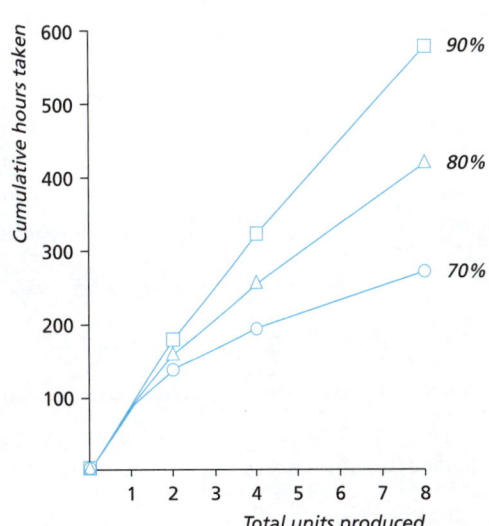

(c) Budgeting, budgetary control and project evaluation all rely upon the preparation of accurate forecasts of production capacity and operating costs. Learning curve theory may be used in such forecasts.

In particular, the learning curve theory may be used when repetitive manual tasks are introduced into a production process. Under these circumstances, application of this theory may result in more accurate prediction of labour time, labour costs, variable overhead costs that are driven by labour usage, and possibly material usage savings. Furthermore, if absorption costing is used, then this theory will enable the relationship between fixed overhead recovery and production rate to be accurately included in the budgeting process.

For budgetary control to be effective, the variances calculated must be based on realistic targets. A constant standard for labour, materials and variable overhead variances is not appropriate when the learning curve effect is present. By incorporating the learning curve theory into the targets, meaningful variances may be calculated and used in budgetary control.

Problems may be experienced in obtaining data on the rate of the learning curve until significant production has taken place. High labour turnover and changes in motivation levels may have significant effects upon the learning process. If there are extensive periods of time between batches of a particular product then the learning effect may be lost. The learning curve does not model long-term behaviour when there are no further productivity gains due to the learning process.

(d) The learning curve models the speeding up of a relatively new production process that involves repetitive manual operations due to labour learning from the experience. It was first documented in the 1920s and 1930s in the aircraft industry in the United States.

The experience curve is used to cover the improvement in a whole organisation's efficiency due to its internal learning effects. This covers functions such as production, research and development, management, marketing, etc. The experience curve is most appropriate in a growth area, or when the organisation operates on a large scale, i.e. it has a significant market share. One reason for taking over a competitor may be to obtain their in-house expertise, i.e. to move rapidly down the experience curve.

Neither effect is likely to be noticeable in well-established organisations that operate in static markets (growth, technology, etc.) and use standardised production facilities and mainly promotional marketing strategies.

Costing Systems

Costing Systems

12

LEARNING OUTCOMES

▸ Explain the concept of life cycle costing and how life cycle costs interact with marketing strategies of the life cycle.

▸ Explain how target costs can be derived from target prices and describe the relationship between target costs and standard costs.

12.1 Introduction

Organisations are facing a need to force down costs while still satisfying customers' requirements, if they are to achieve competitive advantage. The need to be flexible and to maintain the ability to respond quickly to changes in the market place has also become paramount.

Product life cycles have been shortened by increased competition, and the importance of bringing products quickly to market has increased.

Organisations have introduced new technology to enable them to maintain and improve their competitive edge.

In response, the management accounting profession has introduced new costing systems to provide management with the information they need to operate effectively in the modern business environment.

Different production systems need different costing systems and we will begin this chapter by looking at how costing systems have evolved to reflect the manufacturing philosophy.

12.2 Costing systems and manufacturing philosophy

12.2.1 Introduction

The costing system should be designed to complement the operations flow of the particular organisation. It should provide information which management can use to plan and control the operations on a daily, monthly and longer-term basis. The costing system will also reflect the organisation's philosophy and management style. For example, an organisation in a mature industry with a bureaucratic management style will require more operational control measures than a more youthful organisation with a different management approach. A manufacturing organisation will, or should, arrange its physical systems to best advantage, so that materials and production flow from one process to another in the best possible way. This also applies to the flow of operations in service industries.

The first part of this chapter will consider systems which manufacturing organisations, that have the added problem of stock to cope with, may use. The latter part will consider systems applicable to all types of organisations.

The last 15–20 years have seen a considerable change in the way manufacturing facilities and their related systems are organised. This has been due in part to a change in manufacturing philosophy and in part to new technology, such as CAM (computer aided manufacturing) and FMS (flexible manufacturing systems), which has helped facilitate the change. Not every company has undergone this change, but for those that have it has been vital that their information and cost reporting systems change in sympathy. These systems may be radically altered so that they suit and match the new physical systems and management's changed information needs. If the costing systems are not adjusted properly it is very unlikely that the manufacturing changes, whether physical or philosophical, will bring many benefits.

The management accountant needs to be involved with the planned manufacturing changes at an early stage so that the cost accounting and information systems can be suitably amended. This does not merely mean collecting information in a slightly different way, such as automatically from a computerised system rather than manually from a more traditional one. It means completely rethinking what data should be collected and what information should be reported.

The new costing systems are likely to report unit quantities rather than monthly monetary values to production employees, and performance measures based on output rather than hours worked to management.

In order to make the correct changes to the systems the management accountant must keep an open mind and be willing to discuss the existing and proposed systems with other managers and employees.

In this chapter we begin by considering recent changes in manufacturing philosophy and then go on to discuss some of the resulting changes in costing systems.

12.2.2 Traditional manufacturing philosophy

Traditional manufacturing philosophy in the West may be summed up by the following aphorisms:

- time is money, therefore, no worker or resources should be idle;
- as time spent adjusting machinery to cope with different products is time wasted, the production runs of each product should be as long as possible.

In other words, the traditional view is that labour and manufacturing equipment are so valuable that they should not be left idle. They should be kept working at all times and if the resulting components or products are not needed immediately they should be placed in store. In order to increase efficiency and reduce production cost per unit, batch sizes and production runs should be as great as possible. This will reduce costs such as downtime due to resetting equipment.

The traditional view is not wrong. It is just totally one-sided. Yes, machine set-up time is downtime and non-productive, but the answer is not to do away with it by removing product mix and product choice. Instead the answer is to try to reduce it to a minimum by efficient changeover procedures. The downside of long production runs is a build-up of stock. Stock is usually not an asset; instead it is a liability. This is despite the fact that it appears in published accounts as an asset, and financial accountants place considerable emphasis on determining its value 'correctly'. Stock may be considered to be a liability because it takes up valuable space and ties up money that could be invested elsewhere.

When US and UK companies began to switch over to just-in-time practices during the 1980s much of the space that was previously given over to stock became free. It was not unusual for this to amount to one-third of the total production area. Freed space may be used in a variety of ways – not least of which is to increase production capacity by 50 per cent!

Accountants became wise to the effect of the cost of interest on money tied up in stock many years ago and began to delay payment to their suppliers thus negating part of the cost of holding stock. Unfortunately in turn their customers became wise and delayed payment to them and so debtors and creditors were created in vast quantities. These, together with stock, were useful to accountants because they could be manipulated for financial reporting purposes.

Taken as a whole, however, this system has no benefits, it is just abominably wasteful. What is really happening is that money and goods are waiting around covering up and protecting inefficiency. The main reason for keeping stock, apart from coping with seasonal fluctuations in demand, is to cope with inefficient and uneven production methods. Inefficiency and unevenness of machine capacity creates bottlenecks, and in order to overcome these, stock is built up in large quantities. The answer is to solve the production problems and not to hide them. The case of Garrett Automotive (discussed later) illustrates the extent to which machine unevenness can occur in companies which are apparently operating satisfactorily.

Traditional manufacturing philosophy is concerned with balancing two sets of costs: production run costs and stock-holding costs. Long production runs decrease the manufacturing cost per unit but stock-holding costs will increase per unit as a result. Table 12.1 identifies the main costs involved. Each company has its own particular set of costs and can determine its own unique minimum cost per unit, as seen in Figure 12.1.

The traditional philosophy did not have a chance to take root in much of Japanese industry. This was due to the Second World War interrupting the country's development as an industrial nation. After the war there was such a shortage of materials and components in Japan that companies could not afford to use these scarce resources in manufacturing unless they had a customer for the product. This meant that long production runs were impossible. Toyota has been the champion of the new manufacturing philosophy and has developed and refined it painstakingly over the intervening years, resulting in its widely reported just-in-time (JIT) system of today. (This is described later.) However, JIT is an

Table 12.1 Long production run costs

Manufacturing costs per unit	Stock-holding costs per unit
Set-up costs reduced	Space costs increased
Waiting time/costs reduced	Labour costs increased
Production scheduling reduced	Insurance costs increased
Purchasing costs reduced	Interest charges increased
Labour costs reduced	

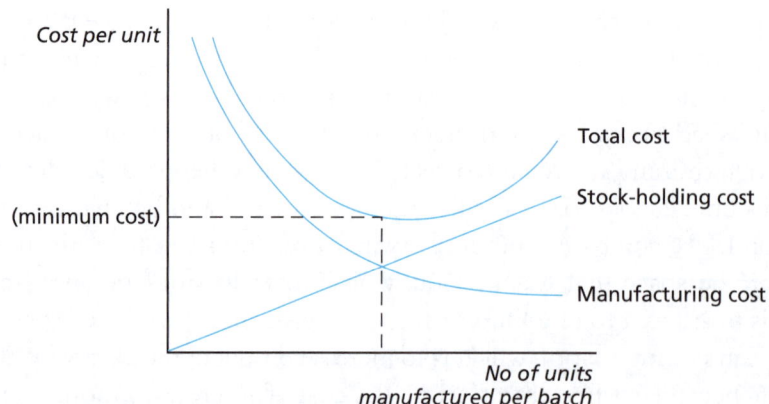

Figure 12.1 The relationship between batch size and cost per unit

extreme philosophy that cannot be attained in less than ten years of constant effort. Neither is a complete JIT system with zero stocks suitable for most Western organisations, but it does contain some very important elements that are included in the modern philosophy outlined in the next paragraph.

12.2.3 Modern manufacturing philosophy

Organisations using traditional manufacturing philosophy can be very efficient but they are rarely effective. Modern manufacturing philosophy places emphasis on smooth, steady production flow (throughput) and not on high individual labour activity and machine efficiency. Its two main aphorisms may be summarised as:

- the parts working together as effectively as possible in order to make the whole effective;
- be flexible and provide exactly what the customer wants, at the moment it is wanted.

The latter approach has grown out of the need to achieve competitive advantage by not only providing value products but providing them as quickly as possible after the customer has realised the need. Thus companies that adopt modern manufacturing philosophy must be responsive, flexible and effective.

In order to be all these things an organisation must offer a relatively wide range of products and produce them on demand. This makes managing the business a more complex affair as it entails more production scheduling, more components to buy, more materials to track, etc. It also means increased unit costs. According to Stalk and Hout (1990), if variety is increased threefold, that is if the products offered increase by 300 per cent, the organisation's breakeven point is likely to double, productivity may be reduced by between 40 and 45 per cent and unit cost may rise by between 40 and 50 per cent.

Thus, increasing the range of products to suit individual customer needs brings severe problems. The company must be ready to produce any product from a wide range at a moment's notice. Therefore, the traditional large batches and long production runs must be replaced by small batches and short production runs.

12.2.4 Volume versus variety

Long production runs (volume) reduce costs, whereas short production runs (variety) increase costs. The result of the traditional approach of long production runs is shown in

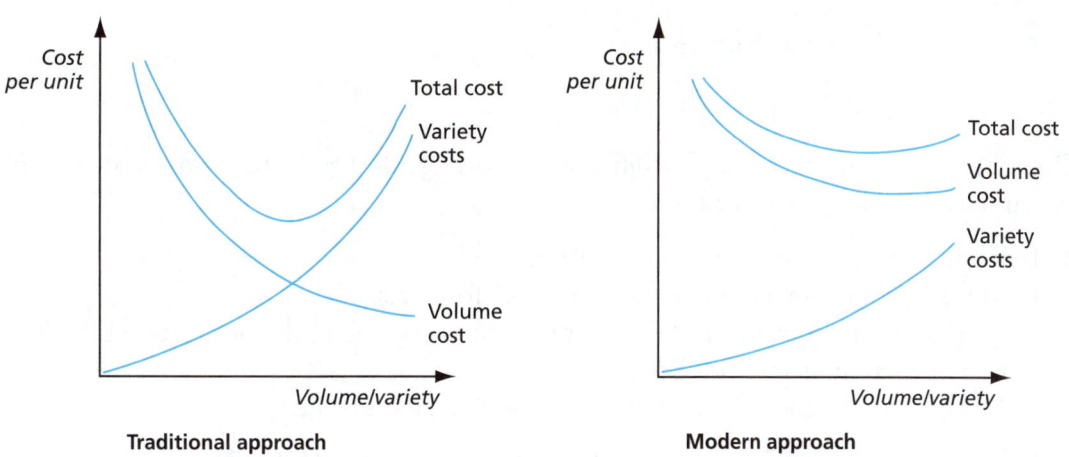

Figure 12.2 The cost relationship between volume and variety

the left-hand graph in Figure 12.2. Research has shown that when volume doubles, the average cost per unit decreases by 15–25 per cent (the experience curve effect, 75–85 per cent of previous cost). This automatic reduction may be considered satisfactory by management and they may not attempt to reduce volume costs further by attempting to control and minimise set-up and waiting-time as they should do. Variety costs behave in the opposite way to volume costs. Stalk and Hout (1990) found that when the variety of products manufactured doubles the average unit costs rise by 20–35 per cent. When a company adopts the modern philosophy and manufactures in variety, therefore, emphasis is inevitably put on controlling costs and minimising set-up and waiting time costs. The result of this emphasis is that variety costs increase more slowly than they would have done had the company adopted the traditional approach. This has the effect of moving the minimum cost to a higher output level which in turn means that this type of company tends to have a competitive edge over its more traditional competitors.

In order to achieve this reduction in cost, increased production capacity needs to be organised by product/process and not by function. For example, traditionally a consumer durable manufacturer would group all metal presses together in one department which would make parts for all models. In order to produce products quickly to suit customers the presses need to be separated and located with other machinery manufacturing a single product line. The path to responsiveness, effectiveness and flexibility may be summarised as follows:

- Minimise the movement of components and products. (For example, one manufacturer managed to reduce product movement between workstations from 300 yards to 18 inches.)
- Organise manufacturing layout by product family and not by production activity or function.
- Production scheduling will be simplified as a result of altering the layout and will therefore be more efficient. This will help compensate for the complication and additional cost of short production runs.
- Waiting time decreases – because movement of components is reduced and scheduling improved.

These methods and benefits are also obtained from a JIT production system.

12.3 Pull systems

12.3.1 Just-in-time (JIT)

Organisations in the West have traditionally used a 'push' production flow system. This system has the following stages:

1. Buy raw materials and put them into stock.
2. Produce a production schedule based on sales forecasts.
3. Withdraw goods from stock and make products according to the production schedule.
4. Put completed units into finished goods store.
5. Sell from finished goods store when customers request products.

Toyota developed a different system known as just-in-time (JIT). This system is not a 'push' system but a 'pull' system (see Figure 12.3). A product is not 'made' until the customer requests it and components are not made until they are required by the next production stage. In a full JIT system virtually no stock is held, that is no raw material stock and no finished goods stock is held, but there will be a small amount of work-in-progress, say one-tenth of a day's production. The system works by the customer triggering the final stage of production, the assembly. As the product is assembled components are used and this in turn triggers the component stage of production and a small amount of work-in-progress is made ready for the next product. So the cycle goes on until the final trigger requests more raw material from the supplier.

If a JIT system is to work satisfactorily suppliers must deliver several times a day and so when the raw material arrives it may go straight into the factory and be used immediately. This means that the production lead-time (i.e. the time from raw materials entering production to the finished goods emerging) should equal the processing time. In many Western organisations in the past it took several months to make a product from start to finish, despite the fact that if worked on continuously it could be made in, say, two days. The difference in time is largely due to work-in-progress waiting to be used in the next process. For example, Morgan cars made just nine cars a week in the mid-1980s but each car took several months to make from start to finish.

JIT requires the following:

- The labour force must be versatile so that they can perform any job within reason to keep production flowing as required.
- Production processes must be grouped by product line rather than by function in order to eliminate stock movements between workstations and to speed flow.
- A simple, infallible information system. Originally the Japanese used a system based on cards which were called kanbans. There would be a small container of components (WIP)

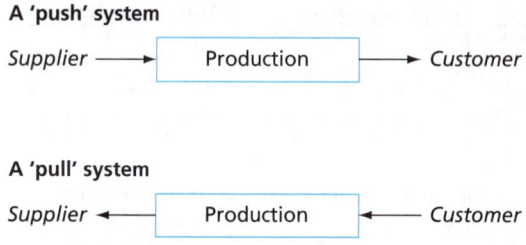

Figure 12.3 Pull and push systems

between each workstation with a kanban resting on top. When the container was taken for use by the following workstation the card would be taken off and left behind. This would act as a trigger for the previous workstation to produce another container of that component. Nowadays computer systems are likely to be used instead of cards but the basic simplicity of the system should not change.

Cases from *Management Today*, November 1999

- The British Institute of Management gave Britax Wingard the award of best factory of 1999. Britax makes components, including mirrors, for Rover, Toyota and Nissan. Their assembly operation is constructed around tightly knit cells that operate on the 'heijunka' principle. With this method manufacturing is focused on 15-minute slots and different coloured ping pong balls are used to denote which kind of mirror the cell must build in the next production slot: left-hand, right-hand, heated, electrically operated, etc. for a particular car model. Thanks to the use of kanban devices the company never makes anything that has not already been sold. Staff do not go home at the end of the day until the heijunka board has been cleared. A machine changeover is completed in just six minutes from last off to first off. The mould tools weigh 930 kg and are changed quickly through quick release tooling, single size Allen keys and adroit handling. Each mould is stored immediately above the machine and electrically hoisted in and out of position.
- Each night the computers at the DIY retailer B & Q's headquarters total the EPOS (electronic point of sale) bar code data on the day's sales throughout the country. The sales of products such as Solvite, Locktite and Copydex are transmitted electronically to Henkel's factory in Winsford, Cheshire. Four hours later the order has been delivered to B & Q's Runcorn distribution depot.
- Giroflex manufactures office chairs, etc. Every product is highly configurable and almost specific to the customer, as there are literally millions of possible product permutations. The factory production schedule operates in customer postcode order each day so as to optimise the distribution process.

12.3.2 Backflush accounting

Traditional cost accounting systems track the sequence of raw materials and components moving through the production systems, and as a consequence are called 'sequential tracking systems'. As JIT is an entirely different system it requires its own cost accounting system. The absence of stocks makes choices about stock valuation systems unnecessary and the rapid conversion of direct material into cost of goods sold simplifies the cost accounting system. The approach is known as backflush accounting.

Backflush accounting delays the recording of costs until after the events have taken place, then standard costs are used to work backwards to 'flush' out the manufacturing costs. There are two events that trigger the records kept in most backflush accounting systems:

- The first is the purchase of raw materials. In a true JIT system where absolutely no raw material stock is held, even this trigger is not relevant and raw materials are 'flushed' when the second trigger is activated.
- The second trigger is either the transfer of goods to finished goods stock or, in a true JIT system, the sale of goods. Two examples of possible backflush accounting systems are given in Tables 12.2 and 12.3 and the corresponding ledger accounts are shown in Figures 12.4 and 12.5.

Table 12.2 System 1
A small stock of raw materials is held but no finished goods stock

	Dr £	Cr £
1. Raw materials are purchased – £3,200		
Stock control	3,200	
Creditors control		3,200
2. Conversion costs are incurred – £3,000		
Conversion cost control	3,000	
Individual a/cs		3,000
3. Goods sold – £6,000 worth at standard cost		
Cost of goods sold	6,000	
Stock control		2,900
Conversion costs allocated		3,100
4. Under- or over-allocation of conversion costs		
Conversion costs allocated	3,100	
Cost of goods sold		100
Conversion costs control		3,000

Table 12.3 System 2
No raw material stock is held but some finished goods stock is held

The figures are the same as for system 1, but the transfer to finished goods is assumed to be £6,000 and the cost of goods sold is £5,900 leaving a finished goods stock of £100.

	Dr £	Cr £
1. Raw materials are purchased – no entry		
2. Conversion costs are incurred – £3,000		
Conversion cost control	3,000	
Individual a/cs		3,000
3. Finished goods units produced £6,000		
Finished goods control	6,000	
Creditors control		2,900
Conversion costs allocated		3,100
4. Finished goods sold – £5,900		
Cost of goods sold	5,900	
Finished goods control		5,900
5. Under- or over-allocation of conversion costs		
Conversion costs allocated	3,100	
Cost of goods sold		100
Conversion costs control		3,000

This is the system used by Toyota in its UK factory. In true Japanese style it manipulates employees to behave in a certain way. First, employees must concentrate on achieving sales because cost of sales is the trigger – nothing gets recorded until the sale is made. Second, there is no benefit in producing goods for stock. In traditional systems, which have a finished goods stock, managers can increase profit by producing more goods than are sold in a period because an increase in finished goods stock reduces the cost of sales in traditional financial accounts.

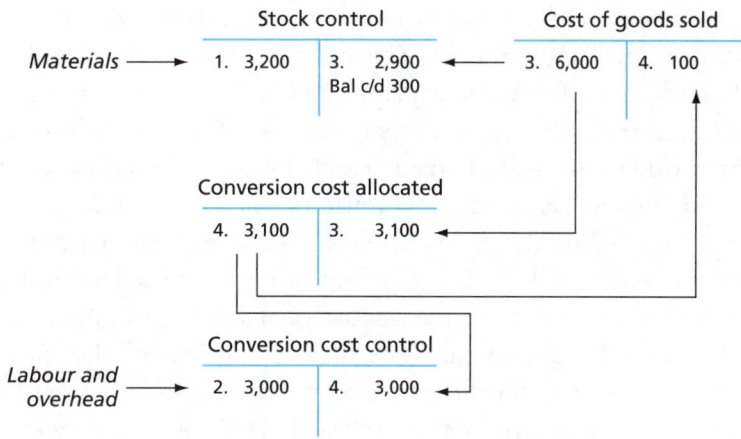

Figure 12.4 Ledger accounts for system 1

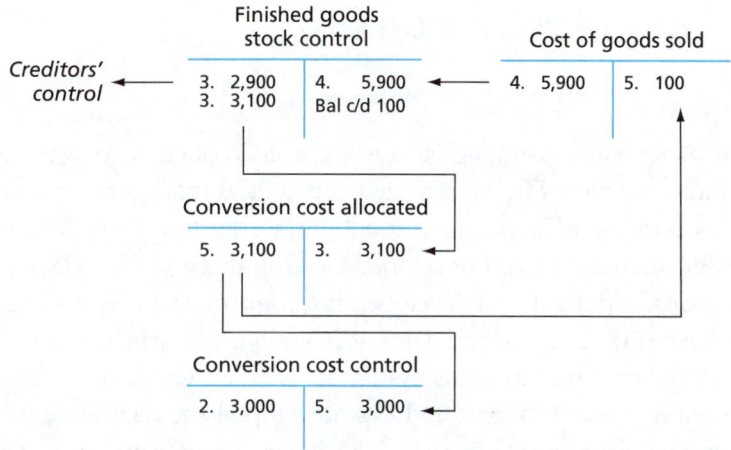

Figure 12.5 Ledger accounts for system 2

The model just described may be altered to cope with work-in-progress in the system by using a raw and in progress account (RIP) in place of the stock control account. All other entries remain the same.

The backflush accounting model cannot be used by all organisations. It can only be used where a JIT-type system is in operation. Where it is used it does have advantages. The traditional system is time consuming and expensive to operate, as it requires a considerable amount of documentation, such as material requisitions and time sheets to support it in order to maintain the WIP records and job cards. If a company operates with low stock levels the benefits of operating the traditional costing system are few. By introducing a backflush system a considerable amount of clerical time is saved.

From the backflush accounting examples it can be seen that JIT eliminates direct labour as a cost category. Instead labour is treated as an indirect cost and is included in conversion cost with the overheads. This is because production is only required when demand requires it and so production labour will be paid regardless of activity. All indirect costs are treated as a fixed period expense. With JIT, failed or rework must be almost eliminated if the system is to work and so no accounts for this will exist in backflush accounting whereas they are required in traditional systems.

The backflush accounting model does not conform to the accepted financial accounting procedures for external reporting in the UK. This is because work-in-progress is treated as an asset in the financial accounts and in backflush accounting it is not shown to exist although in practice a small amount does. This can be countered by claiming, quite rightly, immateriality. If only one-tenth of one day's production is held in work-in-progress then it is immaterial. It can also be claimed that it is immaterial if the work-in-progress does not change from one period to the next as opening and closing stock will cancel each other out.

Backflush accounting can be criticised because of the lack of information that it provides. Some argue, quite rightly, that in reality it is impossible to eliminate all stock as a truck arriving with raw material creates stock until it is moved to and used in production. If backflush accounting is used in a system where a substantial amount of stock is held, a physical stock-take will be needed, because the system does not record the quantity of stock. Instead, it is derived on paper by the difference between the standard cost of material in the goods sold and the amount of materials purchased. This must be checked by a physical stock-take from time to time.

12.4 Throughput accounting

12.4.1 The theory of constraints (TOC)

A new type of management accounting system was needed once the new manufacturing philosophy was put into practice. The most widely recognised management accounting system developed for this purpose is known as throughput accounting (TA). The concept behind the system was first formulated and developed by Goldratt and Cox (1986) in the US in a book called *The Goal*. Goldratt (1990) developed the concept and eventually gave it the name the *theory of constraints* (TOC) by which name it is known today in the US. The theory was picked up and turned into an accounting system in the UK, where it has become known as throughput accounting (TA). Goldratt and Cox developed the technique to help managers improve the overall profitability of the firm. The theory focuses attention on constraints or bottlenecks within the organisation which hinder speedy production. The main concept is to maximise the rate of manufacturing output, that is, the throughput of the organisation. The idea behind TOC is that raw materials should be turned into products that are immediately shipped to customers at the greatest possible speed, in a similar way to the JIT system.

The important concept behind TOC is that the production rate of the entire factory is set at the pace of the bottleneck – the constraining resource. Hence, in order to achieve the best results TOC emphasises the importance of removing bottlenecks or, as they are called in the USA, binding constraints from the production process. If they cannot be removed they must be coped with in the best possible way so that they do not hinder production unduly. In order to do this, network diagrams need to be drawn to identify the bottlenecks or binding constraints. Figure 12.6 illustrates a simple network chart where the assembly and test process is the bottleneck.

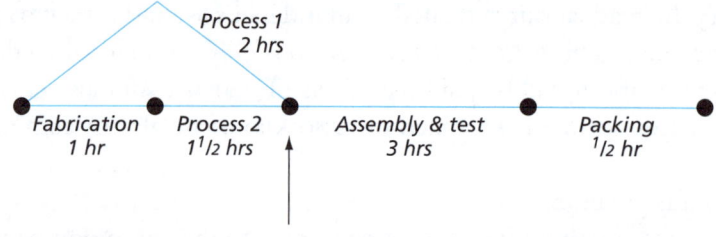

Figure 12.6 Network chart of a manufacturing process

In Figure 12.6 it can be seen that the assembly and test process is the bottleneck and that in order to maximise throughput, a buffer stock is needed prior to the assembly and test process so that its employees never have to wait for components from prior processes.

The aim is to operate what Goldratt terms a drum-buffer-rope system. The bottleneck (drum) dictates the overall pace of work. Stock is only allowed to build up in finished goods and in front of the bottleneck to act as the buffer, which allows the crucial function to continue even if there are breakdowns upstream. The rope links all upstream operations to the pace of the bottleneck, to keep those at the front end of the production process from churning out more than the bottleneck can handle.

TOC identifies three types of cost.

- *Throughput contribution*
    = sales revenue − completely variable costs
  this is usually = sales revenue − direct material cost.
  (Labour costs tend to be partially fixed and are excluded normally. Direct material cost includes purchased components and material handling costs.)
- *Conversion costs*. These are all operating costs, excluding completely variable costs, which are incurred in order to produce the product, that is, labour and overhead, including rent, utilities and relevant depreciation.
- *Investments* which include all stock, raw material, work-in-progress, finished goods, research and development costs, costs of equipment and buildings, etc.

The aim is to increase throughput contribution while decreasing conversion costs and investment costs. TOC is a short-term profit maximising technique that is very similar in approach to marginal costing. The only real difference is that the contribution may be more realistic in that all conversion costs are assumed to be fixed costs. Bottleneck decisions are in reality linear programming decisions as TOC attempts to do the following:

Maximise throughput contribution (sales revenue − direct materials)
Subject to:
Production capacity (supply constraints)
Production demand (demand constraints)

This is discussed later in more detail.

TOC is quite widely used in the USA by companies such as Ford Electronics, General Motors and Avery Dennison, some of which claim that it has revolutionised their business. It is also used by a number of UK companies, sometimes in the form of throughput accounting, discussed next.

12.4.2 Throughput accounting (TA)

In the UK, Galloway and Waldron (1988–89) developed throughput accounting from the theory of constraints. It is very similar in concept to TOC but it is an accounting-based technique whereas TOC is not. Eli Goldratt has always stressed the differences between the two systems. This may have been because he is not over-fond of cost accountants or their methods and at one time one of his sayings was that 'cost accounting is the number 1 enemy of productivity'. TA is an extreme version of variable costing as, like TOC, it treats only direct material as variable and all labour and overhead costs as fixed. It operates through a series of ratios and differs from all other management accounting systems because it emphasises throughput first, stock minimisation second and cost control third.

Throughput accounting's primary concern is the rate at which a business can generate profits. In order to monitor this it focuses on the return on the throughput through the bottleneck resource.

Its key measure is:

$$\text{Return per time period} = \frac{\text{Sales revenue} - \text{Material cost}}{\text{Time period}}$$

[Assuming materials are the only totally variable costs, Balderstone and Keef (1999)]

This ratio measures the value added by the organisation during a specific period of time, normally one hour. As time plays a crucial part in the ratio, managers' attention is automatically drawn to removing bottlenecks that might cause delay in the production process.

If one machine holds up production, because it is inefficient or has inadequate capacity, it is of little use to work the other machines at 100 per cent efficiency as the parts produced will be destined for stock until such time as the bottleneck machine can process them. Eventually when parts are spilling from the storeroom or piled all over the factory floor the efficient machines will have to stop altogether for a time, in order to allow the bottleneck machine to catch up. Therefore, there is nothing to be gained by measuring and encouraging the efficiency of machines that do not govern the overall flow of work. The same applies to the efficiency of production staff working in the non-bottleneck processes. In fact bonuses that are paid to encourage fast working are at best simply wasted and at worst result in increased storage costs. Furthermore, if workers are encouraged to work too quickly they are likely to produce more faulty goods and to waste materials. If the goods are destined for the storeroom, this increase in waste serves no purpose except to increase the average cost per unit.

A minor use of the return per time period ratio is to optimise production in the short term. Product return per time period ratio can be used in the same way as limiting factor ratios are used in order to plan how many units of each product should be made in order to maximise profit. The limiting factor is the first factor that prevents a manufacturing company expanding production towards infinity, and the ratio is contribution/limiting factor. The products are ranked according to this ratio; that is according to their use of the limiting factor, the one with the highest contribution per key or limiting factor being the best financially. In TA the key or limiting factor is the bottleneck. The return per time period ratio can be modified and used in a similar way to the P/V ratio. The amended ratio for ranking products is:

$$\text{Product return per minute} = \frac{\text{Sales price} - \text{Material costs}}{\text{Minutes on key/bottleneck resource}}$$

This is illustrated in detail in the following example.

✋ Exercise – contrasting TA with the limiting factor approach

A company produces two products, A and B, the production costs of which are shown below:

	A £	B £
Direct material cost	10	10
Direct labour cost	5	9
Variable overhead	5	9
Fixed overhead	5	9
Total product cost	25	37

Fixed overhead is absorbed on the basis of direct labour cost.

The products pass through two processes, Y and Z, with associated labour costs of £10 per direct labour hour in each. The direct labour associated with the two products for these processes is shown below:

Process	Time taken	
	Product A	Product B
Y	10 min	39 min
Z	20 min	15 min

Selling prices are set by the market. The current market price for A is £65 and that for B, £52. At these prices, the market will absorb as many units of A and B as the company can produce. The ability of the company to produce A and B is limited by the capacity to process the products through Y and Z. The company operates a two-shift system, giving 16 working hours per day. Process Z is a single-process line and 2 hours in each shift will be downtime. Process Y can process two units simultaneously, although this doubles the requirement for direct labour. Process Y can operate for the full 16 working hours each day.

Requirement

What production plan should the company follow in order to maximise profits?

Solution

In order to find the profit maximising solution in any problem, the constraints which prevent the profit from being infinite must be identified; the greater the number of constraints, the more difficult the problem is to solve. In the simplest case, where there is only one binding constraint, the profit maximising solution is found by maximising the contribution per unit of the scarce resource, that is, the binding constraint. Linear programming may be used to solve the problem where more than one constraint is binding for some, but not all, feasible solutions. Where the number of products is limited to two, and such constraints are relatively few in number, the problem can easily be expressed graphically to reveal the profit maximising solution, and/or the problem can be expressed in the form of a set of simultaneous equations. As the number of potentially binding constraints increases, the use of a computer becomes the only feasible way to solve the necessary number of simultaneous equations.

In this question, the only constraint is the company's ability to process the product. The total daily processing time for processes Y and Z are:

Maximum process time Y = 2 × 16 hours × 60 mins = 1,920 minutes
Maximum process time Z = 12 hours × 60 mins = 720 minutes

So the maximum number that could be produced of each of the two products is:

	Product A Maximum units	Product B Maximum units
Y	$\frac{1,920}{10} = 192$	$\frac{1,920}{39} = 49.23$
Z	$\frac{720}{20} = 36$	$\frac{720}{15} = 48$

In the case of both products, the maximum number of units which can be produced in process Y exceeds the number that can be produced in process Z, and thus the capacity of process Y is not a binding constraint. The problem therefore becomes one of deciding how to allocate the scarce production capacity of process Z in such a way as to maximise profit.

Traditional approach – maximising the contribution per minute in process Z
Contribution of A = £65 (selling price) − £20 (variable cost) = £45
Contribution of B = £52 (selling price) − £28 (variable cost) = £24

Contribution of A per minute in process Z = £45 ÷ 20 = £2.25
Contribution of B per minute in process Z = £24 ÷ 15 = £1.60

The profit maximising solution is therefore to produce the maximum possible number of units of A, 36, giving a contribution of £45 × 36 = £1,620.

Throughput approach – maximising throughput per minute in bottleneck resource Z
Throughput of A = £65 (selling price) − £10 (material cost) = £55
Throughput of B = £52 (selling price) − £10 (material cost) = £42

Contribution of A per minute in process Z = £55 ÷ 20 = £2.75
Contribution of B per minute in process Z = £42 ÷ 15 = £2.80

The profit maximising solution is therefore to produce the maximum number of units of B, 48, giving a throughput of £42 × 48 = £2,016.

It is clear that, given the different solutions, the two approaches cannot both lead to profit maximisation. Which technique is correct depends on the variability or otherwise of labour and variable overheads, which in turn depends on the time horizon of the decision. This type of profit maximization technique is a short-term one and in today's world labour cost is likely to be fixed in the short term and so it can be argued that TA provides the more correct solution. Variable overheads would need to be analysed to assess their variability.

Marginal costing rose to popularity in the 1930s when labour costs were usually variable as the workforce was usually paid on a piece-rate basis. Since then textbooks, at least, have always assumed that labour is a variable cost in the short term. All that has happened with TA is that it tends to recognise the present reality, which is that most costs excluding materials are now fixed in the short term.

The marginal costing approach should of course be modified to accommodate this, as it requires only variable costs to be used to calculate contribution. If only material costs are variable then only those costs should be used in the calculation of contribution. Thus there should be no difference between the two systems in this respect.

Provision of additional resources to bottleneck

The aim of throughput management is to focus attention on bottleneck resources, with the immediate aim of ensuring that such resources are utilised for 100 per cent of their capacity, and the further aim of alleviating the constraint. In this example, Z is the bottleneck resource. If management is able to find a way to enable this machine to work for one extra hour, the maximum number that could be produced of each of the two products becomes:

	Product A Maximum units	Product B Maximum units
Y	$\frac{1,920}{10} = 192$	$\frac{1,920}{39} = 49.23$
Z	$\frac{780}{20} = 39$	$\frac{780}{15} = 52$

Whether a particular constraint is binding now depends on the production plan. The capacity of Y limits production of B, while the capacity of Z limits production of A.

The adoption of a linear programming approach (calculations not shown) reveals that the profit maximising output, if labour and variable overhead are truly variable costs, is to produce units of A only. If the only variable cost is material, the profit maximising output is to produce 48.57 units of B and 2.57 units of A.

If one extra hour could be provided to relieve the bottleneck at Z, the above analysis suggests that, where no costs other than material are variable the effect is to alter the optimal production plan. Y and Z both become bottlenecks in this case, as they are both utilised to 100 per cent of their capacity:

Y: $[48.57 \times 39] + [2.57 \times 10] = 1{,}920$ minutes
Z: $[48.57 \times 15] + [2.57 \times 20] = 780$ minutes

If costs other than material are variable the provision of one extra hour at Z does not alter the optimal production plan, except in so far as additional units of A can now be produced. Z remains a bottleneck, being used to 100 per cent of its capacity, while spare capacity continues to exist in Y. The quality of the decision regarding the appropriate production schedule to follow is thus crucially dependent on the quality of the assumptions on which the decision is based.

The example above is illustrative only, as few organisations would produce and market products based on their short-term profitability. Strategic issues such as stage in product life cycle, future product developments, market developments, etc., need to be considered and are usually more important considerations than short-term profit.

Also, the example is trivial in some respects. It relates to a company producing only two standard products, requiring only two production processes, and with a stable demand for the products. Contrast this with a multi-product, multi-process company, where prices are set by negotiation between the supplier and the buyer, and the demand for products is largely unpredictable. Such situations are difficult to model accurately, even with modern information technology.

The contribution of the throughput accounting approach may lie in the insights it can offer in such a chaotic, but realistic, production condition. A global measure of throughput at factory level may give a clear signal as to the effectiveness of factory management. With a given level of resources (i.e. premises, machinery, employees, etc.) an increase in the throughput period by period would give a simple measure of improvement of the flow of goods through the factory and to the customer. By drawing attention to impediments to that flow – that is, the bottleneck resources – management will focus on alleviating problems which are inhibiting the profitability of the factory as a whole, rather than on sub-units or particular product lines. Managing the throughput of a factory reflects the philosophy of 'management by walking about', that is, bottlenecks related to particular machines or processes are generally much more easily identified by direct observation than by relying on the output of conventional accounting reports. Traditional variance reporting may be harmful as it can encourage the attainment of high levels of local efficiency at the expense of overall efficiency.

12.4.3 Throughput cost control and effectiveness measures

Although the measure of return per period is a valuable measure for speeding up the flow of work and eliminating bottlenecks it ignores the costs involved in running the factory.

There is little to be gained if throughput and, therefore, revenue are increased marginally but in order to achieve this labour and overhead costs increase considerably. The throughput accounting ratio measures this:

$$\text{TA ratio} = \frac{\text{Value added per time period}}{\text{Conversion cost per time period}}$$

$$\text{i.e.} \ \frac{(\text{sales} - \text{materials}) \text{ per time period}}{(\text{labour} + \text{overhead}) \text{ per time period}}$$

This ratio will obviously be greater than one for a profitable company and the aim will be to increase it to an acceptably high level. If a product has a ratio of less than one the organisation loses money every time it is produced.

Traditional efficiency measures such as standard costing variances and labour ratios can no longer be used with TA because traditional efficiency cannot be encouraged. (The labour force must not be encouraged to work to produce for stock.) A process efficiency ratio of throughput/cost can still be used.

Effectiveness is, however, the more important measure:

$$\text{Current effectiveness ratio} = \frac{\text{Standard minutes of throughput achieved}}{\text{Minutes available}}$$

This measures effectiveness and compares it to a current standard.

Traditional variances can also be misleading in a throughput environment. For example, if overtime was worked at the bottleneck to increase throughput an adverse labour rate variance would arise. Generally adverse variances are considered bad. However, in a throughput environment this would be good and would increase profits as long as the extra labour cost was less than the increase in value added. (See the Garrett Automotive case below.)

TA's aim, like JIT, must always be to minimise production time taken and so all non-value added elements in the production lead time need to be eliminated or minimised so that process time approaches the lead time.

Lead time = Set-up time + waiting time + process time + inspection time + move time

12.4.4 Case – throughput accounting at Garrett Automotive Ltd UK

In 1988, Garrett Automotive reorganised its operations. This resulted in the UK factory producing many more product lines in smaller batches than before. The company's management accounting system prior to 1988 was very detailed and cumbersome. It consisted of a 48-page monthly report that largely dealt with detailed variances which, as is often the case, were not properly understood by many managers. As sales and materials were the two largest influences on profit it made sense to introduce a new costing system which concentrated on those two elements. This led to a throughput system being chosen. At the time the company set up the new system it had three production processes, each of which had a single machine. Machine A could produce 30 units an hour and machines B and C, 18 units and 80 units respectively. Clearly the production flow was not in balance. The new system highlighted this. To partially remedy the situation machine D was introduced to perform one of the operations normally carried out by machine B. This raised the capacity at this point to 21 units. Then machine E was purchased for just £6,000 and this further increased the output in that process to 24 units per hour. When machine C became due for replacement shortly afterwards, a new machine with an output of just 26 units an hour was purchased. These adjustments raised the output of the plant from 2,025 to 2,700 units per week and evened out production flow considerably.

Previously Garrett Automotive had used an 'efficiency' report that measured actual departmental direct labour hours against the standard hours allowed for the components produced. If 'efficiency' fell in one section the manager was pressured into improving it. As far as machines A and C were concerned this meant increasing stock, as they were already working at a greater rate than machine B was capable of.

When the company changed to TA, the lengthy monthly report was altered. It was reduced to just five pages so that it consisted of:

- controller's commentary;
- key operating and investment statistics;
- working capital performance;
- schedule adherence summary by production cell.

According to the company, however, the simplification of the information and costing system was not the most important benefit of the introduction of throughput accounting. The most important benefit was that employees began to realise the importance of adhering to the production schedule. For example, if each of the three production processes only managed to achieve an 80 per cent schedule adherence, only 51 per cent of the final customer orders would be met on time (80 per cent $\times$ 80 per cent $\times$ 80 per cent = 51 per cent.) The final page of the monthly report provided regular reinforcement of the importance of sticking to the production schedule. It included new quantitative information on the following measures:

- per cent schedule adherence;
- scheduled quantity;
- scheduled finished;
- per cent mix adherence;
- quantity finished;
- per cent unscheduled.

Better schedule adherence resulted in the stock held being halved. However, because the bottlenecks are critical to production throughput, work-in-progress immediately before the bottleneck was increased so that the bottleneck machines were not held up by a lack of components.

The introduction of TA and adjusting the machinery balance resulted in the company doubling its profits from the same volume of sales. This was done without a large amount of capital expenditure and without reducing the number of employees.

The Garrett Automotive example is an abbreviated version of an original article. An article later deals with this in greater depth and calculates product costs to show how product cost per unit increases but profit goes up because of the larger throughput volume.

12.4.5 Summary of throughput accounting

Table 12.4 highlights the difference between TA and traditional product costing.

So far TA has only been considered in relation to manufacturing organisations but it has been used very successfully in service industries as well. For example, it has been used to

Table 12.4 Difference between throughput accounting and traditional product cost systems

Throughput accounting	Traditional product costing
Value is added when an item is sold	Value is added when an item is produced
Schedule adherence and meeting delivery dates are the key to working effectively	Full utilisation of labour and machine time is the key to working efficiently
Variance analysis only investigates why the scheduled mix was not produced	Variance analysis investigates whether standards were achieved
Labour and traditionally defined variable overheads are not normally treated as variable costs	Labour and traditionally defined variable overheads are treated as variable costs
Stock is valued in the P&L and balance sheet at material cost only (i.e. variable cost)	Stock is valued in the P&L and balance sheet at total production cost

speed up and reduce costs in checking customers' creditworthiness. In one company this process took a long time, often longer than a week, and held up further activities. Before TA was used, over-qualified people were used to make basic credit decisions and this caused the delays in deciding on creditworthiness. Afterwards ordinary members of staff were allowed to make decisions in the majority of cases and only difficult ones were referred to experts. This meant that decisions were made much faster, normally within 24 hours, and the cost of the function was reduced.

TA has been criticised for being unduly short term because all costs apart from material costs tend to be treated as fixed. It could be argued that the use of traditional marginal costing is not always correct because those that use it tend to treat direct labour as a variable cost, which is not realistic. It could be argued, and has been by some, that labour is more fixed than an item of machinery and its associated costs, as that can be removed and sold within a few weeks. Staff cannot be made redundant as quickly and the cost may be greater. Having said that, in the long term all costs are variable and all options possible but TA only considers the current situation and ways of improving it.

Marginal costing and throughput accounting rely on the calculation of contribution (sales − variable cost) and as such there is no difference between them. Because direct labour was paid on a piece-rate, it was largely a truly variable cost when marginal costing was developed early this century. Today, textbooks tend to use the same definition of variable costs for marginal costing purposes even though it is usually no longer relevant. Once this problem has been overcome the two systems are seen to be the same in principle, marginal costing dealing with short-term one-off decisions and throughput accounting providing a planning and control system.

Make or buy decisions should nearly always be made from a strategic viewpoint and not from a short-term marginal cost point of view. But assume for a moment that a short-term decision is needed and marginal costing is used, and that it suggests that the product under consideration should be made rather than bought in. If this product uses valuable capacity on the machine before the bottleneck machine, then the holding of buffer stock could be jeopardised under certain circumstances. This was a real scenario at Allied Signal Ltd. Because throughput accounting was used, management declined the opportunity to make the product under consideration (Darlington, 1995). Again conflict occurred between the two systems, but the consequence of using spare capacity should have been considered in any system; throughput accounting simply drew attention to it.

It is also argued that by concentrating on the relationship between sales and materials TA neglects other costs. This is not a valid criticism as the TA ratio incorporates conversion costs per time period. However the purpose of throughput accounting, and especially TOC, is not so much to control costs as to demonstrate ways of improving profit by increasing production flow. It is an attention-directing system. The criticisms can be countered but nevertheless throughput accounting is not a technique that will suit all organisations.

12.5 Cost planning and reduction over the life cycle

12.5.1 Target costing: a strategic profit management system

Target costing supposedly originated in Japan in the 1960s, where it is known as Genka Kikaku. It is not a costing system but could be considered a profit planning system as it is a comprehensive system to control costs and manage profit over a product's life cycle – from the product concept to the sale of the last spare part years after the product has ceased production. Kato (1993) described target costing this way:

> 'Target costing is an activity which is aimed at reducing the life-cycle costs of new products, while ensuring quality, reliability, and other consumer requirements, by examining all possible ideas for cost reduction at the product planning, research and development, and the prototyping phases of production. But it is not just a cost reduction technique; it is part of a comprehensive strategic profit management system.'

Target costing is an important tool because it promotes cost consciousness and focuses on profit margins, both of which strengthen an organisation's competitive position. It is not a technique that attempts to slash costs by trimming functions or closing departments; it is a steady and never-ending pressure to make sure that costs are always kept to a minimum. It is entirely different from standard costing where managers are expected to keep within predetermined standard costs, and variances are calculated to determine whether they have done so.

Standard costing, as used in the West, does not start with the product concept. Instead it starts as the product goes into production with a predetermined set of circumstances. That is: the organisation is going to make a new product, it will be designed this particular way and as a consequence the costs will be so much – this in turn influences the selling price.

Target costing, as used in the East, starts with a product design concept. From this a selling price is determined for the product and a profit requirement is set. This leads to the development of a target cost, that is the cost that must be met if profit is going to be achieved. Finally the product is designed to achieve the target cost – if this is not possible aspects of the product would be redesigned until the target is met.

The target profit requirement, of say 15 per cent, should be driven by strategic profit planning rather than a standard mark-up. In Japan, this is done after consideration of the medium-term profit plans which reflect management and business strategies over that period. Once it is set the target profit is not just an expectation; it is a commitment agreed by all the people who have any part in achieving it. Therefore, the procedures used to derive a target profit must be scientific, rational and agreed by all staff responsible for achieving it otherwise no one will accept responsibility for achieving it.

Table 12.5 The different nature of standard costing and target costing

	West	East
Product concept stage		Selling price and required profit set. Target cost determined
Design stage	Standard costs determined followed by standard price	Target costing used to keep costs to a minimum
Production stage	Cost control through variance analysis	Constant cost reduction through target costing

The different nature of standard and target costing are shown in Table 12.5. Although both approaches use predetermined measures as controls, the difference between them is absolutely fundamental. The Western approach is always short-term cost control through variance analysis, with no medium-term planning of costs that tie the operational to the long-term strategic plans.

The use of target costing rectifies this weakness as the medium-term strategic position is considered at the start of the process with the product concept and the determination of the required profit. If it is thought that the product cannot generate the required profit it will not be produced. Target costing continues over the product's life and the pressure to reduce costs is continuous as costs are reduced monthly. This is another difference between target and standard costing where standards are often only revised annually.

The target costing approach is a vital total cost control tool because research has shown that up to 90 per cent of costs are 'built in' at the product's design stage. For example, the design stage sets the following:

- *The design specification of the product including extra features.* For example, the specification may be for a basic car with lots of additional extras that may be specified and paid for separately. Alternatively it may be for a product that includes as standard most of the extras desired by customers. Clearly the latter car will be cheaper, but does it meet customer requirements better?
- *The number of components incorporated in the product.* For example, during an anti-dumping argument in the 1980s, the EU accused Amstrad of dumping their audio systems in Europe, that is, selling them at a price less than cost. During a television debate on this, the cover was taken off a Grundig and an Amstrad machine. The former was considerably more expensive and no doubt produced a far better sound for those with discerning ears. The Grundig case was full of wires, soldered elements, etc., and to the untutored eye was a confusing mass of many different parts. The Amstrad case was half-empty. Was this because the designers thought that customers would perceive the product to be inferior if it were smaller? About a quarter of the space was occupied by a box, a single component, to which some wires were attached. Anyone could see that it would be a lot cheaper to produce because assembly time would be only a fraction of the Grundig machine.
- *Design of components.* These should be designed for reliability in use and ease of manufacture. Wherever possible standard parts should be used because they are proven to be reliable and will help reduce stock and handling costs. Where new components are required it is important that their manufacturing process is considered before the component is

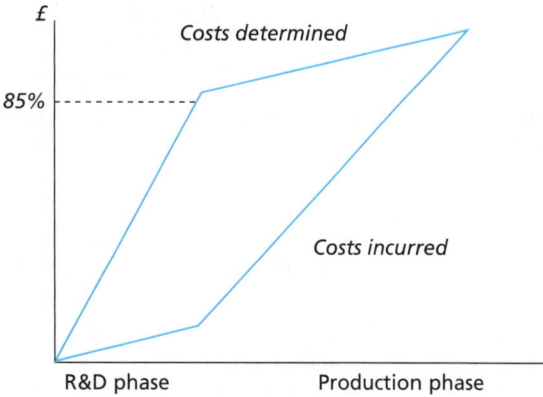

Figure 12.7 Timing of cost determination and occurence

finally designed so that they can be manufactured as cheaply as possible consistent with quality and functionality.
- *Type of packaging required.* This includes product packaging and packing per case and per pallet. The aim is to protect the product and to minimise handling costs by not breaking pallets or cases during distribution.
- *The number of spare parts that need to be carried.* This ties in with the number of components used. Parts must sometimes be held for up to 15 years or so. They may be made while the product is still in production and stored for years, which is costly. The alternative is to disrupt current production to make a small batch of a past component, which is very costly.

The chart in Figure 12.7 shows that, as discussed above, costs are determined before they are incurred and that most costs, 85 per cent in this case, are determined before production starts. This is because they are committed at the various pre-production stages, especially at the design and process planning stages.

12.5.2 Using target costing in the concept and design stages

Target costing is an iterative process that cannot be de-coupled from design. The pre-production stages can be categorised in a variety of different ways; in the detailed discussion below five different stages are used and the different activities are now listed.

1. *Planning.* This includes fixing the product concept and the primary specifications for performance and design. A very brief product concept might be: a small, town car for two people with a large amount of easily accessible luggage space and low fuel consumption – aimed at those in their mid-twenties and so style is important. (In reality the concept would be much fuller.) Value engineering analysis (VE) could be used to identify new and innovative, yet cost effective, product features that would be valued by customers and meet their requirements.

    Once the concept has been developed a planned sales volume and selling price, which depend on each other, will be set, as well as the required profit discussed earlier. From this the necessary target cost (or allowable cost as it is often known) can be ascertained:

    Target cost = Planned selling price − Required profit

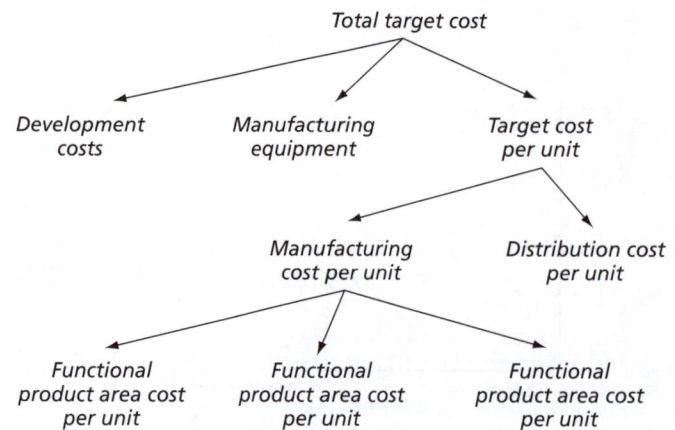

Figure 12.8 The breakdown of target cost

2. *Concept design.* The basic product is designed. The total target cost is split up as illustrated in Figure 12.8. First an allowance for development costs and manufacturing equipment costs are deducted from the total. The remainder is then split up into unit costs that will cover manufacturing and distribution, etc. The manufacturing target cost per unit is assigned to the functional areas of the new product. For example, a functional area for a ballpoint pen might be the flow of ink to the tip and a functional area for a car might be the steering mechanism.
3. *Basic design.* The components are designed in detail so that they do not exceed the functional target costs. Value engineering is used to get the costs down to the target. If one function cannot meet its target, the targets for the others must be reduced or the product redesigned.
4. *Detailed design.* The detailed specifications and cost estimates are set down from the basic design stage.
5. *Manufacturing preparation.* The manufacturing process, including new machines and jigs, etc., is designed in keeping with the target cost.
    Standards for the materials and labour hours that should be used are set. These values are presented to the staff in the factory immediately they are set so that approval can be given.
    The purchasing department negotiates prices for bought-in components.

12.5.3 Target costing for existing products

Cost control is not forgotten once the product goes into production. Manufacturing performance is measured to see if the target is being achieved. The reasons for doing this are:

1. to see who is responsible for any cost excess and to offer them help, and
2. to judge whether the cost planning activities were effective.

If after 3 months the target cost is missed by a large margin an improvement team is organised which will conduct a thorough value analysis (VA) and will stay in existence for about six months.

Although the Japanese use standard costing to some extent they do not consider it to be suitable for on-going cost control. They see standard costing as part of budget accounting where the same value is maintained throughout the budget period, whereas they use target costing to control production cost and as a consequence revise it monthly. Monden and Sakurai (1989) expressed the limitations of standard costing this way:

> Since standard costing systems have constraints from a financial perspective, they are inappropriate measures for management. A typical constraint is the infrequency in which quantity standards, such as processing time per production unit or material requirements, are revised. Normally these standards are maintained at the same level throughout the year.

Target costing, therefore, continues to be used to control costs throughout the product's life. After the initial start-up stage target costs will be set through budgets, which in Japan tend to be set every six months rather than a year. This type of target costing is a different technique in the eyes of the Japanese and they call this Genka Kaizen. It is widely used in Japan; about 80 per cent of assembly environments use it. If a manager cannot meet the target cost for a function, a committee will be set up to help achieve it. All costs including both variable and fixed overheads are expected to reduce on a regular basis, usually monthly.

12.5.4 Target costing support systems

It should be clear that target costing cannot operate in isolation; support systems are needed to feed it information. VE and VA have already been mentioned and in fact a large number of support systems are needed if target costing is to operate in the way intended. Some of the systems are sophisticated computer systems; some are detailed cost systems, etc. Kato (1993) listed the support systems needed in order to operate target costing successfully. They are as follows.

Sales pricing support systems

These are market research systems, which have the following qualities:

- An ability to decompose product functions into sub-functions and supply information on that basis.
- Facilities to convert the value placed on each function into price.
- A value-price conversion table or database.
- A market research toolbox with various forecasting techniques.
- Simulation functions (what-if, sensitivity analysis, etc).

Target profit computation support systems

- Support mechanisms for strategy formulation, profit planning, human resource management and capital investment decision making.
- Product portfolio planning systems, which can calculate the optimal product mix in the future.
- Profit decomposition systems for each product.

Research and development support systems

- Computer graphics, computer aided design (CAD), computer aided engineering (CAE), etc.
- Project management systems to monitor and aid R&D activities based on expert systems or artificial intelligence (AI).

Support systems for infusing target costs into products

- Value engineering (VE) – in Japan these are based on cost tables and cost reduction databases. (Cost tables are widely used in Japan and agencies exist to provide relevant data to

different industries. The tables are extremely important and help accurate cost predictions and allow for a series of 'what if' questions to be asked.)
- Variety reduction.

Although Kato does mention human resource management systems briefly in the list above, perhaps it should be listed as a separate category. (This would be particularly important if a Western organisation wanted to use target costing for the first time.)

Human motivation and resource support systems

Pressure is put on individuals to achieve the required results in their section. If they do not meet the target they are perceived as letting the group down. If this approach is used all employees must operate as a group and cooperate to achieve the best results. The committees used by the Japanese are seen as support activities or systems and not as a sort of punishment. All motivation systems must operate efficiently, as staff must be willing to accept targets in the first place – this is a function of good management and good communications.

12.6 Life cycle costing

12.6.1 Life cycle costing – introduction

Life cycle costing can apply to products, services, customers, projects or assets and, as its name implies, it costs the cost object over its projected life. The aim is to adopt a policy which will maximise the return over the cost object's total life. To a certain extent capital budgeting attempts to do this but often a project's complete life is not costed as a cut-off time is used. For example, any inflows after year 5 or 10 are ignored because they are assumed to be too uncertain or insignificant. More importantly, normal capital budgeting techniques simply project expected costs and revenues in order to make an assessment of profitability in advance of the project. They do not attempt to maximise profit by minimising costs and maximising revenues over the life cycle by applying planning and control techniques. This deliberate attempt to maximise profitability is the key to life cycle costing.

Projecting costs and revenues over the cost object's life span runs counter to traditional accounting, which chops up costs and revenue into time periods – a month, a year, etc. This prevents consideration of the total profitability of an individual product or service and does not allow the total picture to be seen. If a snapshot is taken on one particular day, an organisation will have a number of different projects, products, customers, etc., all of which have different life spans (Figure 12.9).

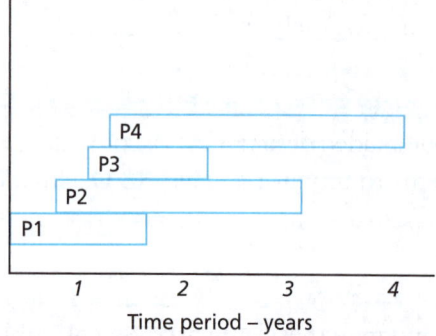

Figure 12.9 Projects per time period

The importance of life cycle costing lies in the consideration of the whole life cycle. When viewed as a whole cost reduction and minimisation opportunities as well as revenue extension opportunities will present themselves. These are unlikely to be found when management is focusing on maximising profit on a period-by-period basis.

The old adage, time is money, still holds true. The management of time is particularly important in life cycle costing if profit is to be maximised. An increase in time during the development stage causes an increase in cost or a decrease in revenue, which in turn causes a reduction in profit. Time is often the causal factor of a reduction in profit whereas an increase in costs is merely the effect or result of an increase in time.

This section will look specifically at life cycle costing for products and customers.

12.6.2 Product life cycle costing

All products have a life cycle chart that looks something like Figure 12.10. In reality the time span may be only a few months or years, as in the case of novelty products and toys, or it may last for more than 100 years, as in the case of products such as binoculars and marmite.

Figure 12.10 shows a product that has a research and development stage prior to the commencement of production in year 4 when revenues begin to be generated. Losses are incurred initially, followed by a profit that gradually tapers off once the product enters its maturity stage.

Figure 12.11 illustrates a product that has several different life cycles; the original life cycle has been extended because the organisation found new uses for the product. One of the classic examples of this is the manufacture of nylon, which was developed just before the Second World War. Its first use was in parachutes for the armed forces, its next use was in ladies' stockings, this was followed by car tyres, carpets and clothes.

Figure 12.12 highlights the danger of product proliferation, when products are updated or superseded too quickly. The product life cycle is cut short so that the product hardly has time to generate a profit. The product barely covers the R&D costs before its successor is launched on the market.

There are a number of factors that need to be managed in order to maximise a product's return over its life cycle. These are:

- maximise the length of the life cycle itself;
- design costs out of the product;

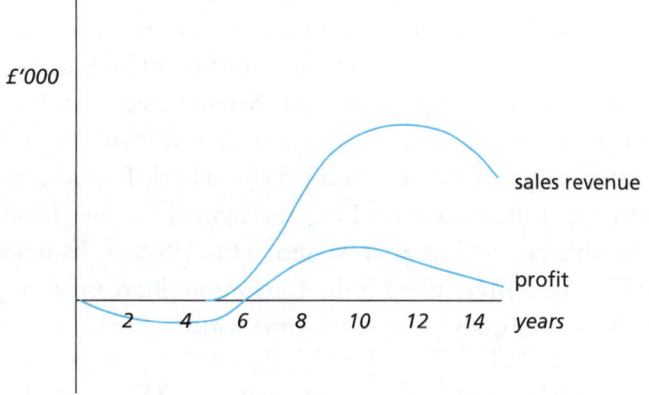

Figure 12.10 The product life cycle

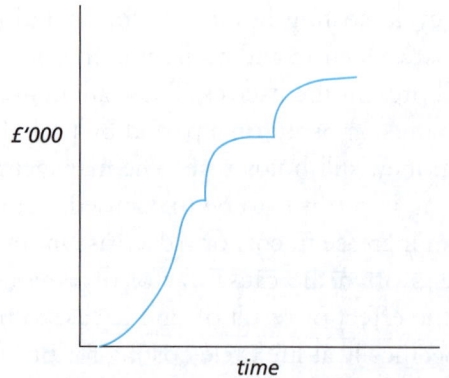

Figure 12.11 Extending the product life cycle

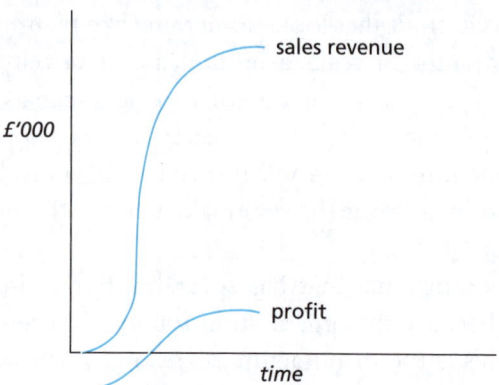

Figure 12.12 Product life cycle when product proliferation occurs

- minimise the time to market;
- manage the product's cash flows.

These factors will be considered in turn.

Maximise the length of the life cycle itself

Generally, the longer the life cycle the greater the profit that will be generated, assuming that production ceases once the product goes into decline and becomes unprofitable. One way to maximise the life cycle is to get the product to market as quickly as possible because this should maximise the time in which the product generates a profit. This is discussed below. Figure 12.11 illustrates another way of extending a product's life, by finding other uses, or markets, for the product. Other product uses may not be obvious when the product is still in its planning stage and need to be planned and managed later on. On the other hand, it may be possible to plan for a staggered entry into different markets at the planning stage. Many organisations stagger the launch of their products in different world markets in order to reduce costs, increase revenue and prolong the overall life of the product. A current example is the way in which new films are released in the US months before the UK launch. This is done to build up the enthusiasm for the film and to increase revenues overall. Other companies may not have the funds to launch world-wide at the same moment and may be forced to stagger it.

Skimming the market is another way to prolong life and to maximise the revenue over the product's life. This was discussed earlier in this text.

Design costs out of the product

It was stated earlier that between 80 and 90 per cent of a product's costs were often incurred at the design and development stages of its life. That is, decisions made then committed the organisation to incurring the costs at a later date, because the design of the product determines the number of components, the production method, etc. It is absolutely vital therefore that design teams do not work in isolation but as part of a cross-functional team in order to minimise costs over the whole life cycle.

Minimise the time to market

In a world where competitors watch each other keenly to see what new products will be launched, it is vital to get any new product into the market place as quickly as possible. The competitors will monitor each other closely so that they can launch rival products as soon as possible in order to maintain profitability. It is vital, therefore, for the first organisation to launch its product as quickly as possible after the concept has been developed, so that it has as long as possible to establish the product in the market and to make a profit before the rival's product is launched.

Often it is not so much costs that reduce profit as time wasted. A McKinsey study revealed that if a product was launched six months behind schedule 33 per cent of after-tax profit was lost. If on the other hand product development cost 50 per cent more than planned, profits reduced by just 3.5 per cent. All new product developments should have a planned time to market and events should be monitored closely to make sure that the planned timing is adhered to. This can be done using Gantt charts. Nowadays simultaneous engineering is often used in the planning, development and testing stages, which allows for several activities to be performed at the same time rather than sequentially, thus speeding the product on to the market. Alternatively cross-functional development teams, which operate simultaneously, are used to shorten the time to market.

Manage the product's cash flows

In order to manage the life cycle of their products Hewlett-Packard developed what they termed the return map. House and Price (1991) describe how this was developed in order to minimise the time to market and to maximise the return over the product's life cycle. It was developed to help employees focus on the issue of developing products that would make the most profit in the least time. The return map measures both money and time (Figure 12.13), and plots the cumulative investment, sales and profit over time. The y-axis

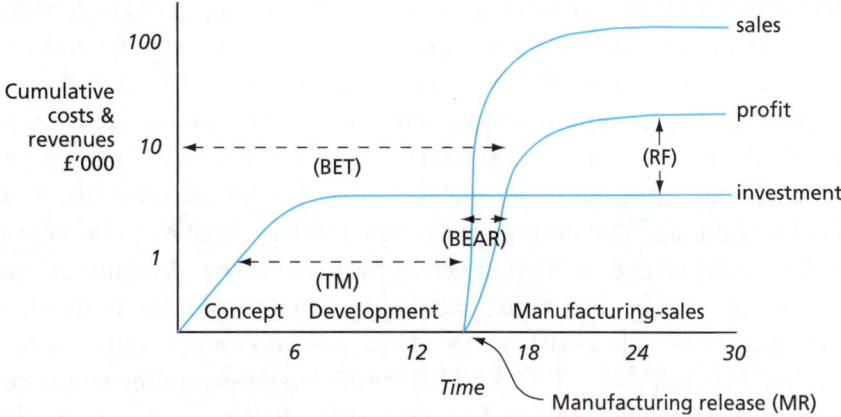

Figure 12.13 The return map

Table 12.6

Measures	Original proposal	Revised proposal	Actual results
Time to market (TM)	9 months	13 months	15 months
Breakeven time (BET)	18 months	22 months	26 months
Breakeven after release (BEAR)	4 months	4 months	6 months
Return factor (RF) 1 year after MR	$7.3m	$7.0m	$5.4m
Time from start to MR	14 months	18 months	20 months

is the measurement of money and is normally drawn on a logarithmic scale to capture cumulative sales and investment adequately.

The return map measures several key time periods, the first of which is the time to market (TM). Other key measures that are shown on the chart in Figure 12.13 are breakeven time (BET), breakeven time after release (that is after the product is launched) (BEAR), and return factor (RF), which is the excess of profit over the investment.

House and Price (1991) recount the history of the ultra-sound machine that had a time to market (TM) of 9 months when the product was proposed. Two months into the project's development, Hewlett-Packard had a breakthrough in technology that would give clearer pictures. The management decided to incorporate this, and so the TM was extended by 4 months despite the fact that the return map showed that the return factor would reduce slightly (Table 12.6). The actual TM was 15 months and there was also a cost overspend as shown in Table 12.6.

Table 12.6 shows that the initial proposal was very profitable with a return of $7.3m in excess of the initial investment one year after the product launch. The modification did not improve profitability but the company felt that customers would appreciate the improvement and so went ahead. The actual results show that not only was the return seriously reduced but that it began to be received 6 months late, and as a consequence the total earnings life cycle of the project was cut by 6 months resulting in a further loss of earnings.

12.6.3 Customer life cycle costing

Not all investment decisions involve large initial capital outflows or involve the purchase of physical assets. The decision to serve and retain customers can also be a capital budgeting decision even though the initial outlay may be small. For example a credit card company or an insurance company will have to choose which customers they take on and then register them on the company's records. The company incurs initial costs due to the paperwork, checking creditworthiness, opening policies, etc., for new customers. It takes some time before these initial costs are recouped. Research has also shown that the longer a customer stays with the company the more profitable that customer becomes to the company. Figure 12.14 shows this and that customers become more profitable year after year. Thus, it becomes important to retain customers, whether by good service, discounts, other benefits, etc. A customer's 'life' can be discounted and decisions made as to the value of, say, a 'five-year-old' customer. Eventually a point arises where profit no longer continues to grow; this plateau is reached between about 5 years and 20 years depending on the nature of the business. Therefore by studying the increased revenue and decreased costs generated by an 'old' customer, management can find strategies to meet their needs better and to retain them.

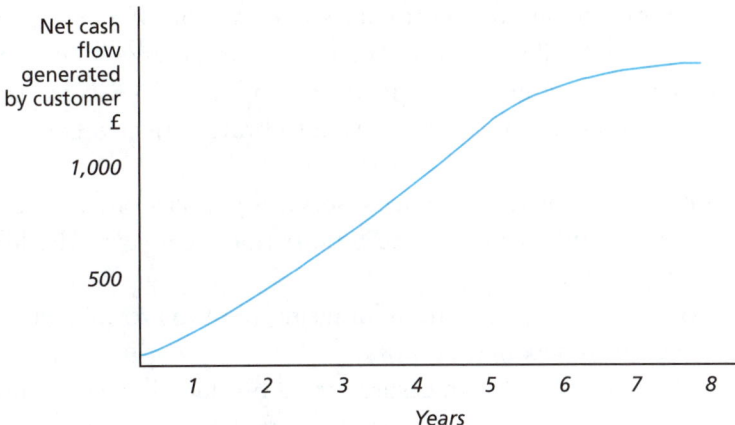

Figure 12.14 Customer cash flow over time

Many manufacturing companies only supply a small number of customers, say between six and ten, and so they can cost customers relatively easily. Other companies such as banks and supermarkets have many customers and cannot easily analyse every single customer. In this case similar customers are grouped together to form category types and these can then be analysed in terms of profitability. For example, the UK banks analyse customers in terms of fruits, such as oranges, lemons, plums, etc. Customers tend to move from one category to another as they age and as their financial habits change. Customers with large mortgages, for example, are more valuable to the bank than customers who do not have a large income and do not borrow money. Banks are not keen on keeping the latter type of customer.

12.7 Summary

This chapter has dealt with costing and accounting systems. Key points are as follows:

- The modern manufacturing philosophy is based on meeting customer needs as quickly as possible through flexible and smooth processes while holding as little stock as possible.
- Costing systems need to be designed to complement and reflect the operations flow of the organisation.
- Backflush accounting can be used with a JIT system. It usually reduces the number of accounting entries considerably, thus saving costs and time.
- The theory of constraints (TOC) focuses on bottlenecks and their removal and aims to maximize throughput contribution.
- Throughput accounting (TA) is a management accounting system based on the theory of constraints. It uses the throughput contribution to calculate the key measure, return per period, and several other ratios.
- TA recognises that most costs, excluding materials, are fixed in the short term.
- Traditional variance reporting may be harmful as it can encourage the attainment of high levels of local efficiency at the expense of overall efficiency.
- Traditional efficiency measures, such as standard costing variances and labour ratios, cannot be used with TA because traditional efficiency cannot be encouraged: the labour force must not be encouraged to produce for stock.
- Traditional variances can also be misleading in a throughput environment.

- Target costing is a tool to minimise cost consistently at both the design and production phases. A predetermined selling price is obtained from an analysis of the market, and from this is deducted the target profit, to determine the target cost. Techniques such as value analysis and value engineering are used to bring expected costs in line with the target cost.
- Life cycle costing views individual products, services and customers over their total life rather than assessing them over the single time period of a year. The life cycle can be managed to maximise profit.
- Designing cost out of the product and minimising the time to market are possibly the most important factors in maximising profit.
- A return map identifies four key measures in a product life cycle: time to market, breakeven time, breakeven after release and return factor.

Readings

12

This article illustrates the benefits to be gained by shortening manufacturing cycle times and moving towards a JIT system.

Manage your costs by managing your cycle times
Tony Brabazon, *Management Accounting,* June 1999

Customers of manufacturing and service companies are becoming ever more demanding in their requirements. As product life cycles shorten and as more firms adopt lean production systems, they are demanding that their suppliers respond quickly to their orders. Because of these pressures, firms are seeking continuous improvements in both their customer response time (CRT) and their on-time delivery rate. CRT represents the length of time between an order being placed and the delivery of the goods or service to the customer. It is a measure of a firm's ability to respond to a customer's request and is especially crucial in industries which have short product life cycles, such as the clothing, toys and high-tech sectors.

In general, the key issues in determining CRT are internal to the firm, namely the delay before work on an order commences and the length of time the order spends in the production process. Both of these are linked in turn to the length of the manufacturing cycle.

What is manufacturing cycle time?
Manufacturing cycle time (MCT) is the length of time between starting and finishing the production of an order. In a typical production process, MCT is composed of four elements:

- Processing time
- Wait time
- Move time
- Inspection time

Processing time consists of the time spent actually working on the order at each stage of production;
Wait time is the time spent by an order between the various stages of the production process;
Move time is the time spent by an order between the various stages;
Inspection time is the time spent ensuring that the output is of the required quality. Although all of these elements lengthen the manufacturing cycle, only the processing time adds value in the eyes of the customer.

The manufacturing cycle time can be expressed in terms of manufacturing cycle efficiency (MCE). This represents, in a ratio format, the proportion of time during which value is being added in the production process. The MCE can be calculated as follows:

$$\frac{\text{Processing time}}{\text{Processing} + \text{Wait} + \text{Move} + \text{Inspection times}}$$

The closer this ratio is to 1, the greater the efficiency of manufacturing operations. The firm can measure the MCE on a global basis, or separately for each of its product lines. It has been suggested that, in traditional manufacturing environments, the MCE is often less than 10 per cent, indicating that a typical manufacturing plant had large (and costly) investments in work-in-progress stocks (WIP)[1]. Often, more than 80 per cent of the cycle time consists of waiting – waiting for raw materials to arrive, waiting for a set-up operation to be performed, waiting between processing departments because of production bottlenecks and waiting for the correction of quality defects caused by earlier production mistakes. The net effect of this waiting is to increase substantially both the complexity of production scheduling and the level of WIP.

In essence, MCE highlights the portion of the cycle time that is represented by 'non value added' (NVA) activities. Many firms have been able to reduce markedly their manufacturing cycle time by reducing or eliminating NVA activities. For example, Ford Motor Company's North Penn factory, which makes electronic engine control units, was able to reduce its average manufacturing cycle time from 7.8 days to 17[2] hours through the elimination of NVA activities.

Why focus on increasing manufacturing cycle efficiency?

If MCE is increased a number of advantages will emerge. First, as orders spend less time in the production process, the level of WIP will tend to decline. Reducing WIP will ultimately lead to a number of benefits: lower stock financing costs; lower risk of obsolescence or damage and lessened storage space requirements. The reduction resulting from an increase in MCE can generally be easily calculated.

Case in Point

Consider a firm that has an average manufacturing cycle time of 15 working days and an annual cost of goods sold of £10,000,000. The average value of WIP is:

£10,000,000 × (15/365) = £410,959.

If the cycle time could be reduced to 12 days, the average value of WIP would shrink to:

£10,000,000 × (12/365) = £328,767

As MCE increases, the firm's ability to respond flexibly to rush orders from customers or to sudden market changes is enhanced. Increased production flexibility can improve the firm's ability to capture either higher margin orders or higher sales volumes. Shortening cycle time enables manufacturers to increase production throughput without increasing plant capacity. This may result in lower costs as overtime is reduced or may enable the firm to chase new business without increasing fixed production costs. Reducing manufacturing cycle time has close links to total quality management (TQM). If cycle times are to be reduced, NVA activities such as rework and inspection must be minimised. The requirement to 'do it right first time' focuses attention on efforts to improve quality, which in turn can lead to cost savings outside the manufacturing process, such as lower post-sale support costs.

Costs of increasing manufacturing cycle efficiency

While the benefits of increasing MCE are evident, it must be remembered that there will be costs associated with the reduction of cycle time. Shortening cycle times may require that the manufacturing process be redesigned and may require investment in new machinery. The net benefits of reducing manufacturing cycle time will depend on the individual circumstances of the firm. Will the improvement in MCE increase sales volumes or margin or reduce costs sufficiently, so as to justify the investment? The decision is well suited to a relevant costing framework. Cost savings resulting from reducing cycle time can be estimated by considering the portion of (for example) labour costs, inventory carrying costs and set-up costs that could be avoided if manufacturing cycle time were reduced. Activity-based costings for each activity in the manufacturing process could be used to assist in the estimation of the avoidable costs. If the decrease in cycle time results in saleable incremental production, an opportunity cost of a cycle hour can be calculated and used to assist in the decision as to whether or not to invest in reduction of cycle time. For example, suppose that business is currently being lost from a number of customers because the firm is unable to achieve a 24-hour turnaround time for orders. This problem is arising because there is a single bottleneck production process in the factory. The average selling price of each of the lost orders is £25,000 and each order gives rise to incremental cash costs of £16,360. The lost cash flow is £8,640 per order, which equates to an opportunity cost per cycle-time hour of £360 (£8,640/24). This opportunity cost provides a financial benchmark against which the cost of reducing cycle time at the bottleneck resource can be assessed. Clearly, as suggested in the above example, reduction of cycle time will not be equally valuable in all production departments. This idea is developed further in the Theory of Constraints (see David Dugdale and Colwyn Jones' article in the 1 December 1997 issue of *Management Accounting*). Ultimately, while the financial costs and benefits of the cycle time reduction will be evaluated, the strategic non-financial aspects of the decision must also be considered. It may be impossible to maintain the status quo with regard to cycle times if competitors are reducing theirs. The cost of not reducing cycle times may be a gradual erosion of sales volume and margin.

Comparison of MCE with JIT

The comparison of MCE with just-in-time (JIT) shows considerable linkage between the two concepts. The basic premise underlying JIT is that production is demand-led. No production starts until a customer demands a unit of finished output.

If a firm follows a strict JIT production philosophy, the following consequences will emerge:

- Stocks will be reduced to zero.
- There will be no stocks of finished goods awaiting sale.
- WP will be greatly reduced because production is demand-led.
- There must be zero defects in production thus ensuring that the product is right the first time.
- Raw material inputs must be of high quality and there will be a need for preventive machine maintenance.
- NVA activities must be eliminated from the production process. Set-up times must be reduced to zero. As set-up times reduce, the delays (with resulting build-up of WIP) between production processes are eliminated. A reduction of set-up times also enhances the flexibility of the firm to switch between products in response to customer demands.

As NVA activities in the production process are eliminated, MCE will naturally increase. The reduction of MCT is a pivotal step in the introduction of a JIT system. However, while JIT has undoubted advantages in certain manufacturing settings, the benefits of increasing MCE apply to all firms, regardless of whether they operate JIT production.

Like performance measurement in a JIT system, the goal of continuous improvement in MCE is inconsistent with some traditional performance measures such as machine utilisation. MCE aims to enhance manufacturing efficiency with respect to the speed of manufacturing response.

The objective is to enable the firm to produce flexibly in response to customer demand rather than for stock.

Finally, in a similar fashion to JIT, the concept of MCE can be extended beyond the boundary of the firm to encompass the supply chain. It may be possible to reduce MCTs by working more closely with suppliers. One example would be to insist on a guaranteed quality of inputs from suppliers and thus minimise production losses due to sub-standard raw materials. A closer partnership with suppliers may uncover other possibilities for the reduction of cycle time. Examples would include altering the packaging on raw material inputs so as to minimise handling time on delivery or the involvement of suppliers in the product design process which will ensure that bought-in components are designed with the requirements of the production process in mind.

Conclusion

The key lesson of MCT is to remind us that production costs are a function of several variables including the length of the manufacturing cycle.

By implementing a policy of seeking continuous improvements in MCT, the costs of production can be reduced and the flexibility of the firm's response to customer requests can be enhanced.

1. Berliner, C and Brimson, J (1988): *Cost Management for Today's Advanced Manufacturing*, Harvard Business School Press.
2. Martin, N. (1996): 'Questions, questions', *Automotive Industries*, June 1996, Vol. 1 76, No 6, pp 84–86.

The article below gives more detail on the example used in the text.

An extract from:
Throughput Accounting: The Garrett Automotive Experience

John Darlington, John Innes, Falconer Mitchell and John Woodward,
Management Accounting, April 1992

Introduction

GAL (a manufacturer of turbochargers for the automotive industry) decided to begin its profit improvement programme by examining its factory throughput. Throughput was defined as the rate at which raw materials were turned into sales. In other words, throughput was defined as sales less material costs per period of time. In conjunction with its new

OPT (optimised production technology) scheduling system this led the accountants to examine the factory bottlenecks and constraints which were defined as follows:

1. A bottleneck is an activity within the organisation where the demand for that resource outstrips its capacity to supply.
2. A constraint is a situational factor which makes the achievement of throughput more difficult than it would otherwise be. Constraints may take several forms such as lack of skilled employees or the need to achieve a high level of quality in product output.

Using GAL's definitions, therefore, a bottleneck is always a constraint but a constraint need not necessarily be a bottleneck. Managers in each department can usually identify their bottlenecks and constraints but these are not normally monitored as part of the formal reporting system. In this particular factory the major constraint was considered to be the customer due date performance, i.e. meeting the delivery schedule for customer orders.

The bottlenecks became certain machines in the factory. Throughput was then related directly to the ability to cope with the constraint and manage the bottlenecks. This focus on throughput forced management to examine both the constraints and the bottlenecks in order to increase throughput.

TA approach

The TA approach is very similar to the approach of contribution per unit of scarce resource. One measurement difference is that throughput is defined as sales less material costs, in contrast to contribution, which equals sales less all variable costs (material, labour and variable overhead costs). The implicit assumption of TA is that all costs except materials can be assumed fixed in relation to changes in throughput in the short run.

However, the identification of bottlenecks which is integral to TA also stimulates managerial action to alleviate the problem. One bottleneck at GAL relating to machine capacity and the actions taken are illustrated in Figure 1. This shows that in this machining line the bottleneck was machine B, with a capacity of only 18 units per hour. The first improvement was to introduce machine D which was already operating in a non-bottleneck part of the factory and to remove one operation from machine B to be performed by machine D.

This raised the capacity of the bottleneck from 18 to 21 units per hour at a cost of £2,000. The second improvement was to buy machine E (costing £6,000), which raised the capacity of the bottleneck from 21 to 24 units per hour. At the same time, when machine C had to be replaced it was replaced by a much smaller machine than previously, with an output of 26 units per hour. With a 125-hour week and 90 per cent utilisation this raised the weekly output from 2,025 to 2,700 units. This example emphasises an important assumption underlying TA and bottlenecks – it assumes that the extra output can be sold which was the case at GAL.

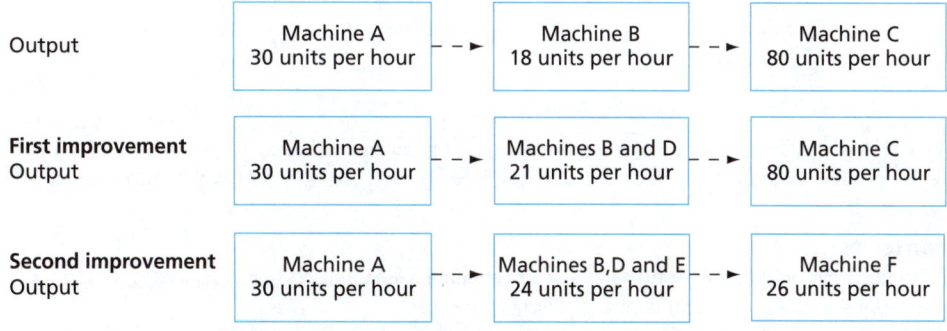

Figure 1 Example of bottleneck improvements

Some observations can be made about the above example:

- GAL used to produce an 'efficiency' report which split the turbocharger into component groups and showed efficiency by measuring total direct labour hours available compared with the standard hours of components produced. If the efficiency of a section fell below what was considered an acceptable level, then managers were pressurised to improve. If you consider this in relation to machine A, you realise the weakness of such an approach. If machine A works faster than machine B to increase its 'efficiency', it is making units which the company does not need. If you measure manufacturing on efficiency, unwanted units may be produced.
- If a manufacturing engineer told us that machine A is getting old and a new machine is needed which would double the output over machine A, our bottleneck analysis would show that such an investment would not improve throughput. An increase in production from machine A will not lead to better company performance at present. Many capital-investment appraisals have been based on a reduction of the fully absorbed or marginal cost by producing more units without considering fully whether these extra units will result in more sales. This concentration on bottlenecks can influence capital-investment decisions. One implication is to give priority to investment in your bottlenecks. However, it is frequently the case that when you solve one bottleneck problem, another will arise. Similarly, a major change in the product mix may change the bottlenecks. Bottlenecks are dynamic and managing the bottlenecks is a process of ongoing improvement.
- The changes in Figure 1 can be considered in the context of their full impact on cost and not simply on throughput. The changes, such as using another machine to perform one particular operation and reducing the capacity of other machines, meant an increased number of material movements, but this gave an increased throughput with an overall cost saving.

Example

Suppose that the product manufactured on machines A, B and C in Figure 1 had the following characteristics:

	Time taken per unit (minutes)	Labour rate (£ per hour)
Machine A	2	6
Machine B (before first improvement)	3.33	9
Machine B (after first improvement)	2.86	9
Machine B (after second improvement)	2.5	9
Machine C	0.75	6
Machine D	1	6
Machine E	1.25	6
Machine F	2.31	6

There is a 1:1 relationship between men and machines, and a uniform overhead recovery rate of 250 per cent on labour cost is operated throughout the plant. The sales price per product unit is £6.00 and its material content £2.00.

Requirements
(a) What would be the product cost of a unit produced under the existing method on machines A, B and C?
(b) What would the product cost become after the 'first improvement'?
(c) What would be the product cost of a unit produced on machines A, B, D, E and F?
(d) How could investment in machines D and E be justified?

Solution

(a) Calculation of labour and overhead cost:

	Machine time per unit hours	Labour cost £	Overhead cost £
A	0.0333	0.2000	0.5000
B	0.0555	0.5000	1.2500
C	0.0125	0.0750	0.1875
		0.7750	1.9375

Total product cost:

	£
Material	2.0000
Labour	0.7750
Overhead	1.9375
	4.7125

(b) Calculation of labour and overhead cost:

	Machine time per unit hours	Labour cost £	Overhead cost £
A	0.0333	0.2000	0.5000
B	0.0477	0.4290	1.0725
C	0.0125	0.0750	0.1875
D	0.0167	0.1000	0.2500
		0.8040	2.0100

Total product cost:

	£
Material	2.0000
Labour	0.8040
Overhead	2.0100
	4.8140

(c) Calculation of labour and overhead cost:

	Machine time per unit hours	Labour cost £	Overhead cost £
A	0.0333	0.2000	0.5000
B	0.0417	0.3753	0.9380
D	0.0167	0.1000	0.2500
E	0.0208	0.1248	0.3120
F	0.0385	0.2310	0.5780
		1.0311	2.5780

Total product cost:

	£
Material	2.0000
Labour	1.0311
Overhead	2.5780
	5.6091

(d) The proponents of 'throughput accounting' are arguing that only relevant costs and revenues should be considered when making decisions. In this respect their advice is not different from that of traditional management accounting texts. They do, however, argue that all operating expense (including 'direct' labour cost) can be regarded as 'fixed' and only material costs are truly variable. On these assumptions investment in machine D could be justified.

Incremental 'throughput' per hour = (£6 − £2) × 3 = £12
Incremental 'throughput' per week = 12 × 125 × 0.9 = £1,350
Investment in machine D would be paid back in less than 2 weeks.
A similar calculation for machine E:
Incremental 'throughput' per hour = (£6 − £2) × 3 = £12
Incremental 'throughput' per week = 12 × 125 × 0.9 = £1,350
Investment in machine E would be paid back in less than 5 weeks.

This example demonstrates how the slavish calculation of product costs in 'traditional' ways can militate against sensible decision-making. (The example does, of course, assume that bottlenecks can be reliably identified and appropriate action taken and that additional throughput can be sold.)

Revision Questions

 Question 1

1.1 Which feature distinguishes backflush accounting from other systems?

(A) Labour costs are not charged to the units produced.
(B) Costs are attached when output is completed or sold.
(C) Cost records reflect the flow of work through the production process.
(D) Entries are not made until the customer pays for goods purchased.
(E) Material entries are made when the material is received and moved.

1.2 Company X produces a single product with the following standard cost per unit:

Material cost	£10
Conversion cost	£12
Total cost	£22

The company operates a backflush costing system with a raw material stock control account. Details for the current month are:

Raw material stock control account opening balance	£500
Raw materials purchased	£4,600
Conversion costs incurred	£5,200
Cost of goods sold at standard cost	£8,998

The closing balance on the raw material stock control account is:

(A) £290
(B) £502
(C) £790
(D) £800
(E) £1,010.

1.3 A company operates a throughput accounting system. The details of product A per unit are:

Selling price	£24.99
Material cost	£8.87
Conversion costs	£12.27
Time on bottleneck resource	6.5 minutes

The return per hour for product A is:

(A) £81.88
(B) £113.26

(C) £117.42
(D) £123.80
(E) £148.80.

1.4 A company produces two products, A and B, which pass through two production processes, J and K. The time taken to make each product in each process is:

	Product A	Product B
Process **J**	6.5 minutes	9 minutes
Process **K**	22 minutes	15 minutes

The company operates a 16-hour day and the processes have an average downtime each day of:

Process **J**	2.5 hours
Process **K**	2 hours.

The costs and revenue for each unit of each product are:

	Product A £	Product B £
Direct materials	15.00	15.0
Direct labour	17.00	12.00
Variable overhead	8.00	6.00
Fixed costs	8.00	6.00
Total cost	48.00	39.00
Selling price	87.50	72.50

Sales demand restricts the output of A and B to 40 and 60 units a day, respectively. The daily production plan that would maximise the *throughput* contribution is

(A) 40 units of A.
(B) 38 units of A.
(C) 36 units of A and 4 units of B.
(D) 34 units of A and 5 units of B.
(E) 56 units of B.

1.5 The selling price of product Z is set at £250 for each unit and sales for the coming year are expected to be 500 units.

If the company requires a return of 15% in the coming year on its investment of £250,000 in product Z, the target cost for each unit for the coming year is

(A) £145
(B) £155
(C) £165
(D) £175
(E) £185.

Question 2

'Many of the topics that come under the heading of modern management philosophies and which appear in CIMA examination syllabuses, once the veneer is removed there is either nothing underneath or else one finds an old friend with a new name. One can become sceptical of all new ideas since some add little to the fount of management accounting knowledge.'

(Extract from a journal article on 'modern' management accounting technique.)

(a) EC Flow Ltd manufactures a product which requires to pass through the cutting department. Owing to lack of cutting machines this is seen as the bottleneck resource. Each unit of the product requires 0.75 cutting machine hours and 200 of these hours are available each week.

Other data relating to the product are:

	£
Selling price per unit	6.00
Direct material cost per unit	3.00
Other factory costs per week	500

Calculate the product's return per factory hour and the throughput accounting ratio.

(b) Explain the term 'throughput accounting'; compare and contrast throughput accounting with 'limiting factor analysis'; explain the circumstances (if any) in which throughput accounting is an effective management accounting technique.

(c) Explain the term 'life cycle costing'; explain the changes in the business environment during the last 10 years that have prompted the development of life cycle costing.

Requirements

(a) Prepare summary journal entries for the last period.
(b) Under an ideal just-in-time system state how your journal entries in (a) above will change.
(c) Explain what backflush costing is and the circumstances (if any) in which the use of backflush costing is appropriate.

Question 3

Disc Sounds Ltd specialises in the manufacture of CD players. It is planning to introduce a new CD player specially designed for young children. Development of the new CD player is to begin shortly, and Disc Sounds Ltd is in the process of preparing a product life cycle budget. It expects the new product to have a life cycle of 3 years and estimates the following costs:

	Year 1	Year 2	Year 3
Units manufactured and sold	50,000	200,000	150,000
CD players per batch	400	500	500
Price per CD player	£45	£40	£35
R&D and design costs	£900,000	£100,000	–
Production costs			
Variable cost per CD player	£16	£15	£15
Variable cost per batch	£700	£600	£600
Fixed costs	£600,000	£600,000	£600,000
Marketing costs			
Variable cost per CD player	£3.60	£3.20	£2.80
Fixed costs	£400,000	£300,000	£300,000
Distribution costs			
CD players per batch	200	160	120
Variable cost per CD player	£1	£1	£1
Variable cost per batch	£120	£120	£100
Fixed costs	£240,000	£240,000	£240,000
Customer service costs			
per CD player	£2	£1.50	£1.50

Ignore the time value of money in your answers.

Requirements

(a) Calculate the budgeted life cycle operating profit for the new CD player.
(b) Market research has indicated that reducing the selling price by £3 each year would result in increased sales volume of 10 per cent each year. If sales increase by 10 per cent, Disc Sounds Ltd plans to increase its production and distribution batch sizes by 10 per cent as well. Assuming all other costs remain the same should the price be reduced by £3?
(c) Explain how an organisation would benefit from a product life cycle costing exercise.

Question 4

You are the Assistant Management Accountant of QXY plc, a food manufacturer. The Board of Directors is concerned that its operational managers may not be fully aware of the importance of understanding the costs incurred by the business and the effect that this has on their operational decision making. In addition, the operational managers need to be aware of the implications of their pricing policy when trying to increase the volume of sales.

You are scheduled to make a presentation to the operational managers tomorrow to explain to them the different costs that are incurred by the business, the results of some research that has been conducted into the implications for pricing and the importance of understanding these issues for their decision making. **The diagram on the opposite page has already been prepared for the presentation.**

Requirement

You are required to interpret the diagram and explain how it illustrates issues that the operational managers should consider when making decisions. (Note: your answer must include explanations of the Sales Revenue, Total Cost and Fixed Cost lines, and the significance of each of the activity levels labelled A, B, C, D). **(10 marks)**

Diagram for Question Four - Costs and Revenues over a range of activity levels

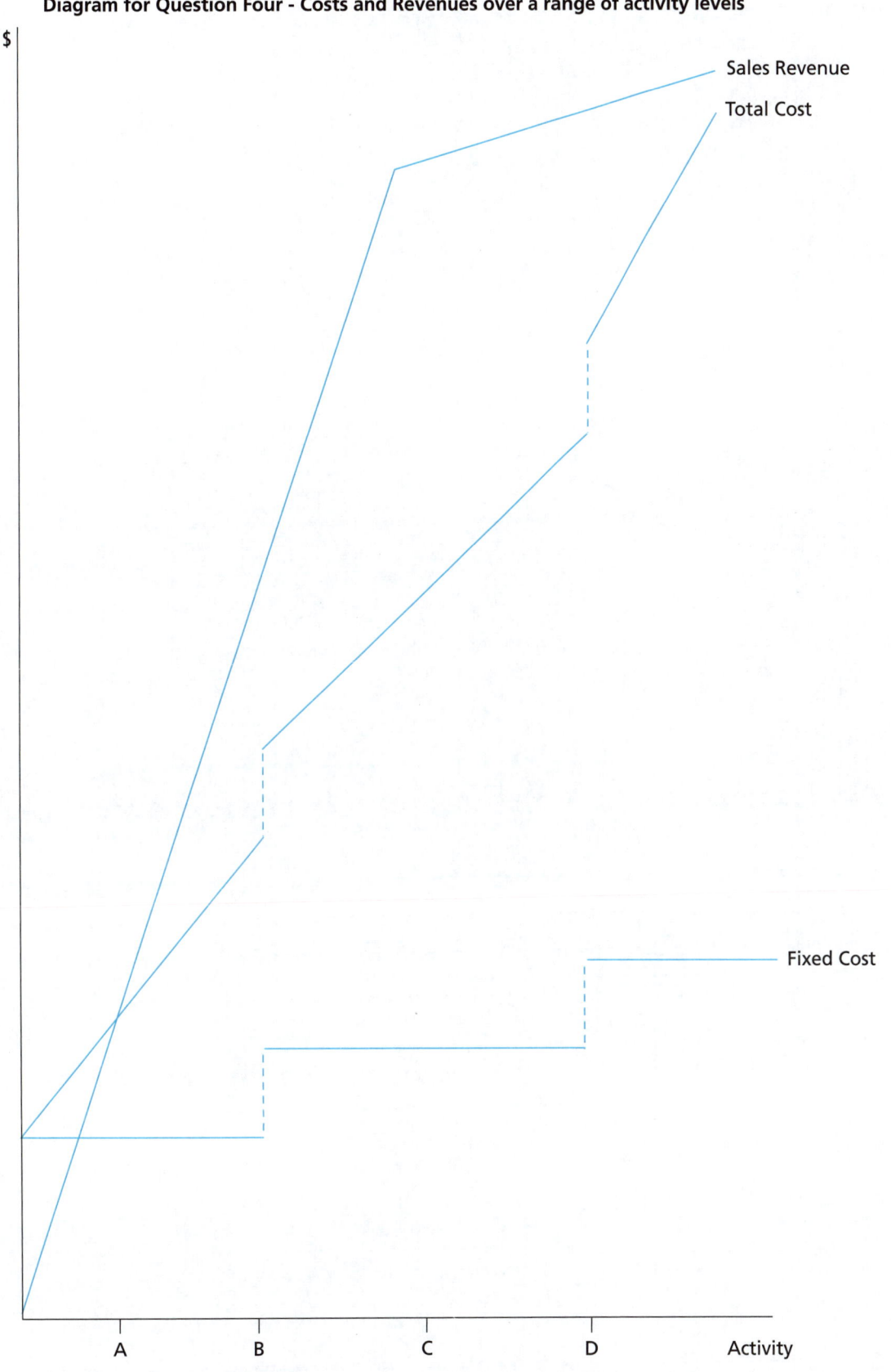

Solutions to Revision Questions 12

Solution 1

1.1 Answer: (B)

Backflush accounting is a method of costing associated with JIT. It delays the recording of costs until after the events have taken place. The recording of costs may be triggered when goods are transferred to finished goods stock or, in a true JIT system, when goods are sold.

1.2 Answer: (E)

Material cost of goods sold = £8,998 × £10/£22 = £4,090

Raw materials stock control account

	£		£
Opening balance	500	Standard cost of goods sold	4,090
Materials purchased	4,600	Closing balance	1,010
	5,100		5,100

1.3 Answer: (E)

	Product A	*Product B*
Throughput of J per day	13.5 hours × $\frac{60}{6.5}$ = 124.62	13.5 hours × $\frac{60}{9}$ = 90
Throughput of K per day	14 hours × $\frac{60}{22}$ = 38.18	14 hours × $\frac{60}{15}$ = 56

So process K is the bottleneck for both products
Contribution per hour of product A = £87.50 − 15.00 = £72.50 × 60 ÷ 22 = £197.73
Contribution per hour of product B = £72.50 − 15.00 = £57.50 × 60 ÷ 15 = £230.00
Processing product B will give the larger contribution per day = 56 units

1.4 Answer: (D)

	£
Sales revenue 500 units @ £250	125,000
Return on investment required 15% × £250,000	37,500
Total cost allowed	87,500
Target cost per unit	£175

467

Solution 2

Tip
- Part (a) of the question is a simple example to test your knowledge of the various throughput ratios.

(a)

$$\text{Return per factory hour} = \frac{\text{Sales} - \text{Direct material costs}}{\text{Usage of bottleneck resource}}$$

$$= \frac{£6.00 - £3.00}{0.75}$$

$$= £4.00 \text{ per hour.}$$

$$\text{Cost per factory hour} = \frac{\text{Total factory costs}}{\text{Bottleneck resource hours available}}$$

$$= \frac{£500}{200}$$

$$= £2.50 \text{ per hour}$$

$$\text{Throughput accounting ratio} = \frac{\text{Return per factory hour}}{\text{Cost per factory hour}}$$

$$= \frac{£4.00}{£2.50}$$

$$= 1.6 : 1$$

(b) Throughput accounting is an approach that concentrates attention on time spent in production or service facilities. For example, costs (other than direct materials) may be charged to products in proportion to the time that those products spend in a 'bottleneck' facility. The performance of products can be ranked according to the sales revenue less direct material costs that they generate per hour in the bottleneck facility.

Throughput accounting and limiting factor analysis are variations on a theme. The former is an approach to management reporting and the latter is a financial analysis tool – the two are not the same.

(c) Conspicuous developments in the business environment have been the increase in product diversity and the shortening of product life cycles. Associated with this has been the replacement of 'mass production' by 'flexible manufacturing'. It has been claimed that the costs of a product are now likely to be largely determined at the outset of its life cycle. Consequently, reporting on costs in any one given period may not be very meaningful. The life cycle approach to costing is to report on costs incurred on each product over the whole course of its life.

 ## Solution 3

Tips
- A long question with a lot of information regarding the new CD player. Candidates should not be put off by the length of the question or the amount of information.

- Part (a) of the question requires you to calculate the life cycle profit – the sum of the three years' data given.
- Part (b) tests your knowledge of sensitivity analysis – a drop in selling price increases demand. What effect would this have on profit given the increased batch sizes?

(a) Life cycle operating profit for the new disc player:

	Year 1 £000	Year 2 £000	Year 3 £000	Life cycle £000
Sales	2,250	8,000	5,250	15,500
R&D and design	(900)	(100)		(1,000)
Production costs				
Variable cost/CD	(800)	(3,000)	(2,250)	(6,050)
Variable cost/batch	(87.5)	(240)	(180)	(507.5)
Fixed costs	(600)	(600)	(600)	(1,800)
Marketing costs				
Variable cost/CD	(180)	(640)	(420)	(1,240)
Fixed costs	(400)	(300)	(300)	(1,000)
Distribution costs				
Variable cost/CD	(50)	(200)	(150)	(400)
Variable cost/batch	(30)	(150)	(125)	(305)
Fixed costs	(240)	(240)	(240)	(720)
Customer service				
Costs/CD	(100)	(300)	(225)	(625)
Operating profit	(1,137.5)	2,230	760	1,852.5

(b) Effect on operating profit when S.P. reduced by £3 and volume increased by 10 per cent:

	Year 1	Year 2	Year 3
New selling price	£42	£37	£32
Sales volume	55,000	220,000	165,000
Production batch size	440	550	550
Distribution batch size	220	176	132

Operating statement

	Year 1 £000	Year 2 £000	Year 3 £000	Life cycle £000
Sales	2,310	8,140	5,280	15,730
R&D and design	(900)	(100)		(1,000)
Production costs				
Variable cost/CD	(880)	(3,300)	(2,475)	(6,655)
Variable cost/batch	(87.5)	(240)	(180)	(507.5)
Fixed costs	(600)	(600)	(600)	(1,800)
Marketing costs				
Variable cost/CD	(198)	(704)	(462)	(1,364)
Fixed costs	(400)	(300)	(300)	(1,000)
Distribution costs				
Variable cost/CD	(55)	(220)	(165)	(440)
Variable cost/batch	(30)	(150)	(125)	(305)
Fixed costs	(240)	(240)	(240)	(720)
Customer service				
Cost/CD	(110)	(330)	(247.5)	(687.5)
Operating profit	(1190.5)	1956	(485.5)	1,251

Overall life cycle profit decreased by £600,000. Price should not be reduced unless there is a reduction in costs through economies of scale due to the 10 per cent increase in volume.

(c) A life cycle costing exercise enables an organisation to appraise the profitability over the whole life of the product rather than a period at a time. Thus, products that are loss making initially but profitable in the longer term will be accepted. A large proportion of the costs are locked in at the design stage – a life cycle costing exercise will enable organisations to reconsider some of these costs at the R&D stage. It also enables management to focus marketing and promotion when required – at certain critical points of the life cycle.

Solution 4

Notes for meeting with Operational Managers: The implications of understanding costs and revenues for decision making

The diagram shows the monetary values of costs and revenues over a range of activity levels.

Fixed costs are costs which are not expected to change in total when there is a change in activity level within the relevant range. The diagram shows that these costs are incurred when there is a zero level of activity. This is usually as a result of making a decision to commence activity and incurring costs such as rent and rates on a business premises. In this case it can be seen that the level of fixed costs changes at certain levels of activity which have been identified as points B and D. This is an example of a stepped fixed cost. Clearly there is a significant increase in the level of costs as soon as these activity levels are reached. This means that for decision making a manager must be aware of these key activity points because otherwise they might accept an order which causes a significant increase in cost for a small amount of additional revenue.

Total costs are the sum of the fixed costs referred to above and the variable costs. Variable costs are incurred in proportion to the level of activity and are most likely to be the ingredients and packing materials used in the food manufacturing process. The diagram shows that the variable costs are constant per unit of activity up to activity level B as the gradient of the line is constant throughout this activity range. Between activity levels B and D the variable costs are constant per unit, but the unit cost is lower than that up to point B possibly due to economies of scale and learning effects. However, above activity level D it can be seen that the gradient of the line increases. This represents a higher unit cost for these units.

Sales revenue increases as the level of activity increases and the rate of increase is constant from the activity level of zero up to activity point C. This implies that the selling price per unit is constant up to this point. However, above point C while the total sales revenue continues to increase, it does so at a decreasing rate. This shows that the market research indicates that in order to sell a volume higher than activity level C the price per unit must be reduced.

The diagram can also be used to identify the level of activity at which profits are maximised. This lies at the activity level where the vertical distance between the sales revenue and total cost lines is greatest.

Activity level A represents the level of activity at which the total revenue and total costs are equal and thus there is neither a profit nor a loss. This is commonly referred to as the breakeven point. This means that at activity levels lower than point A the company makes a loss, but that beyond activity point A profits start to be earned.

Activity level B has already been explained as the point at which the fixed costs and total costs increase due to the step effect. It can be seen that this has a significant effect on the profit being earned.

Activity level C shows the point at which reductions in selling price are required in order to increase the volume of sales being achieved. Beyond this point the slopes of the total cost and sales revenue lines show that total costs are rising faster than total revenues and thus profits are falling.

Activity level D shows the impact of the next step in the fixed costs which has a similar effect on profit as that indicated in relation to activity point B above.

Preparing for the Examination

Preparing for the Examination

This chapter is intended for use when you are ready to start revising for your examination. It contains:

- a summary of useful revision techniques;
- details of the format of the examination;
- a bank of examination-standard revision questions and suggested solutions. These solutions are of a length and level of detail that a competent student might be expected to produce in an examination;
- pilot paper.

Revision technique

Planning

The first thing to say about revision is that it is an addition to your initial studies, not a substitute for them. In other words, do not coast along early in your course in the hope of catching up during the revision phase. On the contrary, you should be studying and revising concurrently from the outset. At the end of each week, and at the end of each month, get into the habit of summarising the material you have covered to refresh your memory of it.

As with your initial studies, planning is important to maximise the value of your revision work. You need to balance the demands for study, professional work, family life and other commitments. To make this work, you will need to think carefully about how to make best use of your time.

Begin as before by comparing the estimated hours you will need to devote to revision with the hours available to you in the weeks leading up to the examination. Prepare a written schedule setting out the areas you intend to cover during particular weeks, and break that down further into topics for each day's revision. To help focus on the key areas try to establish:

- which areas you are weakest on, so that you can concentrate on the topics where effort is particularly needed;
- which areas are especially significant for the examination – the topics that are tested frequently.

Do not forget the need for relaxation, and for family commitments. Sustained intellectual effort is only possible for limited periods, and must be broken up at intervals by lighter activities. And don't continue your revision timetable right up to the moment when you enter the exam hall: you should aim to stop work a day or even two days before the exam. Beyond this point the most you should attempt is an occasional brief look at your notes to refresh your memory.

Getting down to work

By the time you begin your revision you should already have settled into a fixed work pattern: a regular time of day for doing the work, a particular location where you sit, particular equipment that you assemble before you begin and so on. If this is not already a matter of routine for you, think carefully about it now in the last vital weeks before the exam.

You should have notes summarising the main points of each topic you have covered. Begin each session by reading through the relevant notes and trying to commit the important points to memory.

Usually, this will be just your starting point. Unless the area is one where you already feel very confident, you will need to track back from your notes to the relevant chapter(s) in the *Study System*. This will refresh your memory on points not covered by your notes and fill in the detail that inevitably gets lost in the process of summarisation.

When you think you have understood and memorised the main principles and techniques, attempt an exam-standard question. At this stage of your studies you should normally be expecting to complete such questions in something close to the actual time allocation allowed in the exam. After completing your effort, check the solution provided and add to your notes any extra points it reveals.

Tips for the final revision phase

As the exam looms closer, consider the following list of techniques and make use of those that work for you:

- Summarise your notes into more concise form, perhaps on index cards that you can carry with you for revision on the way into work.
- Go through your notes with a highlighter pen, marking key concepts and definitions.
- Summarise the main points in a key area by producing a wordlist, mind map or other mnemonic device.
- On areas that you find difficult, rework questions that you have already attempted, and compare your answers in detail with those provided in the *Study System*.
- Rework questions you attempted earlier in your studies with a view to producing more 'polished' answers (better layout and presentation may earn marks in the exam) and to completing them within the time limits.
- Stay alert for practical examples, incidents, situations and events that illustrate the material you are studying. If you can refer in the exam to real-life topical illustrations you will impress the examiner and may earn extra marks.

Format of the examination

Structure of the paper

The examination for *Management Accounting – Decision Management* is a three-hour written paper and has four sections:

- Section A: objective testing for 20 per cent of the marks.
- Section B: one compulsory question for 30 per cent of the marks.
- Section C: a choice of two questions from three, for 50 per cent of the marks.

Any changes in the structure of the examination or in the format of questions will be indicated well in advance in the appropriate CIMA journals.

Revision Questions

  Question 1 Multiple-choice questions

1.1 The following data has been extracted from the budget working papers of BL Ltd:

	Production volume 1,000 £/unit	2,000 £/unit
Direct materials	4.00	4.00
Direct labour	3.50	3.50
Production overhead department 1	6.00	4.20
Production overhead department 2	4.00	2.00

The total fixed cost and variable cost per unit is:

	Total fixed cost £	Variable cost/unit £
(A)	3,600	9.90
(B)	4,000	11.70
(C)	7,600	7.50
(D)	7,600	9.90

1.2 The adoption of JIT normally requires which one of the following factors to increase:

(A) stock levels;
(B) work-in-progress levels;
(C) batch sizes;
(D) quality standards.

1.3 In the practice of ABTs, a cost driver is:

(A) a reduction in unit cost without any loss of value;
(B) a factor that causes the total cost of an activity to change;
(C) the cost of converting raw materials into finished goods;
(D) a fee paid to the consultants who designed the ABT.

1.4 Functional analysis is:

(A) an approach to the construction of budgets around the functions within a business;
(B) an approach to the examination of the specified purpose of a product;
(C) the separation of the materials mixture variance into component parts;
(D) a method of appraising the performance of cost centres.

1.5 When comparing the performance of two factories, one of which is owned and the other rented, the inclusion of rent as an expense in the profit statement of the factory owned is known as the inclusion of:

(A) a relevant cost;
(B) a notional cost;
(C) a controllable cost;
(D) an indirect cost.

1.6 Q Limited has in stock 10,000 kg of V, a raw material which it bought for £5 per kg 5 years ago. This was bought for a product line which was discontinued 4 years ago. At present, V has no use in its existing state but could be sold as scrap for £1.50 per kg. One of the company's current products (QX) requires 2 kg of a raw material which is available for £4.50 per kg. V can be modified at a cost of £1 per kg so that it may be used as a substitute for this material. However, after modification, 3 kg of V is required for every unit of QX to be produced.

Q Limited has now received an invitation to tender for a product which could use V in its present state.

The relevant cost per kg of V to be included in the cost estimate for the tender is:

(A) £1.00
(B) £1.50
(C) £2.00
(D) £5.00.

1.7 A company operates a throughput accounting system. The details of product A per unit are:

Selling price	£24.99
Material cost	£8.8
Conversion costs	£12.27
Time on bottleneck resource	6.5 minutes

The return per hour for product A is:

(A) £35.54
(B) £117.42
(C) £123.80
(D) £148.80.

1.8 Activity-based costing is:

(A) a method of total costing which attributes costs to cost units using multiple activity drivers;
(B) a method of costing which is used to recognise the effects of changes in output activity and their effect on total costs;
(C) a method of costing which is used to calculate the cost per unit in organisations which have only one single activity;
(D) a method of cost accounting which derives unit costs according to planned outputs.

1.9 In the context of quality costs, training costs and reworking costs are classified as:

	Training costs	Reworking costs
(A)	prevention costs	internal failure costs
(B)	internal failure costs	internal failure costs

(C) internal failure costs   external failure costs
(D) prevention costs   external failure costs

1.10 XY Ltd manufactures two products – the X (which gives a contribution of £4 per unit) and the Y (which gives a contribution of £6 per unit). The X and the Y are budgeted to sell in the proportion two units of X for every one unit of Y. XY Ltd incurs £14,000 fixed costs per period and its production capacity is 3,000 units of X and 1,500 units of Y. XY Ltd's breakeven point is:

(A) 66.66% capacity
(B) 55.55% capacity
(C) 822 units of X and 411 units of Y
(D) 92.31% of capacity.

1.11 In a TQM environment, external benchmarking is preferred to standard costing as a performance measurement technique because:

(A) standard costs quickly become obsolete;
(B) TQM emphasises continuous improvement and reference to a predetermined internal standard gives no incentive to improve;
(C) TQM places an emphasis on employee empowerment, and the concept of a standard cost is alien to this;
(D) the use of standard costs is only possible in a traditional mass-production industry.

Question 2

ABC Ltd manufactures one product in each of its three factories in Anytown. Each factory makes the same complete product. One factory is located to the north of the town, another is in the central area, and a third is located in the south of the town. ABC Ltd owns a warehouse to the east of the town, which it uses as a distribution centre and also to store finished goods. These locations are illustrated below.

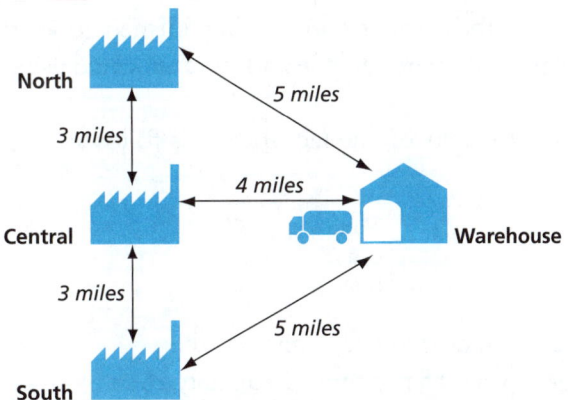

The company is now preparing its budgets for the year to 31 December 2001 and has recognised that demand for its product will be 30 per cent less than its activity during the year ended 31 December 1999. ABC Ltd is therefore considering the resources that it has available and seeks to identify the most profitable way of reducing its activity level. Factory closure is being considered, provided that at least one of the remaining factories is utilised at maximum capacity. All units to be sold in the year ending 31 December 2001 will have to be made in that year because the company has no spare capacity in the year ending

31 December 2000. This is due to its acceptance of some subcontracting work. This contract will be completed on 31 December 2000 and it is not expected to be renewed.

Cost statements for the three factories for the year ended 31 December 1999 are set out below.

	North	Central	South
Number of units produced	100,000	200,000	150,000
	£000	£000	£000
Direct materials	500	1,000	750
Direct wages	800	1,600	1,200
Indirect materials	375	800	530
Indirect wages	250	1,000	750
Indirect expenses	1,000	2,000	750
Administration	300	550	350
Transport	500	800	750
Total cost	3,725	7,750	5,080

Additional information

1. Direct costs are totally variable, and are dependent on the number of units produced.
2. Indirect production costs are semi-variable. The variable element varies in relation to the number of units produced. Analysis has revealed that the variable element in each factory is as follows:

	North	Central	South
	%	%	%
Indirect materials	80	75	85
Indirect wages	20	15	20
Indirect expenses	35	30	40

The fixed cost element of the indirect production costs is avoidable if the factory is closed.

3. The administration costs include £900,000 for head-office costs. These costs have been apportioned to the factories based on the number of units produced. The balance of administration costs are for fixed costs specific to each factory.
4. Transport costs represent the costs of transporting finished goods from the factory to the warehouse. The transport costs are variable and were allocated using 'unit mile' as the cost unit.
5. The annual production capacity of the factories is as follows:

	Units
North	160,000
Central	250,000
South	180,000

It is estimated, based on trade/industry averages, that:
- if production levels exceed 85 per cent of capacity, then there is a 40 per cent increase in specific fixed cost;
- if more than 95 per cent of available capacity is used, then specific fixed cost doubles from its original level.

Requirements

(a) (i) Prepare a cost statement analysing the cost information provided by behaviour.

(6 marks)

(ii) Calculate how the production should be scheduled for the factories of ABC Ltd so as to maximise its profit for the year ended 31 December 2001.
   Show all workings. **(14 marks)**
(b) Prepare a memorandum to the production controller that states other factors that should be considered before making a final decision about how to schedule the production.
(5 marks)
(Total marks = 25)

Question 3

3.1 T plc has developed a new product, the TF8. The time taken to produce the first unit was 18 minutes. Assuming that an 80% lerning curve applies, the time allowed for the fifth unit (to two decimal places) should be

(A) 5.79 minutes
(B) 7.53 minutes
(C) 10.72 minutes
(D) 11.52 minutes.

Note: For an 80% learning curve $y = ax^{-0.3219}$. **(4 marks)**

3.2 Z plc operates an activity based costing (ABC) system to attribute its overhead costs to cost objects.

In its budget for the year ending 31 December 2001, the company expected to place a total of 2,785 purchase orders at a total cost of £94,690. This activity and its related costs were budgeted to occur at a constant rate throughout the budget year, which is divided into thirteen 4-week periods.

During the 4-week period ended 27 October 2001, a total of 202 purchase orders was placed at a cost of £7,318.

The under-recovery of these costs for the 4-week period (to the nearest £1) was

(A) £34
(B) £416
(C) £443
(D) £450. **(2 marks)**

3.3 Which of the following are required to determine the breakeven sales value in a multi-product manufacturing environment?

(i) individual product gross contribution to sales ratios;
(ii) the general fixed cost;
(iii) the product-specific fixed cost;
(iv) the product mix ratio;
(v) the method of apportionment of general fixed costs.

(A) (i), (ii), (iii) and (iv) only.
(B) (i), (iii) and (iv) only.
(C) (i), (ii) and (iv) only.
(D) All of them. **(2 marks)**

3.4 M Limited manufactures four products from different quantities of the same material which is in short supply. The following budgeted data relates to the products:

	Product M1 £/unit	Product M2 £/unit	Product M3 £/unit	Product M4 £/unit
Selling price	70	92	113	83
Materials (£4 per kg)	16	22	34	20
Conversion costs	39	52	57	43
	55	74	91	63
Profit	15	18	22	20
Machine time per unit in minutes	40	40	37.5	45

The conversion costs include general fixed costs that have been absorbed using a rate of £24 per machine hour.

The most profitable use of the raw materials is to make

(A) product M1
(B) product M2
(C) product M3
(D) product M4.

(2 marks)
(Total marks = 10)

Question 4

DP plc assembles computers from bought-in-components, using a computer-controlled robotic assembly line. The assembled computers are then tested by highly qualified computer engineers before they are packaged for despatch to customers.

DP plc currently assembles two different types of computer from different combinations of the same components.

The following budgeted details relate to the computers:

	Computer X	Computer Y
Selling price/unit	£800	£1,200
Component costs per unit	£150	£310
	Minutes per unit	Minutes per unit
Assembly time (S1)	80	130
Testing time (S2)	120	180
Packaging time (S3)	60	30

The following costs are derived from DP plc's budget for the year to 31 December 2001:

Assembly	£180/hour
Testing	£60/hour
packaging	£20/hour

No cost increases are expected until July 2002.

DP plc is now preparing its detailed plans for the 6-month period to 30 June 2002. During this period, it expects that the assembly time available will be limited to 1,000 hours and the testing time available will be limited to 875 hours. The packaging is carried out by part-time workers, and the company believes that there are a number of local residents who would be pleased to undertake this work if the existing packaging staff were unable to complete the level of activity needed. The maximum levels of demand for each computer will be:

300 units of X (S4); and
800 units of Y (S5).

Requirements

(a) Calculate the contribution per unit for each type of computer. **(2 marks)**
(b) determine the mix of computers that will maximise DP plc's profits for the 6 months ending 30 june 2002, using a graphical linear programming solution, and calculate the contribution that will be earned. **(8 marks)**
(c) DP plc now realises that there may be a limit on the number of packaging hours available. A computer package for linear programming has been used and the following solution determined:

Variables	
X	268.75
Y	112.50
Constraints	
S1	23,875.00
S2	1.46
S3	4.75
S4	31.25
S5	687.50
Contribution	£107,437.50

Requirements

Write a report to the management team that interprets the solution produced by the computer package and makes appropriate recommendations.
(*Note*: Do not formulate, or explain the basis of, the computer model.) **(7 marks)**

(d) At the management meeting that discussed the report you produced in part (c) above, the senior computer engineer responsible for the testing of the computers was surprised at the times per unit being used in your calculations.

'It seems to me', she said 'that you have used the testing times per unit that were set as the targets when those models of computer were first assembled. We seem to test them much more quickly than this now.'

Requirements

Explain how the learning effect referred to by the senior computer engineer will affect the calculation of the optimum product mix. Use a 90 per cent learning curve to illustrate your answer but *Do not determine a revised product mix*.
Note: The formula for a 90 per cent learning curve is $y = ax^{-0.1520}$ **(8 marks)**
(Total marks = 25)

 Question 5

AVX Plc assembles circuit boards for use by high technology audio video companies. Due to the rapidly advancing technology in this field, AVX Plc is constantly being challenged to learn new techniques.

AVX Plc uses standard costing to control its costs against targets set by senior managers. The standard labour cost per batch of one particular type of circuit board (CB45) is set out below:

	£
Direct labour – 50 hours @ £10/hour	500

The following labour efficiency variances arose during the first six months of the assembly of CB45:

Month	Number of batches assembled and sold	Labour Efficiency Variance (£)
November	1	Nil
December	1	170.00 Favourable
January	2	452.20 Favourable
February	4	1,089.30 Favourable
March	8	1,711.50 Favourable
April	16	3,423.00 Favourable

An investigation has confirmed that all of the costs were as expected except that there was a learning effect in respect of the direct labour that had not been anticipated when the standard cost was set.

Requirement

(a)
- (i) Calculate the monthly rates of learning that applied during the six months;
- (ii) Identify when the learning period ended and briefly discuss the implications of your findings for AVX Plc. **(10 marks)**

AVX Plc initially priced each batch of CB45 circuit boards on the basis of its standard cost of £960 plus a mark-up of 25%. Recently the company has noticed that, due to increasing competition, it is having difficulty maintaining its sales volume at this price.

The Finance Director has agreed that the long run unit variable cost of the CB45 circuit board is £672.72 per batch. She has suggested that the price charged should be based on an analysis of market demand. She has discovered that at a price of £1,200 the demand is 16 batches per month, for every £20 reduction in selling price there is an increase in demand of 1 batch of CB45 circuit boards, and for every £20 increase in selling price there is a reduction in demand of 1 batch.

Requirement

(b) Calculate the profit maximising selling price per batch using the data supplied by the Finance Director. **(8 marks)**

Note: If Price (P) = a − bx then Marginal Revenue (MR) = a − 2bx

The Technical Director cannot understand why there is a need to change the selling price. He argues that this is a highly advanced technological product and that AVX Plc should not reduce its price as this reflects badly on the company. If anything is at fault, he argues, it is the use of Standard Costing and he has asked whether Target Costing should be used instead.

Requirement

(c)
  (i) Explain the difference between standard costs and target costs;
  (ii) Explain the possible reasons why AVX Plc needs to re-consider its pricing policy now that the CB45 circuit board has been available in the market for six months.

(7 marks)

(Total for Question Five = 25 marks)

Question 6

A health clinic is reviewing its plans for the next three years. It is a not for profit organisation but it has a financial responsibility to manage its costs and to ensure that it provides a value for money service to its clients. The health clinic uses the net present value technique to appraise the financial viability of delivering the service, but it also considers other non-financial factors before making any final decisions.

The present facilities, which incur an annual total cost of £300,000, are only sufficient to meet a low level of service provision so the manager is considering investing in facilities to meet potential higher levels of demand. For the purpose of evaluating this decision the possible levels of demand for the health clinic's services have been simplified to high, medium or low.

The possible demand for the services in the first year and the level of demand that could follow that specific level in the next years, and their expected probabilities, are as follows:

Year 1	Probability	Years 2 and 3	Probability
Low	30%	Low	40%
		Medium	60%
		High	0%
Medium	50%	Low	30%
		Medium	40%
		High	30%
High	20%	Low	0%
		Medium	30%
		High	70%

The level of demand will be the same in years 2 and 3.

The manager is considering two alternative investments in facilities:

Facility A has the capacity to meet the low and medium levels of demand and requires an investment at the start of year 1 of £500,000. Thereafter it incurs annual fixed costs of £100,000 and annual variable costs depending on the level of operation. These annual variable costs are expected to be £150,000 at the low level of operation and £250,000 at the medium level of operation.

Facility B has the capacity to meet all levels of demand and requires an investment at the start of year 1 of £800,000. Thereafter it incurs annual fixed costs of £200,000 and annual variable costs depending on the level of operation. These annual variable costs are expected to be £100,000 at the low level of operation, £150,000 at the medium level of operation and £200,000 at the high level of operation.

Neither of these alternative investments has any residual value at the end of year 3.

If the facilities of the health clinic are insufficient to meet the level of service demand that occurs, the clinic must obtain additional facilities on a yearly contract basis at the following annual costs:

Level of service provision available internally	Level of service provision demanded	Annual cost of additional facilities
Low	Medium	£100,000
Low	High	£250,000
Medium	High	£150,000

These additional facilities are not under the direct control of the health clinic manager.

Note: All monetary values used throughout the question have been stated in terms of their present value. No further discounting is required.

Requirements

(a) Prepare a decision tree to illustrate the investment decision that needs to be made by the manager of the health clinic. (Numerical values are NOT required). **(6 marks)**

(b) Advise the manager of the health clinic which investment decision should be undertaken on financial grounds. **(15 marks)**

(c) Briefly discuss any non-financial factors that the manager should consider before making her final investment decision. **(4 marks)**

(Total for Question Six = 25 marks)

Question 7

 GHK manufactures four products from different combinations of the same direct materials and direct labour. An extract from the flexible budgets for next quarter for each of these products is as follows:

Product	G		H		J		K	
Units	3,000	5,000	3,000	5,000	3,000	5,000	3,000	5,000
	$'000	$'000	$'000	$'000	$'000	$'000	$'000	$'000
Revenue	30	50	60	100	45	75	90	150
Direct Material A (note 1)	9	15	12	20	4.5	7.5	18	30
Direct Material B (note 2)	6	10	6	10	13.5	22.5	36	60
Direct labour (note 3)	6	10	24	40	22.5	37.5	9	15
Overhead (note 4)	6	8	13	19	11	17	11	17

Notes:

1. Material A was purchased some time ago at a cost of $5 per kg. There are 5,000 kgs in inventory. The costs shown in the flexible budget are based on this historical cost. The material is in regular use and currently has a replacement cost of $7 per kg.
2. Material B is purchased as required; its expected cost is $10 per kg. The costs shown in the flexible budget are based on this expected cost.
3. Direct labour costs are based on an hourly rate of $10 per hour. Employees work the number of hours necessary to meet production requirements.
4. Overhead costs of each product include a specific fixed cost of $1,000 per quarter which would be avoided if the product was to be discontinued. Other fixed overhead costs are apportioned between the products but are not affected by the mix of products manufactured.

GHK has been advised by the only supplier of material B that the quantity of material B that will be available during the next quarter will be limited to 5,000 kgs. Accordingly the company is being forced to reconsider its production plan for the next quarter. GHK has already entered into contracts to supply one of its major customers with the following:

500 units of product G
1,600 units of product H
800 units of product J
400 units of product K

Apart from this, the demand expected from other customers is expected to be

3,600 units of product G
3,000 units of product H
3,000 units of product J
4,000 units of product K

The major customer will not accept partial delivery of the contract and if the contract with this major customer is not completed in full, then GHK will have to pay a financial penalty of $5,000.

Requirements

(a) For each of the four products, calculate the relevant contribution per $ of material B for the next quarter. **(6 marks)**

(b) It has been determined that the optimum production plan based on the data above is to produce 4,100 units of product G, 4600 units of product H, 800 units of product J, and 2,417 units of product K. Determine the amount of financial penalty at which GHK would be indifferent between meeting the contract or paying the penalty. **(5 marks)**

(c) Calculate the relevant contribution to sales ratios for each of the four products. **(2 marks)**

(d) Assuming that the limiting factor restrictions no longer apply, prepare a sketch of a multi-product profit–volume chart by ranking the products according to your contribution to sales ratio calculations based on total market demand. Your sketch should plot the products using the highest contribution to sales ratio first. **(6 marks)**

(e) Explain briefly, stating any relevant assumptions and limitations, how the multi-product profit–volume chart that you prepared in (d) above may be used by the manager of GHK to understand the relationships between costs, volume and profit within the business. **(6 marks)**

(Total for Question Seven = 25 marks)

Question 8

BK Chemicals produces three joint products in one common process but each product is capable of being further processed separately after the split-off point. The estimated data given below relate to June:

	Product B	Product K	Product C
Selling price at split-off point (per litre)	£6	£8	£9
Selling price after further processing (per litre)	£10	£20	£30
Post-separation point costs	£20,000	£10,000	£22,500
Output in litres	3,500	2,500	2,000

Pre-separation point joint costs are estimated to be £40,000 and it is current practice to apportion these to the three products according to litres produced.

Requirements

(a) Prepare a statement of estimated profit or loss for each product and in total for June if all three products are processed further. **(5 marks)**

(b) Advise how profits could be maximised if one or more products are sold at the split-off point. Your advice should be supported by a profit statement. **(10 marks)**

(c) Discuss the problems associated with joint cost apportionment in relation to decision making. **(5 marks)**

(Total marks = 20)

Question 9

You are the management accountant of a publishing and printing company, which has been asked to quote for the production of a programme for the local village fair. The work would be carried out in addition to the normal work of the company. Because of existing commitments, some weekend working would be required to complete the printing of the programme. A trainee accountant has produced the following cost estimate based upon the resources required as specified by the production manager:

			£
Direct materials	– paper (book value)		5,000
	– inks (purchase price)		2,400
Direct labour	– skilled	250 hours @ £4.00	1,000
	– unskilled	100 hours @ £3.50	350
Variable overhead		350 hours @ £4.00	1,400
Printing press depreciation		200 hours @ £2.50	500
Fixed production costs		350 hours @ £6.00	2,100
Estimating department costs			400
			13,150

You are aware that considerable publicity could be obtained for the company if you are able to win this order and the price quoted must be very competitive.

The following notes are relevant to the cost estimate above:

1. The paper to be used is currently in stock at a value of £5,000. It is of an unusual colour which has not been used for some time. The replacement price of the paper is £8,000, while the scrap value of that stock is £2,500. The production manager does not foresee any alternative use for the paper if it is not used for the village fair programmes.

2. The inks required are not held in stock. They would have to be purchased in bulk at a cost of £3,000. Eighty per cent of the ink purchased would be used in printing the programmes. No other use is foreseen for the remainder.

3. Skilled direct labour is in short supply, and to accommodate the printing of the programmes, 50 per cent of the time required would be worked at weekends for which the premium of 25 per cent above the normal hourly rate is paid. The normal hourly rate is £4.00 per hour.
4. Unskilled labour is presently under-utilised, and at present 200 hours per week are recorded as idle time. If the printing work is carried out at a weekend, 25 unskilled hours would have to occur at this time, but the employees concerned would be given two hours time off (for which they would be paid) in lieu of each hour worked.
5. Variable overhead represents the cost of operating the printing press and binding machines.
6. When not being used by the company, the printing press is hired to outside companies for £6.00 per hour. This earns a contribution of £3.00 per hour. There is unlimited demand for this facility.
7. Fixed production costs are those incurred by and absorbed into production, using an hourly rate based on budgeted activity.
8. The cost of the estimating department represents time spent in discussions with the village fair committee concerning the printing of its programme.

Requirements
(a) Prepare a revised cost estimate using the opportunity cost approach, showing clearly the minimum price that the company should accept for the order. Give reasons for each resource valuation in your cost estimate. **(16 marks)**
(b) Explain why contribution theory is used as a basis for providing information relevant to decision making. **(4 marks)**
(Total marks = 20)

Question 10

Enterprise Health International plc (EHI) is a commercial healthcare organisation that undertakes the development and marketing of new treatments. EHI is based in the UK and receives patients from around the world. One possible new treatment is under review. The demand for this treatment is very uncertain.

Preliminary research has indicated that the treatment can be developed but there are two alternative approaches to its design. The details of these alternatives are:

- A low-technology route using existing surgical treatment and drugs; this involves a development cost of £800,000 and a variable cost of £40,000 per treatment. This route will take 1 year to develop, with the development cost being paid for 1 year from now.
- A high-technology route using new surgical treatment, drugs and equipment; this involves a development cost of £6,300,000 and a variable cost of £18,000 per treatment. This route will take 3 years to develop, with development costs being paid for in three equal annual instalments, the first of which is 1 year from now.

EHI's managers are uncertain which of the two development alternatives to follow. They are considering an offer from a firm of strategic consultants to advise on the annual level of demand for treatments. For the purpose of appraising this offer it may be assumed that two levels of annual demand for treatments are possible – weak (30 treatments and 0.4 probability), and strong (65 treatments and 0.6 probability). It may be assumed that the consultants have a 92 per cent chance of correctly forecasting each level of demand.

EHI appraises projects using cash flows over a period of 10 years from now and a 10 per cent annual discount rate. It is forecast that the selling price of each treatment will be £43,000.

Requirements

(a) Calculate the minimum number of treatments demanded annually to make:
   (i) the low-technology route viable;
   (ii) the high-technology route viable;
   (iii) calculate the number of treatments demanded annually to make the low- and high-technology routes equally viable. **(9 marks)**

(b) Draw a diagram to illustrate the relative sensitivity of the two alternative routes to the number of treatments demanded annually. **(7 marks)**

(c) Advise EHI's managers on the maximum amount they should pay for the forecast of the annual demand for treatments. **(9 marks)**

(Total marks = 25)

Question 11

A ticket agent has an arrangement with a concert hall that holds pop concerts on 60 nights a year whereby he receives discounts as follows per concert:

For purchase of	He receives a discount of
200 tickets	20%
300 tickets	25%
400 tickets	30%
500 tickets or more	40%

Purchases must be in full hundreds. The average price per ticket is £3.

He must decide in advance each year the number of tickets he will purchase. If he has any tickets unsold by the afternoon of the concert he must return them to the box office. If the box office sells any of these he receives 60 per cent of their price.

His sales records over a few years show that for a concert with extremely popular artistes he can be confident of selling 500 tickets, for one with less known artistes 350 tickets, and for one with relatively unknown artistes 200 tickets.

His records show that 10 per cent of the tickets he returns are sold by the box office.

His administration costs incurred in selling tickets are the same per concert irrespective of the popularity of the artistes.

There are two possible scenarios in which his sales records can be viewed:

Scenario 1: that on average, he can expect concerts with lesser-known artistes;

Scenario 2: that the frequency of concerts will be:

	%
with popular artistes	45
with lesser-known artistes	30
with unknown artistes	25
	100

Requirements

(a) Calculate separately for each of scenarios 1 and 2:
   (i) the expected demand for tickets per concert;
   (ii) • the level of his purchases of tickets per concert that will give him the largest profit over a long period of time;
   • the profit per concert that this level of purchases of tickets will yield.

(12 marks)

(b) For scenario 2, only the maximum sum per annum that the ticket agent should pay to a pop concert specialist for 100 per cent correct predictions as to the likely success of each concert. **(8 marks)**
(Total marks = 20)

Question 12

XYZ manufactures a product called the X. During recent months the X has been sold at a unit price of around £6.25, with small adjustments to this price being made in order to try and find a profit-maximising selling price.

Consultants engaged by XYZ have reported that at a unit price of £10 there is no demand for Xs but that demand increases by 40 Xs for each 1p that the unit price is reduced below £10. The consultants have further reported that 'when demand is at around half its theoretical maximum the elasticity of demand is 1'.

Upon receiving this report XYZ's commercial manager makes the following statement:

Recent experience gained in adjusting the unit selling price of the X suggests that the product has quite an elastic demand structure. Small changes in the unit selling price produce far larger proportionate increases in demand. I do not believe that the elasticity of demand for the X is only 1.

Requirements
(a) Reconcile the consultants' report with the commercial manager's observations concerning the elasticity of demand for the X. **(7 marks)**
(b) The consultants have determined that the profit-maximising price is £5.75. Calculate the following:
  (i) The profit-maximising sales volume for the X;
  (ii) The elasticity of demand for the X at a price of £5.75. **(7 marks)**
(Total marks = 14)

Question 13 - Redo tom

VI plc produces a number of mobile telephone products. It is an established company with a good reputation that has been built on well-engineered, reliable and good-quality products. It is currently developing a product called Computel and has spent £1.5m on development so far. It now has to decide whether it should proceed further and launch the product in one year's time.

If VI plc decides to continue with the project, it will incur further development costs of £0.75 million straight away. Assets worth £3.5m will be required immediately prior to the product launch, and working capital of £1.5m would be required. VI plc expects that it could sell Computel for 3 years before the product becomes out of date.

It is estimated that the first 500 Computels produced and sold would cost an average of £675 each unit, for production, marketing and distribution costs. The fixed costs associated with the project are expected to amount to £2.4m (cash outflow) for each year the product is in production.

Because of the cost estimates, the chief executive expected the selling price to be in the region of £950. However, the marketing director is against this pricing strategy; he says that this price is far too high for this type of product and that he could sell only 6,000 units in each year at this price. He suggests a different strategy: setting a price of £425, at which price he expects sales to be 15,000 units each year.

VI plc has found from past experience that a 70 per cent experience curve applies to production, marketing and distribution costs. The company's cost of capital is 7 percent a year.

Requirements
(a) The chief executive has asked you to help sort out the pricing dilemma. Prepare calculations that demonstrate:
  - which of the two suggestions is the better pricing strategy;
  - the financial viability of the better strategy. **(15 marks)**
(b) Discuss other issues that VI plc should consider in relation to the two pricing strategies. **(5 marks)**
(c) Calculate and comment on the sensitivity of the financially better pricing strategy to changes in the selling price. **(4 marks)**
(d) Discuss the usefulness of the experience curve in gaining market share. Illustrate your answer with specific instances/examples. **(6 marks)**

(Total marks = 30)

Question 14

Delroads Electronics Ltd (DEL) produces a variety of products including an electronic navigational unit for use in ships. Construction of the unit is a delicate assembly operation by a team of highly skilled operatives. Components used in the unit are purchased from outside manufacturers. The unit is sold in relatively small numbers, and a new model is produced each year.

Costs associated with production of the 20X9 model of the unit are:

Fixed costs	£35,000
Variable costs	£20 wages per labour hour worked, plus £20 materials per unit

Production of the first unit of the 20X9 model will take 60 labour hours, and work of the operatives is known to be subject to an 83 per cent learning curve effect. Learning curve effects are achieved only within a model.

Market research has forecast that annual sales of the 20X9 model are associated with unit prices as follows:

1 unit	can be sold at unit price £10,000
500 units	can be sold at unit price £327.80

Requirements
(a) Explain what a learning curve effect is, and suggest reasons for the effect in this particular case. **(6 marks)**
(b) Draw a diagram (accurately to scale) on the graph paper supplied, demonstrating the relationship between units of output, total costs and total revenues in respect of the 20X9 model. Set out sufficient workings to justify your diagram. **(12 marks)**
(c) Use your diagram and supporting workings to identify the profit-maximising units of output and unit price in respect of the 20X9 model. **(7 marks)**

Notes:

In evaluating learning curve effects you should use the cumulative average time equation:

$$y = \frac{a}{x^{0.269}}$$

In evaluating the link between revenue and output you should use the equation:

$$y = ax^n$$

where a = price of first unit
x = output
y = total revenue

(Total marks = 25)

Question 15

The new manufacturing environment is characterised by more flexibility, a readiness to meet customers' requirements, smaller batches, continuous improvements and an emphasis on quality. In such circumstances, traditional management accounting performance measures are, at best, irrelevant and, at worst, misleading.

Requirements

(a) Discuss the above statement, citing specific examples to support or refute the views expressed. **(10 marks)**
(b) Explain in what ways management accountants can adapt the services they provide to the new environment. **(7 marks)**

(Total marks = 17)

Question 16

(a) 'Costing systems attempt to explain how products consume resources but do not indicate the joint benefits of having multiple products.'

Requirement

Explain the statement above and discuss
(i) how the addition of a new product to the product range may affect the 'cost' of existing products;
(ii) the consequences, in terms of total profitability, of decisions to increase/decrease the product range. **(10 marks)**

(b) Telmat is a company that manufactures mobile phones. This market is extremely volatile and competitive and achieving adequate product profitability is extremely important. Telmat is a mature company that has been producing electronic equipment for many years and has all the costing systems in place that one would expect in such a company. These include a comprehensive overhead absorption system, annual budgets and monthly variance reports and the balanced scorecard for performance measurement.

The company is considering introducing:
(i) target costing; and
(ii) life cycle costing systems.

Requirement

Discuss the advantages (or otherwise) that this specific company is likely to gain from these two systems. (15 marks)

(Total marks = 25)

Question 17

PSA Ltd pays its operatives an hourly rate which at the start of 20X2 was forecast to be £10.50 throughout the year. Both hardwood and softwood are used on jobs, the 20X2 costs of which were forecast to be £55 per cubic metre (hardwood) and £9 per cubic metre (softwood). Overheads (absorbed on a labour hour overhead absorption rate [OAR]) for 20X2 were forecast to be £96,000 (fixed) and £72,000 (variable). It was forecast that 24,000 labour hours would be worked on all jobs at an even rate in 20X2. PSA Ltd uses a conventional cost accounting system and reports cost variances at the end of each month, with labour and material variances split into operational and planning components.

At the start of April 20X2 there was no work-in-progress and, during the month, work started on jobs 98, 107 and 109. Jobs 98 and 107 were fully complete by the end of the month. Job 109 was estimated to be 60 per cent complete as regards labour and 80 per cent complete as regards materials. The evaluator had calculated the following requirements for the jobs, based on the original standards specified above:

	Job 98	Job 107	Job 109
Standard labour hours	1,000	600	780
Hardwood (cubic metres)	200	180	120
Softwood (cubic metres)	320	400	300

During April, 2,200 labour hours were worked (wages paid were £24,500), 520 cubic metres of hardwood were used (cost £28,600) and 1,100 cubic metres of softwood were used (cost £9,200). Conditions in the labour market meant that operatives had to be engaged who were less able than those planned for. On average, operatives were able to work only at 4 per cent below the original standard level of efficiency (that is, expected output per hour is 4 per cent less than standard). Hardwood available during 20X2 is 5 per cent below forecast quality (that is, the output per cubic metre is 5 per cent below standard). During March, the standard price of softwood for 20X2 was revised to £8 per cubic metre. April overheads were £7,800 (fixed) and £6,900 (variable).

Rapier Management Consultants have reported as follows:

Your cost system looks like something from an accounting textbook written forty years ago. What you need is backflush costing. Rapier will be delighted to design you a backflush costing system for a modest fee.

Requirements

(a) Explain why conventional cost accounting systems use predetermined OARs.

(5 marks)

(b) Construct PSA Ltd's April cost control report. (12 marks)

(c) Explain what backflush costing is and (as far as you can on the basis of available information) comment on the suitability of PSA Ltd's operation for backflush costing.

(8 marks)

(Total marks = 25)

Question 18

Apollo plc manufactures and sells several products, two of which are Alpha and Beta. Estimated data for the two products for the forthcoming period is as follows:

(i)

Product data	Alpha	Beta	Other products
Production/sales units	5,000	10,000	40,000
	£000	£000	£000
Total direct material cost	80	300	2,020
Total direct labour cost	40	100	660

(ii) Variable overhead cost is £1,500,000 of which 40 per cent is related to the acquisition, storage and use of direct materials and the remainder is related to the control and use of direct labour.

(iii) It is current practice for Apollo plc to absorb the two types of variable overhead cost to products using an overall company-wide percentage based on either direct material cost and direct labour cost as appropriate.

(iv) Apollo are considering the use of activity-based costing. The cost drivers for material and labour related overheads have been identified as follows:

	Alpha	Beta	Other products
Direct material related overheads – cost driver is weight of material			
Weight of material/unit	4	1	1.5
Direct labour related overheads – cost driver is number of labour operations			
Labour operations/unit	6	1	2

(v) Market investigation indicates that market prices for Alpha and Beta of £75 and £95 per unit respectively will achieve the estimated sales shown in (i) above.

(vi) Apollo plc require a minimum estimated contribution: sales ratio of 40 per cent before proceeding with the production or sale of any product.

Requirements

(a) Prepare estimated unit product costs for Alpha and Beta where the variable overhead is charged to product units as follows:
  (i) using the existing absorption rates as detailed above,
  (ii) using an activity-based costing approach. **(5 marks)**

(b) Using the information in (a) prepare an analysis that will help Apollo determine whether both A and B should remain in production.
  Your answer should include relevant calculations and discussion and be prepared in a form suitable for presentation to management. **(10 marks)**

(c) Explain how Apollo could make use of target costing in conjunction with activity-based costing with respect to Alpha and Beta. **(5 marks)**

(Total marks = 20)

Question 19

DEF Ltd produces fuel pumps that are incorporated in petrol engines produced by a number of other companies. At present DEF Ltd produces three different versions of its standard fuel pump – versions D, E and F. Rapier Management Consultants have recently been engaged by DEF Ltd to undertake a value analysis and engineering exercise concerning the design of the fuel pumps.

Rapier have proposed that the three different versions of the fuel pump be replaced by a single general-purpose unit – known as version X. The main features of this proposal are:

- it will be possible to dispose immediately of equipment and buildings at a price of £120,000 and there will be no additional development costs;
- total annual unit sales will initially drop by 25 per cent from their existing level but will thereafter grow at 4 per cent per annum compound;
- it will be possible to make £250,000 initial reduction in the value of component and finished goods stock; stocks will thereafter grow at a rate of 2 per cent per annum compound;
- the variable cost of producing one unit of version X will be £1.75 less than that of producing versions D, E and F.

If the proposal is not adopted and production of units D, E and F continues, then it is forecast that unit sales and stocks will both grow at an annual rate of 3 percent compound. The market price of a fuel pump is £48 and the variable cost of producing one unit of D, E or F is £35. At present (before the Rapier proposal is implemented), DEF Ltd's stocks have a cost of £560,000 and annual sales of D, E and F total 18,000 units.

DEF Ltd appraises projects using a 10 per cent discount rate and an 8-year time horizon.

Requirements

(a) Explain why the redesign of DEF Ltd's product may have the effects claimed for it by Rapier Management Consultants; explain the general principles of value analysis.

(8 marks)

(b) Advise DEF Ltd's management on the merits of the Rapier proposal; support your advice with a full financial evaluation. **(10 marks)**

(c) Draw a diagram to illustrate the sensitivity of the Rapier proposal to the reduction in unit variable cost (claimed to be £1.75); identify the minimum reduction in net variable cost needed to make the proposal viable and indicate this point on your diagram.

(7 marks)
(Total marks = 25)

 Question 20

Trimake Ltd makes three main products, using broadly the same production methods and equipment for each. A conventional product costing system is used at present, although an activity-based costing (ABC) system is being considered. Details of the three products for a typical period are:

	Hours per unit		Material	Volume
	Labour hours	Machine hours	per unit £	units
Product X	0.5	1.5	20	750
Product Y	1.5	1	12	1,250
Product Z	1	3	25	7,000

Direct labour costs £6 per hour and production overheads are absorbed on a machine hour basis. The rate for the period is £28 per machine hour.

Requirements

(a) Calculate the cost per unit for each product using conventional methods. (4 marks)

Further analysis shows that the total of production overheads can be divided as follows:

	%
Costs relating to set-ups	35
Costs relating to machinery	20
Costs relating to materials handling	15
Costs relating to inspection	30
Total production overhead	100

The following total activity volumes are associated with the product line for the period as a whole:

	Number of set-ups	Movements of materials	Number of inspections
Product X	75	12	150
Product Y	115	21	180
Product Z	480	87	670
	670	120	1,000

(b) Calculate the cost per unit for each product using ABC principles. (15 marks)
(c) Comment on the reasons for any differences in the costs in your answers to (a) and (b). (3 marks)

(Total marks = 22)

Question 21

Having attended a CIMA course on activity-based costing (ABC) you decide to experiment by applying the principles to the four products currently made and sold by your company. Details of the four products and relevant information are given below for one period:

Product	A	B	C	D
Output in units	120	100	80	120
Costs per unit	£	£	£	£
Direct material	40	50	30	60
Direct labour	28	21	14	21
Machine hours (per unit)	4	3	2	3

The four products are similar and are usually produced in production runs of 20 units and sold in batches of 10 units.

The production overhead is currently absorbed by using a machine hour rate, and the total of the production overhead has been analysed as follows:

	£
Machine department costs (rent, business rates, depreciation and supervision)	10,430
Set-up costs	5,250
Stores receiving	3,600
Inspection/quality control	2,100
Material handling and dispatch	4,620

You have ascertained that the 'cost drivers' to be used are as listed below for the overhead costs shown:

Cost	Cost driver
Set-up costs	Number of production runs
Stores receiving	Requisitions raised
Inspection/quality control	Number of production runs
Materials handling and dispatch	Orders executed

The number of requisitions raised on the stores was 20 for each product and the number of orders executed was 42, each order being for a batch of 10 of a product.

Requirements

(a) Calculate the total costs for each product if all overhead costs are absorbed on a machine hour basis. **(4 marks)**

(b) Calculate the total cost of each product, using activity-based costing. **(7 marks)**

(c) Calculate and list the unit product costs from your figures in (a) and (b) above, to show the differences and comment briefly on any conclusions which may be drawn which could have pricing and profit implications. **(4 marks)**

(Total marks = 15)

Question 22

In 1994, Hulk Petroleum plc (HPC) constructed an oil production platform known as Claymore 4 (C4). After construction, C4 was positioned in the North Sea and wells were drilled from C4 into an oilfield below. The platform was designed to have a life of 25 years from 1 January 1995, with the original wells being productive for 10 years.

By 2004 the reservoirs in the oilfield tapped by the original wells will be almost exhausted. Untapped reservoirs in the oilfield below C4 are estimated to contain a maximum of 1,500,000 tonnes of extractable oil. Alternative strategies for the continuation of oil production from C4 have been identified as follows:

- low-intensity depletion strategy: involves drilling of new wells at a cost of £105m. These would recover maximum extractable oil at an even rate over 15 years; the annual operating costs will be £3.2 million and the costs of decontaminating and dismantling C4 at year 15 will be £395m.
- high-intensity depletion strategy: involves the drilling of new wells at a cost of £118m. These would recover 1,300,000 tonnes of oil over eight years at an even rate; the annual operating costs will be £3.6m and the costs of decontaminating and dismantling C4 at year 8 will be £280m.

The average market price of oil throughout the period is forecast to be £325 per tonne. It is HPC's normal policy to require all new investment projects to generate an IRR in excess of 10 per cent (which is HPC's cost of money). In the case of mutually exclusive investments, the one with the highest IRR is adopted.

Requirements

(a) Write a memorandum in response to a letter from one of HPC's directors which includes the following statement:

> Since cash flow and profit are the same thing in the long run, we should always adopt courses of action which maximise accounting profit. I do not understand the logic behind our investment appraisal policy.

(5 marks)

(b) Draw a graph in order to illustrate the sensitivity of the two strategies to the choice of discount rate (in the range 0–25 per cent) that may be used to appraise them.

(10 marks)

(c) In the light of your answer to (b), comment on the merits of HPC's existing investment appraisal policy.

(6 marks)

(d) Advise HPC's management on which of the two strategies should be selected.

(4 marks)

(Total marks = 25)

Question 23

H plc is considering purchasing a new machine to alleviate a bottleneck in its production facilities. At present it uses an old machine which can process 200 units of product P per hour. H plc could replace it with machine AB, which is product-specific and can produce 500 units an hour. Machine AB costs £500,000. If it is installed, two members of staff will have to attend a short training course, which will cost the company a total of £5,000. Removing the old machine and preparing the area for machine AB will cost £20,000.

The company expects demand for P to be 12,000 units per week for another 3 years. After this, early in the fourth year, the new machine would be scrapped and sold for £50,000. The existing machine will have no scrap value. Each P earns a contribution of £1.40. The company works a 40-hour week for 48 weeks in the year. H plc normally expects a payback within two years, and its after-tax cost of capital is 10 per cent per annum. The company pays corporation tax at 30 per cent and receives writing-down allowances of 25 per cent, reducing balance. Corporation tax is payable quarterly, in the seventh and tenth months of the year in which the profit is earned, and in the first and fourth months of the following year.

Requirements

(a) Prepare detailed calculations that show whether machine AB should be bought, and advise the management of H plc as to whether it should proceed with the purchase.

Make the following assumptions:

(i) The company's financial year begins on the same day that the new machine would start operating, if purchased.

(ii) The company uses discounted cash flow techniques with annual breaks only.

(iii) For taxation purposes, H plc's management will elect for short-life asset treatment for this asset.

(18 marks)

(b) The investment decision in part (a) is a closely defined manufacturing one. Explain how a marketing or an IT investment decision might differ in terms of approach and assessment. **(7 marks)**

(Total marks = 25)

Question 24

CD Ltd has for some years manufactured a product called the C which is used as a component in a variety of electrical items. Although the C remains in demand, the technology on which its design is based has become obsolete. CD Ltd's engineers have developed a new product called the D which incorporates new technology. The D is smaller and more reliable than the C but performs exactly the same function.

The management of CD Ltd is considering whether to continue production of the C or discontinue the C and start production of the D. CD Ltd does not have the means to produce both products simultaneously.

If the C is produced then unit sales in year 1 are forecast to be 24,000, but declining by 4,000 units in each subsequent year. Additional equipment costing £70,000 must be purchased now if C production is to continue.

If the D is produced then unit sales in year 1 are forecast to be 6,000, but a rapid increase in unit sales is expected thereafter. Additional equipment costing £620,000 must be purchased now if D production is to start.

Relevant details of the two products are as follows:

	C	D
	£	£
Variable cost per unit	25	50
Selling price per unit	55	105

CD Ltd normally appraises investments using a 12 per cent per annum compound cost of money and ignores cash flows beyond five years from the start of investments.

Requirements

(a) Advise CD Ltd's management on the minimum annual growth in unit sales of the D needed to justify starting D production now – using CD Ltd's normal investment appraisal rules. Support your advice with a full financial evaluation. **(11 marks)**

(b) Advise CD Ltd's management on the number of years to which its investment appraisal time horizon (currently 5 years) would have to be extended in order to justify starting D production now if the forecast annual increase in D sales is 2,800 units. **(7 marks)**

(c) State and explain any factors not included in your financial evaluation that CD Ltd should consider in making its decision. **(7 marks)**

(Total marks = 25)

Note: You should ignore inflation, and the residual values of equipment.

Question 25

Anmexsco is a mining company, which has discovered deposits of bauxite beneath Hyde Park in London. Anmexsco has negotiated a possible deal to undertake open-cast bauxite mining in Hyde Park for a 5-year period. This would involve excavating most of the park to a depth of about 2,000 feet but restoring the park to its original condition at the end of the 5 years.

Details of the proposed deal are:

- an initial fee of £9,700,000 would be payable to the government;
- amounts of bauxite extracted are forecast to be:

Year	Tonnes
1	100,000
2	150,000
3	220,000
4	180,000
5	90,000

- the market price of bauxite is £90 per ton;
- annual operating costs will be £3,000,000 throughout;
- the costs of restoring Hyde Park are forecast to be:

Year	£
4	42,000,000
5	1,000,000

Anmexsco's investment appraisal rules require a project to show a minimum IRR of 17 per cent before it is allowed to proceed.

Financial analysts working for Anmexsco prepare a project evaluation, which shows the project yielding an IRR of 23.836 per cent and recommend that the project should proceed. On receiving this evaluation Anmexsco's chief executive makes the following statement:

I have checked these figures using only a pocket calculator and I would place the IRR of the project at around 11.5 per cent. This project is not viable and these analysts do not know what they are doing.

Requirements

(a) Explain and reconcile the two alternative evaluations of the project. **(18 marks)**

(b) Explain how you would use a standard computer spreadsheet to assist in this exercise. **(7 marks)**

(Total marks = 25)

Question 26

ABC Ltd is considering a project for the manufacture and sale of a product known as the widget. ABC Ltd's market share will be small and its output will not influence the market price of the widget. Details of the project are:

Equipment costing £40,000 will have to be purchased at the outset. It is forecast that at the end of the project this equipment will have a residual value of £5,000.

Market research has forecast that the following quantities of widgets can be sold at a price of £103 per widget:

Year	
1	200
2	500
3	1,000
4	1,800
5	2,000
6	1,800
7	1,600
8	1,400

- In any year, cost of sales (excluding depreciation) will be £95 per widget sold.
- At the end of each year, debtors will be 10 per cent of the value of sales in that year. At the start of each year, inventories will be approximately 5 per cent of the cost of forecast sales in that year.

ABC Ltd evaluates projects using the DCF technique, a 15 per cent per annum discount rate and a 9-year time horizon. Ignore taxation.

Requirements
(a) Advise ABC Ltd's managers on whether or not the project is viable. Justify your advice with a full financial evaluation. **(15 marks)**
(b) Draw a diagram on the graph paper provided to illustrate the sensitivity of the project to the selling price per widget. Use the diagram to identify the minimum selling price per widget needed (accurate to the nearest £0.50) to make the project viable. **(10 marks)**

(Total marks = 25)

Question 27

AMG plc is an engine manufacturer. AMG plc's management believes that it can produce one last batch of its K2 engine for sale to customers in an African country next year before the K2 becomes obsolete.

The batch must be in multiples of 1,000 units to a maximum of 5,000 units. The material cost of one K2 is £100. The labour cost of the first K2 in the batch is £2,000 (100 hours at a rate of £20 per hour) and K2 manufacture is subject to an 81.225 per cent learning curve effect. [* see note below]

Market research in the African country indicates that the relationship between revenues (y) and unit sales (x) next year may be represented by the following equations in the circumstances specified:

$$y = 1,000x - \frac{x^{1.90}}{5} \quad \text{[case (1)] if the competing product of another manufacturer is not on sale;}$$

and

$$y = 1,000x - \frac{x^{1.95}}{5} \quad \text{[case (2)] if the competing product is on sale.}$$

It is considered that there is a one in three probability that the competing product will be on sale. The batch has to be produced before it is known whether case (1) or case (2) applies. The unit selling price may be set after it is known which case applies. A business consultant has offered to find out for a fee of £50,000 whether or not the competing product will be on sale.

Requirements

(a) Construct a table to demonstrate the relationship between the K2 batch size, total costs and total revenues (both demand cases). Use the table to identify the profit-maximising batch size in each demand case. **(11 marks)**

(b) Calculate the expected profit that will be generated by the sale of K2 if the company assumes, when deciding what batch size to produce, that case (1) will happen. **(8 marks)**

(c) Advise the company on whether it should assume case (1) will happen or pay the consultant for his forecast. Assume that the consultant is capable of providing a completely accurate forecast. **(6 marks)**

(Total marks = 25)

Note: Learning curve effects should be evaluated using the Cumulative Average Time formula

$$y = \frac{a}{x^{0.3}}.$$

Question 28

TC plc launched a new product in January this year. Expected production was budgeted to be:

January	400 units	April	750 units
February	480 units	May	800 units
March	620 units	June	820 units

The initial costings for the new product at the beginning of January were based on:

- Labour: Rate of pay £4 per hour.
  A trial period run of 100 units at the end of December showed a 70 per cent learning curve and the time taken to produce the first unit of the trial period was 53.47 hours.
- Variable overhead: varies with labour hours and is 300 per cent of labour cost.

TC plc always agrees a learning curve with its employee representatives when a new product is introduced. This governs the payment of a bonus of 15 per cent of pay, if the average actual hours each month are less than the hours expected with the application of the learning percentage. In this case the 70 per cent learning curve was agreed for the first 3 months based on the trial period. The actual learning curve achieved in the first three months plus the trial period would be substituted thereafter for bonus payments.

The labour force experienced some difficulty working with the material, which was not 100 per cent pure. As a result, after the first month of production, the supplier improved the purity of the material supplied.

During January to March, the units produced were as budgeted. The actual labour hours spent making the new product from the beginning of the trial period to the end of March were 2,150.

Requirements

(a) (i) Calculate the budgeted average labour time per unit for all units produced up to the end of March. **(2 marks)**

(ii) Calculate the learning curve percentage, to two decimal places, which would apply from April onwards for the payment of the bonus. **(5 marks)**

(b) Comment on the eligibility of a bonus payment to the employees of TC plc if 460 labour hours were worked to produce 775 units in April. **(12 marks)**
(c) Comment briefly on the suitability of TC plc's accounting systems and staff remuneration policy. **(6 marks)**

(Total marks = 25)

Note: Learning curve effects may be appraised by using the formula $Y = aX^b$.

where Y = the cumulative average time per unit for X units,
a = the time taken to make the first unit,
X = the number of units made, and
b = the index of learning, this is the log of learning rate/log 2.

Question 29

D has recently set up a small business, which manufactures three different types of chair to customer order. Each type is produced in a single batch per week and despatched as individual items. The size of the batch is determined by the weekly customer orders. The three different types of chair are known as the Comfort, the Relaxer and the Scandinavia. The Comfort is a fully leather-upholstered chair and is the most expensive of the range. The Relaxer is the middle-of-the-range chair, and has a comfortable leather seat. The cheapest of the range, the Scandinavia, is purely a wooden chair, but D feels it has great potential and hopes it will provide at least 50 per cent of sales revenue.

D has employed F, an experienced but unqualified accountant, to act as the organisation's accountant. F has produced figures for the past month, April 20X2, which is considered a normal month in terms of costs:

Profit statement for April 20X2

	£	£
Sales revenue		79,800
Material costs	17,250	
Labour costs	27,600	
Overheads	34,500	
		79,350
Profit		450

	Comfort	Relaxer	Scandinavia
Units produced and sold during April	30	120	150
	£	£	£
Selling price per chair	395	285	225
Less: Costs per chair:			
Material	85	60	50
Labour	120	100	80
Overheads absorbed on labour hours	150	125	100
	355	285	230
Profit per chair	40	–	(5)

D hopes to use these figures as the basis for budgets for the next 3 months. He is pleased to see that the organisation has made its first monthly profit, however small it might be. On the other hand, he is unhappy with F's advice about the loss-making Scandinavia, which is, either to reduce its production or to increase its price. D is concerned because this advice goes against the strategy on which he based his business idea. After much discussion F says that he has heard about a newer type of costing system, known as activity-based costing

(ABC), and that he will recalculate the position on this basis. In order to do this, F extracts the following information:

	Comfort	Relaxer	Scandinavia
Wood (metres) per chair	10	9	9
Leather (metres) per chair	4	2	–
Labour (hours) per chair	24	20	16

The overheads included in April's profit statement comprised:

	£
Set-up costs	5,600
Purchasing and checking leather hides	4,000
Purchase of wood	2,400
Quality inspection of leather seating	3,200
Despatch and transport	6,000
Administration and personnel costs	13,300

Requirements

(a) Use the ABC technique to prepare a revised product cost statement for April 20X2 such as F might produce. **(13 marks)**

(b) Explain whether the statement you have prepared in (a) provides an adequate basis to make decisions on the future production volume and price of the Scandinavia. What other information or approach might you seek or adopt? **(5 marks)**

(c) It is just as important for an organisation to determine how individual customers or groups of customers differ in terms of their profitability to the organisation as it is to determine the relative profitability of products. Briefly explain how this can be done. Would you advise D to do this? **(7 marks)**

(Total marks = 25)

Question 30

Note: The following three questions (Questions 30, 31, and 32) are scenario-based questions which were of the sort examinable in the previous syllabus. They have been included here as they are excellent revision questions on throughput accounting. The technical ability required in the current syllabus will be of a similar standard but will not be based on such a detailed scenario.

MN Ltd manufactures automated industrial trolleys, known as TRLs. Each TRL sells for £2,000 and the material cost per unit is £600. Labour and variable overhead are £5,500 and £8,000 per week respectively. Fixed production costs are £450,000 per annum and marketing and administrative costs are £265,000 per annum.

The trolleys are made on three different machines. Machine X makes the four frame panels required for each TRL. Its maximum output is 180 frame panels per week. Machine X is old and unreliable and it breaks down from time to time – it is estimated that, on average, between 15 and 20 hours of production are lost per month. Machine Y can manufacture parts for 52 TRLs per week and machine Z, which is old but reasonably reliable, can process and assemble 30 TRLs per week.

The company has recently introduced a just-in-time (JIT) system and it is company policy to hold little work-in-progress and no finished goods stock from week to week. The company operates a 40-hour week, 48 weeks a year (12 months × 4 weeks) but cannot meet demand. The demand for the next year is predicted to be as follows – this is expected to be typical of the demand for the next 4 years:

	Units per week		Units per week
January	30	July	48
February	30	August	45
March	33	September	42
April	36	October	40
May	39	November	33
June	44	December	30

The production manager has suggested that the company replaces machine Z with either machine F or machine G. Machine F can process 36 TRLs per week and costs £330,000. It is expected that labour costs would increase by £2,500 per week if machine F were installed. Machine G can process 45 TRLs per week and costs £550,000. It is estimated that the variable overhead cost per week will increase by £4,500 if TRLs are made on machine G. The maintenance manager is keen to spend £100,000 on a major overhaul of machine X – he says this will make it 100 per cent reliable.

The management of MN Ltd is wondering whether it should now install a full standard costing and variance analysis system. At present, standard costs are calculated only as part of the annual budgeting process. Management is concerned about implementing so many changes in a short space of time, but feels the system could be very useful.

The company's cost of capital is 10 per cent per annum. It evaluates projects over 4 years and depreciates its assets over 5 years.

Requirements
Using the case of MN Ltd in the scenario:

(a) Calculate the throughput accounting ratio (defined below) for the key resource for an average hour next year.

$$\text{Throughput accounting ratio} = \frac{\text{Return per factory hour}}{\text{Cost per factory hour}}$$

where

$$\text{Return per factory hour} = \frac{\text{Sales price} - \text{material cost}}{\text{Time on key resource}}$$

(5 marks)

(b) Prepare calculations that will help the managers of MN Ltd assess which, if any, of the different machine alternatives should be undertaken. Which alternative appears to be the best from the standpoint of your calculations? (15 marks)

(c) To which, if any, of the estimated figures is your answer in (b) sensitive? (5 marks)

(Total marks = 25)

Question 31

Requirements
Using the case of MN Ltd presented in the scenario where appropriate, and the throughput accounting ratio defined in 30(a), answer the following:

(a) Explain the concept of throughput accounting. (4 marks)
(b) To what uses do advocates of throughput accounting suggest that the ratio be put?
(4 marks)

(c) Suggest two other ratios which may be used by a company operating throughput accounting, and explain the use to which they may be put. **(6 marks)**
(d) Explain how the concept of contribution in throughput accounting differs from that in marginal costing. **(6 marks)**
(e) If MN Ltd has decided to purchase machine G and spend £100,000 on a major overhaul of machine X, the management accountant and the production manager should collaborate to ensure a new focus for monitoring and reporting production activities. What is the new focus? Explain what should be monitored and reported. **(5 marks)**

(Total marks = 25)

Question 32

Requirements

Using the case of MN Ltd presented in the scenario, answer the following:

(a) To date MN Ltd has not operated a procedure of post-project appraisal and audit. Briefly discuss the advantages and disadvantages of such a procedure. Would you advise MN Ltd to use the procedure for the first time on the purchase of either new machine F or G? **(10 marks)**
(b) Explain the term 'value added' and contrast it with the term 'value added activity'.

(5 marks)
(Total marks = 15)

Question 33

J has a sales franchise for skin-care products that are supplied by SPS plc. She buys two products from SPS plc that she normally markets by mail order and door-to-door sales. The details of the two products are:

	Purchase price to J £ per jar	J's retail selling price £ per jar
Wrinkle vanishing cream (WVC)	6.50	11.45
Skin tightening cream (STC)	5.50	10.25

J has had a portable selling stall made at a cost of £1,000 and she plans to set this up within department stores for a week or so at a time. The management of the well-known department store DDS plc has agreed to rent her space during August for one week in each of four of its department stores. They have offered three different methods for calculating their fee:

(i) fixed fee of £600 per week;
(ii) fixed fee of £500 per week plus 5 per cent of sales revenue;
(iii) 25 per cent of sales revenue.

If J decides to go ahead with this scheme, she plans to employ a part-time assistant for £200 per week to staff the stall. The remainder of the time, 20 hours per week, J will staff the stall herself. J considers that she normally earns £10 per hour as an agent. J also thinks that it will take her 5 hours to move and reassemble the stall in the next store.

J has attempted to predict sales and has produced the following probability analysis of sales per week based on the assumption that sales of WVC will be 150 per cent of sales of STC:

High sales – 20 per cent chance of selling 180 jars of WVC and 120 jars of STC
Average sales – 50 per cent chance of selling 150 jars of WVC and 100 jars of STC
Low sales – 30 per cent chance of selling 100 jars of WVC and 67 jars of STC.

Requirements

(a) Calculate which fee alternative J should select, using the expected value approach. Advise J which of the three fee alternatives she should select, if she wishes to minimise financial risk. **(9 marks)**

(b) Draw a graph illustrating the optimum fee choice at varying levels of sales. In what circumstances would you advise accepting fee option (ii)? **(6 marks)**

(c) J is aware that the weather in August will be an important factor in determining sales. If the temperature is above average, sales will be lower than expected; if the temperature is below average, sales will be higher. J has to buy her products two months in advance and store them in a specially provided cold chamber and so predicting the weather will be important if she is to maximise profit as unsold products will probably have to be scrapped. She can buy a long-term monthly weather forecast from the Weather Centre. Basically, the forecast will simply tell her if the temperature is likely to be above average or below average for the month. The Weather Centre is 80 per cent accurate with its forecasts.
Assume that J decides to go ahead with the scheme, and that she selects fee option (iii).

Requirement

Using the following simplified probability analysis of sales, determine how much a favourable weather forecast of below-average temperature from the Weather Centre is worth to her.

    Above-average temperature – 40 per cent chance of selling 150 jars of WVC and 100 jars of STC
                                               – 60 per cent chance of selling 100 jars of WVC and 67 jars of STC
    Below-average temperature – 40 per cent chance of selling 180 jars of WVC and 120 jars of STC
                                               – 60 per cent chance of selling 150 jars of WVC and 100 jars of STC

(10 marks)
(Total marks = 25)

 ## Question 34

Note: The following three questions (Questions 34, 35 and 36) are scenario-based questions which were of the sort examinable in the previous syllabus. They have been included here as they are excellent revision questions on a variety of topics included in the current syllabus. The technical ability required in the current syllabus will be of a similar standard but will not be based on such a detailed scenario.

November 1997

In early November 1997, R Ltd considered manufacturing a new product called Sparkle. Up to that time, £750,000 had been spent on researching the product.

The company estimated that it would take two further years to develop Sparkle to the point of production and by that time it would probably have a lead of 18 months over its chief competitor. R Ltd expected to launch Sparkle on 1 November 1999 and to produce and sell 100,000 units in the first year if £1.5 million was spent on pre-launch advertising. During the first year of production, R Ltd planned to spend £750,000 on advertising; this level of expenditure would be maintained each year.

From the second year onwards, the market was expected to increase to between 160,000 and 200,000 units. Once the competitor entered the market, it was thought that the competitor would win 50 per cent market share very quickly because of its reputation.

The development and engineering costs of Sparkle were estimated to be £6 million, £2 million of which would be incurred in the first year of development, 1997/98. A special piece of equipment costing £500,000 would be required for production and this was to be installed in the month prior to the commencement of manufacture.

R Ltd planned to set a selling price of £249 a unit on the basis that variable manufacturing and distribution costs were expected to be £122 per unit. The company normally sets selling prices so that the contribution/sales ratio is 50 per cent or slightly more. The fixed administrative and space costs that relate to the product, and which would be incurred from the commencement of production, were estimated to be £7.5m per annum. It was also estimated that working capital of £2.5 million would be needed at the start of production in November 1999.

The product was expected to have a life span of about five years at which time the equipment would be scrapped as having no value. The company estimated its cost of capital to be 12 per cent per annum.

November 2000

Development of Sparkle took 6 months longer than planned. This was largely because it proved necessary to employ two extra members of staff in the engineering department for the technical aspects of the product development.

The engineering department did not have a budget for this in year 1 (1997–98) and so employment was delayed until the start of the second year, November 1998, when the budget for the extra funds had been approved. This caused the planned expenditure on development for year 2 to be spread over the 18-month period from the start of year 2 to the middle of year 3. The two new members of staff were employed at salaries of £45,000 each and employment costs were estimated to be 100 per cent of the first year's salary. As a result, production started six months late in May 2000, the pre-launch costs were delayed accordingly and only 55,000 units were sold in the year November 1999 to October 2000.

As expected, the competitor has decided to enter the market and is launching its rival product Glitter this month, November 2000.

R Ltd now predicts the market for 2000/01 to be 150,000 units and its share of this to be 50 per cent. Thereafter the market size will be as forecast previously, that is between 160,000 and 200,000 units each year, and the product life cycle will stop at the same date as planned previously. The monetary value of all expenditures and revenues to date has been very close to the estimates and there is no reason to revise future forecasts in this respect.

Requirements

Using the case of Sparkle in the scenario:

(a) Calculate the net present value of the project as perceived at the beginning of November 1997, when R Ltd decided to manufacture Sparkle. State clearly any assumptions you make. **(11 marks)**

(b) Calculate the revised net present value of the whole project as perceived at the beginning of November 2000. **(8 marks)**

(c) Comment on the position revealed by the figures you have calculated in (a) and (b) and on the events which have taken place. What should the company do now? **(6 marks)**

(Total marks = 25)

Question 35

Requirements

Using the case of Sparkle presented in the scenario as an illustration, answer the following:

(a) Explain the concept of life cycle costing and give reasons why it may be important to use it. **(5 marks)**

(b) Using the figures from the proposal made in November 1997, draw a life cycle chart for Sparkle. (Precision is not required.) **(4 marks)**

(c) Discuss the importance or otherwise of a post-project audit to the successful use of life cycle costing techniques. **(10 marks)**

(d) Discuss the difficulties of using life cycle costing techniques in an organisation with a heavy reliance on periodic reporting. **(6 marks)**

(Total marks = 25)

Question 36

It is usually of little advantage for a company to spend a considerable effort in developing and refining the product cost system for pricing purposes. Rather, the company should spend time and money on researching customer perceptions and requirements.

Requirements

Using the case of Sparkle presented in the scenario as an illustration, answer the following:

(a) Comment on the suitability of R Ltd's pricing policy. **(5 marks)**

(b) Discuss the opening statement. **(7 marks)**

(c) Prepare a memorandum to the chief executive of R Ltd outlining the benefits of target costing. Explain how it functions in relation both to new products and to existing products. **(13 marks)**

(Total marks = 25)

Question 37

LM Hospital is a private hospital, whose management is considering the adoption of an activity-based costing (ABC) system for next year. The main reason for its introduction would be to provide more accurate information for pricing purposes. With the adoption of new medical technology, the amount of time that some patients stay in hospital has decreased considerably, and the management feels that the current pricing strategy may no longer reflect the different costs incurred.

Prices are currently calculated by determining the direct costs for the particular type of operation and adding a mark-up of 135 per cent. With the proposed ABC system, the management expects to use a mark-up for pricing purposes of 15 per cent on cost. This percentage will be based on all costs except facility-sustaining costs. It has been decided that the hospital support activities should be grouped into three categories – admissions and record keeping, caring for patients, and facility sustaining.

The hospital has four operating theatres that are used for 9 hours a day for 300 days a year. It is expected that 7,200 operations will be performed during the coming year. The hospital has fifteen consultant surgeons engaged in operating theatre work and consultancy. It is estimated that each consultant surgeon will work at the hospital for 2,000 hours next year. The expected costs for next year are:

	£
Nursing services and administration	9,936,000
Linen and laundry	920,000
Kitchen and food costs (three meals a day)	2,256,000
Consultant surgeons' fees	5,250,000
Insurance of buildings and general equipment	60,000
Depreciation of buildings and general equipment	520,000
Operating theatre	4,050,000
Pre-operation costs	1,260,000
Medical supplies – used in the hospital wards	1,100,000
Pathology laboratory (where blood tests, etc., are carried out)	920,000
Updating patient records	590,000
Patient/bed scheduling	100,000
Invoicing and collections	160,000
Housekeeping activities, including ward maintenance, window cleaning, etc.	760,000

Other information for next year:

Nursing hours	480,000
Number of pathology laboratory tests	8,000
Patient days	44,000
Number of patients	9,600

Information relating to specific operations for next year:

	ENT (Ear, nose and throat)	Cataract
Time of stay in hospital	4 days	1 day
Operation time	2 hours	0.5 hour
Consultant surgeon's time (which includes time in the operating theatre)	3 hours	0.85 hour

Requirements

(a) Before making the final decision on the costing/pricing system, management has selected two types of operation for review: an ear, nose and throat (ENT) operation and a cataract operation.

   (i) Calculate the prices that would be charged under each method for the two types of operation. (Your answer should include an explanation and calculations of the cost drivers you have used.) **(10 marks)**

(ii) Comment on the results of your calculations and the implications for the proposed pricing policy. **(5 marks)**

(b) Critically assess the method you have used to calculate the ABC prices by selecting two items/categories above which you feel should have been dealt with in a different way. **(5 marks)**

(c) Explain whether the concept of throughput accounting could be used in a hospital. **(5 marks)**

(Total marks = 25)

Question 38

38.1 R Ltd is deciding whether to launch a new product. The initial outlay for the product is £20,000. The forecast possible annual cash inflows and their associated probabilities are shown below.

	Probability	Year 1	Year 2	Year 3
Optimistic	0.20	£10,000	£12,000	£9,000
Most likely	0.50	£7,000	£8,000	£7,600
Pessimistic	0.30	£6,400	£7,200	£6,200

The company's cost of capital is 10 per cent per annum.

Assume the cash inflows are received at the end of the year and that the cash inflows for each year are independent.

The expected net present value for the product is

(A) (£582)
(B) (£1,170)
(C) (£10,660)
(D) £10,430
(E) £22,286.

(3 marks)

38.2 A supermarket is trying to determine the optimal replacement policy for its fleet of delivery vehicles. The total purchase price of the fleet is £220,000.

The running costs and scrap values of the fleet at the end of each year are:

	Year 1	Year 2	Year 3	Year 4	Year 5
Running costs	£110,000	£132,000	£154,000	£165,000	£176,000
Scrap value	£121,000	£88,000	£66,000	£55,000	£25,000

The supermarket's cost of capital is 12 per cent per annum.
Ignore taxation and inflation.
The supermarket should replace its fleet of delivery vehicles at the end of

(A) Year 1
(B) Year 2
(C) Year 3
(D) Year 4
(E) Year 5.

(4 marks)

38.3 A company manufactures four products – J, K, L and M. The products use a series of different machines but there is a common machine, X, which causes a bottleneck.

The standard selling price and standard cost per unit for each product for the forthcoming year are as follows:

	J £	K £	L £	M £
Selling price	2,000	1,500	1,500	1,750
Cost:				
Direct materials	410	200	300	400
Labour	300	200	360	275
Variable overheads	250	200	300	175
Fixed overheads	360	300	210	330
Profit	680	600	330	570
Machine X – minutes per unit	120	100	70	110

Direct materials is the only unit-level manufacturing cost.

Using a throughput accounting approach, the ranking of the products would be:

	J	K	L	M
(A)	1st	2nd	3rd	4th
(B)	1st	2nd	4th	3rd
(C)	2nd	1st	4th	3rd
(D)	2nd	3rd	1st	4th
(E)	3rd	2nd	1st	4th

(3 marks)

38.4 In calculating the life cycle costs of a product, which of the following items would be included?

(i) Planning and concept design costs.
(ii) Preliminary and detailed design costs.
(iii) Testing costs.
(iv) Production costs.
(v) Distribution and customer service costs.

(A) All of the above
(B) (i) to (iv)
(C) (iii) to (v)
(D) (ii) to (iv)
(E) (ii) to (v).

(2 marks)

38.5 S Ltd manufactures components for the aircraft industry. The following annual information regarding three of its key customers is available:

	W	X	Y
Gross margin	£1,100,000	£1,750,000	£1,200,000
General administration costs	£40,000	£80,000	£30,000
Units sold	1,750	2,000	1,500
Orders placed	1,000	1,000	1,500
Sales visits	110	100	170
Invoices raised	900	1,200	1,500

The company uses an activity based costing system and the analysis of customer-related costs is as follows:

Sales visits	£500 per visit
Order processing	£100 per order placed
Despatch costs	£100 per order placed
Billing and collections	£175 per invoice raised

Using customer profitability analysis, the ranking of the customers would be:

	W	X	Y
(A)	1st	2nd	3rd
(B)	1st	3rd	2nd
(C)	2nd	1st	3rd
(D)	2nd	3rd	1st
(E)	3rd	2nd	1st

(4 marks)
(Total marks = 16)

Question 39

X Ltd manufactures and distributes three types of car (the C1, C2, and C3). Each type of car has its own production line. The company is worried by extremely difficult market conditions and forecasts losses for the forthcoming year.

Current operations
The budgeted details for next year are as follows:

	C1 £	C2 £	C3 £
Direct materials	2,520	2,924	3,960
Direct labour	1,120	1,292	1,980
Total direct cost per car	3,640	4,216	5,940
Budgeted production (cars)	75,000	75,000	75,000
Number of production runs	1,000	1,000	1,500
Number of orders executed	4,000	5,000	5,600
Machine hours	1,080,000	1,800,000	1,680,000

Annual overheads

	Fixed £000	Variable £
Sets ups	42,660	13,000 per production run
Materials handling	52,890	4,000 per order executed
Inspection	59,880	18,000 per production run
Machining	144,540	40 per machine hour
Distribution and warehousing	42,900	3,000 per order executed

Proposed JIT system
Management has hired a consultant to advise them on how to reduce costs. The consultant has suggested that the company adopts a just-in-time (JIT) manufacturing

system. The introduction of the JIT system would have the following impact on costs (fixed and variable):

Direct labour	Increase by 20%
Set ups	Decrease by 30%
Materials handling	Decrease by 30%
Inspection	Decrease by 30%
Machining	Decrease by 15%
Distribution and warehousing	Eliminated

Requirements

(a) Based on the budgeted production levels, calculate the total annual savings that would be achieved by introducing the JIT system. **(6 marks)**

The following table shows the price/demand relationship for each type of car per annum.

C1		C2		C3	
Price £	Demand	Price £	Demand	Price £	Demand
5,000	75,000	5,750	75,000	6,500	75,000
5,750	65,000	6,250	60,000	6,750	60,000
6,000	50,000	6,500	45,000	7,750	45,000
6,500	35,000	7,500	35,000	8,000	30,000

(b) Assuming that X Ltd adopts the JIT system that the revised variable overhead cost per car remains constant (as per the proposed JIT system budget), calculate the profit-maximising price and output level for each type of car. **(12 marks)**

Investigations have revealed that some of the fixed costs are directly attributable to the individual production lines and could be avoided if a line is closed down for the year. The specific fixed costs for each of the production lines, expressed as a percentage of the total fixed costs, are:

C1	4%
C2	5%
C3	8%

(c) Determine the optimum production plan for the forthcoming year (based on the JIT cost structure and the prices and output levels you recommended in answer to requirement (b)). **(4 marks)**

(d) Write a report to the management of X Ltd which explains the conditions that are necessary for the successful implementation of a JIT manufacturing system. **(8 marks)**

(Total marks = 30)

Question 40

CH Ltd is a swimming club. Potential exists to expand the business by providing a gymnasium as part of the facilities at the club. The Directors believe that this will stimulate additional membership of the club.

The expansion project would require an initial expenditure of £550,000. The project is expected to have a disposal value at the end of 5 years which is equal to 10 per cent of the initial expenditure.

The following schedule reflects a recent market research survey regarding the estimated annual sales revenue from additional memberships over the project's 5-year life:

Level of demand	£000	Probability
High	800	0.25
Medium	560	0.50
Low	448	0.25

It is expected that the contribution to sales ratio will be 55 per cent. Additional expenditure on fixed overheads is expected to be £90,000 per annum.

CH Ltd incurs a 30 per cent tax rate on corporate profits. Corporation tax is to be paid in two equal instalments: one in the year that profits are earned and the other in the following year.

CH Ltd's after-tax nominal (money) discount rate is 15.5 per cent per annum. A uniform inflation rate of 5 per cent per annum will apply to all costs and revenues during the life of the project.

All of the values above have been expressed in terms of current prices.

You can assume that all cash flows occur at the end of each year and that the initial investment does not qualify for capital allowances.

Requirements
(a) Evaluate the proposed expansion from a financial perspective. **(13 marks)**
(b) Calculate and then discuss the sensitivity of the project to changes in the expected annual contribution. **(5 marks)**

You have now been advised that the capital cost of the expansion will qualify for writing down allowances at the rate of 25 per cent per annum on a reducing balance basis. Also, at the end of the project's life, a balancing charge or allowance will arise equal to the difference between the scrap proceeds and the tax written down value.

(c) Calculate the financial impact of these allowances. **(7 marks)**

(Total marks = 25)

Question 41

P, a multinational organisation, is currently appraising a major capital investment project which will revolutionise its business. This investment involves the installation of an Intranet. [An Intranet is a private Internet reserved for use by employees and/or customers who have been given the authority and passwords necessary to use that network. It is a private network environment built around Internet technologies and standards.]

You have recently been appointed as the Management Accountant for this project and have been charged with the responsibility of preparing the financial evaluation of the proposed investment. You have carried out some initial investigations and find that management currently uses a target accounting rate of return of 25 per cent and a target payback period of 4 years as the criteria for the acceptance or rejection of major capital investments.

You propose to use the net present value method of project appraisal and, having carried out some further investigations, you ascertain the following information for the project:

	£000
Initial outlay	2,000
Cash savings:	
Years 1–3	400 per annum
Years 4–5	500 per annum
Years 6–8	450 per annum
Years 9–10	400 per annum

At the end of the project's life, no residual value is expected for the project.

The company's cost of capital is 15 per cent per annum. All cash savings are assumed to occur at the end of each year.

Ignore taxation and inflation.

Requirements

As Management Accountant for this project,

(a) write a report to the management of P which incorporates the following:
   (i) a full analysis and evaluation of the existing methods of project appraisal and of your proposed method of project appraisal;
   (ii) a recommendation on a purely financial basis as to whether or not the project should be undertaken;
   (iii) a discussion of the difficulties associated with the net present value method when appraising this type of investment; **(15 marks)**
(b) describe how you would undertake a post-completion appraisal for this project and discuss the benefits and drawbacks which the management of P might expect when undertaking such an exercise. **(10 marks)**
(Total marks = 25)

Question 42

42.1 BG plc has recently developed a new product. The nature of BG plc's work is repetitive, and it is usual for there to be an 80 per cent learning effect when a new product is developed. The time taken for the first unit was 22 minutes. Assuming that an 80 per cent learning effect applies, the time to be taken for the fourth unit is nearest to

(A) 9.91 minutes
(B) 9.97 minutes
(C) 14.08 minutes
(D) 15.45 minutes
(E) 17.60 minutes. **(3 marks)**

The following data relates to both questions 42.2 and 42.3

X Ltd can choose from five mutually exclusive projects. The projects will each last for 1 year only and their net cash inflows will be determined by the prevailing market conditions. The forecast annual cash inflows and their associated probabilities are shown below.

Market Conditions	Poor	Good	Excellent
Probability	0.20	0.50	0.30
	£000	£000	£000
Project L	500	470	550
Project M	400	550	570
Project N	450	400	475
Project O	360	400	420
Project P	600	500	425

42.2 Based on the expected value of the net cash inflows, which project should be undertaken?

(A) L
(B) M
(C) N
(D) O
(E) P.

(2 marks)

42.3 The value of perfect information about the state of the market is

(A) Nil
(B) £5,000
(C) £26,000
(D) £40,000
(E) £128,000.

(3 marks)

The following data relates to both Questions 42.4 and 42.5.

An education authority is considering the implementation of a CCTV (closed circuit television) security system in one of its schools.

Details of the proposed project are as follows:

Life of project	5 years
Initial cost	£75,000
Annual Savings:	
Labour costs	£20,000
Others costs	£5,000
Cost of capital	15% per annum

42.4 The internal rate of return for this project is nearest to

(A) 10.13 per cent
(B) 14.87 per cent
(C) 15.64 per cent
(D) 19.88 per cent
(E) 20.13 per cent.

(2 marks)

42.5 The percentage change in the annual labour cost savings that could occur before the project ceased to be viable is

(A) 10.50 per cent
(B) 11.73 per cent
(C) 13.13 per cent
(D) 35.20 per cent
(E) 44.00 per cent.

(3 marks)
(Total marks = 13)

Question 43

Just over 2 years ago, R Ltd was the first company to produce a specific 'off-the-shelf' accounting software packages. The pricing strategy, decided on by the Managing Director, for the packages was to add a 50 per cent mark-up to the budgeted full cost of the packages. The company achieved and maintained a significant market share and high profits for the first 2 years.

Budgeted information for the current year (year 3) was as follows:

Production and sales   15,000 packages
Full cost   £400 per package

At a recent Board meeting, the Finance Director reported that although costs were in line with the budget for the current year, profits were declining. He explained that the full cost included £80 for fixed overheads. This figure had been calculated by using an overhead absorption rate based on labour hours and the budgeted level of production which, he pointed out, was much lower than the current capacity of 25,000 packages.

The Marketing Director stated that competitors were beginning to increase their market share. He also reported the results of a recent competitor analysis which showed that when R Ltd announced its prices for the current year, the competitors responded by undercutting them by 15 per cent. Consequently, he commissioned an investigation of the market. He informed the Board that the market research showed that at a price of £750 there would be no demand for the packages but for every £10 reduction in price the demand would increase by 1,000 packages.

The Managing Director appeared to be unconcerned about the loss of market share and argued that profits could be restored to their former level by increasing the mark-up.

Note: If price = $a - bx$ then marginal revenue = $a - 2bx$

Requirements

(a) Discuss the Managing Director's pricing strategy in the circumstances described above. Your appraisal must include a discussion of the alternative strategies that could have been implemented at the launch of the packages. **(10 marks)**

(b) (i) Based on the data supplied by the market research, calculate the maximum annual profit that can be earned from the sale of the packages from year 3 onwards.

(6 marks)

(ii) A German computer software distribution company, L, which is interested in becoming the sole distributor of the accounting software packages, has now approached R Ltd. It has offered to purchase 25,000 accounting packages per annum at a fixed price of €930 per package. If R Ltd were to sell the packages to L, then the variable costs would be £300 per package.

The current exchange rate is €1 = £0.60.

Requirements

Draw a diagram to illustrate the sensitivity of the proposal from the German company to changes in the exchange rate and then state and comment on the minimum exchange rate needed for the proposal to be worthwhile. **(7 marks)**

(c) R Ltd has signed a contract with L to supply the accounting packages. However, there has been a fire in one of the software manufacturing departments and a machine has been seriously damaged and requires urgent replacement.

The replacement machine will cost £1m and R Ltd is considering whether to lease or buy the machine. A lease could be arranged under which R Ltd would pay £300,000 per annum for 4 years with each payment being made annually in advance. The lease payments would be an allowable expense for taxation purposes.

Corporation tax is payable at the rate of 30 per cent per annum in two equal instalments: one in the year that profits are earned and the other in the following year. Writing-down allowances are allowed at 25 per cent each year on a reducing balance basis. It is anticipated that the machine will have a useful economic life of 4 years, at the end of which there will be no residual value.

The after-tax cost of capital is 12 per cent.

Requirement

Evaluate the acquisition of the new machine from a financial viewpoint. **(7 marks)**
(Total marks = 30)

Question 44

All of the 100 accountants employed by X Ltd are offered the opportunity to attend six training courses per year. Each course lasts for several days and requires the delegates to travel to a specially selected hotel for the training. The current costs incurred for each course are:

Delegate costs:

	£ per delegate per course
Travel	200
Accommodation, food and drink	670
	870

It is expected that the current delegate costs will increase by 5% per annum.

Course costs:

	£ per course
Room hire	1,500
Trainers	6,000
Course material	2,000
Equipment hire	1,500
Course administration	750
	11,750

It is expected that the current course costs will increase by 2.5 per cent per annum.

The Human Resources Director of X Ltd is concerned at the level of costs that these courses incur and has recently read an article about the use of the Internet for the delivery of training courses (e-learning). She decided to hire an external consultant at a cost of

£5,000 to advise the company on how to implement an e-learning solution. The consultant prepared a report which detailed the costs of implementing and running an e-learning solution:

	Notes	£	
Computer hardware	(1)	1,500,000	
Software licences	(2)	35,000	per annum
Technical Manager	(3)	30,000	per annum
Camera and sound crew	(4)	4,000	per course
Trainers and course material	(5)	2,000	per course
Broadband connection	(6)	300	per delegate per annum

Notes

(1) The computer hardware will be depreciated on a straight-line basis over 5 years. The scrap value at the end of the five years is expected to be £50,000.
(2) The company would sign a software licence agreement which fixes the annual software licence fee for 5 years. This fee is payable in advance.
(3) An employee working in the IT Department currently earning £20,000 per annum will be promoted to Technical Manager for this project. This employee's position will be replaced. The salary of the Technical Manager is expected to increase by 6 per cent per annum.
(4) The company supplying the camera and sound crew for recording the courses for Internet delivery has agreed to hold its current level of pricing for the first 2 years but then will increase costs by 6 per cent per annum. All courses will be recorded in the first quarter of the year of delivery.
(5) The trainers will charge a fixed fee of £2,000 per course for the delivery and course material in the first year and expect to increase this by 6 per cent per annum thereafter. The preparation of the course material and the recording of the trainers delivering the courses will take place in the first quarter of the year of delivery.
(6) All of the accountants utilising the training courses will be offered £300 towards broadband costs which will allow them to access the courses from home. They will claim this expense annually in arrears. Broadband costs are expected to decrease by 5 per cent per annum after the first year as it becomes more widely used by Internet users.

X Ltd uses a 14 per cent cost of capital to appraise projects of this nature.
Ignore taxation.

Requirements

As the Management Accountant for X Ltd,

(a) prepare a financial evaluation of the options available to the company and advise the directors on the best course of action to take, from a purely financial point of view;
(Your answer should state any assumption you have made.) **(16 marks)**
(b) (i) using the annual equivalent technique, calculate the breakeven number of delegates per annum taking each of the six e-learning courses that is required to justify the implementation of the e-learning solution;
(Note that you should assume that the number of delegates taking the e-learning courses will be the same in each of the 5 years.) **(6 marks)**
(ii) comment on the implications of the breakeven number you have calculated in your answer to (b) (i). **(3 marks)**
(Total marks = 25)

Question 45

The management team of T Ltd, a small venture capital company, is planning its investment activities for the next five years. It has been approached by four start-up companies from the same industry sector which have presented their business plans for consideration. The forecast cash flows and resulting net present values (NPV) for each start-up company are as follows:

Company	Capital Year 0	Operational cash flows					NPV
		Year 1	Year 2	Year 3	Year 4	Year 5	
	$000	$000	$000	$000	$000	$000	$000
A	(500)	(75)	(40)	50	400	650	60
B	(250)	(30)	(20)	(5)	250	247	0
C	(475)	(100)	(30)	(20)	400	750	77
D	(800)	(150)	(50)	50	900	786	80

The directors of T Ltd use a 12 per cent cost of capital for appraising this type of investment. You can assume that all investments are divisible and that they are not mutually exclusive. Ignore tax and inflation.

Requirements

(a) Advise T Ltd which of the investments, if any, it should invest in. **(3 marks)**
(b) If capital for investment now is limited to $700,000 but T Ltd can raise further capital in one year's time and thereafter at a cost of 12 per cent per annum,
   (i) advise T Ltd how it should invest the $700,000; **(5 marks)**
   (ii) discuss other factors which may affect the decision. **(4 marks)**
(c) T Ltd has now found out that funds will also be restricted in future years and that the constraints are absolute and cannot be removed by project generated incomes. The present values of cash that will be available for future investment are as follows:

	Present value $000
Year 0	700
Year 1	80
Year 2	35

Requirement

Formulate the linear programming model that will maximise net present value and explain the meaning of each variable and the purpose of each constraint you have identified. *(You are not required to attempt a solution.)* **(10 marks)**

(d) Briefly explain the benefits of using a linear programming format in this situation.
(3 marks)
(Total marks = 25)

 ## Question 46

(a) The CS group is planning its annual marketing conference for its sales executives and has approached the VBJ Holiday company (VBJ) to obtain a quotation.

VBJ has been trying to win the business of the CS group for some time and is keen to provide a quotation which the CS group will find acceptable in the hope that this will lead to future contracts.

The manager of VBJ has produced the following cost estimate for the conference:

	$
Coach running costs	2,000
Driver costs	3,000
Hotel costs	5,000
General overheads	2,000
Sub total	12,000
Profit (30%)	3,600
Total	15,600

You have considered this cost estimate but you believe that it would be more appropriate to base the quotation on relevant costs. You have therefore obtained the following further information:

Coach running costs represent the fuel costs of $1,500 plus an apportionment of the annual fixed costs of operating the coach. No specific fixed costs would be incurred if the coach is used on this contract. If the contract did not go ahead, the coach would not be in use for eight out of the ten days of the conference. For the other two days a contract has already been accepted which contains a significant financial penalty clause. This contract earns a contribution of $250 per day. A replacement coach could be hired for $180 per day.

Driver costs represent the salary and related employment costs of one driver for 10 days. If the driver is used on this contract the company will need to replace the driver so that VBJ can complete its existing work. The replacement driver would be hired from a recruitment agency that charges $400 per day for a suitably qualified driver.

Hotel costs are the expected costs of hiring the hotel for the conference.

General overheads are based upon the overhead absorption rate of VBJ and are set annually when the company prepares its budgets. The only general overhead cost that can be specifically identified with the conference is the time that has been spent in considering the costs of the conference and preparing the quotation. This amounted to $250.

Required:
Prepare a statement showing the total relevant cost of the contract. Explain clearly the reasons for each of the values in your quotation and for excluding any of the costs (if appropriate). **(10 marks)**

(b) Now that the quotation has been prepared, it is realised that there is some uncertainty concerning the hotel and the fuel cost. Further investigation has shown that these costs may be higher or lower than the original estimates. Estimated costs with their associated probabilities are as follows:

Estimated hotel cost ($)	Probability %	Estimated fuel cost ($)	Probability %
4,000	20	1,200	10
5,000	50	1,500	50
6,000	30	2,000	40

The following two-way data table shows the effect on the total relevant cost of these alternative values. All figures are in $:

		Hotel		
		$4,000	$5,000	$6,000
	$1,200	−1,300	−300	+700
Fuel	$1,500	−1,0000	0	+1,000
	$2,000	−500	+500	+1,500

Required:

(i) Explain the meaning of the above two-way data table.

(ii) Produce and interpret a table that shows how the two-way data table may be used in conjunction with the probabilities to improve the information available to the manager of VBJ. **(15 marks)**

(Total for Question Six = 25 marks)

Question 47

(a) The Q organisation is a large, worldwide respected manufacturer of consumer electrical and electronic goods. Q constantly develops new products that are in high demand as they represent the latest technology and are "must haves" for those consumers that want to own the latest consumer gadgets. Recently Q has developed a new handheld digital DVD recorder and seeks your advice as to the price it should charge for such a technologically advanced product.

Required:

Explain the relevance of the product life cycle to the consideration of alternative pricing policies that might be adopted by Q. **(10 marks)**

(b) Market research has discovered that the price demand relationship for the item during the initial launch phase will be as follows:

Price (£)	Demand (units)
100	10,000
80	20,000
69	30,000
62	40,000

Production of the DVD recorder would occur in batches of 10,000 units, and the production director believes that 50% of the variable manufacturing cost would be affected by a learning and experience curve. This would apply to each batch produced and continue at a constant rate of learning up to a production volume of 40,000 units when the learning would be complete. Thereafter, the unit variable manufacturing cost of the product would be equal to the unit cost of the fourth batch. The production director estimates that the unit variable manufacturing cost of the first batch would be £60 (£30 of which is subject to the effect of the learning and experience curve, and £30 of which is unaffected), whereas the average unit variable manufacturing cost of all four batches would be £52.71.

There are no-manufacturing variable costs associated with the DVD recorder.

Required:
(i) Calculate the rate of learning that is expected by the production director.
(4 marks)
(ii) Calculate the optimum price at which Q should sell the DVD recorder in order to maximise its profits during the initial launch phase of the product. **(8 marks)**
(iii) Q expects that after the initial launch phase the market price will be £57 per unit. Estimated product specific fixed costs during this phase of the product's life are expected to be £15,000 per month. During this phase of the product life cycle Q wishes to achieve a target monthly profit from the product of £30,000.

Calculate the number of units that need to be sold each month during this phase in order that Q achieves this target monthly profit. **(3 marks)**
(Total for Question Seven = 25 marks)

(Total for Section C = 50 marks)

Question 48

KL manufactures three products, W, X and Y. Each product uses the same materials and the same type of direct labour but in different quantities. The company currently uses a cost plus basis to determine the selling price of its products. This is based on full cost using an overhead absorption rate per direct labour hour. However, the Managing Director is concerned that the company may be losing sales because of its approach to setting prices. He thinks that a marginal costing approach may be more appropriate, particularly since the workforce is guaranteed a minimum weekly wage and has a three month notice period.

Required:
(a) Given the Managing Director's concern about KL's approach to setting selling prices, discuss the advantages and disadvantages of marginal cost plus pricing **AND** total cost plus pricing. **(6 marks)**

The direct costs of the three products are shown below:

Product	W	X	Y
Budgeted annual production (units)	15,000	24,000	20,000
	$ per unit	$ per unit	$ per unit
Direct materials	35	45	30
Direct labour ($10 per hour)	40	30	50

In addition to the above direct costs, KL incurs annual indirect production costs of $1,044,000.

> *Required*:
> (b) Calculate the full cost per unit of each product using KL's current method of absorption costing. **(4 marks)**

An analysis of the company's indirect production costs shows the following:

	$	Cost driver
Material ordering costs	220,000	Number of supplier orders
Machine setup costs	100,000	Number of batches
Machine running costs	400,000	Number of machine hours
General facility costs	324,000	Number of machine hours

The following additional data relate to each product:

Product	W	X	Y
Machine hours per unit	5	8	7
Batch size (units)	500	400	1,000
Supplier orders per batch	4	3	5

> *Required*:
> (c) Calculate the full cost per unit of each product using Activity Based Costing. **(8 marks)**
>
> (d) Explain how Activity Based Costing could provide information that would be relevant to the management team when it is making decisions about how to improve KL's profitability. **(7 marks)**
>
> **(Total for Question Five = 25 marks)**

Question 49

A theatre has a seating capacity of 500 people and is considering engaging MS and her orchestra for a concert for one night only. The fee that would be charged by MS would be $10,000. If the theatre engages MS, then this sum is payable regardless of the size of the theatre audience.

Based on past experience of events of this type, the price of the theatre ticket would be $25 per person. The size of the audience for this event is uncertain, but based on past experience it is expected to be as follows:

	Probability
300 people	50%
400 people	30%
500 people	20%

In addition to the sale of the theatre tickets, it can be expected that members of the audience will also purchase confectionery both prior to the performance and during the interval. The contribution that this would yield to the theatre is unclear, but has been estimated as follows:

Contribution from confectionery sales	Probability
Contribution of $3 per person	30%
Contribution of $5 per person	50%
Contribution of $10 per person	20%

Required:
(a) Using expected values as the basis of your decision, advise the theatre management whether it is financially worthwhile to engage MS for the concert.
(5 marks)
(b) Prepare a two-way data table to show the profit values that could occur from deciding to engage MS for the concert. (5 marks)
(c) Explain, using the probabilities provided and your answer to (b) above, how the two-way data table can be used by the theatre management to evaluate the financial risks of the concert, including the probability of making a profit.
(9 marks)
(d) Calculate the maximum price that the theatre management should agree to pay for perfect information relating to the size of the audience and the level of contribution from confectionery sales. (6 marks)
(Total for Question Six = 25 marks)

Question 50

JK plc prepares its accounts to 31 December each year. It is considering investing in a new computer controlled production facility on 1 January 2007 at a cost of £50 m. This will enable JK plc to produce a new product which it expects to be able to sell for four years. At the end of this time it has been agreed to sell the new production facility for £1 m cash.

Sales of the product during the year ended 31 December 2007 and the next three years are expected to be as follows:

Year ended 31 December	2007	2008	2009	2010
Sales units (000)	100	105	110	108

Selling price, unit variable cost and fixed overhead costs (excluding depreciation) are expected to be as follows during the year ended 31 December 2007:

	£
Selling price per unit	1,200
Variable production cost per unit	750
Variable selling and distribution cost per unit	100
Fixed production cost for the year	4,000,000
Fixed selling and distribution cost for the year	2,000,000
Fixed administration cost for the year	1,000,000

The following rates of annual inflation are expected for each of the years 2008–2010:

	%
Selling prices	5
Production costs	8
Selling and distribution costs	6
Administration costs	5

The company pays taxation on its profits at the rate of 30%, with half of this being payable in the year in which the profit is earned and the remainder being payable in the following year. Investments of this type qualify for tax depreciation at the rate of 25% per annum on a reducing balance basis.

The Board of Directors of JK plc has agreed to use a 12% post-tax discount rate to evaluate this investment.

> *Required*:
> (a) Advise JK pic whether the investment is financially worthwhile.
> (17 marks)
> (b) Calculate the Internal Rate of Return of the investment. (3 marks)
> (c) Define and contrast *(i)* the real rate of return and *(ii)* the money rate of return, and explain how they would be used when calculating the net present value of a project's cash flows. (5 marks)
> **(Total for Question Seven = 25 marks)**

Solutions to Revision Questions

✓ Solution 1

1.1 Answer: (D)

	Fixed £	Variable £/unit
Direct material – the cost per unit is constant so this is a variable cost		4.00
Direct labour – the cost per unit is constant so this is a variable cost		3.50
Production overhead:		
Department 1		
1,000 units, total cost	6,000	
2,000 units, total cost	8,400	
Using high/low method, 1,000 units	2,400	2.40
and, by substitution: £6,000 − (1,000 × £2.40)	3,600	
Department 2		
Since total cost for 1,000 units is equal to that for 2,000 units, this is a fixed cost	4,000	
	7,600	9.90

1.2 Answer: (D)

An increase in quality standards is one of the key factors that allows the other items listed to be reduced.

1.3 Answer: (B)

1.4 Answer: (B)

1.5 Answer: (B)

A notional cost is one which does not involve a flow of funds, which is used for comparison of performance.

A relevant cost is one appropriate to a decision being made.

A controllable cost is one which may be controlled by the person to whom the cost is being reported.

An indirect cost is a cost which cannot be economically attributed to the cost unit.

1.6 Answer: (C)

Answer (A) is the cost of modification.

Answer (B) is the scrap value of the material and is relevant if there is no higher relevant cost.

Answer (D) is the historical cost of material V and is therefore irrelevant. The correct answer is (C):

	£
Cost of alternative material avoided by using V (2 kg × £4.50)	9.00
Modification cost of V (3 kg × £1)	3.00
NET SAVING (per unit of QX)	6.00
Saving per kg of V (£6.00 ÷ 3)	2.00

1.7 Answer: (D)

$$\frac{\text{Selling price} - \text{material cost}}{\text{Time on bottleneck resource}} = \frac{£24.99 - £8.87}{6.5} \times 60 = £148.80.$$

1.8 Answer: (A)

1.9 Answer: (A)

1.10 Answer: (A)

One hundred per cent capacity gives £21,000 contribution – hence 1 per cent capacity gives £210 contribution and 66.66 per cent capacity (that is £14,000/£210) is needed to achieve breakeven.

1.11 Answer: (B)

Solution 2

(a) (i) *Cost analysis*

	North £000	Central £000	South £000
Variable (units)			
Direct materials	500	1,000	750
Direct wages	800	1,600	1,200
Indirect materials	300	600	450.5
Indirect wages	50	150	150
Indirect expenses	350	600	300
	2,000	3,950	2,850.5
Fixed – avoidable			
Indirect materials	75	200	79.5
Indirect wages	200	850	600
Indirect expenses	650	1,400	450
Administration	100	150	50
	1,025	2,600	1,179.5
Variable production cost/unit (£)	20.00	19.75	19.00
Transport cost/unit (£)	5.00	4.00	5.00

(ii) There are six options available. Each option considers the closure of one factory and the relocation of the required production at the remaining factories, in such a way that production is at maximum capacity at one factory, as shown by the following table:

	North units	%	Central units	%	South units	%
Capacity	160,000		250,000		180,000	
1999 activity	100,000		200,000		150,000	
Option (i)	Nil	0	250,000	100	65,000	36
Option (ii)	Nil	0	135,000	54	180,000	100
Option (iii)	160,000	100	Nil	0	155,000	86
Option (iv)	135,000	84	Nil	0	180,000	100
Option (v)	160,000	100	155,000	62	Nil	0
Option (vi)	65,000	41	250,000	100	Nil	0

The costs of each option (£000) are:

Option		North	Central	South	Total
(i)	Variable	Nil	5,937.5	1,560.0	
	Fixed	Nil	5,200.0	1,179.5	
		Nil	11,137.5	2,739.5	13,877
(ii)	Variable	Nil	3,206.25	4,320.0	
	Fixed	Nil	2,600.00	2,359.0	
		Nil	5,806.25	6,679.0	12,485.25
(iii)	Variable	4,000	Nil	3,720.0	
	Fixed	2,050	Nil	1,651.3	
		6,050	Nil	5,371.3	11,421.3
(iv)	Variable	3,375	Nil	4,320.0	
	Fixed	1,025	Nil	2,359.0	
		4,400	Nil	6,679.0	11,079
(v)	Variable	4,000	3,681.25	Nil	
	Fixed	2,050	2,600.00	Nil	
		6,050	6,281.25	Nil	12,331.25
(vi)	Variable	1,625	5,937.5	Nil	
	Fixed	1,025	5,200.0	Nil	
		2,650	11,137.5	Nil	13,787.5

As can be seen from the above, the lowest cost option is option (iv), which is to close the Central factory, maximise capacity at the South factory and increase production at the North factory.

(b) **Memorandum**

To: Production Controller
From: Management Accountant
Subject: Reduction in activity levels
Date: 5 February 2000

Further to our discussions, the cost analysis shows that the largest cost saving is achieved by closing Central and relocating 35,000 units of activity to North and 30,000 to South. Other factors to consider include the following:

- South would be operating at maximum capacity;
- more employees would have to be recruited at North and at South;
- Central employees may relocate;
- employee morale may be reduced if employees believe that profit is the only factor that we consider;

- the closure of Central removes our largest production facility: if demand increases in future we might not be able to satisfy it;
- production methods could be changed;
- the product could be re-engineered;
- there may be costs associated with the closure of Central.

Solution 3

3.1 *For 4 units*
$$Y = ax^{-b}$$
$$Y = 18 \times 4^{-0.3219}$$
$$= 11.52 \text{ minutes}$$

For 5 units
$$Y = ax^{-b}$$
$$Y = 18 \times 5^{-0.3219}$$
$$= 10.72 \text{ minutes}$$

Total times
5 units @ 10.72 minutes = 53.61 minutes
4 units @ 11.52 minutes = 46.08 minutes

Fifth unit only   7.53 minutes

Therefore the answer is (B)

3.2

Cost driver rate
  Budgeted cost
  Budgeted number of orders $\dfrac{£94{,}690}{2{,}785} = £34$ each order

Actual costs incurred   £7,318
Costs recovered:
202 orders × £34   £6,868
Under recovery   450

Therefore the answer is (D)

3.3 The answer is (A).

3.4

Product	M1 £/unit	M2 £/unit	M3 £/unit	M4 £/unit
Conversion costs:				
Total	39	52	57	43
Fixed	(16)	(16)	(15)	(18)
Variable	23	36	42	25
Materials	16	22	34	20
Total variable cost	39	58	76	45
Selling price	70	92	113	83
Contribution	31	34	37	38
Materials each unit	£16.00	£22.00	£34.00	£20.00
Contribution each £1 of material	£1.94	£1.55	£1.09	£1.90
Ranking	1st	3rd	4th	2nd

Therefore the answer is (A)

Solution 4

Requirement (a)

The contribution can be calculated:

Computer	X	Y
	£	£
Selling price	800	1,200
Per unit		
Components	150	310
Assembly	240	390
Testing	120	180
Packaging	20	10
	530	890
Contribution per unit	270	310

Requirement (b)

The following formulae are appropriate for the solution:

Constraints

$$80x + 130y = 60,000$$
$$120x + 180y = 52,000$$
$$0 \leq x \leq 300$$
$$0 \leq y \leq 800$$

Objective function

$$270x + 310y = C$$

For graphical solution, see overleaf. Graphs should show answers approximating to

    X 300 units
    Y 92 units

(the value of Y could vary depending on graphical accuracy, as the mathematical solution is $X = 300$, $Y = 91.667$)

Product contributions	£
X	81,000
Y	28,520
Total =	109,520

(The mathematical solution is £109,416.667)

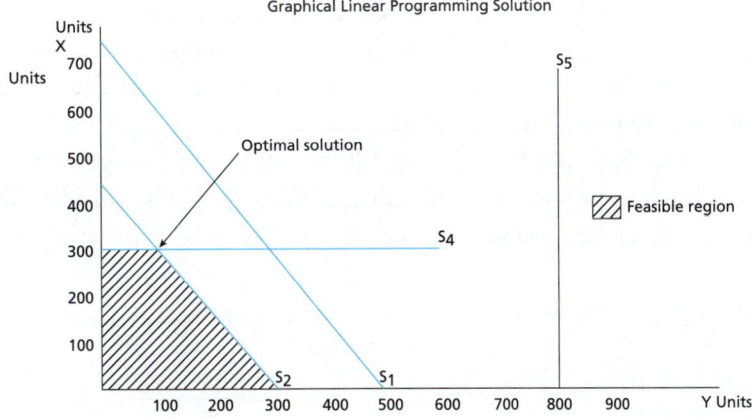

Graphical Linear Programming Solution

Requirement (c)

Report

To: Management Team
From: Management Accountant
Date: 21 November 2001
Subject: Budgeted activity for the 6 months to 30 June 2002

Introduction

Further to our recent meeting, I have considered the implications of the possible shortage of hours in the packaging facility and determined its effect. The results of my findings are summarised below.

Findings

The introduction of the packaging time constraint reduces the budgeted contribution from £109,520 (whole numbers of products) to £107,438. This shows that the packaging time is an effective constraint.

The optimal activity solution shows that we should produce 269 units of computer X and 112 units of computer Y, which results in unsatisfied demand of 31 units of computer X and 688 units of computer Y.

There is a surplus of 23,875 assembly minutes, but there is a shortage of **both** testing time and packaging time. If these could be changed then each extra testing minute would yield an increase in contribution of £1.46 and each extra packaging minute would yield an increase in contribution of £4.75.

Conclusion

We need to consider the alternative use of the assembly workers. If they could be used to test and package the products, after receiving appropriate training, then this would utilise our spare resource and reduce/eliminate our capacity problems.

Signed: Management Accountant.

Requirement (d)

The testing time is one of the factors that limit the activity level of the company. The senior test engineer's statement suggests that the learning period is now ended, but any reduction in the test times taken will affect the solution that has been derived above.

With an 90 per cent learning curve, the average time taken per unit is reduced by 10 per cent each time the cumulative output is doubled so if the original target times are now out of date because of this learning factor, that will affect the possible level of activity. For example, if the time for each unit is based on an initial unit and 128 units were completed before the learning ended, the unit times for X would reduce from 120 minutes to an average of 57.4 minutes with the last unit in the learning period taking 49 minutes. Clearly, this is considerably less than the times allowed for in the earlier calculations, and similar factors will also apply to computer Y.

Solution 5

(a)

Month	Batches		Standard Hours	Actual hours	
	This month	To date	This month	This month	To date
Nov	1	1	50	50	50
Dec	1	2	50	33	83
Jan	2	4	100	54.78	137.78
Feb	4	8	200	91.07	228.85
Mar	8	16	400	228.85	457.70
Apr	16	32	800	457.70	915.40

Month	Average actual hours per batch (year to date)	Comment
Nov	50	
Dec	41.5	83% of November average
Jan	34.445	83% of December average
Feb	28.61	83% of January average
Mar	28.61	100% of February average
Apr	28.61	100% of March average

The learning period ends at the end of month 4; the rate of learning is 83%. This means that subsequent to February the time taken per batch is constant or steady state and therefore decisions involving costs such as profit maximisation and pricing should be based on this constant labour time per batch.

(b) The marginal cost and selling price per batch are as follows:

Marginal cost = £672.72
Demand at price of £1,200 = 16 batches and demand increases by 1 unit for every £20 reduction in selling price.
Therefore, Price = £1,520 − 20q
Marginal Revenue = £1,520 − 40q

Equating marginal cost and marginal revenue:

$672.72 = 1,520 - 40q$
$40q = 847.28$
$q = 21.182$
Price = £1,520 − (20 × 21.182) = £1,096.36

(c) (i) A standard cost is an expected cost based on a measurement of the resources required to deliver a unit of a product or service and the prices expected to be paid for each unit of the resource. It is used as part of a Standard Costing system to control the costs incurred by an organisation.

A target cost is a cost to be achieved by a series of changes so as to achieve a target profit. It is used as part of Target Costing – a technique that identifies the market price of a product or service and determines the target cost to be achieved in order to earn a target profit.

Thus a target cost is driven by an external market price which is not controllable by the organisation whereas a standard cost is an internal control mechanism.

536 SOLUTIONS TO REVISION QUESTIONS P2

(ii) Now that the product has been in the market place for six months it is no longer unique as competitors have been able to purchase the product and reverse engineer it to determine how it works. As a consequence AVX Plc is probably facing competition and hence its difficulty in selling the circuit boards for £1,200 per batch. AVX Plc is no longer able to set its own prices without regard for the actions of its competitors; as a result they have to accept the market price.

Solution 6

(a)

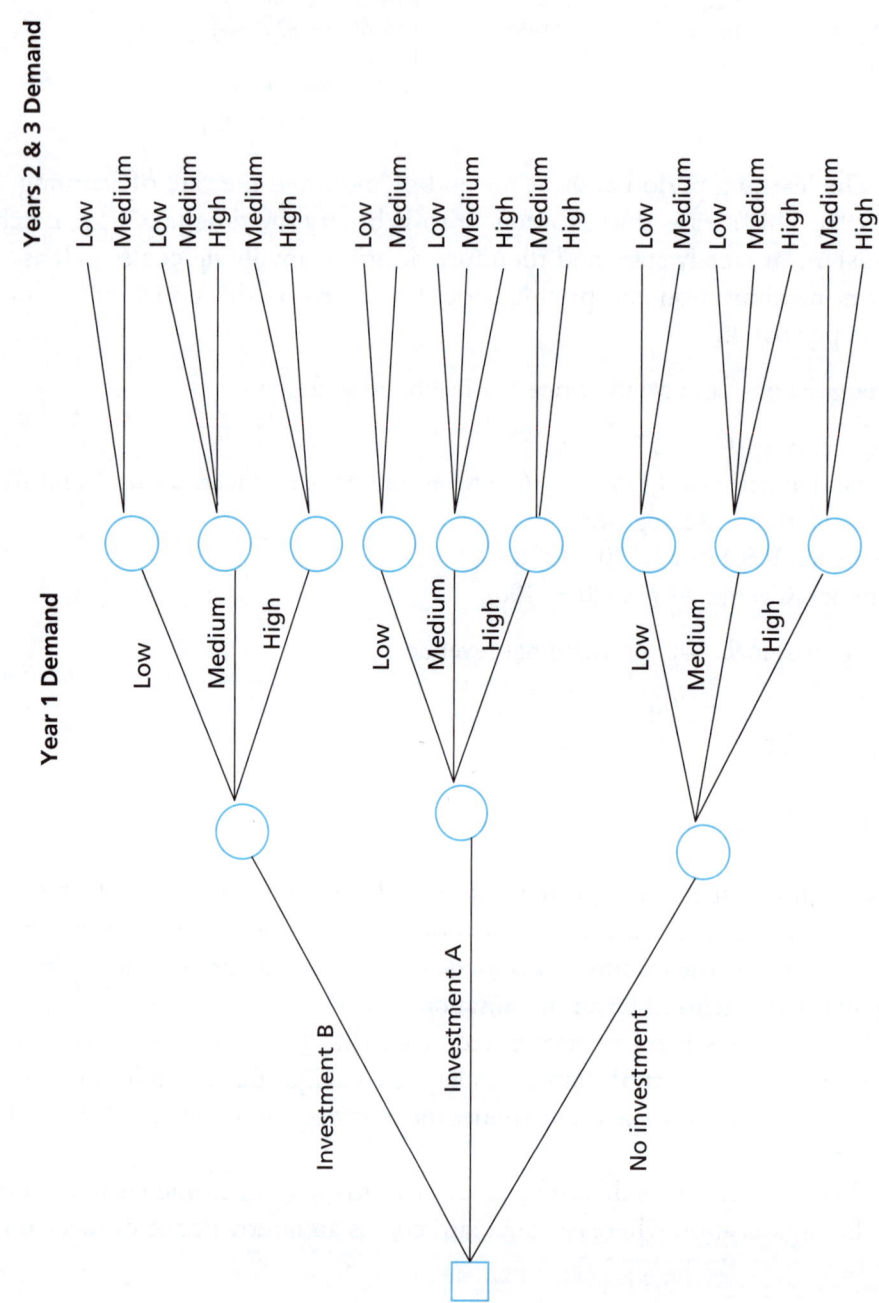

(b)
Investment in Facility B

Year 0 cost		£800,000	£800,000
Year 1 expected cost:			
Low	30% × £300,000 =	£90,000	
Medium	50% × £350,000 =	£175,000	
High	20% × £400,000 =	£80,000	
		£345,000	£345,000
Years 2 & 3 expected cost per year:			
Low	27% × £300,000 =	£81,000	
Medium	44% × £350,000 =	£154,000	
High	29% × £400,000 =	£116,000	
		£351,000	× 2 years = £702,000
Total present value of cost			**£1,847,000**

Investment in Facility A

Year 0 cost		£500,000	£500,000
Year 1 expected cost:			
Low	30% × £250,000 =	£75,000	
Medium	50% × £350,000 =	£175,000	
High	20% × £500,000 =	£100,000	
		£350,000	£350,000
Years 2 & 3 expected cost per year:			
Low	27% × £250,000 =	£67,500	
Medium	44% × £350,000 =	£154,000	
High	29% × £500,000 =	£145,000	
		£366,500	× 2 years = £733,000
Total present value of cost			**£1,583,000**

No further investment

Year 1 expected cost:			
Low	30% × £300,000 =	£90,000	
Medium	50% × £400,000 =	£200,000	
High	20% × £550,000 =	£110,000	
		£400,000	£400,000
Years 2 & 3 expected cost per year:			
Low	27% × £300,000 =	£81,000	
Medium	44% × £400,000 =	£176,000	
High	29% × £550,000 =	£159,500	
		£416,500	× 2 years = £833,000
Total present value of cost			**£1,233,000**

Note: Calculation of probabilities for years 2 and 3

Year 1 demand	Year 2 and 3 demand		Probability	
Low	Low	0.3 × 0.4	0.12	
Medium	Low	0.5 × 0.3	0.15	
High	Low	0.2 × 0.0	0.00	**Total 0.27**
Low	Medium	0.3 × 0.6	0.18	
Medium	Medium	0.5 × 0.4	0.20	
High	Medium	0.2 × 0.3	0.06	**Total 0.44**
Low	High	0.3 × 0.0	0.00	
Medium	High	0.5 × 0.3	0.15	
High	High	0.2 × 0.7	0.14	**Total 0.29**

On purely financial grounds, using the expected cost basis, no further investment should be undertaken.

(c) By not undertaking further investment to increase the ability of the health clinic to service the increasing levels of demand the manager is becoming reliant on the use of other facilities that are not within her direct control. This could lead to a number of problems concerning the quality of the services provided, the reliability of the external service provision, and the vulnerability of the health clinic to increasing fees being charged by the external facility providers.

Furthermore the employees of the health clinic may become less motivated as they see that there is a tendency to utilise external facilities rather than invest within the business. This may illustrate a tendency towards short-term cost control to the detriment of the operation of the health clinic in the longer term.

Solution 7

(a) Relevant contribution per unit

Product	G	H	J	K
	$	$	$	$
Selling Price	10.00	20.00	15.00	30.00
Relevant costs:				
Direct Material A	4.20	5.60	2.10	8.40
Direct Material B	2.00	2.00	4.50	12.00
Direct labour	2.00	8.00	7.50	3.00
Overhead	1.00	3.00	3.00	3.00
	9.20	18.60	17.10	26.40
Relevant contribution	0.80	1.40	(2.10)	3.60
Relevant contribution per $ of Material B	0.40	0.70	(0.47)	0.30

(b) If the contract were not to be completed the material B released would be as follows:

Product	Units	Material B (kgs) per unit	Total (kg)
G	500	0.20	100
H	1,600	0.20	320
J	800	0.45	360
K	400	1.20	480
Total material B released			**1,260**

Products G and H are already being manufactured to satisfy all of the market demand, and product J has a negative relevant contribution per unit so no further production of product J is worthwhile. Therefore the resources released would be used to increase the production of product K.

The non contract demand for product K is 4,000 units of which 1,983 units are currently unsatisfied (4,000 − 2,017). These 1,983 units would require more material B than is released from the contract so the maximum additional units of product K that could be manufactured is 1,050 units.

The relevant contribution that would be earned from 1,050 units of product K is $3,780 (1,050 × $3.60) whereas the contract yields a gross contribution of $2,400 (see below).

Product	Units	Contribution per unit ($)	Total ($)
G	500	0.80	400
H	1,600	1.40	2,240
J	800	(2.10)	(1,680)
K	400	3.60	1,440
Total			**2,400**

From this $1,000 specific fixed cost must be deducted as this would be avoided if product J were not produced so the net relevant contribution from the contract is $1,400. Therefore if the penalty were to be $2,380, the relevant contribution from the additional units of product K less the penalty that would then be payable would be the same as the net relevant contribution from the contract.

(c) The contribution to sales (C/S) ratios of each of the four products based on their relevant contributions is:

G 8%, H 7%, J (14%), K 12%

(d) The general fixed cost attributed to the products excluding their specific fixed costs is:

Product	$
G	2,000
H	3,000
J	1,000
K	1,000
	7,000
Plus specific fixed cost	4,000
	11,000

Therefore if there were to be zero sales there would be a loss of $7,000.

Workings for chart:

Selling products with highest C/S ratios first:

	Profit $	Sales $
No products	(7,000)	Nil
Start K	(8,000)	
K only	7,840	132,000
Start G	6,840	
K & G only	10,120	173,000
Start H	9,120	
K, G and H	15,560	265,000
Start J	14,560	
All	6,580	322,000

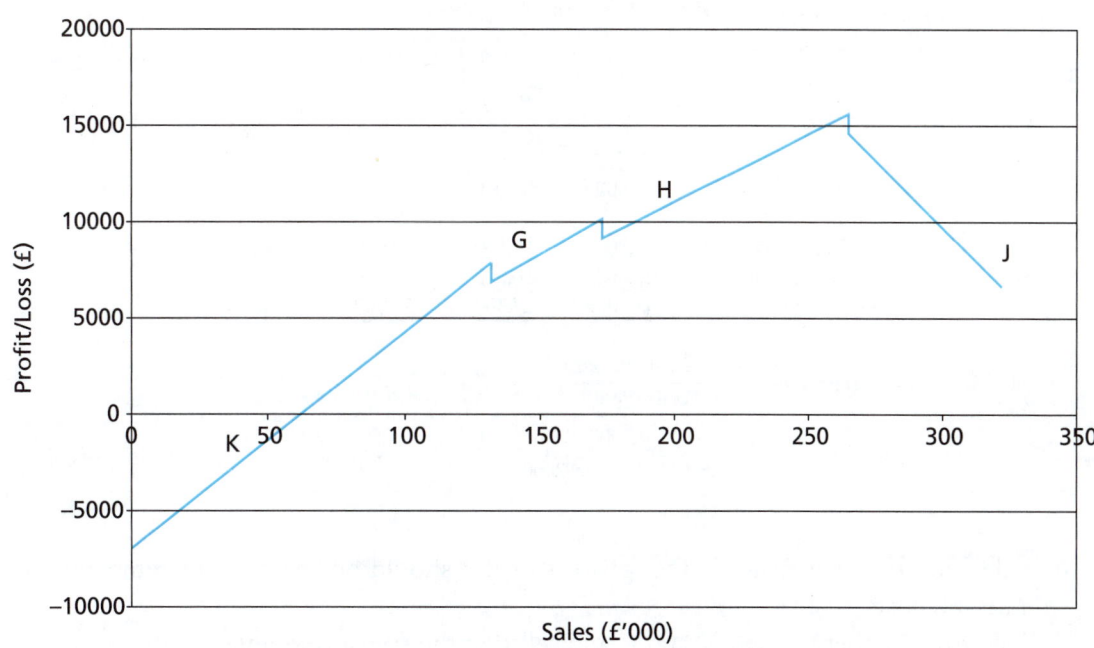

> **Examiner's note:**
> While the chart on the next page is drawn to scale, candidates were only required to prepare a sketch.

(e) The chart shows the effect on the breakeven sales values of alternative sales mixes based on the production plan and using relevant cost. It assumes that all of the products are sold in relation to their contribution to sales ratios, highest first. Any other order of selling the units will result in a different breakeven sales value. The value indicated is the lowest breakeven sales value, the highest will occur if the products were sold in the opposite order, i.e. lowest contribution to sales ratio first.

The manager can use this information to understand the effect on profitability of selling the different products. Some are more worthwhile than others as demonstrated by the solution to part (a) where the products' contribution per unit were calculated and the gradient of their lines. The higher the gradient the greater is the product's contribution to sales ratio. It can clearly be seen that sales of product J are not financially viable. It had a negative contribution to sales ratio and its line is downward sloping. Its continued production needs to be justified on other grounds. The length of each line indicates the value of sales achieved by that product.

The manager can see that if no products were sold at all the business would make a loss (due to the general fixed costs), and that when the production of a product starts there is a further reduction in profit (increase in loss) due to the product's specific fixed cost, but as products that have positive unit contributions are sold these costs are covered by the contribution from the products.

Solution 8

Tip

- Compare incremental revenue and incremental costs when making a decision on whether or not to process further.

(a)

	Product			
	B	K	C	Total
	£	£	£	£
Sales	35,000	50,000	60,000	145,000
Costs				
*Pre-separation	17,500	12,500	10,000	40,000
Post-separation	20,000	10,000	22,500	52,500
Profit/(loss)	(2,500)	27,500	27,500	52,500

$$*\text{Pre-separation cost per litre} = \frac{\text{Pre-separation cost}}{\text{Total output}}$$

$$= \frac{£40,000}{(3,500 + 2,500 + 2000)}$$

$$= £5 \text{ per litre}$$

(b) A decision on whether to further process or not should be based on incremental revenue and costs.

Therefore, further process K and C and sell B at the split-off point.

Profit statement to maximise profits

Product	Incremental revenue £	Incremental cost £	Incremental profit £
B	14,000	20,000	(6,000)
K	30,000	10,000	20,000
C	22,500 (42,000)	22,500	19,500
			33,500

	B £	K £	C £	Total £
Sales	21,000	50,000	60,000	131,000
Costs				
Pre-separation	17,500	12,500	10,000	40,000
Post-separation	–	10,000	22,500	32,500
Profit	3,500	27,500	27,500	58,500

(c) Any apportionment of joint costs is arbitrary and consequently any information provided which incorporates such apportionment is of doubtful value. Decisions can never be reliably made on the basis of apportioned costs because they do not relate to activities or the use of resources.

Solution 9

Tip

- Show clear workings and justify your choice of each cost.

(a) Publishing Company – Revised Cost Estimate

		£
Direct material	Paper	2,500
	Ink	3,000
Direct labour	Skilled	1,125
	Unskilled	–
Variable overhead		1,400
Printing press		600
Fixed production costs		–
Estimating costs		–
		8,625

Reasons for resource valuation

1. *Direct material* – Paper. Current stock value of £5,000 is irrelevant as it is a sunk cost. As there is no other use for this paper, replacement cost is irrelevant. The scrap value of £2,500 is an opportunity cost and relevant.
2. *Direct material* – Ink. As the ink is not in stock the purchase price is relevant. The entire £3,000 is chargeable though only 80 per cent of the ink will be used, as there is no foreseeable use for the remainder.
3. *Direct labour* – skilled. As this is in short supply all labour costs are relevant.

$$
\begin{aligned}
125 \text{ hours @ £4 per hour} &= £500 \\
125 \text{ hours @ £5 per hour} &= £625 \\
& £1,125
\end{aligned}
$$

4. *Direct labour* – unskilled. The weekend work results in 50 hours time off in lieu; this with the 75 (100 − 25) other hours worked totals 125 hours which is less than the 200 hours of idle time which are already being paid for, thus there is no incremental cost.
5. *Variable overhead.* This is a future cost which will be incurred if the work is undertaken and therefore is relevant.
6. *Printing press.* Depreciation of the printing press is a non-cash item and therefore irrelevant. However the use of the press has an opportunity cost – the contribution earned from hiring the press.

$$200 \text{ hours} \times (£6 - £3) = £600$$

7. *Fixed production costs.* These costs are unaffected by the decision and therefore irrelevant.
8. *Estimating costs.* These have already been incurred and are therefore a sunk cost.

(b) Contribution is the difference between sales and variable costs, both of which are dependent on activity. Fixed costs which tend to be largely independent of activity are ignored.

Since most decisions involve changes in the level of activity the relevant costs and revenue are those affected by changes in the level of activity. Thus the net effect of these relevant costs and revenue is contribution.

Solution 10

Tips

- This question involves DCF, sensitivity analysis and probability analysis.
- Remember to make use of cumulative NPV tables where appropriate – this would save you valuable time in an examination.
- Part (b) requires you to draw a diagram to illustrate the sensitivity of the two options to the level of demand. This will involve drawing a graph with Demand on the X axis and NPV on the Y axis.

(a) (i) Low-technology route

Present value (PV) of the development expenditure:

$$£800,000 \times 0.909 = £727,200$$

PV of contribution from the treatments carried out in years 2–10:

$$£3,000^* \times Q \times 5.236 = £15,708Q$$

Thus, for this route to be viable:

$$Q \geq 727.2/15.708$$
$$Q \geq 46.3$$

i.e. the minimum number of treatments is 46.3 per annum.

*Contribution per treatment = £(43,000 − 40,000)
= £3,000

(ii) High-technology route

PV of development expenditure

£2,100,000 × 2.487 = £5,222,700

PV of the contribution from treatments carried out in years 4–10:

£25,000 × Q × 3.658 = £91,450Q

Thus, for this route to be viable:

$Q \geq 5,222.7/91.45$

i.e. the minimum number of treatments is 57.1 per annum.

(iii) For both routes to be equally viable, they must have the same NPV:

$$15,708Q - 727,200 = 91,450Q - 5,222,700$$
$$75,742Q = 4,495,500$$
$$Q = 59.4$$

The number of treatments demanded annually to make the two routes equally viable is 59.4.

(b) For the low-technology route:

$$NPV = £(15,708Q - 727,200)$$

When $Q = 0$, NPV = −£727,200
When $Q = 100$, NPV = £[(15,708 × 100) − 727,200] = £843,600

For the high technology route:

$$NPV = £(91,450Q - 5,222,700)$$

When $Q = 0$, NPV = −£5,222,700
When $Q = 100$, NPV = £[(91,450 × 100) − 5,222,700] = £3,922,300

Sensitivity diagram for low- and high-tech options

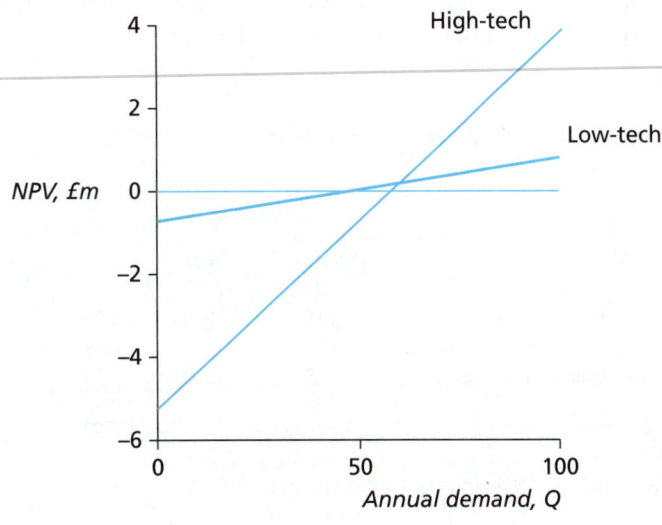

(c) The expected demand is:

$$30 \times 0.4 + 65 \times 0.6 = 51 \text{ treatments}$$

Thus, without the consultant's forecast, the low-tech route would be selected with an NPV of £73,908 [(15,708 × 51) − 727,200 = 73,908].

Using the consultant's forecasts, the following expected value of NPV may be calculated (W = weak; S = strong):

Forecast	Outcome	Working	Probability	NPV £000	Probability × NPV £000
W	W	1.	0.368	0	0
W	S	2.	0.048	0	0
S	W	3.	0.032	−2,479	−79.3
S	S	4.	0.552	722	398.3
Expected value NPV					319.0

The expected value of the NPV after the forecast is £319,000. This is an increase of:

$$£319,000 - £74,000 = £245,000$$

Therefore, the forecast is worth £245,000 to EHI plc.

Workings

1a.	0.40 × 0.92	= 0.368
2a.	0.60 × 0.08	= 0.048
3a.	0.40 × 0.08	= 0.032
4a.	0.60 × 0.92	= 0.552
		1.000

1b. and 2b.   If a weak demand is forecast then development will be cancelled ∴ NPV = 0
3b. and 4b.   If a strong demand is forecast (65 treatments) the high-tech development will be pursued.
3b.   NPV = 91.45 × 30 − 5,222.7 = −2,479
4b.   NPV = 91.45 × 65 − 5,222.7 = 722

Solution 11

Tips

- A straightforward question that involves probability theory and the calculation of expected values.
- Notice that part (b) requires the maximum sum per annum. Don't forget to multiply the amount per concert by the number of concerts each year.

(a) (i) **Scenario 1**

Expected demand = 350 tickets per concert

Scenario 2

	Probability P	Demand X	EV
Popular artistes	0.45	500	225
Lesser known artistes	0.30	350	105
Unknown artistes	0.25	200	50
			380

Expected demand = 380 tickets per concert

(ii) Payoff table showing profit (W1, W2, W3)

		Demand		
		200	350	500
Purchase level	200	120	120	120
	300	(57)	225	225
	400	(204)	219	360
	500	(246)	177	600

Expected values:

	EV
200 tickets 120×1	120
300 tickets $(57) \times 0.25 + 225 \times 0.75$	154.5
400 tickets $(204) \times 0.25 + 219 \times 0.3 + 360 \times 0.45$	176.7
500 tickets $(246) \times 0.25 + 117 \times 0.3 + 600 \times 0.45$	261.6

Scenario 1

If demand is 350 tickets on average, the ticket agent can purchase 200, 300, 400 or 500 tickets. The expected profits will be £120, £225, £219 or £177 respectively.

Optimum purchase level is 300 tickets per concert. This would give an expected profit of £225 per concert.

Scenario 2

The optimum purchase level is 500 tickets per concert, which will give an expected profit of £261.60 per concert.

(b) If demand is going to be 200 tickets for a concert then the optimum purchase level would be 200 tickets and the expected profit would be £120 per concert.

Similarly, if demand is going to be 350 tickets then the best profit would be £225 and if demand is going to be 500 then the best profit would be £600.

If the ticket agent has perfect information he will always make the best decision.

Expected profit	$= 120 \times 0.25 + 225 \times 0.3 + 600 \times 0.45$
	$= £367.50$ given perfect information.
Value of perfect information	$= £367.50 - £261.60$
	$= £105.90$
Annual value $= £105.90 \times 60$	$= £6,354$

Workings

(W1) Profit per ticket at different purchase levels

Purchase level	Discount	Profit per ticket sold
200	20%	$20\% \times £3 = 60p$
300	25%	$25\% \times £3 = 75p$
400	30%	$30\% \times £3 = 90p$
500	40%	$40\% \times £3 = £1.20$

(W2)

Purchase level	Demand	Sales
200	200	200
200	350	200
200	500	200
300	200	200
300	350	300
300	500	300
400	200	200
400	350	350
400	500	400
500	200	200
500	350	350
500	500	500

(W3) Each profit calculation consists of:

1. the profit of the units sold;
2. the cost of the units unsold and returned;
3. the value of the returns.

Value of returns = £3.00 × 60% × 10% = 18p per return

Buy 200 demand 200:   Sales 200 tickets × 60p = £120
Buy 200 demand 350:   Sales 200 tickets × 60p = £120
Buy 300 demand 200:   Sales 200 tickets and returns 100 tickets

	£
Sales 200 tickets × (£3.00 − £2.25)	150
Returns 100 tickets × 18p	18
	168
Cost of returns 100 tickets × £2.25 (30% disc)	(225)
	(57)

Solution 12

Tip

- For part (b) you will need to use the data supplied to determine the demand function for the X.

(a) Since the demand function is linear, the elasticity of demand moves from infinity at a unit price of £10 to nil at a unit price of £nil. The elasticity is 1 at unit price £5.
Consequently, the two observations are consistent. The commercial manager is considering a point on the demand function intermediate between unit price £10 and unit price £5 – hence the elasticity of demand he has observed will be greater than one.

(b) (i) The demand function for the X is given by $q = a - mp$

where q = quantity demanded
p = price

When $p = £10, q = 0$ ∴ $0 = a - 10m$ (i)
When $p = £9, q = 4,000$ ∴ $4,000 = a - 9m$ (ii)
Subtract (ii) − (i) $4,000 = m$
Substitute in (i) $0 = a - 40,000$
     $a = 40,000$

Therefore, the demand function for X is $q = 40,000 - 4,000p$.

When $p = £5.75$, $q = 40,000 - (4,000 \times 5.75)$
$= 17,000$

The profit-maximising sales volume for the X is 17,000 units.

(ii)

$$\text{Elasticity of demand} = \frac{\% \text{ change in quantity demanded}}{\% \text{ change in price}}$$

For a change in price of 1p, the demand will reduce by 40 units.

$$\text{Elasticity of demand} = \frac{40/17,000}{0.01/5.75}$$

$$= 1.35$$

Solution 13

Tips
- This question draws on your knowledge of the experience curve, discounted cash flow, sensitivity analysis and pricing strategy.
- In part (a) you need to begin by using the learning curve formula, $Y = aX^b$. Insert the data given where $Y = £675$ and $X = 500$ to determine the value of a.
- You can then use the formula to calculate the cost per unit for the various output levels.
- Remember that the working capital is recovered at the end of project.

(a) $Y = aX^b$ $\log 0.7 / \log 2 = -0.51457$
Cost of first unit:

$675 = a \times 500^{-0.51457}$

$a = \dfrac{675}{0.0408499} = £16,523.90$

Average cost per unit of 15,000 units: $Y = 16,523.9 \times 15,000^{-0.51457} = 117.279$
Average cost per unit of 30,000 units: $Y = 16,523.9 \times 30,000^{-0.51457} = 82.096$
Average cost per unit of 45,000 units: $Y = 16,523.9 \times 45,000^{-0.51457} = 66.636$

Units	Cost per unit £	Total cost £	Incremental cost £
15,000	117.279	1,759,189	
30,000	82.096	2,462,870	703,681
45,000	66.636	2,998,620	535,750

	Year 1 £	Year 2 £	Year 3 £
Sales revenue			
15,000 × £425	6,375,000	6,375,000	6,375,000
Less:			
Experience curve costs	(1,759,189)	(703,681)	(535,750)
Differential cash flow	4,615,811	5,671,319	5,839,250

Average cost per unit of 6,000 units: $Y = 16{,}523.90 \times 6{,}000^{-0.51457} = 187.927$
Average cost per unit of 12,000 units: $Y = 16{,}523.90 \times 12{,}000^{-0.51457} = 131.549$
Average cost per unit of 18,000 units: $Y = 16{,}523.90 \times 18{,}000^{-0.51457} = 106.777$

Units	Cost per unit £	Total cost £	Incremental cost £
6,000	187.927	1,127,562	
12,000	131.549	1,578,588	451,026
18,000	106.777	1,921,986	343,398

	Year 1 £	Year 2 £	Year 3 £
Sales revenue			
6,000 × £950	5,700,000	5,700,000	5,700,000
Less:			
Experience curve costs	(1,127,562)	(451,026)	(343,398)
Differential cash flow	4,572,438	5,248,974	5,356,602

Therefore, selling 15,000 units at a price of £425 is the better strategy.
(*Note: Only year 1 calculation for 6,000 units is necessary to show this.*)

	Year 1 £	Year 2 £	Year 3 £
Differential cash flow	4,615,811	5,671,319	5,839,250
Less: Fixed costs	2,400,000	2,400,000	2,400,000
Net cash flow	2,215,811	3,271,319	3,439,250

Year	Cash flows £m		Total flow £m	Discount rate	Net present value £m
0	(0.75)	Dev	(0.75)	1.000	(0.75)
1	(3.5)	Asset			
	(1.5)	WC	(5.0)	0.935	(4.675)
2	2.216		2.216	0.873	1.935
3	3.271		3.271	0.816	2.669
4	3.439				
	1.5	WC	4.939	0.763	3.768
					2.947

The option of selling 15,000 units a year at £425 is financially viable and gives an NPV over the project's life of £2.9 million.

(b) Other issues to consider include:
- If VI plc sets a low price it will gain a greater market share. This may be an advantage in the long term and something that the company could build on with the next generation of products – thus increasing future profits.
- On the other hand, VI plc has built its reputation on good-quality products and, presumably, it wishes to retain this image. Selling at a low price could harm the company image, even though the quality of the product is good, because customers may perceive a cheaper product to be inferior.
- A larger production volume may require more in the way of production facilities. Could the additional space and equipment be used more profitably for another product?
- The product is likely to be under attack from competing products and newer technologies. Will VI plc be able to sustain constant demand (especially at the higher level) for 3 years?

(c) Sales revenue each year over years 2 to 4   £6,375,000
This generates a present value of £6,375,000 × £2.452 = £15,631,500

NPV of project is £2,947,000, so at indifference point, present value of sales revenue must be
£15,631,500 − £2,947,000
= £12,684,500

This is a reduction of £2,947,000 ÷ £15,631,500 × 100 = 18.9%
So the sales price could fall by 18.9 per cent to £345.

The project does not appear to be sensitive to a change in selling price. However, it is possible with this type of product, that a competing company could force prices down by this amount if it can utilise large experience curve cost advantages.

(d) The experience curve can assist in setting a low price that can be used to enter a market and gain an acceptable market share within a required time period. It can only be used if an experience curve can be determined from previous experience of similar products/markets. Therefore, it requires a certain amount of economic stability and repetition. However, this does not imply large-volume mass production, as aircraft manufacturers, for example, have used the technique very successfully.

If a company entering a new market sets a high price, not many units will be sold and the entrant will only achieve a relatively small market share. This could mean that the entrant does not achieve the required critical mass within the required time. If a lower price had been set, volume would be higher, the critical mass might well have been achieved and the market would then be profitable for the company. Setting a low price – one lower than initial cost – is possible if the experience curve factor is known. However, this can be a dangerous strategy if it triggers a price war.

A number of Japanese companies used a low-price strategy, based on the experience curve, when entering European markets with electronic/electrical goods for the first time about 30 years ago. Once they became established in the market they could produce a more sophisticated product. This type of product lends itself to this tactic; for example, Amstrad launched its first computer for £399 plus VAT when other computers were selling for about £1,000. Texas Instruments have used this type of tactic. On one occasion, it ended disastrously when competitors lowered their prices aggressively and prevented Texas Instruments from selling the volume they had originally planned and hence cost did not reduce as planned.

Solution 14

Tips

- In part (a) you will earn few marks if you simply write an essay about the learning curve effect, without attempting to relate your answer to the particular case described.
- In part (b) you will need to use the learning curve formula supplied to determine the total hours for a range of batch sizes. Our answer shows one set of workings. A similar approach is used to derive all other data for hours taken.
- Use a piece of graph paper and answer the question properly. It will be good practice at selecting scales, drawing neat and accurate lines, etc.

(a) The learning curve effect is a mathematical expression of the relationship, observed in certain situations, between the reduction in labour hours taken to complete a job as the labour force becomes more familiar with the production process, i.e. as output increases. It is observed in situations where there is little automation, and where the process is complex or requires the application of traditional skills into new areas. Thus, the labour force is able to learn and thereby improve its efficiency as output increases.

The production process for this product is carried out manually and is relatively complex. The manufacturing procedure would appear to require the application of traditional electronic technician skills into a new area. Thus, one would expect learning effects during the production of a new model.

As there will be variations in both production and the process, the efficiency gains may well be lost (unlearned) which is why these effects are not expected to be carried forward from one model to the next.

(b) Relationship between output, costs and revenues

Batch size Units	Total hours Hours	Labour v. costs £	Other v. costs £	Total cost £	Sales price £/unit	Total revenue £	Profit £
0	60	0	0	35,000	0	0	(35,000)
100	1,738.4	34,768	2,000	71,768	794.33	79,433	7,665
300	3,880.9	77,617	6,000	118,617	434.10	130,228	11,611
500	5,637.7	112,753	10,000	157,753	327.80	163,900	6,147

Workings for 100 units

1. *Labour hours*

   Cum. av. labour hours $= y = ax^{-0.269}$

   a = time taken for first unit = 60 hours

   x = cumulative number of units produced = 100

   $y = 60 \times 100^{-0.269}$

   $= 17.384$ hours/unit

   $\therefore$ Total hours for 100 units = 17.384×100

   $= 1738.4$ hours

2. *Selling price*

   Revenue formula

   $y = ax^n$

   a = revenue of first unit = £10,000

   x = output

   At output of 500 units $\quad y = £327.80 \times 500$

   $= 163,900$

   $\therefore 163,900 = 10,000 \times 500^n$

   $\log 163,900 = \log 10,000 + n \log 500$

   $n = \dfrac{(\log 163,900 - \log 10,000)}{\log 500}$

   $n = \dfrac{5.2146 - 4}{2.699}$

   $n = 0.45$

   $\therefore$ Revenue formula $= y = ax^{0.45}$

   Revenue for 100 units $y = 10,000 \times 100^{0.45}$

   $= 10,000 \times 7.9433$

   $= £79,433$

Revenue for 300 units $y = 10{,}000 \times 300^{0.45}$
$= 10{,}000 \times 13.0228$
$= 130{,}228$

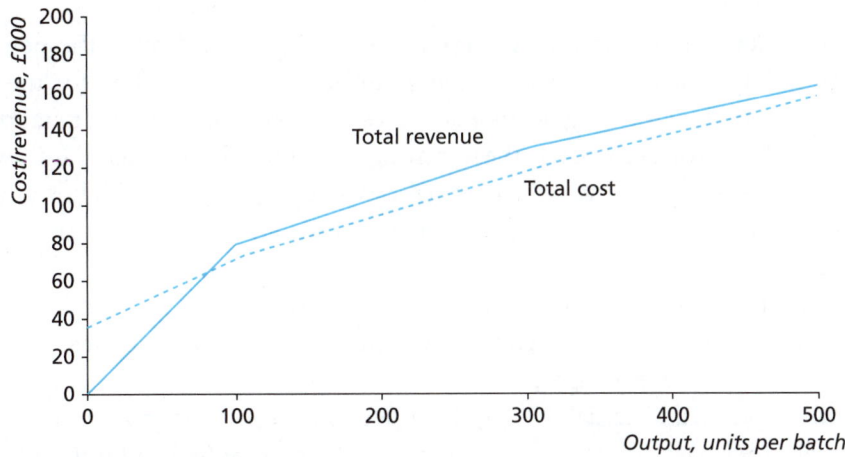

(c) From the graph the maximum profit is apparent between a batch size of 200 to 300 units, at approximately 250 units.

A more exact solution may be obtained by trial and error, using small increments in batch size around the 250-unit position.

At 250 units, the profit may be calculated to be £12,038 at a sales price of £480 and this increases to £12,051 for 240 units at a selling price of £491.

Further calculations would prove that this is the profit-maximising batch size and unit price.

Solution 15

(a) The traditional management accounting performance measures are best suited to a stable environment, which is programmable. These measures include budgetary control and standard costing which relies upon the ability to be able to predict the future with some accuracy. Standards are frequently set based upon past performance, the assumption being that the past is a good predictor of the future.

With the increase in competition in world markets and the ever-increasing rate of change of technology the manufacturing environment has had to become more flexible in order to meet customer needs. Rather than being able to have long batch runs of the same product the emphasis is on small batches and constant product innovation and a requirement to improve and monitor quality.

Traditional management accounting techniques to monitor performance, such as standard costing, are unable to provide the information required because of the need to constantly revise standards. The move to more mechanised and computerised processes has also made the traditional labour variances obsolete because of the insignificant proportion of direct labour in total product cost. Taking the specific example of small batch manufacture, traditional standard costing spreads the set-up costs across the batch so that each item within the batch has a share. With small batch manufacture this cost becomes a much larger proportion of total cost. The traditional costing system also lays little emphasis on the cost of quality and hence the system is not able to provide the information required by management to control this important aspect of modern manufacture. It is therefore true to say that traditional management accounting performance measures are at best irrelevant and at worst misleading in the new manufacturing environment.

(b) There are a number of ways management accounting can adapt to the new environment. Traditional standard costing systems can be modified to allow for the flexibility required. If the industrial engineering schemes are mechanised so that standard times can be calculated for each batch these can be multiplied by the standard cost rate to give the standard cost against which actual costs can be measured. The standard cost rate would not have labour as a separate part, but would consider it as part of variable overhead.

An alternative is to move to a system of actual costing using statistical control charts to monitor costs. This is where a confidence interval is set about the mean and any deviations outside this are investigated.

In both standard and actual costing the move away from labour as the cost driver has meant that other bases of charging costs to products have had to be found. Although such methods have been used for many years, particularly in the metals industry, it has been recently formalised into activity-based costing.

Non-financial performance measures are also being developed to complement or replace the traditional measures. This is particularly true in the area of quality where control is essential for long-term survival.

Solution 16

Tip

- In part (b) your answer must relate to the specific situation of a company that manufactures mobile phones. A general essay on target costing and life cycle costing will not earn many marks.

(a) There are a variety of different costing systems and they all attempt, to a greater or lesser extent, to inform management on the way in which products consume resources. For example, marginal costing relates only variable costs to products. Throughput accounting is a similar technique that focuses on how products use scarce resources. ABC is probably the technique which endeavours to provide the most accurate results by relating costs to activities/resources.

(i) *The effect of the addition of a new product on the 'cost' of existing products*

The total cost of some types of activity/resource depends on the number of batches put through production. Such activities include, for example, machine set-up. If long production runs are used, set-up costs will be less than if many short production runs are used. The same applies to the number of different products manufactured. If only one product is made set-up costs will not be incurred. Two products create the cost and three increase it, and so on. Thus, some resource costs will increase if a company manufactures multiple products. On the other hand, there are a number of benefits from manufacturing a number of products that need to be considered. They are:

- an additional product may help smooth out production peaks and troughs caused by economic or seasonal fluctuations.

- distribution and marketing channels can be used more fully bringing down the cost per unit;
- if a company making a range of products creates a brand name, it can be used to launch a new product more cheaply than if the new product was made by a single product company set up for the purpose.

(ii) *The effect on total profit if the product range is increased/decreased*

All costs (production, distribution, research, marketing and so on) must be considered when making decisions on whether or not to expand the product range. Some companies focus on production costs and so, as a consequence, could overlook cost reduction benefits gained on the marketing side if another product is added. A full product range is almost always an advantage on the marketing side. For example, a brand name for a range of products creates joint benefits for that range of products. The effect of brand names is difficult to measure and could be ignored if only 'hard' costs and benefits are included when making a decision.

Sometimes a full product range is necessary to attract customers – such as a company supplying plumbing pipes and joints, and so on. If one product is withdrawn, because the costing system shows it to be unprofitable, customers may switch to another supplier and the organisation's overall profit may go down as a result.

(b) The modern business environment tends to be an unstable one and is rapidly changing in terms of customer requirements, economic factors, technology, and so on. Telmat is in a particularly unstable business because technology is changing rapidly as digital telephones take over and text messaging develops. Both target costing and life cycle costing are systems which should help the company cope with this. These systems should help Telmat to compete in terms of cost and product development in the competitive telecommunications market.

Their specific advantages are as follows:

(i) *Target costing*

Target costing may replace, and is often compared with, traditional standard costing/variance analysis which has long been in place in the West. Telmat may wish to replace standard costing/variance analysis with target costing for cost control and reduction for the following reasons:

- *It puts pressure on cost* – it can be used as a cost reduction technique unlike standard costing and can incorporate a learning effect. This is likely to be important in the manufacture of phones.
- *Traditional standards may be too rigid for cost control and reduction purposes* for a company such as Telmat as they usually need to be set for a year at a time. Target costing is more flexible and targets can change/reduce from month to month.
- *It considers the market and the price customers are prepared to pay* – so it forces an organisation to be outward rather than inward looking. Telmat needs to consider the final customer as well as the system supplier. (Standard costing tends to focus on internal costs.)
- *It should motivate staff if used correctly and help break down any artificial functional barriers* as it involves staff at all levels and in most functions and forces them to communicate.

- *It leads towards the use of other techniques, such as value analysis and value engineering*, which should simplify production methods and reduce cost. This is particularly important in an industry with short product life cycles.

(ii) *Life cycle costing*
- *The life cycle of Telmat's products is likely to be short* because of changing technology, therefore it is vital that the products begin to generate profits quickly. Estimating life cycle costs and revenues will highlight this.
- *Research and development costs are likely to be quite high* and must be recovered in a short period.
- *Many of Telmat's costs are likely to be 'locked in' during the design stage*, say 80–90 per cent, so it is important to control costs initially in order to maximise the profit over the product's life.
- *It focuses on the time as well as money*. Time to market is often a key factor in generating profit. It is often more important to measure time than money/cost. It may be vital for Telmat to bring new products to market quickly and on time in order to achieve a profit.
- *Monitoring of costs and benefits over the life cycle helps to stop a project early* if events have changed or not turned out as planned.
- *It presents a different perspective* that could be advantageous to Telmat as it is not tied to periodic reporting.

Because of the above it would be advantageous for the company to adopt both of these techniques.

Solution 17

Tip

- When you are calculating the standard allowances for the actual production in part (b) you will need to use the concept of equivalent units for job 109. Since the job is 60 per cent complete as regards labour, the standard labour hours for variance calculations will be 60 per cent of the original standard hours forecast for the job.

(a) Most organisations are required to set the price of their goods or services in advance of manufacturing and/or supplying them. The pricing policy for a product must be developed taking full account of the anticipated market conditions. As part of this decision-making process it is necessary to estimate all the costs involved to determine the profit generated by the forecast sales. This requires the use of a predetermined overhead absorption rate (OAR).

The timeframe used for calculating the OAR is usually the next budget year. Taking such a timescale will tend to even out seasonal or market fluctuations in demand. For example, a gas supply company making monthly calculations of OAR would have a much lower OAR in the winter months than in the summer. These short-term OARs send the wrong pricing signals, suggesting that one might reduce price when demand is high and increase price when demand is low. Alternatively, if the price is held constant, the profit per unit will fluctuate with the seasons. The use of predetermined OARs will almost certainly result in over- or under-absorption. This is shown in variance analysis as the fixed overhead volume variance.

(b) *PSA Ltd – Cost control report for April*

	Standard cost	Actual cost	Variance	
	£	£	£	
Labour	21,714	24,500	2,786	ADV
Hardwood	26,180	28,600	2,420	ADV
Softwood	8,640	9,200	560	ADV
Fixed overheads	8,272	7,800	472	FAV
Variable overheads	6,204	6,900	696	ADV
	71,010	77,000	5,990	ADV

Labour variances

	£		£
Operational efficiency (W1)	483	ADV	
Operational rate (W2)	1,400	ADV	
Planning (W3)	903	ADV	
	2,786	ADV	2,786

Hardwood variances

	£		
Operational usage (W4)	1,045	ADV	
Price (W5)	0		
Planning (W6)	1,375	ADV	
	2,420	ADV	5,206

	£		
Operational usage (W7)	1,120	ADV	
Price (W8)	400	ADV	
Planning (W9)	960	ADV	
	560	ADV	5,766

Overhead variances

	800	FAV	
Expenditure (W11)	100	ADV	
Efficiency (W12)		ADV	
	224	ADV	5,990

Workings
Labour

Std hours = 1,000 + 600 + (780 × 60%) = 2,068, actual hours = 2,200

Actual cost per hour £11.136

Revised std hours $\frac{2,068}{0.96} = 2,154$

(W1) (2,154 − 2,200) × 10.5 = 483 ADV
(W2) 2,200 × (11.136 − 10.5) = 1,400 ADV
(W3) (2,068 − 2,154) × 10.5 = 903 ADV

Hardwood

Std volume = 200 + 180 + (120 × 80%) = 476, actual volume = 520

Actual price $\frac{28,600}{520}$ = £55 per cu. m.

Revised std volume 476/0.95 = 501

(W4) $(501 - 520) \times 55 = 1{,}045$ ADV
(W5) $(55 - 55) \times 520 = 0$
(W6) $(476 - 501) \times 55 = 1{,}375$ ADV

Softwood

Std use $= 320 + 400 + (300 \times 80\%) = 960$ cu. m., actual use $= 1{,}100$ cu. m.

Actual price $\dfrac{9{,}200}{1{,}100} = £8.364$ cu. m.

(W7) $(960 - 1{,}100) \times 8 = 1{,}120$ ADV
(W8) $(8.00 - 8.364) \times 1{,}100 = 400$ ADV
(W9) $960 \times (9 - 8) = 960$ FAV

Overheads

Monthly plan	2,000 labour hours × £4 = £8,000	
Revised plan	2,068 labour hours	
Actual	2,200 labour hours × £3 = £6,600	
(W10)	$(2{,}200 - 2{,}000) \times 4$	= 800 FAV
(W11) Fixed overhead expenditure variance	= 8,000 − 7,800	= 200 FAV
Variable overhead expenditure variance	= 6,600 − 6,900	= 300 ADV
(W12) Fixed overhead efficiency variance	$= (2{,}068 - 2{,}200) \times 4$	= 528 ADV
Variable overhead efficiency variance	$= (2{,}068 - 2{,}200) \times 3$	= 396 ADV

(c) The traditional accounting system presently used by PSA Ltd follows all the costs as they are incurred for each product type, job or unit produced. These costs are classified and recorded forming an extensive database, which allows tight financial control to be exercised on the production process.

Specifically, PSA Ltd prepares a detailed monthly variance analysis as part of its control procedures. Its existing system is both flexible and powerful in that it incorporates adjustable standards to cater for external influences outside the control of PSA Ltd, for example, the quality of labour or materials. The disadvantage of this system is that it is time-consuming and expensive to enter and manipulate the vast amount of data involved. In a modern AMT/JIT environment it may not be necessary to use such a complex system if:

- all forms of stock inventory (raw materials, WIP and finished products) are kept at very low levels;
- production is highly automated and reliable, leading to low labour costs and efficient use of labour time;
- long-term relationships with suppliers ensure reliable delivery and fixed price and quality specifications.

Under these conditions, there will be little variation of input prices or efficiencies and therefore insignificant cost variations. Thus, there would be no need to use the traditional accounting technique, and backflush accounting may be used instead. The CIMA *Official Terminology* defines backflush accounting as 'a method of costing, associated with a JIT production system, which applies cost to the output of a process. Costs do not mirror the flow of products through the production process, but are attached to output produced (finished goods stock and cost of sales), on the assumption that such backflushed costs are a realistic measure of the actual costs incurred'. Thus, conversion costs are only attached to products when they are completed. This system only uses raw, in process and finished goods accounts, which saves costs by reducing the amount of data required and the frequency of data entry, for example, data on materials used only enters the system when a piece of work is completed. However, this system does not enable the valuation of WIP nor any variance analysis.

The variances for PSA Ltd are significant for efficiency of inputs (labour and materials) and there is also a noticeable change in WIP, and the price of inputs. If this is typical, then the proposal should be rejected, as backflush accounting is unsuitable. Rapier, like many consultants, may be too concerned with selling its services than with truly serving its customers.

Solution 18

Tip

- When calculating your absorption rates, don't forget to include the data for 'other products' in your total figures.

(a) (i) *Unit costs using traditional absorption costing*

Material related overhead cost (40% of £1.5m) = £600,000

$$\text{Overhead absorption rate } \frac{£600,000}{£2,400,000} \times 100 = 25\% \text{ of direct material cost}$$

Labour related overhead cost (60% of £1.5m) = £900,000

$$\text{Overhead absorption rate } \frac{£900,000}{£800,000} \times 100 = 112.5\% \text{ of direct labour cost}$$

	Alpha £	Beta £
Direct materials	16	30
Direct labour	8	10
Prime cost	24	40
Material related overhead (25%)	4	7.5
Labour related overheads (112.5%)	9	11.25
Total variable costs	37	58.75

(ii) *Unit costs based on activity-based costing*

	Alpha	Beta	Other
Production units	5,000	10,000	40,000
Weight of direct material (kg)	4	1	1.5
Total weight of material (kg)	20,000	10,000	60,000

$$\text{Mat. related overhead/kg } \frac{£600,000}{20,000 + 10,000 + 60,000} = £6.67/\text{kg}$$

	Alpha	Beta	Other
Production units	5,000	10,000	40,000
Labour operations/unit	6	1	2
Total operations	30,000	10,000	80,000

$$\text{Lab. related overhead/op } \frac{£900,000}{30,000 + 10,000 + 80,000} = £7.50 \text{ per operation}$$

Unit costs based on ABC	Alpha £	Beta £
Direct materials	16	30
Direct labour	8	10
Prime cost	24	40
Material related overhead	26.68	6.67
Labour related overheads	45	7.50
Total variable costs	95.68	54.17

(b)

	Alpha		Beta	
	Traditional £	ABC £	Traditional £	ABC £
Direct material	16	16	30	30
Direct labour	8	8	10	10
Material related overhead	4	26.68	7.50	6.67
Labour related overhead	9	45	11.25	7.50
Total variable cost	37	95.68	58.75	54.17
Selling price	75	75.00	95.00	95.00
Contribution/unit	38	(20.68)	36.25	40.83
C/S ratio	51%	(28)%	38%	43%

Apollo plc require a minimum C/S ratio of 40 per cent. If product costs are determined using the traditional methods Apollo would decide to proceed with the production of Alpha (C/S ratio of 51 per cent) and reject Beta which has a C/S just below the required 40 per cent.

If ABC is used the decision will be reversed. Alpha will be rejected on the basis of a negative C/S ratio and Apollo will proceed with Beta which has a C/S ratio of 43 per cent.

ABC provides a more accurate cost of products unlike the traditional method used, which is a broad-based averaging of costs. ABC attempts to reflect the true consumption of resources.

(c) The use of target costing in conjunction with ABC will enable Apollo to find ways of reducing the costs of Alpha to arrive at a target cost. Cost reduction methods such as value analysis and value engineering could be used to achieve this. Though Beta just meets the required 40 per cent C/S ratio, Apollo could decide to increase margins further by carrying out a similar exercise on Beta. Target costing should also be used to identify selling prices for specific markets.

Solution 17

Tips

- The cash flow figures for the two alternatives must include an allowance for the movement in working capital – an increase in stockholding results in a cash outflow which must be deducted from contribution to give the annual cash flow figure.
- In order to appraise the two options on a completely comparable basis it is necessary to assume that stocks are liquidated at the end of the appraisal period.
- The sensitivity analysis in part (c) requires the construction of a graph with NPV represented on the y axis and the unit variable cost of X on the x axis.

(a) By reducing the variety of products sold, DEF Ltd also reduces the number of different components it must purchase and store. Purchasing and stockholding do not add value to the product, but incur costs to DEF Ltd. Thus, it is likely that DEF Ltd will reduce stockholding of both components and products if it introduces fuel pump X.

Sales are likely to drop in the immediate future as fuel pump X is not totally suitable for all applications presently catered for. However, future sales are expected to increase rapidly as purchasers redesign their engines in order to gain the benefits of using a single fuel pump.

The variable costs should fall if DEF Ltd concentrates on producing a single product as there will be no downtime for changing between products, and labour efficiency should increase when only producing one product, that is, it can specialise on one production process. The surplus equipment and buildings arise from the above savings.

Value analysis is a systematic inter-disciplinary examination of factors affecting the cost of a product or service in order to devise means of achieving the specified purpose most economically at the required standard of quality and reliability. This analysis will lead to savings in work added unnecessarily by design and specification features, work added by inefficient methods of manufacture and unnecessary overheads. The analysis asks the questions:

- What is it?
- What does it do?
- What is it worth?
- What else would work?
- What does the alternative cost?

Thus, unnecessary and costly specifications, designs, procedures and bureaucracy are removed from the project or process.

(b) Cash flow for fuel pumps D, E and F:

Time Years	Contribution £000	Stockholding £000	Total £000	Disc. factor	PV £000
1	241.0	−16.8	224.2	0.909	203.8
2	248.2	−17.3	230.9	0.826	190.8
3	255.7	−17.8	237.9	0.751	178.7
4	263.4	−18.4	245.0	0.683	167.3
5	271.3	−18.9	252.4	0.621	156.7
6	279.4	−19.5	259.9	0.564	146.7
7	287.8	−20.1	267.7	0.513	137.4
8	296.4	688.7	985.1	0.466	459.5
					1,640.9

Example workings

Contribution after one year $= £(48 - 35) \times 18{,}000 \times 1.03 = £241{,}020$

Increased stockholding cost after one year $= £560{,}000 \times 0.03 = £16{,}800$

after two years $= £(560{,}000 + 16{,}800) \times 0.03 = £17{,}304$

Cash flow for fuel pump X:

Time Years	Asset £000	Contr. £000	Stockholding £000	Total £000	Disc. Factor	PV £000
0	120.0		250.0	370.0	1.000	370.0
1		199.1	−6.2	192.9	0.909	175.4
2		207.1	−6.3	200.8	0.826	166.0
3		215.4	−6.5	208.9	0.751	156.9
4		224.0	−6.6	217.4	0.683	148.5
5		232.9	−6.7	226.2	0.621	140.5
6		242.3	−6.8	235.5	0.564	132.9
7		252.0	−7.0	245.0	0.513	125.7
8		262.0	356.1	618.1	0.466	288.3
						1,704.2

Example workings

Contribution after 1 year $= £(48 - 35 + 1.75) \times 18{,}000 \times 0.75$
$= £199{,}125$

Increased stockholding cost after 1 year $= £(560{,}000 - 250{,}000) \times 0.02 = £6{,}200$
after 2 years $= £(310{,}000 + 6{,}200) \times 0.02 = £6{,}324$

As the proposed single fuel pump has a greater NPV than the existing pumps, the proposal should be seriously considered. However, the difference is not great, so a sensitivity analysis should be carried out before making the final decision.

(c) The only variable in the analysis above affected by the unit variable cost of fuel pump X is the contribution for X. The sales price is unchanged and the sales volume is also unchanged. Thus, there is a linear relationship between unit variable cost and contribution:

Contribution = Sales volume × (Price − Variable cost)

A 10p increase in variable cost of X has the following effect upon the NPV:

Time Years	Contribution £000	Reduction £000	Disc. Factor	PV £000
1	197.8	−1.3	0.909	−1.2
2	205.7	−1.4	0.826	−1.2
3	213.9	−1.5	0.751	−1.1
4	222.5	−1.5	0.683	−1.0
5	231.4	−1.5	0.621	−0.9
6	240.6	−1.7	0.564	−1.0
7	250.2	−1.8	0.513	−0.9
8	260.3	−1.7	0.466	−0.8
				−8.1

where 'Reduction' is the revised contribution less the contribution found in part (b). The number of 10p increases required to reduce the NPV for fuel pump X to that for the existing fuel pumps is:

$(1{,}704 - 1{,}641) \div 8.1 = 7.8$

Therefore, the maximum unit variable cost that fuel pump X may have and still remain viable is:

$£35 - 1.75 + 0.78 = £34.03$.

This may be shown diagrammatically as follows:

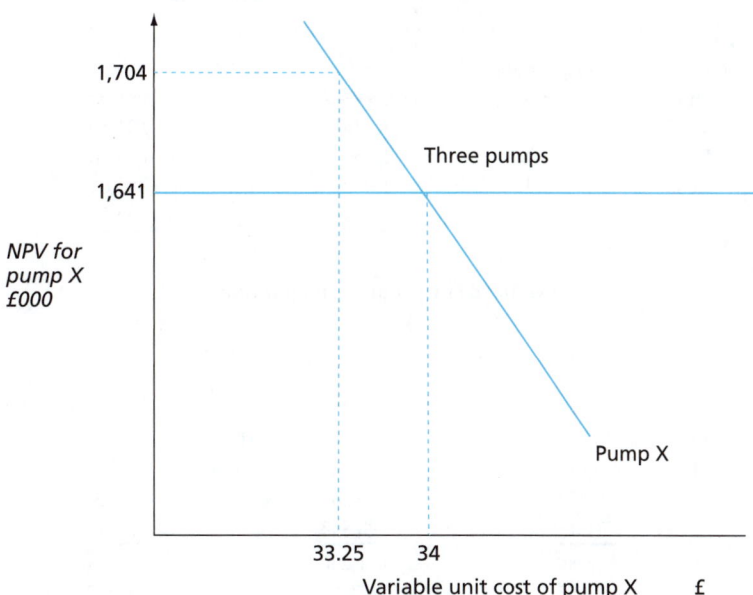

Solution 20

Tip

 To calculate the cost driver rates for part (b) you will need to use the information on machine hours and the machine hour rate to determine the total production overhead. This total can then be analysed, according to the percentages given, to derive the production overhead cost relating to each activity.

(a) **Conventional cost per unit**

	X £	Y £	Z £
Materials	20	12	25
Labour	3	9	6
Direct cost	23	21	31
Production overheads (£28/hour)	42	28	84
Total production cost per unit	65	49	115

(b) **ABC cost per unit**

Analysis of total overheads and cost per unit of activity

	%	Total overhead £	Level of activity	Cost per unit of activity £
Set-ups	35	229,075	670	341.90
Machining	20	130,900	23,375	5.60
Materials movement	15	98,175	120	818.13
Inspection	30	196,350	1,000	196.35
	100	654,500*		

Workings

*Total overheads

	Production units	Machine hours per unit	Total machine hours	OAR	Total overheads
X	750	1.5	1,125	£28	£31,500
Y	1,250	1.0	1,250	£28	£35,000
Z	7,000	3.0	21,000	£28	£588,000
			23,375		£654,500

Total overheads by product and per unit

	X		Y		Z		
Overhead	Activity	Cost £	Activity	Cost £	Activity	Cost £	Total £
Set-ups	75	25,643	115	39,319	480	164,113	229,075
Machining	1,125	6,300	1,250	7,000	21,000	117,600	130,900
Mat. movement	12	9,817	21	17,181	87	71,177	98,175
Inspection	150	29,453	180	35,343	670	131,554	196,350
Total overheads		71,213		98,843		484,444	654,500
No. of units		750		1,250		7,000	
Overhead cost per unit		£94.95		£79.07		£69.21	

Total cost per unit

	X £	Y £	Z £
Direct costs	23.00	21.00	31.00
Overhead costs	94.95	79.07	69.21
Total production cost per unit	117.95	100.07	100.21

(c) Comment

Product	X £	Y £	Z £
Overheads per unit (conventional system)	42.00	28.00	84.00
Overheads per unit (activity-based costing)	94.95	79.07	69.21

A change to activity-based costing results in the overhead costs of X and Y increasing while the overhead cost of Z decreases.

The adoption of ABC provides a fairer unit cost that better reflects the effort required in the manufacture of different products.

This can be illustrated with Z, a major product line which takes longer to produce but once production has begun is simple to administer unlike X and Y which are minor products but still require a fair amount of administrative time. See table below:

Activities per 1000 units	Set-ups	Material movement	Inspections
X	100	16	200
Y	92	17	144
Z	69	12	96

This highlights:
- Product Z has fewer set-ups, material movements and inspections per 1,000 units than X or Y.
- As a consequence product Z's overhead cost per unit for these three activities has fallen.

- The machining overhead cost per unit is still two to three times greater than X or Z. However machining overhead is only 20 per cent of the total overhead.
- The above results in a reduction in Z's overhead cost per unit and an increase for X and Y.

Solution 21

Tip
- This question is very similar to the last one. If you had difficulty then make sure that you work through the data in a systematic way and you should arrive at the correct answer.

(a) Overheads absorbed on machine hour basis

$$\text{Machine hour absorption rate} = \frac{\text{Total overheads}}{\text{Total machine hours}}$$

$$= \frac{£10,430 + £5,520 + £3,600 + £2,100 + £4,620}{(120 \times 4) + (100 \times 3) + (80 \times 2) + (120 \times 3)}$$

$$= \frac{£26,000}{1,300} = £20 \text{ per machine hour}$$

Total costs based on machine hour basis

	A	B	C	D
	£	£	£	£
Direct materials	40	50	30	60
Direct labour	28	21	14	21
Production overhead	80	60	40	60
Production cost/unit	148	131	84	141
Output in units	120	100	80	120
Total production cost	£17,760	£13,100	£6,720	£16,920

(b) Overheads absorbed based on ABC

	Overhead costs	Level of activity	Cost/activity
	£		
Machine department costs	10,430	1,300	£8.02/hour
Set-up costs	5,250	21*	£250.00/run
Stores receiving costs	3,600	80**	£45.00/requisition
Inspection/quality costs	2,100	21*	£100.00/run
Material handling and despatch	4,620	42	£110.00/order

Workings

*No. of production runs = output in units/20

$$= \frac{120 + 100 + 80 + 120}{20}$$

$$= \frac{420}{20} = 21$$

**No. of requisitions raised = No. of products × 20
= 4 × 20 = 80

Total costs based on ABC

	A	B	C	D
	£	£	£	£
Direct materials	40.00	50.00	30.00	60.00
Direct labour	28.00	21.00	14.00	21.00
Machine dept costs	32.09	24.07	16.05	24.07
Set-up costs	12.50	12.50	12.50	12.50
Stores receiving	7.50	9.00	11.25	7.50
Inspection	5.00	5.00	5.00	5.00
Material handling	11.00	11.00	11.00	11.00
Production cost/unit	136.09	132.57	99.80	141.07
Output in units	120	100	80	120
Total production costs	£16,331	£13,257	£7,984	£16,928

(c) Comparison of the two unit costs calculated in (a) and (b) above.

Product	A	B	C	D
	£	£	£	£
Based on machine hour rate	148.00	131.00	84.00	141.00
ABC method	136.09	132.57	99.80	141.07
Difference	11.91	(1.57)	(15.80)	(0.07)

Products A and C have the largest differences. The ABC approach in theory, attributes the cost of resources to each product which uses those resources on a more appropriate basis than the traditional method. The implication is that product A is more profitable than the traditional approach implies, whereas C is less profitable. If selling prices were determined on costs based on the traditional absorption method, the organisation might consider increasing the price of C and reducing that of A.

Solution 22

Tips

- This is an investment appraisal question with multiple IRRs.
- Part (b) requires a graph with NPV on the Y-axis and discount rates on the X-axis.
- You will require a minimum of four data points in order to draw a fairly accurate curve.
- Make use of the cumulative DCF tables where appropriate – this will save you valuable time in an examination and avoids being lost in a mass of calculation.

(a) **Memorandum**

To: Director, Managing Director
From: Management Accountant
Date: 20 November
Re: Maximising accounting profit

Thank you for your letter of 18 November. I appreciate that directors may be more familiar with the concept of profit as opposed to discounted cash flow analysis (DCF), but DCF analysis is the conventional and correct method to use.

The calculation of a profit figure is subjective in that different accounting conventions, such as straight-line or reducing balance depreciation, may be used to calculate the figure.

DCF analysis recognises the true cash flows in a project, the timing of these flows and the time value of money.

By using the internal rate of return, HPC can compare projects of different sizes in an equitable manner, using the DCF approach.

I suggest that we discuss these concepts further at our next meeting.

Signed: Management Accountant

(b) **Workings**

Low-intensity strategy

The annual revenue is $(1,500,000 /15.0) \times £325 = £32.5m$. Thus, the annual net cash flow is $£32.5m - £3.2m = £29.3m$.

Time Years	Cash flow £m	0% DCF	PV £m	10% DCF	PV £m	15% DCF	PV £m	20% DCF	PV £m
0	(105)	1.000	(105.0)	1.000	(105.0)	1.000	(105.0)	1.000	(105.0)
1–15	29.3	15.000	439.5	7.606	222.9	5.847	171.3	4.675	137.0
15	(395)	1.000	(395.0)	0.239	(94.4)	0.123	(48.6)	0.065	25.7
NPV			(60.5)		23.5		17.7		6.3

High-intensity strategy

The annual revenue is $(1,300,000/8) \times £325 = £52.81m$.

Thus, the annual net cash flow is $£52.81m - £3.6m = £49.21m$.

Time Years	Cash flow £m	0% DCF	PV £m	10% DCF	PV £m	15% DCF	PV £m	20% DCF	PV £m
0	(118)	1.000	(118.0)	1.000	(118.0)	1.000	(118.0)	1.000	(118.0)
1–8	49.21	8.000	393.7	5.335	262.5	4.487	220.8	3.837	188.8
8	(280)	1.000	(280.0)	0.467	(130.8)	0.327	(91.6)	0.233	(65.2)
NPV			(4.3)		13.7		11.2		5.6

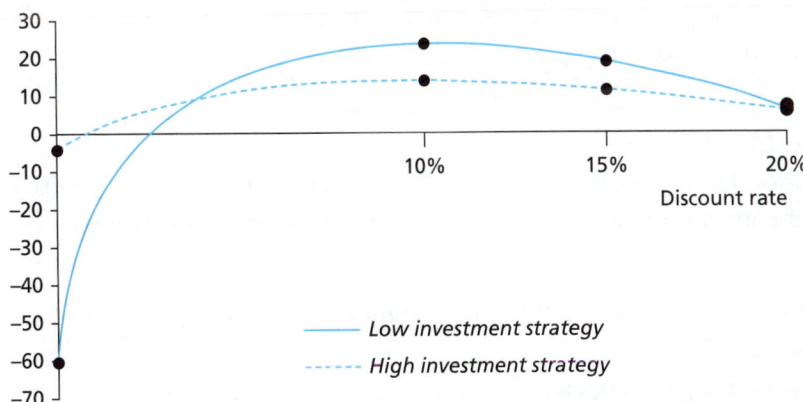

— Low investment strategy
---- High investment strategy

(c) Projects such as marine oil wells and nuclear power stations have negative cash flows at both the commencement and termination of the project. Under these conditions, there is more than one value of IRR that may be calculated for each strategy. Thus, a meaningful conclusion on IRRs is difficult to achieve.

In mutually exclusive options, such as this one, it is important to consider scale as well as a ratio of performance. Thus, the net present values should be compared and their effect on the organisation as a whole should be considered.

The project with the best IRR or NPV may be subject to greater risk than the alternative. Thus, HPC must decide upon its attitude to risks and rewards. In this scenario, the low-intensity strategy is better if the cost of money stays within the range 6–21 per cent per annum.

(d) The high-intensity option extracts the oil in a shorter period. If HPC does not intend to extract oil for the next 15 years this option may be beneficial. Also, if the cost of money is expected to be between 1 and 5 per cent per annum this option is preferable.

If the cost of money is expected to be between 6 and 21 per cent per annum the low-intensity option realises the larger NPV and is preferable. Normally, the project with the largest negative NPV would not be undertaken by a risk-averse company. The low-intensity option has this characteristic, but only if the cost of money is less than 1 per cent – which is very unlikely.

In this scenario, the lower capital investment option potentially offers the higher NPV, so a risk-taking company might choose the low-intensity operation. HPC must define its risk/reward attitude and the likely future cost of money in order to make a rational choice between the projects.

Solution 23

Tips
- Half of each year's tax is payable in the year in which the profit is earned. The other half is payable in the following year.
- As a first step you need to calculate the increase in the annual contribution that the new machine will generate.

(a) Operating hours per year = 40 hours × 48 weeks = 1,920 hours
Units demanded per hour = 12,000 units ÷ 40 hours = 300 units
Units currently produced per hour = 200 units
Increase in units using machine AB per hour = 100 units

Machine AB
Contribution from increased output of P per hour = 100 units × £1.40 = £140
Increased contribution per annum = £140 × 1,920 hrs = £268,800

Tax:
  Year 1 contribution £268,800 − corporation tax (@ 30%) = £80,640:
    50% Year 1 £40,320
    50% Year 2 £40,320, etc.
  Year 0 extra costs £5,000 − tax saving £1,500:
    50% Year 1 £750
    50% Year 2 £750

Writing-down allowance:

	Corporation tax @ 30%	Payable in...				
		Year 1	Year 2	Year 3	Year 4	Year 5
	£	£	£	£	£	£
Purchase price	520,000					
Year 1 WDA @ 25%	130,000	39,000	19,500	19,500		
	390,000					
Year 2 WDA @ 25%	97,500	29,250		14,625	14,625	
	292,500					
Year 3 WDA @ 25%	73,125	21,938			10,969	10,969
	219,375					
Year 4 scrap value	50,000					
Balancing adjustment	169,375	50,813			25,406	25,407
			19,500	34,125	25,594	36,375	25,407

Machine AB: present value calculations:

Year	Machine, etc.	Tax relief on WDA	Contribution	Tax on contribution	Total	Discount factor	Present value
	£	£	£	£	£		£
0	(20,000)						
	(500,000)		(5,000)		(525,000)	1.000	(525,000)
1		19,500	268,800	750			
				(40,320)	248,730	0.909	226,096
2		34,125	268,800	750			
				(80,640)	223,035	0.826	184,227
3		25,594	268,800	(80,640)	213,754	0.751	160,529
4	50,000	36,375		(40,320)	46,055	0.683	31,456
5		25,407			25,407	0.621	15,778
Net present value							93,086

As the NPV is positive the machine should be purchased. However, as the NPV is fairly sensitive to a change in the annual contribution, it can drop by 19.5 per cent, and the project can be shortened by 8 months before the indifference point is reached. Non-discounted payback is reached after around 2 years and 3 months, which is outside the normal requirements, albeit not by a great deal. Assuming that the figures are a fair estimate and that not too much uncertainty surrounds them, the project should go ahead as it produces a return well in excess of 10 per cent.

Calculation of drop in contribution:

		£
Current contribution − present value	£268,800 × 2.487	668,506
Less tax	(£80,640) × 2.373*	(191,359)
		477,147

Percentage drop in net present value required: $\dfrac{£93,086}{£477,147} = 19.5\%$

*Working: $0.909(0.5) + 0.826 + 0.751 + 0.683(0.5)$

(b) In the investment decision in part (a) all costs were tangible and therefore relatively easy to predict. Also, as far as can be ascertained, the decision is to be made in isolation (i.e. on grounds of operational efficiency) with no reference to the organisation's long-term strategy – which is not advisable. The new machine will increase capacity considerably (200 units up to 500 units), which is likely to have strategic implications with such a large increase in market share.

Marketing investment decisions tend to have a large initial outflow followed by rather vague intangible inflows. As a consequence, financial appraisal methods such as discounted cash flow are not often used. Management tends to make leaps of faith when sanctioning an investment, and phrases such as 'improving the company image' and 'meeting strategic aims' are used. It is, of course, very difficult to precisely quantify the impact of a marketing investment and, because there are so many external influences, a post-investment audit may not be worth while. Measures such as an increase in market share are often used to gauge the benefit, but this may be influenced by other factors.

IT investment decisions are not dissimilar to manufacturing ones, but there are probably more benefits and costs to consider. Many of these are difficult to quantify, and a number are intangible. For example, 'improving the organisation's learning' is almost impossible to express in figures. Even training costs are often overlooked or underestimated. The new system under consideration may be for only one department, but other departments may benefit from it – this should be taken into account, but often these benefits are ignored.

Solution 24

Tip

- The key point to appreciate in this question is that each 1,000 unit annual increase in sales of D produces a constant increase in NPV.

(a) **Memorandum**

To:	CD Ltd's Management
From:	Management Accountant
Date:	24 May 20X5
Subject:	Future production policy

The minimum annual growth in unit sales of the new D needed to justify starting production of the D now is approximately 3,400 units per annum.

As existing fixed costs are unaffected by the decision, and the alternatives are mutually exclusive, the relevant cash flows are the extra investment costs for, and contributions from, the D.

Workings for this analysis are attached to this memorandum.

Signed: Management accountant

Workings

Assume that the sales of D increase by 6,000 units per annum. The net investment in the equipment for D is £(620,000 − 70,000) = £550,000.

Time Years	Net investment £	Contribution forgone from C £	Contribution from D £	Net cash flow £	Discount factor	Present value £
0	−550,000			−550,000	1.000	−550,000
1		−720,000	330,000	−390,000	0.893	−348,200
2		−600,000	660,000	60,000	0.797	47,800
3		−480,000	990,000	510,000	0.712	363,000
4		−360,000	1,320,000	960,000	0.636	610,100
		−240,000	1,650,000	1,410,000	0.567	800,100
						922,800

Assume that the sales of D increase by 3,000 units per annum.

Time	Net investment	Contribution forgone from C	Contribution from D	Net cash flow	Discount factor	Present value
Years	£	£	£	£		£
0	−550,000			−550,000	1.000	−550,000
1		−720,000	330,000	−390,000	0.893	−348,200
2		−600,000	495,000	−105,000	0.797	−83,700
3		−480,000	660,000	180,000	0.712	128,100
4		−360,000	825,000	465,000	0.636	295,500
5		−240,000	990,000	750,000	0.567	425,600
						−132,700

This NPV is closer to zero. The minimum annual growth in unit sales of the D required is the increase that causes the NPV to equal zero, which will occur at approximately:

$$\left(1 + \frac{132{,}700}{922{,}800 + 132{,}700}\right) \times 3{,}000 \text{ units} = 3{,}377 \text{ units p.a.}$$

A more accurate figure may be found by further iterations.

(b)

Time	Net investment	Contribution forgone from C	Contribution from D	Net cash flow	Discount factor	Present value
Years	£	£	£	£		£
0	−550,000			−550,000	1.000	−550,000
1		−720,000	330,000	−390,000	0.893	−348,200
2		−600,000	484,000	−116,000	0.797	−92,500
3		−480,000	638,000	158,000	0.712	112,500
4		−360,000	792,000	432,000	0.636	274,500
5		−240,000	946,000	706,000	0.567	400,600
					NPV	−203,100
6		−120,000	1,100,000	980,000	0.507	496,500

Thus, the investment appraisal time horizon is extended by approximately

$$\frac{203{,}100}{496{,}500} = 0.41 \text{ of a year, say 5 months}$$

to 5 years and 5 months.

(c) Further factors to be considered in deciding which product to manufacture are as follows:
- *Technology.* How proven is the technology used to manufacture D? Has a full-scale manufacturing plant been commissioned and operated, or are there potential risks in adopting this technology?
- *Competition.* Are CD Ltd's rivals intending to upgrade their products, or have they already done so? If D truly makes C obsolete and rival firms have an equivalent to D, there may be little choice but to follow suit.
- *Market.* Although the D is smaller and more reliable, it is almost twice the price of the C. Will the companies that presently buy the C prefer to buy the D? They will need to pass this price increase on to their customers. Are these attributes of size and reliability of prime importance to the final customer; will they be willing to pay extra for them? Is the 50 per cent increase in costs significant in terms of the final product cost and the final product profitability? Has sufficient market research been carried out to explore these questions?

570 SOLUTIONS TO REVISION QUESTIONS P2

- *Sensitivity analysis.* The following factors will significantly affect the above calculations and therefore the decision as to which product to manufacture:
  - Sales forecasts for C and D.
  - Cost of capital for CD Ltd.
  - Selling prices for C and D.
  - Variable costs for C and D.

A likely range of each of the above parameters should be established and the sensitivity of the decision to variations across each range should be investigated. This gives some indication of the key parameters and the risk attached to the decision. The investment costs for producing the D are greater than for continuing to produce the C, so a risk-averse organisation might choose to defer introducing the D.

Solution 25

Tip

- Because there are net cash outflows at both the beginning and the end of this project, two separate IRRs will arise.

(a) This is a case of multiple IRRs, as illustrated by the following diagram:

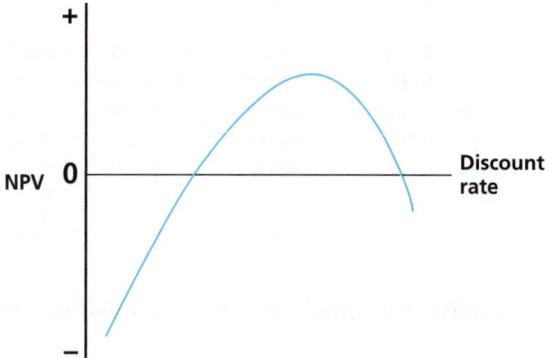

The project is viable because it yields a positive NPV at 17 per cent discount rate. However, it is also true that the cash flows show IRRs at both 11 and 24 per cent approximately and it is evident that in such a case only the NPV gives a reasonable basis for a decision.

Workings
Determination of project cash flows

Year	Initial fee £000	Annual costs £000		Sales value of bauxite £000	Restoration costs £000	Total cash flow £000
0	(9,700)	–		–	–	(9,700)
1		(3,000)	100 × £90	9,000	–	6,000
2		(3,000)	150 × £90	13,500	–	10,500
3		(3,000)	220 × £90	19,800	–	16,800
4		(3,000)	180 × £90	16,200	(42,000)	(28,800)
5		(3,000)	90 × £90	8,100	(1,000)	4,100

Year	Cash flows £000	0%	PVs at 11%	17%	24%
0	(9,700)	(9,700)	(9,700)	(9,700)	(9,700)
1	6,000	6,000	5,405	5,128	4,838
2	10,500	10,500	8,522	7,670	6,828
3	16,800	16,800	12,284	10,489	8,811
4	(28,800)	(28,800)	(18,971)	(15,369)	(12,182)
5	4,100	4,100	2,433	1,870	1,398
		(1,100)	(27)	88	(7)

(b) The cash flows and relevant discount factors for each year could be arranged in vertical columns. The sum of their products is the NPV. By linking the discount factors to an interest rate in a reference cell, considering alternative interest rates is fast and easy. Thus the calculation of precise IRRs is possible and a situation of multiple IRRs quickly established.

Solution 26

Tips

- An unusual aspect of this question is the need to allow for changes in the investment in stocks and debtors each year.
- Remember that the cash flow involved is the increase or decrease in stocks and debtors each year.
- In year 8 the stock brought forward from year 7 will be recovered in cash (1,400 units × £95 × 0.05) = £6,650.
- In year 9 the debtors from year 8 will be recovered in cash (1,400 units × £103 × 0.10) = £14,420.

(a)

Year	Sales less COS £	Debtors £	Stock £	Cash flow £	DF	PV £
0			(950)	(40,950)	1.000	(40,950)
1	1,600	(2,060)	(1,425)	(1,885)	0.870	(1,640)
2	4,000	(3,090)	(2,375)	(1,465)	0.756	(1,108)
3	8,000	(5,150)	(3,800)	(950)	0.658	(625)
4	14,400	(8,240)	(950)	5,210	0.572	2,980
5	16,000	(2,060)	950	14,890	0.497	7,400
6	14,400	2,060	950	17,410	0.432	7,521
7	12,800	2,060	950	15,810	0.376	5,945
8	11,200	2,060	6,650	24,910	0.327	8,146
9		14,420		14,420	0.284	4,095
					NPV	(8,236)

Thus, the project is not economic and should not be pursued.

Workings for year 3

These workings are provided as an example. Figures for other years are calculated in the same way.

Sales less COS = 1,000 × £(103 − 95) = £8,000
Increase in debtors = 0.1 × £103 × (1,000 − 500) = £5,150
Increase in stock = 0.05 × £95 × (1,800 − 1,000) = £3,800

Note: £5,000 residual value added to cash flow in year 8

(b) For a sales price of £104 per widget:

Year	Sales less COS £	Debtors £	Stock £	Cash flow £	DF	PV £
0			(950)	(40,950)	1.000	(40,950)
1	1,800	(2,080)	(1,425)	(1,705)	0.870	(1,483)
2	4,500	(3,120)	(2,375)	(995)	0.756	(752)
3	9,000	(5,200)	(3,800)	0	0.658	0
4	16,200	(8,320)	(950)	6,930	0.572	3,964
5	18,000	(2,080)	950	16,870	0.497	8,384
6	16,200	2,080	950	19,230	0.432	8,307
7	14,400	2,080	950	17,430	0.376	6,554
8	12,600	2,080	6,650	26,330	0.327	8,610
9		14,560		14,560	0.284	4,135
					NPV	(3,231)

For a sales price of £105 per widget:

Year	Sales less COS £	Debtors £	Stock £	Cash flow £	DF	PV £
0			(950)	(40,950)	1.000	(40,950)
1	2,000	(2,100)	(1,425)	(1,525)	0.870	(1,327)
2	5,000	(3,150)	(2,375)	(525)	0.756	(397)
3	10,000	(5,250)	(3,800)	950	0.658	625
4	18,000	(8,400)	(950)	8,650	0.572	4,948
5	20,000	(2,100)	950	18,850	0.497	9,368
6	18,000	2,100	950	21,050	0.432	9,094
7	16,000	2,100	950	19,050	0.376	7,163
8	14,000	2,100	6,650	27,750	0.327	9,074
9		14,700		14,700	0.284	4,175
					NPV	1,773

Sensitivity of NPV to the selling price per widget

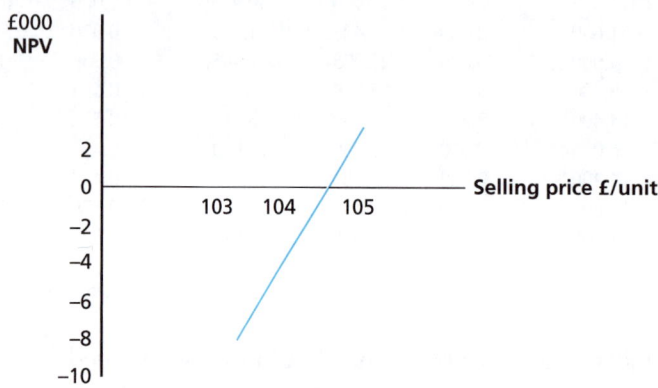

Therefore, the minimum price needed to generate a positive NPV is around £104.50.

Solution 27

Tip
- The calculations in this question are not difficult but you need to be systematic in your application of the formulae.

(a)

Batch size	Revenue 1 £000	Revenue 2 £000	Costs £000	Profit 1 £000	Profit 2 £000
1,000	899.8	858.4	351.8	548.0	506.6
2,000	1,625.9	1,452.9	609.2	1,016.7	843.7
3,000	2,191.7	1,793.8	843.6	1,348.1	950.2
4,000	2,603.8	1,886.3	1,064.8	1,539.0	821.5
5,000	2,866.6	1,734.0	1,277.0	1,589.6	457.0

Workings for 1,000 units
Revenue 1 $= (1{,}000 \times 1{,}000) - (1{,}000)^{1.9}/5 = £899{,}763$
Revenue 2 $= (1{,}000 \times 1{,}000) - (1{,}000)^{1.95}/5 = £858{,}411$
Cumulative average time $= 100 \times (1{,}000)^{-0.3} = 12.59$ hr
Cost $= (12.59 \times £20 \times 1{,}000) + (1{,}000 \times £100) = £351{,}800$

Workings for 2,000 units
Revenue 1 $= (1{,}000 \times 2{,}000) - (2{,}000)^{1.9}/5 = £1{,}625{,}901$
Revenue 2 $= (1{,}000 \times 2{,}000) \times (2{,}000)^{1.95}/5 = £1{,}452{,}936$
Cumulative average time $= 100 \times (2{,}000)^{-0.3} = 10.23$ hr
Cost $= (10.23 \times £20 \times 2{,}000) + (2{,}000 \times £100) = £609{,}200$

Workings for 3,000 units
Revenue 1 $= (1{,}000 \times 3{,}000) - (3{,}000)^{1.9}/5 = £2{,}191{,}723$
Revenue 2 $= (1{,}000 \times 3{,}000) - (3{,}000)^{1.95}/5 = £1{,}793{,}808$
Cumulative average time $= 100 \times (3{,}000)^{-0.3} = 9.06$ hr
Cost $= (9.06 \times £20 \times 3{,}000) + (3{,}000 \times £100) = £843{,}600$

Workings for 4,000 units
Revenue 1 $= (1{,}000 \times 4{,}000) - (4{,}000)^{1.9}/5 = £2{,}603{,}812$
Revenue 2 $= (1{,}000 \times 4{,}000) - (4{,}000)^{1.95}/5 = £1{,}886{,}282$
Cumulative average time $= 100 \times (4{,}000)^{-0.3} = 8.31$ hr
Cost $= (8.31 \times £20 \times 4{,}000) + (4{,}000 \times £100) = £1{,}064{,}800$

Workings for 5,000 units
Revenue 1 $= (1{,}000 \times 5{,}000) - (5{,}000)^{1.9}/5 = £2{,}866{,}596$
Revenue 2 $= (1{,}000 \times 5{,}000) - (5{,}000)^{1.95}/5 = £1{,}733{,}960$
Cumulative average time $= 100 \times (5{,}000)^{-0.3} = 7.77$ hr
Cost $= (7.77 \times £20 \times 5{,}000) + (5{,}000 \times £100) = £1{,}277{,}000$

From the table it can be seen that the profit-maximising batch sizes are:

Case (1) 5,000 units
Case (2) 3,000 units

(b) The maximum profit generated for cases (1) and (2) are £1,589,600 and £950,200 respectively.

The expected profit is based on producing 5,000 units. However if case (2) occurs then sales for that situation should be based on maximum revenue generation. The costs have already been incurred. Revenue 2 is maximised at 4,000 units and has a value of £1,886,300.

The profit forecast if case (2) occurs is therefore:

	£000
Sales revenue (4,000 units sold)	1,886.3
Costs (5,000 units produced)	1,277.0
	609.3

The expected profit is:

$(\frac{2}{3} \times £1{,}589{,}600) + (\frac{1}{3} \times £609{,}300) = £1{,}262{,}800$

(c) If the consultant forecasts case (1) – profit £1,589,600
If the consultant forecasts case (2) – profit £950,200
Thus the new expected profit is:

$$(\tfrac{1}{3} \times £950{,}200) + (\tfrac{2}{3} \times £1{,}589{,}600) = £1{,}376{,}500$$

This is an increase of £113,700, which is greater than the fee of £50,000.

It is less risky to hire the consultant, but if case (1) does ensue the company have spent £50,000 to justify their decision. The company should have a consistent policy for all such decisions as only then will the expected value approach aid decision making.

In my opinion the consultant should be hired.

Solution 28

Tips

- In part (a) (i), do not forget that the cumulative output to the end of March must include the 100 units manufactured during the trial period.
- In part (a) (ii) you will need to substitute the known data into the learning curve formula to derive the index of learning. The log calculations can be performed with tables, or by using the log button on your calculator.
- Once you have derived the learning curve percentage in (a) (ii), this can be used as the basis for the bonus calculation in (b).

(a) (i) Trial period

To the end of March, cumulative units produced = 100 + 400 + 480 + 620
= 1,600

In the learning curve formula, $b = \dfrac{\log 0.7}{\log 2}$

$$= \dfrac{-0.15490}{0.30103}$$

$$= -0.51457$$

Budgeted average labour time for the first three months and the trial period:

$$Y = 53.47 \times 1{,}600^{-0.51457} = 1.20051 \text{ hours}$$

(ii) Actual time taken for first 3 months and the trial period = 2,150 hours

Cumulative average time per unit $\dfrac{2{,}150}{1{,}600} = 1.34375$ hours

Solution for the actual learning curve index b

$1.34375 = 53.47 \times 1{,}600^{b}$ – equation (1)

$1600^{b} = \dfrac{1.34375}{53.47} = 0.0251309$

taking logs

$b \log 1{,}600 = \log 0.0251309$

$$b = \frac{-1.599792}{3.20412} = -0.499292$$

So $-0.499292 = \frac{\log p}{\log 2}$ where p is the learning rate

$\log p = -0.1503$

$p = 0.7075$, i.e. a learning curve of 70.75%

Note: The actual learning curve index b may be obtained by trial and error using equation (1) above.

(b) Using the 70.75% learning curve, $b = -0.499292$ as before

The budgeted cumulative average time $= 53.47 \times (1{,}600 + 775)^{-0.499292}$
$= 1.10323$ hours per unit

Standard labour hours for April
Cum. hours to end of April	$2{,}375 \times 1.10323 = 2{,}620$
Cum. hours to end of March	$1{,}600 \times 1.34375 = \underline{2{,}150}$
Standard time for 775 units	470 hours
Actual time for 775 units	460 hours

As 10 hours were saved in April the employees will be eligible to a bonus.

(c) The labour force may deliberately work slowly during the first three months in order to appear to be more efficient later. This would enable them to earn their bonus payments with a lower output.

The labour force were presumably working more slowly during January due to difficulty with the material supplied. This has now been rectified with better quality material, and in April the production was above target. Therefore, perhaps a better (more demanding) learning curve percentage would be found from using February and March production data.

Apportioning variable overhead on the basis of direct hours will result in less of these overheads being recovered on each subsequent unit produced. This is acceptable if all these overheads are truly driven by direct labour. If not, then a more appropriate cost driver should be developed.

Solution 29

Tip
- Do not fall into the trap of believing that ABC is the panacea for all costing problems. Try to discuss both sides of the argument for a change in the costing system.

(a) The following activity-based cost drivers may be developed:

	Comfort	Relaxer	Scand.	Total
Wood Metres (m)	10×30 = 300	9×120 = 1,080	9×150 = 1,350	2,730
Leather m	4×30 = 120	2×120 = 240		360
Labour hrs	24×30 = 720	20×120 = 2,400	16×150 = 2,400	5,520
Despatch units	30	120	150	300

Overhead cost analysis

	Comfort £	Relaxer £	Scand. £	Total £
Set-up costs (batches)	1,867	1,867	1,867	5,601
Purchase of leather (m)	1,333	2,667		4,000
Purchase of wood (m)	264	949	1,187	2,400
Quality (leather m)	1,067	2,133		3,200
Despatch (units)	600	2,400	3,000	6,000
Admin. (labour hours)	1,734	5,783	5,783	13,300
Total	6,865	15,799	11,837	34,501
Overhead cost per unit	£228.83	£131.66	£78.91	

Product cost statement

	Comfort £	Relaxer £	Scand. £
Selling price	395	285	225
Less: Material costs	85	60	50
Labour costs	120	100	80
Contribution	190 (48%)	125 (44%)	95 (42%)
Less: Overheads	229	132	79
Profit/(Loss)	(39)	(7)	16

(b) This more detailed analysis of overheads shows a different view, that is, that only the simple all-wood chair was making a profit. The more luxurious chairs were making a loss, especially the top of the range 'Comfort' model. This analysis is of more use for mid to long-term planning.

However, for short-term decision making, marginal costing should be used. The analysis in part (a) shows that the ratios of contribution to selling price were all very similar. Therefore, the business plan to make the 'Scandinavian' the high-volume product is the correct long-term decision.

The plan for the two leather chairs needs to be reviewed. Either the overhead costs for purchasing leather and quality control must be reduced and/or the sales prices need to be revised upwards. If these options are not viable, D may need to downsize the business and produce a single product, the 'Scandinavian'.

Therefore, a combination of marginal and absorption costing (ABC) is required to make future decisions about volumes and prices of the products.

(c) Information has not been gathered on the costs of supplying different customers in D's company. Some customers require high levels of service within the product-service package while other customers may only require the product itself. The price charged to each customer should (competition allowing) reflect this different level of requirement. I would advise D to undertake this activity.

ABC may be used to determine the costs to D in providing different levels of service. The costs would comprise elements such as:

Customer development costs	– Number of visits/meetings and the time spent on design of customised service
Production costs	– Batch and order sizes
	– Specials or extras, for example, packaging in a different form
Despatch	– Order time, distance, pattern of deliveries and availability of return loads
After-sales	– Follow-up time required, extra availability or speed of response for spares

Based upon the existing cost analysis, D's business does not appear to incur extra customer costs for: pre-sales costs, production costs, despatch and after-sales costs. These costs are hidden from D at the moment and may be built into the existing cost areas, not only production and despatch, but also administration, quality, etc.

Therefore, D must determine for each customer their price/quality/service profile, that is, some customers may be prepared to pay more for the extra service they are receiving. The information generated by an ABC analysis could and should be used to justify different charges for different packages of product and service.

Solution 30

Tip

- Do not get carried away with the extra capacity available in part (b)! Remember that the output may also be constrained by the weekly demand.

(a) Key source   Machine Z time

Time on key resource $\dfrac{40}{30} = 1.3333$ hr/unit

Return per factory hour $\dfrac{£2,000 - £600}{1.3333} = £1.050$

Cost per factory hour $\dfrac{£13,500 + (£450,000/48)}{40} = £571.88$

Throughout accounting ratio $= \dfrac{£1,050}{£571.88} = 1.84$

(b) The reliability of machine X is $\dfrac{(160 - 17.5) \times 100}{160} = 89\%$

The existing output capacities per week are:

Machine X	Machine Y	Machine Z
40	52	30

The output may be increased to 36 if machine F replaces machine Z or to 40 (machine X limiting) if machine G is purchased or to 45 (180 ÷ 4) if machine X is overhauled. The output may also be constrained by demand.

	Present machinery	Production Machine F	Machine G	Machine G and overhaul
Month				
Jan	120	120	120	120
Feb	120	120	120	120
Mar	120	132	132	132
Apr	120	144	144	144
May	120	144	156	156
Jun	120	144	160	176
Jul	120	144	160	180
Aug	120	144	160	180
Sep	120	144	160	168
Oct	120	144	160	160
Nov	120	132	132	132
Dec	120	120	120	120
	1,440	1,632	1,724	1,788
Additional units each year		192	284	348

Value added per unit	£
Selling price	2,000
Less: Materials	600
	1,400

	Machine F £000	Machine G £000	Machine G and overhaul £000
Additional value added	268.8	397.6	487.2
Less: Additional costs	120.0	216.0	216.0
Net gain each year	148.8	181.6	271.2

Cash flows	Discount factor	Machine F £	Machine G £	Machine G and overhaul £
Year 0				
Machine cost	1	(330,000)	(550,000)	(550,000)
Overhaul	1			(100,000)
Years 1–4				
£148,800	3.170	471,696		
£181,600	3.170		575,672	
£271,200	3.170			859,704
NPV		141,696	25,672	209,704

The combination of machine G and overhauling machine X has the greatest NPV and should be undertaken. The lowest cost option to overhaul machine X is not worthwhile on its own, as machine X is not presently limiting output.

If the overhaul is not possible for any reason then machine F should be purchased.

(c) The analysis is very sensitive to the output figures, that is, sales demand and production capacity used.

For the combination machine G and overhaul, an annual reduction of 4 per cent in output from 1,788 to 1,716.5 units would render the proposal quite uneconomic:

Extra units	276.5
Extra added value	£387,100
Net gain each year	£171,100
NPV	= £171,100 × 3.170 − £650,000 = (£107,600)

A 10% reduction in selling price to £1,800 would be required to render the proposal uneconomic, that is,

$$\text{Extra added value} = £487,200 \times \frac{1,200}{1,400} = £417,600$$

Net gain each year = £201,600

NPV = £201,600 × 3.170 − £650,000 = (£10,928)

Solution 31

(a) Throughput may be defined as:

The rate of production of a defined process over a stated period of time.

CIMA Official Terminology

or as:

Sales revenue less direct material cost.

Goldratt and Cox

The concepts underlying throughput accounting are that:
- In some organisations all labour costs are fixed costs, as are all overhead costs. Therefore, the only variable cost is the cost of direct materials.
- Direct material inventory should be minimised in line with a just-in-time approach. Therefore the direct material cost used by Goldratt and Cox is the purchase cost for the time period not the cost of direct material used in that time period.

The aim of the 'throughput accounting' approach is to ensure that production schedules maximise the 'throughput' value in each time period. This should focus management attention on:
- removing bottlenecks to achieve increased production and hence increased profit;
- maximising the effectiveness of the whole system rather than concentrating on specific components within it;
- manufacturing the optimum product mix as determined by this approach.

(b) The return per factory hour shows the rate of added value or contribution based on the premise that direct material costs are the only variable cost for the organisation. This ratio is used to rank different products that use the same bottleneck resource in the production process. The product with the highest value of this ratio is given highest ranking.

The throughput accounting ratio compares the rate of added value or contribution compared to the rate at which the organisation incurs production costs. If this ratio is greater than one then the organisation is generating contribution at a greater rate than it is generating production costs. Therefore, products should only be produced if this ratio is greater than one.

The proposal that MN Ltd should replace machine Z with machine G and overhaul machine X generates a sizeable NPV using MN's cost of capital. However, the throughput ratio declines from that generated by the present production process. This shows that for this proposal the relative increase in conversion costs is greater than the relative increase in value added. This is equivalent to a declining ROCE for an attractive (NPV) project.

(c) As throughput accounting strives to maximise production of saleable product two further ratios which may be used are availability of machinery/processes and the level of 'on specification' production produced:

$$\text{Availability} = \frac{\text{Process time}}{\text{Scheduled time}} \times 100$$

For the bottleneck in the process, the scheduled time will be the total production time in the period. An availability of less than 100 per cent for the bottleneck-processing step will reduce the throughput, i.e. the profitability of the operation.

If other process steps have availabilities of less than 100 per cent, then buffer stock may need to be held to ensure that the bottleneck-processing step is not deprived of material flow. For processing steps with poor availabilities, there is likely to be an economic incentive (throughput and stock-holding costs) to improve the situation:

$$\text{The level of 'on specification' output} = \frac{\text{Good production}}{\text{Total production}} \times 100$$

Obviously, production that fails to meet quality standards requires reworking, incurring extra costs. A more critical ratio would be the level of 'on specification' output from the bottleneck-processing step, as below quality material will need to use up bottleneck source time to transform it to saleable product. Hence, throughput capacity is lost as well as incurring rework costs.

These two ratios are sub-ratios of the throughput ratio:

$$\text{Throughput ratio} = \frac{\text{Good production}}{\text{Total scheduled time}}$$

$$= \frac{\text{Total units}}{\text{Process time}} \times \text{Availability} \times \text{Level of 'on spec' output}$$

(d) Throughput accounting and contribution (in marginal costing) use the same concept. They both calculate the difference between sales revenue and variable costs to determine a contribution that is used to cover the fixed costs of the organisation. In both approaches, the rate of contribution generated from different products using the same processing sequence can be used to rank the products and determine the optimum production mix.

One of the differences between these two approaches is in what constitutes the variable costs of the organisation. In marginal costing, normally direct labour costs and some overhead production costs are analysed to see if they are variable costs. However, in throughput accounting they are treated as fixed costs.

Furthermore, in throughput accounting there is a disincentive to produce goods unless there is a real demand for them. This disincentive is in the form of deducting the cost of all purchases of direct materials rather than only deducting the cost of direct materials used. The latter is used in marginal costing.

(e) The production manager and the management accountant need to focus on meeting scheduled output and maintaining low levels of inventory. The replacement of machine Z with machine G and the overhaul of machine X will increase capacity by removing existing bottlenecks. The new output constraints are Demand or Capacity, that is,

Machine X	45 units per week
Machine Y	54 units per week
Machine G	45 units per week

Therefore, both machines X and G will become the new bottlenecks during the period June to October. Therefore, the project must be completed and full capacity on these processing steps must be ensured by the first of June. Once the project is completed, the availability and the level of 'on specification' output must be monitored and reported for all the machines, but for these two machines in particular. The return per factory hour based upon these bottlenecks and the throughput ratio will also need to be monitored and reported along with any physical, real-time indicators that aid the workforce in maximising throughput.

✓ Solution 32

(a) Post-project appraisal and audit (PPAA) closes the loop in investment monitoring and control. Many companies have over-stressed the area of capital investment appraisal as a prerequisite of decision making, but failed to review the assumptions made and the success of the project's outcomes with the benefit of hindsight.

The advantages of PPAA are as follows:

- If managers know in advance that projects are going to be subject to PPAA they ensure that the assumptions and plans for the project are more accurate and realistic.
- PPAA has shown that undue haste and the setting of too strict self-imposed deadlines during the investment decision-making phase may result in poor decisions being made.
- PPAA has revealed that only contractors who have relevant experience and sufficient resources should be considered for selection.
- PPAA highlights the reasons for success or failure in previous projects and thereby improves the quality of decision-making.
- It improves the control mechanism for projects and increases the frequency of early modification (or termination) of under-performing projects.

The disadvantages with PPAA may be in the perception and implementation of the procedure rather than in the procedure itself.

- Many organisations outside of the manufacturing sector have failed to see the relevance of PPAA to their organisation.
- Organisations may not bother to carry out a detailed PPAA if the project produces the expected results. However, this may hide two offsetting variations or inaccuracies within the project.

Other disadvantages include slowing down the decision-making process so that opportunities may be missed and the cost of carrying out detailed PPAAs.

The proposals to replace machine Z and overhaul machine X are fairly straightforward, small-scale, efficiency projects that do not depend upon many external factors (cost of money, predicted demand). Therefore, the disadvantages noted above should not be of any consequence.

If the management of MN Ltd are aware in advance that PPAA will be carried out they will certainly take more time and effort to check their predictions of forecast demand and machine capacity. They may also review the contractors who are allowed to tender for the project. If MN have recently upgraded their production process with other replacements and/or overhauls, then carrying out PPAAs on those projects may highlight past problems and produce a better performance for this project.

However, MN need to complete the project by the first of June to maximise the benefit of increased throughput, so carrying out PPAAs on past projects may take too long and result in a rushed and possibly poor investment decision in this case.

Therefore, the decision as to whether to implement PPAA on this project is not clear cut, but for MN as a whole it would appear to be a good idea.

(b) The term 'value added' is simply the difference between sales price and material purchase cost. It is the contribution if material purchase costs are the only variable costs for the organisation.

The term 'value added activity' refers to any activity carried out within the organisation which adds more value to the customer than it costs the organisation to carry out.

For example, if adding machine H to the production process did not increase capacity but increased the quality of MN's output, such that the extra cost per unit was £1, but customers would pay an extra £2 per unit, then this activity (operating machine H) is a value-adding activity.

The two terms have little in common. The former is a very specific term for a very specific area of analysis. The second term is a general principle that should be used to consider all organisational activities using a cross-functional attitude.

Solution 33

Tips

- The expected value approach in (a) begins by calculating the expected revenue and contribution per week using the probabilities provided. Once the expected revenue is known, this can be used to determine the fee payable under options (ii) and (iii).
- Financial risk is minimised by selecting the option that results in the least loss when sales are low.

(a)

	High sales £/week	Average sales £/week	Low sales £/week	Expected sales £/week
Sales revenue	3,291.0	2,742.5	1,831.8	2,579.0
Less: Purchase costs	1,830.0	1,525.0	1,018.5	1,434.1
Contribution	1,461.0	1,217.5	813.3	1,144.9

	Alternative (i) £/week	Alternative (ii) £/week	Alternative (iii) £/week
Rent for expected sales:	600.0	500.0	
Fraction of sales revenue		129.0	644.8
	600.0	629.0	644.8
Contribution for expected sales	544.9	515.9	500.1
Rent for low sales:	600.0	500.0	
Fraction of sales revenue		91.6	458.0
	600.0	591.6	458.0
Contribution for low sales	213.3	221.7	355.3

∴ Alternative (i) should be selected using the expected value approach.

To minimise risk, alternative (iii) should be selected as this gives the maximum contribution (least loss) for low sales.

> **Examiner's note:**
> The contributions calculated above are not essential, but may help with part (c). An alternative approach to part (a) is as follows:
>
> **Best fee option**
> Fee option £600 — pay £600
> Fee option £500 plus 5% sales revenue
>
> | | High sales £/w | Average sales £/w | Low sales £/w |
> |---|---|---|---|
> | Fixed fee | 500 | 500 | 500 |
> | Sales revenue from WVC £11.45 × 180 × 0.05 = | 103 | | |
> | £11.45 × 150 × 0.05 | | 86 | |
> | £11.45 × 100 × 0.05 | | | 57 |
> | Similarly sales revenue from STC | 62 | 51 | 34 |
> | | 665 | 637 | 591 |
> | Multiplied by probability | × 0.2 | × 0.5 | × 0.3 |
> | | 133 | 318.5 | 177.3 |
>
> **Therefore expected payment = £629**
>
> **Fee option —25% sales revenue**
>
> | | High sales £/w | Average sales £/w | Low sales £/w |
> |---|---|---|---|
> | Sales revenue from WVC £11.45 × 180 × 0.25 = | 515 | | |
> | £11.45 × 150 × 0.25 | | 429 | |
> | £11.45 × 100 × 0.25 | | | 286 |
> | Similarly sales revenue from STC | 308 | 256 | 172 |
> | | 823 | 685 | 458 |
> | Multiplied by probability | × 0.2 | × 0.5 | × 0.3 |
> | | 164.6 | 342.5 | 137.4 |
>
> **Therefore, expected payment = £645**

(b) Option (ii) should never be selected as there is always a cheaper option.

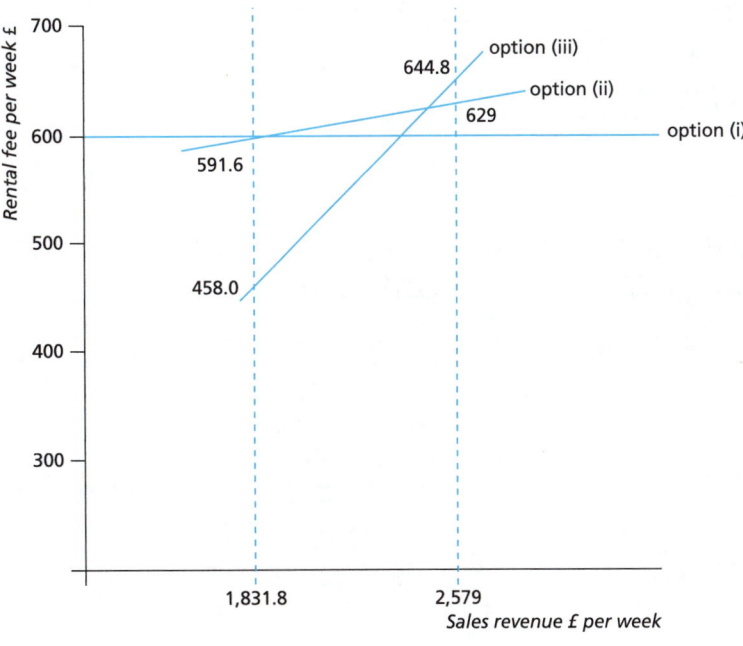

> **Examiner's note:**
> An alternative graph illustrating fee choice at varying sales levels is as follows:

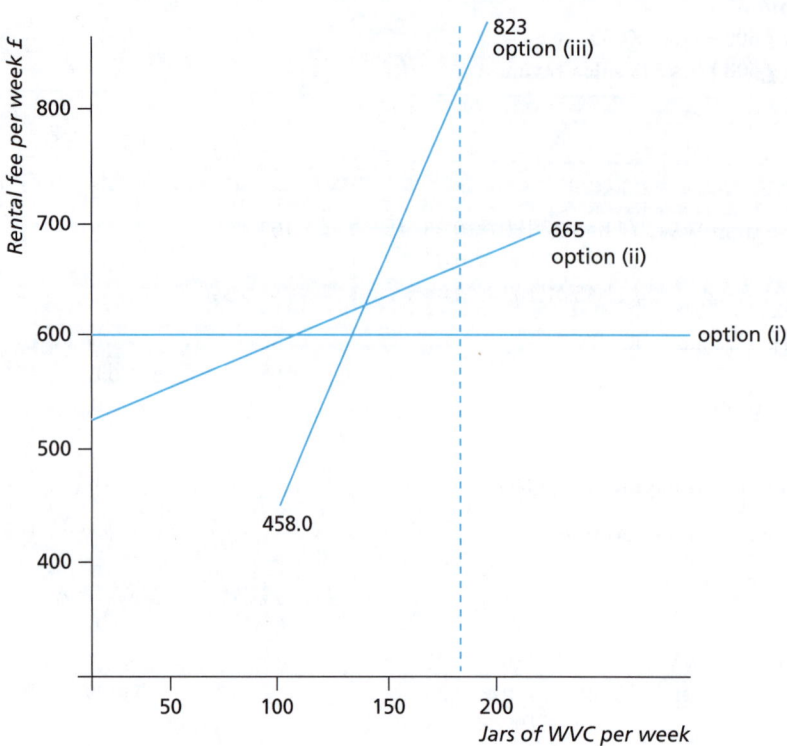

(c) Expected contribution without forecast, for option (iii) = £500.1 (from (a))
Above-average temperature forecast:

If correct	Expected sales
0.8 × 0.4	(150 jars WVC + 100 jars STC)
0.8 × 0.6	(100 jars WVC + 67 jars STC)
If incorrect	Expected sales
0.2 × 0.4	(180 jars WVC + 120 jars STC)
0.2 × 0.6	(150 jars WVC + 100 jars STC)

i.e. 128 jars of WVC
and 86 jars of STC

Contributions:

WVC = £4.95 − (0.25 × £11.45) = £2.09 per jar
STC = £4.75 − (0.25 × £10.25) = £2.19 per jar

Thus, the expected value is:

	£
128 × £2.09	267.52
86 × £2.19	188.34
	455.86

Below-average temperature forecast:

If correct	Expected sales
0.8 × 0.4	(180 jars WVC + 120 jars STC)
0.8 × 0.6	(150 jars WVC + 100 jars STC)
If incorrect	*Expected sales*
0.2 × 0.4	(150 jars WVC + 100 jars STC)
0.2 × 0.6	(100 jars WVC + 67 jars STC)

i.e. 154 jars of WVC
and 102 jars of STC

Thus, the expected value is:

	£
154 × £2.09	321.86
102 × £2.19	223.38
	545.24

Therefore, the extra contribution per week is £545.24 − £455.86 = £89.38 or £358 per 4 weeks compared with a forecast for unfavourable weather. The extra contribution compared with the expected value ignoring weather forecasts is (£545.24 − £500.1) × 4 = £181 per 4 weeks. J should also quantify the financial effects of:

- increased product scrap levels due to overstocking based on demand forecasts that are greater than those actually experienced;
- lost sales, if stocks cannot be replenished at short notice, when demand levels are greater than those forecast.

Solution 34

Tip

- Since the question asks you to state clearly any assumptions, you will lose marks if you do not do so. Furthermore, as long as your assumptions are reasonable you should receive marks even if they are different from our assumptions.

(a)

Year	Capital cost £m	Working capital £m	Marketing costs £m	Sales 000 units	Contribution £m	Cash flow £m	DF	PV £m
1	(2)					(2.00)	0.893	(1.79)
2	(4.5)	(2.5)	(1.50)			(8.50)	0.797	(6.77)
3			(0.75)	100	12.70	11.95	0.712	8.51
4			(0.75)	135	17.15	16.40	0.636	10.43
5			(0.75)	90	11.43	10.68	0.567	6.06
6			(0.75)	90	11.43	10.68	0.507	5.41
7		2.5	(0.75)	90	11.43	13.18	0.452	5.96
								27.81
Less: Present value of fixed costs			7.5 × (4.564 − 1.690)					21.567
Gives an NPV								6.25

The NPV is a significant positive value, thus the proposal appears to be financially worthwhile.

SOLUTIONS TO REVISION QUESTIONS P2

Assumptions

- The amount already spent is not relevant to the proposal (sunk cost);
- The sales figures are the average of the range and the competitor takes 50 per cent of market share after 18 months of sales;
- The equipment has no scrap value after 5 years;
- Working capital is released immediately production ceases.

(b)

Year	Capital cost £m	Working capital £m	Marketing costs £m	Sales 000 units	Contribution £m	Cash flow £m	DF	PV £m
1								(1.79)
2	(2.847)					(2.847)	0.797	(2.27)
3	(1.923)	2.5	(1.875)	55	6.985	0.687	0.712	0.49
4			(0.750)	75	9.525	8.775	0.636	5.58
5								6.06
6								5.41
7								5.96
								19.44
Less: Fixed cost		21.56 − (7.5 × 0.5 × 0.712)						18.89
NPV								0.55

The assumptions are as for part (a), with the following additions:

- Fixed costs assumed to be for one half of year 3;
- Working capital and pre-launch marketing campaign are put back 6 months;
- This delay is seen to severely damage the profitability of the project.

Workings

Capital cost year 2	2.667 plus extra salaries 0.180
Capital cost year 3	1.333 plus extra salaries 0.090 plus equipment 0.5
Marketing cost year 3	1.5 plus (0.75 × 0.5)

(c) The project is extremely sensitive to the sales in early years of the life cycle. These have been severely reduced due to the delay in the project (55,000 versus 100,000 in year 3) and the reduced total sales in year 4 (down 30,000 units). This second reduction may also be attributable to the delay in product launch.

This large loss in profits is due to a budget constraint, which involves a very small increase in the total development budget. The need for and the effects of not spending this small increase should have been made clear early on to avoid this ludicrous situation. If the sales figures in the remaining years are at the lower bound of the forecast, the project may well make a loss.

As the major cash outflows have already taken place (development, operating equipment and pre-launch marketing) the project should continue to reap the positive cash flows forecast for the next 4 years. The company can attempt to improve the size of the future positive cash flows by:

- finding ways to compete with its competitor that holds 50 per cent of the market share;
- further develop the product or market to extend the life cycle of the project;
- an ongoing cost reduction exercise.

Solution 35

Tip

- A number of alternative graphs would be acceptable for part (b), including those shown. Only one graph would be required.

(a) Life cycle costing (LCC) involves collecting cost data for each product from inception, through its useful life and including any end costs. This data is compared with the life cycle budgeted costs for the product. This comparison will show if the expected savings from using new technology or production methods have been realised.

The recognition of the total support required over the life of the product should lead to a more effective allocation of resources and is therefore an improvement on traditional budgeting which focuses on financial years, rather than product life span. Typically 80–90 per cent of the life cycle costs are determined at the design stage. There is also a change in cost focus; LCC gathers costs for each product, whereas traditional costing methods follow costs by function, for example, R&D, production, marketing and so on.

(b) **Life cycle chart for the Sparkle**

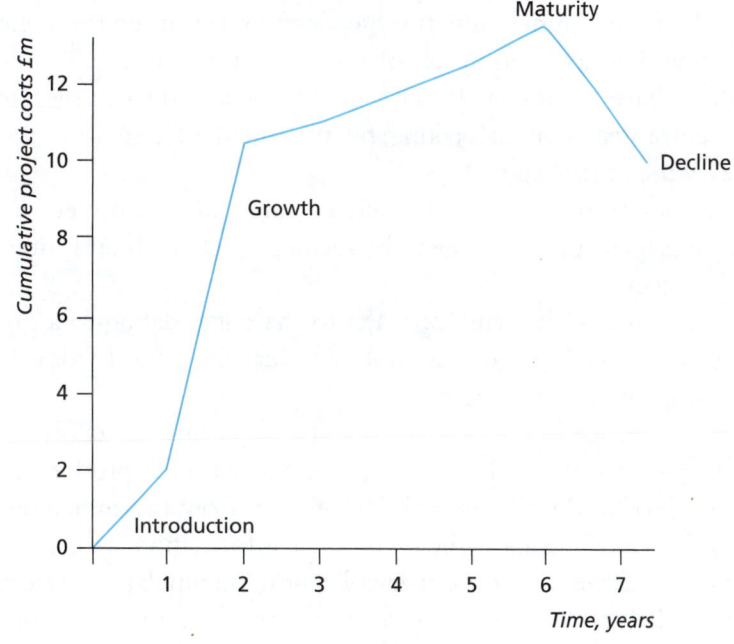

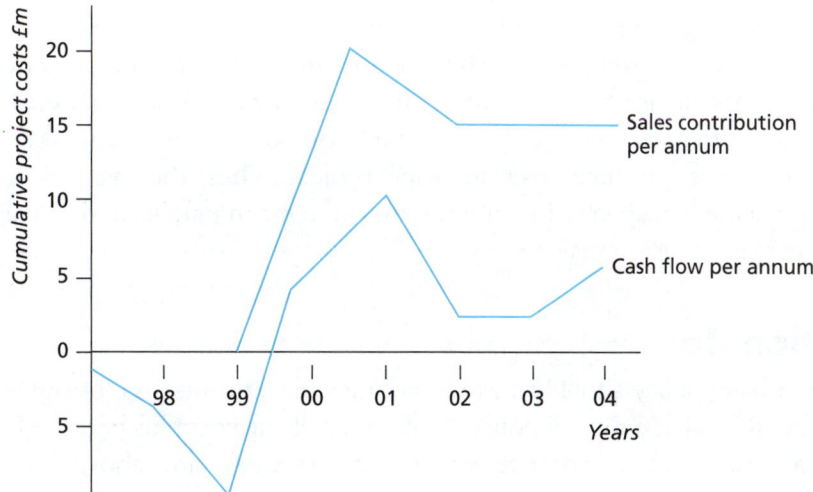

(c) Six potential benefits from using a post-project audit are:
   1. it improves the decision-making process by providing past experience to the decision makers;
   2. it inculcates a more rational approach to project appraisal as the managers are aware that their decisions will be reviewed with the benefit of hindsight;
   3. it improves the project control mechanism by showing areas of weakness;
   4. it enables timely modification of projects by comparing their actual performance against a series of stage targets;
   5. it enables unprofitable projects to be abandoned earlier in their life;
   6. it highlights reasons for success, which may be of use in increasing the benefits from future projects.

   As up to 90 per cent of the life cycle costs may be fully committed by the end of the design stage, it is paramount that the front end of the project is managed using best practice, that is using a post-project audit.

   Potential benefit numbers 3 and/or 4 may have prevented the Sparkle development from overrunning on time due to the annual budget restrictions. This overrun has significantly reduced the expected profit of the project.

   The general points learned from this project, that is the effect of late entry to market on sales volume and on net present value, need to be learned throughout the organisation. This should be achieved by use of a post-project audit.

   Some authors have commented that a post-project audit will discourage initiative and positive entrepreneurial risk-taking by management and thus result in underperformance by the organisation.

   Overall, it can be seen that both life cycle costing and post-project audit attempt to complete the management control cycle by feeding, backwards and forwards, a holistic view on each project.

(d) Life cycle costing uses a different approach to the data relating to a project. It is not constrained to a financial budget period, but covers the period from the commencement to the completion of a project.

   There is also a change in cost focus from the traditional function cost centres, for example R&D, production, marketing, etc., to a cost for each product launched. Thus, the information produced is of a very different form from the annual budget. This will not produce a difficulty so long as the two sets of information are used to complement each other, and if sufficient data and data collection/manipulation systems are in place.

   In the case of R Ltd, the two sets of information are not used to complement each other. The extra development staff were not hired until a new budget year commenced, with their costs included in the budget. This may be due to the failure of the project team to use a life cycle costing approach to identify the cost of this delay, or due to their failure to convince higher management of the consequences of a short-term mindset.

   Most information systems should be capable of adaptation to give the necessary information, that is, produce costs for each project. Thus, the main difficulty may well be convincing management to run the two systems in parallel and to use them to complement their decision making.

✓ Solution 36

(a) A strategic pricing policy should aim to either maximise profits and/or obtain a target market share. R Ltd has a pricing policy which is a variable cost plus policy. This blanket policy for all products does not meet either of the strategic aims above. Furthermore, for some products that have high associated fixed costs, there is no guarantee that this price will cover the total cost of the product.

The price set for a product should be market based and should relate to the stage of the product life cycle. Generally, new products are launched at a relatively high price as demand is likely to be limited to better-off fashion setters (market skimming) and the price will be lowered as part of the ongoing marketing campaign to increase the market and market share. In the case of the Sparkle, the delayed launch and early entry of competition may severely limit R Ltd's ability to skim the market. In later stages of the life cycle, it is more profitable for all competitors if price competition is minimal and marketing promotions, brand image and service facilities are used to compete for market share. Thus, R Ltd should change its policy to one that is market based.

(b) Many organisations have implemented refined product cost systems, such as ABC, in recent years. However, this does not imply that they then use a cost-based pricing policy. The advantage of an accurate product cost system is that management can make better informed decisions in the light of a fuller understanding of the cost, volume, profit relationship for each product and/or each customer. The statement does make a valid point in that this is not the be-all and end-all of the pricing process.

The market-based approach to pricing throughout the product life cycle, referred to in part (a), requires a sound knowledge of customer perceptions and requirements. Different customers have both different values, for example, price versus quality, and different needs, for example, just the product itself versus a complete product/service package.

Furthermore, the actions and reactions of competitors are important considerations regarding pricing for maximum profit or target market share. Thus, the statement is correct in stating that the company should spend time and money on researching customer perceptions and requirements. This should be part of every employee's remit and should be a continuous programme. Hiring in a market research team for a one-off exercise will not suffice.

R Ltd appears to have some feel for the market demand as a function of its recommended price, but has it investigated demand level for different prices? It also seems very sure of its competitor's actions and ensuring market share, but is it expecting its competitor to match its price and quality exactly, hence the 50:50 market split? Perhaps R Ltd needs to consider how the market will react if the competitor enters with a different offering on price, quality, service levels and how it will affect the market share of the Sparkle.

(c) **Memorandum**

To: Chief Executive
From: Management Accountant
Date: 22 November
Re: Target costing

Target costing is complementary to a market-based pricing policy. Selling prices are set based upon what the customer is willing to pay in order for the organisation to obtain a derived level of output (market share). The required profit is deducted from the estimated revenue to leave a target cost.

Target costing for products (Genka Kaizen) has been employed by Japanese industry for more than 30 years. Furthermore, around 80 per cent of Japanese assembly environments use this technique. This form of target costing may be defined as 'an approach to cost reduction which can be applied to the production phase of the life cycle for both new and existing products'.

The Japanese also have a variant of target costing (Genka Kikaku) which may be defined as 'an activity whose aim is that of reducing the life cycle costs of new products, through the examination of all ideas for cost reduction of the product at the pre-production stage'. The aim is to meet customer requirements, such as quality and reliability, at the minimum possible cost.

The English translation 'target' loses an essential part of the meaning of the Japanese term. In Japan, a 'target' cost is an agreed target to which all members have a 100 per cent commitment to achieving. These 'targets' cover the whole life cycle of the product and, although they may be set at different values for different stages of the life cycle, they are never expected to be revised.

The use of target costing is to stimulate innovation and cost cutting in the early stages of the life cycle. This is a period when most of the costs incurred over the whole life cycle are 'designed in' to the project. This could be based on a 6-monthly budgeting and review process which sets target product costs broken down into department costs. These specific cost targets will be set at reduced levels for subsequent budget periods.

A further use is to set ongoing targets for reduction of costs via continuous improvement in the production process.

The limitation of this technique is that if unrealistic, that is unachievable targets are set, then the workforce will either not be committed to the targets, or if they were committed to the targets, then the sense of failure to meet them will demotivate the workforce. If the levels of improvement targeted are too conservative, then they will not motivate the workforce to improve.

I hope this gives you a brief outline of target costing.

Signed: Management Accountant

Solution 37

Tips

- The most difficult part of this question is the initial analysis of cost into cost pools and the identification of appropriate cost drivers.
- A fundamental point to appreciate is that the direct cost of each operation will not be affected by the costing method used.
- You may have selected two different items in your answer to part (b). As long as your discussion is sensible you should earn good marks.

(a) (i)

Direct costs:		
Number of theatre hours	300 days × 4 theatres × 9 hours	=10,800
Theatre cost per hour	£4,050,000 ÷ 10,800	= £375
Pre-operation cost per operation	£1,260,000 ÷ 7,200	= £175
Consultants' fees per hour	£5,250,000 ÷ (2,000 hours × 15)	= £175

Indirect costs:	
Caring for patients:	£000
Nursing	9,936
Linen and laundry	920
Kitchen and food	2,256
Medical supplies	1,100
Pathology laboratory	920
	15,132

Patient care cost per day = £15,132,000 ÷ 44,000 days = £343.91

Admissions and record keeping:	£000
Updating records	590
Patient/bed scheduling	100
Invoicing	160
	850

Admission costs per patient = £850,000 ÷ 9,600 patients = £88.54

Facility-sustaining costs:	£000
Housekeeping	760
Insurance of buildings, etc.	60
Depreciation of buildings, etc.	520
	1,340

The indirect costs have been split into the three categories indicated in the question. The chosen cost driver for caring for patients is patient days, on the grounds that most of the costs placed in this category are dependent on the length of patient stay. Medical supplies and pathology laboratory do not fit well into this category and a more accurate accounting treatment would have been given if the information had been available.

The chosen cost driver for admissions and record keeping is number of patients, on the grounds that these costs vary with the number of patients rather than their length of stay or type of illness.

Facility-sustaining costs have not been given a cost driver because the question says that the mark-up is to cover these costs. Either treatment is acceptable under ABC.

Price for an ENT operation:

	Existing method	ABC	
	£	£	£
Direct costs:			
Operation £375 × 2 hours	750.00		
Pre-operation costs	175.00		
Consultant's fee £175 × 3 hours	525.00		
	1,450.00		1,450.00
Mark-up on direct costs 135%	1,957.50		
ABC: Support costs:			
Patient care cost £343.91 × 4 days		1,375.64	
Admission costs		88.54	
			1,464.18
			2,914.18
Mark-up 15%			437.13
Price	3,407.50		3,351.31

Price for a cataract operation:

	Existing method	ABC	
	£	£	£
Direct costs:			
Operation £375 × 0.5 hours	187.50		
Pre-operation costs	175.00		
Consultant's fee £175 × 0.85 hours	148.75		
	511.25		511.25
Mark-up on direct costs 135%	690.19		
ABC: Support costs:			
Patient care cost £343.91 × 1 day		343.91	
Admission costs		88.54	
			432.45
			943.70
Mark-up 15%			141.56
Price	1,201.44		1,085.26

(ii) The proposed method prices both operations lower than previously. If this is likely to be replicated for most operations, consideration should be given to raising the mark-up to, say, 20 per cent in order to maintain the current total profit. Also, a detailed assessment of facility costs should be undertaken first (if not already done) in order to determine the true mark-up required.

The ENT operation, which is a relatively long-stay operation, does not show a marked difference between the two pricing systems. The cataract operation, which is a short-stay procedure, shows a marked drop in price with ABC because of the low patient care cost. As a consequence, the hospital may be over-pricing this type of operation at present and not winning the business it would like from customers (individuals, private health insurers and the National Health Service).

It should be noted that the cataract operation does not require an overnight stay in hospital and so the patient care cost could be refined and probably reduced in this instance. So it is recommended that all estimated costs are checked carefully and pricing is adjusted with the proviso given in (b) below.

(b) The method used in (a) is a very basic form of ABC utilising very few activities and cost drivers. If it is to be really useful for pricing and other purposes, costs should be divided into a greater number of cost pools so that a more accurate picture is given, and items such as medical supplies are not spread on the basis of patient days. The two items chosen for detailed discussion are 'pathology laboratory' and 'nursing costs'.

Pathology laboratory. This work has been included under patient care costs per day – not all patients require these services. Some patients will make more demands than others on the pathology laboratory and perhaps a specific charge per type of patient admission should be calculated. Alternatively, a simple rate per laboratory test could be calculated and used:

£920,000 ÷ 8,000 tests = £115 per test

However, it would be more accurate to calculate an average cost per type of test and charge this specifically.

Nursing costs. These costs are considerable in relation to the total and should be dealt with as accurately as possible. Different nursing skills are required for different types of care and much nursing is administration work. The costs in this category range from intensive care to just providing room service after a minor operation. Nursing care should be split into a number of different categories dependent on skills/pay and different cost drivers used. The heading 'nursing services and administration' seems to cover much more than just nursing salaries judging by the figure given for nursing hours, and so further analysis is definitely needed.

(c) Yes, it is possible to use throughput accounting in a hospital. The bottleneck facility could be:
- intensive care bed;
- bed occupied;
- operating theatre;
- specialist skill, etc.

This system could help to ensure that the hospital's hard-pressed resources are used to best advantage and that all resources are in reasonable balance.

T However, throughput accounting is often used to speed up flow through facilities, but in a hospital any system that encourages patients to be rushed through the process, endangering their health, is not to be encouraged and would not benefit the hospital in the long run! Therefore, performance measures based on throughput are not advisable, or if used they would have to be counter-balanced by measures such as patient death, recovery, re-admission, etc., as well as qualitative measures. But the system could be of great help if used by top management in planning and balancing resources.

Solution 38

36.1

Year	Cash Flow £	DF	PV £
0	(20,000)	1.000	(20,000)
1	7,420	0.909	6,745
2	8,560	0.826	7,071
3	7,460	0.751	5,602
NPV			(582)

Cash Flow

Year 1

P	x £	Px £
0.2	10,000	2,000
0.5	7,000	3,500
0.3	6,400	1,920
EV		7,420

Year 2

P	x £	Px £
0.2	12,000	2,400
0.5	8,000	4,000
0.3	7,200	2,160
EV		8,560

Year 3

P	x £	Px £
0.2	9,000	1,800
0.5	7,600	3,800
0.3	6,200	1,860
EV		7,460

Therefore the answer is (A)

36.2 Replacement at the end of the first year:

(£220,000 × 1.00) + ((£110,000 − £121,000) × 0.893) = 210,177

$$\text{Annualised equivalent cost} = \frac{£210,177}{0.893} = £235,361$$

Replacement at the end of the second year:

(£220,000 × 1.00) + (£110,000 × 0.893) + ((£132,000 − £88,000) × 0.797) = £353,298

$$\text{Annualised equivalent cost} = \frac{£353,298}{1.69} = £209,052$$

Replacement at the end of the third year:

(£220,000 × 1.00) + (£110,000 × 0.893) + (£132,000 × 0.797) + ((£154,000 − £66,000) × 0.712) = £486,090

$$\text{Annualised equivalent cost} = \frac{£486,090}{2.402} = £202,369$$

Replacement at the end of the fourth year:

(£220,000 × 1.00) + (£110,000 × 0.893) + (£132,000 × 0.797) + (£154,000 × 0.712) + ((£165,000 − £55,000) × 0.636) = £603,042

$$\text{Annualised equivalent cost} = \frac{£603,042}{3.037} = £198,565$$

Replacement at the end of the fifth year:

(£220,000 × 1.00) + (£110,000 × 0.893) + (£132,000 × 0.797) + (£154,000 × 0.712) + ((£165,000 × 0.636) + ((£176,000 − £25,000) × 0.567) = £723,639

$$\text{Annualised equivalent cost} = \frac{£723,639}{3.605} = £200,732$$

The fleet should be replaced at the end of four years.

Therefore the answer is (D)

36.3

	J	K	L	M
	£	£	£	£
Selling price	2,000	1,500	1,500	1,750
Direct materials	410	200	300	400
Throughput	1,590	1,300	1,200	1,350
Machine X (minutes)	120	100	70	110
Throughput per machine (minutes)	$\frac{£1,590}{120}$	$\frac{£1,300}{100}$	$\frac{£1,200}{70}$	$\frac{£1,350}{110}$
	£13.25	£13.00	£17.14	£12.27
Ranking	2nd	3rd	1st	4th

Therefore the answer is (D)

36.4 The answer is (A).

36.5

	W	X	Y
	£000	£000	£000
Gross margin	1,100	1,750	1,200
Less: Customer related costs			
Sales visits	55	50	85
Order processing	100	100	150
Despatch costs	100	100	150
Billing and collections	157.5	210	262.5
Net profit/(loss)	687.5	1,290	552.5
Ranking	2nd	1st	3rd

Therefore the answer is (C)

Solution 39

Requirement (a)

Total savings achieved by implementing JIT	£000	£000
Current situation		
Prime costs:		
C1		273,000
C2		316,200
C3		445,500
Total prime costs		1,034,700
Overheads		
Variable overheads		
Set-ups	45,500	
Materials handling	58,400	
Inspection	63,000	
Machining	182,400	
Distribution and warehousing	43,800	393,100
Fixed overheads		342,870
Total cost		1,770,670
Implement JIT		
Prime costs:		
C1		289,800
C2		335,580
C3		475,200
Total prime costs		1,100,580
Variable overheads		
Set-ups	31,850	
Materials handling	40,880	
Inspection	44,100	
Machining	155,040	271,870
Fixed overheads		
Set-ups	29,862	
Materials handling	37,023	
Inspection	41,916	
Machining	122,859	231,660
Total cost		1,604,110
Conclusion		
Current cost		1,770,670
JIT cost		1,604,110
Cost savings		166,560

Therefore implement the JIT system, as there are substantial savings in costs.

Requirement (b)

Variable cost per car under JIT

	C1	C2	C3
	£	£	£
Prime cost	3,864.00	4,474.40	6,336.00
Variable o/heads (W1)	928.26	1,292.00	1,404.67
Variable cost	4,792.26	5,766.40	7,740.67

Workings

(1) *Variable overheads*

Set up costs £13,000 × 70% = £9,100 per production run

C1 £9,100 × $\frac{1,000}{75,000}$ = £121.33

C2 £9,100 × $\frac{1,000}{75,000}$ = £121.33

C3 £9,100 × $\frac{1,500}{75,000}$ = £182.00

Material handling £4,000 × 70% = £2,800 per order executed

C1 £2,800 × $\frac{4,000}{75,000}$ = £149.33

C2 £2,800 × $\frac{5,000}{75,000}$ = £186.67

C3 £2,800 × $\frac{5,600}{75,000}$ = £209.07

Inspection £18,000 × 70% = £12,600 per production run

C1 £12,600 × $\frac{1,000}{75,000}$ = £168

C2 £12,600 × $\frac{1,000}{75,000}$ = £168

C3 £12,600 × $\frac{1,500}{75,000}$ = £252

Machining £40 × 85% = £34 per machine hour

C1 £34 × $\frac{1,080,000}{75,000}$ = £489.60

C2 £34 × $\frac{1,800,000}{75,000}$ = £816.00

C3 £34 × $\frac{1,680,000}{75,000}$ = £761.60

Variable overheads per car

	C1 £	C2 £	C3 £
Set-up	121.33	121.33	182.00
Material handling	149.33	186.67	209.07
Inspection	168.00	168.00	252.00
Machining	489.60	816.00	761.60
Variable overheads	928.26	1,292.00	1,404.67

The optimum selling price and output level is determined as follows:

C1	Demand	Selling price	Variable cost	Contribution	Total contribution
		£	£	£	£000
	75,000	5,000	4,792.26	207.74	15,581
	65,000	5,750	4,792.26	957.74	62,253
	50,000	6,000	4,792.26	1,207.74	60,387
	35,000	6,500	4,792.26	1,707.74	59,771

Therefore, the optimum level of sales and the corresponding selling price is:

65,000 cars @ £5,750

C2	Demand	Selling price	Variable cost	Contribution	Total contribution
		£	£	£	£000
	75,000	5,750	5,766.40	(16.40)	(1,230)
	60,000	6,250	5,766.40	483.60	29,016
	45,000	6,500	5,766.40	733.60	33,012
	35,000	7,500	5,766.40	1,733.60	60,676

Therefore, the optimum level of sales and the corresponding selling price is:

35,000 cars @ £7,500

C3	Demand	Selling price	Variable cost	Contribution	Total contribution
		£	£	£	£000
	75,000	6,500	7,740.67	(1,240.67)	(93,050)
	60,000	6,750	7,740.67	(990.67)	(59,440)
	45,000	7,750	7,740.67	9.33	420
	30,000	8,000	7,740.67	259.33	7,780

Therefore, the optimum level of sales and the corresponding selling price is:

30,000 cars @ £8,000

Requirement (c)
Consider discontinuing one or more of the car types

	C1	C2	C3
	£000	£000	£000
Loss in contribution	(62,253)	(60,676)	(7,780)
Savings in fixed costs	9,266	11,583	18,533
Overall (loss)/gain	(52,987)	(49,093)	10,753
Decision	Continue	Continue	Discontinue

Recommendation
Continue operations and produce C1 and C2, but discontinue C3. This will minimise the losses for the forthcoming twelve months.

Requirement (d)

Report

To: The Management of X Ltd
Re: Just In Time

From: Management Accountant
Date: 20 November 2002

As identified, the implementation of a JIT manufacturing system would substantially reduce costs for the company. However, beyond the financial savings, consideration must now be given to the conditions necessary for its successful implementation in the company.

Conditions

- There is a need for smooth uniform production rates, that is smooth production flow, as fluctuations in production rates will result in delays and excess work in progress.
- The pull method of coordinating steps in the production process begins at the last stage of the manufacturing process, that is when additional elements are needed for final assembly, the message goes to the immediately preceding centre to send the amount of elements needed. Therefore, nothing is manufactured until it is triggered from the subsequent process.
- There must be multi-skilled workers and flexible facilities in order to produce the different types of cars. Workers should be versatile and capable of moving between production lines in order to keep production flowing. Equipment must be more versatile so that no bottlenecks result.
- There must be good teamwork so that efficiency levels are high and any non-value added costs are eliminated. This can sometimes be achieved through the introduction of an incentive scheme.
- There must be routine checks and preventative maintenance on equipment to avoid downtime.
- There is a need for quick and inexpensive set ups of machinery.
- Purchases of materials and production of sub-assemblies should be in small amounts to avoid stock building up and the costs associated with this.
- High-quality material is needed and a reliable working relationship must be established with the supplier to ensure that the materials are available and can be used straight away.

Meeting the above conditions will help to ensure the successful implementation of a JIT manufacturing system for the company.

Signed: Management Accountant

Solution 40

Requirement (a)

Net Present Value
Cost of capital 10% (W1)

Year	Total cash flow £	DF	PV £
0	(550,000)	1.000	(550,000)
1	200,260	0.909	182,036
2	164,920	0.826	136,224
3	164,920	0.751	123,855
4	164,920	0.683	112,640
5	219,920	0.621	136,570
6	(35,340)	0.564	(19,932)
		NPV	121,393

The above NPV of £121,393, while an expedient calculation, does not allow for the benefit of the lag in the payment of taxation. When this is incorporated the NPV will be slightly larger which is even more in favour of the decision (see alternative below).

Alternative approach

If candidates use the nominal discount rate, and adjust all values for inflation, this reveals a slightly different NPV result because of the time lag of taxation.

Net Present Value
Cost of capital   15.5%

Year	Total cash flow £	DF	PV £
0	(550,000)	1.000	(550,000)
1	210,273	0.866	182,096
2	183,680	0.750	137,760
3	192,864	0.649	125,169
4	202,507	0.562	113,809
5	282,827	0.487	137,737
6	(45,104)	0.421	(18,989)
NPV			127,582

Workings

Project cash Flows	Year 1	Year 2	Year 3	Year 4	Year 5	Year 6
Contribution less fixed overhead		£247,380	£259,749	£272,736	£286,373	£300,692
Scrap value			£70,195			
Total tax payable on corporate profit	(£37,107)	(£76,069)	(£79,872)	(£83,866)	(£88,060)	(£45,104)
Net cash flow	£210,273	£183,680	£192,864	£202,507	£282,827	(£45,104)

Recommendation:

The project should be undertaken as it generates a positive net present value.

Workings

1. Real discount rate $\dfrac{(1 + 0.155)}{(1 + 0.05)} - 1 = 10\%$

2. Total cash flows

Expected value of annual sales

Demand	x £	P	Px £
High	800,000	0.25	200,000
Medium	560,000	0.50	280,000
Low	448,000	0.25	112,000
Expected value			592,000

Expected value of annual sales	£592,000
CS ratio	55%
Contribution	£325,600
Less: Fixed overheads	£90,000
Corporate profit	£235,600
Tax @ 30%	£70,680

Project cash flows	Year 1 £	Year 2 £	Year 3 £	Year 4 £	Year 5 £	Year 6 £
Profit	235,600	235,600	235,600	235,600	235,600	
Scrap value					55,000	
Total tax payable on corporate profit	(35,340)	(70,680)	(70,680)	(70,680)	(70,680)	(35,340)
Net cash flow	200,260	164,920	164,920	164,920	219,920	(35,340)

Requirement (b)
Sensitivity of the project to changes in the expected annual contribution

The net (after tax) present value of the contribution
Cost of capital 10%

Year	Contribution £	Tax payment £	Cash flow £	DF	PV £
1	325,600	(48,840)	276,760	0.909	251,575
2	325,600	(97,680)	227,920	0.826	188,262
3	325,600	(97,680)	227,920	0.751	171,168
4	325,600	(97,680)	227,920	0.683	155,669
5	325,600	(97,680)	227,920	0.621	141,538
6		(48,840)	(48,840)	0.564	(27,546)
			NPV		880,666

The NPV of the project is £121,393. Therefore the PV of the contributions can fall by this amount. This means can fall by £121,393/£880,666, that is, a sensitivity of 13.78%.

Requirement (c)

Writing-Down Allowances schedule

	£	Tax saved @ 30% £	Year 1 £	Year 2 £	Year 3 £	Year 4 £	Year 5 £	Year 6 £
Initial expenditure	550,000							
WDA Year 1, 25%	137,500	41,250	20,625	20,625				
	412,500							
WDA Year 2, 25%	103,125	30,938		15,469	15,469			
	309,375							
WDA Year 3, 25%	77,344	23,203			11,602	11,601		
	232,031							
WDA Year 4, 25%	58,008	17,402				8,701	8,701	
	174,023							
Sale for scrap, year 5	70,195							
Balancing allowance	103,828	31,148					15,574	15,574
Total tax savings			20,625	36,094	27,071	20,302	24,275	15,574
Discount factor (nominal rate)			0.866	0.750	0.649	0.562	0.487	0.42
Present value			17,861	27,071	17,569	11,410	11,822	6,557
Total present value		92,290						

The net present value for the investment will increase by £92,290 due to savings in tax arising from writing down allowances.

> **Examiner's Note:**
> The writing down allowances are not affected by inflation, except to the extent that the final asset value will increase.

Solution 41

Requirement (a)

Report

To: The Management
Re: Investment Appraisal

From: Management Accountant
Date: 20 November 2002

Payback method

The payback method, which is currently used, is one of the simplest methods to understand and apply to capital investment appraisal. it represents the length of time that is required for cash proceeds from an investment to recover the original cash outlay required by the investment.

The payback period for this investment is:

	Cumulative cash flows		Payback
Initial outlay	Years 1–3	Years 4–5	
£000	£000	£000	
2,000	1,200	2,200	4 years 7 months

The company's target payback is 4 years and on this basis, as this project exceeds that target, it would be rejected.

It can be seen, therefore, that this method maintains the organisation's liquidity in that it favours projects with early cash inflow. While managers find this method easy to understand and apply it is flawed, as it does not take into account cash flows that are earned after the payback date which in the case of this project are quite significant. It also fails to take into account the differences in the timing of the proceeds that are earned before the payback date. Unlike discounted cash flow, the payback method ignores the importance of the time value of money, that is future cash receipts are not comparable to cash today. However, in order to overcome the problem associated with the time value of money, discounted payback could be used as an initial screening to assess the length of time the project will take to recoup the initial cash outlay. However, it should not be used as the only methods as, unlike net present value (NPV), it is not an absolute measure as to whether or not the investment will maximise shareholders' wealth.

Accounting rate of return (ARR) method

The ARR method expresses the annual average profit from a project as a percentage of the average annual investment in the project, in order to measure whether or not a project is worthwhile.

The ARR for this investment is:

	£000
Total cash savings	4,350
Less: Depreciation	2,000
Accounting profit	2,350
Project life — years	10
Average annual accounting profit	235
ARR	$\frac{235}{1,000} \times 100$
	23.5%

The company's target ARR is 25 per cent and as this project only yields a return of 23.5 per cent, it would be rejected.

As can be seen, this method uses annual accounting profits, rather than annual net cash flow, and while it allows for difference in the useful lives of the assets being compared, it ignores the time value of money. Also, when this method is used in investment appraisal, even if the benefits from a project come in later years, the averaging out of the profits and investment means that the same ARR will exist providing the cash inflows are the same. This method also measures the impact of the investment on the balance sheet and allows the organisation to select projects that maintain a strong balance sheet, rather than those that maximise shareholder's wealth. This method should not be used for project appraisal purposes as it can produce incorrect results.

Net Present Value (NPV) method

I propose the use of the NPV method as it takes into account the time value of money, that is, it acknowledges that cash received in the future has less value than cash received today. With NPV, all future cash flows from the project will be discounted into present day values based on the company's cost of capital. If the discounted cash inflow exceeds the discounted cash outflow, a positive NPV will arise and the project would be accepted. A positive NPV means that the company has not only returned the desired cost of capital, but also an additional amount which will go towards maximising shareholders' wealth.

When using the NPV method of investment appraisal, there are certain assumptions made:

1. Cash flows during a period are assumed to occur at the end of the period;
2. The discount rate is assumed to represent the company's cost of capital;
3. The initial cash outlay happens in year 0, that is, now.

The net present value for this investment would be:

Cost of capital – 15%

Year	Cash flow £000	DF	PV £000
0	(2,000)	1.000	(2,000.00)
1–3	400	2.283	913.20
4–5	500	1.069	534.50
6–8	450	1.135	510.75
9–10	400	0.531	212.40
NPV			170.85

As the NPV is greater than zero, this means that the investment has returned the desired cost of capital, as well as an additional £170,850 and should, therefore, be undertaken as it increases shareholder wealth.

Unlike the ARR and payback methods, the NPV method takes account of the time value of money and consider all relevant cash flows. The NPV model can also account for risk, taxation and inflation issues.

If we were to follow the target payback and ARR for the company as our methods of appraising capital investments we would have concluded that this investment should not be undertaken. This of course would have been the incorrect decision, as it can be clearly seen that the project's NPV is positive.

However, basing a decision only on a positive NPV does not take account of other factors such as the speed of repayments of the original investment and therefore the discounted payback method should be incorporated in the decision making process. Other difficulties encountered when applying NPV to this type of investment decision are:

The cost of capital being used may be set too high. This would result in a lower NPV, which may make the justification for the investment difficult. To overcome this difficulty the organisation should consider the rate used for similar projects with the same risk element.

The time horizons on this project may be too short. The outlay for the project is large and the benefits will probably come in the long term rather than the short/medium term. If the time horizon is too short, then the danger is that such future benefits are excluded from the calculation. I would recommend that the time horizon be reviewed and should be lengthened if appropriate.

It is sometimes difficult to quantify all of the benefits from this type of investment and therefore the resulting NPV may not be as high as expected and management may take the view not be undertake the investment. All benefits must be quantified, however crude. If there is significant difficulty in quantifying some of the benefits, then the non-quantifiable benefits should be detailed separately, but still considered in the decision making process. Therefore, even if the net present value is zero or negative and the non-quantifiable benefits are significant, then the company should proceed with the investment.

As with all projects, there is always an element of uncertainty when predicting cash flows for a project. Such uncertainty needs to be built into the evaluation process and can be achieved through the use of probabilities. This could be incorporated in the next NPV calculation for this project.

As profits are reported annually to shareholders and yet it is cash flows for numerous projects extending over several years that we discount, this creates a problem for internal reporting purposes when reconciling the two.

I would recommend that this project be undertaken and that for the future we combine the discounted payback and NPV methods for capital investment decisions.

Signed: Management Accountant

Requirement (b)
Post-completion appraisal

A post-completion audit is 'an Objective and independent appraisal of the measure of success of capital expenditure project in progressing the business as planned. The appraisal should cover the implementation of the project from authorisation to commissioning and its technical and commercial performance after commissioning. The information provided is also used by management as feedback which aids the implementation and control of future project.'

When P uses the NPV approach to appraise this investment, it will be highly dependent on accurate cash flow projections. If these projections are inaccurate, they may result in the acceptance of this project which could be undersirable and should probably not be pursued. In order to assess the accuracy of the projections made. P must follow up on the result for this project. This procedure is called post-completion appraisal.

In order to undertake a post-completion appraisal, the management accountant of P must collect information about the actual cash flows, plus the estimated cash flows for the remainder of the project's life. These cash flows should then be compared to the expected cash flows and should be based on the same method of evaluation as was used in making the original investment decision. If the outcome results in an unfavourable situation, then there must be an investigation as to why this has happened.

Such an investigation should indicate exactly what went wrong; for example the predicted cash flows for the project might have been overstated. If the post-completion appraisal is undertaken during the project, it will allows for deviations from the plan to be identified and corrective action to be taken in order to place the project back on track. If the post-completion appraisal is carried out at the end of the project, it will then provide a mechanism whereby experience gained from the project can be fed into the organisation's decision-making process to aid decisions on future projects.

A post-completion appraisal can be a very difficult task. It must be remembered that capital investment decisions are made under uncertain conditions and, despite the use of various techniques to incorporate these conditions, what may have seemed like a good decision at the time may well turn out to be the wrong one.

Despite the difficulties encountered when undertaking a post-completion appraisal, it should be carried out, as it allows for past performance to be used to improve future decision-making.

Benefits
- Under- or over-achieving projects can be rapidly modified.
- Under-achieving projects can be terminated at an early stage.
- Improvement in the quality of future decisions as the process provides valuable information on past project. In other words, it aids organisational learning.
- Managers are more realistic with their projections as they are aware that unrealistic projections will be highlighted through carrying out the post completion appraisal.
- Reasons for successful and unsuccessful projects are highlighted and can then be used in the appraisal of future projects.

Drawbacks
- Costly and time consuming to collect the information needed to carry out the post-completion appraisal.
- Managers may perceive the post-completion appraisal as a policing exercise and this may discourage initiative and cause excessive caution. This may result in managers submitting only those projects that demonstrate a safe investment proposal.
- It can be difficult to estimate the future cash flows expected from a project. This difficulty will be further compounded for P, as the cost and benefits from such a project will be experienced throughout the organisation.

Solution 42

40.1

Cumulative units produced	Average time/unit Minutes	Time for nth unit Minutes
1 unit	22.00	22
2 units	17.60	$13.2 = (17.6 \times 2) - 22$
3 units	15.45	$11.15 = ((15.45 \times 3) - (22 + 13.2))$
4 units	14.08	$9.97 = ((14.08 \times 4) - (22 + 13.2 + 11.15))$

Therefore the answer is (B)

40.2

		EV £000	Ranking
L	(500 × 0.2) + (470 × 0.5) + (550 × 0.3)	500	2
M	(400 × 0.2) + (550 × 0.5) + (570 × 0.3)	526	1
N	(450 × 0.2) + (400 × 0.5) + (475 × 0.3)	432.5	4
O	(360 × 0.2) + (400 × 0.5) + (420 × 0.3)	398	5
P	(600 × 0.2) + (500 × 0.5) + (425 × 0.3)	497.5	3

Therefore the answer is (B)

40.3

Value of perfect information

Market prediction	Project	Profit £000	Pr.	EV £000
Poor	P	600	0.20	120
Good	M	550	0.50	275
Excellent	M	570	0.30	171
EV of profit with perfect information				566
Less the highest EV profit available without perfect information				526
Value of perfect information				40

Therefore the answer is (D)

40.4

NPV – 15%

Years	Cash flow £	DF	PV £
0	(75,000)	1.000	(75,000)
1-5	25,000	3.352	83,800
NPV			8,800

NPV – 20%

Years	Cash flow £	DF	PV £
0	(75,000)	1.000	(75,000)
1–5	25,000	2.991	74,775
NPV			(225)

IRR = 15% + (8800/(8,800 + 225))(20% − 15%) = 19.88%

Alternative solution:

The 5-year annuity factor for the IRR = Investement/cash flow = $\frac{75,000}{25,000} = 3$

Searching the cumulative discount tables along the 5-year line shows that a value of 3 corresponds to a discount rate of just less than 20 per cent.

Therefore the answer is (D)

40.5

Present value of the labour savings:

$$£20,000 \times 3.352 = £67,040*$$

$$\frac{£8,800}{£67,040} = 13.13\%$$

Therefore the answer is (C)

Solution 43

Requirement (a)
Appraisal of the current pricing strategy

Managing Director's current pricing method

	£
Cost	400
50% mark up	200
Selling price	600

Drawbacks
As can be seen, the cost-plus approach adds a mark up to cost to arrive at the selling price. There are many drawbacks asssociated with this pricing method as follows:

- It completely ignores the market, hence the reason why the selling price is out of line with competitors;
- It focuses entirely on internal costs;
- It ignores competitors' reactions which has resulted in the competitors reducing prices as soon as the company released theirs;
- It can result in different selling prices due to the different absorption methods used when determining the total cost;
- It ignores the distinction between incremental and fixed costs;
- It fails to ensure that the quantity produced will be sold since the company does not know if the price is in line with the customer's perceptions of the value of the product;
- It is based on the belief that demand for the software is inelastic, that is an increase in price will not lead to any significant reduction in demand. If this were-true then increasing prices would clearly lead to increased demand. However, this view is not supported by the market research information. Therefore, increasing prices are likely to lead to a fall in demand and hence fall in profitability.

Benefits
There are however, benefits to this method of pricing which include the following:

- It ensures that all costs are covered and a desired profit is achieved. So far this has been achieved with the pricing of the software packages as they have been profitable to date.
- It is easy to calculate, as once cost is determined a simple mark up on these costs identifies the selling price.
- It allows the delegation of the price setting to more junior finance staff.
- It allows the company to avoid the costs involved in seeking information about the level of demand in the market.
- It allows the maintenance of relatively stable prices and any price increases are easier to justify to clients.

Alternative Pricing Strategies
Price skimming This method of pricing sets high initial prices in an attempt to exploit those sections of the market which are relatively insensitive to price changes. As R Ltd's product was the first of its type it could have initially set high prices to take advantage of the novelty appeal of a new product as demand would have been inelastic. If this approach had been used, R Ltd could have subsequently reduced the price to remain competitive in the market.

Penetration pricing This method sets very low prices in the initial stages of a product's life cycle to rapid acceptance of the product and therefore a significant market share. If R Ltd had used this approach it could have discouraged entrants into the market.

Demand-based approach With this method R Ltd could have utilised some market research information to determine the selling price and level of demand to maximise company profits. This method, however, does pose the following drawbacks:

- It is dependent on the quality of the market research information;
- It also assumes a competitive market; that is that the actions of competitors will not impact on actual demand for the software package.
- It is difficult to estimate the demand curve;
- It is difficult to incorporate the effect of competition;
- This method assumes that price is the only factor that influences the quantity demanded – other factors like quality, packaging, advertising, promotion, credit terms, after sales service are ignored;
- The marginal cost curve for our packages can only be determined after considerable analysis and the final results (£320) are only an approximation of the true marginal cost function.

However, this method does benefit from:

- A useful insight that stresses the need for managers to think about price/demand relationships even if the relationship cannot be measured precisely.
- A consideration of the marketplace.
- Considering only incremental costs.

Requirement (b)

(i) **Optimum selling price and maximum annual profit**

Optimum selling price and level of demand can be found when marginal cost equates to marginal revenue:

Marginal revenue	£750 − £0.02X
Marginal cost	£320
Marginal cost = marginal revenue	£320 = £750 − £0.02X
X	= 21,500
Price	= £750 − £10/1,000(21,500)
	= £535

Revised profit		£
Selling price		535
Variable cost		320
Contribution per unit		215
Total contribution	£215 × 21,500	4,622,500
Less: Fixed costs		1,200,000
Profit		3,422,500

(ii) See diagram on next page.

Workings

Current contribution (b) (i)	£4,622,500
Contribution from exporting to L	
((€930 × 0.60) − £300) × 25,000	£6,450,000

R Ltd should sell all of their output to L as it will increase contribution by £1,827,500.

However, if the exchange rate falls to €1 = £0.20 then negative contribution will be generated:

((€930 × 0.20) − £300) × 25,000 (£2,850,000)

Comment

As can be seen from the graph if the exchange rate falls to €1 = £0.52 (i.e. a 13.33% drop) then R Ltd will be indifferent as to whether they sell the accounting packages themselves or export them to L. If the exchange rate falls below €1 = £0.52, then R Ltd should sell the accounting packages themselves. R Ltd needs to assess the likelihood of the Euro falling in value.

(ii)

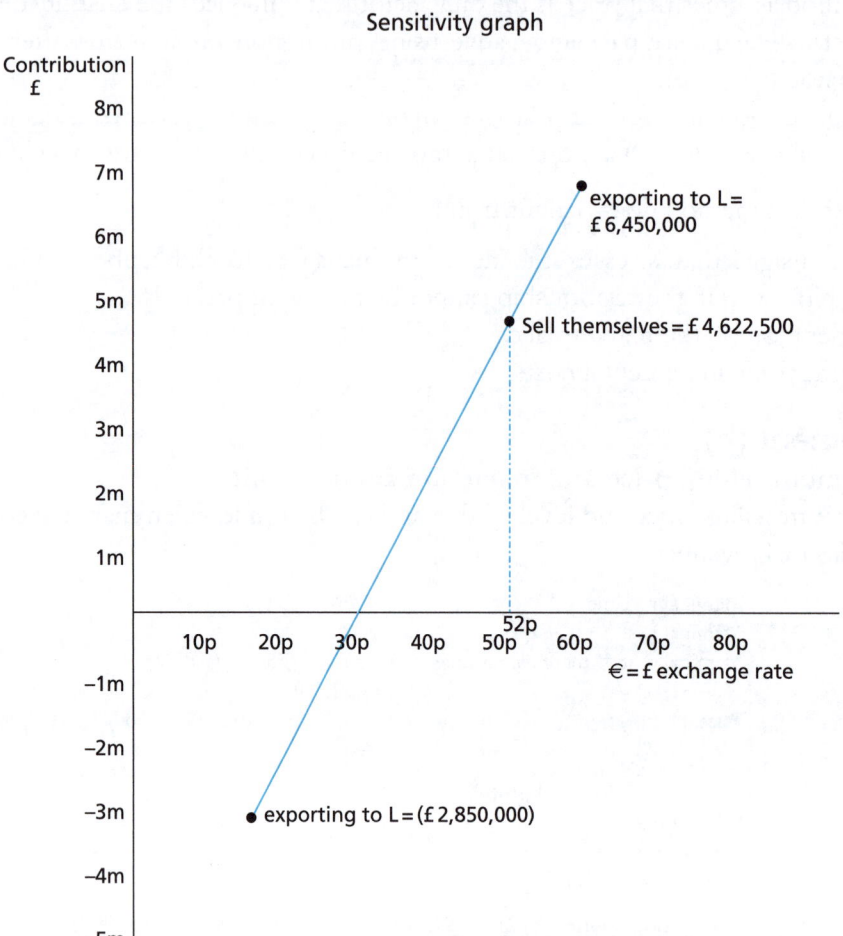

Exporting to L = £6,450,000 in contribution at an exchange rate of 60p
Selling themselves = £4,622,500 in contribution at an exchange rate of 52p
Negative point = £2,850,000 in contribution at an exchange rate of 20p

Requirement (c)

Purchase

Year	Outlay £	Capital allowances £	Tax cash flow £	Net cash flow £	DF £	PV £
0	(1,000,000)			(1,000,000)	1.000	(1,000,000)
1		(250,000)	37,500	37,500	0.893	33,488
2		(187,500)	65,625	65,625	0.797	52,303
3		(140,625)	49,219	49,219	0.712	35,044
4		(421,875)	84,375	84,375	0.636	53,663
5			63,281	63,281	0.567	35,880
						(789,622)

Lease

Year	Payments £	Tax cash flow £	Net cash flow £	DF	PV £
0	(300,000)	45,000	(255,000)	1.000	(255,000)
1	(300,000)	90,000	(210,000)	0.893	(187,530)
2	(300,000)	90,000	(210,000)	0.797	(167,370)
3	(300,000)	90,000	(210,000)	0.712	(149,520)
4		45,000	45,000	0.636	28,620
					(730,800)

Therefore, leasing is the least cost option with savings of £58,822.

Solution 44

Requirement (a)

Current situation

Years	Cash flow £000	DF	PV £000
1	522.00	0.877	457.79
	70.50	0.877	61.83
2	548.10	0.769	421.49
	72.26	0.769	55.57
3	575.51	0.675	388.47
	74.07	0.675	50.00
4	604.29	0.592	357.74
	75.92	0.592	44.95
5	634.50	0.519	329.31
	77.82	0.519	40.39
		NPV	2,207.54

Working

Cost/delegate		£000
Travel	£200	
Accommodation, food and drink	£670	
Total	£870 × 100 delegates × 6 courses per annum	522
Course costs	£11,750 × 6 courses per annum	70.5

	Proposed e-learning solution		
Years	Cash flow	DF	PV
	£000		£000
0	1,535.00	1.000	1,535.00
1	101.00	0.877	88.58
	30.00	0.877	26.31
2	103.52	0.769	79.61
	28.50	0.769	21.92
3	107.63	0.675	72.65
	27.08	0.675	18.28
4	111.99	0.592	66.30
	25.73	0.592	15.23
5	31.61	0.519	16.41
	24.44	0.519	12.68
		NPV	1,952.97

Working

	Year 0	Year 1	Year 2	Year 3	Year 4	Year 5
	£000	£000	£000	£000	£000	£000
Hardware	1,500					(50)
Software		35	35	35	35	35
Technical Manager	30					
Trainers and material	12					
	42	42	44.52	47.19	50.02	53.02
Camera and Sound		24	24	25.44	26.97	28.59
Total	1,535	101	103.52	107.63	111.99	31.61
Broadband connection		30	28.50	27.08	25.73	24.44

Recommendation:
The e-learning solution should be implemented, as it is the least cost option for the company.

Requirement (b)
(i)

	PV of fixed cost	Annual equivalent	PV of variable cost	Annual equivalent	Cost per delegate
	£000	£000	£000	£000	£000
Traditional courses	252.74	73.62	1,954.80	569.41	5.69
E-learning courses	1,858.55	541.38	94.42	27.50	0.28
Saving annualised		467.76			5.41

Breakeven number of delegate $\dfrac{467.76}{5.41} = 86.46$, say 86 delegates.

(ii) Eighty-six out of the 100 delegates would be required to utilise the e-learning solution. This is a high take up number, so the company would need to be assured that all the delegates are in favour of this method of delivery.

Solution 45

Requirement (a)

Company	NPV
	$000
A	60
B	0
C	77
D	80

The management team of T Ltd should invest in companies D, C and A as they generate a positive NPV. The positive NPV forecast to be generated by companies D, C and A means that T Ltd would not only be returned the desired cost of capital (12 per cent), but also an additional amount of $80,000 in the case of company D; $77,000 in the case of company C; and $60,000 in the case of company A. These amounts will go towards maximising shareholders' wealth.

T Ltd will be indifferent as to whether to invest in company B as it generates a zero NPV. The zero NPV forecast to be generated by company B means that T Ltd would only return the desired cost of capital (12 per cent) and no more.

Requirement (b)

(i)

Company	A	B	C	D
	$000	$000	$000	$000
NPV	60	0	77	80
Investment	500	250	475	800
NPV/$1	0.12	0	0.162	0.10
Ranking	2nd	4th	1st	3rd

Invest $475,000 in company C and $225,000 in company A.

(ii) *The riskiness of the product/service that company C and A wish to offer.* If it is very innovative and untested, there will be a higher amount of risk than a product/service being launched which is competitive with another product/service already in the market. For example, company D may be launching a competitive product/service and be less risky than companies C and A.

The experience of the management staff within companies C and A will be important. If the start up team has specific and relevant commercial experience within their industry then this will ensure that the investment will be carefully managed.

T Ltd's attitude to risk will be an important element. This will probably depend on their current portfolio of investments. If there is a large amount already invested in high-risk projects they may decide to lower their exposure by investing in a more reliable, less risky venture.

The speed of the payback period on these investments will also be important. The sooner the funds are repaid the sooner funds will be available for investment in other projects. This may be a factor that T Ltd will consider when finalising their decision.

Requirement (c)

Let $X1$ = Proportional investment in Company A
Let $X2$ = Proportional investment in Company B
Let $X3$ = Proportional investment in Company C
Let $X4$ = Proportional investment in Company D

Maximise = $60X1 + 0X2 + 77X3 + 80X4$

Subject to:

$$500X1 + 250X2 + 475X3 + 800X4 + S1 = 700 \quad \text{(Period 0 Constraint)}$$
$$75X1 + 30X2 + 100X3 + 150X4 + S2 = 89.60 \quad \text{(Period 1 Constraint)}$$
$$40X1 + 20X2 + 30X3 + 50X4 + S3 = 43.91 \quad \text{(Period 2 Constraint)}$$

$$0 < I = X_j < I = 1 \quad (j = 1, \ldots, 3)$$

Our objective function seeks to maximise the NPV from our investment, subject to the investment constraints for each of the three periods. S1, S2 and S3 represent the slack variables (that is, the unused funds for each of the three periods). Xj may take a value from 0 to 1 and ensures that none of the investments can be undertaken more than once, but allows for partial investments to be undertaken.

Requirement (d)
Benefits

- With computer programs a complex investment decision like this can be quickly and efficiently solved. It is also usual for these computer programs to provide as sensitivity analysis of the problem, allowing the decision-makers to identify by how much key variables can change without changing the solution.
- Once the final tableau for this investment decision has been established, the output will provide details of the opportunity costs and the marginal rates of substitution for the scare resources which is useful for decision-making, planning and control purposes.
- Provides a clear plan of action.

Solution 46

(a)

	$	
Coach ($180 × 2 days)	360	(i)
Fuel	1,500	(ii)
Replacement driver ($400 × 10)	4,000	(iii)
Hotel	5,000	(iv)
Total relevant cost	10,860	

(i) this is the cost of the replacement coach as this is the least cost alternative.
(ii) the expected future cost.
(iii) replacement cost to meet existing obligations.
(iv) the expected future cost.

General overheads & profit are ignored because these are not relevant costs. The specific fixed costs are ignored because they have already been incurred and so are sunk costs.

(b) (i) The two-way data table shows the effect on the relevant cost of $10,860 of the hotel and/or fuel costs being different from those originally estimated.
It can be seen that the relevant cost could be as low as $9,560 ($10,860 − $1,300) if the fuel and hotel costs were as low as $1,200 and $4,000 respectively.
However, if these costs were to be $2,000 and $6,000 respectively then the relevant cost would increase to $12,360 ($10,860 + $1,500).

(ii) By introducing the probability values provided the likelihood of different relevant cost values can be determined:

Hotel	Fuel	Probability	Effect	EV
$4,000	$1,200	0.02	−$1,30z0	−$26
$4,000	$1,500	0.10	−$1,000	−$100
$4,000	$2,000	0.08	−$500	−$40
$5,000	$1,200	0.05	−$300	−$15
$5,000	$1,500	0.25	NIL	NIL
$5,000	$2,000	0.20	+$500	+$100
$6,000	$1,200	0.03	+$700	+$21
$6,000	$1,500	0.15	+$1,000	+$150
$6,000	$2,000	0.12	+$1,500	+$180
				+$270

This shows that the expected value of this probability distribution is that the relevant cost will be $270 higher than that predicted using the most likely combination of $5,000 for the hotel costs and $1,500 for the fuel cost.

However, as this is a one-off quotation more useful analysis than EV can be found by considering the probability and effect of each combination occurring. For example, by summing the appropriate probability it can be seen that there is a 50% chance that the relevant cost will be greater than the value of $10,860 and only a 25% chance that it will be less than this value. (There is a 25% chance that it will be $10,860).

Solution 47

(a) The Product Life Cycle comprises 4 stages:

- Introduction
- Growth
- Maturity
- Decline

In the Introduction stage the company needs to price the product to achieve its market strategy using either penetration or skimming pricing policies.

A penetration policy is used with the objective of achieving a high level of demand very quickly by using a low price that is affordable to a large number of potential customers. This has the effect of discouraging new suppliers to the market because the unit profitability is relatively low, but the high volume of sales enables the initial supplier to recover their development costs.

A skimming policy is particular appropriate to a product that has a novelty value or that is technologically advanced. Such a policy uses a price that is high and thus restricts the volume of sales since only high worth customers can afford the product, but the high unit profitability enables the initial supplier to recover their development costs. However, the high unit profitability attracts competitors to the market so that it is important for the initial supplier to be able to reduce the price and prevent new entrants to the market from benefiting from being able to reverse engineer the product and make significant profits from little or no development investment.

The Q organisation is launching a technologically advanced product which will be demanded by high worth customers who are proud to be amongst the first to own such a state of the art product. This is exactly the type of product for which a price skimming policy is appropriate.

The initial price will be high as this will quickly recover the development costs of the product. The high worth customers will not be deterred from buying the product as it will be sold on the basis of its technological value rather than its price.

Competitors will be attracted to the product by its high price and will seek to compete with it by introducing their own version of the product at much lower development costs (by reverse engineering Q's product) so it is important for Q to reduce the price during the growth stage of the product's life cycle. There may be many price reductions during this phase so that the product gradually becomes more affordable to lower social economic groups.

As the product enters the maturity stage the price will need to be lowered further, though a normal contribution ratio would continue to be earned. Oligopolistic competition is often found in this stage, but provided Q has gained market share and survived until this stage the opportunity to make profit and cash surpluses should exist. However, in this type of market the price will tend to be set by the market and Q will have to accept that price. Thus Q will need to focus on the control of its costs to ensure that the product remains profitable.

When the product enters the decline phase a loyal group of customers may continue to be prepared to pay a reasonable price and at this price the product will continue to be profitable, especially as costs continue to reduce. Eventually the price will be lowered to marginal cost or even lower in order to sell off inventories of what is now an obsolete product as it has been replaced by a more technologically advanced item.

(b) (i) Variable costs

Number of units	Total variable costs/unit	Variable costs/unit	
		Affected by learning	Not affected by learning
10,000	£60.00	£30.00	£30.00
20,000	£56.10	£26.10	£30.00
30,000	£54.06	£24.06	£30.00
40,000	£52.71	£22.71	£30.00

The variable cost affected by learning has reduced from £30.00 to £22.71. This new cost is 75.7% of the initial cost of £30.00. This reduction has occurred when the number of units has doubled twice so the rate of learning is the square root of 0.757 = 0.87 or 87%.

(ii) This can then be applied to determine the variable cost per unit values shown in the table above:

$$£30 \times 0.87 = £26.10$$
$$y = ax^b$$
$$y = 30 \times (3^{-0.2010})$$
$$= 24.06$$
$$b = \log 0.87 / \log 2$$
$$= -0.0605/0.3010$$
$$= -0.2010$$

Contributions can now be compared at the respective price/demand levels:

Demand units	Selling price per unit	Variable cost per unit	Contribution per unit	Contribution Total
10,000	£100	£60.00	£40.00	£400,000
20,000	£80	£56.10	£23.90	£478,000
30,000	£69	£54.06	£14.94	£448,200
40,000	£62	£52.71	£9.29	£371,600

The optimum price is £80.

(iii) Target contribution = Fixed costs + Required Profit
= £15,000 + £30,000
= £45,000

The initial launch phase represents the first 20,000 units (as per (b)(ii) above). However the learning effect continues until 40,000 units hence the unit cost decreases (and therefore unit contribution increases) until the 40,000 units have been completed.

The average unit cost of the batch of units from 20,001 – 30,000 is:

$$\frac{(30,000 \times £54.06) - (20,000 \times £56.10)}{10,000} = £49.98$$

thus giving a unit contribution of £57.00 − £49.98 = £7.02 and a monthly sales target of £45,000/£7.02 = 6,410 units.

Once the learning is complete the contribution per unit = £57.00 − [((40,000 × £52.71) − (30,000 × £54.06))/10,000] = £8.34
and thus the sales target = £45,000/£8.34 = 5,396 units.

Solution 48

(a) Absorption costing is a costing system that attributes all production costs to individual cost units. As a consequence its use as part of a cost plus pricing system should ensure that the company is profitable providing the volume of sales provides a mark up that is sufficient to cover the non production costs that are incurred.

Marginal costing is a costing system that only attributes variable production costs to the cost unit. Thus the percentage mark-up that is added as part of a cost plus pricing system must be sufficient to cover the fixed production overhead costs as well as the non production overhead costs before any profit results.

Both systems are used in an environment where market based pricing is either difficult or inappropriate, often because of the uniqueness of the product or service being provided. Thus cost plus pricing enables senior managers to delegate the price setting decision to operational managers.

Both systems have their own problems. The use of absorption cost means that the price is dependent at least in part on the method used to absorb the costs into each cost unit. Furthermore it suggests that this is the cost of the individual item whereas in fact it includes costs that would continue to be incurred if the item were not produced. Thus a manager may reject a sale because the customer is only prepared to pay a price which is less than the absorption cost, but in fact that price would be better than no sale because it exceeds the variable cost and thus makes a contribution to the fixed costs that would be incurred anyway.

The use of marginal costing identifies the variable cost of the item produced and thus provides a clear indication of the minimum price that should be charged so as to avoid a negative contribution. However this approach may mean that managers are persuaded to sell items at too low a price, so that the contribution earned is insufficient to cover the fixed costs of the business. Also it is very difficult to increase the price for a subsequent sale of the same item to the same customer, so the company may find it difficult to break out of the low price arena once they have entered it.

(b)

			Hours
Direct labour hours: W	15,000 × 4		60,000
X	24,000 × 3		72,000
Y	20,000 × 5		100,000
			232,000

Absorption rate $1,044,000/232,000 $4.50 per direct labour hour

Product	W	X	Y
	$/unit	$/unit	$/unit
Direct material	35	45.0	30.0
Direct labour	40	30.0	50.0
Overhead	18	13.5	22.5
Total	93	88.5	102.5

(c) Cost driver rates:

	W	X	Y
Number of batches	30	60	20
Number of supplier orders	120	180	100
Number of machine hours (000)	75	192	140

Material ordering cost $220,000/400 = $550 per supplier order
Machine setup cost $100,000/110 = $909 per batch
Machine running cost $400,000/407,000 = $0.9828 per machine hour
General facility cost $324,000/407,000 = $0.7961 per machine hour

Note: The values shown in the table below are calculated using these cost driver rates. This causes minor differences compared to the total overhead cost because of roundings.

Product	W		X		Y	
	Total	/unit	Total	/unit	Total	/unit
	$	$	$	$	$	$
Direct materials		35		45		30
Direct labour		40		30		50
Material ordering	66,000		99,000		55,000	
Machine setups	27,270		54,540		18,180	
Machine running	73,710		188,698		137,592	
General facility	59,708		152,851		111,454	
	226,688	15	495,089	21	322,226	16
Total cost		90		96		96

(d) The above calculations show that the unit cost of product W is similar under both the current absorption and activity based costing methods. However there are significant differences in the unit costs of product X and product Y. This may provide an opportunity to change the selling prices of these products to reflect their true cost. As a result, profitability may be improved.

Activity Based Costing recognises the causes of costs and attributes the costs to products depending on their utilisation of the activities that cause costs to be incurred. As a consequence it is argued that the attribution of costs is less arbitrary than traditional absorption costing and leads to more accurate unit costs.

The management of KL can use the information provided by the Activity Based Costing approach to identify potential cost savings by changing the method of operation within the company; for example by increasing the size of each batch or standardising on the material suppliers that are used to reduce the number of supplier orders. It may also be appropriate to consider investing in new machines to reduce the number of machine hours.

The effect of Activity Based Costing is often to identify costs as being more controllable because their cause has now been identified. While some facility costs will remain and are truly fixed as they are not driven by any particular future activity, many of the other costs will now become variable depending on the number of times an activity is performed and therefore more controllable.

Solution 49

(a) The expected size of the audience is:
$(300 \times 0.5) + (400 \times 0.3) + (500 \times 0.2) = 370$ people

The expected value of contribution from non-ticket sales is:
$(\$3 \times 0.3) + (\$5 \times 0.5) + (\$10 \times 0.2) = \$5.40$

Ticket price = $25.00

Expected income ($25.00 + $5.40) × 370	$11,248
Less MS fee	$10,000
Expected gain	$1,248

Thus MS should be engaged for the concert.

(b)

	Size of audience		
	300	400	500
Contribution from confectionery sales			
$3	(1,600)	1,200	4,000
$5	(1,000)	2,000	5,000
$10	500	4,000	7,500

All values shown in the cells of the above table are in $

(c) The probabilities can be combined to show the probability of each of the nine possible outcomes occurring. These are shown in the following table:

	Size of audience		
	300	400	500
Contribution from confectionery sales			
$3	15%	9%	6%
$5	25%	15%	10%
$10	10%	6%	4%

By combining the values that have been summarised in these two tables it can be seen that there is a 40% chance of the concert making a loss (and hence a 60% chance of it having a profit). Furthermore it can be seen that the solution found in part (a) is an average value and that the range of possible results is from a loss of $1,600 to a profit of $7,500. The probabilities can also be used to demonstrate that the distribution of possible values is skewed, because the probability of the profit being above the average (expected) value of $1,248 is 41%.

The theatre management can use this information to evaluate their decision more thoroughly. Instead of relying on a single possible value these tables show the range of values that could occur and the likelihood of each of them occurring. The information therefore allows the theatre management to consider the risks associated with their decision.

(d) The maximum price that should be paid for the information is the difference between the expected value that would result from actions taken with the information compared to the expected value calculated without the information (as already calculated above $1,248).

There are two aspects to the information: the size of the audience and the level of contribution from confectionery sales.

The possible combinations/decisions and their probabilities and expected values are as follows:

Audience	Confectionery Contribution ($)	Outcome ($)	Decision	Probability	Expected Value ($)
300	10	500	Yes	0.10	50
300	5	(1,000)	No		
300	3	(1,600)	No		
400	10	4,000	Yes	0.06	240
400	5	2,000	Yes	0.15	300
400	3	1,200	Yes	0.09	108
500	10	7,500	Yes	0.04	300
500	5	5,000	Yes	0.10	500
500	3	4,000	Yes	0.06	240
Total					1,738

The value of the information and therefore the maximum price that should be paid for it is $1,738 less $1,248 = $490.

Solution 50

(a)

	2006 £m	2007 £m	2008 £m	2009 £m	2010 £m	2011 £m
Sales		120.0	132.3	145.5	150.0	
Variable cost:						
Production		75.0	85.1	96.2	102.0	
Sales		10.0	11.1	12.4	12.9	
Fixed cost:						
Production		4.0	4.3	4.7	5.0	
Sales		2.0	2.1	2.2	2.4	
Administration		1.0	1.1	1.1	1.2	
Total cost		92.0	103.7	116.6	123.5	
Pre-tax operating cash flow		28.0	28.6	28.9	26.5	
Tax		2.3	5.2	6.2	4.3	1.0
Post-tax operating cash flow		25.7	23.4	22.7	22.2	(1.0)
Capital cash flow	(50.0)				1.0	
Total cash flow	(50.0)	25.7	23.4	22.7	23.2	(1.0)
DF@12%	1.000	0.893	0.797	0.712	0.636	0.567
PV	(50.0)	23.0	18.7	16.2	14.8	(0.6)

NPV = £22.1 m

The investment has a positive NPV and therefore is financially worthwhile.

Workings:

	Capital allowances £m	Operating profit £m	Taxable profit £m	Tax £m	Payable current year £m	Payable next year £m
2007						
Cost	50					
WDA	12.5	28.0	15.5	4.6	2.3	2.3
2008	37.5					
WDA	9.4	28.6	19.2	5.8	2.9	2.9
2009	28.1					
WDA	7.0	28.9	21.9	6.6	3.3	3.3
2010	21.1					
Disposal	1.0					
Balancing allowance	20.1	26.5	6.4	2.0	1.0	1.0

Note: The tax liability has been rounded so that the tax payments are stated to the nearest £0.1 m

(b) The IRR is found by comparing the NPV at two different discount rates. Since the investment has a positive NPV at 12% then a higher discount rate should be chosen. Using a 20% discount rate results in the following:

Total cash flow (£m)	(50.0)	25.7	23.4	22.7	23.2	(1.0)
DF@20%	1.000	0.833	0.694	0.579	0.482	0.402
PV(£m)	(50.0)	21.4	16.2	13.1	11.2	(0.4)

NPV = £11.5 m

Thus an 8% increase in the discount factor caused NPV to reduce by £10.6 m. The internal rate of return is found when the NPV equals zero so it can be estimated to be approximately:

$$20\% + (11.5/10.6 \times 8\%) = 29\%$$

(c) The difference between the real rate of return and the money rate of return is the annual rate of inflation. The money rate of return includes an allowance for annual inflation whereas the real rate of return does not. Thus the two rates are connected by the formula:

$$(1 + \text{real rate of return}) \times (1 + \text{inflation rate}) = (1 + \text{money rate of return})$$

so that for example if the real rate of return required from a project is 6% per annum and annual inflation is expected to be 4% per annum, the money rate of return required is given by:

$$1.06 \times 1.04 = 1.1024$$

The required money rate of return would thus be 10.24%.

This is slightly more than the result of simply adding together the 6% and 4% together because of the compounding effect.

This can be applied to investment decisions because such decisions usually occur within a real world environment in which inflation exists, so to ignore the effects of inflation is a simplification that may not be appropriate. Most managers when asked to predict future costs and revenues will think in terms of today's price levels and then estimate the inflation that is expected to occur in future periods. This means that the predicted cash flows are stated in terms of future price levels and thus the viability of the investment must be measured using an inflation inclusive cost of capital. However, the exercise of inflating each of the future cash flows can be time consuming. If the rate of inflation to be applied to EVERY element of the investment is the same then the same result can be determined by not inflating ANY of the investment cash flows and discounting instead using the real cost of capital.

PRESENT VALUE TABLE

Present value of £1 ie $(1 + r)^{-n}$ where r = interest rate; n = number of periods until payment or receipt

Interest rates (r)

Periods (n)	1%	2%	3%	4%	5%	6%	7%	8%	9%	10%	11%	12%	13%	14%	15%	16%	17%	18%	19%	20%
1	.990	.980	.971	.962	.952	.943	.935	.926	.917	.909	.901	.893	.885	.877	.870	.862	.855	.847	.840	.833
2	.980	.961	.943	.925	.907	.890	.873	.857	.842	.826	.812	.797	.783	.769	.756	.743	.731	.718	.706	.694
3	.971	.942	.915	.889	.864	.840	.816	.794	.772	.751	.731	.712	.693	.675	.658	.641	.624	.609	.593	.579
4	.961	.924	.888	.855	.823	.792	.763	.735	.708	.683	.659	.636	.613	.592	.572	.552	.534	.516	.499	.482
5	.951	.906	.863	.822	.784	.747	.713	.681	.650	.621	.593	.567	.543	.519	.497	.476	.456	.437	.419	.402
6	.942	.888	.837	.790	.746	.705	.666	.630	.596	.564	.535	.507	.480	.456	.432	.410	.390	.370	.352	.335
7	.933	.871	.813	.760	.711	.665	.623	.583	.547	.513	.482	.452	.425	.400	.376	.354	.333	.314	.296	.279
8	.923	.853	.789	.731	.677	.627	.582	.540	.502	.467	.434	.404	.376	.351	.327	.305	.285	.266	.249	.233
9	.914	.837	.766	.703	.645	.592	.544	.500	.460	.424	.391	.361	.333	.308	.284	.263	.243	.225	.209	.194
10	.905	.820	.744	.676	.614	.558	.508	.463	.422	.386	.352	.322	.295	.270	.247	.227	.208	.191	.176	.162
11	.896	.804	.722	.650	.585	.527	.475	.429	.388	.350	.317	.287	.261	.237	.215	.195	.178	.162	.148	.135
12	.887	.788	.701	.625	.557	.497	.444	.397	.356	.319	.286	.257	.231	.208	.187	.168	.152	.137	.124	.112
13	.879	.773	.681	.601	.530	.469	.415	.368	.326	.290	.258	.229	.204	.182	.163	.145	.130	.116	.104	.093
14	.870	.758	.661	.577	.505	.442	.388	.340	.299	.263	.232	.205	.181	.160	.141	.125	.111	.099	.088	.078
15	.861	.743	.642	.555	.481	.417	.362	.315	.275	.239	.209	.183	.160	.140	.123	.108	.095	.084	.074	.065
16	.853	.728	.623	.534	.458	.394	.339	.292	.252	.218	.188	.163	.141	.123	.107	.093	.081	.071	.062	.054
17	.844	.714	.605	.513	.436	.371	.317	.270	.231	.198	.170	.146	.125	.108	.093	.080	.069	.060	.052	.045
18	.836	.700	.587	.494	.416	.350	.296	.250	.212	.180	.153	.130	.111	.095	.081	.069	.059	.051	.044	.038
19	.828	.686	.570	.475	.396	.331	.277	.232	.194	.164	.138	.116	.098	.083	.070	.060	.051	.043	.037	.031
20	.820	.673	.554	.456	.377	.312	.258	.215	.178	.149	.124	.104	.087	.073	.061	.051	.043	.037	.031	.026

CUMULATIVE PRESENT VALUE OF £1

This table shows the Present Value of £1 per annum, Receivable or Payable at the end of each year for n years $\dfrac{1 - (1 + r)^{-n}}{r}$

Periods (n)	1%	2%	3%	4%	5%	6%	7%	8%	9%	10%	11%	12%	13%	14%	15%	16%	17%	18%	19%	20%
1	.990	.980	.971	.962	.952	.943	.935	.926	.917	.909	.901	.893	.885	.877	.870	.862	.855	.847	.840	.833
2	1.970	1.942	1.913	1.886	1.859	1.833	1.808	1.783	1.759	1.736	1.713	1.690	1.668	1.647	1.626	1.605	1.585	1.566	1.547	1.528
3	2.941	2.884	2.829	2.775	2.723	2.673	2.624	2.577	2.531	2.487	2.444	2.402	2.361	2.322	2.283	2.246	2.210	2.174	2.140	2.106
4	3.902	3.808	3.717	3.630	3.546	3.465	3.387	3.312	3.240	3.170	3.102	3.037	2.974	2.914	2.855	2.798	2.743	2.690	2.639	2.589
5	4.853	4.713	4.580	4.452	4.329	4.212	4.100	3.993	3.890	3.791	3.696	3.605	3.517	3.433	3.352	3.274	3.199	3.127	3.058	2.991
6	5.795	5.601	5.417	5.242	5.076	4.917	4.767	4.623	4.486	4.355	4.231	4.111	3.998	3.889	3.784	3.685	3.589	3.498	3.410	3.326
7	6.728	6.472	6.230	6.002	5.786	5.582	5.389	5.206	5.033	4.868	4.712	4.564	4.423	4.288	4.160	4.039	3.922	3.812	3.706	3.605
8	7.652	7.325	7.020	6.733	6.463	6.210	5.971	5.747	5.535	5.335	5.146	4.968	4.799	4.639	4.487	4.344	4.207	4.078	3.954	3.837
9	8.566	8.162	7.786	7.435	7.108	6.802	6.515	6.247	5.995	5.759	5.537	5.328	5.132	4.946	4.772	4.607	4.451	4.303	4.163	4.031
10	9.471	8.983	8.530	8.111	7.722	7.360	7.024	6.710	6.418	6.145	5.889	5.650	5.426	5.216	5.019	4.833	4.659	4.494	4.339	4.192
11	10.368	9.787	9.253	8.760	8.306	7.887	7.499	7.139	6.805	6.495	6.207	5.938	5.687	5.453	5.234	5.029	4.836	4.656	4.486	4.327
12	11.255	10.575	9.954	9.385	8.863	8.384	7.943	7.536	7.161	6.814	6.492	6.194	5.918	5.660	5.421	5.197	4.988	4.793	4.611	4.439
13	12.134	11.348	10.635	9.986	9.394	8.853	8.358	7.904	7.487	7.103	6.750	6.424	6.122	5.842	5.583	5.342	5.118	4.910	4.715	4.533
14	13.004	12.106	11.296	10.563	9.899	9.295	8.745	8.244	7.786	7.367	6.982	6.628	6.302	6.002	5.724	5.468	5.229	5.008	4.802	4.611
15	13.865	12.849	11.938	11.118	10.380	9.712	9.108	8.559	8.061	7.606	7.191	6.811	6.462	6.142	5.847	5.575	5.324	5.092	4.876	4.675
16	14.718	13.578	12.561	11.652	10.838	10.106	9.447	8.851	8.313	7.824	7.379	6.974	6.604	6.265	5.954	5.668	5.405	5.162	4.938	4.730
17	15.562	14.292	13.166	12.166	11.274	10.477	9.763	9.122	8.544	8.022	7.549	7.120	6.729	6.373	6.047	5.749	5.475	5.222	4.990	4.775
18	16.398	14.992	13.754	12.659	11.690	10.828	10.059	9.372	8.756	8.201	7.702	7.250	6.840	6.467	6.128	5.818	5.534	5.273	5.033	4.812
19	17.226	15.679	14.324	13.134	12.085	11.158	10.336	9.604	8.950	8.365	7.839	7.366	6.938	6.550	6.198	5.877	5.584	5.316	5.070	4.843
20	18.046	16.351	14.878	13.590	12.462	11.470	10.594	9.818	9.129	8.514	7.963	7.469	7.025	6.623	6.259	5.929	5.628	5.353	5.101	4.870

Index

Abandonment, investment appraisals, 458
ABC *see* Activity-based costing (ABC)
ABM *see* Activity-based management (ABM)
Abnormal costs, 6
Absorbed fixed overheads, 66
Absorption costing:
    activity-based costing, 24–6, 161, 332, 333, 335, 336–49
    concepts, 24
    example, 24–5
    historical background, 336, 340
    marginal costing, 22–5, 27
    over- or under-absorption, 21, 22, 30
    profit reconciliation, 29
    recent developments, 24–6
Accounting rate of return (ARR), 222–4, 248
    concepts, 222
    usage statistics, 222
Accounting, backflush accounting, 429–32
Activity-based costing (ABC):
    activity categories, 339
    benefits, 342
    concepts, 161–2, 336–7
    customers, 368
    definitions, 337–9
    examples, 339–41
    historical background, 332–3
    information, 336–7
    Pareto analysis, 350–1
    problems, 349
    purposes, 342
    services, 332
    stages, 342
Activity-based management (ABM):
    benefits, 342
    concepts, 274
    strategic activity management, 347–8
Activity cost drivers, 343, 344
Activity cost pools, 26
Administration costs, 6
Amstrad, 442
AMTs *see* Automated Manufacturing Technologies (AMTs)
Annuity rates, 248
Answer reports, 125
Appraisal costs, 310, 311, 326, 327
ARR *see* Accounting rate of return (ARR)
Assets:
    replacement cycles, 227–30
    return on investment, 222–4
AT&T, 348–9
Audits, post-completion audits, 254, 603
Automated Manufacturing Technologies (AMTs), 305
Avoidable costs, 68

B & Q, 429
Backflush accounting, 429–32
Batch level activities, 339, 386
Batch sizes, costs, 323, 411, 424, 464, 549
Bellis-Jones, Robin, 347, 368
Benefit types, investment appraisals, 242–4
Bernoulli, 189
Binding, linear programming, 119–21
Boeing, 402
Bottlenecks, 456–7
BP, 244
BPR *see* Business process re-engineering
Brabazon, Tony, 453
Branding, 351
Brantjes, Mathijs, 244, 254
Breakeven analysis:
    calculating the breakeven point, 35–6
    contribution, 35, 37, 39
    contribution to sales ratio, 37–8
    economist's breakeven chart, 43
    limitations, 42–3
    margin of safety, 36
    multi-product CVP analysis, 46–8
    profit–volume charts, 40–2
    proposal evaluation, 44–6
Breakeven charts, 38, 42, 56, 60, 61
Britax Wingard, 429
British Telecom, 318
Budgeting, capital budgeting, 211, 212, 263, 267–70, 367, 446, 450
Bundling, 154–5
Business process re-engineering, 313

C/S *see* Contribution to sales (C/S) ratio
CAD *see* Computer aided design (CAD)
CAE *see* Computer aided engineering (CAE)
CAM *see* Computer aided manufacturing (CAM)
Capacity:
    linear programming, 119–21
    proposal evaluation, 44
Capital budgeting, 212, 263, 268–70, 367, 446, 450
Capital investment appraisals, 293, 295, 581, 601
    see also Investment appraisals
Capital rationing, 230–1
Cash flows:
    discounted cash flow, 215, 227, 232
    investment appraisals, 458
    product life cycles, 313, 317, 453, 468, 554
Change:
    breakeven analysis, 35–8
    costs, 154
    manufacturing philosophy, 423–7
    total quality management, 310–13
CIMA Insider, 81, 143, 193, 259, 315

Committed costs, 66
Committees, 318, 446
Compensation, quality failure cost, 313
Competitive advantages, 306
Complementary products, price elasticity, 145
Compliance costs, 315, 316
Composite cost units, 4
Computer aided design (CAD), 445
Computer aided engineering (CAE), 445
Computer aided manufacturing (CAM), 445
Computer systems *see* Information technology (IT)
Conformance costs, 315
Constraints:
  graphical solutions, 137
  linear programming, 136
  specifying, 109
  see also Limiting factors
Continuous improvement, 303
Contribution:
  breakeven analysis, 35, 37, 39
  concepts, 26–7, 39–40
  limiting factors, 70, 72, 151
  linear programming, 107
  marginal costing, 26
Contribution to sales (C/S) ratio, 37–8
Controllable costs, 6
Controlled prices, 157
Cooper, Robin, 365
Corporation tax, investment appraisals, 238
Cost accounting:
  classifications, 5–6
  concepts, 3–6
  elements of cost, 13–14
  fixed costs, 7
  high-low method, 11–12
  scattergraph method, 12–13
  semi-variable costs, 10–13
  variable costs, 6
Cost behaviour, 7–13
Cost centres, 5
Cost drivers, 26, 162, 338, 343–4, 348–9, 352, 358, 365–6
Cost objects, 331
Cost of capital, 214
Cost of Quality Report, 313, 316
Cost-plus pricing, 148–51
Cost units, 4
Cost-volume-profit (CVP) analysis, 35–6
  see also Breakeven analysis
Costing systems:
  absorption costing, 24–6
  activity-based costing, 24–6
  change, 154
  customer life cycle costing, 450–1
  just-in-time system, 306
  life cycle costing, 446–51
  manufacturing philosophy, 423–4
  product life cycle costing, 447–50
  pull systems, 428–32
  standard costing, 444–5
  target costing, 441
  throughput accounting, 456
  see also Marginal costing
Costs:
  activity-based management, 341–2
  batch sizes, 323, 411, 424, 464, 549
  behaviour, 7–13
  changes, 154

classification, 5–6
concepts, 3–6
decision making, 43–4
drivers, 338, 343–4, 348, 352
economies of scale, 43, 50, 146,. 172, 469, 470
elements, 13–14
experience curves, 401–406
learning curves, 409–13
mark-ups, 148–51
minimisation, 112–13
nature classification, 5–6
non-relevant, 6, 43, 65–6
overhead allocation, 17–18
planning, 442
pricing strategies, 148–52
product variety issues, 426–7
production run costs, 425
purpose classification, 6
relevant, 6, 43, 65–6
semi-variable, 10
short-term decision making, 44
stock holding costs, 425
theory of constraints, 432–3
throughput accounting, 432–3
total quality management, 310–12
variable, 6, 8–10
volumes, 35, 43, 141–2
see also Fixed costs; Marginal costing; Overhead costs
Cox, J., 432
Creditworthiness checks, 440, 450
Cross-elasticity of demand, 141–5
Customer service, 306, 317
Customers:
  activity-based costing, 24–5, 336
  life cycle costing, 450–1
  Pareto analysis, 351–2
  profits, 368
CVP *see* Cost-volume-profit (CVP) analysis

Darlington, John, 440
DCF *see* Discounted cash flow (DCF), concepts
Decision grid analysis (DGA), 371
Decision making:
  absorption costing, 31
  breakeven analysis, 35, 37, 39
  capital budgeting, 212, 263, 268–70, 367, 446, 450
  decision-maker types, 176
  information, 13
  investment appraisals, 265
  limiting factors, 70–3
  linear programming, 119–21, 433
  Pareto analysis, 351–2
  post-completion appraisals, 242–8
  risk, 193–5
  short-term, 44, 65–6, 576
  total quality management, 310–12
Decision trees:
  concepts, 180
  considerations, 182
Decision variables, linear programming, 109
Demand:
  elasticities, 141–3, 150
  pricing, 141–5
  product life cycles, 145–7
Depreciation, 66, 92, 223
DGA *see* Decision grid analysis (DGA)
Differential costs, 68

Differentiated products, 145
Direct costs, 4, 288, 299
    attributable fixed costs, 67
    labour, 8, 9, 19, 333, 355, 405, 486, 497
    materials, 8, 20
    wages cost percentage, 20
Direct product profitability (DPP):
    concepts, 333–6
    historical background, 333
Discount rates, investment cash flow, 620
Discounted cash flow (DCF), concepts, 242, 248
Discounted payback (DPB), 217
Discounted payback index (DPBI), 217–18
Discounts, 156–7
Disposable income, price elasticity, 145
Distribution channel profitability, 346–7
DPB *see* Discounted payback (DPB)
DPBI *see* Discounted payback index (DPBI)
DPP *see* Direct product profitability (DPP)

Economies of scale, 43, 50, 146172, 469, 470
Economists:
    breakeven chart, 43
    profit maximisation issues, 161, 436
Effectiveness measures, throughput
    accounting, 437–8
Efficiencies, 311, 323, 343, 365, 372, 556
EFTPOS, 335
Eije, Henk von, 254
Elasticities of demand, 141–5
EPOS, 335, 429
Eusman, Frans, 254
Examinations:
    format/paper structure, 475
    preparation, 473–6
    revision questions, 477–528
    revision technique, 473–4
    solutions to revision questions, 529–622
Excel software, 123, 125, 128
Expected values, 178, 186
Experience curves, 406–408
Extra features, pricing, 155–7

Facility level activities, 339
Feasible region, linear
    programming, 110, 119–21
Financial Management, 364
Fixed costs:
    breakeven analysis, 35–40
    overhead problem, 331–2
    per unit, 8
    short-term decision making, 44, 576
    throughput accounting, 432
Fixed-overhead absorption rates, 20
Flexible manufacturing systems (FMS), 424
Florida Power and Light Company, 318
Fordham, David, 263
Functional analysis, 305
Future costs, 66

Galloway, David, 433
Garrett Automotive, 425
Genka kikaku, 441, 590
Goldratt, Eli, 432, 433
Gourdie, Stephanie, 364
Grocery trade, 333
Grundig, 442

Hansen, Don, 365
Heijunka principle, 429
Heineken Nederland, 255–8
Hewlett-Packard, 449–50
High-low method, 11–12
Historical cost depreciation, 66
Historical data, semi-variable costs, 10–12
Human resources:
    direct labour, 19, 21
    learning curves, 409–13
    target costing, 304, 441

Idle time, 192
Income:
    elasticity of demand, 141–5
    price elasticity, 141, 145
Incremental costs, 68–9
Incremental revenues, 69
Indifference point, 232
Indirect costs, 6
Inefficiencies, 323, 343, 372
Inflation, 236–7
    breakeven analysis, 35–62
    semi-variable costs, 10–12
Information:
    activity-based costing, 24–5, 336
    perfect information, 184–5
    pricing decisions, 142–4
Information technology (IT):
    direct product profitability, 333–6
    linear programming, 119–21
    Simplex method, 119–21
    spreadsheets, 263, 267, 366
Innes, John, 456
Internal failure costs, 326
Internal rate of return (IRR), 218, 221
    concepts, 219
    multiple IRRs, 220–1
    usage statistics, 218–9
Investment appraisals:
    abandonment considerations, 244–8
    benefit types, 242–4
    concepts, 159
    corporation tax, 238
    inflation, 236–7
    post-completion, 242–8
    return on investment, 222–4
    risk, 193–5
    sensitivity analysis, 232–5
    taxation, 238–40
    uncertainty, 185
    see also Net present value (NPV)
IRR *see* Internal rate of return (IRR)
IT *see* Information technology (IT)

Japan, 236, 390, 425, 441, 445, 590
Joint products, 81–9
Just-in-time (JIT) system, 306–308
    concepts, 306–308
    historical background, 385
    production, 325
    purchasing, 307
    suppliers, 309–10
    total quality management, 310–12

Kaizen costing, 304
Kanbans, 428

Kaplan, R., 232, 343, 365
Kato, 441, 445, 446
Knowledge *see* Information

Labour:
   absorption costing, 24, 31, 332–3, 336–43, 387, 391, 420, 575, 617
   linear programming, 107–28
Lead times, 307, 308, 428, 438
Learned behaviour, 405
Learning curves:
   concepts, 409
   definition, 409
   formula, 403
   uses, 405
Learning organisations, 254, 255, 257
Ledger accounts, backflush accounting, 429–32
Life cycle costing:
   concepts, 446–7, 554
   product life cycle costing, 447–8
Limiting factors, 362–6
   linear programming, 123–8
   short-term decision making, 70–3
Linear programming, 107–28
   concepts, 107
   constraints, 113–14, 136
   decision variables, 109
   formulation of model, 108–109
   graphical solutions, 109–13
   limiting factors, 123–8
   multiple solutions, 114–17
   non-negativity conditions, 109
   opportunity costs, 118–19
   relative loss, 121–2
   shadow prices, 118–19
   Simplex method, 119–21
   slack and surplus, 117–18
   specifying constraints, 109
   throughput accounting, 432–9
   worth, 121–2
Linear variable costs, 8
Loss leaders, 154
Lucas, Mike, 152, 159

Machine hour rate, 19, 21, 26
Management:
   activity-based, 341–2
   by walking about, 437
   project management, 375, 445
   strategic activity, 347–8
   see also Planning; Total quality management (TQM)
Management Accounting, 455
Management Today, 429
Manufacturing:
   cost hierarchy, 339
   lead time, 307, 308, 428, 438
   philosophy changes, 426
Manufacturing cycle efficiency (MCE), 454, 455
Manufacturing cycle time (MCT), 453–5
Margin of safety, 36
Marginal cost-plus pricing, 151–2
Marginal costing, 17–31
   absorption costing, 24, 26, 27, 31
   concepts, 18
   contribution, 26
   historical background, 436
   marginal revenues, 147, 159, 165
   profit statements, 28

Marginal revenues, 147, 159, 165
Marginal utilities, 189
Mark-ups, 148–51
Market shares, product life cycles, 313, 317, 423, 453, 468, 554
Market skimming pricing strategies, 152–3
Marshall, S. Brooks, 263
Materials:
   absorption costing, 332
   linear programming, 107–28
Maximised profit issues, 147, 151
MCE *see* Manufacturing cycle efficiency (MCE)
MCT *see* Manufacturing cycle time (MCT)
Minimum price quotations, 44, 70
Mitchell, Falconer, 456
Modified internal rate of return (MIRR), 221–2
Monetary cost of capital, 236, 237
Monopolies, 82, 88
Monte Carlo techniques, 191
Mowen, Maryanne, 365
Multi-product CVP analysis, 46–8
Multiple IRRs, 220–1
Multiple solutions, linear programming, 114–17

Naidoo, Selvan, 374
Net present value (NPV):
   asset replacement cycles, 227
   capital rationing, 230–1
   concepts, 213–14
   discount rates, 214
   indifference point, 232–3, 549, 563
   inflation, 236–41
   realistic approaches, 243
   sensitivity analysis, 232
   taxation, 238–41
   unequal lives, 226–7
   usage statistics, 213
Network diagrams, theory of constraints, 432–3
Non-binding resources, 127
Non-controllable costs, 6
Non-financial factors, 44, 75, 76
Non-linear variable costs, 42
Non-negativity conditions, 62
Non-relevant costs, 6, 65–6
Normal costs, 6
Notional costs, 66, 68
NPV *see* Net present value (NPV)

OARs *see* Overhead absorption rates (OARs)
Objective functions, 108
Objective variables, 108
Opportunity costs:
   linear programming, 107–28
   short-term decision making, 70–3
Optimum defects level, 312, 317
Over-absorption, 20, 21, 29, 30
Overhead absorption rates (OARs), 20–1
   predetermined, 20
Overhead costs, 20, 365, 369, 372
   absorption costing, 332–3
   activity-based costing, 24–5
   allocation, 17–18, 162
   apportionment, 17–18
   concepts, 17, 18
   over- or under-absorption, 335, 554
   Pareto analysis, 350–1
   problems, 331–2
   short-term decision making, 44, 70–3

P/V *see* Profit-volume (P/V) ratio
Pareto analysis, 350
   activity-based costing (ABC), 336–7
   concepts, 350
   uses, 351–2
Past costs, 65
Pay-off, decision trees, 181
Payback (PB), 215–17
   concepts, 215–16
Penetration pricing, 153
Perfect information, 184–5
Planning, 443, 473–4
   see also Management
Post-completion appraisals, 242–8
   abandonment considerations, 244–8
   benefits, 604
Post-completion audits, 240, 244, 254, 603
Predetermined overhead absorption rates, 20–2
Premium pricing, 152
Prevention costs, 311, 326
Price elasticity of demand, 141–5
   concepts, 143
   influencing factors, 145
   product life cycles, 145–7
   Pricing, 148–51, 152
   bundling strategies, 154–5
   controlled prices, 157
   cost-based strategies, 159
   cost-plus pricing, 148–50
   demand, 153–4
   differentiation, 153–4
   discounts, 156
   experience curves, 406–408
   extra features, 155
   learning curves, 401–405
   loss leaders, 154
   mark-ups, 148–51
   market skimming strategies, 152–3
   penetration pricing, 153
   premium pricing, 152
   price differentiation, 153–4
   product life cycles, 145–7, 423, 453, 468
   profit maximisation issues, 161, 436
   psychological considerations, 143
   regulating bodies, 143
   skimming strategies, 152
   target costing, 304, 441
   volume interactions, 127–31
Prime cost percentage, 20
Prins, Wout, 254
Printer's Cost Finding System, 332
Privatisations, 157
Probabilities, 175–80
   calculation examples, 159–62
   decision trees, 162–7
   expected values, 160–8
Processing time, 453
Product contribution, Pareto analysis, 352
Product costing, 20, 341, 342, 364, 439, 440, 496
Product level activities, 339
Product life cycles, 145–7, 423, 453, 468
   cash flow management, 449
   concepts, 145–6
   costing, 148–9
   design costs, 449
   price elasticity of demand, 153–4
   returns maps, 449, 450

   target costing, 304, 441
   time to market issues, 449
Product-specific fixed costs, 67
Production, 272, 274
   absorption costing, 332–3
   costs, 364, 459
   just-in-time system, 306
   lead times, 308
   plans, 70, 191, 193, 437
   run costs, 364, 425
Products:
   bundling, 154–5
   differentiation, 153–4
   direct product profitability, 333–6
   experience curves, 406–408
   extra features, 155–7
   returns per minute, 434
   variety explosion, 425, 427
   see also Pricing
Profit statements, costing, 27, 28
Profitability index, 217, 231
Profits:
   breakeven analysis, 232
   concepts, 35
   constraints, 35–6
   customers, 368
   direct product profitability, 333–6
   life cycle costing, 447–8
   mark-ups, 148–51
   maximisation, 161, 436
   pricing, 148–51, 152
   product life cycles, 145–7
   reconciliation, 429
   return on investment, 222–4
   strategic issues, 437
   target costing, 304, 441
   see also Revenues
Profit-volume (P/V) ratio, 37
Projects:
   abandonment considerations, 244–8
   investment appraisals, 247
   management, 375
   post-completion, 242–8
Proposal evaluation, 44–6
Psychological considerations, price changes, 143
Pull principle, 309
Pull systems, 306, 428
Purchasing, just-in-time system, 307, 324
Push-through systems, 309

Quality issues, 270, 274, 326
   absorption costing, 332–3
   premium pricing, 152
   see also Total quality management (TQM)

Random numbers, 191–3, 267, 268, 270
Rate per unit, 19
Raw and in progress accounts (RIPs), 431
Real cost of capital, 248, 628
Reconciliation, profits, 29
Rectification costs, 311, 313
Regulating bodies, 157
Relative loss, linear programming, 121–2
Relevant costs, 65–7
   decision making, 43–4
   short-term decision making, 65–80

Research and development (R&D):
    target costing, 553–4
    value chain, 305–6
Resource cost drivers, 338
Resources *see* Constraints
Retailers:
    activity-based costing, 24–31
    direct product profitability, 368
Return on investment (ROI), 222–4
Returns:
    accounting rate of return, 222–4
    internal rate of return, 218–20
    maps, 449, 450
    per time period ratio, 434
    product returns per minute, 434
Revenues, 121–2
    expected values, 178, 186, 273, 618
    life cycle costing, 447–8
    marginal revenues, 147, 159, 165
    product life cycles, 145–7
    short-term decision making, 65–80
    see also Profits
Revision technique, 473–5
RIPs *see* Raw and in progress accounts (RIPs)
Risk, 175, 193–5
    attitudes, 194
    breakeven analysis, 232
    concepts, 175
    decision-maker types, 180
    investment appraisals, 185
    standard deviations, to measure, 186
    see also Uncertainty
ROI *see* Return on investment (ROI)
Routines, 248, 405, 474

Sales:
    breakeven analysis, 232
    volume interactions, 141–2
Sanyo, 344
Scattergraph method, 12–13
Segmentation, 154
Selling costs, 30, 147
Semi-variable costs, analysis, 10–12
Sensitivity analysis, 183, 232
    concepts, 232
    definition, 232
Sensitivity reports, 126
Sequential tracking systems, 429
Services:
    activity-based costing, 24–31
    direct product profitability, 333–6
Shadow prices, 118–19
Short-term decision making, 65–80
    accept/reject order decision, 73
    closure decision, 77–6
    incremental revenues, 69
    limiting factors, 70–3
    make or buy decision, 440
    minimum price quotations, 70
    opportunity costs, 67–8
Simplex method, 119–121
Simulations, 191–3
Skimming pricing strategies, 152–3
Slack, linear programming, 117–18
Split-off point, 79
Spreadsheets, 263, 267, 366
Standard costing, 324, 441, 442, 445

Standard deviations, 186
Steering committees, 375
Stepped fixed costs, 7, 8
Steven, Grahame, 123
Stock:
    breakeven analysis, 232
    holding costs, 325, 391, 425
    just-in-time system, 428
    Pareto analysis, 350–2
Strategic activity management, 342, 347
Strategic issues, 437
Strict equalities, 110, 114
Sunk costs, 7, 79, 151, 290
Suppliers, just-in-time system, 309, 324
Support systems, target costing, 445–6
Surplus, linear programming, 117–18

TA *see* Throughput accounting (TA)
Target costing, 304, 441
    breakdown, 305, 308, 309, 433
    concepts, 441
    existing products, 444–5
    human resources, 304, 441
    plannin g, 441, 443
    support systems, 445–6
Taxation, investment appraisals, 238–9
Technical committees, 376
Test data, 127
Theory of constraints (TOC), 432–3
Throughput accounting (TA), 432–4
    case study, 438
    concepts, 432–4
    criticisms, 441
    effectiveness measures, 437–8
    limiting factors, 434
    product costing, 20, 341, 342, 364, 440
Time value of money, 183
TOC *see* Theory of constraints (TOC)
Top-down strategies, 375
Total cost-plus pricing, 148–51
Total quality management (TQM), 310–13
    costs, 335–6
    just-in-time system, 306
    practice, 312–13
    quality concept, 310–11
    value chain, 305–306
Toyota, 425, 428–9
TQM *see* Total quality management (TQM)

Uncertainty, 175–88
    concepts, 175
    investment appraisals, 185
    perfect information, 184
    reduction techniques, 441–3
    standard deviations, to measure, 186
    tools, 263–6
    see also Risk
Under-absorption, 21, 22, 30, 554
Uniform costing *see* Absorption costing
Unit level activities, 339
Unit variable costs, 42, 167
United States of America (USA), 236, 390, 432, 433
Utility theory, 176, 189

Value analysis (VA), 304–5
Value chains, 305–306
Value engineering (VE), 445–6

Variable costs, 559
  breakeven analysis, 232
  per unit, 6, 42, 167
  short-term decision making, 65–80
Variances, 554
Variety explosion, products, 425, 427
VE *see* Value engineering (VE)
Volume interaction:
  pricing, 148–51, 152
  sales, 141–2
  variety, cost relationship, 427

Waldron, David, 433
WCM *see* World-class manufacturing (WCM)
WDA *see* Writing-down allowances (WDA)
Wealth distribution, 350
Wedgwood, Josiah, 153
Woodward, John, 456
Working forums, 376
Workshops, 376
World-class manufacturing (WCM), 306
Worth, linear programming, 121–2
Writing-down allowances (WDA), 238–40

Get 10% Discount and Free P&P
off your next order

Quote APP6 when ordering or add it to the offer code box online.

Order Form
For CIMA Official Study Materials for 2008 Exams

Post this form to:

CIMA Publishing Customer Services
Elsevier
FREEPOST (OF 1639)
Linacre House, Jordan Hill
OXFORD, OX2 8DP, UK

Or **FAX** +44 (0)1865 314 572
Or **PHONE** +44 (0)1865 474 014
Email: cimaorders@elsevier.com
www.cimapublishing.com

QTY	PAPER	TITLE	ISBN-13	PRICE	TOTAL
CIMA Official *Learning Systems*					
	P1	Performance Evaluation	978 0 7506 8430 9	£35.00	
	P2	Decision Management	978 0 7506 8535 1	£35.00	
	P3	Risk and Control Strategy	978 0 7506 8497 2	£35.00	
	P4	Organisational Management & Information Systems	978 0 7506 8428 6	£35.00	
	P5	Integrated Management	978 0 7506 8540 5	£35.00	
	P6	Business Strategy	978 0 7506 8467 5	£35.00	
	P7	Financial Accounting and Tax Principles	978 0 7506 8541 2	£35.00	
	P8	Financial Analysis	978 0 7506 8429 3	£35.00	
	P9	Financial Strategy	978 0 7506 8538 2	£35.00	
	P10	TOPCIMA	978 0 7506 8445 3	£35.00	
CIMA Official *Exam Practice Kits*					
	P1	Performance Evaluation	978 0 7506 8401 9	£14.99	
	P2	Decision Management	978 0 7506 8403 3	£14.99	
	P3	Risk and Control Strategy	978 0 7506 8410 1	£14.99	
	P4	Organisational Management & Information Systems	978 0 7506 8332 6	£14.99	
	P5	Integrated Management	978 0 7506 8376 0	£14.99	
	P6	Business Strategy	978 0 7506 8400 2	£14.99	
	P7	Financial Accounting and Tax Principles	978 0 7506 8394 4	£14.99	
	P8	Financial Analysis	978 0 7506 8373 9	£14.99	
	P9	Financial Strategy	978 0 7506 8390 6	£14.99	
	P10	TOPCIMA	978 0 7506 8329 6	£14.99	
CIMA Official *Revision Cards*					
	P1	Performance Evaluation	978 0 7506 8123 0	£8.99	
	P2	Decision Management	978 0 7506 8124 7	£8.99	
	P3	Risk and Control Strategy	978 0 7506 8120 9	£8.99	
	P4	Organisational Management & Information Systems	978 0 7506 8121 6	£8.99	
	P5	Integrated Management	978 0 7506 8122 3	£8.99	
	P6	Business Strategy	978 0 7506 8119 3	£8.99	
	P7	Financial Accounting and Tax Principles	978 0 7506 8126 1	£8.99	
	P8	Financial Analysis	978 0 7506 8125 4	£8.99	
	P9	Financial Strategy	978 0 7506 8118 6	£8.99	
Books					
		Principles of Business Taxation	978 0 7506 8457 6	£49.99	
		CIMA: Pass First Time!	978 0 7506 8396 8	£12.99	
		Better Exam Results	978 0 7506 6357 1	£12.99	
			Postage and packing		£2.95
			TOTAL		

Name:

Organisation:

Invoice Address:

Postcode:

Phone number:

Email:

Delivery Address if different:

FAO

Address

Postcode

Please note that all deliveries must be signed for

1. Cheques payable to Elsevier.

2. Please charge my:

☐ Visa/Barclaycard ☐ Access/Mastercard
☐ American Express ☐ Diners Card
☐ Switch   Issue No._____

Card No.

Expiry Date

Cardholder Name:

Signature:

Date:

Elsevier Ltd, Science & Technology Books, retains certain personal information about you in hard copy and on computer. It will be used to inform you about goods and services available from Elsevier Ltd and its offices worldwide in which you may be interested.
Please tick the box if you do NOT wish to receive this information. ☐

CIMA Official *Learning Systems*

These comprehensive workbooks are the only texts written and endorsed by the CIMA Faculty. As writers of the new syllabus and exams, nobody is better qualified to explain how to pass.

- Step-by-step subject coverage directly linked to CIMA's learning outcomes
- Extensive question practice throughout
- Complete revision section
- Q&As, complete with examiner's solutions

CIMA Official *Revision Cards*

- Pocket-sized books for learning all the key points – especially for students on the move
- Relevant, succinct and compact reminders of all the bullet points and diagrams needed for the new CIMA exams
- Break down the syllabus into memorable bite-size chunks

CIMA Official *Exam Practice Kits*

Supplement the Learning Systems with a bank of additional questions focusing purely on applying what has been learnt to passing the exam. Ideal for independent study or tutored revision courses. Prepare with confidence for exam day, and pass the new syllabus first time.

- Avoid common pitfalls with fully worked model answers
- Type and weighting of questions match the format of the exam by paper, helping you prepare by giving you the closest available preview of the exam
- Summaries of key theory

Get **10% Discount** and **Free P&P** off your next order

Quote APP6 when ordering or add it to the offer code box online.

Science & Technology Books, Elsevier Ltd.
Registered Office: The Boulevard, Langford Lane, Kidlington, OXON, OX5 1GB
Registered in England: 1982084

Give CIMA Publishing Your Feedback and Win a Prize

Win your choice of 3 further *Learning Systems* or an iPod

Help us to improve our product for next year by telling us of your experience using this product. All feedback forms returned will be entered into a prize draw. The first three forms drawn on 30 November 2007 will receive either three *Learning Systems* of their choice or an 2Gb iPod Nano. The winners will be notified by email.

Feedback form:

CIMA Official *Learning Systems*
2008 Editions

Name:

Address:

Email:

■ **How did you use your CIMA Official *Learning System*?**

☐ Self-study (book only)

☐ On a full course?
How long was the course?
Which college did you attend?

☐ On a revision course?
Which college did you attend?

☐ Other

Additional comments:

■ **How did you order your CIMA Official *Learning System*?**

☐ Carrier sheet from CIMA Financial Management magazine

☐ CIMA Publishing catalogue found in Financial Management magazine

☐ Order form from the back of a previous *Learning System*

☐ www.cimapublishing.com website

☐ Bookshop
Name
Branch

☐ Other

Additional comments:

Your ratings and comments would be appreciated on the following aspects. Please circle your response, where one indicates an excellent rating and four a poor rating.

	Excellent			Poor
☐ Topic coverage	1	2	3	4
☐ Accuracy	1	2	3	4
☐ Readings	1	2	3	4
☐ End of chapter questions and solutions	1	2	3	4
☐ Revision section	1	2	3	4
☐ Layout/Presentation	1	2	3	4
☐ Overall opinion of this study system	1	2	3	4

Additional comments:

■ Would you recommend CIMA Official *Learning Systems* to other students?

Please circle: Yes   No

Additional comments:

■ Which CIMA Publishing products have you used?
☐ CIMA Official *Learning Systems*
☐ Q&As
☐ CIMA eSuccess CDs
☐ CIMA Revision Cards
☐ CIMA Exam Practice Kits

Additional comments:

■ Are there any related products you would like to see from CIMA Publishing? If so, please elaborate below.

■ Please note any further comments or errors found in the space below.

Thank you for your time in completing this questionnaire. We wish you good luck in your exam.

Please return to:
Claire Lawlor
CIMA Publishing
FREEPOST – SCE 5435
Linacre House
Jordan Hill
Oxford, OX2 8DP, UK

Or Fax: FAO C. Lawlor to: +44 (0) 1865 314572

Stay Informed with CIMA Publishing eNews

Visit
www.cimapublishing.com
and register for our monthly email to keep up to date with:

Regular discounts on CIMA Publishing products

Knowledge of our latest releases:
■ CIMA's Official *Learning Systems*
■ Q&As with examiners' answers
■ CIMA research reports
■ CIMA eSuccess CDs
■ CIMA Revision cards
■ Related accountancy and management books

News and critical deadline remnders from CIMA
Prize draws and competitions

MAY 07 Q&A

To access the May 07 Q&A for the book you have bought please follow these instructions:

Go to
http://cimapublishing.com/QandA

- Enter in the passcode found on the back cover of the book

- Fill in the registration form

- Download the PDF for immediate access to Q&A